*Richard Baxter and
the Mechanical Philosophers*

OXFORD STUDIES IN HISTORICAL THEOLOGY

Richard Baxter and the Mechanical Philosophers

DAVID S. SYTSMA

OXFORD
UNIVERSITY PRESS

OXFORD
UNIVERSITY PRESS

Oxford University Press is a department of the University of Oxford. It furthers the University's objective of excellence in research, scholarship, and education by publishing worldwide. Oxford is a registered trade mark of Oxford University Press in the UK and certain other countries.

Published in the United States of America by Oxford University Press
198 Madison Avenue, New York, NY 10016, United States of America.

CIP data is on file at the Library of Congress
ISBN 978-0-19-027487-0

1 3 5 7 9 8 6 4 2
Printed by Sheridan Books, Inc., United States of America

For Hiroko

There is a good measure of knowledge necessary to make some men to know their ignorance. What can shew a man his error, but the contrary truth? This is it therefore that hinders men's conviction, and makes them confident in their most false conceits; seeing they want both that Light, and that Humility which should take down their confidence. We have as much ado to make some men know, that they do not know, as to make them know, that which they know not, when once they will believe that they do not know it.

—RICHARD BAXTER, *The Arrogancy of Reason against Divine Revelations, Repressed*

Contents

Preface

THE PRESENT STUDY is the fruit of an intellectual journey that began as a student at Calvin Theological Seminary. It was there, through course papers on Samuel Clarke and Joseph Priestley (seminal figures in the development of eighteenth-century Trinitarian heterodoxy), that I first took notice of the theological importance of changing notions of substance and causality generated by seventeenth-century mechanical philosophy. This initial sentiment was confirmed by further study of Edward Stillingfleet's debate with John Locke in a course with Daniel Garber at Princeton University. Having already explored late seventeenth- and eighteenth-century developments, I wished to study the interaction between theology and philosophy during the earlier seventeenth-century period of transition when varieties of both the older Christian Aristotelianism and mechanical philosophy were in play. The result of this inquiry was my doctoral dissertation on Richard Baxter, written under the kind supervision of Elsie McKee and Ken Appold of Princeton Theological Seminary, which now, in significantly revised and expanded form, constitutes the present book.

All historical research is in a sense *actus entis in potentia*, and the present book represents a further actualization of my dissertation. I have added and revised entire chapters, while incorporating additional primary sources, both in manuscript and print. These changes have not only helped to clarify more precisely the chronology of Baxter's works under discussion, but also reinforced my opinion that Baxter's mind is in many respects a moving target. Baxter's correspondence with Matthew Hale, for example, shows him changing his mind on matters of substance (literally!) under the force of Hale's reply. In light of the importance of chronology to Baxter's intellectual development and engagement with philosophy, I have included an appendix on the chronology of Baxter's post-Restoration writings relating to philosophy. As every student of Baxter's large corpus of printed and manuscript works is aware, a complete comprehension of his works is an elusive goal. I have focused on a narrow set of topics that seemed relevant to the present study. Further evidence relating to the topics of the present book will no doubt surface over the course of time. I ask the reader's indulgence for what is inevitably an imperfect approximation of Baxter's large corpus and complicated intellectual development.

The reader will observe in the present study discussion of philosophical trends beyond Baxter's own works. Most notably, chapter 2 contains a large survey of the English reception of the Pierre Gassendi's Christian Epicurean philosophy. This wider view is intentional. I have sought to bring to light those aspects of mechanical philosophy that help to explain the philosophical situation faced by Baxter. Thus the second half of the title of this book: "and the Mechanical Philosophers." Moreover, given that the issues dealt with in this book straddle matters of concern to both historians of philosophy and theology, I have tried to orient readers to important concerns and literature in both fields with a mind to facilitating interdisciplinary awareness. The seventeenth-century theologians and philosophers whom we study do not oblige our modern disciplinary specializations, and historians of theology and philosophy have much to learn from each other. My sense is that the historians of philosophy have done a better job thinking through theological connections to their field than vice versa. Accordingly, I have generally erred on the side of greater discussion of philosophical context for the sake of the theological reader.

Thanks are also due to the Dr. Williams's Library and Lambeth Palace Library in London for permission to cite excepts from their manuscript holdings. Baxter's manuscripts in the appendices have been transcribed and printed with the permission of Dr. David Wykes, on behalf of the Trustees of Dr Williams's Library.

I am grateful to a great many people for their advice and encouragement. To professors Richard Muller, John Cooper, and John Bolt of Calvin Theological Seminary, and Elsie McKee and Ken Appold of Princeton Theological Seminary, I offer my sincere thanks for their instruction over many years. I am also grateful to Daniel Garber of Princeton University for his instruction in seventeenth-century philosophy. Thanks are due to Mordechai Feingold, Richard Muller, Albert Gootjes, Aza Goudriaan, Matthew Gaetano, and Jordan Ballor for their helpful suggestions and encouragement on drafts of the present book. Simon Burton and Todd Rester also helped with specific questions relating to the book. Alison Searle graciously assisted me with queries on Baxter's manuscript correspondence. I am thankful for the wise counsel of Stephen Grabill on many matters. The theological librarians at Calvin College, Paul Fields and Lugene Schemper, along with Kate Skrebutenas of Princeton Theological Seminary, have made my researches over the years a pleasant experience. More than anyone, I am grateful to my wife, Hiroko, who has been a constant support and faithful companion.

David S. Sytsma
Tokyo, Japan

Abbreviations

AT   René Descartes, *Oeuvres de Descartes*. Edited by Charles
Adam and Paul Tannery. 13 vols. Paris: Léopold Cerf,
1897–1913.

CCRB   *Calendar of the Correspondence of Richard Baxter*. Edited by
N. H. Keeble and Geoffrey F. Nuttall. 2 vols. Oxford: Clarendon
Press, 1991.

CD   Richard Baxter, *A Christian Directory: Or, A Summ of Practical
Theologie, and Cases of Conscience*. London: Robert White, 1673.
Reference is to part and page numbers.

CHSP   *The Cambridge History of Seventeenth-Century Philosophy*. Edited by
Daniel Garber and Michael Ayers. 2 vols. Cambridge: Cambridge
University Press, 1998.

CSEL   *Corpus Scriptorum Ecclesiasticorum Latinorum*. Vienna, 1866–.

CSM   René Descartes, *The Philosophical Writings of Descartes*. Translated
by John Cottingham, Robert Stoothoff, and Dugald Murdoch.
3 vols. Cambridge: Cambridge University Press, 1985–1991.

CT   Richard Baxter, *Catholick Theologie: Plain, Pure, Peacable: For the
Pacification of the Dogmatical Word-Warriours*. London: Robert
White, 1675.

DWL BC   Dr. Williams's Library, London, Baxter Correspondence (MS 59,
vols. 1–6). Reference is to volume and folio numbers.

DWL BT   Dr. Williams's Library, London, Baxter Treatises (MS 59, vols.
7–13, and MS 61, vols. 1–6, 11–18). Reference is to volume, item,
and folio numbers, cited according to the consecutive sequence
of 22 volumes as classified by Roger Thomas, *The Baxter Treatises*
(London: Dr. Williams's Trust, 1959), 4a.

JNIR   *The Judgment of Non-conformists, of the Interest of Reason, in Matters
of Religion*. London, 1676.

LPL   Lambeth Palace Library, London.

MT	Richard Baxter, *Methodus theologiae christianae*. London: M. White & T. Snowden, 1681. Reference is to part and page numbers.
ODNB	*Oxford Dictionary of National Biography*. Oxford: Oxford University Press, 2004.
PG	*Patrologiae Cursus Completus: Series Graeca*. Edited by J. P. Migne. 161 vols. Paris, 1857–1866.
PL	*Patrologiae Cursus Completus: Series Latina*. Edited by J. P. Migne. 221 vols. Paris, 1844–1864.
PRRD	Richard A. Muller, *Post-Reformation Reformed Dogmatics*. 2nd ed., 4 vols. Grand Rapids, MI: Baker Academic, 2003.
Rel. Bax.	Richard Baxter, *Reliquiae Baxterianae: Or, Mr. Richard Baxter's Narrative of the most Memorable Passages of his Life and Times*. Edited by Matthew Sylvester. London: T. Parkhurst et al., 1696. Reference is to part and page numbers.
RCR	Richard Baxter, *The Reasons of the Christian Religion*. London: R. White, 1667.
SER2	Richard Baxter, *The Saints Everlasting Rest*. 2nd ed. London: Thomas Underhill, 1651.
TKL	Richard Baxter, *A Treatise of Knowledge and Love Compared*. London: Tho. Parkhurst, 1689.

Note on Style of Citation

When citing manuscripts, I have sought to preserve paleographical fidelity as much as possible. Although the long "s" and ligatures such as æ and œ have been modernized, other contractions such as yᵉ (the) and wᶜʰ (which) have not been modified. Insertions are marked as <text>, deleted words as ~~text~~, illegible words as [?], editorial conjectures as [?text], editorial insertions as [text], and page breaks as /fol. 1r/. Foreign words and underlined words are written in *italics*.

*Richard Baxter and
the Mechanical Philosophers*

I

Richard Baxter as Philosophical Theologian

RICHARD BAXTER DESERVES to be better known as a philosophical theologian. In 1852, George Park Fisher wrote, "We feel bound to enter a protest against the extraordinary liberty which has been taken with the writings of this great divine. While Baxter is regarded by the multitude as a man of saintly piety, his intellectual traits are poorly appreciated."[1] Over a century and a half after Fisher penned these words, they have lost little of their force. Baxter is still one of the most famous Puritans, but he is almost exclusively known as a practical theologian or Pietist.[2] With few exceptions, Baxter's major theological works, *Catholick Theologie* (1675) and *Methodus theologiae christianae* (1681), which by his own account "expressed my maturest, calmest thoughts,"[3] remain little studied.[4] One recent study contrasts

---

1. George Park Fisher, "The Writings of Richard Baxter," *Bibliotheca Sacra and American Biblical Repository* 9 (1852): 324.

2. F. Ernest Stoeffler, *The Rise of Evangelical Pietism* (Leiden: E. J. Brill, 1965), 88–96; N. H. Keeble, *Richard Baxter: Puritan Man of Letters* (Oxford: Clarendon Press, 1982), 39–41; Carl Trueman, "Lewis Bayly (d. 1631) and Richard Baxter (1615–1691)," in *The Pietist Theologians: An Introduction to Theology in the Seventeenth and Eighteenth Centuries*, ed. Carter Lindberg (Malden, MA: Blackwell, 2005), 52–67. Baxter was the "most important writer of British devotional books" in German translation for the period 1651–1700, during the birth of German Pietism. See Edgar C. McKenzie, "British Devotional Literature and the Rise of German Pietism" (PhD diss., University of St. Andrews, 1984), 228.

3. Richard Baxter, *The True History of Councils Enlarged and Defended* (London: T. Parkhurst, 1682), 240.

4. Notable exceptions include George Park Fisher, "The Theology of Richard Baxter," *Bibliotheca Sacra and American Biblical Repository* 9 (1852): 135–69; J. I. Packer, "The Redemption and Restoration of Man in the Thought of Richard Baxter" (PhD diss., Oxford University, 1954), published as *The Redemption & Restoration of Man in the Thought of Richard Baxter: A Study in Puritan Theology* (Vancouver: Regent College Publishing, 2003); Hans Boersma, *A Hot Pepper Corn: Richard Baxter's Doctrine of Justification in Its*

Baxter's practical orientation with his "scorn for scholastic quibbling," but makes no reference to Baxter's *Methodus theologiae*.[5] Such scholarly neglect puts asunder what Baxter himself joined together. Baxter intended his *Methodus theologiae* and *Christian Directory* (1673), on the model of William Ames's *Medulla theologiae* and *Cases of Conscience*, as "one Compleat Body of Theology, The *Latin* one the Theory, and the *English* one the Practical part."[6] Neglect of Baxter's theoretical works also obscures the quality of his intellect. Baxter's impressive nine-hundred-page *Methodus theologiae* rivals contemporary theological systems such as Francis Turretin's *Institutio theologiae elencticae* (1679–1685) in scholastic subtlety and erudition, and arguably surpasses Turretin's grasp of the patristic and medieval tradition with respect to the doctrine of the Trinity.[7] Furthermore, despite the fact that Baxter's *Methodus theologiae* and other works contain extensive philosophical argumentation, among theological studies little attention has been given to Baxter's engagement with early modern philosophy.[8]

In his own lifetime and for at least a generation after his death, Baxter was not valued merely as a practical or devotional theologian. Much modern scholarship, often citing Baxter's autobiographical remark that "most lay [the *Methodus theologiae*] by as too hard for them, as over Scholastical and exact,"[9] has assumed that Baxter's scholastic theology fell on deaf ears. As Frederick Powicke wrote, "Overdone books like his *Catholic Theology*, and *Methodus Theologiae* were not read at all."[10] Such assertions, which have reinforced the perceived irrelevance

Seventeenth-Century Context of Controversy (Zoetermeer: Uitgeverij Boekencentrum, 1993); Carl R. Trueman, "A Small Step Towards Rationalism: The Impact of the Metaphysics of Tommaso Campanella on the Theology of Richard Baxter," in *Protestant Scholasticism: Essays in Reassessment*, ed. Carl R. Trueman and R. Scott Clark (Carlisle: Paternoster, 1999), 181–95; and Simon J. G. Burton, *The Hallowing of Logic: The Trinitarian Method of Richard Baxter's Methodus Theologiae* (Leiden: Brill, 2012).

5. Dewey D. Wallace, *Shapers of English Calvinism, 1660–1714* (Oxford: Oxford University Press, 2011), 177. Baxter's *Methodus theologiae* does not appear in the bibliography.

6. *Rel. Bax.*, III.190. Cf. *CD*, fol. A2r.

7. *MT*, I.79–123. Cf. Burton, *Hallowing of Logic*, 201–52. This is the best treatment of Baxter's scholastic theology.

8. Except for Trueman, "Small Step," 181–95; Burton, *Hallowing of Logic*, 95–200.

9. *Rel. Bax.*, III.190.

10. Frederick J. Powicke, *The Reverend Richard Baxter under the Cross (1662–1691)* (London: Jonathan Cape, 1927), 253, also 62–64. Cf. Hugh Martin, *Puritanism and Richard Baxter* (London: SCM Press, 1954), 128; James McJunkin Phillips, "Between Conscience and the Law: The Ethics of Richard Baxter (1615–1691)" (PhD diss., Princeton University, 1958), 106; Packer, *Redemption*, 85. Baxter's *Catholick Theologie* and *Methodus theologiae* are not mentioned in Geoffrey F. Nuttall, *Richard Baxter* (Stanford, CA: Stanford University Press, 1965).

of Baxter's scholastic theology, cannot withstand historical scrutiny. Baxter's *Methodus theologiae* was cited by theologians from both the British Isles and the Continent well into the eighteenth century.[11] The *Methodus theologiae* was also used at many nonconformist academies, where tutors and students, in the estimation of Herbert McLachlan, "both read and admired it."[12] Among the tutors known to have used the *Methodus theologiae* are John Woodhouse (c. 1627–1700), John Ker (c. 1639–1713), Thomas Doolittle (1630/1633–1707), Benjamin Robinson (1666–1724), and Stephen James (c. 1676–1725).[13] The *Methodus theologiae* is also listed in a

---

11. Thomas Doolittle, *The Lord's Last-Sufferings Shewed in the Lords Supper* (London: John Dunton, 1682), fol. C3v; Willem Salden, *Otia theologica* (Amsterdam: H. & T. Boom, 1684), 373, 480; Willem Salden, *De libris, varioque eorum usu et abusu libri duo* (Amsterdam: H. & T. Boom, 1688), 328–29; Paul Anton, *De autoritate ecclesiae, qua mater est, positiones theologicae* (Leipzig: Christopher Gunther, 1690), §LIX (E2r); Timothy Manlove, *The Immortality of the Soul Asserted and Practically Improved* (London: R. Roberts, 1697), 9, 108, 116–17; Vincent Alsop, *A Vindication of the Faithful Rebuke to a False Report* (London: John Lawrence, 1698), 147; Thomas Edwards, *The Paraselene Dismantled of her Cloud. Or, Baxterianism Barefac'd* (London: Will. Marshal, 1699), passim; Thomas Gipps, *Tentamen novum continuatum* (London: Tho. Warren, 1699), 55; Daniel Williams, *An End to Discord* (London: John Lawrence and Tho. Cockeril, 1699), 67–68; Samuel Clifford, *An Account of the Judgment of the Late Reverend Mr. Baxter* (London: John Lawrence, 1701), 8; Friedrich Ernst Kettner, *Exercitationes historico-theologicae de religione prudentum* ([Jenae]: Bielke, 1701), 23; Stephen Nye, *The Doctrine of the Holy Trinity, and the Manner of our Saviour's Divinity* (London: Andrew Bell, 1701), 19; Nye, *Institutions, Concerning the Holy Trinity, and the Manner of our Saviour's Divinity* (London: J. Nutt, 1703), 6; Nye, *The Explication of the Articles of the Divine Unity, the Trinity, and Incarnation* (London: John Darby, 1703), 12–13, 86–87, 93, 162; Edmund Elys, *Animadversiones in aliqua C. Jansenii, Guillielmi Twissi, Richardi Baxteri, et Gerardi de Vries, dogmata* (London: E. P., 1706), 27–29; Barthold Holzfus, *Dissertatio theologica, de libero hominis arbitrio . . . praeside Bartholdo Holtzfus* (Frankfurt: Christopher Zeitler, 1707), 9, 16, 23–24; John Maxwell, *A Discourse Concerning God* (London: W. Taylor, 1715), 41; Johan Henrich Reitz, *Historie der Wiedergebohrnen*, vol. 3 ([Itzstein]: [Haug], 1717), 78, 87, 89, 91, 94, 96; William Staunton, *An Epistolary Conference with the Reverend Dr. Waterland*, 2nd ed. (London: E. Curll, 1724), 31; Isaac Watts, *Dissertations Relating to the Christian Doctrine of the Trinity, The Second Part* (London: J. Clark and R. Hett, 1725), 66–67, 103–4; Francis Iredell, *Remarks upon some Passages* (Dublin: S. Powell, 1726), 25; John Anderson, *A Dialogue between a Curat and a Country-Man* (Edinburgh, 1728), 14; John Enty, *A Preservative Against Several Abuses and Corruptions of Reveal'd Religion* (Exon: Andrew Brice, 1730), 95–96; John Brine, *A Vindication of some Truths of Natural and Revealed Religion* (London: Aaron Ward, 1746), 307, 328–29, 351, 354, 355, 359; Daniel Williams, *Discourses on Several Important Subjects* (London: James Waugh, 1750), 5:79–82; John Fletcher, *A Vindication of the Rev. Mr. Wesley's Last Minutes* (Bristol: W. Pine, 1771), 78–79.

12. Herbert McLachlan, *English Education under the Test Acts: Being the History of the Nonconformist Academies 1662–1820* (Manchester: Manchester University Press, 1931), 303.

13. Mark Burden, "Academical Learning in the Dissenters' Private Academies" (PhD diss., University of London, 2012), 232–33, 238–39; Burden, "A Biographical Dictionary of Tutors at the Dissenters' Private Academies, 1660–1729" (London: Dr. Williams's Centre for Dissenting Studies, 2013), 290, 536, http://www.qmulreligionandliterature.co.uk/wp-content/uploads/2015/11/bd.pdf; McLachlan, *English Education*, 46–47, 88, 303; [Benjamin Robinson], *A Plea for the Late Accurate and Excellent Mr. Baxter* (London: J[ohn] Lawrence,

catalogue of books used under Richard Frankland (1630–1698), who trained at least three hundred students.[14] The numerous students who possibly came into contact with Baxter's works would have been impressed not only by his practical works, but also his works of a scholastic and theoretical nature. Doolittle recommended Baxter's *Reasons of the Christian Religion, Catholick Theologie,* and *Methodus theologiae* to his students at the private academy in Islington, where "near thirty pupils" were being instructed at one time in the early 1680s.[15] There is a strong likelihood that these books were read by Doolittle's most famous student, Matthew Henry (1662–1714), who attended Doolittle's academy with the commendation of Baxter.[16] In 1690, eleven students from Ker's academy at Bethnal Green, where Baxter's *Methodus theologiae* was in use, signed a letter to Baxter praising him as the "most sought after supporter of doctrine" (*exquisitissimus doctrinae cultor*) and "patron and pattern of piety" (*pietatis fautor et exemplar*).[17]

To a great extent, the neglect of Baxter's scholastic theology and philosophical thought can be attributed to the practical focus in the eighteenth- and nineteenth-century nonconformist reception of Baxter's works, resulting in part from the publication of *The Practical Works* (1707) and in part from a general transition away from older scholastic theology.[18] Philip Doddridge (1702–1751), one of the most influential nonconformists of the eighteenth century, found his heart strangely warmed by the "devotion, good sense, and pathos" of *The Practical Works*.[19] At the same time, Doddridge described Baxter's *Methodus theologiae* as "unintelligible,"[20] thereby registering not only a decline of interest in Baxter's

1699), 3–11, 73, 108–10, 120, 123. The authorship of Robinson's work was noted by John Cumming, *A Funeral Sermon on Occasion of the Death of the Late Reverend and Learned Mr. Benjamin Robinson* (London: John Clark, 1724), 52; and Edmund Calamy, *An Historical Account of My Own Life,* ed. John Towill Rutt (London: Henry Colburn, 1830), 1:397.

14. McLachlan, *English Education,* 68. Cf. See Burden, "A Biographical Dictionary," 195.

15. Burden, "Academical Learning," 72, 236–38.

16. Burden, "Academical Learning," 273–74; Burden, "A Biographical Dictionary," 143.

17. [Students at Bethnal Green] to Baxter, 26 Sept. 1690, in *CCRB,* 2:306–7 (no. 1212).

18. Richard Baxter, *The Practical Works,* 4 vols. (London: Thomas Parkhurst, 1707). Cf. Trueman, "Small Step," 185.

19. Philip Doddridge, *The Correspondence and Diary of Philip Doddridge,* ed. J. D. Humphreys (London: Henry Colburn & Richard Bentley, 1829–1831), 1:378 (5 May 1724); cf. 1:345 (3 Mar. 1724), 368 (13 Apr. 1724), 426–27 (22 Oct. 1724), 460 (8 Dec. 1724), 2:58 (5 Aug. 1725), 3:9, 5:275, 282, 291, 293, 296, 298, 306, 320 (1 Jan. 1732).

20. Doddridge, *Correspondence,* 1:397 (29 May 1724). On Doddridge's reception of Baxter, see Geoffrey F. Nuttall, *Richard Baxter and Philip Doddridge: A Study in a Tradition* (London: Oxford University Press, 1951), 17–19; and Robert Strivens, *Philip Doddridge and the Shaping of Evangelical Dissent* (Farnham: Ashgate, 2015).

scholastic theology, but also an important theological and philosophical shift in early eighteenth-century nonconformity. Doddridge regarded himself as in some sense a Baxterian and "in all the most important points, a Calvinist," but his relation to Baxter's theology was in fact highly eclectic.[21] In contrast to the earlier tutors who used and recommended Baxter's *Methodus theologiae*, the work made no noticeable impact on Doddridge's mature *Course of Lectures*. Both Doddridge and Baxter interacted heavily with philosophy, particularly on the nature of the soul, but Doddridge took as his point of departure Cartesian and Lockean philosophy.[22]

Doddridge's practical bias toward Baxter's works was shared and perpetuated into the nineteenth and twentieth centuries by his disciples and other nonconformists.[23] Benjamin Fawcett, who has been called "a favourite pupil of Dr. Doddridge,"[24] produced a wildly successful abridgement of Baxter's *The Saints Everlasting Rest* (1759), on which most later editions were based.[25] In this abridgement, Fawcett removed all of Baxter's prefaces, excised sections of the work that were heavily philosophical, and replaced Baxter's extensive marginal apparatus of patristic and scholastic authorities with biblical footnotes.[26] For the multitude of nineteenth- and twentieth-century evangelicals who encountered *The Saints Everlasting Rest* through Fawcett's "mutilated edition,"[27] Baxter appeared as an exclusively biblical thinker, devoid of traditional precedent, and free of philosophical assumptions.

---

21. Strivens, *Philip Doddridge*, 44–45.

22. Philip Doddridge, *A Course of Lectures on the Principle Subjects in Pneumatology, Ethics, and Divinity* (London: J. Buckland, et al., 1763), 1–4. Cf. Strivens, *Philip Doddridge*, 67–82 on Locke.

23. Job Orton, *Memoirs of Life, Character and Writings of the Late Reverend Philip Doddridge, D.D. of Northampton* (Salop: J. Cotton and J. Eddowes, 1766), 26, 63, 257; Andrew Kippis, "Doddridge (Philip)," in *Biographia Britannica*, 2nd ed. (London, 1793), 5:266–315, at 271, 274, 314–15; Samuel Palmer, preface to *The Reformed Pastor; A Discourse on the Pastoral Office*, by Richard Baxter (London: J. Buckland, 1766), vi; Robert Philip, "An Essay on the Genius, Works, and Times of Richard Baxter," in *The Practical Works of Richard Baxter*, ed. Robert Philip (London: George Virtue, 1838), 1:xxi–lx.

24. William Orme, *The Life and Times of Richard Baxter: With a Critical Examination of His Writings* (London: James Duncan, 1830), 1:168.

25. Frederick J. Powicke, "Story and Significance of the Rev. Richard Baxter's 'Saints' Everlasting Rest,'" *Bulletin of the John Rylands Library* 5 (1920): 473–74.

26. Richard Baxter, *The Saints Everlasting Rest*, abridged by Benjamin Fawcett (Salop: J. Cotton and J. Eddowes, 1759). Sections that Fawcett excised include the following: "A Premonition" prefacing the entire work; part 2, chap. 6 ("This Rest tryed by nine Rules in Philosophy or Reason, and found by all to be the most excellent state in general"); the preface to part 2 on the relation between reason and faith; and the entirety of part 2 on the authority of Scripture.

27. Fisher, "Writings of Richard Baxter," 318.

Needless to say, readers of an estimated eighteen thousand copies of the twelve editions of *The Saints Everlasting Rest* that circulated in the seventeenth century encountered a different work, filled with citations to at least 150 authorities, such as Irenaeus, Clement of Alexandria, Athanasius, Augustine, Aquinas, Scotus, and Bradwardine.[28]

William Orme, who edited a new edition of the *Practical Works* (1830), formed a more balanced evaluation of Baxter's systematic and metaphysical thought than Doddridge, even while perpetuating a practical bias. Unlike Doddridge, Orme did not find Baxter's *Methodus theologiae* to be "unintelligible" but rather as displaying "considerable ingenuity and vast labour." On the one hand, Orme described Baxter's *Methodus theologiae* as containing much that is "fanciful and hypothetical ... and, taken as a whole, it is more calculated to amuse as a curious speculation or effort of genius, than to answer any important practical purpose."[29] On the other hand, Orme judged Baxter's *Methodus theologiae* to be a work of genius. He declared,

> The work shows that the author is entitled to rank high among the metaphysico-theological writers of the period.... Whatever may be thought of his opinions, Baxter, in point of genius, as a metaphysician, is not unworthy of a place on the same roll with Cudworth, and Leibnitz, and Clarke; and is unquestionably superior to Bramhall and Tenison, Wilkins, Cumberland, and More.[30]

Despite this praise, Orme still followed Doddridge in encouraging his readers to read Baxter's works through the prism of his practical writings,[31] while avoiding those aspects of his works that he deemed "disputatious," "scholastic," and "metaphysical."[32] Orme revised Baxter's practical works in a new edition, which excluded the *Methodus theologiae* and *Catholick Theologie*.[33] If Fawcett's abridgement perpetuated Baxter's Pietist reputation for a popular audience, Orme's

---

28. Powicke, "Story and Significance," 468. Given no less than 1,500 copies per edition, Powicke estimated "a circulation of 18,000 copies for the twelve editions" (470).

29. Orme, *Life*, 2:70–71.

30. Orme, *Life*, 2:71.

31. Orme, *Life*, 2:82. Of Doddridge, Orme wrote, "Few men were capable of forming a better or more candid opinion of Baxter than Dr. Doddridge" (Orme, *Life*, 2:448).

32. Orme, *Life*, 2:84.

33. Richard Baxter, *The Practical Works of Richard Baxter*, ed. William Orme, 23 vols. (London: James Duncan, 1830).

biography and edition of Baxter's practical works had a similar effect on the scholarly world.[34]

A bias toward Baxter's practical thought is less evident among historians of philosophy and science. Historians of seventeenth-century philosophy generally have paid more attention to theological context than historians of theology have paid to philosophical context.[35] This is also true of studies on Baxter. Long ago, Baxter was recognized as an early critic of Herbert of Cherbury's *De Veritate*.[36] In the twentieth century, Baxter has been interpreted both as a protagonist and antagonist to the rise of early modern science. In his influential thesis arguing for the Puritan origins of early modern science, Robert Merton followed Max Weber in utilizing Baxter's *Christian Directory* as "a typical presentation of the leading elements in the Puritan ethos."[37] In contrast to Merton, others have noted Baxter's negative response to mechanical philosophy and his place as one of the earliest contributors to the controversial literature at the beginning of the Royal Society.[38]

---

34. See, e.g., Stoeffler, *Rise of Evangelical Pietism*, 88–96, who relied on Orme's biography.

35. Richard A. Muller, "Thomas Barlow on the Liabilities of 'New Philosophy'. Perceptions of a Rebellious *Ancilla* in the Era of Protestant Orthodoxy," in *Scholasticism Reformed: Essays in Honour of Willem J. van Asselt*, ed. Maarten Wisse, Marcel Sarot, and Willemien Otten (Leiden: Brill, 2010), 179–95, at 179.

36. Charles de Rémusat, *Histoire de la philosophie en Angleterre depuis Bacon jusqu'à Locke*, 2nd ed. (Paris: Didier et cie, 1875), 1:371–89. More recently, see Richard Serjeanston, "Herbert of Cherbury before Deism: The Early Reception of the *De veritate*," *The Seventeenth Century* 16, no. 2 (2001): 217–38.

37. Robert K. Merton, "Science, Technology and Society in Seventeenth Century England," *Osiris* 4 (1938): 360–632, at 418–19. This foundational monograph-length article was later reprinted with a new preface as *Science, Technology & Society in Seventeenth Century England* (New York: Harper & Row, 1970). Cf. Max Weber, *The Protestant Ethic and the Spirit of Capitalism*, trans. Talcott Parsons (New York: Charles Scribner's Sons, 1958), 155–83, which draws heavily on Baxter's *Christian Directory* (cf. 224–25n30, 229n47, 236n84, etc.). Merton's reading of Baxter was followed by John Dillenberger, *Protestant Thought and Natural Science* (Garden City, NY: Doubleday, 1960), 129–30, 132, among others. For an introduction to this literature, see John Henry, "The Scientific Revolution in England," in *The Scientific Revolutions in National Context*, ed. Roy Porter and Mikuláš Teich (Cambridge: Cambridge University Press, 1992), 178–209; and Joseph W. Dauben, "Merton Thesis," in *Reader's Guide to the History of Science*, ed. Arne Hessenbruch (Chicago: Fitzroy Dearborn, 2000), 469–71.

38. Richard Foster Jones, *Ancients and Moderns: A Study of the Rise of the Scientific Movement in Seventeenth-Century England*, 2nd ed. (St. Louis: Washington University, 1961), 229, 322–23n2; Richard S. Westfall, *Science and Religion in Seventeenth-Century England* (New Haven, CT: Yale University Press, 1958), 22; Michael R. G. Spiller, *"Concerning Natural Experimental Philosophie": Meric Casaubon and the Royal Society* (The Hague: Martinus Nijhoff, 1980), 23–25; Spiller, "Die Opposition gegen die Royal Society," in *Die Philosophie des 17. Jahrhunderts*, ed. Jean-Pierre Schobinger (Basel: Schwabe, 1988), vol. 3, bk. 2, *England*, 444; Howard Jones, *The Epicurean Tradition* (London: Routledge, 1980), 206–7; Michael Hunter, *Science and Society in Restoration England* (Cambridge: Cambridge University Press, 1981), 173–74; B. C. Southgate, "'Forgotten and Lost': Some Reactions to Autonomous

Baxter's polemical correspondence with Henry More is now taken seriously for illustrating the importance not only of differing theological assumptions for philosophy, but also for the significance of medical philosophy, including vitalist matter theories, in philosophical and theological debate.[39]

Despite the importance attributed to Baxter by these studies, he remains underappreciated in the wider literature on the early Enlightenment.[40] In this respect, he has shared a similar fate as other early modern theologians and philosophers deemed "outsiders" from a modern canonical standpoint.[41] English theologians such as Thomas Barlow, Edward Stillingfleet, and John Howe, or philosophers such as Alexander Ross, Sir Kenelm Digby, and Theophilus Gale, although famous in their own day for their learning, have been "barely mentioned or dismissed as less than cognizant of the demands of modernity, whether scientific or cultural."[42] Yet an accurate historical assessment of theological and philosophical change requires attention to such figures, who provide a valuable contemporary index by which to evaluate both controversial figures and ideas. Among seventeenth-century theologians concerned with the impact that new philosophy would have on theology, Baxter deserves special attention for a number of reasons.

Science in the Seventeenth Century," *Journal of the History of Ideas* 50, no. 2 (1989): 258–60, 262–63; Richard W. F. Kroll, *The Material Word: Literate Culture in the Restoration and Early Eighteenth Century* (Baltimore: The Johns Hopkins University Press, 1991), 46–47, 96, 125; and Jon Parkin, *Science, Religion and Politics in Restoration England: Richard Cumberland's* De legibus naturae (Woodbridge: The Boydell Press, 1999), 123–27.

39. John Henry, "Medicine and Pneumatology: Henry More, Richard Baxter, and Francis Glisson's *Treatise on the Energetic Nature of Substance*," *Medical History* 31 (1987): 15–42, at 17. See also John Henry, "A Cambridge Platonist's Materialism: Henry More and the Concept of Soul," *Journal of the Warburg and Courtauld Institutes* 49 (1986): 172–95, at 183–89; and John Henry, "The Matter of Souls: Medical Theory and Theology in Seventeenth-Century England," in *The Medical Revolution of the Seventeenth Century*, ed. Roger French and Andrew Wear (Cambridge: Cambridge University Press, 1989), 87–113, at 93, 109–110.

40. Baxter is not mentioned in Jonathan I. Israel, *Radical Enlightenment: Philosophy and the Making of Modernity, 1650–1750* (Oxford: Oxford University Press, 2001); Jonathan I. Israel, *Enlightenment Contested: Philosophy, Modernity, and the Emancipation of Man 1670–1752* (Oxford: Oxford University Press, 2006).

41. Cf. G. A. J. Rogers, Tom Sorell, and Jill Kraye, eds., *Insiders and Outsiders in Seventeenth-Century Philosophy* (New York: Routledge, 2010).

42. Muller, "Thomas Barlow," 179. On Stillingfleet and Howe, see Richard H. Popkin, "The Philosophy of Bishop Stillingfleet," *Journal of the History of Philosophy* 9, no. 3 (1971): 303–19; Sarah Hutton, "Edward Stillingfleet and Spinoza," in *Disguised and Overt Spinozism around 1700*, ed. Wiep van Bunge and Wim Klever (Leiden: E. J. Brill, 1996), 261–74; Reita Yazawa, "John Howe on Divine Simplicity: A Debate Over Spinozism," in *Church and School in Early Modern Protestantism: Studies in Honor of Richard A. Muller on the Maturation of a Theological Tradition*, ed. Jordan J. Ballor, David S. Sytsma, and Jason Zuidema (Leiden: Brill, 2013), 629–40. On Digby and Gale, see Rogers et al., eds., *Insiders and Outsiders*.

Along with John Owen, Baxter was one of the most famous and influential Puritans of the second half of the seventeenth century. At the Restoration, Baxter was offered the bishopric of Hereford, and although he declined it, he exercised a comparable spiritual leadership among the nonconformists. Shortly after Baxter's death, Stephen Nye wrote somewhat hyperbolically, "[Baxter] found himself *Archbishop* of a whole Party, and therefore (I think) cared not to be *Bishop* only of a *Diocess.*"[43] This reputation is well deserved, for Baxter was easily the most prolific Puritan of the seventeenth century.[44] In just over forty years, he published at least 135 works and left behind a mass of manuscripts for posterity. His unpublished correspondence alone fills six folio volumes of manuscripts, while his various other unpublished tracts and treatises fill some twenty-two volumes.[45]

Due to his prominent place in the history of Puritanism and nonconformity, Baxter is also one of the most important figures to consider (as Merton recognized long ago) on the larger question of the relation of Puritanism to the rise of modern science.[46] Beginning in the 1680s, some tutors at nonconformist academies started to incorporate Cartesian logic and physics alongside an Aristotelian course of study, and by the early eighteenth century many (though not all) tutors were adopting Lockean and Newtonian philosophy.[47] At the same time, Baxter's works were well read at dissenting academies until the beginning of the eighteenth century. As such, Baxter's thoughts on philosophy provide a point of comparison by which change within Puritanism and nonconformity can be evaluated in a more historically accurate way.

Furthermore, despite his lack of university training, as an autodidact Baxter was unusually well read by comparison with contemporary Puritans. Baxter himself remarked that in his youth, "in order to the Knowledge of *Divinity* my inclination was most to *Logick* and *Metaphysicks*, with that part *Physicks* which treateth of

---

43. Nye, *Explication of the Articles*, 86.

44. Cf. Orme, *Life*, 2:466: "Baxter was beyond comparison the most voluminous of all his contemporaries."

45. A list of his published works is found in N. H. Keeble, *Richard Baxter: Puritan Man of Letters* (Oxford: Clarendon Press, 1982), 157–69. For manuscripts, see *CCRB*; and Roger Thomas, *The Baxter Treatises: A Catalogue of the Richard Baxter Papers (Other than the Letters) in Dr. Williams's Library*, Dr. Williams's Library Occasional Paper 8 (London: Dr. Williams's Trust, 1959).

46. Merton, "Science, Technology and Society," 418–19.

47. Burden, "Academical Learning," 144–93; David L. Wykes, "The Contribution of the Dissenting Academy to the Emergence of Rational Dissent," in *Enlightenment and Religion: Rational Dissent in Eighteenth-Century Britain*, ed. Knud Haakonssen (Cambridge: Cambridge University Press, 1996), 99–139, at 111–21; Alan P. F. Sell, *Philosophy, Dissent and Nonconformity* (Cambridge: James Clarke & Co, 2004), ch. 2; Strivens, *Philip Doddridge*, ch. 3.

the Soul, contenting my self at first with a slighter study of the rest: And these had my *Labour* and *Delight*." This led him "to read all the School men I could get; (for next *Practical Divinity*, no Books so suited with my Disposition as *Aquinus, Scotus, Durandus, Ockam,* and their Disciples."[48] Despite downplaying the relative importance of such scholastic learning in comparison to the essentials of catechetical doctrine,[49] Baxter consistently employed such a wide array of scholastic authors and distinctions that readers of his works from the seventeenth century to the present have expressed admiration for his erudition. In 1654, the elderly Puritan scholar Thomas Gataker (1574–1654), whose own works were praised "for the rare extraction of all manner of knowledge from almost all Authors,"[50] remarked to Baxter, "Sir, I stand amazed, when I consider, how amids such continual infirmities & pains as you complain of, you should be <able> to <read> so manie (Autors that I never heard of but by reading of them in your works) & write so much as you have done, & do stil."[51] Recently, Baxter's knowledge of the medieval scholastics has been called "remarkable, possibly second to no other Protestant in the seventeenth century."[52] According to his biographer, "though lacking in formal qualifications and without the benefit of educational supervision, through omnivorous reading Baxter became one of the most learned of seventeenth-century divines."[53]

Baxter not only read widely in medieval and early modern scholasticism; he also kept current with new philosophical trends. The remains of his personal library of some 1,400 books (representing only a fraction of his acquisitions) and the books recommended in his *Christian Directory* demonstrate familiarity with a broad range of modern authors on logic, physics, metaphysics, the soul, and anatomy.[54] His knowledge extended beyond familiar names to include a host of less familiar works (still rarely studied today), such as Honoré Fabri's *Tractatus physicus de motu locali* (1646), Jean-François Le Grand's *Dissertationes philosophicae et criticae* (1657), and Samuel Parker's *Tentamina de Deo* (1665).[55] Moreover, Baxter acquired his

---

48. *Rel. Bax.*, I.6. Cf. *Rel. Bax.*, I.126; *TKL*, 9.

49. See, e.g., *Rel. Bax.*, I.126.

50. Simeon Ashe, "The Narrative of the Life and Death of Mr Gataker," in *Gray Hayres Crowned with Grace* (London: A. M., 1655), 55.

51. Gataker to Baxter, 1 Mar. 1654, cited in *CCRB*, 1:129–30 (no. 166).

52. Trueman, "Small Step," 184.

53. N. H. Keeble, "Richard Baxter," in *ODNB*.

54. Geoffrey F. Nuttall, "A Transcript of Richard Baxter's Library Catalogue: A Bibliographical Note," *Journal of Ecclesiastical History* 2, no. 2 (1951): 207–21 and 3, no. 1 (1952): 74–100; *CD*, III.195, 198 (q. 173).

55. *RCR*, 516 (Le Grand), 519 (Fabri, cited as Mousnerius), 579 (Parker). Fabri is discussed in chapter 5 below. On the complete neglect of Parker's *Tentamina*, see Dmitri Levitin,

knowledge rapidly, often responding to new works within a year of publication. He was corresponding about Hobbes's *Leviathan* (1651) by February of 1652. As Baxter communicated to Robert Boyle, he had read Boyle's *Some Considerations Touching the Usefulness of Experimental Naturall Philosophy* (1663) and *Occasional Reflections* (1665) in June of 1665.[56] He was also writing about John Wallis's *Mechanica* (1670) and Henry More's *Enchiridion metaphysicum* (1671) around 1671–1672, Spinoza's *Tractatus theologico-politicus* (1670), and Thomas Willis's *De anima brutorum* (1672) in 1672, and Francis Glisson's *De natura substantiae energetica* (1672) and Robert Boyle's *Essays of the Strange Subtilty, Great Efficacy, Determinate Nature of Effluviums* (1673) in 1673.[57] Early in his career, while confessing to a youthful infatuation with philosophy, Baxter declared, "I love philosophy lesse & Scr[ipture] more, y^n ev[er] I did."[58] If Baxter's subsequent rapid acquisition of philosophical knowledge represents diminished love for philosophy, his love for Scripture must have been great indeed!

Baxter was also both well placed and well connected in relation to individuals involved with new philosophical trends. With a life spanning most of the seventeenth century (1615–1691), Baxter lived through the decline of Aristotelian philosophy and the rise of mechanical philosophy. At the Restoration in 1660, he moved to London just as English scientific circles were coalescing around the foundation of the Royal Society in London (Nov. 1660–1663). Baxter's correspondents included Robert Boyle, John Beale, Henry More, Joseph Glanvill, Edward Stillingfleet, and Matthew Hale. He developed a close relationship with Hale, with whom he carried on conversations about philosophy and exchanged manuscripts on the nature of the soul.[59] Baxter remained engaged with others about philosophy to the end of his life. In the early 1680s, he reported, "I have met lately with University-men, that cry'd up *Cartesius* as if they had been quite above *Aristotle* and *Plato*; and when I tryed them, I found that they knew not what *Aristotle* or *Plato* said (nor what *Cartesius* neither.)"[60] Around the same time, Baxter told More, "I

"Rethinking English Physico-theology: Samuel Parker's *Tentamina de Deo* (1665)," *Early Science and Medicine* 19 (2014): 28–75, at 30.

56. *CCRB*, 1:74 (Hobbes); Baxter to Boyle, 14 June 1665, in Robert Boyle, *The Correspondence of Robert Boyle*, ed. Michael Hunter and Antonio Clericuzio (Burlington, VT: Pickering & Chatto, 2001), 2:473; *CCRB*, 2:43–45.

57. DWL BT XIX.351, fols. 125r–143r (Willis), 143v (More); LPL MS 3499, fols. 92v, 100v, 105v (Glisson), 96v (Boyle); *CD*, III.923 (Wallis), 925 (More); *TKL*, 20, 28 (Glisson), 47, 66 (Spinoza). For dates of these works, see Appendix A.

58. Baxter to Thomas Hill, 8 Mar. 1652 (DWL BC III.272v).

59. See chapter 2 below.

60. Richard Baxter, *Catholick Communion Defended against both Extreams* (London: Tho. Parkhurst, 1684), 15.

have talkt with divers high pretenders to Philosophy here of the new strain, and askt them their judgment of Dr Glissons Book [*Tractatus de natura substantiae energetica* (1672)], and I found that none of them understood it, but neglected it as too hard for them and yet contemned it."[61]

Finally and most importantly, while other major Puritan theologians of his generation such as John Owen remained largely silent about philosophical transition, Baxter directly addressed ideas of the most influential and controversial mechanical philosophers of the seventeenth century, including René Descartes, Pierre Gassendi, Robert Boyle, Thomas Hobbes, and Benedict de Spinoza. Mechanical philosophy was the most successful anti-Aristotelian natural philosophy in the seventeenth century—ultimately winning out over other alternatives to Christian Aristotelian philosophy such as chymical philosophy and Italian naturalism.[62] Although a transhistorical definition of mechanical philosophy still eludes consensus and is fraught with difficulties,[63] when the term was first popularized in the 1660s by Robert Boyle (and so understood by Baxter), he used it synonymously with "corpuscular" philosophy to describe the ideal shared by the major parties, Cartesians and atomists, "in deducing all the Phaenomena of Nature from Matter and local Motion" (rather than the substantial forms and qualities of scholastic Aristotelian philosophy). Because "Motion and other Affections of the minute Particles of Matter" are "obvious and very powerfull in Mechanical Engines," wrote Boyle, "I sometimes also term it the Mechanical Hypothesis or

---

61. Richard Baxter, *Of the Nature of Spirits; Especially Mans Soul. In a Placid Collation with the Learned Dr. Henry More* (London: B. Simmons, 1682), 6. John Henry sees this remark as indicative of a wider trend "that mechanical philosophers—particularly the less serious minded of them—were constitutionally unable to understand the older ways of philosophizing" (Henry, "Matter of Souls," 93n17).

62. Daniel Garber, "Physics and Foundations," in *The Cambridge History of Science*, ed. Katherine Park and Lorraine Daston, vol. 3, *Early Modern Science* (Cambridge: Cambridge University Press, 2006), 21–69.

63. William R. Newman, *Atoms and Alchemy: Chymistry and the Experimental Origins of the Scientific Revolution* (Chicago: University of Chicago Press, 2006), 175–80. For recent discussion, see Daniel Garber, "Remarks on the Pre-history of the Mechanical Philosophy," in *The Mechanization of Natural Philosophy*, ed. Daniel Garber and Sophie Roux (Dordrecht: Springer, 2013), 3–26; and Alan Gabbey, "What Was 'Mechanical' about 'The Mechanical Philosophy'?," in *The Reception of the Galilean Science of Motion in Seventeenth-Century Europe*, ed. Carla Rita Palmerino and J. M. M. H. Thijssen (Springer: Kluwer Academic, 2004), 11–23. Most scholars have viewed Newton as moving beyond mechanical philosophy, since he incorporates action at a distance, but there are also good arguments for continuity, on which see Hylarie Kochiras, "The Mechanical Philosophy and Newton's Mechanical Force," *Philosophy of Science* 80, no. 4 (2013): 557–78; and Peter Hans Reill, "The Legacy of the 'Scientific Revolution': Science and the Enlightenment," in *The Cambridge History of Science*, vol. 4, *The Eighteenth Century*, ed. Roy Porter (Cambridge: Cambridge University Press, 2003), 23–43, at 26–28.

Philosophy."[64] Thus, as Boyle used the term mechanical philosophy, it denoted the explanatory reduction of nature to material particles characterized by size, shape, local motion, and texture (ordering of the parts), and the use of mechanical devices such as clocks and levers as analogues for understanding nature.[65]

Some scholars have argued that Gassendi and Boyle were not strictly mechanical since they retained explanations involving seminal and chymical powers.[66] Against this, William R. Newman has countered that Boyle himself "spent the better part of his life trying to justify a set of scientific beliefs that he himself dubbed 'the mechanical philosophy,'" so that such terminological revisionism is historically unwarranted and reveals an implicit Cartesian bias.[67] Moreover, Boyle described the powers of aggregate material particles as "mechanical affections" or "textures," so that his understanding of mechanical philosophy includes compound corpuscles that admit of intermediate chymical explanations.[68] Others have persuasively argued that various mechanical philosophers, including Boyle and Robert Hooke, retained traditional terminology such as "occult qualities" and "seminal principles," while replacing Aristotelian explanations of such qualities and principles with alternative mechanical explanations. Accordingly, the retention of traditional terminology was entirely compatible with profound theoretical change.[69] It should also be observed that Gassendi himself said of his *semina* that "each one of them is a little machine [*machinula*] within which are enclosed in a way incomprehensible almost innumerable [other] little machines [*machinulae*], each with its own little motions."[70] Gassendi's willingness to refer to life as

---

64. Robert Boyle, Preface to "Some Specimens of an Attempt to make Chymical Experiments Usefull to Illustrate the Notions of the Corpuscular Philosophy," in *Certain Physiological Essays* (London: Henry Herringman, 1661), fol. P4v.

65. Peter R. Anstey, *The Philosophy of Robert Boyle* (New York: Routledge, 2000), 1–4; Newman, *Atoms and Alchemy*, 181–89.

66. See especially Antonio Clericuzio, "A Redefinition of Boyle's Chemistry and Corpuscular Philosophy," *Annals of Science* 47 (1990): 561–89; Clericuzio, *Elements, Principles and Corpuscles: A Study of Atomism and Chemistry in the Seventeenth Century* (Dordrecht: Kluwer Academic, 2000), 63–71, 103–48.

67. Newman, *Atoms and Alchemy*, 175–89, at 178.

68. Newman, *Atoms and Alchemy*, 180–89.

69. Peter R. Anstey, "Boyle on Seminal Principles," *Studies in History and Philosophy of Science* 33 (2002): 597–630; Anstey, *Philosophy of Robert Boyle*, 21–24; Mark E. Ehrlich, "Mechanism and Activity in the Scientific Revolution: The Case of Robert Hooke," *Annals of Science* 52, no. 2 (1995): 127–51; Cees Leijenhorst, *The Mechanisation of Aristotelianism: The Late Aristotelian Setting of Thomas Hobbes' Natural Philosophy* (Leiden: Brill, 2002), 2–3, et passim.

70. Pierre Gassendi, *Opera omnia* (Lyon: Laurentius Anisson & Joan. Bapt. Devenet, 1658), 2:267a, with trans. in Howard B. Adelmann, *Marcello Malpighi and the Evolution of*

a complex of "little machines" ought to caution us from overly rigid definitions of mechanical philosophy that would exclude Gassendi's active atoms and seeds as imperfectly mechanical. This study will refer to mechanical philosophy in the historically warranted sense given by Boyle, broadly inclusive of Gassendi and Descartes, with the ideal of replacing Aristotelian forms and qualities with alternative reductionist explanations.

The introduction of a philosophy that aimed to reduce "all the Phaenomena of Nature," as Boyle put it, to mechanical explanation at the expense of Aristotelian forms and powers naturally raised serious concerns for theologians whose discipline used concepts of substance and causality. When Cartesian philosophy arose in the Netherlands, some of the most important debates surrounded conceptions of substance, secondary causality, and the soul.[71] Baxter was certainly concerned with similar issues. Yet although Baxter agreed with his Reformed brethren in the Netherlands on the largely problematic nature of Descartes's philosophy, particularly his laws of motion, Baxter showed a relatively greater concern with Gassendi's Christian Epicurean philosophy, particularly as it pertained to the nature and immortality of the soul. Thus, Baxter illustrates the relatively greater importance of Gassendi and Christian Epicureanism in England by comparison with the Dutch Reformed response to Cartesianism.

As will be shown in the present book, for Baxter the chief problem of mechanical philosophy involved the reduction of motion to local motion and the corresponding evacuation of intrinsic principles of motion from active natures and principally living forms. Baxter could not accept the reduction of activity in nature to explanations of matter in motion, however complex such explanations might be. This issue framed both his critique of mechanical philosophy and the extent of his willingness to accommodate it within his philosophical theology. The present study identifies three major areas on which Baxter focused his objections to mechanical philosophy: the nature of motion and its relation to God, the nature of the soul and the threat of materialism, and the potentially radical implications for ethics as exemplified by Hobbes and Spinoza. Although Baxter reacted strongly against mechanical philosophy in these areas, his critique was not simply based on a conservative Aristotelian reaction to the new philosophy. Rather, Baxter was attuned to recent experimental discoveries and open to philosophical change at a theoretical level. He developed a highly original Trinitarian natural philosophy as an alternative to the mechanization of the living world. This Trinitarian natural

---

Embryology (Ithaca, NY: Cornell University Press, 1966), 2:806. Cf. Antonia LoLordo, *Pierre Gassendi and the Birth of Early Modern Philosophy* (Cambridge: Cambridge University Press, 2007), 201.

71. Aza Goudriaan, *Reformed Orthodoxy and Philosophy, 1625–1750: Gisbertus Voetius, Petrus van Mastricht, and Anthonius Driessen* (Leiden: Brill, 2006), 113–25, 143–44, 233–59.

philosophy incorporated an eclectic blend of philosophical concepts, and, while drawing on Aristotelian accounts of the soul and its faculties, it also accommodated mechanical and atomist notions. Baxter's response to mechanical philosophy thus represents a targeted critique by a theologian conversant with old and new philosophies.

Baxter's eclectic, yet largely negative, response to mechanical philosophy has implications for various larger theses on the relation of Protestantism—or more narrowly Reformed (Calvinist) and Puritan theological traditions—to the rise of early modern science and philosophy. There are many theses that posit some form of strong link between new philosophy and one of these theological traditions, as if the theology of Protestantism or Puritanism was intrinsically supportive of new philosophy, and in particular mechanical philosophy. One author argues that Protestant Reformers' "radical sovereignty of God" paved the way for mechanical philosophy in that "the Reformers' view of God rendered Aristotelian essentialism pointless by denying that essences contribute causality or purpose to nature."[72] Another similarly states, "[T]he Calvinist God in His remote majesty resembles the watchmaker God of the mechanical universe, suggesting that the Calvinist tenor of English theology helped to make the mechanical hypothesis congenial to English scientists."[73] Others posit a "happy marriage" and "intrinsic compatibility" between "Puritanism and New Philosophy,"[74] or state, "Puritans as a whole felt that the 'new philosophy' was consistent with the reformed Christian faith."[75] Still others argue that "univocal metaphysical assumptions" of Protestants likely contributed to the "disenchanted natural world" brought about by modern science,[76] or likewise, that Protestant literalist hermeneutics "entailed a new,

---

72. Gary B. Deason, "Reformation Theology and the Mechanistic Conception of Nature," in *God and Nature: Historical Essays on the Encounter between Christianity and Science*, ed. David C. Lindberg and Ronald L. Numbers (Berkeley: University of California Press, 1986), 167–91, at 177–78.

73. Westfall, *Science and Religion*, 5.

74. Reijer Hooykaas, *Religion and the Rise of Modern Science* (Edinburgh: Scottish Academic Press, 1972), 143, in agreement with Merton, "Science, Technology and Society," 495.

75. Charles Webster, *The Great Instauration: Science, Medicine and Reform, 1626–1660* (New York: Holmes & Meier, 1976), 498. Similarly, see Perry Miller, *The New England Mind: The Seventeenth Century* (New York: Macmillan, 1939), 217–23; and Perry Miller, *The New England Mind: From Colony to Province* (Cambridge: Harvard University Press, 1953), 437–38; Dillenberger, *Protestant Thought*, 128–32.

76. Brad S. Gregory, *The Unintended Reformation: How a Religious Revolution Secularized Society* (Cambridge, MA: Harvard University Press, 2012), 41. This was suggested by Amos Funkenstein, *Theology and the Scientific Imagination: From the Middle Ages to the Seventeenth Century* (Princeton, NJ: Princeton University Press, 1986), 70–72, on whom Gregory relies (*Unintended Reformation*, 5, 39, 55).

non-symbolic conception of the nature of things," and this loss of symbolism in nature allowed for a "new scheme of things, [where] objects were related mathematically, mechanically, causally, or ordered and classified according to categories other than those of resemblance."[77]

Baxter's critique of mechanical philosophy casts doubt on such sweeping theories. It renders problematic the argument for an intrinsic compatibility between Puritanism and the theoretical direction toward mechanical philosophy taken by the English scientific movement after the Restoration. Here a distinction between empirical and theoretical developments is important. Although it is certainly the case that Baxter, along with many other Puritans, kept an open mind with respect to new experimental discoveries,[78] this should not be confused with a general acceptance of the theoretical underpinnings of mechanical philosophy. Indeed, acceptance of experimental discoveries did not necessarily correlate with the acceptance of mechanical philosophy, as can be seen in the contrast between the discoveries of the earth's magnetism and circulation of the blood, which were made independently of mechanical theories, and the subsequent mechanical explanations given to these discoveries.[79] In response to the above claims, it should be observed that Baxter found the denial of the causal efficacy of secondary formal causes to be among the most problematic aspects of mechanical philosophy, and his retention of the causal efficacy of forms constitutes a point of continuity with John Calvin and the eclectic yet predominately Aristotelian character of Reformed philosophical education that flourished well into the seventeenth century.[80]

---

77. Peter Harrison, *The Bible, Protestantism, and the Rise of Natural Science* (Cambridge: Cambridge University Press, 1998), 114–15.

78. See the discussion of Copernicanism in chapter 5 below.

79. Thomas Fuchs, *The Mechanization of the Heart: Harvey and Descartes*, trans. Marjorie Grene (Rochester, NY: The University of Rochester Press, 2001); Roger French, *William Harvey's Natural Philosophy* (Cambridge: Cambridge University Press, 1994); Robert G. Frank Jr., *Harvey and the Oxford Physiologists* (Berkeley: University of California Press, 1980); Stephen Pumfrey, "Mechanizing Magnetism in Restoration England—the Decline of Magnetic Philosophy," *Annals of Science* 44 (1987): 1–22.

80. See, e.g., John Calvin, *Treatises against the Anabaptists and against the Libertines*, ed. and trans. Benjamin Farley (Grand Rapids, MI: Baker, 1982), 243: "Nevertheless, this universal operation of God's does not prevent each creature, heavenly or earthly, from having and retaining its own quality and nature and from following its own inclination." Contra Deason, "Reformation Theology," 177–78. On Calvin and Aristotelianism, see *PRRD*, 1:365–66; Richard A. Muller, *The Unaccommodated Calvin: Studies in the Formation of a Theological Tradition* (New York: Oxford University Press, 2000), 156–57; Muller, "Scholasticism, Reformation, Orthodoxy, and the Persistence of Christian Aristotelianism," *Trinity Journal* NS 19, no. 1 (1998): 81–96, at 92–93; Christopher Kaiser, "Calvin's Understanding of Aristotelian Natural Philosophy: Its Extent and Possible Origins," in *Calviniana: Ideas and Influence of Jean Calvin*, ed. Robert V. Schnucker (Kirksville, MO: Sixteenth Century Essays and Studies, 1988), 77–92; A. N. S. Lane, introduction to *The Bondage and Liberation*

Baxter also forms a counterexample to the claim that Protestant "univocal metaphysical assumptions" or a Protestant nonsymbolic view of nature contributed to a disenchanted modern world. At least among Reformed theologians, there was widespread rejection of Scotist univocity in favor of a Thomistic doctrine of analogy with respect to the creator-creature relation,[81] and Protestants continued to employ allegory, with many drawing directly on Aquinas's hermeneutics by the end of the sixteenth century.[82] Although Baxter's doctrine of analogy is somewhat more eclectic and he favored Scotus in many respects,[83] he shared with his Reformed contemporaries an analogical understanding of the relation of God and creatures, and this doctrine of analogy forms an important doctrinal component to his objection to mechanical philosophy.[84]

The present study also highlights the highly variegated nature of the response to the new philosophy within the English Reformed tradition, including

---

of the Will: A Defense of the Orthodox Doctrine of Human Choice against Pighius, by John Calvin, ed. A. N. S. Lane, trans. G. I. Davies (Grand Rapids, MI: Baker, 1996), xxiv–xxvi. On Aristotle and the wider Reformed tradition, see *PRRD*, 1:360–82; David S. Sytsma, "'As a Dwarfe set upon a Gyants shoulders': John Weemes (ca. 1579–1636) on the Place of Philosophy and Scholasticism in Reformed Theology," in *Die Philosophie der Reformierten*, ed. Günter Frank and Herman J. Selderhuis (Stuttgart: Frommann-Holzboog, 2012), 299–321, at 303–4; Luca Baschera, "Aristotle and Scholasticism," in *A Companion to Peter Martyr Vermigli*, ed. T. Kirby, E. Campi, and F. A. JamesIII (Leiden: Brill, 2009), 133–59; Donald Sinnema, "Aristotle and Early Reformed Orthodoxy: Moments of Accommodation and Antithesis," in *Christianity and the Classics: The Acceptance of a Heritage*, ed. Wendy Helleman (New York: University Press of America, 1990), 119–48; Joseph Prost, *La philosophie à l'académie protestante de Saumur (1606–1685)* (Paris: Paulin, 1907); M. J. Petry, "Burgersdijk's Physics," in *Franco Burgersdijk (1590–1635): Neo-Aristotelianism in Leiden*, ed. E. P. Bos and H. A. Krop (Amsterdam: Rodopi, 1993), 83–118; Sarah Hutton, "Thomas Jackson, Oxford Platonist, and William Twisse, Aristotelian," *Journal of the History of Ideas* 39, no. 4 (1978): 635–52.

81. Richard A. Muller, "Not Scotist: Understandings of Being, Univocity, and Analogy in Early-Modern Reformed Thought," *Reformation & Renaissance Review* 14, no. 2 (2012): 127–50.

82. Jitse M. van der Meer and Richard J. Oosterhoff, "God, Scripture, and the Rise of Modern Science (1200–1700): Notes in the Margin of Harrison's Hypothesis," in *Nature and Scripture in the Abrahamic Religions: Up to 1700*, ed. Jitse M. van der Meer and Scott Mandelbrote (Leiden: Brill, 2008), 2:363–96; *PRRD*, 2:477–82; David S. Sytsma, "Thomas Aquinas and Reformed Biblical Interpretation: The Contribution of William Whitaker," in *Aquinas among the Protestants*, ed. David VanDrunen and Manfred Svensson (Hoboken: Wiley-Blackwell), forthcoming.

83. Baxter to Thomas Hill, 8 Mar. 1652: "To yo[u]^r Quest[io]^n 'who I like best of Concourse, Contingency, Attributes &c' I answ[er]. None Satisfyeth me: wch I speake in Accusation of my owne Incapacity. I like Scotus well in much. And I thinke Durandus is ofter chidd<en> y^n well confuted" (DWL BC III.272r). On Scotistic aspects, see Burton, *Hallowing of Logic*, 11–12, 275–77, 308, 322, 326, 349–52, 357.

84. See chapters 4 and 5 below.

Puritanism.[85] That the advent of Cartesianism in the Netherlands produced varying reactions among Reformed theologians ranging from strong rejection to enthusiastic adoption is well known.[86] The introduction of the new philosophy in England generated a similar diversity of opinion. On the one side, there were a variety of theologians, especially early Latitudinarians, but also Puritans and Reformed Anglicans, who were intimately involved in the promotion of the new philosophy both during the interregnum and the Restoration.[87] Even though John Wilkins shared characteristics with the Latitudinarians, both he and Robert Boyle, who were among the leaders of the mid-century experimental community and early Royal Society, held distinctly Reformed theological beliefs.[88] On the other side, it was also reported that the introduction of the new philosophy during the interregnum "was as great a bug-beare to the Presbyterians as a Crosse or Surplisse," and that Presbyterians had argued that "*Philosophy* and *Divinity* are so inter-woven by the School-men, that it cannot be safe to separate them; *new Philosophy* will bring in *new Divinity*; and freedom in the one will make men desire a liberty in the other."[89] After the Restoration, a variety of theologians—including the Arminian conformist Peter Gunning, Reformed conformists Robert Crosse, Thomas Barlow,

---

85. On diversity in general, see Richard A. Muller, "Diversity in the Reformed Tradition: A Historiographical Introduction," in *Drawn into Controversie: Reformed Theological Diversity and Debates within Seventeenth-Century British Puritanism*, ed. Michael A. G. Haykin and Mark Jones (Gottingen: Vandenhoeck & Ruprecht, 2011), 11–30.

86. Aza Goudriaan, "Theology and Philosophy," in *A Companion to Reformed Orthodoxy*, ed. Herman J. Selderhuis (Leiden: Brill, 2013), 27–63, at 43–53; Yoshiyuki Kato, "*Deus sive Natura*: The Dutch Controversy over the Radical Concept of God, 1660–1690" (PhD diss., Princeton Theological Seminary, 2013); Theo Verbeek, *Descartes and the Dutch: Early Reactions to Cartesian Philosophy, 1637–1650* (Carbondale: Southern Illinois University Press, 1992); Ernst Bizer, "Die reformierte Orthodoxie und der Cartesianismus," *Zeitschrift für Theologie und Kirche* 55 (1958): 306–72; Bizer, "Reformed Orthodoxy and Cartesianism," trans. Chalmers MacCormick, *Journal for Theology and the Church* 11 (1965): 20–82; Thomas A. McGahagan, "Cartesianism in the Netherlands, 1639–1676: The New Science and the Calvinist Counter Reformation" (PhD diss., University of Pennsylvania, 1976).

87. Latitudinarians are discussed in chapter 2. For others, see Christoph J. Scriba, "The Autobiography of John Wallis," *Notes and Records of the Royal Society* 25 (1970): 17–46; Theodore Hornberger, "Samuel Lee (1625–1691), a Clerical Channel for the Flow of New Ideas to Seventeenth-Century New England," *Osiris* 1 (1936): 341–55; Rick Kennedy, "Thomas Brattle and the Scientific Provincialism of New England, 1680–1713," *New England Quarterly* 63, no. 4 (1990): 584–600; Kennedy, "The Alliance between Puritanism and Cartesian Logic at Harvard, 1687–1735," *Journal of the History of Ideas* 51, no. 4 (1990): 549–72; Arthur Daniel Kaledin, "The Mind of John Leverett" (PhD diss., Harvard University, 1965).

88. Stephen Hampton, *Anti-Arminians: The Anglican Reformed Tradition from Charles II to George I* (Oxford: Oxford University Press, 2008), 16–18, 122–23.

89. S[imon] P[atrick], *A Brief Account of the new Sect of Latitude-Men, Together with some reflections upon the New Philosophy. By S. P. of Cambridge. In answer to a Letter from his Friend at Oxford* (London, 1662), 14, 22–23. Cf. John Gascoigne, *Cambridge in the Age of*

and Robert South, and Reformed nonconformists Robert Ferguson, Samuel Gott, and Thomas Hill (d. 1677)—continued to oppose the new philosophy associated with Descartes and Gassendi.[90] There were also a fair number of theologians who attempted eclectic syntheses of old and new philosophy, a point of view reflected in the eclectic choice of textbooks in many early dissenting academies.[91] This diversity of approaches continued until around 1700, when Samuel Palmer remarked, "Some [nonconformist] *Tutors* are more inclin'd to the *Philosophy* of *Aristotle*, others to the *Cartesian Hypothesis*, while my own had a due Regard for both, but strictly adhered to neither."[92] Baxter's targeted critique of mechanical philosophy, combined with an eclectic appropriation of certain aspects of the new philosophy, places him in continuity with the critics and eclectic synthesizers, but in discontinuity with those characterized by Palmer as "more inclin'd" to Cartesianism.

If theologians exhibited a diverse spectrum ranging from proponents to critics of the new philosophy, the critics themselves admitted of some significant diversity with respect to the subject matter of their criticisms.[93] The seventeenth-century philosophical transition challenged prevailing notions of cosmology, epistemology, metaphysics, physics, the soul, and ethics, among other topics. Although it is possible to find theologians reacting to change regarding any one of these topics, Baxter focused on problems pertaining to the soul and related questions in physics, metaphysics, and ethics. There is little indication that Baxter worried much about Copernicanism as a theological problem, and although he clearly

---

the Enlightenment: Science, Religion and Politics from the Restoration to the French Revolution (Cambridge University Press, 1989), 53.

90. R. H. Syfret, "Some Early Reactions to the Royal Society," *Notes and Records of the Royal Society* 7, no. 2 (1950): 207–58, at 219–49; Gascoigne, *Cambridge*, 55–56; Muller, "Thomas Barlow," 179–95; Robert Ferguson, *The Interest of Reason in Religion* (London: Dorman Newman, 1675), 41–46, 248–67; Samuel Gott, *The Divine History of the Genesis of the World Explicated and Illustrated* (London: E. C. & A. C. for Henry Eversden, 1670), 3–6; Edmund Calamy, *A Continuation of the Account* (London: R. Ford, 1727), 2:856 (on Hill). On the Reformed conformity of Barlow and South, see Hampton, *Anti-Arminians*, 10–12.

91. M. A. Stewart, *Independency of the Mind in Early Dissent* (London: The Congregational Memorial Trust, 2004), 21–27; McLachlan, *English Education*, 46, 69, 87. For philosophical eclecticism, see also Marjorie Grene, "Aristotelico-Cartesian Themes in Natural Philosophy: Some Seventeenth-Century Cases," *Perspectives on Science* 1, no. 1 (1993): 66–87; and Christia Mercer, "The Seventeenth-Century Debate between the Moderns and the Aristotelians: Leibniz and *Philosophia Reformata*," in *Leibniz' Auseinandersetzung mit Vorgängern und Zeitgenossen*, ed. Ingrid Marchlewitz and Albert Heinekamp (Stuttgart: Franz Steiner Verlag, 1990), 18–29.

92. Samuel Palmer, *A Vindication of the Learning, Loyalty, Morals, and Most Christian Behaviour of the Dissenters toward the Church of England* (London: J. Lawrence, 1705), 23–24.

93. Aza Goudriaan, "Introduction," in *Jacobus Revius: A Theological Examination of Cartesian Philosophy: Early Criticisms (1647)* (Leiden: Brill, 2002), 10.

disliked Cartesian methodological doubt and distrust of the senses, his sporadic comments on such epistemological issues lacked the sustained attention he gave to the physical and metaphysical aspects of mechanical philosophy.[94] Baxter thus represents a different emphasis from English and Dutch theologians for whom Copernicanism and Cartesian epistemology remained highly controversial and biblically suspect. Moreover, Baxter's polemical focus on physics and metaphysics rather than epistemology supports the claim of those who have argued that the priority given to epistemology (along with the bifurcation into rationalism and empiricism) in narratives of early modern philosophy is inherently flawed.[95]

The following chapters provide a chronological and topical analysis of Baxter's involvement with mechanical philosophy. Chapter 2 is arranged chronologically and provides context for all of the subsequent chapters. It situates Baxter's writings against the backdrop of the rise of mechanical philosophy with particular attention to the English reception of Gassendi's philosophy and the revival of interest in Epicurean ideas and writings. Here, Baxter's relationship and correspondence with figures such as Glanvill, Boyle, Hale, and More are discussed with attention to their importance for his polemics and positive intellectual development. Both Boyle and Hale contributed positively in different respects to Baxter's mature thought, while Glanvill and More sparked polemical exchanges with Baxter that shed light on his thought by way of contrast.

Chapters 3 and 4 together explain Baxter's own understanding of philosophy and nature, and constitute topical background to his polemics. Chapter 3 addresses Baxter's general approach to philosophy. Here Baxter's explanation of the noetic effects of sin, the interaction of intellect and will, and the relation of reason and revelation are shown to lead to an eclectic and somewhat ambivalent approach to philosophical sects. Chapter 4 discusses Baxter's view of the relation between God and creation that came to expression in his uniquely Trinitarian approach to nature. Baxter's eclectic use of old and new philosophy in his views on substance, causality, and the soul are explained in light of his participation in a Reformed tradition of Mosaic physics and his attribution of God's communicable attributes to the realm of living beings through the notion of *vestigia Trinitatis*.

The remaining three chapters focus on Baxter's specific objections to mechanical philosophy. Chapter 5 addresses Baxter's response to new doctrines of motion.

---

94. On Copernicanism, see chapter 5. On Cartesian epistemology, see chapter 3.

95. S. P. Lamprecht, "The Role of Descartes in Seventeenth-Century England," in *Studies in the History of Ideas* (New York: Columbia University Press, 1918–1935), 3:181–240, esp. 183–87; Stephen Gaukroger, *The Collapse of Mechanism and the Rise of Sensibility: Science and the Shaping of Modernity* (Oxford: Clarendon Press, 2010), 155–57; Alberto Vanzo, "Empiricism and Rationalism in Nineteenth-Century Histories of Philosophy," *Journal of the History of Ideas* 77 (2016): 253–82.

Although Baxter recognized advances in astronomy and the study of motion, he raised a series of objections against the philosophies of Descartes, Gassendi, and More. Chapter 6 turns to the doctrine of the soul, where Baxter raised objections to ideas promoted by More, Gassendi, and Thomas Willis, and expressed a suspicion that the mechanical philosophy of Gassendi and Willis would lead to a completely materialistic account of the soul. Chapter 7 focuses on Baxter's criticisms of Hobbes and Spinoza with respect to ethics. Baxter, whose own doctrine of natural law is shown to derive in important ways from Francisco Suárez, viewed the philosophies of Hobbes and Spinoza as an outworking of the principles of mechanical philosophy and therefore as exemplifying its potential danger of overturning traditional Christian morality and leading to philosophical necessitarianism.

Sometime in late 1666 or early 1667, Baxter penned his opening salvo against mechanical philosophy: "The Conclusion [of *The Reasons of the Christian Religion*], Defending the Soul's Immortality against the Somatists or Epicureans, and other Pseudophilosophers."[96] Near the end of this conclusion, Baxter commented on Bishop Tempier's famous condemnation of philosophical theses in 1277. Baxter disapproved of that manner of "too hastily and peremptorily" condemning as heretics those who hold dangerous philosophical opinions. But he went on to remark, "I think that in this age, it is one of the devils chief designs, to assault Christianity by false Philosophy."[97] With these reflections, Baxter may have glimpsed that he was living in a unique age of philosophical transition analogous to the reintroduction of Aristotle's complete corpus in thirteenth-century Latin Christendom. For Baxter, this was an age fraught with new challenges and dangers for Christianity. What did Baxter think was so dangerous about the philosophy of his age? What follows is an attempt to answer this question.

---

96. *RCR*, 489–604.

97. *RCR*, 588.

2

Baxter and the Rise
of Mechanical Philosophy

LIVING AS WE do in the aftermath of nineteenth-century controversies over Darwinism and narratives of "conflict" or "warfare" between religion and science,[1] it is difficult to imagine that the great philosophical changes of the seventeenth century could be accompanied or even motivated by the appeal to religion and antiquity. Yet many bright scholars who lived in the immediate aftermath of these changes did not share our modern prejudices. Sir Richard Blackmore (1654–1729), who received a doctorate in medicine from the University of Padua, was elected fellow of the Royal Society of Physicians, and appointed physician-in-ordinary to William III, viewed religion and antiquity as highly relevant for the explanation of seventeenth-century philosophical transition. In the preface to his *Creation: A Philosophical Poem* (1712), which went through sixteen editions, Blackmore looked back on the previous generation of "Patriots of the Commonwealth of Learning" who had "combin'd to reform the Corruptions, and redress the Grievances, of Philosophy." In their attempt to "pull down the Peripatetick Monarchy, and set up a free and independent State of Science," Blackmore wrote, these patriots "had recourse to the *Corpuscularian Hypothesis*, and reviv'd the obsolete and exploded System of *Epicurus*." Blackmore went on to explain, "When these first Reformers of *Aristotle*'s School had espoused the Interest of *Epicurus*, and introduc'd his Doctrines, that his Hypothesis might be

---

1. John W. Draper, *History of the Conflict between Religion and Science* (New York: Appleton, 1874); and Andrew D. White, *History of the Warfare of Science with Theology in Christendom*, 2 vols. (London: Macmillan, 1896). For the historiographical place of these works and the subsequent shift away from a conflict model with respect to the seventeenth century, see Margaret J. Osler, "Religion and the Changing Historiography of the Scientific Revolution," in *Science and Religion: New Historical Perspectives*, ed. Thomas Dixon, Geoffrey Cantor, and Stephen Pumfrey (Cambridge: Cambridge University Press, 2010), 71–86.

receiv'd with the less Opposition, they thought it necessary to remove the igno-minious Character of Impiety, under which their Philosopher had long lain." Blackmore highlighted the work of Pierre Gassendi as a major factor in this transi-tion: "The Learned *Gassendus* is eminent above all others for the warm Zeal he has express'd, and the great Pains he has taken, to vindicate the Honour of *Epicurus*, and clear his Character from the Imputation of Irreligion."[2]

In the middle of the eighteenth century, the Lutheran historian of philosophy Johann Jakob Brucker (1696–1770) composed his *Historia critica philosophiae* (1742–1744; 2nd ed., 1766–1767), one of the most influential historical texts of that time.[3] Brucker divided the history of philosophy into three great periods. The third period—that of the "revival of letters" since the thirteenth century—he saw as a time characterized by (1) a revival of ancient philosophical sects, (2) attempts at new philosophical methods, and (3) the improvement of philosophy according to "the true eclectic method" of the moderns.[4] His account of the revival of an-cient philosophical sects is notable both for the attention it gives to "the revival of the Democritan-Epicurean philosophy" and for the significance it attaches to that revival.[5] Brucker singled out Pierre Gassendi as the most successful reviver of Epicurus, and after some discussion of his life and influence, concluded that Isaac Newton embraced the Epicurean doctrine of atoms and void in opposition to Descartes's physics.

Brucker's account, like that of Blackmore, is notable in at least two respects. First, he recognized that rather than explaining the seventeenth century as a simple conflict of ancients *versus* moderns,[6] the appeal to antiquity, and particularly the antiquity of the ancient atomists, could support the moderns as they sought to supplant the views of other ancients, particularly Aristotle. Second, unlike many later surveys of early modern philosophy, he gave significant weight both to the

---

2. Richard Blackmore, preface to *Creation. A Philosophical Poem. Demonstrating the Existence and Providence of a God* (London: S. Buckley, 1712), xiv–xvi. For biography, see Flavio Gregori, "Blackmore, Sir Richard," in *ODNB*.

3. It has been referred to as "a mammoth work that influenced generations of German scholars and which Kant explicitly cites in the *Critique*" (Daniel Garber and Béatrice Longuenesse, "Introduction," in *Kant and the Early Moderns*, ed. Garber and Longuenesse [Princeton, NJ: Princeton University Press, 2008], 4). On Brucker, see Mario Longo, "A 'Critical' History of Philosophy and the Early Enlightenment," in *Models of the History of Philosophy*, vol. 2, *From the Cartesian Age to Brucker*, ed. Gregorio Piaia and Giovanni Santinello (Dordrecht: Springer, 2011), 477–577.

4. For a synopsis of the contents, see the English abridgment: Johann Jakob Brucker, *The History of Philosophy*, trans. William Enfield (London: J. Johnson, 1791), 1:xxv–xxvii.

5. Johann Jakob Brucker, *Historia critica philosophiae*, 2nd ed. (Leipzig, 1766), 4:503–35; Brucker, *History of Philosophy*, 2:463–67.

6. Thus, Jones, *Ancients and Moderns*.

revival of Epicureanism alongside revivals of other ancient philosophical sects and to the role of Gassendi in that revival.[7] Both of these points have in the last generation of scholarship received abundant confirmation from a more detailed examination of the primary sources.[8]

While mechanical philosophy benefited from new instruments such as the telescope and microscope, which increasingly discredited prevailing Aristotelian assumptions regarding both the macro- and micro-cosmos,[9] at the theoretical level mechanical philosophy also benefited from the revival of select ancient philosophies and texts. Mechanical philosophy grew partly from the soil of the discipline of mechanics, which had been understood (along with astronomy, optics, and music) as a kind of "mixed mathematics" or "middle science" that treated artificial things within a larger Aristotelian framework of physics. Two ancient texts, pseudo-Aristotle's *Mechanica problemata* and Archimedes's *On the Equilibrium of Plains*, were studied in this mixed discipline of mechanics. In a sense, the transition to mechanical *philosophy* involved the transposition or re-imagination of a subdiscipline, mechanics, as a model for the entire natural order.[10]

---

7. Observe the marginal place of Gassendi in Johann Eduard Erdmann, *A History of Philosophy*, trans. W. S. Hough, 2nd ed. (London: Swan Sonnenschein & Co., 1891), 1:604–5; Frederick C. Copleston, *A History of Philosophy*, vol. 3, *Late Medieval and Renaissance Philosophy* (London: Burns, Oates & Washbourne, 1953), 263–64. Cf. Margaret J. Osler, "Becoming an Outsider: Gassendi in the History of Philosophy," in *Insiders and Outsiders in Seventeenth-Century Philosophy*, ed. G. A. J. Rogers, Tom Sorell, and Jill Kraye (New York: Routledge, 2010), 23–42.

8. The importance of the appeal to antiquity as an agent of philosophical change is becoming increasingly recognized. See Dmitri Levitin, *Ancient Wisdom in the Age of the New Science: Histories of Philosophy in England, c. 1640–1700* (Cambridge: Cambridge University Press, 2015); Lynn Sumida Joy, *Gassendi the Atomist: Advocate of History in an Age of Science* (Cambridge: Cambridge University Press, 1987); Michael Hunter, "Ancients, Moderns, Philologists, and Scientists," *Annals of Science* 39 (1982): 187–92; and William E. A. Makin, "The Philosophy of Pierre Gassendi: Science and Belief in Seventeenth-Century Paris and Provence" (PhD diss., The Open University, 1985), 2:556–67.

9. Albert Van Helden, "The Birth of the Modern Scientific Instrument," in *The Uses of Science in the Age of Newton*, ed. John G. Burke (Berkeley: University of California Press, 1983), 49–84; John Henry, *The Scientific Revolution and the Origins of Modern Science*, 3rd ed. (New York: Palgrave Macmillan, 2008), 36; Albert Van Helden, "Galileo, Telescopic Astronomy, and the Copernican System," in *Planetary Astronomy from the Renaissance to the Rise of Astrophysics, Part A: Tycho to Newton*, ed. René Taton and Curtis Wilson (Cambridge: Cambridge University Press, 1995), 81–105; Catherine Wilson, *The Invisible World: Early Modern Philosophy and the Invention of the Microscope* (Princeton, NJ: Princeton University Press, 1995), 56–60. The telescope's importance increased dramatically after Galileo's *Sidereus nuncius* (1610), and the microscope after Robert Hooke's *Micrographia* (1665).

10. Daniel Garber, "Descartes, Mechanics, and the Mechanical Philosophy," *Midwest Studies in Philosophy* 26 (2002): 185–204; also Sylvia Berryman, *The Mechanical Hypothesis in Ancient Greek Natural Philosophy* (Cambridge: Cambridge University Press, 2009), 236–49.

A second theoretical development associated with mechanical philosophy involved the revival of ancient Epicureanism in the early seventeenth century. An interest in more innovative philosophers like Descartes often went hand in hand with an interest in ancient atomism or Epicureanism. Indeed, Descartes developed his initial thoughts on the nature of motion in conversation with Isaac Beeckman (1588–1637),[11] who drew inspiration from Lucretius's *De rerum natura*,[12] and Descartes's later formulation of the first law of motion (the persistence of inertial motion) contained the key phrase "as far as it is in itself" (*quantum in se est*), which is found four times in Lucretius's *De rerum natura*.[13] Beeckman's revival of ancient atomism also impressed Gassendi to such an extent that he once referred to Beeckman as "the best philosopher I have yet met."[14] Another reviver of ancient atomism, David Gorlaeus (1591–1612), exercised some influence through his posthumous *Exercitationes philosophicae* (1620). This work, in the estimation of one historian of Dutch Cartesianism, was "in everybody's hands."[15] Moreover, both early modern historians and Dutch opponents of Descartes saw strong similarities between the thought of Gorlaeus and Descartes, which, while not establishing lines of influence on Descartes's own development, still illustrates an affinity between their respective natural philosophies that is important for understanding Descartes's reception and intellectual appeal.[16] One leading scholar on Descartes goes so far as to state that, despite Descartes's unique views, "There can be no question but that Descartes was deeply influenced by the atomist tradition, either directly or through one or another of its later followers; the obvious

---

11. Klaas van Berkel, *Isaac Beeckman on Matter and Motion: Mechanical Philosophy in the Making* (Baltimore: The Johns Hopkins University Press, 2013), 109–16, 123–29; Richard Arthur, "Beeckman, Descartes and the Force of Motion," *Journal of the History of Philosophy* 45, no. 1 (2007): 1–28; Frédéric de Buzon, "Beeckman, Descartes and Physico-Mathematics," in *The Mechanization of Natural Philosophy*, ed. Daniel Garber and Sophie Roux (Dordrecht: Springer, 2013), 143–58; Daniel Garber, *Descartes' Metaphysical Physics* (Chicago: The University of Chicago Press, 1992), 9–12, 197.

12. See van Berkel, *Isaac Beeckman*, 130–34, who emphasizes the eclectic use of Lucretius.

13. I. Bernard Cohen, "'Quantum in se est': Newton's Concept of Inertia in Relation to Descartes and Lucretius," *Notes and Records of the Royal Society of London* 19, no. 2 (1964): 131–55, at 143–44.

14. LoLordo, *Pierre Gassendi*, 11. On Beeckman's relation to Gassendi and Descartes, see van Berkel, *Isaac Beeckman*, 165–73; and Harold J. Cook, "The New Philosophy in the Low Countries," in *The Scientific Revolution in National Context*, ed. Roy Porter and Mikuláš Teich (Cambridge: Cambridge University Press, 1992), 115–49, at 127–29.

15. Verbeek, *Descartes and the Dutch*, 9. There is ample evidence for Verbeek's remark: Christoph Lüthy, *David Gorlaeus (1591–1612): An Enigmatic Figure in the History of Philosophy and Science* (Amsterdam: Amsterdam University Press, 2012), 139–40.

16. Lüthy, *David Gorlaeus*, 15–17, 150–53.

correspondence between his program and that of other mechanists, ancient and modern, can be no accident."[17]

Given a certain affinity between the philosophy of Descartes and ancient atomism, it is not surprising that an interest in Cartesian mechanical philosophy was paralleled by an interest in Gassendi's revival of Epicureanism. Gassendi's philosophical project, long relegated to the shadows of the history of philosophy, is increasingly appreciated as a major motor of intellectual change in the seventeenth century. As Richard Popkin already recognized in 1967, Gassendi's philosophy was "one of the major and most influential theories of the scientific and philosophical revolutions of the seventeenth century. Gassendism rivaled Cartesianism as a new alternative to Scholasticism and as a way of interpreting the findings of the scientists."[18] More recently, G. A. J. Rogers has observed that Gassendi's "reputation has grown with the increasing recognition of the importance of the atomist revival to science and philosophy in the early modern period and the spill-over of Epicurean philosophy into virtually all aspects of intellectual enquiry in the course of the [seventeenth] century."[19] Indeed, the reception of Gassendi and Epicureanism was particularly strong in midseventeenth-century England, and this reception provides an important context for the particularly English development of mechanical philosophy.

The Reception of Gassendi's Christian Epicureanism in England

While the first polemics over mechanical philosophy began in the Netherlands with the introduction of Cartesian philosophy in the Reformed universities at Utrecht (from 1639) and Leiden (from 1643),[20] Cartesian philosophy quickly spread to Reformed centers of learning in France, Germany, and Switzerland.[21]

---

17. Garber, *Descartes' Metaphysical Physics*, 119.

18. Richard H. Popkin, "Gassendi, Pierre," in *The Encyclopedia of Philosophy*, ed. Paul Edwards (New York: The Macmillan Co., 1967), 3:269–73, at 272.

19. G. A. J. Rogers, "Gassendi and the Birth of Modern Philosophy," *Studies in History and Philosophy of Science* 26, no. 4 (1995): 681–87, at 681.

20. Verbeek, *Descartes and the Dutch*; McGahagan, "Cartesianism in the Netherlands"; Israel, *Radical Enlightenment*, 23–29.

21. Israel, *Radical Enlightenment*, 29–34; Michael Heyd, *Between Orthodoxy and the Enlightenment: Jean-Robert Chouet and the Introduction of Cartesian Science in the Academy of Geneva* (The Hague: Martinus Nijhoff, 1982), ch. 4; Heyd, "Un rôle nouveau pour la science: Jean-Alphonse Turrettini et les débuts de la théologie naturelle à Genève," *Revue de théologie et philosophie* 112 (1980): 25–42; Heyd, "From a Rationalist Theology to Cartesian Voluntarism: David Derodon and Jean-Robert Chouet," *Journal of the History of Ideas* 40, no. 4 (1979): 527–42; Martin I. Klauber, "Reason, Revelation, and Cartesianism: Louis Tronchin

Cartesian philosophy also passed across the channel to England.[22] However, the English reception of Descartes was often highly eclectic,[23] and Gassendi received an equal if not warmer reception as Descartes.[24] To some extent, we may attribute this warm reception of Gassendi to a native English interest in atomism already evident from the early seventeenth century.[25] Be that as it may, the works of both Gassendi and Descartes were "widely discussed" at English universities from the

and Enlightened Orthodoxy in Late Seventeenth-Century Geneva," *Church History* 59, no. 3 (1990): 326–39; Wolfgang Rother, "Zur Geschichte der Basler Universitätsphilosophie im 17. Jahrhundert," *History of Universities* 2 (1982): 153–91; Rother, "The Teaching of Philosophy at Seventeenth-Century Zurich," *History of Universities* 11 (1992): 59–74.

22. Marjorie Nicolson, "The Early Stage of Cartesianism in England," *Studies in Philology* 26 (1929): 356–74; Lamprecht, "Role of Descartes," 181–240; John Laird, "L'Influence de Descartes sur la philosophie anglaise du xvi siècle," *Revue Philosophique de la France et de l'Étranger* 123, no. 5–8 (May–August 1937): 226–56; G. A. J. Rogers, "Descartes and the English," in *The Light of Nature: Essays in the History and Philosophy of Science Presented to A. C. Crombie*, ed. J. D. North and J. J. Roche (Dordrecht: M. Nijhoff, 1985), 281–302; Arrigo Pacchi, "Die Rezeption der cartesischen Philosophie," in *Die Philosophie des 17. Jahrhunderts*, ed. Jean-Pierre Schobinger (Basel: Schwabe, 1988), vol. 3, bk. 1, *England*, 293–97, with bibliography, 308–9.

23. Lamprecht, "Role of Descartes," 182; Rogers, "Descartes and the English," 302.

24. For the following account of Gassendi and Epicureanism in England, I have drawn upon C. T. Harrison, "Bacon, Hobbes, Boyle, and the Ancient Atomists," *Harvard Studies and Notes in Philology and Literature* 15 (1933): 191–218; Harrison, "The Ancient Atomists and English Literature of the Seventeenth Century," *Harvard Studies in Classical Philology* 45 (1934): 1–79; Thomas Mayo, *Epicurus in England (1650–1725)* (Dallas: The Southwest Press, 1934); Meyrick H. Carré, *Phases of Thought in England* (Oxford: Clarendon Press, 1949), 245–49; Danton B. Sailor, "Moses and Atomism," *Journal of the History of Ideas* 25, no. 1 (1964): 3–16; Robert Kargon, *Atomism in England from Hariot to Newton* (Oxford: Clarendon Press, 1966); W. R. Albury, "Halley's Ode on the *Principia* of Newton and the Epicurean Revival in England," *Journal of the History of Ideas* 39, no. 1 (1978): 24–43; Spiller, *"Concerning Natural Experimental Philosophie,"* 80–104; Jones, *The Epicurean Tradition*, 186–213; John Henry, "Die Rezeption der atomistischen Philosophie," in *Die Philosophie des 17. Jahrhunderts*, ed. Jean-Pierre Schobinger (Basel: Schwabe, 1988), vol. 3, bk. 2, *England*, 370–82; Kroll, *Material Word*; Catherine Wilson, "Epicureanism in Early Modern Philosophy: Leibniz and His Contemporaries," in *Hellenistic and Early Modern Philosophy*, ed. Jon Miller and Brad Inwood (Cambridge: Cambridge University Press, 2003), 90–115; Catherine Wilson, *Epicureanism at the Origins of Modernity* (Oxford: Oxford University Press, 2008).

25. Kargon, *Atomism*, 5–42; Kargon, "Thomas Hariot, the Northumberland Circle and Early Atomism in England," *Journal of the History of Ideas* 27, no. 1 (1966): 128–36; and Stephen Clucas, "Corpuscular Matter Theory in the Northumberland Circle," in *Late Medieval and Early Modern Corpuscular Matter Theories*, ed. Christoph Lüthy, John E. Murdoch, and William R. Newman (Leiden: E. J. Brill, 2001), 181–207. Bacon's early works were more favorable to ancient atomism, although his mature works were unfavorable. See now Silva A. Manzo, "Francis Bacon and Atomism: A Reappraisal," in *Late Medieval and Early Modern Corpuscular Matter Theories*, ed. Christoph Lüthy, John E. Murdoch, and William R. Newman (Leiden: E. J. Brill, 2001), 209–43; also Kargon, *Atomism*, 43–53; and Harrison, "Bacon, Hobbes, Boyle," 192–200.

early 1650s,[26] and at least at Oxford (where there was more initial interest in the new philosophy than at Cambridge), "Gassendi may have exceeded Descartes in popularity."[27] This trend was also reflected in the Scottish universities during the second half of the seventeenth century, where Gassendian or Epicurean concepts about physics rivaled Cartesian concepts as the major mechanist alternative to Aristotle, although likely due to the strong connections between Scottish and Dutch universities, Descartes was often preferred over Gassendi.[28]

While Descartes's mature account of the mechanical foundations of physics, *Principia philosophiae*, appeared in 1644, Gassendi's mature works took longer to appear. In his *Animadversiones in decimum librum Diogenis Laertii* (1649), Gassendi set forth a systematic treatment of Epicurean canonics (or logic), physics, and ethics in the form of a massive 1,768-page philological and philosophical commentary on book 10 of Diogenes Laertius's *De vitis philosophorum*. To this was appended the short *Philosophiae Epicuri syntagma*, which systematically arranged Epicurus's own views. The initial treatment of logic, physics, and ethics in the *Animadversiones* was expanded in the even larger *Syntagma philosophicum*, which appeared posthumously in volumes one and two of Gassendi's *Opera omnia* (1658).

Of course, a wholesale revival of ancient Epicureanism would have been just as problematic to early modern Christian systems of thought as a wholesale revival of Aristotle, who notoriously held the world to be eternal. Accordingly, just as in the process of the medieval reception of Aristotle's corpus Christians selectively appropriated Aristotelian philosophy so as to harmonize it with Christian doctrines such as creation ex nihilo, special providence, and the soul's immortality, so also Gassendi sought to purify ancient atomist and Epicurean philosophy in order to make this ancient alternative to Aristotle acceptable to early modern Christians. Indeed, Gassendi explicitly appealed to the historical reception of Aristotle—from initial antipathy in the early church to the status of handmaiden in the medieval

26. Kargon, *Atomism*, 78.

27. Mordechai Feingold, "The Mathematical Sciences and New Philosophies," in *The History of the University of Oxford*, IV, *Seventeenth-Century Oxford*, ed. Nicholas Tyacke (Oxford: Clarendon Press, 1997), 405–6. On Cambridge, see Gascoigne, *Cambridge*, 58. For further evidence, see Hornberger, "Samuel Lee," 345–46, 348–49; Phyllis Allen, "Scientific Studies in the English Universities of the Seventeenth Century," *Journal of the History of Ideas* 10, no. 2 (1949): 219–53, at 235, 241, 248; Jones, *Ancients and Moderns*, 110–11, 223, 295n34; Barbara J. Shapiro, "The Universities and Science in Seventeenth Century England," *The Journal of British Studies* 10, no. 2 (1971): 47–82, at 73; A. Rupert Hall, "Cambridge: Newton's Legacy," *Notes and Records of the Royal Society of London* 55, no. 2 (2001): 205–26, at 206–7.

28. Christine King, "Philosophy and Science in the Arts Curriculum of the Scottish Universities in the 17th century" (PhD diss., University of Edinburgh, 1974), 210–76, 334–38. Cf. John L. Russell, "Cosmological Teaching in the Seventeenth-Century Scottish Universities, Part 1," *Journal for the History of Astronomy* 5 (1974): 122–32, at 128–29.

period—as justification for his own similar attempt to turn Epicurus into the handmaiden of Christianity.[29] Scholars now speak of the Christian Aristotelianism of the medieval and early modern periods,[30] and it is appropriate to speak of a Christian Epicureanism in the seventeenth century.

While Gassendi accepted much from ancient Epicureanism, his Christian Epicurean project was not a simple repristination of the ancient Epicurus, but involved significant theological and philosophical modification. Theologically, he argued against Epicurus for a more traditional monotheism consisting of God's omniscience and omnipotence, creation ex nihilo, the providential direction of atoms (no longer considered infinite in number or random in motion), the soul's immortality, and a hedonistic ethics that integrated Christian salvation.[31] Philosophically, Gassendi revised ancient Epicureanism with a more sophisticated understanding of matter according to which the weight (*gravitas*) of atoms is omni-directional (not simply downward), their speed is variable (not constant), and their activity both intrinsic and divinely endowed.[32] Moreover, Gassendi's account of composite bodies was more complex, incorporating a theory of texture, Galilean motion, and compound molecules and *semina* (complex organic matter with the power to develop according to patterns).[33] The sincerity of Gassendi's private beliefs has been the subject of recurring debate, with some placing him in continuity with French freethinkers, and one historian even arguing that while

29. Pierre Gassendi, *Syntagma philosophicum*, "De philosophia universe," cap. 2, in *Opera omnia*, 1:5a; with translation in Barry Brundell, *Pierre Gassendi: From Aristotelianism to a New Natural Philosophy* (Dordrecht: Kluwer Academic, 1987), 52. Cf. E. J. Dijksterhuis, *The Mechanization of the World Picture*, trans. C. Dikshoorn (Oxford: Oxford University Press, 1961), 425 (sec. 231); and Margaret J. Osler, *Divine Will and the Mechanical Philosophy: Gassendi and Descartes on Contingency and Necessity in the Created World* (Cambridge: Cambridge University Press, 1994), 45.

30. *PRRD*, 1:367–82. On the strength of Protestant and Catholic Aristotelianism, see Charles B. Schmitt, *Aristotle and the Renaissance* (Cambridge, MA: Harvard University Press, 1983), 26.

31. Osler, *Divine Will*, 36–77, esp. 45; Osler, "Fortune, Fate, and Divination: Gassendi's Voluntarist Theology and the Baptism of Epicureanism," in *Atoms, Pneuma, and Tranquillity: Epicurean and Stoic Themes in European Thought*, ed. Margaret J. Osler (Cambridge: Cambridge University Press, 1991), 155–74; Osler, "Baptizing Epicurean Atomism: Pierre Gassendi on the Immortality of the Soul," in *Religion, Science, and Worldview: Essays in Honor of Richard S. Westfall*, ed. Margaret J. Osler and Paul L. Farber (Cambridge: Cambridge University Press, 1985), 163–83.

32. LoLordo, *Pierre Gassendi*, 142–43.

33. LoLordo, *Pierre Gassendi*, 153–82, 186–89; and on *semina*, Clericuzio, *Elements, Principles and Corpuscles*, 63–71; and Hiro Hirai, "Le concept de semence de Pierre Gassendi entre les théories de la matière et les sciences de la vie au XVII e siècle," *Medicina nei Secoli* 15, no. 2 (2003): 205–26.

"[p]ublicly baptising Epicurus, Gassendi privately Epicureanised Jehovah."[34] Yet regardless of his personal sincerity, Gassendi's public philosophical project included modifications necessary for its acceptance by a Christian audience. For the historical reception of his work in the seventeenth century, the question of sincerity is less relevant.

The mechanical philosophy of Gassendi and Descartes made its way quickly across the channel into English hands. A scholarly network surrounding Charles and William Cavendish, the so-called Newcastle circle, was in close contact with Gassendi and Descartes in Paris during the 1640s. This circle—which included the important philosophers Thomas Hobbes, Sir Kenelm Digby, and Margaret Cavendish, as well as John Pell and William Petty—promoted their writings almost immediately.[35] Hobbes was a personal friend of Gassendi, and although Hobbes's version of mechanical philosophy was sui generis, his physics in De corpore (1655) was constructed in dialogue with both Gassendi and Descartes.[36] Lady Margaret Cavendish, sister-in-law to Sir Charles and well connected in her own right, promoted a thoroughly atomist physics in her Poems and Fancies (1653) and Philosophicall Fancies (1653), in which she explained the faculties of the human soul in terms of changes produced by eternally existing matter and motion.[37] A steady stream of similar works and new editions followed these initial works of hers for over a decade.

Gassendi's philosophy received a particularly strong spokesman in another member of the Newcastle circle, Walter Charleton (1620–1707), physician-in-ordinary to both Charles I and II.[38] Against the materialistic tendencies of Hobbes and Lady Margaret, he followed Gassendi in promoting a version of Epicureanism

---

34. Makin, "Philosophy of Pierre Gassendi," 2:535. Contrast Osler, Divine Will, 45–47, who summarizes the debate.

35. See Jean Jacquot, "Sir Charles Cavendish and His Learned Friends," Annals of Science 8 (1952): 13–28, 175–92; Helen Hervey, "Hobbes and Descartes in the Light of Some Unpublished Letters of the Correspondence between Sir Charles Cavendish and Dr. John Pell," Osiris 10 (1952): 67–90; Stephen Clucas, "The Atomism of the Cavendish Circle. A Reappraisal," The Seventeenth Century 9, no. 2 (1994): 247–73; Lisa T. Sarasohn, "Thomas Hobbes and the Duke of Newcastle: A Study in the Mutuality of Patronage before the Establishment of the Royal Society," Isis 90, no. 4 (1999): 715–37; Kargon, Atomism, 66–67. Cf. Alexander Ross, "Epistle Dedicatory," in The Philosophicall Touch-stone (London: James Young, 1645) on Kenelm Digby's "French sauce"; and Alexander Ross, Arcana Microcosmi: Or, the hid Secrets of Mans Body disclosed (London: Thomas Newcomb, 1651), 255–67 on Gassendi's Epicureanism.

36. Kargon, Atomism, ch. 6.

37. Margaret Cavendish, Philosophicall Fancies (London: Tho. Roycroft, 1653), 1–3, 30–33, 52–53. Cf. Kargon, Atomism, 73–75.

38. Robert Kargon, "Walter Charleton, Robert Boyle and the Acceptance of Epicurean Atomism in England," Isis 55, no. 2 (1964): 184–92; G. A. J. Rogers, "Charleton, Gassendi, et la reception de l'atomisme," in Gassendi et l'Europe, 1592–1792, ed. Sylvia Murr (Paris: J. Vrin, 1997), 213–25. For biography, see John Henry, "Charleton, Walter," in ODNB; Emily Booth, 'A Subtle and Mysterious Machine': The Medical World of Walter Charleton (1619–1707)

purged of heretical or atheistic doctrine. Charleton deliberately prepared the way for the acceptance of his subsequent Epicurean physics with *The Darkness of Atheism Refuted by the Light of Nature: A Physico-Theologicall Treatise* (1652), which had two principal objects: (1) to prove the existence of God, and (2) to defend the doctrines of creation ex nihilo and God's general and special providence against Epicurus's impious "doctrine of the worlds spontaneous result from a *Chaos* of *Atoms*."[39] In constructing this apologetic, Charleton admitted that he drew on Descartes's proof for God's existence, and for the doctrine of divine providence, he drew on a variety of medieval and modern authors, but "chiefly" Gassendi's *Animadversiones* (1649).[40] Charleton included in his treatise a short *"Digression, winnowing the Chaffe from the Wheat"* of Epicurus's theory of atoms. In that digression, while he affirmed the "great advantages" of atomism over other theories, he listed four Epicurean positions that should be rejected: (1) atoms were eternal; (2) atoms were not created ex nihilo; (3) atoms were disposed to the "order and figure" that make up bodies by fortune rather than by "artifice"; and (4) atoms have their motion by an eternal faculty of motion rather than from an external principle (i.e., God).[41]

Charleton completed his project of constructing a Christian Epicureanism over the next several years. In his *Physiologia Epicuro-Gassendo-Charltoniana* (1654), Charleton presented an atomist physics built on Gassendi's *Animadversiones*, in which he treated both general principles built upon the supposition of atoms and infinite void (books 1–2), explained the five senses and their objects according to these general principles (book 3), and finally provided an atomist alternative to Aristotle's doctrines of generation, corruption, and motion (book 4).[42] In his *Epicurus's Morals* (1656), he published a translation of the ethical section of Gassendi's *Philosophiae Epicuri syntagma* (1649), to which he prefaced "An Apologie for Epicurus," where he defended the reputation of Epicurus as no worse

(Dordrecht: Springer, 2005), 1–31; Nina R. Gelbart, "The Intellectual Development of Walter Charleton," *Ambix* 18, no. 3 (1971): 149–68; Lindsay Sharp, "Walter Charleton's Early Life 1620–1659, and Relationship to Natural Philosophy in Mid-Seventeenth Century England," *Annals of Science* 30 (1973): 311–40.

39. Walter Charleton, "A Preparatory Advertisement to the Reader," in *The Darkness of Atheism Refuted by the Light of Nature: A Physico-Theologicall Treatise* (London, 1652), a2v, 5, 40 (marginal note). Cf. Margaret J. Osler, "Descartes and Charleton on Nature and God," *Journal of the History of Ideas* 40, no. 3 (1979): 452.

40. Charleton, "A Preparatory Advertisement," in *Darkness of Atheism*, b3r–b4v.

41. Charleton, *Darkness of Atheism*, 43–47.

42. Walter Charleton, *Physiologia Epicuro-Gassendo-Charltoniana: Or a Fabrick of Science Natural, Upon the Hypothesis of Atoms, Founded by Epicurus, Repaired by Petrus Gassendus, Augmented by Walter Charleton* (London: Thomas Newcomb, 1654).

than other ancient philosophers with respect to the immortality of the soul, the conception of deity, and suicide.[43] Finally, in *The Immortality of the Human Soul, Demonstrated by the Light of Nature* (1657), Charleton defended the soul's immortality in the manner of a dialogue between Lucretius and Athanasius.[44]

Others continued the importation of Epicurean ideas initiated by Charleton. John Evelyn produced the first English translation of Lucretius's *De rerum natura* (book 1) in 1656. Like Charleton's apology for Epicurus, Evelyn's preface defended Lucretius as no worse than other ancient philosophers, pleaded for an eclectic use of the good amidst the evil in Lucretius's text, and concluded with a citation from Gassendi's *De vita et moribus Epicuri* (1647) to the same effect.[45] In his "Animadversions" on Lucretius's text, Evelyn recommended Gassendi's Epicurean doctrine of atoms and void space as "exactly translated by Dr. *Charleton.*"[46] A postscript following the "Animadversions" concluded with an epitaph of "the admirable *Gassendus,* who for being so great an Assertor of *Epicurus's Institution,* the *Doctrine* delivered by *Carus,* and a person of such excellent *erudition,* deserves highly to be remembred by Posterity." Even as Evelyn eulogized Gassendi, Thomas Stanley published *The History of Philosophy* (3 vols., 1655–1660), which was clearly biased in favor of Gassendi's Epicureanism. It contained a section on "the Epicurean sect" that incorporated both the first two books of Gassendi's *De vita et moribus Epicuri* (1647) and Gassendi's *Philosophiae Epicuri syntagma* (1649). In contrast with the sections on Plato (118 pages) and Aristotle (99 pages), the section on Epicurus was substantially longer (170 pages).[47] Stanley even

---

43. Walter Charleton, "An Apologie for Epicurus," in *Epicurus's Morals* (London: W. Wilson, 1656).

44. Walter Charleton, *The Immortality of the Human Soul, Demonstrated by the Light of Nature* (London: William Wilson, 1657). All of Charleton's arguments, according to Fred S. Michael and Emily Michael, were drawn from Gassendi's *Animadversiones* with the exception of one argument from Descartes. See "A Note on Gassendi in England," *Notes and Queries* 37, no. 3 (1990): 297–99.

45. John Evelyn, "The Interpreter to Him that Reads," in *An Essay on the First Book of T. Lucretius Carus* De rerum natura (London: Gabriel Bedle and Thomas Collins, 1656). Cf. Kroll, *Material Word,* 140–42; Kargon, *Atomism,* 89–92; Mayo, *Epicurus,* 43–51.

46. Evelyn, "Animadversions upon the First Book of T. Lucretius Carus *De rerum natura,*" in *Essay,* 135, also 138, 172.

47. Stanley's treatment of Epicurus was also more than fifty pages longer than Aristotle and later Aristotelians put together. See Thomas Stanley, "Epicurus, His Life and Doctrine. Written by Petrus Gassendus," in *The History of Philosophy, The Third and Last Volume, in Five Parts* (London: Humphrey Moseley and Thomas Dring, 1660), 105–275. See by contrast Thomas Stanley, *The History of Philosophy. The Fift Part, Containing the Academic Philosophers* (London, 1656), 1–118 (on Plato) and *The History of Philosophy. The Sixth Part, Containing the Peripatetick Philosophers* (London, 1656), 1–118 (on Aristotelians); both are printed in

acknowledged that in writing his history of philosophy, "the Learned *Gassendus* was my precedent."[48]

We can gather some indication of the influence this Epicurean revival exerted by the broad readership of the aforementioned works. Stanley's *History* was among the books in the personal libraries of Evelyn, Locke, and Newton,[49] while Joseph Glanvill also made use of it.[50] Charleton's *Physiologia* was also widely read,[51] and along with Descartes's *Principia philosophiae* was among the important works in Newton's early intellectual formation while at Cambridge.[52] It is also possible to detect a growing English interest in the ideas of both Epicurus and Gassendi through London reprints of Gassendi's works. Gassendi's short synthesis of Epicurean ideas, *Philosophiae Epicuri syntagma*, was reprinted in London in 1660 and 1668, while the *Institutio logica* was reprinted in London in 1668 (together with the *Philosophiae Epicuri syntagma*) and at Oxford in 1718.[53]

As important as this Epicurean literature was in the general spread of Epicurean ideas, the personal influence exercised by the authors themselves on experimental scientific societies was equally important for the heightened reputation of atomism and Gassendi.[54] As Charles Webster observed, "The strength of the new science and philosophy lay outside formal studies, in the scientific clubs which had sprung up in both universities during the interregnum."[55] Charleton was among the active members of the College of Physicians, while both Charleton and Evelyn were involved with the group of experimentalists at Gresham College (1659–1660). Another highly influential member of the Oxford medical community and founding member of the Royal Society, Thomas Willis (1621–1675), is

The History of Philosophy, The Second Volume (London: Humphrey Moseley and Thomas Dring, 1656).

48. Thomas Stanley, "To My Honoured Uncle John Marsham, Esq," in *The History of Philosophy. The First Volume* (London: Humphrey Moseley and Thomas Dring, 1655).

49. See Kroll, *Material Word*, 152.

50. Jackson I. Cope, *Joseph Glanvill: Anglican Apologist* (St. Louis: Washington University, 1956), 133–35.

51. Kargon, *Atomism*, 89; King, "Philosophy and Science," 211, 235, 271–73.

52. Richard S. Westfall, "The Foundations of Newton's Philosophy of Nature," *British Journal for the History of Science* 1 (1962–1963): 171–82, at 172; Geoffrey Gorham, "Newton on God's Relation to Space and Time: The Cartesian Framework," *Archiv für Geschichte der Philosophie* 93 (2011): 281–320.

53. Cf. Kroll, *Material Word*, 155.

54. Cf. Hansruedi Isler, *Thomas Willis, 1621–1675: Doctor and Scientist* (New York: Hafner, 1968), 19.

55. Webster, *Great Instauration*, 144.

known to have referred to Gassendi "quite often," and some of his main concepts on the soul derive from Gassendi.[56] Both Charleton and Evelyn were also among the most active members of the early Royal Society (1660–1663), and Stanley was an active fellow of the Society from 1663.[57] Evelyn was a close friend of John Wilkins,[58] who, as warden of Wadham College (1648–1659), led the "experimental philosophy club" at Oxford, and subsequently became a founding member and secretary of the Royal Society.[59] When John Webster, an advocate of chymical and Hermetic philosophy, launched an attack on scholastic education in his *Academiarum Examen* (1654), John Wilkins and Seth Ward, both leading members of the Oxford club, came to the defense of Oxford with their *Vindiciae Academiarum* (1654).[60] Ward, who wrote the body of the defense, did not concede to the accusation that Baconian experimentalism and new philosophy were neglected at Oxford.[61] Instead, demonstrating familiarity with the works of Gassendi, Ward identified a list of places from Gassendi's *Exercitationes paradoxicae adversus Aristoteleos* (1649) that he accused Webster of plagiarizing.[62] Moreover, in response to Webster's accusation that the schools are ignorant of "Atomicall Learning," Ward replied that in fact those at Oxford "whose studies are toward Physick or Philosophy" are "all employed to salve Mechanically" natural phenomena, and "have in some parts advanced the Philosophy" of atomical learning.[63]

By the time of the Restoration, Robert Boyle became an even more important leader of experimental science through his participation in the Oxford "experimental philosophy club," the meetings at Gresham College, and finally the Royal Society.[64] In this capacity, Boyle surely played a large role during the interregnum

---

56. Isler, *Thomas Willis*, 19–20. We will have occasion to discuss Willis in more detail below and in chapter 6.

57. Webster, *Great Instauration*, 92, 94; *ODNB*, s.v. "Stanley, Thomas."

58. Barbara J. Shapiro, *John Wilkins, 1614–1672: An Intellectual Biography* (Berkeley and Los Angeles: University of California Press, 1969), 116, 122.

59. Shapiro, *John Wilkins*, 118–47, 191–223. For a list of the Oxford club's members, see Webster, *Great Instauration*, 166–69.

60. [Set]h [War]d, *Vindiciae Academiarum* (Oxford: Leonard Lichfield, 1654), with introduction by "[Joh]N. [Wilkin]S." On this debate, see Allen G. Debus, "The Webster-Ward Debate of 1654: The New Philosophy and the Problem of Educational Reform," in *L'univers á la Renaissance: Microcosme et macrocosme* (Brussels: Presses Universitaires de Bruxelles, 1970), 33–51.

61. [War]d, *Vindiciae*, 46, 49–50.

62. [War]d, *Vindiciae*, 33.

63. [War]d, *Vindiciae*, 34, 36.

64. Webster, *Great Instauration*, 92, 94, 155–56.

in stimulating interest in Gassendi's philosophy among members of the various experimental societies. Positive references to Gassendi are scattered throughout his *Works*,[65] and his mature concept of "corpuscularism" was closer to Gassendi than Descartes.[66] As a medical student at Christ Church, Oxford, John Locke became acquainted with Boyle by May 1660 and over the next few years embarked on a reading program in mechanical philosophy that included not only almost everything that Boyle was publishing, but also Descartes's *Principia philosophiae* (Parts 2–4) and the physics of Gassendi's *Syntagma philosophicum* (Sec. 1, Bk. 2).[67] Locke subsequently attended lectures by Willis on neuroanatomy and psychology, where it is quite likely that he was exposed to Gassendian ideas on the soul.[68] Locke is just one example of how "the old boy network," as Robert Frank refers to the Oxford scientific community, generated interest in the works of Gassendi and Descartes.[69] Through their personal relationships and involvement in English experimental societies, active members such as Charleton, Evelyn, Willis, and Boyle were instrumental to the growing reputation of Gassendi, Descartes, and mechanical philosophy.

The revival of interest in Descartes and Gassendi was not confined to the Newcastle circle or members of experimental societies, but also affected the Church of England through the early Latitudinarians. This was a group of divines that largely, though not entirely, originated at Cambridge during the civil wars and interregnum in opposition to the theological dogmatism of the day, or "that

---

65. Boyle's *Works* cite Gassendi's writings at least fifty times. See Margaret J. Osler, "The Intellectual Sources of Robert Boyle's Philosophy of Nature: Gassendi's Voluntarism and Boyle's Physico-Theological Project," in *Philosophy, Science, and Religion 1640–1700*, ed. Richard Kroll, Richard Ashcraft, and Perez Zagorin (Cambridge: Cambridge University Press, 1992), 178–98, at 182; cf. Harrison, "Bacon, Hobbes, Boyle," 210.

66. Antonio Clericuzio, "Gassendi, Charleton and Boyle on Matter and Motion," in *Late Medieval and Early Modern Corpuscular Matter Theories*, ed. Christoph Lüthy, John E. Murdoch, and William R. Newman (Leiden: E. J. Brill, 2001), 467–82, at 469: "far from being a *via media* between Descartes' theory of matter and Gassendi's atomism, Boyle's philosophy had much more in common with the latter's views than with the former's." Cf. Antonio Clericuzio, "L'atomisme de Gassendi et la philosophie corpusculaire de Boyle," in *Gassendi et l'Europe, 1592–1792*, ed. Sylvia Murr (Paris: J. Vrin, 1997), 227–35; and Clericuzio, *Elements, Principles and Corpuscles*, 74.

67. See John R. Milton, "Locke at Oxford," in *Locke's Philosophy: Content and Context*, ed. G. A. J. Rogers (Oxford: Clarendon Press, 1994), 29–47, at 37–38; Milton, "Locke and Gassendi: A Reappraisal," in *English Philosophy in the Age of Locke*, ed. M. A. Stewart (Oxford: Clarendon Press, 2000), 87–109, at 89, 92, 97; and Milton, "Locke, John," in *ODNB*.

68. See Isler, *Thomas Willis*, 30–31, 174–81. Locke's relation to Willis is discussed in chapter 6 below.

69. Frank, *Harvey*, 59.

hide-bound, strait-lac'd spirit that did then prevail."[70] According to Gilbert Burnet, early Latitudinarians could be divided into two generations. The first genera-tion was mostly composed of Cambridge divines such as Henry More and Ralph Cudworth, but also included John Wilkins at Oxford. The second-generation, or "those who were formed under them," included such famous men as Simon Patrick, John Tillotson, Edward Stillingfleet, and Joseph Glanvill.[71] Thomas Burnet (c.1635–1715), author of the controversial *Telluris theoria sacra* (1681, 1689; *Sacred Theory of the Earth* [1684, 1690]), and a man whom Gilbert Burnet praised as "the most considerable among those of the younger sort" at Cambridge,[72] probably also belonged to these second-generation Latitudinarians. Thomas Burnet literally fol-lowed Cudworth from Clare to Christ's in 1654, and as a fellow of Christ's (1657–1678) became colleagues with More and Cudworth for two decades.[73]

The Latitudinarians were distinguished by a number of characteristics, which, while generally applicable to most individuals, admit of certain exceptions.[74] In the-ology, they tended to emphasize the role of reason, doctrinal minimalism, practical

---

70. P[atrick], *A Brief Account*, 5. See Martin I. J. Griffin Jr., *Latitudinarianism in the Seventeenth-Century Church of England*, ed. Lila Freedman (Leiden: E. J. Brill, 1992); Patrick Müller, *Latitudinarianism and Didacticism in Eighteenth Century Literature: Moral Theology in Fielding, Sterne, and Goldsmith* (Frankfurt am Main: Peter Lang, 2009), 15–44; and Norman Sykes, *From Sheldon to Secker: Aspects of English Church History 1660–1768* (Cambridge: Cambridge University Press, 1959), ch. 5. The most important primary sources for our knowledge of the main figures and their beliefs are P[atrick]., *A Brief Account*, 14–24; Edward Fowler, *Principles and Practices of Certain Moderate Divines of the Church of England* (London: Lodowick Lloyd, 1670); Joseph Glanvill, "Anti-Fanatical Religion, and Free Philosophy. In a Continuation of the New Atlantis," in *Essays on Several Important Subjects in Philosophy and Religion* (London: J. D., 1676); Jackson I. Cope, "'The Cupri-Cosmits': Glanvill on Latitudinarian Anti-Enthusiasm," *The Huntington Library Quarterly* 17, no. 3 (1954): 269–86; Gilbert Burnet, *History of My Own Time*, ed. Osmund Airy (Oxford: Clarendon Press, 1897), 1:331–41; Gilbert Burnet, *A Supplement to Burnet's History of My Own Time*, ed. H. C. Foxcroft (Oxford: Clarendon Press, 1902), 45–46, 463–64; and William Baron, *An Historical Account of Comprehension, and Toleration. From the Old Puritan to the New Latitudinarian; with their continued Projects and Designs, in Opposition to our more Orthodox Establishment* (London: J. Chantry and Church Simmons, 1706). Baron (b. 1636) has been generally ignored, but he speaks from personal experience as a graduate of Caius College, Cambridge (BA, 1658–1659; MA, 1662). See John Venn, *Biographical History of Gonville and Caius College, 1349–1897* (Cambridge: Cambridge University Press, 1897), 1:390.

71. Burnet, *History*, 1:335. Cf. Alan Gabbey, "Cudworth, More and the Mechanical Philosophy," in *Philosophy, Science, and Religion 1640–1700*, ed. Richard Kroll, Richard Ashcraft, and Perez Zagorin (Cambridge: Cambridge University Press, 1992), 109–27, at 109–10; and Frederic B. Burnham, "The Latitudinarian Background to the Royal Society, 1647–1667" (PhD diss., The Johns Hopkins University, 1970), 17–18. With the exception of Gabbey, "Cudworth, More," 122n5, Burnham's dissertation has been ignored in the secondary literature.

72. Burnet, *Supplement*, 463–64.

73. Gascoigne, *Cambridge*, 66.

74. Cf. Griffin, *Latitudinarianism*, 43–44.

morality, and anti-Calvinist soteriology. These theological tendencies dovetailed in many cases with an attraction to Arminianism, particularly the works of the Dutch Remonstrant, Simon Episcopius (1583–1643).[75] In philosophy, the connections between the early Latitudinarians and the new philosophy were particularly strong.[76] Yet interest in the new philosophy was not exclusive to the Latitudinarians, and some prominent second-generation Latitudinarians such as Edward Fowler displayed little interest in the new philosophy or science, so it must be acknowledged that the "circles of Latitudinarianism and of the new science intersected but did not coalesce,"[77] and attempts to identify an exclusive "Latitudinarian" ideology for the Royal Society are untenable.[78] Still, recent efforts to dispute the "prominent place" of interest in new science and philosophy among Latitudinarians, and relegate it to a peripheral concern, are unconvincing.[79] The testimony of contemporaries who perceived strong connections between early Latitudinarians and

---

75. Griffin, *Latitudinarianism*, vii. Wilkins constitutes an important exception to this generalization; on his Reformed theology, see Hampton, *Anti-Arminians*, 9, 16–17. The Arminian aspect is highlighted by John Gascoigne, "Isaac Barrow's Academic Milieu: Interregnum and Restoration Cambridge," in *Before Newton: The Life and Times of Isaac Barrow*, ed. Mordechai Feingold (Cambridge: Cambridge University Press, 1990), 250–90, at 257–61; John Spurr, "'Latitudinarianism' and the Restoration Church," *The Historical Journal* 31, no. 1 (1988): 61–82; and Hampton, *Anti-Arminians*, 60–75, 211–19. For evidence of the impact of Episcopius, see Burnet, *History*, 1:334; Herbert Thorndike, *The Theological Works of Herbert Thorndike* (Oxford: John Henry Parker, 1854–1856), 5:343, 439, 6:241–2; Thomas Birch, *The Life of the Most Reverend Dr. John Tillotson*, 2nd ed. (London: J. and R. Tonson et al., 1753), 219–20; William Baron, *An Historical Account*, 50; cf. Rosalie Colie, *Light and Enlightenment: A Study of the Cambridge Platonists and the Dutch Arminians* (Cambridge: Cambridge University Press, 1957), 22–48; Sykes, *From Sheldon to Secker*, 107, 142–43.

76. Gascoigne, *Cambridge*, 40–68; Griffin, *Latitudinarianism*, 25, 38–39, 45; also J. E. Saveson, "Differing Reactions to Descartes among the Cambridge Platonists," *Journal of the History of Ideas* 21 (1960): 560–67; Gabbey, "Cudworth, More," 109–27; John Tulloch, *Rational Theology and Christian Philosophy in England in the Seventeenth Century*, 2nd ed. (Edinburgh: W. Blackwood, 1874), 2:17–23, 368–97; and Hans Aarsleff, "John Wilkins," in *Dictionary of Scientific Biography*, ed. Charles C. Gillispie (New York: Charles Scribner's Sons, 1976), 14:361–8n160.

77. Griffin, *Latitudinarianism*, 45.

78. Michael Hunter, *Establishing the New Science: The Experience of the Early Royal Society* (Woodbridge: Boydell Press, 1989), 45–72.

79. Spurr, "'Latitudinarianism,'" 75–76. Spurr is followed by Levitin, *Ancient Wisdom*, 14; and Susan McMahon, "Constructing Natural History in England (1650–1700)" (PhD diss., University of Alberta, 2001), 120. For critical responses to Spurr, see John Marshall, *John Locke: Resistance, Religion and Responsibility* (Cambridge: Cambridge University Press, 1994), 39–40; Isabel Rivers, *Reason, Grace, and Sentiment: A Study of the Language of Religion and Ethics in England, 1660–1780* (Cambridge: Cambridge University Press, 1991), 1:26; Nicholas Tyacke, "From Laudians to Latitudinarians: A Shifting Balance of Theological Forces," in *The Later Stuart Church, 1660–1714*, ed. Grant Tapsell (Manchester: Manchester University Press, 2012), 46–67, at 64n11; and Müller, *Latitudinarianism*, 42.

the new philosophy cannot be easily dismissed. Burnet observed that the original Cambridge men "allowed a great freedom both in philosophy and in divinity."[80] Glanvill's original manuscript for "Anti-Fanatical Religion and Free Philosophy" (1676) referred to the subjects of his narrative with the term "latitudinarian."[81] In the first account of the "Latitude-men," the Latitudinarian S. P. responded to an inquiry in early 1662 from a certain G. B. of Oxford, who had heard of "a certain new sect of men called Latitude-men" that "had their rise at Cambridge, and are followers for the most part, of the new Philosophy."[82] In S. P.'s reply, he acknowledged that "the greatest part" of the Latitudinarians originated at Cambridge and that they "have introduced a new Philosophy; Aristotle and the Schoolemen are out of request with them."[83] Furthermore, S. P. continued, the "new and free philosophy" that the Latitudinarians introduced was actually "antienter than Aristotle" and equivalent to "atomicall" philosophy or the "atomical Hypothesis."[84] These Latitudinarian witnesses are corroborated by others who looked unfavorably upon these developments. William Baron (b. 1636), himself a graduate of Caius College, Cambridge (BA, 1658–1659; MA, 1662), wrote in retrospect of the early Latitudinarians, "I ever observed them to be no less prejudic'd in their *New Courses* both of *Philosophy* and *Divinity*, than those Old *Scholastick Aristotelians* whom they so industriously indeavoured to Expose. . . . Nothing could be of Value with them but the great *Des Cartes*."[85] John North (1645–1683), who matriculated at Jesus College, Cambridge in 1661 (BA, 1664; MA, 1666) and later served as Master of Trinity College, Cambridge (1677–1683), was likewise well placed to make an informed judgment. According to North, "It hath been observed that the Latitudinarians are generally Cartesians."[86] The accounts of Baron and North are confirmed by Baxter, who observed that "those that were called *Latitudinarians*" were at first "*Cambridge Arminians,* and some of them not so much; and were much for new and free Philosophy, and especially for *Cartes*."[87] Elsewhere Baxter

---

80. Burnet, *History*, 1:334.

81. Cope, " 'The Cupri-Cosmits,' " 271.

82. P[atrick]., *A Brief Account*, 3. "S. P." is traditionally identified as Simon Patrick (1626–1707). See T. A. Birrell, introduction to *A Brief Account of the New Sect of Latitude-Men* (1662; repr., Los Angeles: University of California, 1963), i. On Patrick, see Johannes van den Berg, "Between Platonism and Enlightenment: Simon Patrick (1625–1707) and His Place in the Latitudinarian Movement," *Dutch Review of Church History* 68, no. 2 (1988): 164–79.

83. P[atrick]., *A Brief Account*, 5, 14.

84. P[atrick]., *A Brief Account*, 19–20, 24.

85. Baron, *An Historical Account*, 49. On Baron's career, see Venn, *Biographical History*, 1:390.

86. British Library, Add. 32514, fol. 176v, as cited in Gascoigne, *Cambridge*, 63.

87. *Rel. Bax.*, III.19–20.

wrote, "A second sort of Conformists were those called *Latitudinarians*, who were mostly *Cambridge*-men, *Platonists* or *Cartesians*, and many of them *Arminians* with some Additions."[88]

As such examples demonstrate, contemporaries consistently asserted a connection between innovation in theology and philosophy. One of the clearest ways these areas converged was in the polemic against "enthusiasm." The Latitudinarians, beginning with Henry More, promoted the use of mechanical philosophy as an antidote to "enthusiasm" understood as claims to direct supernatural inspiration. Reacting strongly against enthusiasm of the interregnum in all its varieties—both religious (Quakers and religious radicals) and philosophical (the Hermetic or alchemical quest for hidden natural powers)—the early Latitudinarians, particularly More, appealed to the regular order of nature to argue that forms of enthusiasm are products of physiological processes and therefore not of supernatural origin.[89] This anti-enthusiast polemic had a large influence on Restoration Anglicans, and became a part of early Royal Society apologetics. By showing that effects otherwise believed to be extraordinary supernatural events are actually the "inward workings of things," "common Instruments of Nature," and bodily influences on the imagination, Royal Society apologist Thomas Sprat argued in a succinct restatement of the interregnum apologetic, the experimental philosopher would not "be forward to assent to Spiritual Raptures, and Revelations."[90] Sprat's argument was shortly thereafter echoed in Joseph Glanvill's *Philosophia Pia*, written as an apology for the Royal Society, according to which "a *Philosophical* use of *observation*, and the *knowledge of humane nature* by *it*, helps us to distinguish between the *effects* of the adorable *Spirit*, and *those* of an hot,

---

88. *Rel. Bax.*, II.386. Cf. a remark made to John Beale in 1669 that Cambridge "is entirely Anti-Calvinian, & Anti-Aristotelian, generally Cartesian, a great growth there in Mathematics, & not without a Club of Phylosophicall Chemists," as cited in Mordechai Feingold, "Isaac Barrow: Divine, Scholar, Mathematician," in *Before Newton: The Life and Times of Isaac Barrow*, ed. Mordechai Feingold (Cambridge: Cambridge University Press, 1990), 1–104, at 25.

89. George Williamson, "The Restoration Revolt against Enthusiasm," *Studies in Philology* 30, no. 4 (1933): 571–603; Michael Heyd, "The Reaction to Enthusiasm in the Seventeenth Century: Towards an Integrative Approach," *The Journal of the History of Ideas* 53, no. 2 (1981): 258–80; Frederic B. Burnham, "The More-Vaughan Controversy: The Revolt Against Philosophical Enthusiasm," *Journal of the History of Ideas* 35, no. 1 (1974): 33–49; Fouke, *Enthusiastical Concerns*; Cope, "'The Cupri-Cosmits,'" 269–86.

90. Thomas Sprat, *The History of the Royal Society, for the Improving of Natural Knowledge* (London: T. R., 1667), 358–59; P. B. Wood, "Methodology and Apologetics: Thomas Sprat's *History of the Royal Society*," *British Journal for the History of Science* 13 (1980): 1–26, at 16–21; Fouke, *Enthusiastical Concerns*, 231–32; Burnham, "Latitudinarian Background," 233–37; Michael Heyd, *"Be Sober and Reasonable": The Critique of Enthusiasm in the Seventeenth and Early Eighteenth Centuries* (Leiden: Brill, 1995), 157–58.

distemper'd fancy; which is no small advantage for the securing the *purity, honour,* and *all* the interests of *Religion.*"[91]

We can further illustrate the conjunction between Latitudinarians and the new philosophy through specific examples from Henry More, Joseph Glanvill, and Edward Stillingfleet. In the 1640s, the Cambridge divine Henry More began eagerly promoting Cartesian philosophy, albeit as useful to his own apologetic enterprise.[92] Although More is generally known for his highly influential role in the spread of Cartesianism in England,[93] his reception of mechanical philosophy was quite eclectic and incorporated various atomist doctrines. More espoused a uniquely conceived infinite void and atoms while rejecting the Cartesian equation of body with material extension.[94] Significantly, in the prefatory remarks to his early poem entitled *Democritus Platonissans,* he appealed to the "noble patronage" of the "ancients, Epicurus, Democritus, Lucretius, &c." before appending the authority of Descartes—"that sublime and subtil Meckanick too."[95] Although these remarks antedate Gassendi's major works and should not be read as evidence of Gassendian influence, they indicate, as Alan Gabbey remarks that More "saw [Descartes's] *Principia* as a striking contemporary revival of cosmological ideas originally due to the ancient Atomists."[96] These remarks also anticipate the appeal to antiquity and the melding of atomism, Cartesianism, and Platonism that would come to characterize the philosophizing of a segment of Latitudinarian divines.

---

91. Joseph Glanvill, *Philosophia Pia, Or, A Discourse of the Religious Temper, and Tendencies of the Experimental Philosophy, which is profest by the Royal Society* (London: J. Macock, 1671), 64. The far-reaching consequences of this anti-enthusiast polemic are suggested by Fouke, *Enthusiastical Concerns,* 232–33; and Keith Thomas, *Religion and the Decline of Magic* (London: Weidenfeld and Nicolson, 1971), 145–46, and on Baxter's more traditional position, 130–32.

92. Alan Gabbey, *"Philosophia Cartesiana Triumphata:* Henry More (1646–1671)," in *Problems of Cartesianism,* ed. Thomas M. Lennon, John N. Nicholas, and John W. Davis (Toronto: McGill-Queens University Press, 1982), 171–250; see also Alan Gabbey, "Henry More and the Limits of Mechanism," in *Henry More (1614–1687): Tercentenary Studies,* ed. Sarah Hutton and Robert Crocker (Dordrecht: Kluwer, 1990), 19–35; and Gabbey, "Cudworth, More," 109–127.

93. Nicolson, "Early Stage," 356–74; Feingold, "Isaac Barrow," 25.

94. More initially conceived of the void, unlike ancient Epicureanism, without a vacuum, and in his mature writings he retracted his original view of an infinite corporeal universe, maintaining instead an extra-mundane void. See Jasper Reid, *The Metaphysics of Henry More* (Dordrecht: Springer, 2012), 44–63. Older studies include Robert Crocker, *Henry More, 1614–1687: A Biography of the Cambridge Platonist* (Dordrecht: Kluwer, 2003), 68–70; and Harrison, "Ancient Atomists," 41–42.

95. Henry More, "To the Reader," in *Democritus Platonissans, or, An Essay upon the Infinity of Worlds out of Platonick Principles* (Cambridge: Roger Daniel, 1646), A2r.

96. Gabbey, *"Philosophia Cartesiana Triumphata,"* 181.

One of the early Latitudinarians, Joseph Glanvill, who has been described as "a kind of final, living synthesis of the latitudinarianism of Cambridge and Oxford,"[97] painted a revealing picture of the interregnum Latitudinarians in his "Anti-Fanatical Religion, and Free Philosophy."[98] The narrative, cast in the form of a utopian fulfillment of Bacon's *New Atlantis*, describes the early Latitudinarian reaction to interregnum enthusiasm and Calvinist theology, and explains that they overcame the problematic scholasticism of the day by returning to ancient sources—both in philosophy and in theology. In philosophy, they perfected the ancients with the help of modern discoveries in anatomy, mathematics, natural history, and mechanics, and experimental philosophy. In theology, they returned to the ancient faith and practice of the church fathers from the first three centuries after the apostles.[99]

After describing in some detail the anti-Calvinist theology of the Latitudinarians, Glanvill turned to their philosophy. According to Glanvill, the Latitudinarians saw the Aristotelian philosophy of the schools as a corruption of Aristotle's own philosophy. Moreover, they viewed the scholastics' foundational principles of *materia prima*, substantial forms, and qualities as groundless, making the entire superstructure of philosophy "fantastical, and useless." By contrast, the Latitudinarians held that "the *Corpuscular Philosophy* was the *eldest*, and most accountable Doctrine: That it was as *ancient* as *Natural Philosophy* it self," and that by comparison the Aristotelian philosophy was "novel." In this context, Glanvill noted that they read both Gassendi's philosophy, "which restor'd, and amplified the *Atomical Doctrine*," and Descartes, "that other great man of your World." Although they "consider'd, and studied much" Descartes's philosophy, which "they thought to be the nearest *Mechanical* System of things that appear'd in the World," yet they "entertain'd what they thought *probable*, and *freely dissented* in other matters."[100]

When it came to metaphysical questions, Glanvill observed that the Latitudinarians were divided on the one hand between a Platonic and Cartesian

97. Burnham, "Latitudinarian Background," 238.

98. Joseph Glanvill, "Anti-Fanatical Religion, and Free Philosophy. In a Continuation of the New Atlantis," in *Essays on Several Important Subjects in Philosophy and Religion* (London: J. D., 1676). Cf. Cope, "'The Cupri-Cosmits,'" 269–86; Burnham, "The Latitudinarian Background," 31–44; G. A. J. Rogers, "Locke and the Latitude-Men: Ignorance as a Ground of Toleration," in *Philosophy, Science, and Religion 1640–1700*, ed. Richard Kroll, Richard Ashcraft, and Perez Zagorin (Cambridge: Cambridge University Press, 1992), 240–42; Griffin, *Latitudinarianism*, 34–36; and Crocker, *Henry More*, 80–81.

99. Glanvill, "Anti-Fanatical Religion," in *Essays*, 4–11. On interest in the early church fathers, cf. Milton, "Locke at Oxford," 42; and P[atrick]., *A Brief Account*, 24.

100. Glanvill, "Anti-Fanatical Religion," in *Essays*, 50. On the antiquity of "new philosophy," cf. P[atrick]., *A Brief Account*, 14; Sailor, "Moses and Atomism," 10; Reid, *Metaphysics of Henry More*, 21–22.

explanation of the nature of spirits, and on the other hand over whether to introduce a Platonic world soul to account for nonhuman phenomena or rely on Cartesian mechanism:

> They had different thoughts, as other Philosophers have; *Some* of them supposing that the *Platonical* Opinions are very fit to be admitted, to give assistance to the *Mechanical* Principles; which they think very defective of themselves. And *Others* judging, That the *Cartesian Hypotheses* are *probable,* and *Mechanism* sufficient to account for the *Phaenomena;* and that there is no *need* of introducing so hopeless, and obscure a Principle, as the *Soul* of the World.[101]

Glanvill's description is remarkable in at least two respects. First, he observed a split between Latitudinarians who supported a purer mechanical philosophy and those who advocated what Henry More would call a "mixt Mechanicall Philosophy," which supplemented mechanism with a Platonic animating principle (More's "Spirit of Nature").[102] Glanvill's understanding of early Latitudinarianism was not exhausted by what came to be called Cambridge Platonism, but included both Platonizing and non-Platonizing supporters of the new philosophy.[103] Second, despite the important place accorded Descartes, it is noteworthy that Glanvill framed the entire discussion of mechanical philosophy in terms of the probability and antiquity of philosophical principles. For at least some early Latitudinarians, the reception of Cartesianism would be subsumed within a historical frame of reference that privileged an amalgam of ancient atomism and ancient Christianity. And for others, following in the steps of More and Cudworth, this reception would be supplemented by Platonic philosophy.

Edward Stillingfleet provides a good illustration of the early Latitudinarian reception of Gassendi and Descartes within the context of increasing interest in Epicureanism. Having studied at St. Johns, Cambridge in the 1650s, Stillingfleet became a leading post-Restoration Anglican and was eventually elected bishop of Worcester in 1689.[104] Gilbert Burnet placed him among the "most eminent"

---

101. Glanvill, "Anti-Fanatical Religion," in *Essays,* 53.

102. See Reid, *Metaphysics of Henry More,* 298–99.

103. Cf. *Rel. Bax.,* II.386: "those called *Latitudinarians,* who were mostly *Cambridge-men, Platonists* or *Cartesians.*" The difference between Platonizing and non-Platonizing Latitudinarians has often "puzzled scholars" (Barbara J. Shapiro, *Probability and Certainty in Seventeenth-Century England: A Study of the Relationships between Natural Science, Religion, History, Law, and Literature* [Princeton, NJ: Princeton University Press, 1983], 106).

104. *ODNB,* s.v. "Stillingfleet, Edward."

of second-generation Latitudinarian divines.[105] In Stillingfleet's popular apologetic for Christianity, *Origines Sacrae* (1662), which went through five editions by 1680 and has been called "the earliest and most systematic description of the Latitudinarian theology of faith and reason,"[106] he addressed traditional topics of God's existence, the soul's immortality, the origin of the universe, and providence.[107] Throughout his discussion of all of these topics, Stillingfleet was deeply concerned with the problem of Epicureanism in its unmodified ancient form, which he took as tending to atheism. By contrast, he only dealt briefly with Descartes's natural philosophy.[108] Although Cartesian ideas made a favorable appearance (the proof for God's existence and laws of nature),[109] in his refutation of ancient Epicureanism, Gassendi was more frequently cited. After having criticized Descartes's denial that we can know final causes in creation,[110] Stillingfleet drew on Gassendi's mature *Syntagma philosophicum* (1658) for the argument from design in creation.[111] He also drew on both the logical and physical parts of the *Syntagma philosophicum* to argue for the internal incoherence of unmodified ancient Epicurean physics.[112] While Stillingfleet approved of the revival of atomism so long as it supposed God's creation and providence, and favored Gassendi's account of the manner of God's creative act over that of Descartes, he was also critical of Gassendi's revival of Epicurean ethics.[113] Thus, although Stillingfleet was more polemical toward Epicureanism than were Gassendi and Charleton, he likewise participated in the growing reputation of Gassendi's Christian Epicureanism with respect to the doctrines of creation and providence.

As the case of Stillingfleet illustrates, the revival of Epicurean ideas associated with Gassendi could evoke both hostility and eclectic reception, with the result that the rhetoric surrounding "Epicureanism" during the interregnum and following the Restoration would inevitably include a broad semantic range. On the one hand, such rhetoric could be used as a polemical tool to refer to the unmodified ancient teachings of the Epicureans. The antiprovidential

---

105. Burnet, *History*, 1:335.

106. Griffin, *Latitudinarianism*, 23.

107. Edward Stillingfleet, *Origines Sacrae* (London: R.W., 1662), III.i–iii.

108. Stillingfleet, *Origines Sacrae*, 466–69 (on Descartes), 447–66 (on Epicurean natural philosophy).

109. Stillingfleet, *Origines Sacrae*, 400, 457.

110. Stillingfleet, *Origines Sacrae*, 403.

111. Stillingfleet, *Origines Sacrae*, 405.

112. Stillingfleet, *Origines Sacrae*, 456, 458.

113. Stillingfleet, *Origines Sacrae*, 448, 454, 469.

materialism inherent in this view naturally led contemporaries—whether for or against mechanical philosophy—to associate Epicureanism with Hobbes and atheism.[114] On the other hand, even in the midst of such polemics, many were often drawing—either silently or publicly—on Gassendi's Christian Epicureanism, with the result that, particularly in physics, Epicurus could carry a positive signification for proponents of mechanical philosophy. Moreover, given the similar appeal to explain phenomena by matter and motion among various anti-Aristotelian philosophers, the label "Epicurean" could also provide convenient shorthand for a common anti-Aristotelian endeavor. Thus, among proponents of mechanical philosophy, Henry Oldenburg could write to Spinoza that Boyle used "Epicurean principles" regarding "innate motion in particles" as hypotheses in his experiments,[115] while Gottfried Wilhelm Leibniz could refer to modern philosophers such as Galileo, Bacon, Gassendi, Descartes, Hobbes, and Digby as revivers of Democritus and Epicurus.[116] Newton nicely summed up the desire to resuscitate ancient Epicurean philosophy while purging it of its atheistic reputation with the remark, "The philosophy of Epicurus and Lucretius is true and old, but was wrongly interpreted by the ancients as atheism."[117] Baxter, as we shall see, exploited the wide semantic range of Epicureanism to polemical advantage.

Baxter's Early Response to Hobbes's Leviathan

Baxter did not take an active interest in the early dissemination of the thought of Gassendi and Descartes during the 1650s. However, his later response to

114. Harrison, "Bacon, Hobbes, Boyle," 200; Kargon, Atomism, 82–83; Samuel I. Mintz, The Hunting of Leviathan (Cambridge: Cambridge University Press, 1962), 39–40; Jon Parkin, Taming the Leviathan: The Reception of the Political and Religious Ideas of Thomas Hobbes in England 1640–1700 (Cambridge: Cambridge University Press, 2007), 260, 393; Spiller, Meric Casaubon, 93–94; Shapiro, John Wilkins, 233; J. J. Macintosh, "Robert Boyle on Epicurean Atheism and Atomism," in Atoms, Pneuma, and Tranquillity: Epicurean and Stoic Themes in European Thought, ed. Margaret J. Osler (Cambridge: Cambridge University Press, 1991), 197–219; Tulloch, Rational Theology, 2:248–50.

115. Oldenburg to Spinoza, 3 Apr. 1663, in Benedict de Spinoza, Complete Works, trans. Samuel Shirley, ed. Michael Morgan (Indianapolis: Hackett, 2002), 786.

116. Gottfried Wilhelm Leibniz, "The Confession of Nature against Atheists [1669]," in Philosophical Papers and Letters, trans. and ed. Leroy E. Loemker, 2nd ed. (Dordrecht: Kluwer Academic, 1989), 110. Of course, Leibniz recognized specific differences between the "modern followers" of Epicurus like Gassendi and other mechanical philosophers (112).

117. Albury, "Halley's Ode," 39.

mechanical philosophy was surely colored by the publication of Hobbes's *Leviathan* (1651). Baxter was among the earliest critics of the *Leviathan*, and in the opinion of one scholar, a "leading opponent of Hobbes' work."[118] During February and March 1652, Baxter corresponded with Thomas Hill, a Master of Trinity College, Cambridge, about Hobbes's *Leviathan*. Baxter's immediate concern in this correspondence was Hobbes's teaching in *Leviathan* chapters 41–42 that Christ's office is merely to teach while princes govern, so that the governance of Christ and ministers on earth is subordinate to civil authority.[119] Baxter's concerns regarding the *Leviathan* soon expanded. By December 1654, he was petitioning Parliament to burn the *Leviathan* to "manifest a disowning" of books that are "against the Fundamentals or Essentials of Christianity; and that slander or reproach Magistracy, Ministry, or the Ordinances of Christ."[120]

By 1655 it was clear that Baxter saw Hobbes's *Leviathan* as indicative of a rising tide of "infidelity" in England, for which a renewed apologetic enterprise was necessary. In his preface to *The Unreasonableness of Infidelity* (1655), which he intended as a supplement to the apologetic Part 2 of *The Saints Everlasting Rest*,[121] Baxter presented a narrative of the growth of interregnum sects from his own experience. Due to the "prevailing giddyness, unruliness and levity of these times," as well as the "great ignorance, loosness, or ungodly violence of too many Ecclesiasticks," Baxter wrote, the Church of England lost its authority in the eyes of many, who became suspicious of ministers' teaching and condemned the Church's government.[122] From this arose two main kinds of sects: "Pelagian Anabaptists" and "Antinomian Anabaptists," the latter including Familists, Seekers, Ranters, and Quakers.[123] From this "Gulf of Infidelity" came forth "hotter or less reserved minds" who "vent themselves more freely" against the ministry of the Church and various truths of supernatural revelation, especially the immortality of the soul.[124] Baxter claimed to have had conversations with many of such opinions,

---

118. Parkin, *Taming the Leviathan*, 112.

119. Baxter to Thomas Hill, 8 Mar. 1652 (DWL BC III.272v); *CCRB*, 1:74–76; cf. Parkin, *Taming the Leviathan*, 112–14.

120. Richard Baxter, *Humble Advice: Or the Heads of those Things which were Offered to Many Honourable Members of Parliament by Richard Baxter at the End of his Sermon, Decemb. 24. at the Abby in Westminster* (London: Thomas Underhill and Francis Tyton, 1655), 7.

121. Richard Baxter, "The Preface," in *The Unreasonableness of Infidelity* (London: R. W. for Thomas Underhill, 1655), C3r; *Rel. Bax.*, I.116.

122. Baxter, "The Preface," in *Unreasonableness*, Av.

123. Baxter, "The Preface," in *Unreasonableness*, C1r–C1v.

124. Baxter, "The Preface," in *Unreasonableness*, C1v–C2r.

and that even the educated were being convinced of such opinions after reading Hobbes's *Leviathan*. In Baxter's account, "I have perceived that some persons of considerable quality and learning, having much conversed with men of that way, and read such Books as *Hobbs* his *Leviathan*, have been sadly infected with this mortal pestilance."[125] He hoped that by publishing *Unreasonableness of Infidelity*, he would help those who might be tempted by the arguments of Hobbes, among others.

For the next decade (1655–1665), although Baxter was clearly aware of Descartes's writings,[126] he remained relatively silent about mechanical philosophy in general. But along with almost the entire Church of England, he continued to attack Hobbes's *Leviathan* in connection with the perceived spread of infidelity.[127] This silence may be attributed to various factors. Baxter had other pressing matters on his mind. During the years 1660–1661, Baxter was busy leading negotiations between the Presbyterians and the Church of England in an attempt to retain ecclesiastical unity.[128] Moreover, at least until 1656, he still assumed that the philosophy of Aristotle held sway in the schools, for he spoke of the common practice of "using *Aristotle* as a help in Naturals,"[129] and still referred to "Aristotles school" as a synonym for philosophy.[130] In addition, Gassendi's works were not as accessible as they would be following the publication of his *Opera omnia* (1658). As we shall see, the growing popularity of Gassendi's mature philosophy alarmed Baxter. This growing appreciation of Gassendi's philosophy, as it happens, coincided with the formation of the Royal Society.

---

125. Baxter, "The Preface," in *Unreasonableness*, C2r.

126. Richard Baxter, *The Reduction of a Digressor: or Rich. Baxter's Reply to George Kendall's Digression in his Book against Mr. Goodwin* (London: A. M. for Thomas Underhill, 1654), 126 (Descartes, Digby, White, and Hobbes on visible *species*); Richard Baxter, *Of Justification* (London: R. W. for Nevil Simmons, 1658), 196 (Descartes on vibration).

127. Richard Baxter, *Gildas Salvinus; The Reformed Pastor* (London: Robert White for Nevil Simmons, 1656), 271; Baxter, *Confirmation and Restauration* (London: A.M. for Nevil Simmons, 1658), 81; Baxter, *The Crucifying of the world, by the Cross of Christ* (London: Joseph Cranford, 1658), 101; Baxter, *Of Justification*, 195; Baxter, *A Key for Catholicks* (London: R. W. for Nevil Simmons, 1659), 335; Baxter, *A Holy Commonwealth, or, Political Aphorisms, Opening the true Principles of Government* (London: Thomas Underhill and Francis Tyton, 1659), 225; Baxter, *An Accompt of all the Proceedings of the Commissioners of both Perswasions* (London, 1661), 72. Cf. the polemic against Hobbes at this time in Parkin, *Taming the Leviathan*; and Mintz, *Hunting of Leviathan*.

128. Nuttall, *Richard Baxter*, 85–90.

129. Baxter, *Reduction*, 9.

130. Baxter, *Gildas Salvinus*, 129; also 265. Cf. Isler, *Thomas Willis*, 30, who notes the testimony of Edward Bagshaw in 1661: "He [Aristotle] has driven out all other philosophers, and rules supreme, especially in Christ Church [Oxford]."

The Beginning of Baxter's Restoration Polemics

It was not until mechanical philosophy began to be publicly promoted in association with the establishment of the Royal Society that Baxter entered the fray. After the initial efforts of Charleton, Evelyn, Stanley, and others to translate and adapt ancient Epicureanism and Gassendi's ideas for an English audience in the 1650s, an increasing number of works in the early 1660s demonstrated the growing popularity of the philosophy of Gassendi and Descartes. Despite the Royal Society's diversified constituency and lack of an explicit corporate "ideology" other than experimentation,[131] an influential segment of its fellows were dedicated to the mechanical philosophy and recognized by their contemporaries as such.[132] While the Society's public affirmations of mechanical philosophy remained initially muted in favor of Baconian experimentalism, by the 1670s such restraint gave way to more open affirmations of mechanical philosophy, as evident in the Society's minutes.[133]

Even though the Royal Society was composed of a diverse membership, it is possible to detect a growing perception that its members were in one way or another associated with mechanical or Epicurean philosophy. The Royal Society began from meetings held at Gresham College during 1660–1663, and an anonymous "Ballad of Gresham College" from the early 1660s connected a preference for Epicurus over Aristotle with this early group:

> Thy Colledg, Gresham, shall hereafter
> Be the whole world's Universitie,
> Oxford and Cambridge are our laughter;
> Their learning is but Pedantry.
> These new Collegiates doe assure us
> Aristotle's an Asse to Epicurus.[134]

In 1661, Joseph Glanvill stated that while "the more excellent *Hypotheses* of *Democritus* and *Epicurus* have long lain buryed under neglect and obloquy," yet "the ingenuity of this age recall'd them from their *Urne*."[135] In 1662, the early

---

131. Hunter, *Establishing the New Science*, 45–72.

132. Hunter, *Establishing the New Science*, 208–9.

133. Theodore Brown, *The Mechanical Philosophy and the 'Animal Oeconomy'* (New York: Arno Press, 1981), 115–18.

134. Dorothy Stimson, "Ballad of Gresham Colledge," *Isis* 18, no. 1 (1932): 109; Kargon, *Atomism*, 134.

135. Joseph Glanvill, *The Vanity of Dogmatizing* (London: E. C., 1661), 146.

Latitudinarians, many of whom were among the earliest fellows of the Royal Society, were being publicly identified with the "new philosophy" or "mechanical philosophy."[136] This was the same year in which Stillingfleet wrote that the "*Atomical* or *Epicurean Hypothesis*" "makes most noise in the World," and that "many of the *Phænomena* of the Universe, are far more intelligibly explain'd by Matter and Motion than by substantial Forms, and real Qualities, few free and unprejudic'd Minds do now scruple."[137] Burnet reported of his visit to Cambridge in the following year, "the new philosophy was then much in all people's discourse, and the Royal Society was much talked of."[138] By 1665, Glanvill was publicly praising the members of the Royal Society, "that some of you ... publickly own the Cartesian, and Atomical Hypothesis."[139] The Frenchman Samuel Sorbière (1615–1670), a friend of Gassendi and honorary Royal Society fellow from 1663, published in 1664 an account of his journeys to England, in which he stated that the mathematicians of the Royal Society preferred Descartes while other writers ("les literateurs") preferred Gassendi.[140] This public association of Descartes and Gassendi with the Royal Society elicited a response from Thomas Sprat (1635–1713), also a Royal Society fellow from 1663, who did his best to disassociate the Society from reliance on particular philosophical sects or books. He emphasized that "neither of these two men bear any sway amongst them: they are never named there as Dictators over men's Reasons; nor is there any extraordinary reference to their judgments."[141] Sorbière's judgment, in retrospect, was much closer to the truth.[142] Indeed, Henry Oldenberg wrote privately to Spinoza in 1661 that "our Philosophical Society" was conducting experiments with the intention of showing

---

136. P[atrick]., *A Brief Account*, 14–24.

137. Stillingfleet, *Origines Sacrae*, 447–48. Gassendi's works are cited throughout this section on the origin of the universe (452, 456, 458). Cf. Kroll, *Material Word*, 371n37; Harrison, "The Ancient Atomists and English Literature," 56.

138. Burnet, *Supplement*, 46–47, as noted in Sykes, *From Sheldon to Secker*, 145.

139. Joseph Glanvill, "To the Royal Society," in *Scepsis Scientifica: Or, Confest Ignorance, the Way to Science* (London: E. Cotes, 1665), A1v. On Glanvill as apologist for the Royal Society, see Bernard Fabian, "Ein Apologet der Royal Society: Joseph Glanvill," in *Die Philosophie des 17. Jahrhunderts*, ed. Jean-Pierre Schobinger (Basel: Schwabe, 1988), vol. 3, bk. 2, *England*, 435–41; and Cope, *Joseph Glanvill*.

140. Samuel Sorbière, *Relation d'un voyage en Angleterre* (Cologne: Pierre Michel, 1666), 76: "les simples Mathematiciens inclinent plus vers M. Descartes que vers M. Gassendi, d'autre costé les literateurs semblent plus portez vers cestui-cy."

141. Thomas Sprat, *Observations on Monsieur de Sorbier's Voyage into England* (London: John Martyn, 1665), 241.

142. Jon Parkin, *Science, Religion and Politics in Restoration England: Richard Cumberland's De legibus naturae* (Woodbridge: The Boydell Press, 1999), 125–26; Kroll, *Material Word*, 144–46.

that "all Nature's effects are produced by motion, figure, texture and various combinations, and that there is no need to have recourse to inexplicable forms and occult qualities, the refuge of ignorance."[143]

Despite Sprat's apologetic for a merely empirical Royal Society devoid of "any sway" from Descartes and Gassendi, the printed works of a number of its influential members demonstrate that mechanical philosophy had gained significant traction. Willis paid significant attention to atomism in his initial chapter, "On the principles of natural things," in the *Diatribae duae medico-philosophicae* (1659). In this popular book on the nature of fermentation, which had already gone through six editions by 1665,[144] Willis placed the atomist theory of the elements (which he associated with the mechanical) alongside Aristotelian and chymical theories, and noted that "the opinion of Democritus and Epicurus" was "now revived anew in our time."[145] Robert Hooke, assistant first to Willis in the 1650s, assistant to Boyle from 1658 (through the introduction of Willis), and from 1662 the Royal Society's Curator of Experiments, sought to provide empirical evidence for the "Mechanick Knowledge, to which this Age seems so much inclined" through the microscopic observations set forth in his *Micrographia* (1665).[146] Similarly, Henry Power (ca. 1623–1668), whose title page to *Experimental Philosophy* (1664) advertised the "Avouchment and Illustration of the now famous Atomical Hypothesis," was sure that with the microscope, "you may see what the illustrious wits of the Atomical and Corpuscularian Philosophers durst but imagine, even the very Atoms."[147] Samuel Parker (1640–1688), elected as fellow of the Royal Society in 1666, likewise equated the "mechanical hypothesis" with Democritus while praising the experimental method of the Royal Society.[148] If the public association of mechanical philosophy with the experimentation of the Royal Society was not obvious by this time, it was hard to ignore when Robert Boyle published his *The Origine of Formes and Qualities* (1666). Joseph Glanvill shortly thereafter wrote

---

143. Oldenburg to Spinoza, 27 Sept. 1661, in Spinoza, *Complete Works*, 765.

144. London, 1659, 1660, 1662, 1677; Hague, 1662; Amsterdam, 1663, 1665, 1669; Leiden, 1680.

145. Thomas Willis, *Diatribae duae medico-philosophicae* (London: Tho. Roycroft, 1659), 3–4. Cf. Isler, *Thomas Willis*, 27.

146. Robert Hooke, preface to *Micrographia* (London: Jo. Martin, and Ja. Allestry, Printers to the Royal Society, 1665), a[2]v. Cf. William T. Lynch, *Solomon's Child: Method in the Early Royal Society of London* (Stanford: Stanford University Press, 2001), 70–115.

147. Henry Power, preface to *Experimental Philosophy* (London, 1664), b2r. On Hooke and Power, see Wilson, *Invisible World*, 65–66; Charles Webster, "Henry Power's Experimental Philosophy," *Ambix* 14 (1967): 150–78.

148. Samuel Parker, *A Free and Impartial Censure of the Platonick Philosophie* (Oxford: W. Hall, 1666), 41, 45.

of this work, "In *this* Treatise he lays the *Foundations* and delivers the *Principles* of the *Mechanick Philosophy*, which he strengthneth and illustrates by several very *pleasant* and *instructive Experiments*."[149]

Baxter appears to have been following the growing interest in mechanical philosophy and activities of the Royal Society during his stay at Acton on the western outskirts of London (1663–1669). In 1664, Baxter made a passing jibe at "Democritists" who would ascribe the being, power, and perfections of creatures to atoms, "and think that the Motes did make the Sun."[150] He also seems to have been interested in early experiments associated with the Royal Society. He mentioned the "late-discovered trick of passing all the blood of one *animal* into another," a reference to the successful blood transfusions between dogs first carried out by Richard Lower at Oxford, and then by Edmond King and Thomas Coxe on 14 November 1666 at the direction of the Royal Society.[151] Yet, aside from his dismissal of "Democritists," Baxter provided little public notice of the polemic against mechanical philosophy that was to commence in 1667.

From 1661 to 1670, Baxter carried on an amicable correspondence with Joseph Glanvill. Glanvill himself looked up to Baxter with great admiration from Baxter's Kidderminster years, and sent his works to Baxter for comment.[152] Baxter's own view of his young admirer was courteous but less flattering: he censured Glanvill's *Lux Orientalis* (1662) for its doctrine of the pre-existence of souls and described Glanvill as one who "had a too excessive estimation of me."[153] Nonetheless, Glanvill and Baxter found cause for occasional collaboration. In 1670, Baxter requested that Glanvill send him a manuscript on natural theology, *Theologia Philosophica* (now lost), by Joseph Alleine, which was in Glanvill's possession. Both men were also interested in collecting stories of spiritual phenomena such as witchcraft and

---

149. Joseph Glanvill, *Plus Ultra: Or, the Progress and Advancement of Knowledge since the Days of Aristotle* (London: James Collins, 1668), 100–101.

150. Richard Baxter, *The Divine Life* (London: Francis Tyton and Nevil Simmons, 1664), 15.

151. *RCR*, 562. Cf. Robert Boyle, "Tryals Proposed by Mr. Boyle to Dr. Lower, to be Made by Him, for the Improvement of Transfusing Blood out of One Live Animal into Another," *Philosophical Transactions* 1, no. 22 (1665–1666): 385–88 (11 Feb. 1666); [Richard Lower], "The Method Observed in Transfusing the Bloud out of One Animal into Another," *Philosophical Transactions* 1, no. 20 (1665–1666): 353–58 (17 Dec. 1666); Thomas Birch, *The History of the Royal Society of London* (London: A. Millar, 1756), 2:115, 123; Simon Schaffer, "Regeneration: The Body of Natural Philosophers in Restoration England," in *Science Incarnate: Historical Embodiments of Natural Knowledge*, ed. Christopher Lawrence and Steven Shapin (Chicago: University of Chicago Press, 1998), 83–120, at 96–97.

152. *CCRB*, 2:21–22, 25–26, 33, 37–38, 55, 101 (nos. 683, 692, 705, 710, 711, 740, 822); Cope, *Joseph Glanvill*, 6–10.

153. *Rel. Bax.*, II.378; Rhodri Lewis, "Of 'Origenian Platonisme': Joseph Glanvill on the Pre-existence of Souls," *Huntington Library Quarterly* 69, no. 2 (2006): 267–300.

apparitions in order to present arguments against mechanical atheism, and Baxter provided Glanvill with reports of such phenomena.[154]

Baxter also corresponded with Robert Boyle. According to William Bates, Boyle and Baxter were "dear Friends," a judgment corroborated by their life and writings.[155] The two of them were mutually interested in missionary efforts to spread the gospel in America, and corresponded both on that topic and cures for Baxter's physical pains.[156] In 1655, Boyle sent Baxter several of his works. Among them were *Some Motives and Incentives to the Love of God* (1659), *Some Considerations Touching the Style of the H. Scriptures* (1661), *Some Considerations Touching the Usefulness of Experimental Naturall Philosophy* (1663), and *Occasional Reflections* (1665). In reply, Baxter expressed nothing but praise for Boyle's works. The philosophical works, Baxter told Boyle, were a "profitable pleasure," while the theological works "make me put off my hatt, as if I were in the Church. . . . I read your Theologie as the Life of your Philosophie, & your Philosophie as animated & dignifyed by your Theologie; yea indeed as its first Part."[157] Baxter shared with Boyle a basically Reformed theological orientation, and his praise of Boyle was likely due to their common interest in joining traditional theological concerns of creation and providence to philosophy and science.[158] Boyle had not yet published his *Origine of Formes and Qualities*, so one might think that Baxter did not yet at this point fully appreciate the extent of Boyle's support for mechanical philosophy or Gassendi. But in fact even after Boyle's *Origine of Formes* appeared, Baxter continued to respect Boyle and keep an open mind regarding his natural philosophy. By 1672, Baxter had integrated some aspects of Boyle's corpuscularism from the *Origine of Formes* into his explanation of inanimate elements (see chapter 4).

---

154. See Appendix B; and Moody E. Prior, "Joseph Glanvill, Witchcraft, and Seventeenth-Century Science," *Modern Philology* 30, no. 2 (1932): 167–93.

155. William Bates, *A Funeral Sermon for the Reverend, Holy and Excellent Divine, Mr. Richard Baxter* (London: Brab. Aylmer, 1692), A3r.

156. Baxter to Boyle, 20 Oct. 1660, in Boyle, *Correspondence*, 1:435; Baxter to Boyle, 15 Dec. 1668, in Boyle, *Correspondence*, 4:124–26; Baxter to Boyle, 29 Aug. 1682, in Boyle, *Correspondence*, 5:332–33. For further evidence of Baxter's relation to Boyle, see William M. Lamont, *Puritanism and Historical Controversy* (London: UCL Press, 1996), 166–67.

157. Baxter to Boyle, 14 June 1665, in Boyle, *Correspondence*, 2:473; *CCRB*, 2:43–45. Baxter cited *Some Considerations* positively in *CD*, IV.48 ("Mr. Boyles Experiment. Philos p. 303, 304").

158. On Baxter, see chapter 4. On Boyle's Reformed theology, see Hampton, *Anti-Arminians*, 18–19, 122–24, 242–43. On Boyle's pious philosophy, see Muller, "God and Design," 87–111; Jan W. Wojcik, "The Theological Context of Boyle's *Things above Reason*," in *Robert Boyle Reconsidered*, ed. Michael Hunter (Cambridge: Cambridge University Press, 1994), 139–55; Harold Fisch, "The Scientist as Priest: A Note on Robert Boyle's Natural Theology," *Isis* 44, no. 3 (1953): 252–65; and Westfall, *Science and Religion*, 40–44. On Boyle's early "moralistic" period, see Michael Hunter, "How Boyle Became a Scientist," *History of Science* 33 (1995): 59–103.

For his part, Boyle was pleased with Baxter's warm reply and accurately noted Baxter's relatively greater open-mindedness in comparison with many contemporaries: "And there are divers things that speake you to be none of those narrow-Sould Divines, that by too much suspecting Naturall Philosophy, tempt Its Votaries to suspect Theology."[159] Baxter continued to maintain good relations with Boyle and stay up to date on Boyle's works. Shortly after Boyle published his 1673 treatise on effluvia, Baxter wrote to Matthew Hale that Boyle "tell[s] us strange things of Invisible effluvia" that are "exceeding subtile."[160] To the extent that Baxter disagreed with Boyle's overall promotion of mechanical philosophy and the works of Gassendi and Descartes, Baxter kept such disagreement to himself. This silence is surely indicative of the great personal respect Baxter had for Boyle.[161]

Despite his friendly relations with Glanvill and Boyle, Baxter decided to initiate polemics against mechanical philosophy with his appendix to *The Reasons of the Christian Religion* (1667), entitled "The Conclusion, Defending the Soul's Immortality against the Somatists or Epicureans, and other Pseudophilosophers."[162] Baxter intended this conclusion as an expansion of his apologetic in the *Reasons* for the soul's immortality, but at over one hundred pages, it is a substantial treatise in itself. While framed as a defense of the soul's immortality, the work opened with a reply to the objection, "Matter and Motion, without any more, may do all that which you ascribe to souls." Baxter's reply to this objection canvased general problems with mechanical philosophy. He listed ten "general Reasons to distrust this sort of Philosophers above others," followed by "particular reasons which disswade me from believing the *Epicurean* sufficiency of *Matter* and *Motion*."[163] The "Somatists or Epicureans," who constituted the target of Baxter's polemic, were closely identified with the philosophies of Gassendi, Descartes, and Hobbes. In his *Christian Directory* (1673), Baxter listed "our late Somatists" alongside Gassendi, Hobbes, Descartes, and Cartesians such as Claudius Berigardus and Henricus Regius, as those who "give so much more to meer Matter and Motion, than is truly due."[164]

---

159. Boyle to Baxter, late June 1665, in Boyle, *Correspondence*, 2:486; *CCRB*, 2:45.

160. LPL MS 3499, fol. 96v. Cf. Robert Boyle, *Essays of the Strange Subtilty, Great Efficacy, Determinate Nature of Effluviums* (London: W. G. for M. Pitt, 1673).

161. Cf. *RCR*, 601, where he vigorously disagrees with Roger Boyle, *Inquisitio in fidem Christianorum hujus saeculi* (1665), but declines to name the author out of respect for the name. Roger was Robert Boyle's brother.

162. *RCR*, 489–604. Cf. Burton, *Hallowing of Logic*, 101–6.

163. *RCR*, 499.

164. *CD*, III.919 (q. 173, §15).

What motivated Baxter to this sudden attack on mechanical philosophy? In an autobiographical comment, Baxter himself ascribed the occasion of his polemic to the rising popularity of Gassendi and others of like mind: "And the Philosophy of *Gassendus*, and many more besides the Hobbians, now prevailing, and inclining men to Sadducism, induced me to write the *Appendix* to it [*Reasons*], about the *Immortality* of the Soul."[165] We have already observed the growing popularity of Gassendi in the early 1660s. The question remains as to the identity of the "many more besides the Hobbians," which may have triggered Baxter's appendix. One group that Baxter associated around this time with "Sadducism" is the court of Charles II. He referred in 1670 to "the Sadducees (at court and the Innes of Court),"[166] and in an undated manuscript associated "Atheisme, Bestiality & Infidelity" with "Courts, & nobles & gentry."[167] While these remarks do not specify individuals, Baxter may have had in mind the promotion of Gassendian and Epicurean ideas by Walter Charleton, physician to Charles II, and Margaret Cavendish, duchess of Newcastle.

But Baxter was also worried about specific recent publications. Among recently published works that may have triggered Baxter's response are Samuel Parker's *Tentamina de Deo* (1665), Parker's *A Free and Impartial Censure of the Platonick Philosophie* (1666), and Glanvill's *Scepsis Scientifica* (1665), a revision of *Vanity of Dogmatizing* (1661). In his appendix to the *Reasons*, Baxter identified adherents of "the *Epicurean* (or *Cartesian*) Hypothesis" as mostly "the younger sort of ingenious men, who have received prejudice against the *Peripateticks*, *Platonists* and *Stoicks*, before they did ever throughly study them; but reverencing more some person noted for much ingenuity, by his authority have been drawn to defend, what they scarce understand themselves."[168] Baxter seemed irritated by a younger generation of academics who sympathized with Gassendi's works. Glanvill fit this description well enough.[169] So did Parker, whose *Tentamina* was in many ways derivative of Gassendi, particularly with respect to the providential modification of Epicurus's atomism and the *semina* theory of the soul.[170] Parker's

---

165. *Rel. Bax.*, III.61. Note the contemporary association of Hobbesian materialism with "Sadducism" in Joseph Glanvill, *A Blow at Modern Sadducism* (London: E. C., 1668); cf. Cope, *Joseph Glanvill*, 92–94.

166. DWL BC II.138r.

167. DWL BT VI.204, fols. 281r, 282r.

168. *RCR*, 498.

169. As noted in Thomas White, *Sciri, sive, sceptices & scepticorum jure disputationis exclusio* (London, 1663), 13–14.

170. Samuel Parker, *Tentamina physico-theologica de Deo* (London: A. M., 1665), 33–43, 108, 115. Cf. Levitin, "Rethinking English Physico-theology," 42–43, 52–53.

Censure not only attacked Platonist philosophy, as implied by the title page, but also Aristotelian and Stoic philosophy, including a specific attack on the metaphysics of both Platonic and Aristotelian forms.[171] In his *Reasons*, Baxter associated Glanvill's *Vanity of Dogmatizing* and Parker's *Censure* with the arguments of Gassendi. He also had Parker's *Tentamina* in his hands. Since Baxter was already aware of Glanvill's sympathies, Jon Parkin appears correct in his estimation that the additional publication of Parker's works seems to have tipped Baxter over the edge into controversy.[172]

Baxter's rhetoric of "Somatists or Epicureans" was surely designed to cast mechanical philosophy, broadly understood to include the thought of Gassendi and Descartes, in a morally repugnant light. But contrary to one scholar's interpretation, this conflation of Epicureanism with recent mechanical philosophy does not indicate an ignorant "misunderstanding" of contemporary trends.[173] Rather, as another scholar has more correctly observed, Baxter's critique "offers a highly intelligent, deeply informed but unsympathetic appraisal of midcentury natural philosophy, a criticism not only of Hobbes but also of the two other greatest figures on the Anglo-French intellectual scene, Gassendi and Descartes."[174] Baxter's contention, of course, was that Gassendi's philosophy was a slippery slope to a Hobbesian denial of immortality. This concern was not without contemporary precedent. We have at least one notorious contemporary example of mechanical philosophy leading to heterodoxy in the person of Daniel Scargill, a Cambridge student who, after imbibing mechanical philosophy under the tutelage of Thomas Tenison, privately confessed in 1668 to believing that "the soule of man is but a trembling atome" and in 1669 made a public recantation of his "Hobbism."[175]

Baxter's insinuation that the adoption of mechanical philosophy could lead to "Sadducism" or the denial of the soul's immortality caused leading members of the Royal Society to take notice. In December 1667, Henry Oldenburg, secretary of the Royal Society, alerted Robert Boyle to the concern of John Beale (also a Royal Society fellow) over Baxter's polemic.

---

171. Parker, *A Free and Impartial Censure*, 41–42, 58–65.

172. *RCR*, 496–97, 579 (citing *Tentamina*); Parkin, *Science, Religion and Politics*, 123.

173. Contra Spiller, *Meric Casaubon*, 23. Spiller asserts that "it does not seem that [Baxter] was aware of the propagandist writings of Sprat and Glanvill" in the appendix, but Baxter in fact cites Glanvill's *Vanity of Dogmatizing* (*RCR*, 496), and Sprat's *History of the Royal Society* was not published until 1667.

174. Kroll, *Material Word*, 46.

175. Jon Parkin, "Hobbism in the Later 1660s: Daniel Scargill and Samuel Parker," *The Historical Journal* 42, no. 1 (1999): 86–96; James L. Axtell, "The Mechanics of Opposition: Restoration Cambridge v. Daniel Scargill," *Bulletin of the Institute of Historical Research* 38 (1965): 102–11.

Dr Beale writes me word, that Dr Baxter inveighes in his Book, written to assert the reasons of the Christian religion, against the Corpuscularian (called by him, the Somatical) Philosophy, and traduces it as if it supplanted our future Estate. This our good friend, who presents his humble service to you, would fain have obviated and rightly stated, to prevent ill effects, like to follow the popular discoursing of a popular man.[176]

Although neither Beale nor Boyle responded to Baxter's polemic, clearly Baxter's reputation as a "popular man" caused some concern that if his critique was left unanswered, "ill effects" would follow—that is, the reputation of the Royal Society would suffer from the association of mechanical philosophy with Hobbesian heterodoxy.[177] Thomas Sprat's *History of the Royal Society*, published in the same year 1667, was a notable testament to such anxieties, as it included a defensive apologetic against the Royal Society's detractors.[178] In an effort to assuage fears that the new philosophy would usher in new and heretical divinity, Sprat included an extensive defense of the usefulness of experimental philosophy for traditional Christian doctrine and practice.[179] Unfortunately for Sprat, his effort was not able to assuage a number of divines, who in following years unleashed a steady stream of polemics against the new philosophy associated with the Royal Society.[180]

In the midst of these polemics, Glanvill took up the mantle of Sprat's apologetic for the Royal Society. The apologetic theme of the usefulness of the new philosophy to Christian doctrine came to the most mature expression in Glanvill's *Philosophia Pia* (1671). Of this work it has been remarked, "No document of the Restoration better portrays the Royal Society as a handmaiden to the Church of England."[181] In *Philosophia Pia*, Glanvill went beyond Sprat's more ambiguous defense of experimental philosophy to a defense of the usefulness of specific authors, including Descartes and Gassendi. Like Baxter's appendix to *Reasons*, Glanvill included a chapter against "Sadducism" by which he also meant the denial of spirits and immortal souls.[182] The content of Glanvill's argument, however, was

---

176. Oldenburg to Boyle, 24 Dec. 1667, in Boyle, *Correspondence*, 3:386.

177. Cf. Michael Hunter, *Science and Society in Restoration England* (Cambridge: Cambridge University Press, 1981), 173–74; Parkin, *Science, Religion and Politics*, 124–25.

178. See Hunter, *Establishing the New Science*, 45–72.

179. Sprat, *History of the Royal Society*, 345–78 (III.14–23). Note the similar fear addressed in [Patrick], *A Brief Account*, 22–23; also see Gascoigne, *Cambridge*, 64.

180. Parkin, *Science, Religion and Politics*, 132–33; Gascoigne, *Cambridge*, 54–56; Jones, *The Epicurean Tradition*, 207–9. Muller, "Thomas Barlow," 179–95.

181. Cope, *Joseph Glanvill*, 32.

182. Glanvill, *Philosophia Pia*, 25–40 (ch. 3).

the opposite of Baxter. Glanvill argued that a mechanical philosophy such as that of Descartes "is an excellent antidote against *Sadducism*," while by contrast the Aristotelian doctrine of substantial forms contributes to it. That this contrast was by design is readily inferred from a later chapter, in which Glanvill singled out Baxter's appendix to the *Reasons* for censure.[183] Baxter, complained Glanvill, unaccountably lumped together ancient Epicureanism (and Hobbes) with the pious atomism of the moderns:

> And therefore I cannot but wonder that a person of so much reason, learning, and ingenuity as Mr. *Baxter*, should seem to conclude those *Modern Philosophers* under the name, and notion of such *Somatists*, as are for *meer matter*, and *motion*, and exclude *immaterial* beings; This, I take it, he doth in his *Defence* of the *Souls Immortality*, at the end of his *Reasons of Religion*: whereas *those* Philosophers, though they owne *matter*, and *motion* as the *material* and *formal* causes of the *Phaenomena*; They do yet acknowledge Gods *efficiency*, and *Government* of all things, with as much seriousness, and contend for it with as much zeal, as any *Philosophers* or *Divines* whatsoever.[184]

In case there was any doubt who Glanvill was defending against Baxter's polemic, he continued,

> So that methinks that Reverend Author hath not dealt so *fairly* with the great names of *Des-Cartes*, and *Gassendus*, where he mentions them promiscuously with the meer *Epicurean* and *Hobbian Somatists*, without any note to distinguish them from *those Sadduces*; For both those celebrated men have laboured much in asserting the grand Articles of Religion against the *Infidel*, and *Atheist*.[185]

Although it is true, as Glanvill remarked, that Baxter's polemic blurred the lines between "Hobbian" Somatists and Gassendi and Descartes, Glanvill's response did not deal "so fairly" with Baxter either. For in the years immediately preceding the publication of *Philosophia Pia*, Glanvill had sent Baxter a letter (no longer extant) in which he objected to a number of points from Baxter's appendix to the *Reasons*. In November of 1670, Baxter replied with a response to his objections, including an explicit denial that he had ever attributed atheism to Gassendi

---

183. Glanvill, *Philosophia Pia*, 105–13.

184. Glanvill, *Philosophia Pia*, 109–10.

185. Glanvill, *Philosophia Pia*, 110–11.

or Descartes. In Baxter's words, "I no where cast any reflexion of Atheisme on Gassendus or Cartesius. Nor accuse them as excluding all immateriall beings."[186] Moreover, Baxter went on to clarify the sense in which he thought their philosophy contributed indirectly to a denial of the soul's immortality (see chapter 6). Perhaps Glanvill did not wait to receive Baxter's reply before he had already written the manuscript for *Philosophia Pia*. Or perhaps Glanvill did receive the reply but thought that Baxter's own explanations were either unconvincing or inappropriate for his apologetic treatise. In either case, Glanvill's published explanation of Baxter's position ignored Baxter's own unpublished clarifications from their correspondence.

Matthew Hale and the Growth of Baxter's Polemics

During his time at Acton, Baxter developed a friendship with Sir Matthew Hale, Chief Baron of the Exchequer from 1660 and Chief Justice of the King's Bench from 1671, which was to last until Hale's death in 1676. This relationship had a significant impact on Baxter's writings during this period. According to Baxter's account, Hale moved to Acton in 1667, where he attended the same church as Baxter "for many weeks" before Baxter approached him. They struck up a friendship and, shortly thereafter, Hale decided to buy Baxter's house.[187] Hale was a judge by vocation, but a man of various interests by avocation. Having been raised and educated by Puritans, he was particularly interested in matters of religion and natural philosophy, as both his published writings and unpublished manuscripts testify.[188] Until Baxter left Acton for Totteridge in 1669, the two of them carried on lively conversation about the soul's immortality and other philosophical topics, which Baxter found "so edifying, that his very Questions and Objections did help me to more light than other mens solutions."[189] As Baxter relates, Hale mostly initiated the subjects of these conversations, preferring to talk mostly about the nature and immortality of the soul.[190] In general, Baxter was incredibly fond of the

---

186. Baxter to Glanvill, 18 Nov. 1670 (DWL BC II.138r).

187. Richard Baxter, *Additional Notes on the Life and Death of Sir Matthew Hale* (London: Richard Janeway, 1682), A3r, 3–4.

188. Alan Cromartie, *Sir Matthew Hale 1609–1676: Law, Religion and Natural Philosophy* (Cambridge: Cambridge University Press, 1995); David S. Sytsma, "General Introduction," in Matthew Hale, *Of the Law of Nature*, ed. David S. Sytsma (Grand Rapids, MI: CLP Academic, 2015), ix–lv.

189. *Rel. Bax.*, III.47.

190. Baxter, *Additional Notes*, 6.

judge. "I cannot easily praise [him] above his worth," he wrote. "And I scarce ever conversed so profitably with any other person in my Life."[191]

These conversations between Baxter and Hale bore fruit in the weight that Baxter gave to his treatment of philosophy in the *Methodus theologiae christianae*. Even though Baxter did not publish his *Methodus theologiae* until 1681, he had begun work on it in 1668–1669 sometime before his brief imprisonment in June 1669.[192] After he was forced to leave Acton, in late 1669 Baxter sent Hale the manuscript to his "Scheme of the Creation" of the *Methodus theologiae*. According to Baxter's autobiography, Hale "received it with so great Approbation, and importuned me so by Letters, to go on with that work, and not to fear being too much on Philosophy, as added somewhat to my Inclinations and Resolutions."[193] Baxter's account of Hale's response in the preface to the *Methodus theologiae* is still more clear: "when he [Hale] had read the ontology (Ὀντολογίαν) with my *Catholick Theologie*, he not only approved of it (perhaps too much), but often & seriously urged me to add more things concerning physics."[194] Baxter subsequently "finished all the Schemes, and half the Elucidations [of the *Methodus theologiae*] in the end of the Year 1669. and the beginning of 1670."[195] Both Baxter and Hale "greatly disliked the principles of *Cartesius* and *Gassendus*,"[196] and this dislike is apparent in Baxter's discussion of ontology in the *Methodus theologiae*. In the table of contents, Baxter refers to this section of the *Methodus theologiae* as a "compendium of all philosophy" (*Totius Philosophiae compendium*) containing "philosophical elucidations where certain things [are written] against Descartes, Gassendi, etc." Indeed, much of the section is taken up with responses to these two philosophers on fundamental questions relating to substance and motion.[197]

A second fruit of Baxter's conversations with Hale was an unpublished manuscript on the soul, "Of the Nature and Immortality of Humane Soules."

---

191. Baxter, *Additional Notes*, 6.

192. *MT*, "Praefatio," [A5r].

193. *Rel. Bax.*, III.70.

194. *MT*, "Praefatio," [A6r]: "Tres amici, Theologi eximii, haec scripta perlegerunt, taliaque approbarunt: Quartus autem (Magnus ille Matthaeus Haleus, Justitiarius Angliae Primarius) propositi mei conscious, quando Ὀντολογίαν, cum *Theologiâ meâ Catholicâ* legisset, non solum ea (fortasse nimium) approbavit, sed ut de Physicis plura adderem, saepe & seriò me incitavit."

195. *Rel. Bax.*, III.70. Cf. *MT*, "Praefatio," [A5v]: "in paucis mensibus Tabulas descripsi Elucidationes vero & Disputations tardiuscule postea adjunxi."

196. Baxter, *Additional Notes*, 6.

197. *MT*, I.131–53.

Baxter wrote this 281-page, ready-for-press manuscript—complete with a title page, preface, and postscript—shortly after his initial work on the *Methodus theologiae*. The body of the text was written ca. 1669, while the preface and postscript were added sometime during 1672.[198] In multiple places, Baxter attributed the inspiration for this work to Hale. In his autobiography, he stated, "Oft Conference with the Lord Chief Baron *Hale*, put those Cases into my mind, which occasioned the writing of another short Piece, of the *Nature* and *Immortality* of the Soul, by way of Question and Answer (not printed)."[199] Elsewhere Baxter wrote that Hale's "many hard questions, doubts and objections to me, occasioned me to draw up a small Tract of the *Nature* and *Immortality* of *mans Soul*, as proved by *Natural light alone* (by way of Questions and Answers)."[200] Baxter intended this manuscript as a supplement to his anti-Epicurean appendix to the *Reasons*. In the preface to the manuscript, he stated that the work presupposed the earlier appendix.[201] Like the appendix to *Reasons*, "Of the Nature and Immortality of Humane Soules" was also more concerned with Gassendi than with Descartes. Baxter placed Gassendi with the "Sadducees" and reiterated his view that Gassendi's philosophy tends toward materialism.[202]

In the postscript to "Of the Nature and Immortality of Humane Soules," Baxter launched into a new polemic against Christian Epicureanism with a response to Thomas Willis's *De anima brutorum quae hominis vitalis ac sensitiva est* (1672). Willis, a member of the Royal Society, was by this time among the most renowned anatomists in England, and his *De anima brutorum* with the *Pathologiae cerebri, et nervosi generis specimen* (1667) "were the first comprehensive books on the brain and nervous system to be published in Europe."[203] The *De anima brutorum* was the culminating work of a decade of writing on neurology and its relation

---

198. For dates, see Appendix A. A transcription of the postscript appears in Appendix C.

199. *Rel. Bax.*, III.61.

200. Baxter, *Additional Notes*, 11.

201. DWL BT XIX.351, fol. 3r: "I presuppose wᵗ I have written in yᵉ End of my *Reas. of yᵉ Christ. Relig*: agᵗ yᵉ Somatists, yᵗ know nothing in yᵉ world but *matter* & *motion* at least besides God. And yet I heare further prove yᵗ Mans soule (& all soules) have an *essential Virtus Vitalis formalis*, yᵉ Cause of its owne motion."

202. For Gassendi, see DWL BT XIX.351, fol. 4r–4v: "And I have observed ~~not only Gassendus, but~~ divers ~~others~~ who laid downe first such principles as tend to inferre yᵗ yᵉ soule is nothing but *moved atomes*"; DWL BT XIX.351, fol. 140r: "And then yᵉ Sadducees were in yᵉ right ~~(& I thinke Gassendus meant as they)~~ yᵗ there were neither Angels nor spirits, but God & bodies were all yᵉ universe." Baxter (presumably) crossed out Gassendi's name in the MS in both of these cases.

203. *ODNB*, s.v. "Willis, Thomas."

to mind-body problems.[204] In that work, Willis followed Gassendi's division of the nature of the soul into essentially two kinds—rational and animal—and described the animal soul as "corporeal."[205] It was this Gassendi-inspired mechanization of the *anima brutorum* that aroused Baxter's indignation. In his postscript to "Of the Nature and Immortality of Humane Soules," Baxter connected Willis's work to Gassendi's larger philosophical project and specifically responded to chapters 2 and 6 from Willis's *De anima brutorum*.

Soon after completing "Of the Nature and Immortality of Humane Soules," Baxter sent a copy to Hale and requested his commentary. This generated further discussion by way of correspondence between them. In a letter dated 1 January 1673, Hale replied to Baxter's request with extended comments on Baxter's entire treatise, including advice on the title page, preface, and postscript. After having "longe since perused" Baxter's "learned treatise touchinge the immortallity of the soule," Hale wrote, "I made these notes upon it upon my second readinge of them in Christmasse last [1672]."[206] Baxter in turn replied to Hale in September with a letter of thanks and annotations on Hale's comments.[207] Baxter's treatise made quite an impression on Hale, who praised it as among the best works he had read:

> It is true that the papers which you have sent mee have given mee the greatest light that ever I had touchinge the nature of the soule and your natural reasons and explications both for it and of the manner of the soules subsistence and operations both on the body and after its seperation are the best and most perspicuous of any thinge that I ever read of that subject.[208]

This was no small compliment from someone who himself had written over half a dozen manuscripts on the soul.[209] According to Baxter, before reading his

204. Robert G. Frank Jr., "Thomas Willis and His Circle: Brain and Mind in Seventeenth-Century Medicine," in *The Languages of Psyche: Mind and Body in Enlightenment Thought*, ed. G. S. Rousseau (Berkeley: University of California Press, 1990), 107–46, at 108–9.

205. Frank, "Thomas Willis," 130–31.

206. LPL MS 3499, fol. 82r. Hale's letter (fols. 82–115) is dated "1 January 1672" [i.e., 1673] (fol. 115r). Hale's comments appear on the recto pages. The comments follow quite closely the sequence of pages found in DWL BT XIX.351.

207. Baxter to Hale, 20 Sept. 1673 (LPL MS 3499, fol. 81v). Baxter's annotations appear both in the margins of Hale's comments on the recto pages and spill over onto the facing verso pages.

208. LPL MS 3499, fol. 65v.

209. There are at least seven extant manuscripts by Hale on the soul in the Lambeth Palace Library: "Tentamina de anima et ejus immortalitate" (MS 3499, fols. 1–36); "De ortu hominis

appendix, Hale "seemed to reverence and believe the opinion of Dr. *Willis*, and such others, *de Animis brutorum*, as being not spiritual substances," but after he read Baxter's refutation of Willis, "he seemed to acquiesce, and as far as I could judg, did change his mind."[210]

Even though Baxter's manuscript "Of the Nature and Immortality of Humane Soules" was complete and Hale praised its quality, Baxter refrained from publishing it. The reason he withheld publication can be traced back to his reticence to publish the work in English where it would reach a popular, rather than academic, readership. In his preface, Baxter stated, "My first purpose was to have published this in Latine, because I have bawlked no difficult objections, but raised more than ye reader will find elsewhere." He feared that the book's accessibility to "ordinary wits" would "perplexe & stall" them and "so it may do more harme than good." Baxter consulted "ye wisest men" in London, and over his objections they advised him to publish since "ye number is growne <so great> of such as deny ye life to come, & yet understand not ye Latine tongue." Besides, they reasoned with Baxter, such people were already familiar with the objections set forth by Baxter, while those unfamiliar with the content and terminology of his work would not really understand it anyhow, so it would do more good than harm. "In this judgment," Baxter concluded, "though with hesitancie, I acquiesced."[211]

After receiving Hale's comments on his manuscript, however, Baxter changed his mind. Hale remarked that he wished the work "had rather been in Latine than in English for ignorant persons will bee perplexed" by its contents.[212] Hale also advised that with respect to the "method and forme" of the work, "I thinke in regard of the abstrusenes of the subject and manner of handlinge it it were fitter in Latine then in English bycause fitter for the learned then the ordinary persons." He further counseled Baxter to reorganize the work into chapters with headings and brief introductory remarks, and to remove sections that raise doubtful questions that are not fully resolved.[213] Hale's methodological advice was enough to convince Baxter to scuttle plans for publication of the English version of the work. As Baxter later explained, although Hale "thought I had sufficiently answered all

---

secundario seu generatione naturali" (MS 3499, fols. 39–62); "De homine" (MS 3499, fols. 116–214); "Meditationes Itinerarie" [1 July 1665] (MS 3509, fols. 18–52); "De generatione vegetabilium et animalium" [27 Mar. 1672] (MS 3504); "Tentamina de ortu, natura et immortalitate animae" [25 July 1673] (MS 3500); MS 3498, fols. 21–78. See also Matthew Hale, *A Discourse of the Knowledge of God, and of our Selves* (London: B. W. for William Shrowsbery, 1688), 39–60.

210. Baxter, *Additional Notes*, 12.

211. DWL BT XIX.351, fols. 8r–v.

212. LPL MS 3499, fol. 77r.

213. LPL MS 3499, fol. 82r.

the Objections, yet ordinary Readers would take deeper into their minds such hard Objections as they never heard before, than the Answer (how full soever) would be able to overcome: Whereupon, not having leisure to translate and alter it, I cast it by."[214] Thus, the weight of Hale's opinion and methodological concerns prevented publication of one of Baxter's more academic treatises. And without publication, knowledge of Baxter's postscript against Willis's *De anima brutorum* remained buried in the archives for over three centuries.

On the "Epicurean" Ethics of Hobbes and Spinoza

In the early 1670s, Baxter moved beyond his polemic on the nature of basic categories of substance and motion (reflected in *Methodus theologiae*) and the nature of the soul (reflected in the appendix to *Reasons*) to a broader discussion of philosophy in general. A general discussion of philosophy, and indeed knowledge in general, is found both in *A Christian Directory* and more extensively in the opening chapters of *A Treatise of Knowledge and Love.*[215] Although the *Treatise* was not published until 1689, the entire book had been "written long ago,"[216] and based on internal evidence, we can conclude that the first ten chapters were written circa 1672–1673, just as he was putting the finishing touches on the *Christian Directory.*[217]

One of the striking features of the *Treatise* is the emergence of a new threat— Benedict de Spinoza. Many theologians and philosophers in England read Spinoza in light of the controversy over Hobbes, and Spinoza was therefore often received as perpetuating similar errors as Hobbes.[218] Baxter was no exception to this trend. Although Spinoza's *Tractatus theologico-politicus* had only been published in 1670, by 1672 Baxter was at least aware of it and was adding Spinoza's name to his list of most disreputable philosophers. By this time, he was referring to Hobbes as Gassendi's "brother" and Spinoza as a "second" brother.[219] This reception of

---

214. Baxter, *Additional Notes*, 12.

215. *CD*, III.907–8 (q. 158), 3.917–20 (q. 173); *TKL*, I.i–iii.

216. *TKL*, "To the Reader," A2r.

217. For dating, see Appendix A.

218. Rosalie L. Colie, "Spinoza in England, 1665–1730," *Proceedings of the American Philosophical Society* 107, no. 3 (1963): 183–219. Edward Stillingfleet, on the other hand, "regarded Spinozism as an outgrowth of Cartesianism" (Hutton, "Edward Stillingfleet and Spinoza," 266).

219. *TKL*, 47. On p. 66, Baxter mentions Spinoza's discussion in the *Tractatus theologico-politicus* of numerical discrepancies in Scripture.

Spinoza through the lens of Gassendi and Hobbes continued throughout the 1670s and until Baxter's death.[220] In the *Catholick Theologie*, for example, Baxter read Spinoza as perfecting Hobbes's deterministic philosophy,[221] while in his notes on Hale's life, Baxter recalled that while Hale and himself "greatly disliked" Gassendi's and Descartes's principles, they disliked "much more [the principles] of the Bruitists, *Hobs* and *Spinoza*."[222] By 1680, Baxter appears to have concluded that Spinoza was a "Cartesian."[223] The range of these rhetorical associations of Spinoza variously with Gassendi, Descartes, and Hobbes shows that Baxter saw affinities between these mechanical philosophers and Spinoza, and indicates that his earlier polemics over mechanical philosophy colored his interpretation of Spinoza.

While Baxter clearly disliked Spinoza as much as Hobbes, he did not write an extensive refutation of either Spinoza or Hobbes as he had done with Willis. Yet in the late 1670s he composed brief refutations of both Spinoza and Hobbes on natural law. These appeared in *The Second Part of the Nonconformists Plea for Peace* (1680). The immediate occasion of this volume was the accusation that nonconformity was seditious to both civil and ecclesiastic authority. Baxter had written many of the essays contained therein many years earlier, some as early as 1668, but had been dissuaded from publishing them at the time lest they stir up even more opposition to the nonconformists. The sections on Spinoza and Hobbes were then added sometime in the late 1670s. In any event, he wished to publish them before he died in order to vindicate nonconformity from any association with the conspiracy of the Popish Plot (1678–1681). Among the informants involved in the conspiracy, Thomas Dangerfield claimed the existence of a "Presbyeterian Plot" against the king, and Baxter sought to refute the accusation that the nonconformists were "plotting a new war."[224] Baxter sought to vindicate the nonconformists from seditious principles by contrasting the radical philosophies of Spinoza and Hobbes with the principles of nonconformity (his

---

220. Richard Baxter, *The Certainty of Christianity without Popery* (London: Nevil Simons, 1672), 3; Baxter, *More Proofs of Infants Church-membership and Consequently their Right to Baptism* (London: Nevil Simmons, 1675), 307; Baxter, *Church-History of the Government of Bishops and their Councils Abbreviated* (London: B. Griffin, 1680), "The Preface," A2r; Baxter, *The Defence of the Nonconformists Plea for Peace* (London: Benjamin Alsop, 1680), 139, 144.

221. *CT*, II.152; I/3.108.

222. Baxter, *Additional Notes*, 6.

223. Richard Baxter, *The Second Part of the Nonconformists Plea for Peace* (London: John Hancock, 1680), "The Preface," a4v: "Is it the new Philosophers; such Cartesians as Spinosa, and such as Hobbes that you prefer?"

224. Baxter, *Second Part*, "The Preface," A2r–A2v; *Rel. Bax.*, III.188. Cf. John Pollock, *The Popish Plot: A Study in the History of the Reign of Charles II* (London: Duckworth and Co., 1903), 207–12.

own) on natural law and political rule. Such a contrast, Baxter believed, would show that these radical philosophies constituted the real threat to the state.

In his discussion of both Spinoza and Hobbes, Baxter interprets their principles of law and the foundations of government as an outgrowth of Neo-Epicureanism. In this interpretation, Baxter reflected a more widely held view. As Catherine Wilson observes, Spinoza's *Ethics* was "certainly received as an Epicurean work, by Leibniz, amongst others."[225] After summarizing chapter 16 of Spinoza's *Tractatus*, Baxter wrote that "the root of all this mans inhumanity is his Epicurean principles of Philosophy about God and *Nature*."[226] Likewise, he regarded the principles of Hobbes's *De cive* as "mostly the same with Spinosa's."[227] Unfortunately, Baxter only acquired a copy of Spinoza's *Opera posthuma* (1677), which contains the *Ethics*, after he had already written his evaluation of the *Tractatus*. Yet, Baxter included a brief synopsis, or what he called the "marrow" of the *Opera posthuma* together with his discussion of Hobbes's *De cive*. We thus have at least some record of Baxter's opinion about Spinoza's *Ethics*. In Baxter's mind, the publication of Spinoza's *Opera* only reinforced the congruity between Spinoza and Hobbes, for he wrote of the *Opera*, "To which Hobbes much agreeth."[228] For Baxter, then, Spinoza and Hobbes represented the application of a Neo-Epicurean worldview to the foundations of morality with radical and seditious consequences.

Baxter and Henry More

Henry More was among the earliest enthusiasts for Cartesian philosophy in England. He introduced Descartes to his students at Cambridge and praised Descartes in his *Antidote against Atheism* (1653) and *Conjectura Cabbalistica* (1653). He was also conversant with scientific circles and was elected a fellow of the Royal Society in 1664. But his main interest in Descartes's mechanical philosophy was apologetic. More was attracted to Descartes's dualistic separation of matter and mind, and thought that Descartes's mechanical philosophy showed the need for the existence of God and the spiritual realm.[229] Although More's apologetic use of mechanical philosophy remained constant throughout his life, in the 1660s he grew wary of how Descartes's philosophy was put to use by later Cartesians and thus of the potential drift toward atheism when Cartesian ideas were used in a

---

225. Wilson, "Epicureanism," 98.

226. Baxter, *Second Part*, 6.

227. Baxter, *Second Part*, 126.

228. Baxter, *Second Part*, 111.

229. Crocker, *Henry More*, 66–70; Reid, *Metaphysics of Henry More*, 283–98.

more radical way. This threat of potentially atheist mechanical philosophy resulted in a public critique of Cartesianism in More's preface to *Divine Dialogues* (1668), a critique that More continued in the *Enchiridion metaphysicum* (1671).[230]

Baxter shared many of More's interests. He appreciated More's interpretation of the Antichrist and shared his concern to demonstrate the existence of spirits by various accounts of apparitions and witchcraft.[231] After More's critique of Cartesianism, Baxter also became somewhat favorable toward his metaphysics. Thus, in his postscript to the unpublished "Of the Nature and Immortality of Humane Soules," Baxter concluded the work by referring the reader to "two new excellent bookes"—More's *Enchiridion metaphysicum* and Samuel Gott's *The Divine History of the Genesis of the World* (1670)—where "The Reader yᵗ will find fuller satisfaction about Im[m]ateriall beings, or spirits, may have much."[232] Since Baxter had finished the early part of the *Methodus theologiae* dealing with ontology and human nature by this time, More's *Enchiridion metaphysicum* likely had little impact on the development of Baxter's *Methodus theologiae*. Rather, Baxter probably recommended the *Enchiridion metaphysicum* because he appreciated More's anti-Cartesian turn.

More and Baxter did not correspond until after Baxter published his *Methodus theologiae* in 1681. Baxter apparently sent More a copy of it and asked him to look over his section on human nature, since More's first letter to Baxter thanked him for receiving the *Methodus theologiae*. More went on to inquire of Baxter as to his thoughts on More's own discussion of spirit printed in Glanvill's first edition of *Saducismus Triumphatus* (1681). More indicated that after he had heard back from Baxter and had leisure to examine Baxter's thoughts on human nature, he would "briefly give you my thoughts of it, and how farre you and I differe or agree according as you desire in your letter."[233]

After this initial friendly correspondence, the relationship between the two theologians quickly turned sour. As More requested, Baxter sent him his thoughts on the nature of spirits in a "hasty"[234] letter in November of 1681.[235] However, More

---

230. Crocker, *Henry More*, 145–51.

231. As noted in William M. Lamont, *Richard Baxter and the Millenium* (London: Croom Helm, 1979), 45; and Crocker, *Henry More*, 171.

232. DWL BT XIX.351, fol. 143v.

233. More to Baxter, 25 Sept. 1681 (DWL BC III.286r). Baxter recounts More's initial letter in Richard Baxter, *Of the Immortality of Mans Soul, And the Nature of it, and other Spirits* (London: B. Simons, 1682), "The Preface," §3. On the exchange, see also Crocker, *Henry More*, 170–76.

234. Baxter, *Of the Immortality of Mans Soul*, "The Preface," §3.

235. Baxter to More, 17 Nov. 1681, in Richard Baxter, *Of the Nature of Spirits; Especially Mans Soul. In a Placid Collation with the Learned Dr. Henry More* (London: B. Simmons, 1682).

so vehemently disagreed with Baxter that he decided to reply to Baxter in public with a longer treatise. More published his reply to Baxter as *An Answer to a Letter of a Learned Psychopyrist Concerning the True Notion of a Spirit*, which was included in Joseph Glanvill's second edition of *Saducismus Triumphatus* (1682).[236] As the title indicates, More understood Baxter to be among those philosophers who "make the Essence or Substance of all created Spirits to be Fire, for so the word Psychopyrist signifies."[237] Unfortunately, More neither consulted Baxter before taking their friendly correspondence into the public light nor published Baxter's private response in full. Instead, More replied to select excerpts from Baxter's letter with no indication to the reader of Baxter's argument as a whole. As if to add insult to injury, after More's response had already gone to press, More sent Baxter a letter in February in which he notified Baxter that his answer was already in the press and he had deliberately proceeded without Baxter's knowledge lest Baxter had delayed the printed response.[238]

Baxter was furious with More. He shot back with *Of the Nature of Spirits; Especially Mans Soul. In a Placid Collation with the Learned Dr. Henry More* (1682). Baxter included his original reply to More from November in its entirety. In the introduction, Baxter noted that More's accusation of "Psychopyrist" was off the mark: in his own writings, Baxter observed, the soul is called fire "not *formaliter*, or *univoce*, but only *eminenter* and *analogice*."[239] Baxter's work responded to each section of More's *Answer* in kind, and addressed topics such as substance, soul, motion, and the Platonic world soul. Much of the work thus repeats or clarifies the contents of the *Methodus theologiae*,[240] but also highlights Baxter's disagreement with More's use of mechanical philosophy. At one point in his letter, More had

---

236. Henry More, *An Answer to a Letter of a Learned Psychopyrist Concerning the True Notion of a Spirit* (London: S. Lownds, 1681), in *Saducismus Triumphatus*, 2nd ed. (London: Tho. Newcomb, 1682).

237. More, "To the Reader," in *Answer to a Letter*, Q3v.

238. More to Baxter, 10 Feb. 1682 (DWL BC III.284r): "And out of my presumption that you also have a reall Zeal for the common good, and that this Answer of mine will appear such to you, I have published it without acquainting you with my designe, wch might either have much delayed the buisinesse (and the presse was then agoing on the second <edition>) or, because of your over much modesty and shynesse, have frustrated it. But now it is done, when the Book is quite finished I will order Mr [Samuel] Lowndes to present you with a copy of this second Edition [of *Saducismus Triumphatus*]." Cf. Baxter, *Of the Immortality of Mans Soul*, "The Preface," §3: "It seemed good to the worthy Dr. [More] to desire my thoughts of his Description of a Spirit . . . which I gave him in a hasty letter, which he thought meet, without my knowledge, to publish an answer to, in his second Edition of Mr. Glanvile['s *Saducismus Triumphatus*]."

239. Baxter, *Of the Nature of Spirits*, 2; also 72–73.

240. As Baxter himself noted in *Of the Immortality of Mans Soul*, "The Preface," §3: "[*Of the Nature of Spirits*] explaineth some passages in my *Methodus Theologiae*."

defended the "atomic philosophy" as the best explanation for nature (excepting God and spirits) with the comment "in this industrious and searching Age it is most universally received by free and considering Philosophers."[241] To this, Baxter responded that More had not adequately considered alternative philosophies: "I thought you that so extol the Atomists Doctrine, would have deigned to read at least some of the Leaders of the various Sects: And my undervaluing them is no excuse to you."[242]

More concluded their polemics with a "Digression" on Baxter's *Placid Collation* that was printed in More's anonymous *Annotations* on George Rust's *Discourse of Truth* (1682).[243] By this time, their relationship had so deteriorated that More's response included large doses of ad hominem polemic. At one point, More openly questioned Baxter's philosophical prowess, and suggested that he stick to writing devotional literature. "He has bewildered and lost himself in multifarious, and mostwhat needless points in Philosophy or Scholastick Divinity," wrote More. "He had better have set up his Staff in his *Saints everlasting Rest*, and such other edifying and useful Books as those, than to have set up for either a *Philosopher* or *Polemick Divine*. But it is the infelicity of too many, that they are ignorant."[244] And in that hostile spirit both More and Baxter continued for the remainder of their lives.[245]

The clash between Baxter and More over philosophy ended in 1682, but Baxter was preparing for another fight that was cut short by More's death in 1687 and Baxter's in 1691. In a manuscript, originally entitled "Revived Origenisme" but revised as "The State of soules moderately examined," Baxter took aim at More's late treatise, *A Brief Discourse of the Real Presence of the Body and Blood of Christ in the Celebration of the Holy Eucharist* (1686). Baxter's manuscript, as the title page advertises, was "Written by the provocation of Dr H. More," and as the preface indicates, was composed by Baxter while in prison in 1686 (the preface is

---

241. More, *Answer to a Letter*, 40.

242. Baxter, *Of the Nature of Spirits*, 67.

243. Henry More, "Annotations," in *Two Choice and Useful Treatises: the One Lux Orientalis; Or An Enquiry into the Opinions of the Eastern Sages Concerning the Praeexistence of Souls. Being a Key to unlock the Grand Mysteries of Providence. In Relation to Man's Sin and Misery* [by Joseph Glanvill]. *The Other, A Discourse of Truth, By the late Reverend Dr. Rust, Lord Bishop of Dromore in Ireland. With Annotations on them both* [by Henry More] (London: J. Collins and S. Loundes, 1682), 202. For the attribution of these annotations to Henry More, see Johannes van den Berg, *Religious Currents and Cross-Currents: Essays on Early Modern Protestantism and the Protestant Enlightenment*, ed. Jan de Bruijn, Pieter Holtrop, and Ernestine van der Wall (Leiden: Brill, 1999), 65.

244. More, "Annotations," 188–89.

245. For an account of Baxter's polemics with More on the Apocalypse from 1684, see Lamont, *Richard Baxter*, 22–23 and chapter 1.

dated 16 May 1690). Along with More's *Brief Discourse*, Baxter took exception to the Trinitarian theology of Peter Sterry's *A Discourse of the Freedom of the Will* (1675) and John Turner's *A Discourse Concerning the Messias* (1685), particularly Turner's "making yᵉ second Person to be an *Im[m]ateriall Creature*, & yᵉ *Holy Ghost* or *third Person* to be yᵉ *Prime Created matter*."[246] Like More, Turner was a fellow of Christ's College, Cambridge (1673–1681),[247] and his *Discourse* was a probable source for William Sherlock's Cartesian reformulation of the persons of the Trinity using language of "self-consciousness."[248] Baxter saw the treatises of More and Turner as indicative of a growing rationalism in theology.[249] After his preface, Baxter opened his work with the words, "There is lately revived a method of Theologie, by some deep students who are verst in yᵉ Platonike Philosophy, & thinke yᵗ *Reason* must know more of the *Divine being* than Scripture revealeth."[250] He also warned that "to venture on peremptory determinations, beyond plaine scripture revealations, on pretense of greater naturall evidence than wee have, is but yᵉ way of dangerous heresie, by overvaluing our owne wits."[251] Given the subsequent controversy caused by Sherlock's *A Vindication of the Holy and Blessed Trinity* (1690),[252] as well as the positive reception in eighteenth-century nonconformity of new speculation on the Logos associated with the thought of More,[253] Baxter's warning was remarkably prescient.

In order to prevent others from "venturing by presumption too farre in their Reason or Philosophy,"[254] Baxter listed a series of sixty points that constitute the body of the treatise. Points 15 and 16 consist of brief one-paragraph critiques of

---

246. DWL BT IV.87, fol. 228r–229r, citation at 229r. Cf. John Turner, Epistle Dedicatory to *A Discourse Concerning the Messias, in Three Chapters* (London: T. B., 1685), cliv–clxi. Baxter may have known Turner personally: "Lately I have a neighbour John Turner Hospitaller at Sᵗ Thomas in Southworke, son to Melchizedek Turner, late fellow of Christs Colledge in Cambridge" (228v).

247. John Venn, *Alumni Cantabrigienses* (Cambridge: Cambridge University Press, 1927), I/ 4:275.

248. Udo Thiel, "The Trinity and Human Personal Identity," in *English Philosophy in the Age of Locke*, ed. M. A. Stewart (Oxford: Clarendon Press, 2000), 217–43, here 228–31, discussing Turner, *Discourse*, cxxii, cxxvii, cliii, Appendix 71.

249. DWL BT IV.87, fols. 228r–230r. Cf. Richard Baxter, *The Glorious Kingdom of Christ* (London: T. Snowden, for Thomas Parkhurst, 1691), 24, 27; Richard Baxter, *An End of Doctrinal Controversies* (London: John Salisbury, 1691), xviii–xix.

250. DWL BT IV.87, fol. 228r.

251. DWL BT IV.87, fol. 231r. Cf. Baxter, *Of the Nature of Spirits*, 4–5.

252. *PRRD*, 3:123–29.

253. Strivens, *Philip Doddridge*, 61–62.

254. DWL BT IV.87, fol. 230r.

Gassendi and Cartesians.[255] Just as Baxter's attitude toward More hardened over time, so too did his evaluation of "new philosophers." Yet he still found the Trinitarian speculations of those such as More and Turner, who are "for an *eternity of spirit & matter*," more tolerable than the more purely Cartesian philosophers, who are "for an eternity of only *Motion & Matter*." According to Baxter, "You may call these men *New Philosophers*, or *Cartesians*, but for my part I shall take them for proved fooles, fitter for Bedlam than for a Schoole of Philosophy. And I would not have them yᵗ are for an *eternity of spirit, matter & motion*, likened to these *Epicurean Somatists & Sots*."[256] As Baxter was preparing such remarks for publication a year before his death, it is fair to say that he remained a consistent critic of the mechanical philosophy represented by Gassendi and Descartes until the bitter end.

Conclusion

Baxter's controversy with More concluded decades of polemic that began with anxiety over Hobbes's *Leviathan* in the interregnum. After the rise of mechanical philosophy and Christian Epicureanism, and their public association with members of the Royal Society in the 1660s, Baxter launched his initial polemics against Gassendi and Descartes, which later extended to the ethics of Hobbes and Spinoza. Baxter was also drawn into controversy with the leading Latitudinarian divines Glanvill and More, where he reiterated his critique of mechanical philosophy. At the same time, Baxter maintained a friendly relationship with Boyle and, as we shall see, incorporated some aspects of Boyle's mechanical philosophy without jettisoning the concept of substantial form.

While there is some indication that nonconformists carried forward Baxter's polemics, such criticism would become an increasingly diminishing voice amid accommodation to the rising tide of mechanical philosophy.[257] By the early decades of the eighteenth century, leading English nonconformists and American

---

255. DWL BT IV.87, fols. 232v–233r.

256. DWL BT IV.87, fol. 233r.

257. See William Bates, *Considerations on the Existence of God and the Immortality of the Soul* (London: J. D. for Brabazon Aylmer, 1676), 51–70 (on Epicureanism); John Howe, *The Living Temple, or, A Designed Improvement of that Notion, that a Good Man Is the Temple of God* (London: John Starkey, 1675), 81–91 (on Descartes) and 98–118, 226–35 (on Epicureanism); and Howe, *The Living Temple, Part II. Containing Animadversions on Spinoza, and a French Writer pretending to Confute him* (London: Thomas Parkhurst, 1702). In *The Living Temple* [Part I], Howe attacks Descartes on animal souls (81–91) and cites Baxter's appendix to the *Reasons* (97), but he also appears to hold a more accommodating attitude to Descartes (e.g., 50–51, 90) and Henry More (e.g., 40–43, 97, 271–72, 279, 287), reflective of the influence of the Cambridge Platonists from his education at Christ's College, Cambridge. See *ODNB*, s.v. "Howe, John (1630–1705)." These sources are briefly discussed in Wallace, *Shapers*, 179–80. Note that Wallace claims that Bates argued against Descartes's conception of animal souls,

Puritans, including Philip Doddridge and Jonathan Edwards, were accepting new philosophical ideas regarding substance, causality, and psychology to a degree that Baxter would likely have found shocking.[258] Late in life, Baxter himself attributed neglect of his *Methodus theologiae* in part to the influence of antischolastic and anti-Aristotelian polemic on a younger generation. He complained in the 1680s that his *Methodus theologiae* was neglected by "ye multitude of younger students uncapable of things very accurate & methodicall, (& crying downe Aristotle & the Schoolmen to hide their ignorance of their Learning)."[259] Having begun his career in a time dominated by Puritan religion and Aristotelian philosophy, Baxter lived to see not only the re-emergence of anti-Calvinist Anglicanism among both Laudians and Latitudinarians, but also the favorable reception among a new generation of students of philosophical trends he had opposed. The tables, indeed, had turned.

---

but in the places from Bates's *Considerations*, 2nd ed. (1677), cited by Wallace (295n48), Bates nowhere mentions Descartes.

258. Strivens, *Philip Doddridge*, ch. 3; Richard A. Muller, "Philip Doddridge and the Formulation of Calvinistic Theology in an Era of Rationalism and Deconfessionalization," in *Religion, Politics and Dissent, 1660–1832: Essays in Honour of James E. Bradley*, ed. Robert D. Cornwall and William Gibson (Farnham: Ashgate, 2010), 65–84; Sebastian Rehnman, "Towards a Solution to the 'Perennially Intriguing Problem' of the Sources of Jonathan Edwards' Idealism," *Jonathan Edwards Studies* 5, no. 2 (2015): 138–55; Richard A. Muller, "Jonathan Edwards and the Absence of Free Choice: A Parting of Ways in the Reformed Tradition," *Jonathan Edwards Studies* 1, no. 1 (2011): 3–22.

259. DWL BT VII.229, fol. 68v. This MS was written after *The Catechizing of Families* (1683), which is mentioned therein.

3

Reason and Philosophy

RICHARD BAXTER INITIALLY gained his fame through the publication of the devotional classic *The Saints Everlasting Rest*. There is some irony then in the fact that the author of devotional literature has been consistently described as a protorationalist divine anticipating later Lockean, Socinian, and Deist trends. William Orme wondered whether later rationalistic trends in eighteenth-century Presbyterianism toward Unitarianism "may not be traced in some degree to the speculative and argumentative writings of Baxter," in part since he "wished to place a variety of theological truths on grounds belonging rather to philosophy or metaphysics, than revelation."[1] Alexander Gordon argued that Baxter was a "precursor" to Locke's more rationalist Christianity, and remarked, "Locke's *Reasonableness of Christianity as delivered in the Scriptures* (1695) owes more than its title to Baxter's *Reasons for the Christian Religion* (1667)."[2] Major biographers of Baxter followed in Gordon's footsteps. Powicke was of the opinion that Baxter's apologetic method in the *Reasons for the Christian Religion* "anticipated, if he did not initiate," that apologetic later worked out in Deism.[3] Both Nuttall and Keeble agreed with Gordon's assessment, while Keeble reiterated that Baxter's apologetic works such as *Unreasonableness of Infidelity* and *Reasons* "set Baxter in the line of developing rationalism which was to lead to John Locke and the deists."[4] This line of thought has been followed by Carl Trueman, who agreed with Nuttall that

---

1. Orme, *Life*, 2:84.

2. Alexander Gordon, *Heads of English Unitarian History* (London: Philip Green, 1895), 99, also 31–32.

3. Powicke, *Reverend Richard Baxter Under the Cross*, 247.

4. Nuttall, *Richard Baxter*, 123; N. H. Keeble, "Baxter, Richard," in *ODNB*. Cf. Keeble, *Richard Baxter*, 30–31, esp. 191n36. See also Roger Thomas, "The Break-Up of Nonconformity," in *The Beginnings of Nonconformity* (London: James Clarke, 1964), 33–60, at 52–53; Roger Thomas, "Parties in Nonconformity," in *The English Presbyterians: From Elizabethan Puritanism to Modern Unitarianism* (Boston: Beacon Press, 1968), 104, 108–12; Thomas, "Presbyterians in

"Baxter, with his constant appeals to human reason, represents something of a transitional figure between the old-style Reformed Orthodoxy and the theology of the age of the Enlightenment."[5] Trueman has even gone so far as to claim that Baxter "has certain affinities with the Socinian method" in his use of reason.[6] Most recently, Dewey Wallace has argued for a strong continuity between Baxter and the Anglican Latitudinarians on the use of reason. Although he observes several distinctive features in the dissenting apologetics of Baxter and others,[7] Wallace claims similarity between Baxter and Latitudinarians in their preference for antischolastic, even Cartesian, clear reasoning over against "scholastic quibbling."[8]

The view of Baxter as a protorationalist has not gone unchallenged. Simon Burton, basing his opinion on the most detailed study of Baxter's *Methodus theologiae* to date, has argued that "the perception of Baxter as a rationalist and modalist is ultimately mistaken,"[9] and Baxter's Trinitarian theology was neither a " 'small step' or even a 'giant leap' toward Enlightenment rationalism," but instead "a fascinating Augustinian and medieval scholastic synthesis."[10] David Zaret argues that Baxter "opposed the growing appeal of natural religion" as evidenced in his *The Arrogancy of Reason against Divine Revelations* (1655). Comparing Baxter to older Puritan attitudes toward rationality, Zaret states, "Baxter adhered instead to the general reformed tradition that limited the scope and efficacy of human reason."[11] Katherine Calloway likewise questions a protorationalist reading of Baxter. "While at one level he seems relentlessly rational," Calloway writes, "Baxter relies on

---

Transition," in *The English Presbyterians: From Elizabethan Puritanism to Modern Unitarianism* (Boston: Beacon Press, 1968), 137–40.

5. Carl R. Trueman, "Richard Baxter on Christian Unity: A Chapter in the Enlightening of English Reformed Orthodoxy," *Westminster Theological Journal* 61 (1999): 53–71, at 70 (citing Nuttall, *Richard Baxter*, 123–24).

6. Carl R. Trueman, "Small Step," 194. Cf. Carl R. Trueman, "Reformed Orthodoxy in Britain," in *A Companion to Reformed Orthodoxy*, ed. Herman Selderhuis (Leiden: Brill, 2013), 261–91, at 290.

7. Wallace, *Shapers*, 198–202. Wallace highlights the appeal to affections, the reality of original sin, the necessity of Christ's atonement, and the effect of holiness.

8. Wallace, *Shapers*, 177.

9. Burton, *Hallowing of Logic*, 202; also 74.

10. Simon J. G. Burton, "Faith, Reason, and the Trinity in Richard Baxter's Theology: Incipient Rationalism or Scholastic *Fides Quarens Intellectum?*," *Calvin Theological Journal* 49 (2014): 85–111, at 88.

11. David Zaret, "The Use and Abuse of Textual Data," in *Weber's Protestant Ethic: Origins, Evidence, Contexts*, ed. Hartmut Lehmann and Guenther Roth (Washington, DC: German Historical Institute, 1993), 269–70. See John Morgan, *Godly Learning: Puritan Attitudes towards Reason, Learning, and Education, 1560–1640* (Cambridge: Cambridge University Press, 1986), 41–61.

divine revelation in a way that would have looked to more latitudinarian minds like enthusiasm."[12]

There are at least three methodological problems with the interpretation of Baxter as a protorationalist. First, most of the literature has evaluated Baxter's view of reason and faith almost entirely on the basis of his apologetic writings (particularly the *Reasons*), to the neglect of his *Methodus theologiae*, where Baxter includes an entire section on the role of reason in matters of faith. Such an oversight in the secondary literature is analogous to basing an evaluation of Aquinas's doctrine solely on the *Summa contra gentiles* to the complete neglect of the *Summa theologiae*. Second, claims of Baxter's continuity with Latitudinarian divines have been made without sufficient attention to his own pedigree or his own evaluation of Latitudinarians. Baxter's shared interest with More and Glanvill in evidences of spirits and apparitions was not derived from them, but rather antedated their works, as evident in his early comments on Girolamo Zanchi's *De operibus Dei*.[13] Likewise, Baxter's interest in evidences for the authority of Scripture also antedated Latitudinarian works, and was already a well-established feature of Reformed theology.[14] On the closely related question of the internal testimony of the Holy Spirit, Baxter differed from the Latitudinarians. Unlike Latitudinarians such as Edward Fowler, who denied that "an *internal* Testimony, or a secret powerful persuasion" of the Holy Spirit was ordinarily necessary for assent to the authority of Scripture (a view contemporaries attributed to Socinians and Remonstrants),[15] Baxter affirmed that "all true Christians" acknowledge the truth of Scripture by the

---

12. Katherine Calloway, *Natural Theology in the Scientific Revolution: God's Scientists* (London: Pickering & Chatto, 2014), 58.

13. *SER2*, II.269–77, citing Girolamo Zanchi, *Omnium operum theologicorum* (Geneva, 1619), 3:191 (IV.xi), and with him Augustine and Aquinas. Among the other sources is Zurich theologian Ludwig Lavater (1527–1586), whose *Of Ghostes and Spirites, Walking by Night* was an early modern publishing phenomenon. Cf. Richard Baxter, *The Nature and Immortality of the Soul Proved. In Answer to one who professed perplexing Doubtfulness* (London: B. Simons, 1682), 68. Baxter also discussed the topic of apparitions with Matthew Poole. See *CCRB*, 1:260–65, 380. Contra Wallace, *Shapers*, 188–89.

14. *SER2*, II.192–285. These arguments are intended for "the consolation and edification of the Saints, and not the information and conversion of Pagans" (192). He notes David Pareus and Amandus Polanus as precedents (preface to *Unreasonableness*, c8r). Cf. *PRRD*, 2:255–85.

15. Fowler, *Principles and Practices*, 54–57; cf. Joseph Glanvill, *Some Discourses, Sermons, and Remains* (London: Henry Mortlock, 1681), 419–20; Gilbert Burnet, *An Exposition of the Thirty-nine Articles of the Church of England* (London: R. Roberts, 1699), 79. On the Socinian and Remonstrant associations, see Ferguson, *Interest of Reason*, 145–46; Robert Ferguson, *A Sober Enquiry into the Nature, Measure, and Principles of Moral Virtue* (London: D. Newman, 1673), 259–62; John Wilson, *The Scriptures Genuine Interpreter Asserted* ([London]: T. N. for R. Boulter, 1678), 35, 130, "Appendix," 12–13; Kęstutis Daugirdas, "*Ratio recta scripturae interpres*: The Biblical Hermeneutics of Simon Episcopius before 1634 and Its Impact," *Bulletin annuel de l'Institut d'histoire de la Réformation* 32 (2010–2011): 37–49.

Spirit's renewal of the will and illumination of the mind.[16] Baxter himself viewed More and Glanvill as excessively rationalistic,[17] and he offered a critique of the rational "method of Theologie" specifically associated with More and John Turner of Christ's College, Cambridge.[18] Third, insufficient attention has been given to Baxter's own response to contemporary worries that he was "too neer the Socinian way" in making use of reason. His response does not indicate a theologian heading in a new rationalist direction, but rather someone immersed in the works of Reformed scholastics who dealt at length with matters of reason and faith. In particular, Baxter directed readers to Nicolaus Vedel's (1596–1642) *Rationale theologicum* in order to understand "how far Reason and Natural Principles may be used in Disputes of Divinity."[19] Vedel was a professor of philosophy at Geneva (1618–1630), and professor of theology at Deventer (1630–1639) and Franeker (1639–1642), and an ardent critic of the Remonstrants.

When one examines Baxter's precise treatment of the nature of reason and inquires into his use of scholastic sources and distinctions as found in works such as *The Saints Everlasting Rest* and *Methodus theologiae*, it is apparent that the contours of his thought approximate Reformed orthodox attitudes toward the use and limits of reason.[20] This is a position that stands in contrast to the increasing confidence in reason in later eighteenth-century theology.[21] This chapter will demonstrate that Baxter maintained a traditionally Reformed insistence on the noetic effects of sin, rejected Cartesian skepticism of the senses, and developed an approach to the acquisition of knowledge framed within an account of

---

16. Richard Baxter, *More Reasons for the Christian Religion and No Reason Against It* (London: Nevil Simmons, 1672), 135–36, for which he is praised by Wilson, *Scriptures Genuine Interpreter*, "Appendix," 20 (separately paginated). Cf. Baxter, *More Reasons*, 30–41; *RCR*, 282–83, 349–50, 601–2; *MT*, I.21, III.124; *CD*, I/1.42, 319. For a succinct statement of the doctrine, see Westminster Confession of Faith, I.v–vi (Philip Schaff, ed., *The Creeds of Christendom* [New York: Harper & Brothers, 1877], 3:602–3); cf. *PRRD*, 2:266–67.

17. Baxter, *Of the Nature of Spirits*, 4–5.

18. DWL BT IV.87, fols. 226r–255v. Cf. *TKL*, 2: "A mixture of Platonick Philosophy with Christianity, made up most of the Primitive Hereticks, (and for want of a due digestion of each, too much corrupted many of the Greek Doctors of the Church.)"

19. *SER2*, preface to Part II, 8v–9v, citing Nicolaus Vedel, *Rationale theologicum seu de necessitate et vero usu principiorum rationis ac philosophiae in controversiis theologicis* (Geneva: Jacob Chouet, 1628); Robert Baron, *Ad Georgii Turnebulli Tetragonismum pseudographum apodixis catholica* (Aberdeen: Edward Raban, 1631); and André Rivet, *Catholicus orthodoxus* (Geneva: Jacob Chouet, 1644).

20. Cf. *PRRD*, 1:360–405.

21. Cf. *PRRD*, 1:122, 145–46, 305–7; Sell, *Philosophy, Dissent and Nonconformity*, 33–34; Alan P. F. Sell, *Testimony and Tradition: Studies in Reformed and Dissenting Thought* (Eugene, OR: Wipf & Stock, 2005), 104–6.

the faculties of intellect and will eclectically taken from medieval scholasticism. Baxter's understanding of the relation between reason and will incorporated doctrines from Duns Scotus, while his understanding of the relation between reason and revelation drew on the works of Thomas Aquinas. This account of the nature and limitations of reason yielded a cautious and eclectic approach to philosophical knowledge and sects, which, while giving greater preference to Platonic and Aristotelian philosophy over Epicurean and mechanical philosophy, also acknowledged deficiencies in every philosophical tradition and the need for philosophical reform.

Works on Reason

Since most evaluations of Baxter's views on reason and philosophy rest on a partial reading of the available evidence, we will first identify the most important sources on the subject. Besides the apologetic *Reasons*, Baxter set forth his view of the matter in several places. Already in the second edition to *The Saints Everlasting Rest* (1651) Baxter added a preface to Part 2, in which he responded to various objections, among them certain contemporary accusations that his use of reason was "too neer the Socinian way."[22] In Part 2 he also discussed the relation between reason and revelation.[23] In the preface to *Unreasonableness of Infidelity* (1655), he again took up the same objections as four years previously. In that preface, he indicated that *Unreasonableness* was a response to the growth of radical sects. This turbulent period also included an onslaught by radical reformers on the traditional divinity of the schools, culminating in John Webster's *Academiarum Examen, or the Examination of the Academies* (1654).[24] The fourth part of Baxter's *Unreasonableness, The Arrogancy of Reason against Divine Revelations, Repressed* (1655), where he addressed the noetic effects of sin, likely had such radical attacks on the learned ministry in mind, since the preface to *Unreasonableness* refers to radical groups as rejecting the need for teachers.[25] Baxter certainly shared the concerns and perspective of Thomas Hall, whose *Vindiciae Literarum, The Schools Guarded* (1654) offered a representative Reformed response to the radical reformers.[26]

---

22. *SER2*, preface to Part II, 8v.

23. *SER2*, II.203–5.

24. Webster, *Great Instauration*, 178–202.

25. Baxter, "The Preface," in *Unreasonableness*. Westfall thought this work was a response to "the very temper of scientific research" (*Science and Religion*, 22), but Wojcik seems more correct in viewing it as targeting Socinianism ("Theological Context," 143).

26. Thomas Hall, *Vindiciae Literarum, The Schools Guarded* (London: W. H., 1654).

After the Restoration, Baxter's most important occasional writings include *A Treatise of Knowledge and Love* (1689) and the manuscript,[1] "The State of soules moderately examined" (1686). The first several chapters of *A Treatise of Knowledge and Love*, originally composed around 1672, consist of a doctrinal exposition of 1 Corinthians 8:2–3. The scope of this passage, according to Baxter, is the depression of "pretended knowledge" or a "proud unhumbled understanding."[27] He uses this exegetical locus to initiate a discussion of the role of philosophy in theology (Part 1), as well as the proper relationship between truth and love (Part 2). These themes permeate the entire treatise, even though he also addresses various practical questions including catechizing and ecclesiastical divisions. Since the early chapters of the *Treatise* were written only a few years after Baxter began his polemics over mechanical philosophy, they are the most proximate source for Baxter's general opinions on philosophy, as they inform those very polemics. Baxter composed "State of soules" at the end of his life as a final response to Henry More. This work is of interest for Baxter's comments on reason and revelation. Since both the *Treatise* and "State of soules" were written in the context of Baxter's Restoration polemics, they are of special interest to our study.

Baxter's most systematic statement on reason, however, is found at the beginning of the *Methodus theologiae*, where he addressed the question, "What are the functions of REASON concerning things of Faith & the Christian Religion?"[28] Baxter's reply to this question in the *Methodus theologiae* appeared as a separate tract—with some alteration—five years prior to the *Methodus theologiae* itself as *The Judgment of Non-conformists, of the Interest of Reason, in Matters of Religion* (1676). It is possible that *Judgment of Non-conformists* was translated from the Latin manuscript of the *Methodus theologiae* that Baxter had already been drafting circa 1669–1670.[29] Lacking any attribution of authorship on the title page, *Judgment of Non-conformists* simply concluded with fifteen signatories, including noteworthy Puritans Thomas Manton (d. 1677), William Bates (1625–1699), and Thomas Case (d. 1682), a former member of the Westminster Assembly, who affirmed its doctrine.[30] This "party manifesto" for English dissenters, as Perry

---

27. *TKL*, 1.

28. *MT*, I.16–27: "Quaenam sunt RATIONIS Partes circa res Fidei & Religionis Christianae?" (Pars I, Cap. 1). Cf. Baxter, *End of Doctrinal Controversies*, xxxi–xxxiv.

29. For dating, see Appendix A. To my knowledge, this relation between the *Methodus theologiae* and *Judgment of Non-conformists* has gone unnoticed until now.

30. *JNIR*, 21: "We, whose Names are Subscribed, (not undertaking that no Individual Person is otherwise minded,) do, our selves, believe the real Concord of Protestants, as it is here expressed. Th. Manton, W. Bates, Tho. Case, Gabriel Sangar, Rich. Baxter, Math. Pemberton, Mat. Silvester, Henry Hurst, Roger Morice, Edw. Lawrence, Benjam. Agas, James Bedford, Sam. Fairclough, John Turner, Joseph Read."

Miller once observed, was representative enough of the wider Puritan tradition that "it is clear that all New England divines could have signed the endorsement."[31] Its immediate political context was a polemic started by establishment Latitudinarians Simon Patrick, Edward Fowler, and Joseph Glanvill, who accused nonconformists of disdaining "rational discourses" and characterized them as "unreasonable, ill-minded, and wild-headed men."[32] Following the nonconformist rejoinders of Samuel Rolle and Robert Ferguson, Baxter's *Judgment of Non-conformists* sought to vindicate nonconformists from politically damaging allegations of irrationality.[33] Thus, Baxter's discussion of reason in the *Methodus theologiae* carried with it the express approval of leading Puritan divines, and, if Perry Miller is to be believed,[34] was quite representative of the wider Puritan tradition.

The Nature and States of Reason

Due in part to the post-Reformation growth of theology in an academic context in relation to other philosophical disciplines, and in part to the problem of Socianism that was perceived to buttress traditionally heretical doctrine with rational argument, from the early seventeenth century the topic of reason emerged as an important locus in theological literature.[35] Thus, while earlier generations of theologians in the sixteenth century may have been content to discuss the relation of reason and faith in an occasional and abbreviated manner in the context of exegesis of *loci classici* such as Colossians 2:8 and 1 Corinthians 1:23, theologians of the seventeenth century regularly treated the question of the role of reason in theology as a distinct topic, where they addressed both the nature of the faculty

---

31. Miller, *New England Mind: The Seventeenth Century*, 71.

32. Richard Ashcraft, "Latitudinarianism and Toleration: Historical Myth versus Political History," in *Philosophy, Science, and Religion in England 1640–1700*, ed. Richard Kroll, Richard Ashcraft, and Perez Zagorin (Cambridge: Cambridge University Press, 1992), 151–77, at 157–61. See Simon Patrick, *A Friendly Debate between a Conformist and Non-Conformist* (London, 1669); Fowler, *Principles and Practices* (1670); and Joseph Glanvill, *ΛΟΓΟΥ ΘΡΗΣΚΕΙΑ: Or, A Seasonable Recommendation and Defence of Reason in the Affairs of Religion* (London: J. M., 1670), appended to *Philosophia Pia* (1671).

33. Samuel Rolle, *A Sober Answer to the Friendly Debate Betwixt a Conformist and a Nonconformist* (London, 1669); and Ferguson, *Interest of Reason* (1675), written under "[John] Owen's tutelage" (*ODNB*, s.v. "Ferguson, Robert (d. 1714)").

34. Miller, *New England Mind: The Seventeenth Century*, 71–72.

35. *PRRD*, 1:388–98; Klaus Scholder, *The Birth of Modern Critical Theology: Origins and Problems of Biblical Criticism in the Seventeenth Century*, trans. John Bowden (London: SCM Press, 1990), 26–45.

of reason itself and its relation to sin and grace.[36] Baxter was no exception to this trend. In the *Methodus theologiae*, he addresses these issues in a manner typical of the scholastic theology of his day.[37]

It was commonplace by the middle of the seventeenth century for Reformed theologians to distinguish between reason in an objective or subjective sense. By this, some theologians meant to distinguish the essential nature of reason in humanity from dispositions or accidents that vary among individuals and states.[38] Others used the distinction between objective and subjective reason to distinguish the objective extramental object from the subjective agent.[39] Baxter's way of using the distinction follows this latter sense of dividing reason into its objective and subjective aspects, corresponding to object and agent. Objectively taken (*ex parte objecti*), reason refers to the evidence of truth. Baxter divides this objective evidence into the evidence of the thing itself, the means, and the consequence. He distinguishes the evidence of the thing itself into sensible and intelligible objects, and divides the means into either natural or supernatural means that convey the said things.[40]

Subjectively taken (*ex parte subjective agentis*), reason may refer to the faculty of reason itself (*facultas*), or reason's act (*actus*), habit (*habitus*), or external expression (e.g., words and writing).[41] This definition of reason in the subjective agent obviously assumes a basic commitment to Aristotelian psychology in which the metaphysical categories of potency and act are applied to various human functions. According to this psychology, *facultas* is a power to produce acts; *habitus*

---

36. *PRRD*, 1:388–405; Martin I. Klauber, "The Use of Philosophy in the Theology of Johannes Maccovius (1578–1644)," *Calvin Theological Journal* 30, no. 2 (1995): 376–91; Sebastian Rehnman, *Divine Discourse: The Theological Methodology of John Owen* (Grand Rapids, MI: Baker Academic, 2002), 109–28; Rehnman, "Alleged Rationalism: Francis Turretin on Reason," *Calvin Theological Journal* 37, no. 2 (2002): 255–69; Stephen Grabill, "Natural Law and the Noetic Effects of Sin: The Faculty of Reason in Francis Turretin's Theological Anthropology," *Westminster Theological Journal* 67 (2005): 261–79; Goudriaan, *Reformed Orthodoxy and Philosophy*, 29–83.

37. For a complementary account of the following discussion, as it relates to the *Methodus theologiae*, see Burton, *Hallowing of Logic*, 72–78; and Burton, "Faith, Reason, and the Trinity," 88–93.

38. E.g., Gisbertus Voetius, "De ratione humana in rebus fidei," in *Selectarum disputationum theologicarum* (Utrecht: Johannes a Waesberge, 1648–1669), 1:2. For a translation of this disputation, see Willem J. van Asselt, *Introduction to Reformed Scholasticism*, trans. Albert Gootjes (Grand Rapids, MI: Reformation Heritage Books, 2011), 225–47.

39. E.g., Francis Turretin, *Institutio theologiae elencticae* (Geneva, 1679–1685), I.viii.1; *PRRD*, 1:399–400.

40. *MT*, I.17; *JNIR*, 3–4.

41. *MT*, I.17; *JNIR*, 4.

is a disposition or quality of the faculty that is acquired by repeated acts but also continues to exist apart from any concrete acts; and *actus* is any concrete act of the *facultas*.[42] These Aristotelian categories furnish Baxter—and of course most of his scholastic contemporaries—with stable ontic continuities that underlie a theological description of discontinuity in human nature in its various states of creation, fall, and regeneration. Although Baxter's description of objective and subjective reason is quite similar to that of the contemporary Genevan theologian Francis Turretin, Baxter's further subdivision of objective reason into the thing, medium, and consequence, and of subjective reason into faculty, act, habit, and expression, represents a somewhat more detailed description than the famous Genevan scholastic.[43]

Reformed theologians typically emphasized the noetic effects of the fall by drawing on New Testament passages that speak of the human mind as blind and darkened (e.g., Eph. 4:18) or in need of being made obedient to Christ (e.g., 2 Cor. 10:3–5).[44] At the same time, they also recognized that in other passages there are various appeals to knowledge or the exercise of judgment (e.g., Mt. 7:15; Acts 17:11; 1 Thess. 5:21).[45] The proper harmonization of such texts generated a distinction, already in place among early Reformers such as Calvin and Vermigli, between corrupt and sound reason (or philosophy).[46] When addressing the topic of reason in a more scholastic fashion, seventeenth-century Reformed theologians typically distinguished at least three states of reason: a prelapsarian state of innocence, a postlapsarian or corrupted state, and a renewed state of grace[47]—although some also included the fourth state of glory or perfection.[48] The placement of anthropology within a framework of four states can be traced to Augustine and Bernard

---

42. Cf. W. J. van Asselt, J. Martin Bac, and Roelf T. te Velde, eds., *Reformed Thought on Freedom: The Concept of Free Choice in Early Modern Reformed Theology* (Grand Rapids, MI: Baker Academic, 2010), 44, 212.

43. Cf. Turretin, *Institutio*, I.viii.1.

44. Samuel Maresius, *Collegium theologicum*, 6th ed. (Geneva: Joannes Antonius et Samuel de Tournes, 1662), I.xv (p. 5); Turretin, *Institutio*, I.viii.5. See similarly for Puritans, John Morgan, *Godly Learning*, 65–67. For a general account of Reformed hamartiology, which emphasizes the variegated nature of the tradition, see Luca Baschera, "Total Depravity? The Consequences of Original Sin in John Calvin and Later Reformed Theology," in *Calvinus clarissimus theologus*, ed. Herman J. Selderhuis (Göttingen: Vandenhoeck & Ruprecht, 2012), 37–58.

45. Maresius, *Collegium theologicum*, I.xvi; Turretin, *Institutio*, I.x.4.

46. *PRRD*, 1:365.

47. Turretin, *Institutio*, I.viii.1; I.ix.14; I.x.1.

48. Voetius, *Selectarum disputationum theologicarum*, 1:2; cf. Goudriaan, *Reformed Orthodoxy and Philosophy*, 41.

of Clairvaux, and was also applied by early modern scholastics to the nature of free choice.[49] In his various works, Baxter assumes a fourfold division, although he only outlines the first three explicitly.[50]

Using categories of power, disposition, and act drawn from Aristotelian psychology, Baxter outlines the various states of reason, beginning with the state of innocence (*status naturae seu innocentiae*). In all three categories—in its power, disposition, and act—reason was originally without sin or error. As a faculty, reason was "sound." Reason acquired wisdom through distinct acts, and through these acts it became "Habitually more prompt to Act." Thus, reason gained wisdom through a virtuous cycle of acts and habits.[51] Yet even in its original state, reason would have experienced ignorance (albeit not sinful) both in habit and act, due to its natural limitations. It would not have been able "to know without an object," "to know an unrevealed or too distant object," or "actually to know all things knowable at once."[52]

While Baxter has comparatively little to say about reason in the state of innocence, his works contain far more elaboration on corrupted reason.[53] According to the *Methodus theologiae*, in the postlapsarian state of sin (*status peccati*), reason as a faculty is both "blind" and "undisposed" toward rightly or savingly discerning spiritual things. This is due both to its own corruption and to the will's inclination, which, as the beginning of practice (*exercitii principium*), moves reason. Both the reason's corruption and the will's inclination with respect to the intellect lead to "false judging, especially to practical error." Due to the corrupted nature of the faculty of reason, its acts are ignorant, erroneous, and prejudiced against spiritual goods. As reason repeatedly acts in a corrupted manner, its acts lead to a "*habitually* more, and more depraved" state both in terms of lack of disposition (*privativâ*) and positive disposition.[54]

---

49. Van Asselt et al., eds., *Reformed Thought on Freedom*, 44–45, 120–24, 138–43, 173.

50. MT, I.18: "De Lumine perfectissimo Gloriae hic dicere non opus est"; *JNIR*, 5. Cf. Richard Baxter, *The Mischiefs of Self-Ignorance, and the Benefits of Self-Aquaintance* (London: R. White, 1662), 5–6.

51. MT, I.17; *JNIR*, 4.

52. CD, I.96 (Dir. 8, §3).

53. See below, "Reason in the State of Sin."

54. MT, I.17; *JNIR*, 4–5; also MT, I.21; *JNIR*, 9. Contra Thomas, "Parties in Nonconformity," 104, who argued that for Baxter "reason was not dismissed as 'carnal' or 'corrupt,'" but ignored this paragraph while citing from other sections of the same work (110–11). Baxter defines a privation as "the absence of the thing *owed to its non-being*" (MT, I.6). It is a negative contrary, or absence, of a habit or disposition. See Thomas Spencer, *The Art of Logick, Delivered in the Precepts of Aristotle and Ramus* (London: John Dawson, 1638), 92–96.

The third state, that of renewal or renewed reason (*ratio reparata*), consists of the illumination of the mind by both Word and Spirit. Baxter divides this illumination into common and special light that in either case works on the reason in the "first disposition," "exercise," and "habit." The common light either prepares for saving light or makes people useful to each other. The special light refers to either saving or extraordinary light. Special saving light initially enlightens with efficacious calling and then increases love in the process of sanctification. Extraordinary special light simply refers to "visions and prophetic inspiration for miracles, infallibility, or extraordinary offices."[55]

Although Baxter does not address reason in the state of glory in any depth, he does provide some indication of his thoughts on this matter. In the state of glory, writes Baxter, the intellects of the blessed will be perfected. They will come to see "such *Reasons* for all the parts of Religion; even the *Trinity, Incarnation*, and *Resurrection*, as will delight them everlastingly, as seeing the admirable Harmony of all the sacred Truths, and Works of God." Furthermore, they will admire Christ as God's essential wisdom (1 Thess. 1:10–11), so that their knowledge will be like that currently enjoyed by the "principalities and powers in heavenly places" (Eph. 3:9–10).[56]

Reason and Will

Even apart from the noetic effects of the fall, Baxter's approach to philosophy is significantly affected by his perspective on the relation of the will to the intellect. A common view held that the intellect and will were interdependent faculties in which the will, being a blind faculty, depended on the intellect for the proper knowledge or specification of the good, while the intellect was directed by the will in its exercise of the pursuit of the good.[57] Baxter agreed with this basic psychological paradigm and cited the well-known maxim of Aquinas that the will begets actions "as far as the exercise of the act" (*quoad exercitium actus*) but the intellect is also a source of actions "as far as the specification of the act" (*quoad actus specificationem*).[58]

---

55. *MT*, I.17–18; *JNIR*, 5.

56. *MT*, I.24–25; *JNIR*, 15–16.

57. Franco Burgersdijck, *Idea philosophiae, tum moralis, tum naturalis* (Oxford: Ioh. Lichfield, 1631), disp. XXVI.5 (p. 99); Bartholomaeus Keckermann, *Systema ethicae* (London, 1607), 25; John Weemes, *The Portraiture of the Image of God in Man*, 3rd ed. (London: Thomas Cotes for John Bellamie, 1636), 97.

58. *SER2*, IV.178 (IV.viii.2), marginal note: "For (as *Aquinas* and others) the Wil is the Beginning of our Actions, *quoad exercitium Actus*, though the understanding be the beginner, *quoad specificationem*." Cf. *MT*, I.200, 207, 214; *CT*, II.76; *RCR*, 516–17. See Thomas

Within this commonly accepted paradigm there was also significant disagreement among both theologians and philosophers. One question concerned the relative nobility of the intellect or will, which related to whether the final goal of humanity consisted in knowledge or love. Another question concerned whether actions were ultimately rooted in the intellect or will as the first mover. Still another question concerned whether the will was determined by the specification of the intellect's last judgment of the good in the present circumstance (hic et nunc) or if it could rather suspend its activity in relation to the intellect's specification of the good.[59] While Thomists would generally favor the intellect on all these disputed questions, and Scotists would favor the will, Reformed theologians were not bound by dogmatic loyalty to either party, and could thus be quite eclectic in their solutions. For example, the Scottish Hebraist John Weemes agreed with Aquinas that the will was determined by the last judgment of the practical intellect, but also sided with voluntarists (explicitly against Aquinas) on the ultimate priority of the will as the first mover of the soul.[60]

Baxter also reflected this eclecticism of his Reformed contemporaries, albeit with a greater preference for Scotus. In his early period, while he cited Aquinas on the intellect's specification of the will, he also preferred Scotus's views with respect to the greater dignity of the will and the will's freedom in the face of the intellect's practical judgment concerning the good. Already in his *The Saints Everlasting Rest* he cited Scotus's interpretation of John 17:3 that ultimate beatitude consists in knowledge joined with love and enjoyment of God.[61] There he also disagreed with the Thomist position of "those divines" who hold that the will "ever followeth the last dictate of the practical understanding."[62] In his mature writings, he maintained

---

Aquinas, *Summa theologiae*, IaIIae, q. 9, art. 1; q. 13, art. 6; Étienne Gilson, *The Christian Philosophy of St. Thomas Aquinas*, trans. L. K. Shook (New York: Random House, 1956), 246–47; and Robert Sleigh Jr., Vere Chappell, and Michael Della Rocca, "Determinism and Human Freedom," in *CHSP*, 2:1198–99.

59. Cf. Gerard Smith, *Freedom in Molina* (Chicago: Loyola University Press, 1966), 68–89; David Gallagher, "Thomas Aquinas on the Will as Rational Appetite," *Journal of the History of Philosophy* 29 (1991): 571.

60. Weemes, *Portraiture*, 99, 102. Cf. David S. Sytsma, "The Harvest of Thomist Anthropology: John Weemes's Reformed Portrait of the Image of God" (ThM thesis, Calvin Theological Seminary, 2008), 139–42, 145–49.

61. *SER2*, I.36 (I.iii.6), marginal note: "*Scoti glossa est vera, viz. ut cognoscant te Amando & Fruendo. Vide Scotum in 4. senten. distinct. 48. Q. 1. p. 256.*" See Duns Scotus, *Ordinatio IV*, dist. 48, q. 1, in *Opera omnia* (Paris: Vives, 1894), 20:515. Although neither Packer nor Burton refer to this note on John 17:3, they rightly point to the Scotistic influence on Baxter's voluntarism. See Packer, *Redemption*, 86, 114, 333; Burton, *Hallowing of Logic*, 176–84, 377–81.

62. *SER2*, IV.182 [misprinted as p. 202] (IV.viii.6). See also *MT*, I.213. Cf. Burton, *Hallowing of Logic*, 181.

a preference for Scotus when compared to Aquinas, but distanced himself from both in light of his newly constructed Trinitarian anthropology. As he wrote in *Catholick Theologie*,

> I suppose that the *Thomists* grossly err in placing beatitude chiefly in the Intellect, and their Reasons (especially as *Medina* useth them) are very weak; and the Scotists are more sound, who place it in the Will, and those other most sound who place it in the perfection of the whole man actively; but objectively in God.[63]

Having constructed a Trinitarian anthropology of vital activity, willing, and knowing (see chapter 4), he placed the first principle of human acts neither in the will or intellect, but rather in the soul's vital activity or principle of living motion, which precedes both intellect and will in begetting action. As Baxter summarizes, "Since the object is first considered as *One* or *Existent* rather than as *True*, and first as *True* rather than as *Good*: therefore one should say that the *Vital Power* is the first faculty in acting, and the Intellect second, and the Will third."[64] Even with this Trinitarian development, Baxter maintained that the soul's acts culminate in the perfection of the will's delight in the goodness of God.[65]

The impact of Baxter's eclectic voluntarism on his approach to philosophy was quite profound. On the one hand, the will's great influence over reason in action meant that the corruption of the will in the state of sin exercised a contaminating influence over the intellect that was only partially cured by grace. On the other hand, the priority of love over knowledge of God as the highest end of life meant that Baxter was constantly evaluating philosophy in terms of its usefulness to eternal felicity.[66] While these factors would lead Baxter to exercise a cautious or ambivalent attitude toward philosophy, the fact of the will's dependence on the intellect for the specification of its act, together with Baxter's affirmation of the natural knowledge of God reflected in the creation, ensured that philosophy remained a useful handmaiden in the service of theology.

---

63. *CT*, II, "A Premonition," 25. See also *CD*, I.182; *TKL*, 211, 304; *CT*, III.12–13; and Baxter, *Divine Life*, 239.

64. *MT*, I.200: "Quoniam autem objectum priùs consideratur ut *Unum* vel *Existens* quàm ut *Verum*, & priùs ut *Verum* quàm ut *Bonum*: ideo dicendum est *Potentiam Vitalem* esse facultatem primam in agendo, & Intellectum secundam, & Voluntatem tertiam."

65. See Burton, *Hallowing of Logic*, 379–81.

66. *TKL*, 210–34.

Reason in the State of Sin

Of the four states of reason outlined in the *Methodus theologiae*, the states that most occupied his attention throughout his works were the states of sin and renewal. These states were of course the most relevant for his interaction with philosophical problems, since they relate to the more practical question of the present situation of humanity rather than what might have been (*status naturae seu innocentiae*) or what might be (*status gloriae*). Here we will take up the question of the noetic effects of the fall in the state of sin.

Baxter's sketch of corrupted reason in the *Methodus theologiae* is somewhat more filled out in the *Christian Directory*. There he identifies five kinds of "diseases" of the mind based on reason's relation either to the immediate evidence of a thing or to the means of another's testimony (i.e., belief). The first disease, ignorance, results from a privation of act or disposition in the reason with respect to immediate evidence. The second disease, error, comes from a privation of the rectitude of the act (also with respect to immediate evidence). These two differ just like not-seeing versus seeing-falsely. The diseases of belief are threefold. First, unbelief is the privation of the act of knowing by testimony. Second, disbelief is the privation of the rectitude of the act of knowing by testimony. Third, mis-belief is belief of a testimony that should not be believed. In sum, corrupt reason principally concerns either direct or indirect knowledge of things, corresponding to the ignorant, erroneous, and prejudiced acts that we already noted in the *Methodus theologiae*.[67]

In the *Christian Directory*, Baxter addresses the question "How the understanding can be the subject of sin?"[68] For Baxter, it is not immediately obvious that the faculty of reason itself can be sinful. This is because sin requires liberty, but reason is necessitated by knowledge. His solution to this question is that the subject of sin is not properly reason itself, but rather the entire human being as it makes use of reason. In particular, since the nature of free choice (*liberum arbitrium*) consists of a conjoined act of intellect and will with respect to judgment (*arbitrium*) and spontaneous freedom (*liberum*),[69] reason participates in the will's sinfulness and becomes, as it were, guilty by association. Reason is therefore dependent on the will, as it is commanded by it. On this basis, Baxter argues that ignorance that is "naturally, originally, and unalterably" necessary is entirely amoral. Such ignorance occurs entirely apart from the influence of the will and is therefore not

---

67. *CD*, I.96 (Dir. 8, §4). Cf. *TKL*, 175–76.

68. *CD*, I.95.

69. For discussion of *liberum arbitrium* with respect to the Reformed tradition, see Van Asselt et al., eds., *Reformed Thought on Freedom*, 64–66, 79–82, 98–99, 110, 129, 135, 175–76.

sinful. Yet when reason participates in the influence of a sinful will, it contracts a corruption that can be called sinful from its "originally and remotely voluntary" nature. These contracted corrupt dispositions of reason then become "immediately natural and necessary" to fallen humanity. Although the will can positively divert reason from evidence of truth, Baxter himself thinks that the most common way in which the will corrupts reason is by privation, that is, a neglect or suspension of its duty in directing reason toward evidence.[70]

Long before the outline of postlapsarian reason found in the *Christian Directory* and *Methodus theologiae*, Baxter already addressed the noetic effects of the fall in *The Arrogancy of Reason* (1655). His *Arrogancy* provides a far more detailed description of postlapsarian reason than the *Methodus theologiae*. Baxter frames *Arrogancy* as an exposition of John 3:9, "Nicodemus answered and said unto him, 'How can these things be?'" He takes this text as a representative example, among numerous others in Scripture, of the way in which reason is corrupt with respect to spiritual things.[71] The main doctrinal point that he gleans from the text is that "the corrupt nature of man is more prone to question the truth of God's Word, then to see and confess their own ignorance and incapacity; and ready to doubt, whether the things that Christ revealeth are true, when they themselves do not know the nature, cause, and reason of them."[72] Although Baxter frames his discussion with the scriptural example of Nicodemus, his following exposition of the "nature and workings" of corruption integrates scholastic psychology and logic. He makes use of the same scholastic psychology of intellect and will, habit, and act, which we find in his later *Christian Directory* and *Methodus theologiae*.[73] But he also utilizes various terms pertaining to substance (existence and quiddity),

---

70. *CD*, I.95–96 (Dir. 8, §3). Cf. *MT*, I.214. See also Gavin John McGrath, "Puritans and the Human Will: Voluntarism within Mid-Seventeenth Century English Puritanism as Seen in the Works of Richard Baxter and John Owen" (PhD diss., University of Durham, 1989), 219–20, who recognizes the impact of the fallen will on the intellect. A similar account of the impact of original sin on the intellect is found in Voetius. See Goudriaan, *Reformed Orthodoxy and Philosophy*, 43–44.

71. Richard Baxter, *The Arrogancy of Reason against Divine Revelations, Repressed* (London: T. N. for Tho. Underhill, 1655), 5–13, exposits the story of Nicodemus's encounter with Jesus (John 3:1–15); while *Arrogancy*, 14–15, cites Jer. 43:1–2 and John 6 (a "full instance of the like corrupt disposition") as further examples.

72. Baxter, *Arrogancy*, 13.

73. Baxter, *Arrogancy*, 9: "we still have the same natural powers of understanding and willing [in regeneration]; But it is the change of Disposition, Habits, and Acts of those faculties"; and 31: "The *Dispositive* blindness of the best Convert, is cured but in part, much less his *actual* blindness."

causality, and the relation between whole and part, which were commonly found in logical textbooks of his day.[74]

Baxter argues that reason more easily grasps the existence of a thing than any other aspect of it, so that the first mode of inquiry into any matter should be *whether* it is. However, like Nicodemus, fallen reason tends to begin at the "wrong end of the Book" by asking other questions prior to that concerning its existence.[75] Reason is often ignorant of the "quiddity" or essence of a thing and will then conclude from this ignorance that it does not exist. Thus some doubt *whether* the soul exists because they do not know *what* it is.[76] Likewise, when reason cannot understand the various causes of a thing, it will doubt its existence. Thus many doubt or deny God's decrees of predestination, the work of creation, the soul's immortality, or the effects of grace, because they cannot understand their causes.[77] When reason cannot discern how various things can be harmonized with one another (i.e., ignorance of the whole "method" or body of truth), it casts one or the other particular aside. Thus, in the matter of grace and free will, many ancients excluded "too much" of God's grace, and many moderns exclude the will's natural liberty, while in the matter of the sufficiency of Christ's satisfaction and humanity's inherent righteousness, many deny one or the other.[78]

Baxter's prioritization of the knowledge of existence over essence is rooted in a widespread scholastic assumption, deriving from Aristotle's *Posterior Analytics* II.8–10. According to Aristotle, knowledge of a thing's existence is a necessary prerequisite for knowledge of a thing's nature.[79] Aristotle was followed on this point by Aquinas and a variety of late scholastics, including Pedro da Fonseca, Francisco de Toledo, and Francisco Suárez.[80] This Aristotelian order of intellectual inquiry was also reflected in the medieval and early modern scholastic method. The scholastic method would typically begin with the question "does it exist" (*an sit*), then move on to "what is it" (*quid sit*), before asking further questions pertaining to

---

74. See, e.g., Franco Burgersdijck, *Institutionum logicarum* (Cambridge, 1637), cap. 4, 14, 15; and Spencer, *Art of Logick*, 16–17, 26–27.

75. Baxter, *Arrogancy*, 44.

76. Baxter, *Arrogancy*, 16.

77. Baxter, *Arrogancy*, 18.

78. Baxter, *Arrogancy*, 22.

79. Aristotle, *Posterior Analytics*, 93a16–29, 93b29–37. Cf. David Demoss and Daniel Devereux, "Essence, Existence, and Nominal Definition in Aristotle's 'Posterior Analytics' II 8–10," *Phronesis* 33, no. 2 (1988): 133–54.

80. Jorge Secada, *Cartesian Metaphysics: The Late Scholastic Origins of Modern Philosophy* (Cambridge: Cambridge University Press, 2000), 7–8.

its kind (*qualis*), quantity (*quantum*), mode (*quomodo*), and so forth.[81] Baxter likewise advises that *an sit* should be asked prior to *quid sit* and the subsidiary questions of causality and method.[82] We might say that for Baxter the fallen mind, by tending to ask the Nicodemean question "how can this be?" before it asks the logically prior question "does it exist?" reflects a fundamentally antischolastic methodological bias.

For both Baxter and the late scholastics, the prioritization of existence over essence was directly related to the origin of knowledge in sense perception.[83] According to Baxter and other non-Cartesian contemporaries, not only does all ordinary (nonrevelatory) knowledge begin with the senses, but when exercised under the right conditions, the senses provide a more certain form of knowledge than that from the rational deduction of the discursive intellect.[84] This results in a hierarchy of certainties, which Baxter expressed in a list of "degrees of certainty":

1. Sense perceiving the *Object* and it *self*, is the first perceiver; and hereof the surest.
2. Imagination receiving from Sense, hath more requisites to its Certainty.
3. Intellection about things sensible, hath yet more requisites to its Certainty; *viz.* 1. That the Object be true; 2. The Evidence sensible; 3. That the Sense be sound, and the Medium and other Conditions of Sense be just; 4. That the Imagination be not corrupt. That the Intellect it self be sound.
4. But Intellection about *It self* and *Volition* hath the highest Certainty.
5. We are surer of the *Quod* than the *Quid* and *Quale*; as that *we Think*, than *What* and *How*.
6. We are certainer of self-evident Principles than of the Consequences.
7. Consequences have various degrees of Evidence and Certainty.[85]

Whereas the *essence* of things in all cases "are but imperfectly evident to us," the *existence* of corporeal things immediately present to the senses are "fully evident," and the *existence* of things beyond the senses are known only to the discursive

---

81. J. A. Weisheipl, "Scholastic Method," in *New Catholic Encyclopedia*, 2nd ed. (Washington, DC: Catholic University of America, 2003), 12:747–49; Richard A. Muller, *After Calvin: Studies in the Development of a Theological Tradition* (Oxford: Oxford University Press, 2003), 28; Keith Stanglin, *Arminius on the Assurance of Salvation: The Context, Roots, and Shape of the Leiden Debate, 1603–1609* (Leiden: Brill, 2007), 59.

82. Cf. his remarks on scholastic method, *Rel. Bax.*, I.6.

83. Cf. Secada, *Cartesian Metaphysics*, 10–11.

84. See Baxter, *More Reasons*, 141–42; and on the priority of the senses: *MT*, I.189. Cf. Turretin, *Institutio*, I.xi.7.

85. *TKL*, 31. Cf. *MT*, I.189–90.

intellect, which must make use of "borrowed evidences from Causes or Signes." Those objects not immediately present and apprehended by sense or intellect, but rather by discursive intellect, are things distant, things past, and things future. Such absent, past, or future objects are most subject to uncertainty and doubt. This doubt stems from three problems that cloud the process of discursive thought. First, natural principles are sometimes obscure. Second, the connections between things are often obscure. Third, a long series of arguments increase doubt. Yet it is precisely in such absent, past, and future matters that religion is most concerned. Thus fallen reason fails in those invisible and remote realities that are of most importance to religion.[86]

Given Baxter's prioritization of sense perception and existence (over essence), it is hardly surprising that he found Descartes's skepticism with regard to the senses problematic. Descartes prioritized the knowledge of essence over existence and accordingly argued vigorously to liberate the mind's dependence on sensation. As Jorge Secada observes, "One of the main purposes, if not the main purpose, of Cartesian scepticism is to draw the mind away from the senses towards the intellectual grasp of essences existing within it."[87] As measured against Baxter's account on the fallen mind, which begins at the "wrong end of the Book" by asking "what is it?" before "does it exist?" Cartesian epistemology would amount to the normalization or legitimization of a significant noetic effect of the fall. Accordingly, although Baxter did not dwell much on Cartesian epistemology, his scattered comments are generally unsympathetic. "In short," Baxter said, "I am an Adversary to their Philosophy, that vilifie Sense, because it is in Brutes."[88] He regarded Cartesian doubt as generally conducive of infidelity,[89] a position consistent with his view that "the certainty of sensation is a prerequisite for the certainty of faith."[90] Baxter likewise viewed Cartesian doubt of the senses as an "inhuman faith" that undermined not only the certainty of the senses, but also the certainty of the intellect that presupposes the senses.[91] One of the examples that Descartes said "weakened any faith that I had in the senses" was that "[t]owers that had seemed round from afar occasionally appeared square at close quarters."[92] Baxter

---

86. Baxter, *More Reasons*, 142–44.

87. Secada, *Cartesian Metaphysics*, 16.

88. Richard Baxter, "Epistle to the Reader," in *Poetical Fragments* (London: T. Snowden, 1681), A4r.

89. Richard Baxter, *Naked Popery* (London: N. Simmons, 1677), 132.

90. *MT*, I.192–93. Cf. Turretin, *Institutio*, I.xi.

91. *MT*, I.193.

92. René Descartes, *Meditations, Objections, and Replies*, ed. and trans. Roger Ariew and Donald Cress (Indianapolis: Hackett, 2006), 43.

responded that the reliability of senses refers to *"objects duly scituate* and *qualified,"* so that the weakness of one sense can be overcome by resituating the sense (e.g., drawing closer), comparing with other senses, or multiplying observers.[93]

Despite Baxter's criticism of Descartes on sense perception, he was not completely dismissive of Cartesian epistemology. Baxter once mentioned Descartes as a positive reference alongside numerous scholastics to support the opinion that both the senses and intellect are active (and not merely passive).[94] When it came to the mind's self-perception, he agreed with Descartes that one's own thoughts ("act of Intellection") are better perceived than objects, and showed a qualified acceptance of Cartesian "ideas" for knowledge of an intuitive grasp of one's own powers, inclinations, and habits that do not require an externally sensed object.[95] This positive statement regarding Cartesian "ideas" was nonetheless limited to a narrow epistemological point, for elsewhere he wrote dismissively of the metaphysics of the *"Cartesians* and *Cocceians,"* who "say that *God* and *Angels,* and *Spirits,* are but a Thought, or an *Idea.*"[96]

In addition to the "nature and workings" of corrupt reason characterized by a kind of antischolastic disorder leading to doubt, Baxter elaborates on several intimately related "causes" of doubting spiritual truths. First, he affirms the famous opening line to Aristotle's *Metaphysics:* "All men by nature desire to know."[97] In corrupt reason, however, this natural inclination to know for oneself leads to impatience with knowing on account of another, that is, believing. In this sense, fallen humanity is like doubting Thomas (John 20:25). Baxter was unsure how far a desire for knowledge was from God versus corrupt nature, but he remained sure that this inclination is "a preparative Reason of our doubting and dis-satisfaction, if not a proper cause."[98] A "desire to know," he reflected in an early work, "was the beginning of our misery [in Adam], so is it the continuance." Late in life, he reiterated that a sinful desire for knowledge is "p[er]haps one of ye subtilest & dangerousest & com[m]onest sins in ye world: And y^t wch in our first parents was mans fall, & so is propagated to corrupt posterity."[99] With such comments, Baxter

---

93. Richard Baxter, *Full and Easie Satisfaction which is the True and Safe Religion* (London: Nev. Simmons, 1674), 92–93. Cf. *MT,* I.193.

94. Baxter, *Of Justification,* 196–97.

95. *RCR,* 548–49. Cf. *MT,* I.86–87, comparing Descartes's *cogito* to Ockham. As Burton notes, the positive reception of Descartes here is due to Baxter's agreement with Ockham on intuitive perception. See Burton, *Hallowing of Logic,* 172–73.

96. Baxter, "Epistle to the Reader," in *Poetical Fragments,* A4v.

97. Aristotle, *Metaphysics,* 980a22.

98. Baxter, *Arrogancy,* 28–29.

99. DWL BT IV.87, fol. 230v.

indicated general agreement with the longstanding and widespread Christian suspicion of *curiositas*, which theologians as various as Augustine, Aquinas, Calvin,
and Voetius all regarded as a vice.[100]

Second, and related to this natural inclination to know, Baxter echoes
Aristotle's notion that the mind is potentially all things (*On the Soul*, III.4–5)
when he affirms "a certain infiniteness in knowledge" whereby humanity "would
know all that is knowable." This infinite capacity of reason, when joined to its
natural inclination to know, leads reason to remain unsatisfied until it sees "the
whole, and comprehend[s] all things with all their Reasons, Causes, and Modes."
Thus, an insatiable inclination to know all leads to doubting even partial or imperfect knowledge.[101] When Baxter adds that reason is originally in "darkness" and
"blindness" to spiritual things, as well as lacks diligence and patience in coming
to understand them, he paints a fairly bleak picture of reason in its state of sin.[102]
For although human reason remains constitutionally inclined to know all things,
in its fallen state it is frustrated in its imperfect perception of the "highest mysteries," including those "about God, and Mans Soul, and our Redemption, and our
Everlasting State."[103]

Although Baxter paints a highly negative picture of postlapsarian reason in
relation to spiritual "mysteries," this negative evaluation applies less to other
nonspiritual things. Already before Baxter's time, the Synod of Dordt (1618–1619),
easily the most internationally representative Reformed synod ever to meet in the
early modern era, had set forth a summary of noetic ability remaining in the postlapsarian state. In their *Articuli* and *Judicia* upon which the Canons of Dordt were
ultimately based, the synodical delegates were concerned to deny that the light of
nature itself, apart from the special bestowal of grace, could either lead one to salvation or rightly to interpret the spiritual matters found in Scripture.[104] However,

---

100. Cf. Peter Harrison, "Curiosity, Forbidden Knowledge, and the Reformation of Natural
Philosophy in Early Modern England," *Isis* 92, no. 2 (2001): 265–90, with discussion
(among many others) of Augustine, *Confessions*, trans. Maria Boulding (Hyde Park, NY: New
City Press, 1997), X.35; Aquinas, *Summa theologiae*, IIaIIae, q. 167, art. 1–2; John Calvin,
Commentaries on the first book of Moses, called Genesis, trans. John King (Edinburgh: Calvin
Translation Society, 1847), 1:151 (Gen. 3:5); and Calvin, *Institutes of the Christian Religion*, ed.
John T. McNeill, trans. Ford Lewis Battles (Philadelphia: Westminster Press, 1960), II.ii.12.
See also Voetius, *Selectarum disputationum theologicarum*, 3:683–84, citing Aquinas.

101. Baxter, *Arrogancy*, 29–30.

102. Baxter, *Arrogancy*, 30–32.

103. Baxter, *Arrogancy*, 27.

104. See Aza Goudriaan, "The Synod of Dordt on Arminian Anthropology," in *Revisiting the
Synod of Dordt (1618–1619)*, ed. Aza Goudriaan and Fred van Lieburg (Leiden: Brill, 2011), 81–
106; and reflected in *Canons of Dort*, III/IV, art. 1–3, *rejectio errorum* 5 (*Creeds of Christendom*,
ed. Schaff, 3:564, 569).

they also affirmed that postlapsarian reason "retains certain notions about God, natural things, and the difference between honorable and shameful things."[105] Baxter's works reflect this consensus statement in his use of (nonsalvific) natural theology, in his treatment of matters relating to natural philosophy (see chapters 4, 5, and 6), and in his use of natural law in ethics (see chapter 7).

For Baxter, the theological foundation for this affirmation of a postlapsarian light of reason is based on the created constitution of human nature, which, despite the fall, remains constitutionally the same as far as the nature of its faculties are concerned. A favorite phrase of Baxter is "we are men before we are Christians."[106] The postlapsarian rational faculty, according to Baxter, is gifted with numerous common notions (*notitiae communes*), "without which a man is scarce a man, but unman'd."[107] Although he speaks of these *notitiae* throughout his works, he elaborated on them at great length in his *More Reasons*, where he offered a corrective to Lord Edward Herbert of Cherbury's theory of *notitiae communes* in *De veritate* (1624). After acknowledging the usefulness of "most of [Herbert's] Rules and Notions," Baxter faulted Herbert not only for placing divine revelation among probable truths (*veresimilia*) rather than "Certain Verities,"[108] but also for his insufficient enumeration of common notions about religion. Interestingly, Baxter places the darkness of the mind, by which humanity is aware of its ignorance and imperfect knowledge of nature, as well as its need for "a further supernatural Revelation," among the *notitiae communes*.[109] He states that while the intellect is born with "no actual Knowledge" (i.e., it is *tabula rasa*) and is "able or disposed" to know *notitiae communes*, the awareness of them varies due to objective and subjective factors. The intellect must receive some objective evidence of a thing before any *notitiae* form in the mind. Yet some are in a better position to acquire these *notitiae* than others, as they have more favorable conditions. Moreover, the *notitiae* become more certain over time and with the multiplication of particular acts of the intellect.[110] Thus, the *notitiae* are for Baxter not entirely static or uniform, but vary depending on the capacities and exercise of those in whom they arise.

---

105. *Canons of Dort*, III/IV, art. 4 (*Creeds of Christendom*, ed. Schaff, 3:565).

106. Richard Baxter, *The Life of Faith* (London: R. W., 1670), 81; *TKL*, 34; *MT*, I.21; DWL BT XIX.351, fol. 2r.

107. Baxter, *More Reasons*, 119.

108. Baxter, *More Reasons*, A3r. Cf. Serjeanston, "Herbert of Cherbury," 227.

109. Baxter, *More Reasons*, 123.

110. Baxter, *More Reasons*, 127–28. Cf. *MT*, I.189; *TKL*, 33; and Baxter, "Advertisement," in *Unreasonableness*, a4r on the mind as initially *tabula rasa*.

Baxter's theory of *notitiae communes* also incorporates the epistemological priority of the senses and degrees of certainty sketched above. He speaks of the most certain notions as consisting in objects of sense, one's own thinking and willing, and the mind's awareness (though not comprehension) of God:

> Next to the *Act* of *Cogitation* and *Volition* itself, and to the most certain *Objects of Sence*, there is nothing in all the World so *Certain*, that is, so *Evident to the Intellect*, as the Being of God: He being that to the *Mind* which the Sun is to the *Eye*, certainliest *known*, though *little of him* be *known*, and no Creature comprehend him.[111]

Accordingly, Baxter thinks notions closer to immediate objects (particularly of sense, but also of the mind) are more certain than notions of things absent, past, or future. He calls *notitiae communes* the "very lowest degree of knowledge" and argues that there are many other certainties beyond them, including the certainty of faith, which is of greater certainty than all other kinds of knowledge. Moreover, *notitiae communes* are insufficient for the perfection of humanity, which also requires the perfection of the will and life. For Baxter, to make *notitiae communes* the measure of the intellect would be analogous to making an infant the judge of the scholar. The measure of the *power* of the soul ought instead to be gathered from its greatest *acts*, and thus from the wisest minds.[112]

Reason and Revelation

The noetic effects of sin provide an important backdrop to Baxter's general framework for the relation between reason and revelation. His basic position, set forth already in *The Saints Everlasting Rest* and reiterated throughout his later writings, was that the fall renders reason depraved and blind toward spiritual things.[113] Yet, the work of grace begins to restore both the reason and will concurrently, thereby not only convincing the mind of the truth of revelation, but also moving the will with its goodness.[114] To use Thomistic phrases that Baxter was particularly fond of employing, grace "presupposes" nature, and revelation is the "perfection of our

---

111. *TKL*, 39; cf. *TKL*, 43.

112. Baxter, *More Reasons*, 128–31, 133–34.

113. *MT*, I.21; *SER2*, II.280–82 (II.vii.6–7). Baxter later held out hope of salvation for Gentiles prior to Christ, but thought this must proceed "totally from *Gods will and love*" (*RCR*, 399; cf. *More Reasons*, 101) and is a matter lacking certainty (*End of Doctrinal Controversies*, 199).

114. Baxter, *More Reasons*, 135; *MT*, I.24; *Judgment of Non-conformists*, 14; *Divine Life*, 245.

reason."[115] As Baxter's use of such Thomistic phrases indicates, his sympathies with Scotus's voluntarism need not preclude a favorable reception of Aquinas on matters relating to reason and revelation. In fact, Baxter refers to Aquinas as among the "best Schoolmen" while citing his account of the nature of revelation,[116] and directs readers to Aquinas's *De veritate*, where Aquinas writes "most accurately about the definition of truth and verity."[117] He also draws positively on multiple chapters from Aquinas's *Summa contra gentiles* (I.iii–vi, ix), as we shall see. While many theologians in the seventeenth century drew on a paradigm of grace presupposing and perfecting nature,[118] Baxter's detailed elaboration on the relation of reason and revelation provides some unique accents within an inherited theological framework.

We have seen above that Baxter considers reason both objectively or subjectively. His account of reason's relation to revelation likewise has both objective and subjective aspects.[119] With respect to the objective aspect, Baxter thinks in a similar manner to Aquinas that the objects of reason and revelation overlap and, what is more, cannot contradict one another.[120] Like his Reformed contemporaries, Baxter holds that there are also truths of a "mixed" nature, in which one naturally known truth is combined with another premise from Scripture, yielding a conclusion that is partially known and partially believed.[121]

Yet while reason and revelation deal with similar objects, their order and end differ significantly. Baxter distinguishes between the order and dignity of the principles of reason and revelation, with reason prior or superior in order,

---

115. *MT*, "Praefatio," [A5r], I.21, 152, 192, 265; *CD*, III.907 (q. 158); *TKL*, 157, 166; Baxter, *Church History of the Government of Bishops and Their Councils Abbreviated* (London: Thomas Simmons, 1681), 28; *SER2*, preface to Part II, dd2r.

116. *SER2*, II.235 (II.iv.4): "Few of God's extraordinary Revelations have been immediate; (The best Schoolmen think none at all) but either by Angels, or by Jesus himself, who was Man as well as God." The marginal note reads, "Aquin. Sum. 3. q. 55. c. 2."

117. *SER2*, III.3 (III.xi.6): "*Lege* Aquin. *sum. de Veritate. c.* 1 & 2, &c. *accuratissimè de Veri &* Veritatis definitione."

118. See *PRRD*, 1:403–4; Sytsma, "'As a Dwarfe,'" 308–9, esp. 309n49; Johann Heinrich Alsted, *Theologia naturalis* (Frankfurt: Antonius Hummius, 1615), 4; Vedel, *Rationale theologicum*, 549, 552–53; Ferguson, *Interest of Reason*, 20.

119. *MT*, I.21; *JNIR*, 8–9.

120. *MT*, I.21–22; *JNIR*, 10. Cf. Aquinas, *Summa theologiae*, Ia, q. 1, art. 8; Aquinas, *Summa contra gentiles*, I.vii. This also reflects the so-called problem of double truth. See *PRRD*, 1:382–87.

121. *SER2*, II.213 (II.iii.2); also *MT*, I.21; *JNIR*, 9–10; *TKL*, 43–44. Cf. *PRRD*, 1:402–3; Vedel, *Rationale theologicum*, 84–87.

and Scripture as superior "in point of excellency."[122] For example, while revelation "begins with physics" in Genesis and "often repeats" such things (e.g., in the Psalms and Job), and thus indicates that "physics is presupposed for theology," it is the task of the theologian to look into those same creatures for the goal of glorifying God with a focus on their relation to "holiness and heavenly matters."[123] Again, despite the usefulness of languages, logic, and philosophy for interpreting and organizing the contents of the Scriptures, these ought to be subordinated to the goal of morality, which "is the *subject and business* of the Scriptures."[124] These examples reflect the impact of Baxter's views on the relation of intellect and will discussed above. When considered as objects of knowledge, reason and revelation overlap as far as their contents are concerned; when considered with respect to matters of will and beatitude (holiness, ethics, and heaven), the objects known to reason (logic and philosophy) hold a subordinate place.

If Baxter's perspective on the relation of the objects of reason and revelation are reminiscent of Aquinas, his general framework for the subjective aspect of reason, as far as it concerns the insufficiency of philosophy for attaining revealed truths, is explicitly derived from Aquinas. Although Baxter drew on Reformed commentaries on Romans 1–2 for his discussion of the natural knowledge of God,[125] he also made use of Aquinas's argument for the necessity of revelation. Referring directly to Aquinas's *Summa theologiae* and *Summa contra gentiles*, Baxter reiterates Aquinas's opinion that even those theological truths that reason can discover on its own could only be learned slowly, by a few, and with a mixture of many errors, so that the Scriptures are necessary to make theological truth easier, more common, and more certain.[126] From this use of Aquinas, it is fair to conclude that while the general contours of Baxter's view of the will owe more to Scotus, his framework for the relation between reason and revelation is generally Thomistic.

---

122. *SER2*, preface to Part II, dd2r–v.

123. *MT*, "Praefatio," [A5r, A6v].

124. *TKL*, 157.

125. *SER2*, II.282 (II.vii.7), refers to "particularly Dr. *Willet*, on *Rom.* 1.14.20. &c." to distinguish between knowledge of God's eternal power and "knowing sufficient to salvation." See Andrew Willet, *Hexapla: that is, A Six-fold Commentarie upon the most Divine Epistle of the holy Apostle S. Paul to the Romanes* (London: Cantrell Legge, 1611), 59–60, 117–18. According to Edward Leigh, *A Treatise of Divinity Consisting of Three Books* (London: E. Griffin, 1646), 73, the best Reformed exegetes on Romans were Vermigli, Pareus, and Willet. Leigh repeats Gisbertus Voetius, *Exercitia et bibliotheca studiosi theologiae* (Utrecht: Willem Strick, 1644), 521.

126. *SER2*, II.280–81 (II.vii.6): "*Aquin. Sum. prima* 1ᵃᵉ. *Art.* 1. *Q.* 1. *&* 2ᵃ. 2ᵃᵉ. *Q* 2. *Art.* 3 4. But more fully *Cont. Gentiles li.* I. c. 4, 5, 6."

But just as Baxter modifies a received Scotistic paradigm with respect to the will, he also modifies this Thomistic position on reason and revelation. While accepting the Thomistic point that there are truths above human reason,[127] he further divides such truths into two categories. Some theological truths are completely above reason with respect to their probability, existence, and futurity. Others truths are above reason with respect to their existence and futurity, but still can be known to reason as possible and probable.[128] Perhaps Baxter deduced this category of truths above reason, yet still probable to reason, through his reading of Aquinas's *Summa contra gentiles* (I.ix).[129] In any case, the distinction between the two kinds of truths above reason appears to be a unique contribution to a commonly received paradigm.

This Thomistic paradigm receives a further modification with respect to truths discernible to reason apart from revelation. We already observed Baxter's view that fallen reason, despite its greater natural certainty of existence over essence, begins at the "wrong end of the Book" by asking "what is it?" (*quid sit*) before "does it exist?" (*an sit*). In a parallel manner to this general epistemological view, and reflecting a nearly identical position as John Davenant's explanation of Colossians 2:8, Baxter states that reason in its fallen state is most adept at understanding the *existence* of theological realities, while it is least able to understand the *nature* and *manner* of those same realities. For example, while people can naturally come to know that God exists, that there is some state of immortality, and that our nature is depraved, yet *what* God is or *how* he should be worshipped, *what* immortality consists of or *how* it ought to be gained, and *how* our nature came to be depraved or *how* it can be restored, is beyond the reach of fallen reason.[130]

In continuity with this account of the limitations of reason, Baxter places a strong emphasis on the uncertainty, apart from revelation, of inquiry into truths above reason. This is a view that derives in part from his conviction of "the infinite distance between God and man" as expressed in the scholastic dictum,

127. E.g., *End of Doctrinal Controversies*, xxxii–xxxiii.

128. *SER2*, II.204 (II.iii.1). Cf. Baxter's response to the traditional question of the eternality of the world: "And indeed Reason it self doth make that at least very probable, as Revelation makes it certain [that the world is not eternal]" (*RCR*, 585).

129. See *SER2*, II.196 (II.ii.1), citing *Summa contra gentiles*, I.ix; and Baxter, *Certainty of Christianity without Popery*, 100, citing *Summa contra gentiles*, I.ix and *Summa theologiae*, Ia, q. 1, art. 8 *ad* 2.

130. *SER2*, II.280 (II.vii.6); also *RCR*, 196. Cf. John Davenant, *Expositio epistolae D. Pauli ad Colossenses* (Cambridge: Thomas and John Buck, 1630), 181 (Col. 2:8); translated as *An Exposition of the Epistle of St. Paul to the Colossians*, trans. Josiah Allport (London: Hamilton, Adams, & Co., 1831), 1:393; Matthew Hale, "Of the Chief End of Man," in *The Works, Moral and Religious*, ed. Thomas Thirwall (London: H. D. Symonds, 1805), 2:321–22.

"between finite and infinite there is no proportion."[131] It is probable that this emphasis on God's transcendence indicates a positive relation to late medieval theology,[132] but Baxter also refers to Aquinas's *Summa contra gentiles* (I.iii) in support of the intellect's incomprehension of God, so we should not dismiss a possible early Thomist influence.[133] Baxter often warns against excessive speculation into God's nature and acts, and consistently draws on the distinction between God's hidden will (*voluntas arcana*) and revealed will (*voluntas revelata*) in order to curb speculation into "unrevealed things."[134] He wields this antispeculative sword against theological speculation into God's immanent acts (a continuity with John Davenant),[135] as well as the "boldness of Philosophers."[136] Of his own practice, Baxter writes, "[I] bridle my understanding from presuming to enquire into unrevealed things," and "I endeavour to confine my enquiries to things revealed."[137]

In addition to the uncertainty involved in inquiry into truths above reason, Baxter also thinks there are many secrets of nature that God did not intend to reveal, on account of which one must confess ignorance and uncertainty. He appears to have shared with Reformed theologians such as Lambert Daneau (1530–1595) and Gisbertus Voetius (1589–1676) a perspective of "learned

---

131. Baxter, *Reduction*, 7; *RCR*, 20.

132. Cf. *PRRD*, 1:227–28, 261–65; Burton, *Hallowing of Logic*, 14–15, 33.

133. *SER2*, I.45 (I.iv.10), citing Aquinas, *Summa contra gentiles*, I.iii, "where more appears on this matter [of God's incomprehensibility]." Aquinas also holds that there is no proportion of the finite to the infinite (*Summa theologiae*, Ia, q. 12, art. 1 *ad* 4; *De veritate*, q. 2, art. 3 *ad* 4).

134. Baxter, *Reduction*, 7–8; *CD*, I.322, III.726–27 (§16), 763, 919 (§12); Baxter, *Life of Faith*, 172–73. On the distinction, which has exegetical roots in Deut. 29:29, see *PRRD*, 3:439–40, 461–63.

135. Baxter, *Reduction*, 6–11. Cf. Davenant's antipathy for speculation on God's immanent acts (especially priorities and posteriorities), in John Davenant, *Dissertationes duae* (Cambridge: Roger Daniel, 1650), 108–9, 209; John Davenant, *Animadversions Written by the Right Reverend Father in God, John Lord Bishop of Sarisbury, upon a Treatise Intituled, Gods Love to Mankinde* (London: John Partridge, 1641), 14–15, 21–22, 74. Baxter agreed with Davenant against speculation on predetermination of the will from an early date (Baxter to Thomas Hill, 1652 [ca. Jan.–Feb.], DWL BC III.268r, citing Davenant, *Animadversions*, 116–17; cf. *CT*, I/1.58, 61), and also against speculation on priorities and posteriorities in God (*CT*, I/1.68; II.44; cf. Burton, *Hallowing of Logic*, 285–89). Baxter also regarded the notion that justification is an immanent eternal act of God to be a pillar of antinomianism. See Boersma, *Hot Pepper Corn*, 69.

136. Baxter, *Of the Nature of Spirits*, 4–5, citing Deut. 29:29. Cf. DWL BT IV.87, fols. 230v–231r; *TKL*, 14, citing Deut. 29:29.

137. Baxter, *Of the Nature of Spirits*, 4–5.

ignorance," which Voetius describes as "the knowledge of our ignorance and [a knowledge] of things as unknown or unknowable as such."[138] In a similar way, Baxter writes,

> The Lord teach us to use well ye Faculties wch we have, & a little time will open to us ye mysteries of their nature. God never meant to teach me his Artifice of *making men* or *soules*; And I can know nothing but y^t wch I was made to know: And when I read many voluminous pretensions of men, y^t take on y^m confidently to know w^t they know not, & call their presumptions by ye name of Philosophy & Physicks, I am forced to confesse y^t I am ignorant of w^t they pretend to know, & am quiet in my ignorance, when I find y^t I was not made to know it.[139]

This perspective also appears in the *Methodus theologiae*, where Baxter prefaces his discussion of creation with a list of thirty-seven "uncertainties" relating to the origin and nature of the world, and a plea not to confound uncertain and certain things.[140] Likewise, in the midst of his critique of the philosophy of Descartes and Gassendi, Baxter emphasizes the inscrutability of God's works and God's selective revelation of them to the human mind. God as creator of the world knows the mysteries of creation, but he chooses to reveal primarily their use and not their secrets. Baxter likens God to an architect or maker of a clock who teaches the buyer its use but not the art of building. Human knowledge of the phenomena of nature is accordingly filled with ignorance and error, and it is better to confess ignorance than pretend to knowledge of uncertain things.[141] Contrary to the impression one might get from such remarks, Baxter does not advocate a close-minded attitude, "which too hastily and peremptorily condemneth all [philosophical conjectures]" after the manner of Bishop Tempier's Parisian condemnations of 1277.[142] But he insists that speculation about God and his works beyond "plainly revealed" matters should be held as probable and uncertain: "I condemn not modest enquirees,

---

138. Lambert Daneau, *Physice christiana, sive, christiana de rerum creatarum origine, & usu disputatio*, 4th ed. (Geneve: Ex officina Vignoniana, 1602), 50; Gisbertus Voetius, *Selectarum disputationum theologicarum*, 3:668–92, at 670; Theo Verbeek, "From 'Learned Ignorance' to Scepticism: Descartes and Calvinist Orthodoxy," in *Scepticism and Irreligion in the Seventeenth and Eighteenth Centuries*, ed. Richard H. Popkin and Arjo Vanderjagt (Leiden: E. J. Brill, 1993), 31–45; Goudriaan, *Reformed Orthodoxy and Philosophy*, 39.

139. DWL BT XIX.351, fol. 143r.

140. *MT*, I.126–27.

141. *MT*, I.149–50. Cf. *TKL*, 13.

142. *RCR*, 588.

y^t have faire probability, & neither pretend to y^t certainty wch they have not, nor contradict any certaine naturall or scripture truth."[143]

The Use of and Limits of Philosophy

Given his modified Thomistic approach to the relation between reason and revelation, it is unsurprising that Baxter displayed great interest in the writings of philosophers. If grace presupposes nature, as Baxter was fond of arguing, philosophy should be learned at the very least in order to understand the Scriptures.[144] Yet beyond this basic reason, Baxter was also motivated by his concern for the conversion of unbelievers and increasing the certainty of believers' faith. If reason and revelation have overlapping objects, and the objects of belief contain an admixture of rational premises for mixed articles, it follows that reason can play a role in either preparing nonbelievers for faith or confirming the beliefs of Christians. He addressed both of these concerns in his various apologetic writings. Thus, in his greatest and most mature apologetic work, *The Reasons of the Christian Religion* (1667), he included multiple prefaces addressed to Christians, doubters, and unbelievers.[145]

The modified Thomistic perspective inherent in Baxter's view of the relation between reason and revelation certainly undergirded his apologetics. Citing Aquinas's *Summa contra gentiles* (I.ix), Baxter argued that the starting point of debate with non-Christians is those common principles that both could agree upon.[146] He also thought that probable arguments for things in the Scriptures typically precede their "belief of certainty," and thus are "a good preparative" for belief.[147] Most importantly, in both the *Reasons* and *More Reasons*, he reiterated Aquinas's argument (without citation) that apart from revelation, philosophers could only obtain theological truths slowly, and even then by only a few and with a mixture of many errors.[148] Given that nature is "now a very hard book," Baxter

---

143. DWL BT IV.87, fols. 233r.

144. *CD*, III.907 (q. 158).

145. *RCR*, "To the Christian Reader"; "To the Doubting and the Unbelieving Readers"; "To the Hypocrite Readers; Who have the Name of *Christians*, and the Hearts and Lives of *Atheists* and *Unbelievers*."

146. *SER2*, II.196 (II.ii.1), citing Aquinas, *Summa contra gentiles*, I.ix. Cf. Baxter, *More Reasons*, 137.

147. *SER2*, II.213 (II.iii.2). Similarly, on p. 237 in the context of the relation of miracles to faith, Baxter cites Aquinas, *Summa contra gentiles*, I.vi.

148. *RCR*, 192–93; Baxter, *More Reasons*, 144. Cf. *SER2*, II.280–81, citing Aquinas, *Summa theologiae*, Ia, q. 1, art. 1; IIaIae, q. 2, art. 3–4; and "more fully" *Summa contra gentiles*, I.iv–vi.

thought that although revealed truths were practically impossible to arrive at by natural reasoning, they were "plain to us as the high-way" when once grasped with the aid of revelation.[149] Thus, in a similar methodological manner to Aquinas's *Summa contra gentiles*, in his own *Reasons* Baxter presented rational arguments and classical non-Christian authorities for natural and supernatural truths already gathered from Christian revelation. In so doing, he was following an approach to apologetics and natural theology argued by other Reformed predecessors.[150]

Since philosophers exercising fallen reason—particularly through discursive thought—often mix errors with truth, Baxter insists on caution with respect to all sects of philosophers. Appealing to the Pauline *locus classicus* on philosophy, Colossians 2:8, Baxter advises that every system of philosophy, whether of physics or metaphysics, and every philosophical sect, whether ancient or modern, contains "so much errour, darkness, uncertainty and confusion" that the Christian must exercise discernment in distinguishing the "certain and useful parts" from the rest.[151] Likewise, the difficulties inherent in the "meer natural way of Revelation," according to Baxter, have manifested themselves in the multiplication of sects of philosophers, which produced as many controversies as divisions.[152] Indeed, following the apologetic appeal to the priority of Mosaic wisdom established by the early Christian apologists, Baxter argues that ancient philosophers approximated certain Christian doctrines about God by borrowing them from God's prophets. Thus "*Plato* read the Writings of *Moses*," which led Numenius to refer to him as *Moses Atticus* (according to Origen and Clement of Alexandria), and it "is more than probable" that Seneca "had heard or read *Pauls* Doctrine."[153] When Baxter expressed this view early in *The Saints Everlasting Rest*, it was still the dominant perspective; but as the century wore on, it was called increasingly into question.[154]

---

149. *RCR*, 193.

150. Cf. Alsted, *Theologia naturalis*, 1–10; Philippe de Mornay, preface to *A Worke Concerning the Trunesse of Christian Religion* (London: George Purstowe, 1617).

151. *CD*, III.907–8 (q. 158). Cf. Baxter, *Gildas Salvinus*, 129, 271.

152. *RCR*, 194. Cf. Baxter, *More Reasons*, 144–45.

153. *SER2*, II.281 (II.vii.6). On the early apologetic tradition, see Daniel Ridings, *The Attic Moses: The Dependence Theme in Some Early Christian Writers* (Göteborg: Acta Universitatis Gothoburgensia, 1995); and Arthur Droge, *Homer or Moses? Early Christian Interpretations of the History of Culture* (Tübingen: J. C. B. Mohr, 1989). Other Reformed authors who held similar views include Girolamo Zanchi, Lambert Daneau, John Owen, and Theophilus Gale. See Sinnema, "Aristotle and Early Reformed Orthodoxy," 133–34, 140; Levitin, *Ancient Wisdom*, 146–53; and Wallace, *Shapers*, 96–101.

154. On the critique and decline of this perspective, see Levitin, *Ancient Wisdom*, 138–80; and Israel, *Enlightenment Contested*, 473–77.

Baxter did not merely assert the necessity for discernment in general terms; he also provided examples from which the reader can gather a sense of the strengths and weaknesses of philosophical sects both ancient and modern. The Platonists "made very noble attempts" with respect to spiritual realities, but "they run into many unproved fanaticisms, and into divers errours, and want the desirable helps of true method." For Baxter, Renaissance anti-Aristotelians—figures such as Francesco Patrizi, Bernardino Telesio, and Tommaso Campanella—were similarly characterized by erroneous "fanaticisms." Patrizi was "but a Platonist" who based his natural philosophy on light "in fanatical terms," while Telesio "doth the like by *Heat and Cold, Heaven and Earth*," and "hath much that is unsound and of ill consequence." Tommaso Campanella, whose metaphysics of primalities Baxter found useful (see chapter 4), still does not escape his censure. Although Campanella "improved" on Telesio, and had "hints" of better philosophical principles than others, "he phanatically runs them up into so many unproved and vain, yea and mistaken superstructures, as that no true Body of Physics can be gathered out of his works." Aristotle marked an improvement in the scope and method of philosophy. He "was wonderful for subtility and solidity. His knowledge vast; His method (oft) accurate." But he also introduced "many precarious, yea erroneous conceptions and assertions" that had "a corrupting influence into all the rest" of his philosophy. The more Aristotelian of the contemporary natural philosophers—such as Julius Caesar Scaliger, Jacob Schegk, Marcus Friedrich Wendelin, and Daniel Sennert— Baxter first praises as "great men" with "many excellent things," but then critiques as overly reliant on Aristotle. The ancient Epicureans and Democritists, who were "justly the contempt of all the sober sects," and other moderns such as Gassendi and Descartes, give "so much to meer Matter and Motion" while neglecting spirits and other principles of motion, "that they differ as much from true Philosophers, as a Carkass or a Clock from a living man." The Stoics had "noble Ethical principles" but their works are mostly lost, and what little we know of their physics had errors. With respect to Hermetic philosophy, Baxter is generally dismissive: they "have no true method of Philosophy," their philosophy is defective by its omissions, and their principles only "trifle" but do not satisfy "judicious minds."[155]

Despite Baxter's criticism of Aristotle's "erroneous conceptions and assertions," his praise of Aristotle's method provides a notable contrast to Cartesian methodological doubt. Aristotle's method is typified by a nonskeptical approach to knowledge, in which both the senses and ordinary concepts provide a dependable starting point for reflection on phenomena. Moreover, Aristotle placed great importance on the credible opinions (*endoxa*) of predecessors in his own reflection, which explains why he often surveyed the opinions of other philosophers in

---

155. *CD*, III.919 (q. 173, §15); cf. *CD*, III.907–8 (q. 158); *MT*, "Praefatio," [A5r]; *TKL*, 46–48.

his books.[156] Baxter not only shared with Aristotle an antiskeptical affirmation of the reliability of sense perception (as we saw above), but also a similar appreciation of the development of philosophy through consideration of the credible opinions of predecessors. He advised young students,

> In studying Philosophy, 1. See that you neither neglect any helps of those that have gone before you, under pretence of taking nothing upon trust, and of studying the naked Things themselves: (For if every man must begin all a new, as if he had been the first Philosopher, knowledge will make but small proficiency). 2. Nor yet stick not in the bare Belief of any Author whatsoever, but study all things in their *naked natures* and proper *evidences* though by the helps that are afforded you by others. For it is not *science* but *humane belief*, else, whoever you take it from.[157]

In addition to the anti-Cartesian thrust of the first point, Baxter's advice balances the need for both tradition and reform. This advice also approximates Baxter's own procedure, which retained many Aristotelian concepts, especially with respect to the soul and causality, while allowing a degree of philosophical innovation, especially with respect to the elemental realm (see chapter 4). His regard for both tradition and reform is likewise evident in his habit of reading both old and new natural philosophy, as when he writes, "in Physicks, I more regard one *Aristotle, Scotus, Honoratus Faber, Campanella,* Mr. *Boyle,* &c. before all them that never studied them."[158]

In light of the revival of ancient Epicureanism during the interregnum, it is significant that Baxter reserved his harshest criticisms for the Epicurean sect, whose doctrine he construed broadly to include contemporary mechanical philosophers who attributed operations of the soul to matter and motion. Baxter's general hostility to Epicureanism in comparison with other ancient philosophies constitutes an important point of continuity not only with the wider Christian tradition reaching back to the early church,[159] but more specifically with his Reformed heritage going

---

156. Christopher Shields, "Aristotle," *The Stanford Encyclopedia of Philosophy* (Fall 2015 Edition), accessed July 25, 2016, http://plato.stanford.edu/archives/fall2015/entries/aristotle/.

157. *CD*, III.919 (q. 173, §14).

158. Richard Baxter, *Two Disputations of Original Sin* (London: Robert Gibbs, 1675), 46; cf. *CD*, III.923, 927 (q. 174). Note that Baxter's list of authorities for metaphysics is more scholastic and less modern.

159. Clement of Alexandria, *Stromateis*, I.xi; Augustine, *De civitate Dei*, VIII.v.

back to Calvin and Vermigli.[160] In the appendix to the *Reasons*, Baxter enumerated a number of reasons to call into question the authority of this philosophical
perspective. These include the fact that most other philosophical sects rejected
and ridiculed Epicurean notions, that those who adhere to this mechanical hypothesis are largely the "younger sort of ingenious men" who gravitated toward novel
ideas without studying the other ancient philosophical sects thoroughly, and that
in their earnest study of material things, "they quite over-look the noblest natures"
or study only the organ while neglecting the agent and its nature.[161] Specifically,
this kind of philosophizing, Baxter asserted, was leading to ignorance of the philosophy of Aristotle and Plato. An increasing number of younger scholars, Baxter
later observed, were so biased toward the new philosophy that "when I tryed them,
I found that they knew not what *Aristotle* or *Plato* said."[162] He observed a related
problem in theology. Late in life Baxter came to view the "crying downe Aristotle
& the Schoolmen" as linked with the inability of "younger students" to understand
scholastic theology such as his own *Methodus theologiae*, with the result that many
of the younger generation "passe it by as too scholastike."[163]

Of all the disciplines of philosophy, Baxter thought that the student of theology should pay particular attention to the study of natural philosophy—broadly
construed in its early modern sense as inclusive of the topic of the soul. This was
a fairly traditional point, reflective of the importance placed on natural philosophy (alongside logic) in early modern Reformed curricula, even as metaphysics
remained controversial.[164] In addition to appealing to the example of various
Reformed theologians who integrated natural philosophy with their theology (see

---

160. *PRRD*, 1:67–69, 376–77; Nicolaas H. Gootjes, "Calvin on Epicurus and the
Epicureans: Background to a Remark in Article 13 of the Belgic Confession," *Calvin Theological
Journal* 40 (2005): 33–48; David C. Steinmetz, "Calvin as Biblical Interpreter among the
Ancient Philosophers," *Interpretation* 63, no. 2 (2009): 142–53, at 146–47; Charles Partee,
Calvin and Classical Philosophy (Leiden: Brill, 1977), 104; John Patrick Donnelly, *Calvinism
and Scholasticism in Vermigli's Doctrine of Man and Grace* (Leiden: Brill, 1976), 30–31; Joseph
C. McLelland, "Translator's Introduction," in Peter Martyr Vermigli, *Philosophical Works: On
the Relation of Philosophy to Theology*, trans. and ed. Joseph C. McLelland (Kirksville,
MO: Truman State University Press, 1996), xxx.

161. *RCR*, 496–99. Cf. Spiller, *"Concerning Natural Experimental Philosophie,"* 135–37, 180.

162. Baxter, *Catholick Communion Defended*, 15.

163. DWL BT VII.229, fol. 68v.

164. M. J. Petry, "Burgersdijk's Physics," in *Franco Burgersdijk (1590–1635): Neo-Aristotelianism
in Leiden*, ed. E. P. Bos and H. A. Krop (Amsterdam: Rodopi, 1993), 83–118, at 98, 101; J. P.
Dray, "The Protestant Academy of Saumur and Its Relations with the Oratorians of Les
Ardilliers," *History of European Ideas* 9, no. 4 (1988): 465–78, at 472–73; Joseph Prost, *La
philosophie à l'académie protestante de Saumur (1606–1685)* (Paris: Paulin, 1907), 55–56; John
Gascoigne, "A Reappraisal of the Role of the Universities in the Scientific Revolution,"
in *Reappraisals of the Scientific Revolution*, ed. David C. Lindberg and Robert S. Westman

chapter 4), he provided at least two reasons for the study of natural philosophy. First, the Scriptures begin with God's creation so that nature is presupposed for both morality and grace.[165] Second, the knowledge of one's own soul is, besides the knowledge of God, the most important topic for theology.[166] For this reason, Baxter himself recounted, "I read through almost all the writings *on the soul* that I could get hold of," and learned the most from those authors that "*explain most clearly the operations of the human soul.*"[167] In the study of natural philosophy, Baxter advised that the Christian should study it in relation to God as the beginning and end of all things and not as if it were in some sense an independent principle.[168] "[J]oin together the study of Physicks and Theologie," he told ministers, "and take not your Physicks as separated from or independant on Theologie; But as the study of God in his works, and of his *works* as leading to himself. Otherwise you will be but like Scrivener and Printer, who makes his Letters well, but knoweth not what they signifie."[169]

Conclusion

Baxter's approach to reason and philosophy has often been characterized as one stop on the way to the rationalism of the Enlightenment. Upon closer examination, Baxter provides an eloquent and extensive account of the noetic effects of sin that does not oblige an easy assimilation to later rationalist trends. Baxter assumes that the will's fallen desires contaminate reason in the exercise of free choice as a composite act of reason and will, so that the current state of reason is not neutrally disposed toward knowledge. Moreover, he developed his own view of the faculties of intellect and will within parameters inherited from the medieval scholastics. While his voluntarism certainly manifests the influence of Scotus, his approach both to the relation of reason and revelation and to apologetics is clearly indebted to the arguments of Aquinas, and specifically the *Summa contra gentiles* (I.iii–ix). Baxter eclectically draws on these medieval figures while defining the nature and limitations of reason in a similar manner to Reformed authors such as Gisbertus Voetius and John Davenant.

(Cambridge: Cambridge University Press, 1990), 207–60, at 212; Edward Reyner, *A Treatise of the Necessity of Humane Learning for a Gospel-Preacher* (London: John Field, 1663), 107.

165. *MT*, "Praefatio," [A5r, A6v]; *MT*, I.155.

166. *CD*, III.726 (III.vi, §13.2); *MT*, I.154–55; Baxter, *Gildas Salvinus*, 266.

167. *MT*, "Praefatio," [A5r].

168. Baxter, *Gildas Salvinus*, 265–71.

169. *CD*, III.918 (q. 173, §7).

While in the following chapters we will examine specific areas relating to mechanical philosophy, the present chapter has identified some general features of Baxter's thought that frame his polemics. Baxter's insistence on the reliability and priority of sense perception contrasts with the depreciation of the senses, particularly as found in Cartesian philosophy. His account of the fallibility of the fallen intellect and discursive reason—particularly with respect to absent, past, and future realities—results in a highly cautious and generally eclectic approach toward philosophical systems, which Baxter assumes contain a mixture of error. Likewise, Baxter's view of the limitations of the mind with respect to "unrevealed things" leads him to frequently distinguish certain from uncertain knowledge when discussing philosophical topics. His account of the overlapping relation between reason and revelation requires that philosophy be evaluated in light of revelation when they discuss similar objects, particularly objects further removed from immediate empirical perception. More significantly, as far as his polemics are concerned, Baxter highlights the importance of physical knowledge and the soul as a great priority for the theologian. And so it is to his views of the physical order that we turn in the next chapter.

4

A Trinitarian Natural Philosophy

THE PREVIOUS CHAPTER concluded by observing the high priority Baxter placed on the physical order and the soul for the theologian. In the present chapter, we will set forth the main characteristics of Baxter's unique Trinitarian natural philosophy. An understanding of this aspect of Baxter's thought is necessary, since much of Baxter's critique of mechanical philosophy is rooted in his theological understanding of nature. We will first assess some of Baxter's theological motivations and developments before turning to the way these came to be expressed in his understanding of nature. This section will show that Baxter resisted trends in seventeenth-century theology to separate the domains of theology and natural philosophy, but rather sympathized with a tradition of "Mosaic physics" that was popular among Calvinists in the seventeenth century. In addition, Baxter agreed with an older medieval theological tradition of identifying traces of the Trinity (*vestigia Trinitatis*) in the natural order. This medieval aspect of his thought was long ago highlighted by George Park Fisher,[1] and represented a relatively more positive evaluation of the tradition of *vestigia Trinitatis* than many of his Reformed contemporaries.[2] Baxter's agreement with this *vestigia Trinitatis* tradition also led him to distinctly Trinitarian views of the analogy of being and divine causality.

The remainder of the chapter will turn to Baxter's thoughts on causality, substance, and the soul, which he modified in light of his Trinitarian theological motivations. Although Tommaso Campanella's metaphysics of nature certainly played an important role in Baxter's construction of a Trinitarian natural philosophy,[3] the reception of Campanella's philosophy was eclectic and critical and should be judged in light of his prior theological motivations. While searching for traces of God's power, wisdom, and goodness in the created order, Baxter also divided

---

1. Fisher, "Theology of Richard Baxter," 157.

2. Cf. *PRRD*, 4:162.

3. Trueman, "Small Step," esp. 187, 192–93.

reality into passive and active natures, and this division allowed him to accommodate Robert Boyle's corpuscular philosophy in the inorganic realm while retaining a nonmechanical concept of form for other aspects of reality. Accordingly, Baxter's mature theory of nature attempts to balance tradition and reform through the preservation of Aristotelian and scholastic concepts of the soul, the reimagining of living and active things in light of God's power, wisdom, and goodness, and a limited accommodation of corpuscular matter theory. In the construction of this natural philosophy, Baxter displays a great deal of eclecticism controlled by an overarching Trinitarian theological vision.

Theological Motivations
God's Two Books

Although the Bible lacks any reference to the world as a "book," it did not take long for Christians to apply their concept of reading God's revelation in the Bible to the world at large. Augustine has often been credited with coining the metaphor, but in fact it preceded him and found acceptance in the east with Maximus the Confessor and later in the west with Hugh of St. Victor, Bonaventure, and many other medieval theologians.[4] The metaphor survived the Reformation and had an enduring influence in the Reformed tradition after being enshrined in the Belgic Confession.[5] While natural philosophers of the seventeenth century appealed to the concept to bring theological significance to their work, theologians generally distinguished between the knowledge of God's power and wisdom, available through study of the book of nature, and God's salvific will, only available through the book of Scripture.[6]

While post-Reformation Protestants distinguished in principle between two books, and thus two sources, of revelation, in practice Scripture often functioned as a normative guide to the interpretation of philosophy. For example, at the Reformed academy of Herborn, the statutes mandated that philosophy professors disprove philosophical doctrines that disagreed with Scripture.[7] This interest in the integral relation of the two books in light of the rule of Scripture is perhaps most visible in the commentary tradition on Genesis that developed in the

---

4. G. Tanzella-Netti, "The Two Books Prior to the Scientific Revolution," *Annales Theologici* 18 (2004): 51–83.

5. Gisbert van den Brink, "A Most Elegant Book: The Natural World in Article 2 of the Belgic Confession," *Westminster Theological Journal* 73, no. 2 (2011): 273–91.

6. Harrison, *The Bible, Protestantism, and the Rise of Natural Science*, 199–204.

7. Howard Hotson, *Johann Heinrich Alsted (1588–1638): Between Renaissance, Reformation, and Universal Reform* (Oxford: Clarendon Press, 2000), 139.

sixteenth and seventeenth centuries. The exegetes of this period, observes Arnold Williams, "incorporated within their work a larger amount of what they took to be science than any exegetes before or since their day."[8] Francis Bacon perhaps had this commentary tradition in mind when he complained of the corrupting influence of the widespread "admixture of theology" upon philosophy, and called for the "inhibition and repression" of "some moderns" who "attempt to found a system of natural philosophy on the first chapter of Genesis, on the book of Job, and other parts of the sacred writings."[9] Yet, Bacon did not absolutely oppose any integration between the realms of theology and natural philosophy, for he affirmed that the study of nature reveals God's power, albeit not his essence or will.[10] After Bacon's inchoate remarks, fully developed objections to the use of Scripture in natural philosophy came from English proponents of the new philosophy and Dutch Cartesians.

John Wilkins, leader of the "experimental philosophy club" at Oxford and later the first (unofficial) president and (official) secretary of the Royal Society, addressed the general question of the relation of Scripture to philosophy in the context of his argument for Copernicanism and the habitability of the moon.[11] In chapter 3 of *A Discourse Concerning a New Planet*, Wilkins made positive use of Calvin's widely used principle of accommodation to support reading the Genesis creation narrative in a popular (and therefore philosophically imprecise) way.[12] But in chapter 4, he took the more radical step of censuring the broader Christian tradition for its practice of looking to Scripture for natural knowledge with the proposition, "That divers learned men have fallen into great absurdities, whilest they

---

8. Arnold Williams, *The Common Expositor: An Account of the Commentaries on Genesis 1527–1633* (Chapel Hill: The University of North Carolina Press, 1948), 174.

9. Francis Bacon, *New Organon*, trans. Fulton H. Anderson (Indianapolis: Bobbs-Merrill, 1960), I.65 (p. 62); also I.89. Cf. Ann Blair, "Mosaic Physics and the Search for a Pious Natural Philosophy in the Late Renaissance," *Isis* 9, no. 1 (2000): 32–58, at 42; Williams, *Common Expositor*, 176.

10. Steven Matthews, *Theology and Science in the Thought of Francis Bacon* (Burlington, VT: Ashgate, 2008), 110–14. Bacon's reference to "some moderns" remains obscure, but it is possible that his criticisms were limited to the "school of Paracelsus" (111).

11. John Wilkins, *A Discourse Concerning a New Planet. Tending to Prove, That 'Tis Probable Our Earth Is One of the Planets* (London: R. H. for John Maynard, 1640). This work was printed as the second book of *A Discourse Concerning a New world & Another Planet in 2 Bookes* (London: John Maynard, 1640).

12. Wilkins, *New Planet*, 50–51, 54. The accommodation principle was widespread and not limited to later Copernicans. See David S. Sytsma, "Calvin, Daneau, and *Physica Mosaica*: Neglected Continuities at the Origins of an Early Modern Tradition," *Church History and Religious Culture* 95, no. 4 (2015): 457–76, at 473–74.

have looked for the grounds of Philosophy from the words of Scripture."[13] After citing multiple examples of theological misinterpretation of natural phenomena (including Calvin), obviously calculated to instill a skeptical disposition toward the use of Scripture in philosophy, Wilkins concluded that the examples "may sufficiently manifest, how frequently others have been deceived, in concluding the points of Philosophy from the expressions of Scripture."[14] Wilkins's distaste for deriving general points of philosophy from Genesis were shared by others. Thomas Sprat, a protégé of Wilkins, argued for a "divorce" between philosophy and Christianity in his apology for the Royal Society, which was at least partially supervised by Wilkins.[15] Thomas Burnet, in his influential *Telluris Theoria Sacra* (1681), which attempted a reconciliation of Cartesianism with Scripture, was notable for placing emphasis on the Flood, while "barely mentioning the Hexameron or the fall of man in Eden," and suggesting that the early chapters of Genesis ought to be interpreted allegorically.[16] Such ideas were, however, still unpopular in seventeenth-century England, and Burnet's *Theoria Sacra* was widely criticized.[17]

The most explicit attack upon the use of Scripture in natural philosophy came later from Dutch Cartesians. Descartes's own natural philosophy was conspicuous mostly for its indifference to Scripture and the opening chapters of Genesis.[18] But it was the following generation of Dutch Cartesians who explicitly championed the freedom of philosophy. Accordingly, Dutch Cartesians such as Johannes de Raey (1622–1707) and Christoph Wittich (1625–1687) argued for a strict separation between the realms of philosophy and theology, on the basis that philosophy teaches speculative truth grasped by the intellect, whereas Scripture teaches practical knowledge grasped by ordinary experience and faith—an important context for Spinoza's assertion of the separation of philosophy and theology.[19] This later

---

13. Wilkins, *New Planet*, 76–89 (Prop. IIII).

14. Wilkins, *New Planet*, 88. Cf. Levitin, *Ancient Wisdom*, 125–26.

15. Sprat, *History of the Royal Society*, 353–56. On Wilkins's supervision, see Hunter, *Establishing the New Science*, 45–72; and John Morgan, "Sprat, Thomas," in *ODNB*.

16. William Poole, "Sir Robert Southwell's Dialogue on Thomas Burnet's Theory of the Earth: 'C & S discourse of Mr Burnetts Theory of the Earth' (1684): Contexts and an Edition," *The Seventeenth Century* 23, no. 1 (2008): 72–104, at 73.

17. Poole, "Sir Robert Southwell's Dialogue," 72–104.

18. CSM 3:349–50; J. A. van Ruler, *The Crisis of Causality: Voetius and Descartes on God, Nature, and Change* (Leiden: E. J. Brill, 1995), 257. Van Ruler argues that Cartesianism "by disengaging philosophical from theological discourse threatened the accepted interdisciplinary links" (318).

19. Alexander Douglas, *Spinoza and Dutch Cartesianism: Philosophy and Theology* (Oxford: Oxford University Press, 2015), 36–63; Alexander Douglas, "Spinoza and the Dutch Cartesians on Philosophy and Theology," *Journal of the History of Philosophy* 51, no.

Cartesian argument for the freedom of philosophy from theology was among Petrus van Mastricht's (1630–1706) principal criticisms of the later Cartesians (including Spinoza), whom he distinguished from Descartes's own greater subjection to theological considerations.[20]

In England, a different and more influential alternative to the Cartesian separation of philosophy and theology arose in the 1690s in the form of the genre of physico-theology, which in reaction to Descartes's denial of a knowledge of final causes, integrated mechanical and experimental philosophy with explicitly Christian notions of creation and providence.[21] Boyle's *Disquisition about the Final Causes of Natural Things* (1688), for example, was an important source for this new genre, and in it Boyle upheld many traditional theological assumptions regarding creation ex nihilo and providence.[22] But physico-theology grew largely from the soil of Latitudinarians with their concern to provide a new apologetic that fit the exigencies of mechanical philosophy.[23] Unlike the earlier tradition of natural

---

4 (2013): 567–88. See also Theo Verbeek, "Tradition and Novelty: Descartes and Some Cartesians," in *The Rise of Modern Philosophy*, ed. Tom Sorrell (Oxford: Clarendon Press, 1993), 167–96; Scholder, *Birth*, 121–32; Bizer, "Reformed Orthodoxy and Cartesianism," 52–58; Kenneth J. Howell, *God's Two Books: Copernican Cosmology and Biblical Interpretation in Early Modern Science* (Notre Dame, IN: University of Notre Dame Press, 2002), 173–78; Israel, *Radical Enlightenment*, 25–26, 28–29. Wittich expressly objected to the tradition of Mosaic physics discussed below. See Christoph Wittich, *Dissertationes duae quarum prior de S. Scripturae in rebus philosophicis abusu* (Amsterdam: L. Elzevirius, 1653), 2–3; Wittich, *Theologia pacifica*, 3rd ed. (Leiden: C. Boutesteyn, 1683), II.xvii (pp. 13–14); cf. Vermij, *Calvinist Copernicans*, 258; Scholder, *Birth*, 126.

20. See Petrus van Mastricht, *Novitatum Cartesianarum gangraena* (Amsterdam: Janssoons van Waesberghe, 1677), 34–49; with discussion in Goudriaan, *Reformed Orthodoxy and Philosophy*, 57–60; and on Spinoza, see Kato, "*Deus sive Natura*," 192–204.

21. Rienk H. Vermij, "The Beginnings of Physico-Theology: England, Holland, Germany," in "*Grenz-Überschreitung*". *Wandlungen der Geisteshaltung, dargestellt an Beispielen aus Geographie und Wissenschaftshistorie, Theologie, Religions- und Erziehungswissenschaft, Philosophie, Musikwissenschaft und Liturgie. Festschrift zum 70. Geburtstag von Manfred Büttner*, ed. Henyo Kattenstedt (Bochum: Brockmeyer, 1993), 173–84. On the development of this tradition, see Wolfgang Philipp, "Physicotheology in the Age of Enlightenment: Appearance and History," *Studies on Voltaire and the Eighteenth Century* 57 (1967): 1233–67; and Sara Stebbins, *Maxima in minimis: zur Empirie- und Autoritätsverständnis in der physikotheologischen Literatur der Frühaufklärung* (Frankfurt am Main: P. D. Lang, 1980).

22. See Muller, "God and Design," 105, also 101. Boyle is among those forerunners acknowledged in Ray's preface to *The Wisdom of God Manifested in the Works of Creation*.

23. Ray's *Wisdom of God* abounds with citations from Henry More's *An Antidote against Atheism* (1653), Ralph Cudworth's *The True Intellectual System of the Universe* (1678), and John Wilkins's *Of the Principles and Duties of Natural Religion* (1675). The two principal problems addressed are the "Epicurean Hypothesis" of unguided creation (13–20) and Descartes's denial of final causes (20–40). The general connection of physico-theology to Latitudinarianism is observed by Vermij, "Beginnings of Physico-Theology," 178–79, 181; and the specific relation of Ray to the Cambridge Platonists is noted in C. E. Raven, *John Ray,*

theology that it replaced, physico-theology "emphasized not the immediately perceptible regularities of the heavens and the *scala naturae* but, instead, the intricate contrivances of living organisms."[24] The domains of revelation and philosophy were still related through the principle of a wise creator, but the wisdom of creation concerned not so much analogies from the perfections of creation within a ladder of being (*scala naturae*), but the discovery of the complex machinery of efficient causes and material parts that combine to produce various divinely ordained ends.[25] This approach gave rise in the eighteenth century to a proliferation of specific "theologies" of birds (*Petino-theologie*), fishes (*Ichthyo-theologie*), insects (*Insecto-theologie*), plants (*Phyto-theologie*), and even grass (*Chorto-theologie*) and stones (*Litho-theologie*).[26]

Baxter's view of the relation between the books of nature and Scripture stands in contrast both to seventeenth-century trends toward making the two books independent of one another and to the later tradition of physico-theology. By relating the natural world to the Trinity through the medieval tradition of *vestigia Trinitatis*, he brings the two books close together, but does so in a manner controlled by (Trinitarian) theological and metaphysical concerns regarding the nature of substance that distinguish him from later physico-theology. In his *Reasons*, Baxter does affirm, in a similar manner as later physico-theologians, that "[t]he effects in the admirable frame and nature, and motions of the Creation, declare that the Creator is *infinitely wise*," and the heavens declare God's omnipotence.[27] He can even wonder at the "harmony of an in[n]umerable multitude of parts" using the analogy of a watch or clock.[28] But this is a subordinate

---

Naturalist: His Life and Works (Cambridge: Cambridge University Press, 1942), 454, 458–61; Neal C. Gillespie, "Natural History, Natural Theology, and the Social Order: John Ray and the 'Newtonian Ideology,'" *Journal of the History of Biology* 20, no. 1 (1987): 1–49, at 38–39; Webster, *Great Instauration*, 150; and Gascoigne, *Cambridge in the Age of the Enlightenment*, 65, 67. See also Richard Olson, "On the Nature of God's Existence, Wisdom, and Power: The Interplay Between Organic and Mechanistic Imagery in Anglican Natural Theology," in *Approaches to Organic Form: Permutations in Science and Culture*, ed. Frederick Burwick (Dordrecht: D. Reidel, 1987), 1–48.

24. Brian W. Ogilvie, "Natural History, Ethics, and Physico-Theology," in *Historia: Empiricism and Erudition in Early Modern Europe*, ed. Gianna Pomata and Nancy G. Siraisi (Cambridge, MA: MIT Press, 2005), 75–103, at 95. Cf. Wilson, *Invisible World*, 176–80; and on the greater theological importance attributed to microscopic over telescopic observation, see 181–83.

25. Cf. Robert Boyle, *A Disquisition about the Final Causes of Natural Things* (London: H. C. for John Taylor, 1688), 229–34.

26. Philipp, "Physicotheology," 1242–47.

27. *RCR*, 22, 28.

28. DWL BT XIX.351, fol. 75v: "As many peeces goe to make up one watch or clocke, so do they to make up one man. The particles of man are never to be numbred by yᵉ most curious

emphasis,[29] and it is balanced by his insistence that God reveals the use but not the art of his creation.[30] Indeed, Baxter is far more concerned with the affirmation that God and his wisdom are reflected "formally and eminently" in the analogical essential perfections of the *scala naturae*, rather than the machinery of matter and efficient causation.[31]

Baxter's approach to the relation of reason and revelation (see chapter 3) is integrally related to his approach to finding traces of God's perfections in nature. In this view, while reason is a weak or lesser light with respect to revealed things, when the contents of the book of Scripture and the book of nature overlap, it then becomes the theologian's task to interpret the book of nature through the lens of the book of Scripture. Baxter's view of this matter remained consistent throughout his published corpus. In his early *Reformed Pastor* (1656), Baxter argued that the "book of the Creatures" differs from the book of Scripture in that it "represents [God] to us in more sensible appearances, to make our knowledge of him the more intense and operative," yet because the book of Scripture is "the easier book," one ought to begin with Scripture in order to rightly see God in nature.[32] After starting with the easier book of Scripture, Baxter advised, "address your selves cheerfully to the study of his works, that you may there see the Creature it self as your Alphabet, and their Order as the Composure of syllables, words and sentences and God as the subject matter of all, and the respect to him as the sense or signification."[33] Baxter reiterated this same perspective two decades later in the *Methodus theologiae*, where he wrote that although God "makes himself available in all his works as if observed in a mirror," yet "the Redeemer is necessary to reveal the Creator more clearly, & to teach us by the *book of Scripture* a truer exposition & use of the *book* of nature."[34] Thus, in Baxter's view, although the book of nature symbolically represents divine reality, the book of Scripture should guide the understanding of this symbolism. This affirmation of nature as symbolic of divine (and Trinitarian) perfections, furthermore, forms a counterexample to the supposition that "the literalist mentality" of Protestants "precluded the possibility of assigning meanings

---

Anatomist. The many hundred veines & arteries & nerves, besides all other partes in every animall, & ye great diversity of humours, chyle, blood, ly[m]pha, semen, bilis, oleum nervosum, sperma &c, do all proclaime y^t God delighteth in ye harmony of an in[n]umerable multitude of parts."

29. Cf. Calloway, *Natural Theology*, 62–63.

30. *MT*, I.149–50. See chapter 3.

31. *RCR*, 22. Cf. generally, *RCR*, 16–28; and Baxter, *Mischiefs of Self-Ignorance*, 12.

32. Baxter, *Gildas Salvinus*, 268–69.

33. Baxter, *Gildas Salvinus*, 269.

34. *MT*, I.152.

to natural objects," with the result that "only words refer; the things of nature do not."[35]

Mosaic Physics

Baxter adduced both biblical and traditional precedent for a theological reading of nature. The biblical precedent came from the Old Testament books of Genesis, Job, and the Psalms. As Baxter stated more than once, "The beginning of Genesis, the books of Job and the Psalms may acquaint us that our Physicks are not so little kin to Theology as some suppose."[36] When Baxter wrote that the Bible is "no particular revelation or perfect Rule of natural Sciences, as Physicks, Metaphysicks, &c.,"[37] he was denying that the Bible constitutes a revelation of the specifics of physics and metaphysics, but he was not denying the relevance of biblical or theological sources in the study of nature. In the interregnum, he was quite critical of the established academic curriculum, which began studies with philosophy and ended them with theology. In Baxter's estimation, this resulted in "unsanctified Teachers" who instead of "reading Philosophy like Divines . . . read Divinity like Philosophers," and also produced philosophers such as Campanella, Thomas White (ca. 1592–1676), Hobbes, and Herbert of Cherbury, who "reduce all their Theologie to their Philosophy." By contrast, Baxter wished that tutors would "teach all their Philosophy in habitu Theologico,"[38] and urged that "our Physicks and Metaphysicks must be reduced to Theologie; and nature must be read as one of Gods books, which is purposefully written for the revelation of himself."[39] Against those who objected that the "Physicks in Gen. 1 are contrary to all true Philosophy, and suited to the vulgars erroneous conceits"—a probable reference to contemporary Cartesians who posited accommodation to popular error—Baxter replied, "No such matter: there is sounder doctrine of Physicks in Gen. 1 than any Philosopher hath who contradicteth it."[40]

In addition to his appeal to Scripture, Baxter adduced various recent precedents for a theological reading of nature. In his Methodus theologiae, he appealed to the theological systems of Girolamo Zanchi and Amandus Polanus, which

---

35. Harrison, The Bible, Protestantism, and the Rise of Natural Science, 4.

36. Baxter, Gildas Salvinus, 270; cf. MT, "Praefatio," [A6v]: "Ex Physicis S. Scripturae Theologia incipit, Gen. 1. & in libro Jobi, Psalmorum, &c. saepe talia repetuntur."

37. CD, III.886 (q. 130).

38. Baxter, Gildas Salvinus, 271.

39. Baxter, Gildas Salvinus, 269.

40. RCR, 415. On accommodation to error, see Goudriaan, Reformed Orthodoxy and Philosophy, 133–41.

contained discussions of physics.[41] From among his contemporaries he recommended his "old," "learned," and "worthy" friend Samuel Gott's *The Divine History of the Genesis of the World* (1670) on multiple occasions.[42] He contrasted the "excellent Philosophy" of Gott's *Divine History* with "Ignorants and Cabalists"—a likely reference to those such as Paracelsus, Jakob Boehme, and Robert Fludd, who constructed Mosaic philosophy through allegory and individual inspiration.[43] Another important example for Baxter was the "pious" philosopher and theologian Johann Amos Comenius (1592–1670), whose short introduction to physics Baxter valued as having "much that is of worth," even if it came "far short of accurateness."[44] Baxter considered Comenius part of his own tradition, referring to him as "our Commenius."[45] In a letter to Boyle, after stating that "God himselfe begineth the holy scriptures with the doctrine of Physicks," Baxter singled out Comenius's pansophic project as a source of inspiration: "He that will justly frame a *Pansophie* (as Commenius Calls it) must begin with Ontologie, of which *God* & *Man* are the parts which we are most Concerned to Know."[46]

Of all the precedents that Baxter adduced for his Scriptural philosophy of nature, Zanchi, Polanus, and Comenius were all possible influences on Baxter's early intellectual development. Gott's *Divine History* appeared in 1670, and Baxter's earliest known reference to it appeared in his postscript to "Of the Nature and Immortality of Humane Soules" (ca. 1672), after he had already drafted the doctrine of creation in the *Methodus theologiae* (ca. 1669). A more likely influence than Gott during Baxter's period leading up to the *Methodus theologiae* is

---

41. *MT*, "Praefatio," [A5r, A6v].

42. Baxter, *Of the Nature of Spirits*, 39: "My old Friend Mr. *Sam. Got*"; DWL BT XIX.351, fol. 143v: "my worthy friend"; *CD*, III.919 (q. 173): "My worthy, Learned and truly pious friend Mr. *Sam. Gott* in his new Book on *Gen.* 1. hath many excellent notions."

43. *TKL*, 167. Cf. DWL BT IV.87, fol. 233r: "And y^m y^t dare on pretense of Gnostike Cabalisme reduce all Scripture, to the poppets or fictions of their owne braines, I reject, & from *such turne away*." On Paracelsus, Boehme, and Fludd, see Blair, "Mosaic Physics," 36; and Wilhelm Schmidt-Biggemann, "Robert Fludd's Kabbalistic Cosmos," in *Platonism at the Origins of Modernity: Studies on Platonism and Early Modern Philosophy*, ed. Douglas Hedley and Sarah Hutton (Dordrecht: Springer, 2008), 75–92.

44. *CD*, III.919 (q. 173), surely referring to Comenius's *Physicae ad lumen divinum reformatae synopsis* (1633).

45. Baxter, *Of the Nature of Spirits*, 25.

46. Baxter to Boyle, 14 June 1665, in Boyle, *Correspondence*, 2:473. Baxter expressed continued anticipation of Comenius's pansophic project in *TKL*, 199. On *pansophia*, see Johann Amos Comenius, *A Reformation of Schooles* (London: Michael Sparke, 1642), 18–21; Webster, *Great Instauration*, 28–30, 49–50, 110–114; and Burton, *Hallowing of Logic*, 60–63. On the varying reactions, see Dagmar Čapková, "The Reception Given to the *Prodromus pansophiae*, and the Methodology of Comenius," *Acta Comeniana* 7 (1987): 37–59.

Matthew Hale, who provided feedback on a draft of the section on creation from the *Methodus theologiae* and encouraged him to expand it.[47] Hale's views, although perhaps influenced late in life by Baxter, antedated his relationship to Baxter. In *A Discourse of the Knowledge of God, and of Our Selves* (composed ca. 1639–1641), a work reflective of his early Puritan education, Hale stated that the many disputes regarding natural philosophy "we may with satisfaction read, resolved in the First of *Genesis*, and in no Book in the World beside, but what hath been borrowed from thence."[48] Yet Hale's works on these matters were not published until later, and more importantly, the substance of Baxter's views were in place by October of 1666 (when he completed the *Reasons*), the year before he met Hale in Acton. Thus, although Hale and Gott may have altered Baxter's views on some details late in life, and certainly shared affinities with Baxter, a precedent for drawing natural philosophy from the Scriptures derives from earlier sources, likely Zanchi, Polanus, and Comenius.

By identifying himself with such theologians and philosophers who looked to the Bible, and particularly the Genesis account of creation, as a source for truths of natural philosophy, Baxter was placing himself in continuity with an early modern tradition of so-called Mosaic physics.[49] This tradition, as Ann Blair has argued, consisted more in a "set of shared theoretical tenets than as a uniform system of natural philosophical explanation."[50] The theologians and philosophers who espoused this perspective shared an opposition to double truth (i.e., an affirmation of the unity of rational and revealed truths), the use of the Bible (particularly Genesis, Job, and the Psalms) for deriving truths about nature where sense or reason were most inclined to ignorance or error (e.g., things far removed in place or time), and a desire to reform Aristotelian philosophy according to the

---

47. For these details of dating, see Appendix A. The similarities between Baxter, Hale, and Gott are discussed in Burton, *Hallowing of Logic*, 109–15.

48. Hale, *A Discourse of the Knowledge of God*, 101.

49. For a good introduction, see Blair, "Mosaic Physics," 32–58. In addition to the literature cited by Blair, see Voetius, *Exercitia*, 383–84; Johann Heinrich Zedler, "Moses Vielwissenheit," in *Grosses vollständiges Universal Lexicon aller Wissenschafften und Künste* (Halle & Leipzig: J. H. Zedler, 1739), 21:1888–97, esp. 1890–91; van Ruler, *Crisis of Causality*, 30–31, 76–84, 316; Goudriaan, *Reformed Orthodoxy and Philosophy*, 85–86, 104–33; *PRRD*, 1:370; Peter Harrison, *The Fall of Man and the Foundations of Science* (Cambridge: Cambridge University Press, 2007), 107–25; Peter Harrison, *The Bible, Protestantism, and the Rise of Natural Science*, 121–29, 138–60; Eric Jorink, "Reading the Book of Nature in the Seventeenth-Century Dutch Republic," in *The Book of Nature in Early Modern and Modern History*, ed. Klaas van Berkel and Arjo Vanderjagt (Leuven: Peeters, 2006), 45–68; Markku Leinonen, "*De Physica Mosaica Comeniana*: The Academic Thesis of Anders Lundbom," *Acta Comeniana* 15–16 (2002): 107–25; Cees Leijenhurst, "Space and Matter in Calvinist Physics," *The Monist* 84, no. 4 (2001): 520–41; and Howell, *God's Two Books*, 169.

50. Blair, "Mosaic Physics," 47.

standards of sense perception, reason, and Scripture.[51] This did not entail deriving all the details of natural philosophy from the Bible, but rather using the Genesis account—interpreted with the help of the patristic hexameron literature—to inform the most general part relating to nature's principles and causes, and then supplementing this general knowledge with philosophers' observations of the particular natures and qualities of things.[52] While various theological traditions participated in this project of constructing a Mosaic physics, those of the Reformed confession apparently predominated.[53] Comenius, who in the estimation of Blair was "[p]robably the most articulate and most widely read" of this group, mentioned Lambert Daneau (1530–1595), Otto Casmann (1562–1607), Cort Aslakssøn (1564–1624), and his own former teacher Johann Heinrich Alsted (1588–1638) as notable examples.[54] Moreover, other authors looked to Daneau and Zanchi as important examples for their own efforts,[55] and Daneau built up part of his theory in continuity with Calvin's early remarks on Genesis and accommodation.[56] Indeed, a great many of those Dutch Reformed theologians and philosophers who

---

51. See Blair, "Mosaic Physics," 47–57, who bases her argument largely on Comenius's preface and prolegomena to his *Physicae ad lumen divinum reformatae synopsis* (1633), translated as Johann Amos Comenius, *Naturall Philosophy Reformed by Divine Light; or, A Synopsis of Physicks* (London, 1651), sigs. 1r–A7r, 1–8. Cf. Comenius, *Reformation of Schooles*, 17–19, 52–53. The three sources of sense, reason, and Scripture were already mentioned in Daneau, *Physice christiana*, 49; and Johann Heinrich Alsted, *Scientiarum omnium encyclopaediae* (Lyon: J. A. Huguetan & M. A. Ravaud, 1649), 1:72.

52. See Daneau, *Physice christiana*, 29, 36 (general physics taken from Gen. 1; particular physics from philosophers), 31, 38 (citing the hexameron literature of Basil, Chrysostom, and Ambrose, as well as Augustine's *De doctrina christiana* and *De Genesi ad litteram*). Cf. van Ruler, *Crisis of Causality*, 72; Johann Heinrich Alsted, *Physica harmonica* (Herborn, 1616), 13 (citing Daneau on Gen. 1 and general physics); and Alsted, "Physica sacra," in *Triumphus bibliorum sacrorum* (Frankfurt: Bartholomaeus Schmidt, 1625), 61–74.

53. Blair, "Mosaic Physics," 47, notes a "preponderance of Calvinists."

54. Comenius, *Naturall Philosophy*, sig. 11r–11v; Blair, "Mosaic Physics," 43–46. Although Cort Aslakssøn (1564–1624) was Lutheran, he studied at various Reformed academies before teaching at Copenhagen, and his *Physica et ethica mosaica* shows strong Reformed influences. See Cort Aslakssøn, *Physica et ethica mosaica* (Hanoviae, 1613), where he cites Philippe Du Plessis Mornay (10), Zanchi (20, 74, 102, 116, 119, 125, 139, 155, 161, 172), Casmann (20, 74, 116, 172), Franciscus Junius (22, 119, 177, 178, 185), Daneau (24, 45, 125, 172), Polanus (36, 78, 119), Johann Buxtorf (119), Immanuel Tremellius (178, 185), et al. Another Lutheran, Daniel Wülfer (1617–1685), repeatedly cites Daneau in his *De physica christiana exercitio* (Nürnberg: Christophor Gerhard, 1656). John Prideaux, Regius Professor of Divinity at Oxford (1615–1642), named Daneau and Alsted as important representatives of *philosophia dogmatica sacra*; see his *Hypomnemata logica, rhetorica, physica, metaphysica, pneumatica, ethica, politica, oeconomica* (Oxford: Leonar. Lichfield, 1650), 216.

55. Blair, "Mosaic Physics," 42n18, 43n20; van Ruler, *Crisis of Causality*, 76–84.

56. Sytsma, "Calvin, Daneau, and *Physica Mosaica*," 457–76.

opposed Christoph Wittich's Cartesian Copernicanism drew upon this Reformed tradition of Mosaic physics.[57]

Although Polanus, cited by Baxter along with Zanchi, does not appear in Blair's account of Mosaic physics, there is good reason to place him in this tradition. Voetius counted Polanus, together with Danaeu and Zanchi, as among the "systematicians" (*systematici*) of "physico-theology" (*Physico-Theologi*), and specifically the best after Zanchi among those who "explain scriptural physics" in their theological work.[58] Polanus's locus on creation attempted to harmonize general principles of natural philosophy with the creation account of Genesis. He organized his treatment of creation in his *Syntagma* according to the standard textbook division of physics into general principles of nature and particular kinds of constituted matter. He first treated God's relation to the most general "internal principles of nature" (*principia interna naturae*) while drawing on both Genesis 1 and Aristotle's four causes, and discussed the particular kinds of creatures according to the days of the creation in Genesis 1, before turning to the doctrine of humanity.[59]

Baxter's treatment of the doctrine of creation in the *Methodus theologiae* followed a similar pattern as that of Polanus and Zanchi, inasmuch as he organized his Ramist table on creation according to the days of creation.[60] In his elucidations on the table, Baxter likewise first treated general principles of nature (I.iii–iv) before proceeding to the various particular kinds of creatures (I.v–xii).[61] However, unlike Polanus and Zanchi, who moved from the lower forms of creation up to humanity, in these elucidations Baxter moved from a discussion of humanity and its higher faculties (I.v–ix) down to the sensitive, vegetative, and passive aspects of creation (I.x–xii). This order perhaps reflects the importance Baxter gave to the rational soul, which in his estimation as the image of God reflects the *vestigia Trinitatis* more than either the lower part of the soul or the rest of creation.[62]

---

57. These included the Leiden professor of medicine Albert Kyper and the theologians Johannes Beusechum, Petrus van Mastricht, Anthonius Driessen, and Melchior Leydekker. See Vermij, *Calvinist Copernicans*, 135, 263; Goudriaan, *Reformed Orthodoxy and Philosophy*, 85.

58. Voetius refers specifically to Polanus's *Syntagma theologiae christianae*. See Voetius, *Exercitia*, 383–84: "*Physico-Theologi*: qui sunt I. *systematici*, qui vel peculiari syntagmate, ut *Daneus*; vel in cursu theologico physicam scripturariam explicant, ut *Zanchius*; & post eum Polanus in syntagmate." Voetius acknowledges others who treat physics in the midst of their theology (Musculus, Martyr, Hyperius, and Tilenus), but they "were not so elaborately and professedly superior." I owe this reference to Van Ruler, *Crisis of Causality*, 71.

59. Amandus Polanus von Polansdorf, *Syntagma theologiae christianae* (Hanau, 1610), V.xiv–xxxv (cols. 1842–2152).

60. *MT*, I.125. Cf. Burton, *Hallowing of Logic*, 110–11.

61. *MT*, I.124–56.

62. Baxter's doctrine of *imago Dei* is discussed in Burton, *Hallowing of Logic*, 193–200.

In his *Reasons* and *Methodus theologiae*, Baxter provided two complementary sketches of biblically informed natural philosophical principles drawn from the six days of creation. The *Methodus theologiae* also lists a number of uncertainties pertaining to Genesis 1, including the precise meaning of "beginning" (1:1), "heavens" (1:1, 8), the Chaos (1:2), the Spirit of God (1:2), light, the elements, and vegetative and sensitive souls.[63] According to Baxter, the creation of the heavens and the earth on the first day establishes the superior and inferior parts of world. Following Basil's *Homilies on Genesis*, Baxter interprets the first day to imply the creation of an "Intellectual Superiour" realm or "pure simple intellectuals" in the superior part (which Basil had derived by cross-reference to Col. 1:16). The inferior part, paraphrased as an "unformed Mass or Chaos" (*RCR*) or "Chaos and watery Abyss, without form" (*MT*), establishes "the *matter* of the Elementary world" (*RCR*) or *materia passiva* (*MT*). The creation of light on the first day is interpreted as the creation of the element of fire, "the noblest active element, which is able to work on passive matter" (*MT*). On the second and third days, passive matter was distinguished into passive elements. On the second day, God created the element of air, "the greatest of the passive elements, joined to fire" (*MT*). On the third day, God separated the remaining passive elements, water and earth, "into their proper place and bounds" (*RCR*) or "formed and limited" them (*MT*). He also made vegetation with "their specifick forms and virtue of generation" (*RCR*), which Baxter also describes as their "seminative" (*seminativa*), "fructifying" (*fructifica*), and "nutritive" (*nutritiva*) powers (*MT*). The creation of the sun, moon, and stars on the fourth day involved the ordering of the previously made element of fire into luminaries, although the Mosaic account left much obscure—we remain ignorant of the luminaries' composition and are only told their uses related to our realm below (*MT*). The fifth day introduced the "inferiour Sensitives," with the "power of generation and multiplication" (*RCR*). On the sixth day God made the "sensitive" terrestrial animals, followed by humanity made in the image of God and endowed with the power of multiplication (*MT*).[64] A number of important principles of natural philosophy emerge from this reading of the six days: a distinction between the (superior) intellectual and (inferior) material world, a distinction between active and passive elements, the existence of "specifick forms" of creatures, a distinction between sensitive animals, humanity, and other creatures, and the power of generation for all living things.

---

63. *MT*, I.126–27.

64. *RCR*, 415–16; *MT*, I.125. In *RCR*, one marginal note reads, "Lege Basilii Hexamer. & Greg. Nysseni addit."; a second marginal note reads, "Basil *saith, that* In principio *is in the beginning of time; but that the intellectual world is here presupposed.*" Baxter cites Basil, *Hom. in Hexaemeron*, I.5 (*PG* 29:13–14).

While those influenced by Descartes in the Netherlands were arguing for a strong separation between natural philosophy and Scripture, Baxter identified with Reformed proponents of Mosaic physics, and along with them patristic commentaries on the hexameron (particularly Basil's *Homilies on Genesis*), as he sought to reconcile general principles of natural philosophy with the opening chapters of Genesis. Although, as we shall see, Baxter's approach to *vestigia Trinitatis* resulted in a unique natural philosophy, in his agreement with the tradition of Mosaic physics, there is general similarity to the Voetian party in the Netherlands who vigorously opposed the Cartesian party's disjunction between philosophy and Scripture.

Vestigia Trinitatis

One of the most important developments in Baxter's theology is the increasing importance he gave to the doctrine of the Trinity in his writings beginning around the early 1660s.[65] In the interregnum, Baxter had briefly discussed the Trinity using analogies from nature. Just as there were a variety of triunities in nature (vegetative, sensitive, rational faculties in humanity; power, understanding, will in the soul; power, light, heat in the sun), he reasoned, so likewise there was no contradiction of a Trinity of persons in God.[66] Yet by the time Baxter began composing his *Christian Directory* (ca. 1664–1665), he was conceptualizing God's relation to all of creation in a Trinitarian fashion. In the *Directory*, he provided a one-page table delineating both God's threefold nature "in Himself" and as "Related to his Creatures."[67] Subsequently he labored to demonstrate in his apologetic *Reasons* that God's three attributes of power, wisdom, and goodness are reflected in the realm of nature. In this work, he hinted at the direction his future works would take when he stated, "He that could write a perfect method of Physics and Morality, would shew us Trinity in Unity through all its parts from first to last."[68] Over the next several years, Baxter worked more closely to approximate such a "perfect method" in the *Life of Faith* (1670) and *Methodus theologiae*, which both featured elaborate Trinitarian title pages. Just about every detail of the *Methodus theologiae*

---

65. In what follows, I provide a brief sketch of this development in Baxter's life. The background and influences leading Baxter from Ramist dichotomous to trichotomous method is discussed at length in Burton, *Hallowing of Logic*, ch. 2.

66. Baxter, *Arrogancy*, 75.

67. *CD*, I.82 (I.iii, Dir. 4). Cf. Baxter to John Eliot, 30 Nov. 1663, in *Rel. Bax.*, II.297: "If we had a right Scheme of Theology (which I never yet saw) Unity in Trinity would go through the whole Method."

68. *RCR*, 31.

was trichotomized to reflect Baxter's belief that all of reality was patterned in some way on the Trinity.

Baxter himself provided an explanation for this development in his theology in the *Reasons, Methodus theologiae*, and the autobiographical *Reliquiae Baxterianae*. According to the *Reliquiae*, Baxter had been dissatisfied with the dichotomizing method of most dogmatic systems for twenty-six years, since they failed to do justice to the "Divine Trinity in Unity" expressed "in the whole Frame of Nature and Morality."[69] Assuming that these remarks from Part III of the *Reliquiae* date from shortly after 1670,[70] then according to Baxter's own account, his quest for a Trinitarian alternative to existing systems of theology dates back to the mid-1640s, just as he began his publishing career. We find a similar explanation of his Trinitarian development in the preface to the *Methodus theologiae*, written about a decade later. After describing his preference for organizing his theology according to a Trinitarian method, he likewise noted that for "almost forty years I devoted not the least part of my studies to seeking out the *true method* of theology."[71]

During these years of study for a true Trinitarian method, Baxter sifted through numerous authors. Among his contemporaries, Baxter looked to Comenius, Campanella, and Francis Glisson (d. 1677) as good examples for a Trinitarian method in nature, and to George Lawson's *Theo-politica* (1659) as a good example for a Trinitarian method in theology. In the domain of nature, Baxter found that Campanella, "and *Commenius* after him," had "made the fairest Attempt that I ever saw made" toward the expression of a Trinitarian method.[72] Most other philosophers, he complained, overlooked Trinitarian aspects to nature. However, Baxter found even these positive examples wanting. Campanella drew "ill-gathered consequences," while Comenius's natural philosophy was "undigested, with the mixture of crudities and mistakes," and Glisson "confound[ed] Spirits and Bodies."[73] Even Lawson, who had surpassed others in his Trinitarian method in theology, "had not hit on the true Method of the *Vestigia Trinitatis*."[74]

---

69. *Rel. Bax.*, III.69.

70. *Rel. Bax.*, III.1: "*Novemb.* 16. 1670. I began to add the Memorials following." Most of the *Reliquiae Baxterianae* was written in the mid-1660s. See N. H. Keeble, "Autobiographer as Apologist: *Reliquiae Baxterianae* (1696)," *Prose Studies* 9, no. 2 (1986): 105–19, at 110.

71. *MT*, "Praefatio," [A5r].

72. *Rel. Bax.*, III.69. Cf. Baxter, *Of the Nature of Spirits*, 25.

73. *TKL*, 20.

74. *Rel. Bax.*, III.69. Here Baxter also notes that Campanella had "many subsequent notions [beyond his three Principles], which were not provable or coherent." On Lawson's influence with respect to theological system, see Burton, *Hallowing of Logic*, 79–83.

Of these four authors, Comenius and Campanella certainly exercised the earliest influence and had a lasting impact on Baxter. Glisson's *Tractatus de natura substantiae energetica* (1672) and Lawson's *Theo-politica* (1659) appeared long after he began his search for a Trinitarian method. By contrast, Campanella's *Metaphysica* appeared in 1638, and Comenius's *Physicae ad lumen divinum reformatae synopsis* first appeared in 1633 (and in English translation in 1651). The earliest known positive reference to Campanella's Trinitarian metaphysics appears in *A Holy Commonwealth* (1659), a fact which suggests that Baxter began seriously considering Campanella in the late 1650s.[75]

Given Baxter's professed admiration for Comenius's pansophic project,[76] it is quite possible that Baxter was drawn to Campanella through his reading of Comenius. Indeed, in his *Physicae* Comenius himself described how he had eagerly read over Campanella's earlier works—including *Prodromus philosophiae instaurandae* (1617), *Realis philosophiae epilogisticae* (1623), and *De sensu rerum et magia* (1620)—only to be subsequently turned off by their lack of a Trinitarian approach to nature. "For his [i.e. Campanella's] very foundation, that all things were made up of two contrary principles onely, offended me. (For I was already most fully perswaded of the number of three principles out of the divine Book of *Genesis* ...)."[77] Although Comenius's evaluation antedates Campanella's *Metaphysica* (1638), his suggestive remarks could have directed Baxter to Campanella's *Metaphysica*, published shortly after Comenius's *Physicae* (1633). Baxter thus shared Comenius's interest both in Campanella and a Trinitarian approach to nature, but also saw Campanella's primalities in the *Metaphysica* (discussed below) as an improvement on Comenius's natural philosophy.

Besides the contemporary philosophical projects of Comenius, Campanella, and Glisson, Baxter was also well aware of the larger Augustinian roots of the Western *vestigia Trinitatis* tradition and drew positively on various medieval theologians. Given Baxter's preference for an integration between theology and natural philosophy as reflected in the tradition of Mosaic physics, it is unsurprising that he would find greater kinship with medieval scholastics than many modern philosophers. While the scholastics "contaminated sacred doctrine with their empty subtleties," Baxter wrote, echoing a long refrain among Reformed theologians, "I found no better philosophers than the scholastics."[78] Indeed, Baxter identified his

---

75. Baxter, *A Holy Commonwealth*, 131.

76. Baxter to Boyle, 14 June 1665, in Boyle, *Correspondence*, 2:473.

77. Comenius, *Naturall Philosophy*, sig. 3v. See also Comenius, *Reformation of Schooles*, 47, which mentions Campanella more briefly, and is discussed in Burton, *Hallowing of Logic*, 62.

78. *MT*, "Praefatio," [A5r]. On the scholastics' alleged corruption of theologial dogma, see *PRRD*, 1:195–97.

Trinitarian method not only with Campanella and Glisson, but also with "many of the scholastics."[79] The inspiration for Baxter's Trinitarian method, then, was not limited to philosophers such as Campanella but included the larger medieval scholastic tradition.

It is difficult to pin down exactly which of the medievals exercised the most influence on Baxter, since he engages with so many. Based on Baxter's comment that he "long ago read Lullius and many of his commentators"[80] and his reference to Ramon Lull's *Articula Fidei* and Ramon de Sebonde's *Theologia Naturalis* as examples of authors who identified the Trinity with the principles of power, wisdom, and goodness,[81] along with the assumption that Campanella fits into a broadly Lullist tradition, one scholar argues that Baxter's "decisive breakthrough" is a "Lullist turn as much as a Campanellan one."[82] Yet there is reason to be skeptical of such a specific "Lullist turn" in Baxter's development. Baxter referred to Lullist doctrine as "drowned in a multitude of irregular arbitrary notions," "palpably uncertain, and full of certain errours," among other critical remarks.[83] Moreover, in the same place in the *Reasons* where Baxter refers to Lull and Sebonde, he refers to numerous other patristic and medieval authors who make the same point.[84] Among these sources are *De statu domus Dei* of Potho Prumiensis (d. ca. 1170), *Speculum Ecclesiae* of Edmund of Canterbury (1175–1240), and *De tribus appropriatis personis in Trinitate* of Richard of St. Victor (d. 1173), all of whom Baxter cites at length.[85] He later advised readers "especially to peruse" these same medieval writers as cited in the *Methodus theologiae*.[86] In his *Life of Faith* (1670), Baxter singled out these three works, along with Ambrose, Origen, John of Damascus, and Bernard of Clairvaux, but to the exclusion of Lull and Sebonde.[87] If Lull had such a decisive influence on Baxter's thought, one naturally wonders why Baxter stressed these authors to a greater degree.

---

79. *MT*, "Praefatio," [A5v].

80. Richard Baxter, *Richard Baxter's Answer to Dr Edward Stillingfleet's Charge of Separation* (London: Nevil Simmons, 1680), 47–48.

81. *RCR*, 374, 377, 453.

82. Burton, *Hallowing of Logic*, 87.

83. Burton, *Hallowing of Logic*, 83. See *TKL*, 20, 48, 254; and *CD*, III.907–8, 919.

84. Burton, *Hallowing of Logic*, 86, 206–7.

85. *RCR*, 372–74. Cf. Richard of St. Victor, *De tribus appropriatis*, in *Opera* (Cologne: Apud Ioannem Gymnicum, 1621), 420–23. A 1650 edition was also available.

86. Baxter, *End of Doctrinal Controversies*, xx, citing *MT*, I.103.

87. Richard Baxter, *The Life of Faith* (London: R. W., 1670), 202.

Baxter interacts with the larger medieval tradition most fully in the *Methodus theologiae*.[88] While Baxter left "the many and exceedingly rash questions of the scholastics untouched,"[89] he moved quickly to the subject of the *vestigia Trinitatis* with the question: "Is there a trace of the Trinity [*Trinitatis Vestigium*] in created things, & in the Image [of God] in humanity?" His reply to this question refers to the authority of the church fathers, Augustine, Lombard, Aquinas, and most of the scholastics:

> So almost all the Fathers thought, especially Augustine [in] *De Trinitate* book 10 & 11 & 14, especially book 10, chapter 11, & almost all the Scholastics [on] Lombard, [*Sentences*, I,] dist. 3, especially [sections] F. G. pages 8, 9 [and] Aquinas [*Summa theologiae*,] I qu. 93, art. 1, 2, 4, 5, 6, 7, 8, where he shows that the *natural Image* of God is in *all things*, the *holy* Image is in the *Saints*, and the *glorious* Image is in the *glorified*; yet the *Image* of the Trinity is only in the *mind*; but in the same way a *trace* [*vestigium*] is in the lower faculties in other Creatures; and so there is no need to count almost all the interpreters of Master [Lombard], and to cite words or pages.[90]

Although Baxter appealed to this larger medieval tradition of *vestigia Trinitatis*, his account departed from the larger tradition on several points. He minimized differences between the *imago Dei* in humanity and the *vestigia* in the rest of the animate realm. In humanity, he gave preference to the triad of power, understanding, and will over Augustine's triad of memory, understanding, and will.[91] He was also critical of Augustine, Lombard, and those who followed them for denying that power, wisdom, and love could be attributed to the divine persons. Instead, Baxter was attracted to medieval theologians such as Guitmond of Aversa, Potho Prumiensis, Edmund of Canterbury, and Richard of St. Victor, who allowed an

---

88. *MT*, I.79–123 ("Disput. *De Trinitate Principiorum (seu Essentialitatem) & Personarum*").

89. *MT*, I.79.

90. *MT*, I.80: "Qu. III. *Utrum Trinitatis Vestigium in Creatis, & Imago in homine est? Resp.* Ita omnes ferè Patres statuerunt, & praecipuè Augustinus de Trinit. li. 10. & 11. & 14. praecipuè l. 10. cap. 11. & omnes ferè Scholastici. Lombard. dist. 3. praecipuè F. G. pag. 8, 9. Aquin. I. qu. 93. ar. 1, 2, 4, 5, 6, 7, 8. ubi probat *Imaginem* Dei *naturalem* esse in *omnibus*, Imaginem *Sanctam* in *Sanctis*, & *gloriosam* in *glorificatis*; etiam Trinitatis *Imaginem* esse in *mente* tantum; *vestigium* autem in facultatibus inferioribus sicut in aliis Creaturis; Et ita omnes ferè Magistri Interpretes quos enumerare, & verba aut paginas citare, non opus est." The reference to "F. G." is to sections F and G in Lombard's *Sentences*, I, dist. 3: "Quomodo in creaturis in apparet vestigium Trinitatis" (F) and "Quomodo in anima sit imago Trinitatis" (G). See, e.g., Peter Lombard, *Libri quatuor Sententiarum* (Paris: Jacob Du-puys, 1574), 9–10. I am grateful to Simon Burton for this clarification.

91. Burton, *Hallowing of Logic*, 197–98, 234.

appropriation of attributes to persons, although Baxter himself did not favor an exact identification between attributes and persons.[92]

The background to Baxter's doctrine of *vestigia Trinitatis* was not limited only to such medieval theologians, but included various Reformed precedents as well. It would appear that, despite the objections of a number of theologians to demonstrating the Trinity in a rational way, others took a more positive approach to natural analogies and the use of *vestigia*.[93] As Baxter's contemporary Robert Ferguson acknowledged to his personal dismay, "many" Reformed theologians, although granting that reason could not initially discover the doctrine of the Trinity, "yet being once Revealed, they contend that Reason cannot only Illustrate, but Demonstrate it."[94] Baxter was certainly aware of these theologians and noted that Bartholomäus Keckermann (c.1571–1608) "walks faithfully along with the *vestigia* of the Scholastics."[95] As we have already noted, he was also aware of Comenius's natural philosophy, which attributes power, wisdom, and goodness respectively to the Father, Son, and Spirit.[96]

As a young Puritan, Baxter would have also encountered the *vestigia* tradition among many of the early seventeenth-century English authors who sought to find vestiges of the Trinity in every part of the world. For example, in a sermon from 1620, John Donne preached, "It is a lovely and religious thing, to find out *Vestigia Trinitatis*, Impressions of the Trinity, in as many things as we can." These English authors found traces of the Trinity especially in the nature of the soul and in the structure of the natural world.[97] There exists at least one instance where Baxter

---

92. *MT*, I.103; Baxter, *End of Doctrinal Controversies*, xx; Burton, *Hallowing of Logic*, 205–6. On medieval approaches to attribution, see also Gilles Emory, *The Trinitarian Theology of Saint Thomas Aquinas*, trans. Francesca Aran Murphy (Oxford: Oxford University Press, 2007), 312–37.

93. *PRRD*, 4:157: "As with other doctrinal topics, one is impressed by the variety of formulation within confessional limits [on the *vestigia Trinitatis*]—belying the understanding, typical of the older scholarship, of Reformed orthodoxy as 'rigid' and monolithic."

94. Ferguson, *Interest of Reason*, 35, citing as examples of this view "Mornaeus, Keckerman, Claubergius, Bisterfield, &c." Ferguson personally finds their arguments "palpably Fallacious." Cf. Heinrich Heppe, *Reformed Dogmatics*, ed. Ernst Bizer, trans. G. T. Thomson (London: Allen & Ulwin, 1950), 106–9, and note the citation from Petrus van Mastricht (109): "Nor are there lacking some of ours who endeavour, if not to prove at least to declare the Trinity from the three primary attributes of God, power, wisdom and goodness; so, the Father is as it were God mighty, the Son wise, and H. Spirit good."

95. *MT*, I.114.

96. Comenius, *Naturall Philosophy*, 9, 24. There is a possible influence on Comenius from Campanella's primalities of power, wisdom, and goodness here. See Jaromír Cervenka, *Die Naturphilosophie des Johann Amos Comenius* (Hanau: Werner Dausien, 1970), 159n2.

97. Dennis R. Klinck, "*Vestigia Trinitatis* in Man and His Works in the English Renaissance," *Journal of the History of Ideas* 42, no. 1 (1981): 13–27, at 13. In addition to Klinck's examples,

explicitly drew on these native English sources. A marginal note in the *Methodus theologiae* cites a passage from the Cambridge Hebraist Joseph Mede's *Diatribae pars IV. Discourses on Sundry Texts of Scripture* (1652).[98] In the context of an exegesis of Jeremiah 10:11, Mede touched on the topic of natural theology, which he believed to be implied by the prophet in that place. This natural theology, claimed Mede, included an ascent by analogy from the faculties of humanity—understanding, will, and "faculties of working"—to the "threefold" perfections of their objects in wisdom, goodness, and power. Mede argued that by the "ordinary use of reason" all people can arrive at a conception of deity that includes wisdom, goodness, and power, but that they err both in the one to whom they ascribe such attributes and in whether the attributes belong to one or many deities.[99] We have here an adumbration of the type of argument from analogy that would come to characterize Baxter's writings several decades later.

Baxter's familiarity with both the wider scholastic tradition, contemporaries such as Comenius, and English authors such as Mede provides an important background to his positive reception of Campanella. Given the existence of this body of literature prior to Baxter, it is reasonable to assume that the arguments of medieval and early modern theologians for *vestigia Trinitatis* formed the theological context for Baxter's use of the Trinitarian metaphysics of Campanella. Such an explanation also agrees with Baxter's autobiographical comments that he longed for a Trinitarian method since the 1640s, long before he began employing Campanella's metaphysics in the 1660s.

Before proceeding to Baxter's construction of a Trinitarian view of the world, we should address Trueman's charge that by placing the doctrine of the Trinity "within the framework of a generalized metaphysics of being, a natural theology," Baxter opened the door toward a rationalist approach to the Trinity, whereby one might construct "a speculative doctrine of the Trinity on purely rational principles independent of special revelation."[100] In contrast to John Owen, who maintained a strict separation between knowledge of God the creator through reason and knowledge of the Trinity through faith, Trueman claims

---

see Nicholas Mosley, *ΨΥΧΟΣΟΦΙΑ: or, Natural and Divine Contemplations of the Passions & Faculties of the Soul of Man* (London: Humphrey Mosley, 1653), 38–43, who saw the tripartite Aristotelian soul as "an Embleme of the trine-une-God."

98. *MT*, I.33, citing Joseph Mede, *Diatribae pars IV. Discourses on Sundry Texts of Scripture* (London: J. F. for John Clark, 1652), 69.

99. Mede, *Diatribae*, 69.

100. Trueman, "Small Step," 192–93. Cf. Burton, *Hallowing of Logic*, 9–10, 202; Burton, "Faith, Reason, and the Trinity," 87–88, 99–100.

that Baxter represents "a distinctive move towards a more rationalistically oriented theology."[101] The citation that Trueman provides from Baxter's *Catholick Theologie* seems to lend support to this rationalist reading. After identifying the three "divine principles" of life, knowledge, and love (or *potentia-actus, intellectus,* and *voluntas*) as the "same with the Three Persons or Subsistences" of the Trinity, Baxter goes on to claim that these three principles "are so certainly evident to Natural Reason itself, that no understanding person can deny them, we have no Reason to think the Trinity of Eternal Subsistences incredible, and a thing that the Christian faith is to be suspected for, but quite the contrary; though they are mysteries above our reach (as all of God is, as to a full or formal apprehension)."[102]

At first glance, this statement appears rationalistic, as Baxter seems to indicate that the Trinity is "clearly evident to Natural Reason." However, on closer inspection, Baxter does not claim that the *persons* of the Trinity are known to reason, but only that some divine *attributes* (life, knowledge, and love) are available to human reason, which makes the Trinity more easy to believe ("no Reason to think the Trinity . . . incredible").[103] This reading is confirmed by a comparison with Baxter's *Reasons*, where he addresses the issue of the credibility of the Trinity. In answer to the anticipated objection "Will you pretend to prove the Trinity by natural reason?" Baxter responds,

> 1. It is one thing to *prove* the Sacred Trinity of Persons, by such reason (or to undertake *fully to open* the mystery) and it is another thing to prove that the Doctrine is neither *incredible* nor *unlikely* to be true; and that it implieth *no contradiction* or *discordancy*, but rather seemeth *very congruous* both to the frame of nature, and of certain moral verities. This only is my task against the Infidel.
>
> 2. It is one thing to shew in the creatures a clear demonstration of this Trinity of Persons, by shewing an effect that fully answereth it, and another thing to shew such *vestigia*, adumbration or image of it, as hath those dissimilitudes which must be allowed in any created image of God. This is it which I am to do.[104]

---

101. Trueman, "Small Step," 194. By 'rationalism' Trueman means "an unrestrained use of human reason and logic as the primary criteria for doctrinal construction and evaluation" (193).

102. *CT*, I/1.5.

103. *CT*, I/1.5.

104. *RCR*, 375.

Baxter goes on to dissent from those who believe that the Trinity "is no other than this uncontroverted Trinity of Essential Principles."[105] This is a position he repeats in his *Methodus theologiae*:

> That the Trinity of essentialities is the same as the Trinity of persons I have never affirmed in words, nor in my mind, and nor do I think it should be affirmed. I assert only this: while this Trinity of essentialities or primalities shows its footsteps through the whole nature of things, if it is not the Trinity of persons yet it renders it easily credible to mortals. For no reason can be given, when one Trinity in the unity of essence is most known to God from the light of nature, why another should remain in any way incredible.[106]

In other words, while the doctrine of the Trinity of persons is a mystery not demonstrable by natural reason, yet some effects of the Trinity in creation point to some distinctions in the Godhead—viz., power, wisdom, and goodness—that can be known to reason, and make the Trinity more credible. This basic intention to make mysteries (even the Trinity), first discovered apart from reason, later credible to reason, was hardly a novel idea. As Burton points out, this strategy "fits neatly into what Paul Thom has referred to as the 'Augustinian project' of demonstrating the logical consistency of the Trinity."[107] As Baxter noted approvingly, Aquinas reflected a similar perspective when he denied that the paternity, filiation, and procession of the divine persons could be known to reason, while "essential attributes appropriated to the persons" (power, wisdom, and goodness) were available to philosophical inquiry.[108] This is a view also found, for example, in Philippe de Mornay's preface to *De la verité de la religion chrestienne* (1581), an apologetic work commended by Baxter.[109] It also, of course, fits with Baxter's understanding of the relation between reason and revelation, according to which reason provides probable arguments for revealed truths (see chapter 3).

---

105. *RCR*, 377.

106. *MT*, I.121, as cited in Burton, "Faith, Reason, and the Trinity," 109; Burton, *Hallowing of Logic*, 244–45.

107. Burton, "Faith, Reason, and the Trinity," 97, citing Paul Thom, *The Logic of the Trinity: Augustine to Ockham* (New York: Fordham University Press, 2012), 20, 143.

108. Aquinas, *Summa theologiae*, Ia, q. 32, art. 1 ad 1, cited in *MT*, I.106. Cf. Emory, *Trinitarian Theology of Saint Thomas Aquinas*, 322–31.

109. Mornay, preface to *Trunesse*, B5v: "the reason I say (whereunto those mysteries were invisible afore) maketh them credible unto us." Mornay then provides the example of the Trinity (B6r). Cf. Richard Baxter, "A Premonition," in *SER2*, b4r; and *SER2*, II.194.

This nonrationalist reading of Baxter is further confirmed by his negative reaction to contemporary Trinitarian speculations, particularly the mystical speculations of John Pordage (1607–1681). This was a manifestation of his general polemic, expressed elsewhere, against claims to personal revelations independent of Scripture.[110] As a consistent critic of Pordage throughout his life, Baxter had no sympathy for the Trinitarian speculations and analogies of Pordage, "his Leader *Jacob Behmen*," and "other of the *German* Prophets, going near the same way."[111] After summarizing various Trinitarian notions from Pordage's *Theologia mystica, or, The Mystic Divinitie of the Aeternal Invisibles* (1683), Baxter objected in principle to mystics who "pretend to know such Mysteries by *Vision* and [personal] *Revelation.*" For his part, Baxter resolved "to take Christ for my sufficient and infallible Teacher; and to pretend to know no more of the Deity and unseen World, than he hath thought meet to reveal."[112] The priority of Scripture over personal or philosophical speculation is a point he reiterated against the Platonist speculations of Henry More and John Turner. He thought that their opinions were the result of overconfidence in rational speculation beyond supernatural revelation, and contained "a mixture of *Platonisme, Origenisme & Arrianisme*, not having *all* of any of these, but somewhat of *all.*"[113]

Baxter's polemics against Pordage, More, and Turner demonstrate that Baxter himself was wary of proceeding farther in his Trinitarian speculation than he believed to be warranted from Scriptural revelation.

Trinitarian Analogy of Being

While Baxter certainly drew on an older tradition of *vestigia Trinitatis*, he also grounded this relation in a doctrine of analogy between God and creation. For those familiar with the medieval debates over whether God is conceived in an equivocal, univocal, or analogical way, Baxter's approach to this matter is, at first sight, somewhat puzzling.[114] On the one hand, in a seemingly anti-Scotist move, he argues that all of God's attributes are either equivocal or

110. For Baxter's general objection to personal revelations, see his *The Cure of Church-Divisions* (London: Nevil Symmons, 1670), 164–68.

111. Baxter, *End of Doctrinal Controversies*, xxi.

112. Baxter, *End of Doctrinal Controversies*, xxi–xxii. On Baxter's evaluation of Pordage, see Ariel Hessayon, *'Gold Tried in the Fire'. The Prophet Theaurau John Tany and the English Revolution* (Burlington, VT: Ashgate, 2007), 306–7, 329.

113. DWL BT IV.87, fol. 228r. See chapter 2.

114. For medieval background, see E. J. Ashworth, "Analogy and Equivocation in the Thirteenth-Century: Aquinas in Context," *Mediaeval Studies* 54 (1992): 94–135; Ashworth, "Analogy, Univocation, and Equivocation in Some Early Fourteenth-Century Authors," in *Aristotle in Britain during the Middle Ages*, ed. John Marenbon (Belgium: Brepols, 1996), 233–47; Stephen Dumont, "Scotus's Doctrine of Univocity and the Medieval Tradition of

analogical, while disavowing any univocal relationship between God and creatures. On the other hand, he argues that the concept of being (*ens*) is said univocally of God and creatures, and cites Scotus. A clear statement of this view is found in his *End of Controversies* (1691), where he asserts that our conceptions of God "are called analogical, aequivocal, metaphorical, or by similitude. Neither *Substantia, Vita, Perfectio, Potentia, Actus, Intellectus, Voluntas, Love, Truth, Goodness, Mercy* &c. are formally and univocally the same in God and the Creature: *Scotus* excepteth only *ENS*. Which is true, as *ENS* is only a Logical term, signifying no more than *EST* or *Quoddity*, and not *QUID est*, or Quiddity."[115] The basic elements of this perspective date all the way back to his *Reduction of a Digressor* (1654), which constitutes not only the earliest but also the most detailed discussion of the matter.[116] There he defended the proposition that God's "Acting, and Understanding, and Willing are by a very, very, very low remote Analogy ascribed to him."[117] Throughout his later manuscripts and published works, Baxter consistently maintained this view.[118]

It has been argued that since Baxter cites Scotus and later Scotists, his view of analogy between God and creatures expressed here is basically Scotist and in harmony with the views of Scotus himself.[119] However, against this stands the fact that, unlike Baxter, Scotus held that not only *ens* but also other attributes such as wisdom, intellect, and will are conceived univocally of God and creatures.[120] Moreover, in his *Reduction*, Baxter affirms, citing with approval Aquinas's *De veritate* and Zanchi's *De natura Dei*, that God and creatures are conceived neither *univocè* nor *purè aequivocè*, but rather according to analogy of proportionality

Metaphysics," in *Was ist Philosophie im Mittelalter?*, ed. Jan Aertsen and Andreas Speer (Berlin: De Gruyter, 1998), 193–212; Timotheus A. Barth, "Being, Univocity, and Analogy According to Duns Scotus," in *John Duns Scotus, 1265–1965*, ed. John K. Ryan and Bernardine M. Bonansea (Washington, DC: CUA Press, 1965), 210–62; and Richard Cross, "Where Angels Fear to Tread: Duns Scotus and Radical Orthodoxy," *Antonianum* 76 (2001): 7–41.

115. Baxter, *End of Doctrinal Controversies*, viii.

116. Baxter, *Reduction*, 29–37. On p. 70, Baxter anticipates his later Scotist exception of the univocity of *ens*.

117. Baxter, *Reduction*, 29.

118. DWL BT VI.194; DWL BT XIX.351, fols. 41v, 71v–72v, 122r; DWL BT IV.87, fols. 231v–232r; Baxter, *Of the Nature of Spirits*, 42–43, 51, 74–75, 82; *CT*, I/1.2; II.6; III.25; *MT*, I.31, 82, 118.

119. Burton, *Hallowing of Logic*, 210–15; Burton, "Faith, Reason, and the Trinity," 108–9.

120. E.g., Duns Scotus, *Ordinatio* I, dist. 3, q. 2, in *Opera omnia*, 9:21; Duns Scotus, *Philosophical Writings*, ed. and trans. Alan Wolter (Indianapolis: Hackett, 1987), 25. Cf. Richard Cross, *Duns Scotus* (Oxford: Oxford University Press, 1999), 38; William E. Mann, "Duns Scotus on Natural and Supernatural Knowledge of God," in *The Cambridge Companion to Duns Scotus*, ed. Thomas Williams (Cambridge: Cambridge University Press, 2003), 238–62, at 245–48. I am grateful to Richard Muller for clarification on this point.

(*analogiam proportionalitatis*) and not analogy of attribution.[121] These are Thomist points.[122] Baxter's use of Zanchi indicates his early affirmation of Reformed scholastics on this point. Zanchi and a host of other Reformed scholastics, as Richard Muller has recently demonstrated, identified with Aquinas over against Scotus on analogy of being.[123]

If Baxter's position disagrees with Scotus's affirmation that creaturely wisdom and will should be attributed univocally to God, while also citing Thomistic points on analogy favorably, how are we to understand his positive citations to Scotists, particularly his assertion that "*Scotus* excepteth only *ENS*"?[124] The solution would appear to be that Baxter was drawing upon certain later Scotists, such as Peter of Aquila (d. 1361), who attempted a harmonization of Aquinas and Scotus on analogy. Accordingly, Baxter downplays differences between Scotists and Thomists on analogical concepts and reduces their controversy to the concept of being: "Whether the being [*ens*] of God and creatures is said univocally or only analogically is debated among Thomists and Scotists: But for the rest, it is agreed among all that no formal and univocal concepts of God are to be found in the intellect of mortals but only analogical."[125] Elsewhere Baxter says of the debate between the Scotists and "other schoolmen": "I am apt thus to comprimize it" by denying that univocity applies in a physical sense ("*ens physicum*") to whatness ("ad *Quid*"), understood as the "constitutive cause as a Genus to *substantia* et *Accid[?ens]*," but affirming that it applies in a logical sense to the affirmation of existence ("equall to *Est*").[126] Additionally, Baxter agreed with various Scotists that there is no mean between equivocation and univocity, with the result that analogy should be understood as a species of equivocation.[127]

---

121. Baxter, *Reduction*, 35.

122. Muller, "Not Scotist," 142–43. Cf. Joshua P. Hochschild, *The Semantics of Analogy: Rereading Cajetan's De nominum analogia* (Notre Dame, IN: University of Notre Dame Press, 2010), 122–60.

123. Muller, "Not Scotist," 127–50.

124. Baxter, *End of Doctrinal Controversies*, viii.

125. *MT*, I.31. The marginal note cites Scotus "in 1. Sent. d. 3. q. 2"; Aquinas, *Summa theologiae*, Ia, q. 13, art. 5; "Aquil. Scotel. in 1 Sent. d. 3. q. 1. p. 46, &c." (Peter of Aquila, *Scotellus. Ubi non tantum ad Scoti subtilitates, sed etiam ad D. Thomae, reliquorumque scholasticorum doctrinam facilis via paratur* [Paris: Nicolaum Nivellium 1585], 46–57); "Phil. Fabr. Favent. Phil. Scot. de Ente." (Filippo Fabri, *Philosophia naturalis Ioan. Duns Scoti, ex quatuor libris sententiarum et quodlibetis collecta* [Venice: Bertonus, 1606], 654–74 [Theorem. 95]); among others. On Peter of Aquila, see Stephen D. Dumont, "Transcendental Being: Scotus and Scotists," *Topoi* 11 (1992): 135–48, at 143–44.

126. DWL BT IV.87, fols. 231v–232r.

127. *MT*, I.46, 118, as noted in Burton, *Hallowing of Logic*, 212–13.

Baxter's doctrine of analogy is thus an eclectic harmonization, or, as he himself calls it, a "comprimize," of the views of Thomists and Scotists. He appears to allow for a limited univocal conception of God's being as quoddity or "thatness" (not quiddity or "whatness"), while arguing for an explicitly non-univocal, analogical approach to all other concepts of God, which presses Thomistic analogy into the category of equivocity—all the while arguing with Aquinas against purely equivocal concepts of God. Although this leans in a Thomist direction, it is not purely Thomist, for Baxter does identify *ens* as a univocal concept for God and creatures. Nor is it identical with the teaching of Scotus, for whom wisdom, intellect, and will are considered univocal concepts. Yet despite this eclecticism, the fact that Baxter, like many of his Reformed contemporaries, endorsed an analogical understanding of the divine attributes, renders problematic the view of Brad Gregory that Protestants generally held a univocal doctrine of divine knowledge leading to a "disenchanted natural world."[128]

We should also note that Baxter modifies the view of Reformed contemporaries who held to a Thomist paradigm with respect to the three *viae* of knowing God: the way of causality (*via causalitatis*), the way of eminence (*via eminentiae*), and the way of negation (*via negationis*).[129] In place of this, Baxter presents three kinds of knowledge of God: general concepts, the way of eminence (*via eminentiae*), and the way of negation (*via negationis*). Baxter equates the way of eminence with "Metaphorical Conceptions by way of Similitude," so this second way derives, as it does with the wider tradition, from his doctrine of analogy. The first way of general concepts, he explains, is not a univocal notion of God's substance, but is also by "similitude," thereby in effect subsuming this first way as a special case of *via eminentiae*.[130] The priority of an analogous general concept of God's substance here may derive from the priority Baxter places on the knowledge of existence over that of essence.[131]

While Baxter thus shared a broadly analogical approach with the wider Reformed tradition, he thought that nature reflects a particularly Trinitarian analogy of God's power, wisdom, and goodness. Once Baxter was convinced that the activity of God *ad extra* reflected God's *ad intra* perfections of power, wisdom,

---

128. Gregory, *Unintended Reformation*, 41. Gregory's claim seems to derive in part from a similar argument in Funkenstein, *Theology and the Scientific Imagination*, 70–72. See Gregory, *Unintended Reformation*, 5, 39, 55. For a devastating critique of Gregory on this point, see Muller, "Not Scotist," 127–50, esp. 128–30, 146.

129. *PRRD*, 3:166–67, 216–17, 220–21.

130. Baxter, *End of Doctrinal Controversies*, i–iv, ix.

131. See chapter 3.

and goodness,[132] his analogical approach led logically to the conclusion that something reflecting these three attributes should be discoverable in every aspect of nature. As he wrote in more than one place, "[I]t is a most great and certain Truth, that this Sacred Trinity of Divine *Principles*, have made their impress communicatively upon the *Frame of Nature*, and most evidently on the *noblest Parts*, which are in excellency nearest their Creator."[133] The "noblest parts" that Baxter has in mind are human souls, which, along with the rest of creation, reflect God's communicable attributes. With respect to nature in general, Baxter understands the being and motion of things as reflective of God's power, the order of things as reflective of God's wisdom, and the goodness and perfections of things as reflective of God's will or love. Likewise, he views humanity's being, nature, and natural motion as reflecting God's power, human order and wisdom as reflecting God's wisdom, and human perfection and love as reflecting God's goodness or love.[134]

While it is true, as we shall discuss below, that Baxter drew upon Campanella's primalities as a philosophical expression of this Trinitarian analogical communication of God's attributes, the theological antecedents to this aspect of Baxter's thought in the Reformed tradition have been inadequately appreciated. By Baxter's time, a triad of communicable attributes was already well established in Reformed dogmatics: life, intellect, and will.[135] Philippe de Mornay, in his apologetic *De la verité de la religion chrestienne* (1581), which Baxter took as an example for his own apologetics, even anticipated Baxter by stating that, beyond the other *vestigia*, the soul's life (or power), intellect, and will constitute a "much more lively, and more expresse" "image and likenesse of the Trinitie."[136] For the Reformed, life includes activity and self-motion, while intellect includes wisdom and knowledge, and will includes freedom and goodness. This triad was ready-made for Baxter's Trinitarian theology.

If the selection of these attributes, and particularly the *vita Dei*, reflect the "results of Reformation-era exegesis" that sought to develop the divine attributes explicitly on biblical terms,[137] Baxter was no exception. He consistently opposed theological speculation about God's nature and acts apart from revelation (see chapter 3), and his use of biblical terminology for God's attributes is consistent

---

132. Cf. *MT*, I.134; *RCR*, 376–77. He agrees with Reformed orthodoxy that works *ad extra* are undivided. See Baxter, *More Reasons*, 97: "True: *Opera Trinitatis ad extra sunt indivisa*." Cf. *PRRD*, 4:267–74.

133. Baxter, *Life of Faith*, 202. Cf. *RCR*, 374; *MT*, "Praefatio," [A5v].

134. *CT*, II.230.

135. *PRRD*, 3:365–68.

136. Mornay, *Trunesse*, 65. Cf. note 109 above.

137. *PRRD*, 3:373.

with this position. He referred to the frequently appearing biblical terms *life, light,* and *love* to support his choice of vital power, intellect, and will as foundational to his understanding of God and humanity. As he concluded his preface to *Methodus theologiae*:

> I generally better attend to the world, where the essential, first, infinite LIFE, LIGHT, LOVE, will perfectly communicate *life, light, love,* (1) John 5.26. & 1.4. Rev. 11.11. Col. 3. (2) 1 John 1.5. Rev. 22.5. (3) 1 John 4.7, 8, 12, 16. *Amen.*[138]

Later in the *Methodus theologiae,* he referred to an even more expansive list of biblical references.[139] Many of these passages recur throughout the writings of other Reformed orthodox authors as biblical grounds for these communicable attributes.[140]

Baxter's continuity with the Reformed tradition's identification, ordering, and biblical support of the three main divisions of communicable attributes is striking. Yet this aspect of Baxter's continuity with the Reformed tradition has been neglected by those who have rightly also noted similarity in this respect with Campanella, thereby producing a rather one-sided picture of Baxter's thought in this matter as derived entirely from philosophical antecedents extrinsic to his own Reformed tradition.[141] Instead, Baxter's continuity in this respect with the wider Reformed tradition can further explain his attraction to, and eclectic use, of Campanella. For it is most likely that Baxter, having been immersed in Reformed theology long before showing any interest in Campanella, discovered in Campanella's primalities a structural similarity with the Reformed approach to the communicable attributes.

Baxter complemented his understanding of a threefold analogy of power, wisdom, and goodness with a closely related concept of threefold causality in God's relation to creation. That is, God acts as the efficient creating cause, the governing

---

138. *MT,* "Praefatio," [A6v]. Cf. Baxter, *End of Doctrinal Controversies,* v–vi.

139. *MT,* I.31–32: on *vita Dei* (John 5:26; 1:4; 14:6; 1 John 1:2; Num. 14:21, 28; Isa. 49:18; Jer. 22:24; Ezek. 5:11; 14:16, 18, 20; 16:48; 33:11, 27); on light or wisdom (1 John 1:5; James 1:17; Proverbs [8]; John 1:4); on love or will (1 John 1:8, 16).

140. See, e.g., *PRRD,* 3:373–78 (John 1:4 and 5:26 on *vita Dei*), 394 (1 John 1:5 on light as knowledge).

141. Trueman, "Small Step," 189–92, assumes an entirely Campanellian influence. Burton, *Hallowing of Logic,* 216–17, offers a more balanced approach, noting these three communicable attributes, their Scriptural justification, and similarity to Campanella. Cf. Burton, "Faith, Reason, and the Trinity," 100–103, 106.

cause of all wisdom and order, and the final cause of goodness and perfection.[142] Throughout his life—and already in the *Reformed Pastor*—Baxter was fond of referring to those passages in Scripture that refer to God as the Alpha and Omega (Rev. 1:8), in whom we live and move and have our being (Acts 17:28), and from whom and through whom and to whom are all things (Rom. 11:36; 1 Cor. 8:6).[143] He appealed especially to Romans 11:36 to support God's threefold causal relation to the world. For example, in the *Catholick Theologie*, he wrote,

> God's Causal Relations to his Creatures, are in General those named by St. *Paul, Rom.* 11.36. OF HIM and THROUGH HIM and TO HIM are all things. And his is, 1. The first EFFICIENT, 2. The supream DIRIGENT, 3. The Ultimate FINAL Cause of all things.[144]

This reading of Romans 11:36 as implying causal relations had various traditional precedents. Thomas Aquinas, for example, read the verse as indicating God as efficient cause (appropriated to the Father), formal cause (appropriated to the Son), and final cause (appropriated to the Holy Spirit).[145] In Reformed biblical commentaries, exegetes often discussed the Trinity and God's causal relation to the world in their interpretation of Romans 11:36. Over against any hint of Arian subordination of Christ in the work of creation, these exegetes typically followed the church fathers in their view that the entire Trinity is the efficient and final cause of the world. However, they dissented from those fathers who ascribed the prepositions "from" (ἐξ, *ex*), "through" (διὰ, *per*), and "to" (εἰς, *in*) to particular persons of the Trinity; the patristic exegesis on this point appeared to them "forced" (Vermigli) or "too curious" (Willet, Alting).[146] It is not entirely clear

---

142. *MT*, I.15, 30–31, 244, 252; *MT*, II.85, 94, 156, 258.

143. Baxter, *Gildas Salvinus*, 265, 269–70; *MT*, I.30; also *MT*, I.87, 252, 267. Cf. Comenius, *Reformation of Schooles*, 21.

144. *CT*, I.5. Cf. Baxter, *End of Doctrinal Controversies*, iii; Richard Baxter, *A Paraphrase on the New Testament with Notes, Doctrinal and Practical* (London: B. Simmons and Tho. Simmons, 1685), Rom. 11:36, *loc. cit.*

145. Aquinas, *Summa theologiae*, Ia, q. 39, art. 8. Cf. Emory, *Trinitarian Theology of Saint Thomas Aquinas*, 313, 318, 350.

146. Wolfgang Musculus, *In epistolam apostoli Pauli ad Romanos commentarii* (Basel: ex officina Hervagiana, 1562), 206; Peter Martyr Vermigli, *In epistolam S. Pauli apostoli ad Romanos* (Zürich, 1559), 870; David Pareus, *In divinam S. Pauli apostoli Romanos epistolam commentarius* (Frankfurt: Jona Rhodius, 1608), cols. 1143–44; Willet, *Romanes*, 518; Jacob Alting, *Opera omnia theologica analytica, exegetica, practica, problematica & philologica* (Amsterdam: Gerardus Borstius, 1686), 4:169–71. On patristic interpretations, see Lewis Ayres, "From Him, through Him and in Him," in *Augustine and the Trinity* (Cambridge: Cambridge University Press, 2010), 42–71.

whether Baxter went so far as to attribute the prepositions to particular persons such as one finds in Aquinas, but he clearly shared with Reformed theologians and the wider tradition a reading of Romans 11:36 as indicating God's causal relation to the world.

Trinities in Nature
Baxter's Eclectic Reception of Tommaso Campanella

Although the attempt to identify *vestigia Trinitatis* in nature already had a long pedigree prior to Baxter, the systematic construction of a Trinitarian metaphysics was a difficult proposition in an era dominated by Aristotelian metaphysics. Aristotle's dichotomy of *potentia* and *actus* and fourfold causality are not easily conformed to a Trinitarian mold. Tommaso Campanella (1568–1639), who from an early age absorbed the anti-Aristotelian philosophy of Bernardino Telesio (1509–1588), freely broke with Aristotelian metaphysics and natural philosophy.[147] He was therefore able to radically reconstruct metaphysics and natural philosophy in a curious mix of Trinitarian notions and Telesio's philosophy. Campanella took from Telesio the doctrine of panpsychism or pansensism (in which all creatures from humans to stones are endowed with sense perception) and a view of nature in which heat and cold operating on passive matter, rather than Aristotelian form, are responsible for physical change.[148] At the same time, he reconceptualized the nature of being as consisting of essentially three "primalities" or principles of being: power, knowledge, and love. For Campanella, these principles correspond on the one hand to three faculties in all beings—potential, cognitive, and volitional—and on the other hand to three objects—being, truth, and goodness. This Trinitarian metaphysics is linked to the theory of pansensism through the primality of knowledge, which forms the metaphysical basis for the presence of perception in every being.[149]

Despite this radical reconstruction of being, Campanella did not construct de novo his theory of the causal activity of these principles. In fact, he manipulated Aristotelian fourfold causality to conform to three basic genera corresponding to the activity of the three primalities. He linked the primality of power with efficient

---

147. Germana Ernst, "Telesius me delectavit," in *Tommaso Campanella: The Book and the Body of Nature*, trans. David L. Marshall (Dordrecht: Springer, 2010), 1–14.

148. Bernardino M. Bonansea, *Tommaso Campanella: Renaissance Pioneer of Modern Thought* (Washington, DC: The Catholic University of America Press, 1969), 15, 156–61, 193.

149. Bonansea, *Campanella*, 144–65. The full explication of the three primalities is found in Tommaso Campanella, *Metaphysica* (Paris, 1638; repr., Torino: Bottega D'Erasmo, 1961), Pars 2, VI.v (first primality); VI.vii–ix (second primality); VI.x (third primality); and VI.xi (treating all three in summary). The treatise on the second primality contains two separate chapters on pansensism (VI.viii–ix).

and material causes, which produce respectively the effects of action and quantity. He joined the primality of knowledge to the ideal cause constituting the pattern according to which things are made (reflecting the Platonic and Augustinian divine ideas tradition) and the formal cause that produces quality. He linked the primality of love to the final cause according to which an agent acts in itself and the perfective cause according to which a thing is perfected even apart from its own activity.[150] This latter distinction between final and perfective cause reflects the scholastic distinction of the end of the work (*finis operis*) and end of the one who works (*finis operantis*).[151] Thus, Campanella's theory of causality joins four causes derived from Aristotle and two derived from scholastic tradition, and places them upon a Trinitarian frame of being.

Baxter was hardly impressed with Campanella's philosophy as a whole. This is not surprising, given not only Baxter's view of the noetic effects of the fall resulting in errors and uncertainties among philosophers, but also the importance of revelation for philosophy as reflected in his endorsement of Mosaic physics. Thus he advised an eclectic attitude toward natural philosophy. "Choose out so much of the *Certainties* and *Useful* parts of *Physicks* as you can reach to," he counseled his readers, "and make them know their places in subserviency to your holy principles and ends."[152] As we noted in chapter 3, Baxter dismissed most of the anti-Aristotelian natural philosophy running from Francesco Patrizi (1529–1597) to Telesio and Campanella as "Phanatical." Baxter specifically referred to Campanella's "mistaken superstructures, as that no true Body of Physicks can be gathered out of all his works."[153] Such sentiments are repeated in the *Methodus theologiae*, albeit with a more positive indication of what sources Baxter found useful to his eclecticism.

> From the reading of Campanella (especially his Metaphysics) there suddenly appeared to me a considerable amount of light: I perceived that his *primalities*, or three principles of active things, did not lack reason & evidence. But I concluded that his doctrine (and of Telesius himself) on the efficiency of *heat* and *cold*, as well as on the sense of passive things, with several other worthless consequences, and fanatical or rancorous assumptions, must be entirely rejected. But if those things which D. Glisson wrote on the *life of nature*, are applied to *active natures* alone, as distinct from the merely passive natures; and those things could be singled out which

---

150. Bonansea, *Campanella*, 183–89. See Campanella, *Metaphysica*, Pars 1, II.ii.2, for a summary of the causes and II.iii.2 on the divine ideas tradition.

151. Bonansea, *Campanella*, 186; Campanella, *Metaphysica*, Pars 1, II.ix.1–2.

152. *CD*, III.919 (q. 173).

153. *CD*, III.919 (q. 173).

Mousnerius with others rightly said of *motion, Telesius* and *Campanella* of *heat*, and *Patricius* of *light*, and *L. Le Grand* of *fire*, while taking away the bad additions, I certainly think this would constitute an outstanding work, provided that it were arranged by a method suitable to the topics.[154]

As these passages make plain, Baxter was unimpressed with most of Campanella's natural philosophy, with the important exception of Campanella's primalities (power, knowledge, and love). And even with respect to the primalities, he did not altogether accept Campanella's doctrine. Baxter was only interested in Campanella's doctrine of the primalities as it applied to the realm of living and active things and as stripped of pansensism.[155] This discriminating and eclectic appropriation of Campanella's philosophy points to the importance of prior theological commitments with respect to *vestigia Trinitatis*, and prior philosophical commitments in his division of active and passive things. Campanella's primalities provided Baxter with a useful metaphysical expression of his desire to find a reflection of the Trinity in the realm of "active things."

Threefold Causality

We have already seen that Baxter appealed to Romans 11:36 as a basis for God's causal relation to the world. This triune causality also had its analog in the

---

154. *MT*, "Praefatio," [A5r]: "Ex lectione Campanellae (praecipue ejus Metaphysices) lucis nonnihil mihi emicuit: *Primalitates* ejus, seu trina rerum activarum principia ratione & probatione non carere percepi. Ipsius autem (& Telesii sui) doctrinam de *Caloris* & *Frigoris* efficientiâ, *de sensu rerum* etiam passivarum, cum pluribus aliis consequentiis inanibus, & fanaticis seu melancholicis praesumptionibus, omnino reprobandam duxi. Sin autem quae D. Glissonus de *Vita Naturae* scripsit, ad *Naturas Activas* solas, ut à mere passivis distinctas, applicentur; & quae *Mousnerius* cum aliis de *Motu, Telesius* & *Campanella* de *Calore*, & *Patricius* de *Lumine*, & L. *Le Grand de Igne* recte dixêrunt seligantur, malis additionibus amputatis, egregium quidem opus haec constituta existimo, modò Methodo rebus congruâ componeretur." Petrus Mousnerius, student of the Jesuit Honoré Fabri (c.1607–1688), transcribed lectures by Fabri in *Tractatus physicus de motu locali* (Lyon: Joannes Champion, 1646). The attribution of authorship on the title page of this work reads, "*Auctore Petro Movsnerio Doctore Medico: cvncta excerpta Ex praelectionibus R. P. Honorati Fabry, Societatis Iesv.*" Thus, although Fabri's doctrine was properly the source of this work, Baxter attributed it to Mousnerius. "L. Le Grand" is Jean-François Le Grand, whose *Dissertationes philosophicae et criticae* (Paris: Petrus Menard, 1657) Baxter cites in *RCR*, 516.

155. DWL BT XIX.351, fol. 133r: "For neither *culinary* nor *vegetative* fire shew yᵉ least signes of *Sensation* or *Intellection* (wᵗever Campanella say *de Sensu Rerum*)"; *RCR*, 513. Cf. Guido Giglioni, "Pansychism versus Hylozoism: An Interpretation of Some Seventeenth-Century Doctrines of Universal Animation," *Acta Comeniana* 11 (1995): 25–45, at 40: "Like Comenius (and Glisson, to a certain extent), Baxter refers to Campanella's metaphysics, in particular to his three first *primalities*. Unlike Comenius, he rejects Campanella's cosmic pansensism, attributing active qualities only to spiritual substances."

domain of creaturely secondary causality. Baxter discussed the nature of causality in various places, but his most extensive treatment is found in chapter 1 of the *Methodus theologiae*, even before he discussed the relation between faith and reason. Sebastian Rehnman has remarked on this chapter, "I have never seen such extensive use of causality as that found in Baxter."[156] Baxter's treatment of causality reflects both an original attempt to impose Trinitarian order on reality and his use of rather traditional scholastic terminology and definitions.

Although Baxter retained the explanatory force of all four of the Aristotelian causes in that he explained the principles of change by reference to the elements of agency (efficient), matter, form, and end, in his foundational schema of causality he combined explanations of form and matter into what he called the "constitutive" (*constitutiva*) cause. Thus, he holds that there are essentially three causes: efficient, constitutive, and final.[157] Drawing on a scholastic distinction between univocal and equivocal causes, Baxter states that these causes, whether inaccurately enumerated as fourfold or correctly as threefold, are not univocal but rather equivocal.[158] Scholastics thought of equivocal causes as nobler, universal, or prior kinds of causes that produce effects of a different kind, whereas univocal causes are particular causes that produce effects of the same kind. Aquinas, for example, referred to the sun as the equivocal cause of fire, whereas fire is the univocal cause of fire.[159] Baxter's elaboration of causality in chapter 1 of the *Methodus theologiae* therefore refers to causality in this most universal sense.

In his account of efficient causality, Baxter does not entirely depart from the scholastics, but instead imprints a distinctive Trinitarian stamp upon common scholastic distinctions. He begins by distinguishing between primary and subordinate (derivative) efficient causes.[160] He also uses a scholastic distinction

---

156. Rehnman, *Divine Discourse*, 32n58. Cf. Burton, *Hallowing of Logic*, 130–46.

157. *MT*, I.4.

158. *MT*, I.4, 9. Baxter does not call his causes univocal, as stated by Burton, *Hallowing of Logic*, 130. Cf. *Rel. Bax.*, Appendix, 24, where Baxter contrasts *causum univocum* as an equal cause with *causam equivocam* as unequal.

159. Thomas Aquinas, *The Power of God*, trans. Richard J. Regan (Oxford: Oxford University Press, 2012), q. 7, art. 1 ad 8 (p. 195); *Summa theologiae*, Ia, q. 13, art. 5 ad 1; q. 25, art. 2 ad 2; Francisco Suárez, *On Efficient Causality: Metaphysical Disputations 17, 18, and 19*, trans. Alfred J. Freddoso (New Haven, CT: Yale University Press, 1994), 32 (Disp. XVII.ii.21); Christopher Scheibler, *Metaphysica* (Geneva: Jacob Stoer, 1636), 290–91; Rodolphus Goclenius, *Lexicon philosophicum* (Frankfurt: Matthew Becker, 1613), 357–58 (s.v. "Causa Univoca & Aequivoca"); Johannes Micraelius, *Lexicon philosophicum terminorum philosophis usitatorum* (Jena: J. Mamphrasius, 1653), col. 213 (s.v. "Causa").

160. *MT*, I.4. Cf. Scheibler, *Metaphysica*, 292–93.

between necessary and moral efficient causes to distinguish different ways in which efficient causes manifest themselves.[161] Efficient causes effect *necessarily* by means of power (the "most famous" sense), but *morally* by means of wisdom and love. As coordinated with the Campanellan primalities of power, wisdom, and love, efficient causes effect by forces of power (*per vires potentiae*), by the light of wisdom (*per lumen sapientiae*), and by love or goodness (*per amorem seu bonitatem*). The effect by the light of wisdom refers to the primary illumination of the mind by evidence, while the effect by love refers to the secondary effect of volitional attraction to objective goodness. In this way, Baxter applies a Trinitarian order of power, wisdom, and love to the distinction between efficient causes that involve the exercise of free choice and those that work from necessity.[162]

Baxter refers to the constitutive cause as an "Effect of the Efficient," that is, what is produced by the efficient cause. Constitutive causes signify a range of realities, whether simple or composite things, spiritual or corporeal things, substantial or accidental forms. He also uses constitutive causes synonymously with the various principles of a substance, as when he describes passive natures as having "three Principles or Constitutive Causes" (matter, disposition, form).[163] Although the attribution of "cause" to the constituted union of matter and form was rather untraditional, Baxter's choice of the term *constitutiva* was by no means unique. For example, in his account of Mosaic physics, Alsted described the internal "constitutive principle" (*principium constitutivum*) of nature as "partly prime matter and partly form."[164]

While we will discuss the active and passive natures of constitutive causes in more detail below, a few words are in order about his thoughts on final causality. Baxter's understanding of final causality has much in common with contemporary accounts, well represented by Francisco Suárez, which, while assuming that nature acts for an end, place an emphasis on efficient causality as the source of motion.[165] Suárez held that the final cause is a "metaphorical motion" and limited final causality to rational agents. In contrast to efficient causality, which

---

161. See Suárez, *On Efficient Causality*, 16–17, 269–300 (Disp. XVII.ii.6; XIX.i–ii); Micraelius, *Lexicon philosophicum*, col. 213 (s.v. "causa").

162. *MT*, I.4–5. Cf. Suárez, *On Efficient Causality*, 280 (Disp. XIX.i.12); Burton, *Hallowing of Logic*, 132–34.

163. *MT*, I.5.

164. Alsted, *Physica harmonica*, 17: "*Principium constitutivum est tum Materia prima, tum Forma.*"

165. See Mary Richard Reif, "Natural Philosophy in Some Early Seventeenth Century Scholastic Textbooks" (PhD diss., Saint Louis University, 1962), 191–210, who discusses a number of Reformed philosophers.

Suárez argued properly bestows *esse* on an effect, the final cause "causes only by means of a metaphorical motion insofar as it is an end."[166] By this "metaphorical motion," Suárez did not deny the reality of final causality, and he arguably even held to the priority of final over efficient causality. The final cause exercises causality by the attractive power of the end, even though the actual causality is brought about by the efficient cause.[167] And although Suárez restricted final causality to rational agents, he included a teleological account of irrational nature through its participation in the agency of God who created things with dispositions for ends.[168] The notion that irrational agents are directed toward their proper ends by the agency of God who works by instilling instincts and inclinations in creatures was also shared by Reformed philosophers, including Gilbert Jacchaeus and Alsted.[169]

Although the exact source of his views on final causality remain obscure, Baxter indicates continuity with these features of Suárez's thought on final causality. Like Suárez, Baxter thinks that the efficient cause should be more properly considered a cause than the final cause, which leads by attraction.[170] In this respect, Baxter objects somewhat to William Twisse's description of the final cause as the object that induces, whereas Baxter thinks the nature of the final cause is not in the object as such, but rather in the "apprehended *attracting Goodness*" of the object.[171] Baxter also mirrors Suárez's relegation of final causality to rational agents: "The *Final Cause* is not attributed to inanimates and brutes except very improperly, but it is proper to *Intellectual* agents."[172] Yet Baxter affirms that God had created nonrational agents with teleological order, and gave "a *specific Appetite*

---

166. Suárez, *On Efficient Causality*, 10 (Disp. XVII.i.6). This is grounded in his more basic definition of a cause as "a *per se* principle from which being flows into another." See Tad M. Schmaltz, *Descartes on Causation* (Oxford: Oxford University Press, 2008), 29.

167. See Sydney Penner, "Final Causality: Suárez on the Priority of Final Causation," in *Suárez on Aristotelian Causality*, ed. Jakob Leth Fink (Leiden: Brill, 2015), 122–49, who disagrees with the common opinion represented by Schmaltz, *Descartes on Causation*, 33–34, that Suárez taught a "priority of efficient causes."

168. Penner, "Final Causality," 137–43.

169. Reif, "Natural Philosophy," 209–10.

170. *MT*, I.9.

171. *MT*, I.9, in contrast to Twisse's "often" used words: "Memini quidem Doctissimum Dom. Twissum saepe dicere, 'Suadentem operari in genere Causae finalis per modum proponentis objectum.'" Cf. William Twisse, *Vindiciae gratiae, potestatis ac providentiae Dei* (Amsterdam: Joannes Janssonius, 1648), 28b, 224a, 463b, 570a, 751a (who derives this saying approvingly from Bellarmine).

172. *MT*, I.6.

to every active vital nature, which is the *principle* [*principium*] and as it were *weight* [*pondus*] of its own movements."[173] Thus, while Baxter shared with Suárez a restricted sense of final causality as applied only properly to rational agents, he also retained with Suárez and other Reformed philosophers a divinely ordered teleology even with respect to the irrational natural realm.

Passive Nature

Baxter understood the world as composed of various "constitutive causes." By this, he meant a range of passive and active natures or forms.[174] He divides forms into simple and composite. Of these, he subdivides simple forms into active and passive, and composite forms into substantial and respective forms, which manifest degrees of activity and order.[175] Baxter's account of simple passive forms incorporates atomism, while his account of composite forms incorporates a hierarchy of being and substantial forms. He thus allows for an atomic structure to the elements and things composed of elements, while retaining essentially different forms and a version of hylomorphism for composite substances.

At the foundation of Baxter's understanding of created reality is the division between passive and active nature. "Every simple created thing," Baxter sets down categorically, "is either a thing of active or passive nature."[176] This is a division that resonates somewhat with the philosophy of Aristotle, who divided all powers of substance into active (the ability to produce change) and passive (the ability to suffer change),[177] and likewise characterized the elements and qualities as predominantly passive (earth, water; dry, wet, cold) or active (fire; hot) in relation to compound bodies.[178] But whereas Aristotle referred to active and passive principles in things, Baxter understands natures or substances as either active or passive. This is also a division, as we observed above, that Baxter thought was implied

---

173. *MT*, I.7. The term *pondus* may derive from Augustine, who thought of it analogously to final causality. See Montague Brown, "Augustine and Aristotle on Causality," in *Augustine: Presbyter Factus Sum*, ed. Joseph T. Lienhard, Earl C. Muller, and Roland J. Teske (New York: Peter Lang, 1993), 465–76.

174. *MT*, I.5.

175. *MT*, I.137.

176. *MT*, I.5.

177. Aristotle, *Metaphysics*, IX.1 (1046a11–13), in *The Complete Works of Aristotle*, ed. Jonathan Barnes (Princeton, NJ: Princeton University Press, 1984), 2:1651; also *Metaphysics*, V.xii (1019a20–23), in *Complete Works*, 2:1609.

178. Aristotle, *Meteorology*, IV.5 (382a31–382b9), IV.11 (389a29–32), in *Complete Works*, 1:613–14, 623. Cf. Mary Louise Gill, *Aristotle on Substance: The Paradox of Unity* (Princeton, NJ: Princeton University Press, 1989), 81–82.

in the Genesis creation narrative. The creation of light on the first day, according to Baxter, introduced fire, "the noblest active element, which is able to work on passive matter," thereby creating a distinction between active and passive things.[179] The general difference between active and passive nature he explains as follows:

> Supposing the word *"Nature"* to signify in general "Quoddity and Quiddity" I first distinguish *"Nature"* into *Active* and *Passive*: By *Active* I mean that Nature which hath a formal Power, Virtue, and Inclination to Activity. By *Passive* I mean that *Nature* which having no such Active form, is formed to receive the Influx of the Active. I refuse not to call the first *Spirit*: but because they so greatly differ, I choose rather the common name of *Active Nature*; being not metaphorical.[180]

Thus, passive natures are so named because they do not have in themselves an active source of motion, but instead are the recipients of the activity of active natures.

Baxter's enumeration and description of passive natures, as one might expect, follows a threefold pattern. The passive natures are the elements of air, water, and earth. The element of fire, by contrast, is not passive but active. The passive natures consist of a threefold composite of matter, its disposition (privation), and form.[181] While this composite (matter, disposition, form) reflects standard Aristotelian terminology for substance,[182] Baxter's description of the matter and form of passive natures is, as Burton notes, "something at odds with Aristotle."[183] The matter of these passive natures are atoms, and their forms are "special constitutions of Atoms or parts, whence special Dispositions arise." Moreover, "Matter's specific contexture constitutes each [passive] element's form or specific difference."[184] Baxter states,

> As to ye three passive elements (for so I must yet distinguish y^m.) most philosophers suppose y^m to be but ye various shapes of y^e *materia prima*: w^{ch}

---

179. *MT*, I.125.

180. Baxter, *Of the Nature of Spirits*, 84.

181. *MT*, I.5–6. Baxter refers to Aristotle and the "scholastics" while defining privation as a disposition of matter. See also *CT*, I.173: "*Aristotle* maketh *Privatio* to be one of his three Principles in Physicks. By *Privation* must be meant, not *Absentia formae, sed Dispositio materiae*."

182. See, e.g., Suárez, *On the Formal Cause of Substance*, 21, 82 (Disp. XV.i.6; XV.vi.5).

183. Burton, *Hallowing of Logic*, 145.

184. *MT*, I.140; also *MT*, I.5.

many call by ye name of *Atomes*, wch speaketh nothing but ye divisibility into minute p[ar]ts (And they might as well call it by a more coherent name, seeing the coherence & aggregation is so naturall to y^m).[185]

The concepts of atoms, material parts, shapes, and contexture all contribute to Baxter's understanding of the form of passive elements. It is hard to deny that Baxter adopts a kind of corpuscularism. The elements of air, water, and earth arise from the size, shape, and contexture of material particles.[186] With this concept of passive nature, Baxter allows for a mechanical understanding of a large portion of the inorganic realm, with the notable exception of fire.

Although affirming the corpuscular nature of passive substance, Baxter did not wish to speculate too much on the nature of the atoms from which passive natures arise. With respect to the passive elements of earth, water, and air, he did affirm that "Impenetrability and Divisibility" are parts of the "contexture, and various modes" of the disposition of matter (*materiae dispositio*).[187] In his *Reasons*, however, he points out that moderns have reached no agreement on either the number, nature, or qualities of the elements. For all the speculation of Gassendi and others about the shapes and combinations of atoms, they are still limited only to the affirmation "that what ever bodies God made, they are divisible into *atoms*, that is, into parts by man indivisible."[188] By contrast with the uncertainty regarding the details of passive substance, Baxter states that knowledge of the active nature of the soul is far more immediate and certain: "And because we have more use for the faculties of our souls, than for fire and water, or any outward thing, [God] hath given us the *first* and *surest* knowledge of them; whatsoever self-contradicting *Somatists* say, to depress this knowledge, and advance that knowledge of Bodies, which their own disagreements do confute."[189]

Passive and active natures, Baxter held, ought to be strictly distinguished in terms both of their natures and their relations to each other. Baxter was willing to concede that the line dividing passive substances from each other was relatively porous, in that air, water, and earth could transform into different passive forms. However, he saw a firm distinction between passive and

---

185. DWL BT XIX.351, fol. 59r.

186. Cf. Boyle, *Origine of Formes and Qualities* (1666), 37–38.

187. Baxter, *Of the Nature of Spirits*, 19.

188. *RCR*, 554.

189. *RCR*, 555.

active substances: "But it seems altogether improbable, that passive Nature ever changed into *Active*, or active into passive: and of course Air into Fire or Soul; or Fire or Soul into Air."[190] This does not mean that active and passive natures are incapable of unity. The active natures are responsible for bringing about changes in the passive natures as they act upon them either accidentally (e.g., sun producing heat) or essentially to change their forms (e.g., the soul processing food).[191]

Baxter provided some indication of possible sources for his doctrine of passive nature in his published works. In his *Christian Directory*, Baxter recommends familiarity with an eclectic range of early modern authors on physics, many of whom espoused some form of atomism and who could have contributed to this aspect of Baxter's thinking. Daniel Sennert, who incorporated atomism into a larger Aristotelian account of forms, is one likely early source for Baxter's atomism.[192] The particular line dividing passive elements (earth, water, air) from active (fire) may have been derived from Jean-François Le Grand, who accepted an atomic explanation of the three passive elements while retaining fire as a uniquely active element. Baxter cited Le Grand's general division positively in his *Reasons*, and he cited Le Grand's account of fire positively in his *Methodus theologiae*.[193]

Sometime after having established a general division between active and passive natures, Baxter filled in the explanation of passive elements with Boyle's corpuscularism. In the appendix to his unpublished "Of the Nature and Immortality of Humane Soules," Baxter revealed that Boyle was the source of his mature view on the nature of passive substance. In the midst of a description of the nature of forms, he wrote,

---

190. *MT*, I.140. Cf. Baxter's comment in LPL MS 3499, fol. 100v: "1° The transmutation of Passive elements is to me scarce probable, God hath so fixed ye various nature of beings: 2° But ye transmutation of Matter into spirits much more improbable."

191. *MT*, I.140.

192. *CD*, III.923 (q. 174), on secondary books (following the primary theologial) for a pastor's library: "For Physicks: 1. *Magyrus, Combachius, Burgersdicius, Wendeline*, and *Sennertus*. 2. *Commenius*. 3. Mr. *Gott*. 4. *Bacon* and Mr. *Boile*." *CD*, III.927 (q. 174), on tertiary books: "To Physicks, *Philoponus, Telesius, Le Grand, Cartesius, Regius, Hereboord, Sckeggius, Gassendus, Patricius, K. Digby, White*." On Sennert, see Emily Michael, "Daniel Sennert on Matter and Form: At the Juncture of the Old and the New," *Early Science and Medicine* 2, no. 3 (1997): 272–99.

193. *RCR*, 516, citing the first three essays in Le Grand, *Dissertationes*, 1–134. Baxter approves of Le Grand's account of fire as a unique active element in *MT*, "Praefatio," [A5r]; DWL BT XIX.351, fols. 83r, 141r; and Baxter, *Of the Nature of Spirits*, 57–58, 70. But this approval is qualified by criticism of Le Grand's "excess" who "over-magnifieth Fire" along with Telesio and Campanella. See Baxter, *Of the Nature of Spirits*, A5r, 67; and cf. DWL BT XIX.351, fols. 58v–59r.

8° A meere *Body* or *Matter* is meerly *passive,* & hath no *self-moving power;* but if it be moved it is moved by another; wch is *originally* by some *Active spirituall being.*

9° Meere *Bodyes* are distinguished but by their magnitude, shape, site, weight, motion & contexture &c. of wch see Mr Boile of formes.[194]

Here passive natures are equated with "Meere Bodyes" in the sense given by Boyle in his treatise against Aristotelian substantial forms, *The Origine of Formes and Qualities* (1666). In relatively short order, Baxter had incorporated Boyle's views into his own writings, for the appendix to "Of the Nature and Immortality of Humane Soules" was written in 1672, shortly after he drafted the first chapters of the *Methodus theologiae.*[195] Perhaps Baxter found Boyle's treatise acceptable because Boyle professed to limit the scope of his inquiries to the realm of nonliving things.[196] Whatever the case, it is clear that Baxter's views on passive natures (the elements of air, water, and earth) align with Boyle's anti-Aristotelian treatise.

Active Nature

Although Baxter accepted aspects of the mechanical conception of nature with respect to passive substances, this did not amount to an endorsement of mechanical philosophy with respect to nature in general. Besides the simple passive elements, Baxter believed the element of fire to be a simple active nature, characterized by a threefold "*Active, Illuminative, Heating* Virtue."[197] In the created world, the passive elements "are no where found *unmixt;* nor without a participation of *fire,* & its effects uppon them,"[198] thereby rendering the actual world highly active. Other than fire, passive elements are acted upon by various other active forms, which give rise to composite substances. Composite substances are characterized by two kinds of forms: substantial forms, which animate and specify the composite substance, and respective forms, which consist of the order of the parts. Whereas the natures of the passive elements appear to play a determining role in the case of respective forms, active natures play a determining role in the case of substantial forms. While we will return to the concept of substantial form in chapter 5, here we will expand on Baxter's account of the hierarchy of active natures.

---

194. DWL BT XIX.351, fol. 130r.

195. For dating, see Appendix A.

196. See Boyle, *Origine of Formes and Qualities* (1666), "Preface," B3v–B4r, where he expresses his intention to forgo any discussion of the reasonable soul and the realm of living animals.

197. *MT,* I.138.

198. DWL BT XIX.351, fol. 130r.

For Baxter, active natures are most analogous to God, who is life and pure act (*purus actus*).[199] They are the manifestation of *vestigia Trinitatis*. As he puts it, "The analogous SUBSTANCE of things with VIRTUE communicated by way of Creation, is the *Image* of this Glorious God shining forth in Creatures."[200] With the exception of fire, which Baxter viewed in contrast to the other elements as a special active element, these active natures are identical with the world of living beings. Although Baxter to a certain degree accepted Boyle's corpuscularism in the realm of passive natures, when he came to active and living beings, he adopted a concept of form at odds with corpuscular explanation. Active natures have three basic inadequate concepts or principles: substantiality (*Substantialitas*), disposition of substance (*Substantiae peculiaris dispositio*), and power or formal power (*Virtus, seu Vis Formalis*).[201] He refers to "active form" as a synonym for formal power, and this form can be considered according to its power (in the first concept), immanent act (in the second concept), and action *ad extra* (in the third concept).[202] Baxter argues that we come to know the natures of active substances from observing their acts and inferring corresponding powers, and since there must be something behind the powers (nothing can do nothing), we must conclude there also exists a substance that has such powers. He also thinks the powers are more easily known than their substance.[203] In connecting the observation of acts to the knowledge of powers, Baxter reflects an orientation shared by Aristotelian philosophers, who similarly thought powers are inferred by experience of their acts. For example, from the experience of observing an animal eating, moving, or seeing, one can infer powers of nourishment, self-motion, and sight.[204]

In enumerating the various kinds of forms and powers, Baxter follows the standard Aristotelian hierarchy of natural forms that was ready-made for trichotomization: vegetative, animate, and rational forms. Each of these kinds of forms in turn manifests three kinds of powers or virtues. Vegetative forms have vital active (*activa*), discretive (*discretiva*), and appetitive (*appetitiva*) powers. The vital power underlies acts of motion, the discretive power underlies generation and growth,

---

199. On God as *purus actus*, see *MT*, I.8, 28, 35, 133; *RCR*, 20, 376.

200. *MT*, I.131.

201. *MT*, I.5, 132. Cf. Baxter, *Catholick Communion Defended*, 19; Baxter, *Of the Nature of Spirits*, 18–20; Baxter, *Of the Immortality of Mans Soul*, 33. For a detailed account, see Burton, *Hallowing of Logic*, 137–44.

202. *MT*, I.138. These acts were also called immanent or transeunt. See Scheibler, *Metaphysica*, 164, 813–14.

203. *MT*, I.132; DWL BT XIX.351, fol. 10r; Baxter, *End of Doctrinal Controversies*, iv; *RCR*, 2.

204. Dennis Des Chene, *Life's Form: Late Aristotelian Conceptions of the Soul* (Ithaca, NY: Cornell University Press, 2000), 23, 120.

and the attractive power assimilates nutrients. Sensitive forms have more vital active (*activior*), apprehensive (*apprehensiva sensitiva*), and appetitive (*appetitiva sensitiva*) powers. The apprehensive and sensitive powers correspond to acts of sensation and appetite. The rational human soul, as a living, moving, generating, sensitive, and appetitive being, of course shares in the powers already enumerated. However, it is distinguished by a most active vital power (*virtus vita activissima*), intellect (*intellectus*), and will (*voluntas*).[205]

While Baxter spills much ink in further subdividing every form, power, and act into further trichotomies, his discussion of the soul's powers often repackages and recycles older scholastic commentary on the soul. Within the standard Aristotelian tripartite soul (vegetative, sensitive, rational), it was common fare to distinguish powers of nutrition, growth, and generation in plants, as well as powers of locomotion, sense, and appetite in animals.[206] Baxter agreed with this Aristotelian approach to the nature of living things. At the end of his life he stated as a matter of fact, "*Aristotle* defineth the Soul to be *Entelechia*, or the *Entitative Act and Form of a Physical organized Body, capable of being Animated by it.*"[207] With respect to the details of the various powers, he had clearly digested a wide range of scholastic materials. In the previous chapter, we already observed his use of Aquinas and Scotus on the faculties of intellect and will. On the scholastic debate over whether the power of sensation is merely passive or also active, Baxter had decided from an early date that it is active.[208] His detailed account of the apprehensive power of the sensitive appetite included a division between imagination (*phantasia*), common sense (*sensus communis*), and particular senses.[209] He also divided the power of the sensitive appetite into concupiscible and irascible appetites, expanded Aquinas's eleven passions to fifteen, and then arranged each of these into groups of three.[210]

---

205. *MT*, I.153–54.

206. Aristotle, *On the Soul*, II.3, in *Complete Works*, 1:659–60; Des Chene, *Life's Form*, 155–56.

207. Richard Baxter, *Against the Revolt of a Foreign Jurisdiction, Which would be to England its Perjury, Church-ruine, and Slavery* (London: Tho. Parkhurst, 1691), 377.

208. Baxter, *Of Justification*, 194–98. This short excursus on the topic displays extraordinary knowledge of scholastics and modern philosophers. Cf. *MT*, I.226.

209. *MT*, I.223.

210. *MT*, I.225. The acts of the concupiscible appetite are either toward good (*amare, concupiscere, gaudere*) or against evil (*odi, fugere, tristari*). The acts of the irascible appetite are toward good *positively* (*considere, audere, sperare*) or *privatively* (*diffidere, despondere, desperare*), or against evil (*ira, timor, pudor*). Baxter adopts Aquinas's six concupiscible passions without modification, but then significantly expands on Aquinas's enumeration of five irascible passions (*spes, desparatio, timor, audacia, ira*). For Aquinas's own enumeration, see his *Summa theologiae*, IaIIae, q. 23, art. 2, 4. On the appropriation of Aquinas's treatise on the passions by Reformed theologians, see David S. Sytsma, "The Logic of the Heart: Analyzing the Affections in Early Reformed Orthodoxy," in *Church and School in Early*

Unlike his account of passive substance that accommodated Boyle's corpuscularism, Baxter's account of the active substance of the soul thus preserves in a broad sense the various forms, powers, and acts of the scholastic approach to the soul based largely on Aristotle's *On the Soul*.

In addition to Baxter's use of scholastic accounts of the higher functions of the soul (intellect, will, passions), one also finds in Baxter an eclectic use of contemporary medical accounts of the relation between the vegetative soul and the element of fire. Since antiquity, the nature of life had been associated with heat and therefore in some way with the traditional element of fire. Aristotle's theory of innate heat held that although vital heat is not identical with fire, it is analogous to it. Galen went further than Aristotle in closely identifying fire and innate heat. Locating the center of innate animal heat in the heart, both Aristotle and Galen viewed innate heat as the power behind most of the basic functions of life, including digestion, nutrition, and generation.[211] The idea of innate heat persisted into the seventeenth century and was still espoused by William Harvey, but gradually gave way to alternative chemical and mechanical theories.[212] Baxter assumed the validity of this longstanding tradition stemming from Aristotle and Galen, for which Henry More labeled him a "psychopyrist"—or one who "would make all created Spirits a kinde of fire."[213] Baxter's view in this respect also sets him apart from both Descartes and Boyle, who reduced fire and heat to mechanical explanation.[214] For Baxter, fire serves as "a bond between what is Animate or Vital & what is Inanimate." Baxter was not sure whether the vegetative soul was in fact fire or rather something distinct from it, but he was sure that it was at least analogous to fire.[215] This explains why Baxter typically referred to the vegetative soul as

Modern Protestantism: Essays in Honor of Richard A. Muller on the Maturation of a Theological Tradition, ed. Jordan J. Ballor, David S. Sytsma, and Jason Zuidema (Leiden: Brill, 2013), 471–88.

211. Everett Mendelsohn, *Heat and Life: The Development of the Theory of Animal Heat* (Cambridge, MA: Harvard University Press, 1964), 8–26.

212. Mendelsohn, *Heat and Life*, 27–107.

213. Henry, "Medicine and Pneumatology," 34; Henry, "Matter of Souls," 109–10. As Henry observes, "analogies between fire and the soul were almost as common in theology as they were in medical writings" (110).

214. Fuchs, *Mechanization of the Heart*, 139; William R. Eaton, *Boyle on Fire: The Mechanical Revolution in Scientific Explanation* (London: Continuum, 2005).

215. *MT*, I.126, 138. Cf. DWL BT XIX.351, fols. 130v–131r. Note that by fire Baxter meant "not y^t composition of various things, wch we call a *flame*, a *coale*, a *candent matter* &c. & wch ye vulgar call *Fire*: But y^t *pure Virtuous Substance* wch in this is y^e *Active principle of Motion, Light & Heate*. And wch is by others called aether" (DWL BT XIX.351, fol. 131v).

the "fiery vegetative nature" (*Natura IGNEA Vegetativa*).[216] Fire, as a unique active element, was "as a lower soul to the passive matter, and a thing almost middle between a spirit and a body."[217]

Baxter also drew on the contemporary philosophy of life of the influential physician and philosopher Francis Glisson (d. 1677).[218] Glisson's metaphysical treatise *De natura substantiae energetica* (1672) posited that all matter was inherently alive and thus endowed with motion, perception, and appetite. Since Glisson held living matter responsible for producing vegetative and sensitive forms of life, he had no need for a separate principle of life in animals and accordingly rejected the notion of a substantial soul in animals, instead claiming that animal souls were "essential and vital modes of matter" (*modos materiae essentiales, & simul vitales*).[219] As John Henry first pointed out, although Baxter disagreed with Glisson's understanding of living matter, he also defended aspects of Glisson's theory against Henry More's vigorous critique, and stated that there is no logical impossibility for God to endow matter with life in Glisson's sense.[220] Even so, Baxter's reception of Glisson was both highly eclectic and quite late in terms of the development of Baxter's theory of nature. Given Baxter's understanding of the passive nature of the elements other than fire, he could not agree with Glisson's attribution of life and self-motion to passive natures,[221] and Baxter's acceptance of substantial forms for active natures (including animals and humans) stands opposed to Glisson's view that animal souls are "essential and vital modes of matter." In fact, by the time Glisson published his *De vita naturae* in 1672, Baxter had already developed his division between active and passive natures, and had

---

216. E.g., *MT*, I.153.

217. *RCR*, 542; cf. *RCR*, 559, 561.

218. On Glisson, see Guido Giglioni, "The Genesis of Francis Glisson's Philosophy of Life" (PhD diss., Johns Hopkins University, 2002); and French, *William Harvey's Natural Philosophy*, 286–309.

219. Francis Glisson, *De natura substantiae energetica* (London: E. Flesher, 1672), "Ad Lectorem," fols. a4v–b1v (sec. 7–8); cf. Giglioni, "Genesis of Francis Glisson's Philosophy of Life," 287; Henry, "Medicine and Pneumatology," 21.

220. See Henry, "Medicine and Pneumatology," 32–38, who admits to finding Baxter's references to Glisson in the *Methodus theologiae* "somewhat obscure" (33), and notes Baxter's disagreement with Glisson's doctrine of living matter (36).

221. *MT*, I, "Praefatio," [5]: "The doctrine of the Most learned old D. Glisson on the *Life of all simple things*, as far as *substantial* & *vital forms*, that the atoms of every thing are inadequate concepts, & thus every nature is essentially *Active*, seems to me to be not at all proven." See similarly *TKL*, 20; Richard Baxter, *The True and Only Way of Concord of all the Christian Churches* (London: John Hancock, 1680), 14; and LPL MS 3499, fol. 105v. Henry overlooked these negative reference to Glisson. See previous note.

already begun writing the section on ontology in the *Methodus theologiae*.[222] We must therefore assume that what most attracted Baxter to Glisson's work was his account of three faculties in vegetative life that harmonized neatly with Baxter's own agenda for a Trinitarian natural philosophy. Baxter thus took Glisson's suggestion that all things have three faculties of motion, perception, and appetite, and transposed it to the spiritual realm, thereby severing the link between Glisson's matter theory and the traditional hierarchy of souls (vegetative, sensitive, and rational). Or, as he put it, "So that what Glisson saith of every clod and stone, I say only of Spirits."[223]

Baxter's affirmation of a hierarchy of active forms ranging from fiery natures to various souls and finally God as purely immaterial stands in striking contrast the dualism of Cartesian extension and thought. In this respect, John Henry has drawn attention to the Neoplatonic resemblance of Baxter's view of the world, which he contrasts with the more Cartesian perspective of Henry More. In Henry's estimation, Baxter "seems to have had a much clearer sense [than Henry More] of the philosophical shortcomings of any dualist system."[224] Baxter did in fact cite Plotinus's *Enneads* in the context of elaborating a hierarchy of forms, thus indicating at least a limited agreement with Neoplatonism (which of course also blended Aristotelian and Platonic philosophy).[225] Yet, given Baxter's general critique of the "unproved fanaticisms" and "divers errours" of the Platonists, such continuity should not be exaggerated as an endorsement of a particular Platonist philosophical system.[226] While Baxter remained committed to a hierarchy of forms, he filled in the details of this hierarchy with a variety of sources, including Aristotle's understanding of the soul as tripartite and the entelechy of the body.

---

222. Burton, *Hallowing of Logic*, 138–39, assumes a strong influence of Glisson's *De vita naturae* (1672) on the *Methodus theologiae*, but the original date of composition for the ontological section (ca. 1669; see Appendix A) mitigates Glisson's importance. Other important works where Baxter discusses the nature of substance, including his manuscript "Of the Nature and Immortality of Humane Soules" and *Reasons*, also preceded the appearance of Glisson's *De vita naturae*.

223. Baxter, *Of the Nature of Spirits*, 7. Cf. *MT*, "Praefatio," [A5r].

224. Henry, "Medicine and Pneumatology," 36–37.

225. *RCR*, 559, citing Plotinus, *Enneads* 4.3, in *Plotini Platonicorum coryphaei opera quae extant omnia per Marsilium Ficinum* (Basel: Ludovicus Rex, 1615), 384, with Ficinus's marginal note XVII. Plotinus is also cited in *RCR*, 514, 535, 568, 571, 575, 578–79, 588. Baxter lists Plotinus among authors of secondary importance on the soul. See *CD*, III.927 (q. 174).

226. See *CD*, III.919 (q. 173, §15), discussed in chapter 3 above.

Conclusion

Baxter's general view of the created world involved a diverse array of ancient, modern, theological, and philosophical sources that all contributed to a sui generis Trinitarian natural philosophy. On the one hand, Baxter remained quite traditional when discussing the realm of living things by adopting the scholastic notion of substantial form while also following the main contours of the tripartite soul with its various powers, which could be found in commentaries on Aristotle's *On the Soul*. At the same time, he accepted Boyle's conception of corpuscular matter in the realm of passive, inanimate substances. In his theological approach, he identified with the early modern Reformed tradition of Mosaic physics, which explains his desire to make natural philosophy conform in its foundational principles to revealed truths and his sharp criticism of philosophers who constructed natural philosophy apart from revelation. However, he departed from most of his Reformed colleagues in the extent to which he agreed with certain church fathers, medieval scholastics, and moderns like Campanella on the tradition of *vestigia Trinitatis*. The result of this confluence of theological and philosophical ideas is a highly eclectic Trinitarian natural philosophy.

5

A Commotion over Motion

AS WE SAW in the previous chapter, Baxter sought to frame his understanding of nature in light of a commitment to an analogical relation between God and creation, reflecting *vestigia Trinitatis* in all aspects of created reality, and in dialogue with seventeenth-century Reformed works on "Mosaic physics" and Campanella's metaphysics. This reflection led Baxter to adapt Aristotelian accounts of causality and substance to better fit a Trinitarian mold. Although he allowed for a corpuscular account of the elements of earth, water, and air in what he called passive substance, he also believed that the Genesis creation narrative implied the creation of inherently active substances ranging from fire to all kinds of living souls, which ought not be reduced to corpuscular explanation. It was on this latter aspect of the active and living part of creation that Baxter staked out his polemical ground against mechanical philosophers. The entire controversy turned on the nature of motion and its relation to the agency of secondary causes. The status of motion was an issue of intense and intersecting interest to traditional Aristotelian philosophers, modern philosophers such as Descartes and Gassendi, and theologians such as Baxter.

Since the thirteenth century, when Aristotle's physics were recovered for use in the West in Latin translation, the topic of motion was a central concern in natural philosophy. The scholastic philosophers who followed Aristotle's definition of nature (φύσις) as "a principle of motion and rest,"[1] often included motion in their definition of natural philosophy. Albertus Magnus understood the subject of natural philosophy as "mobile body" (*corpus mobile*), and Aquinas understood it as "mobile being" (*ens mobile*).[2] Given the continuous commentary tradition on

---

1. Aristotle, *Physics*, II.1 (192b21), in *Complete Works*, 1:329.

2. Roger Ariew and Alan Gabbey, "The Scholastic Background," in *CHSP*, 1:433. Cf. James Weisheipl, "The Interpretation of Aristotle's *Physics* and the Science of Motion," in *The Cambridge History of Later Medieval Philosophy*, ed. Norman Kretzmann, Anthony Kenny, and Jan Pinborg (Cambridge: Cambridge University Press, 1982), 425–53, at 524.

Aristotle's text into the seventeenth century, motion (conceived most generally as natural change) remained a central concern for the broader early modern Aristotelian philosophical tradition. As one historian observes with respect to early modern commentaries on Aristotle's *Physics*, "The first and most basic [theme] is that of *natural change* and *agency*."[3] Indeed, early modern manuals on natural philosophy often cited Aristotle's dictum from the opening of the third book of *Physics*: "If motion were unknown, nature itself would be unknown" (*Ignorato motu, natura ipsa ignorabitur*).[4]

Motion was also a central concern of seventeenth-century mechanical philosophers. Of the "two grand and most Catholick Principles of Bodies, Matter and Motion," Robert Boyle thought that "Local Motion seems to be indeed the Principal amongst Second Causes, and the Grand Agent of all that happens in Nature." By contrast, "Bulk, Figure, Rest, Situation, and Texture" are "in many Cases Effects, and in many others, little better then *Conditions*, or *Requisites*, or Causes *sine quibus non*" of operations.[5] Descartes was especially concerned about the nature of motion. While twentieth-century philosophers inherited a picture of Descartes as primarily concerned with epistemology and as the author of the *Meditations*,[6] early modern historians of philosophy now recognize that the *Meditations* were preparatory to the *Principia philosophiae* and have accorded a much greater place to Descartes's natural philosophy in his philosophy.[7] In fact, Descartes designed his *Principia philosophiae* as a response to and replacement for the Aristotelian natural

---

3. Dennis Des Chene, *Physiologia: Natural Philosophy in Late Aristotelian and Cartesian Thought* (Ithaca, NY: Cornell University Press, 1996), 3.

4. Reif, "Natural Philosophy," 210. See Aristotle, *Physics*, III.1 (200b14–15), in *Complete Works*, 1:342.

5. Boyle, *Origine of Formes and Qualities* (1666), 6, 8.

6. On this, as well as the similarly problematic bifurcation of early modern philosophy into rationalism and empiricism, see Lamprecht, "Role of Descartes," 183–86; also Laurens Laudan, "The Clock Metaphor and Probabilism: The Impact of Descartes on English Methodological Thought, 1650–65," *Annals of Science* 22, no. 2 (1966): 73–104, at 76, 82; David Fate Norton, "The Myth of 'British Empiricism,'" *History of European Ideas* 1, no. 4 (1981): 331–44; and Vanzo, "Empiricism and Rationalism," 253–82.

7. On the relation of the *Principia* to scholastic philosophy, see Roger Ariew, "Les *Principia* et la *Summa Philosophica Quadripartita*," in *Descartes: Principia Philosophiae (1644–1994)*, ed. Jean Robert Armogathe and Giulia Belgioioso (Napoli: Vivarium, 1996), 473–89; Alan Gabbey, "The *Principia Philosophiae* as a Treatise in Natural Philosophy," in *Descartes: Principia Philosophiae (1644–1994)*, ed. Jean Robert Armogathe and Giulia Belgioioso (Napoli: Vivarium, 1996), 517–29; Garber, *Descartes' Metaphysical Physics*, 24–25, 58–62; and Des Chene, *Physiologia*, 255–398. Descartes himself said the *Meditations* "contain all the foundations of my physics" (AT 3:298; CSM 3:173). He compared philosophy to a "tree" in which metaphysics was the "root" of the "trunk" of physics, from which grow the "branches" of "all the other sciences" of medicine, mechanics, and morals (AT 9B:14; CSM 1:186).

philosophy of the schools, and such a project required the provision of a compelling account of motion.[8]

The topic of motion was also a matter of concern to Christian theologians, who had to affirm that God created living moving creatures (Gen. 1:21, 28) and confess with the apostle Paul, "In him we live and move and have our being" (Acts 17:28). While philosophers both old and new were interested in theology at least to account for the origin and continuance of motion in the world, theologians for their part were interested in the topic of motion as far as it related to the doctrines of creation and providence.[9] At issue for the theologian were the questions of God's causal relation to the world and of the status of creatures as secondary agents in relation to God. Baxter himself had integrated the concept of motion into *The Saints Everlasting Rest*, where philosophical definitions of motion and rest are among the stated presuppositions of the saint's "rest."[10] Whether or not Funkenstein is correct in his general assessment that "[n]ever before or after [the seventeenth century] were science, philosophy, and theology seen as almost one and the same occupation,"[11] both philosophers and theologians during this time argued about the nature and sources of motion as a matter of common concern. As one scholar puts it, "The philosophy of nature [in the early modern period], in fact, was a kind of clearinghouse in which physics, metaphysics, and theology could meet and negotiate their claims."[12]

As the present chapter will show, the manner in which Baxter negotiated the claims of theology and philosophy with respect to motion is distinct from the major Reformed responses in the Netherlands, which had been polarized over the question of Copernicanism. Unlike the Dutch Reformed, Baxter did not evidence an intense polemical interest in Copernicanism. At the same time, he expressed profound concern regarding the deleterious effects of new ideas of substance and motion, particularly recent philosophers' denial of substantial form and Descartes's laws of motion. While past scholarship has noted Baxter's usage of voluntarist arguments in philosophical debate,[13] his polemic as a whole reveals a greater focus on God's analogical relation to creation, and specifically a desire to

---

8. See Garber, *Descartes' Metaphysical Physics*, chs. 6–9, who devotes more than half his exposition of Descartes's physics to Descartes's definition of motion and its laws.

9. Cf. Van Ruler, *Crisis of Causality*.

10. *SER2*, I.6 (I.ii.1), I.17 (I.iii.8), I.24 (I.iv.i). Cf. Trueman, "Small Step," 186.

11. Funkenstein, *Theology and the Scientific Imagination*, 3.

12. Des Chene, *Physiologia*, 3.

13. John Henry, "Voluntarist Theology at the Origins of Modern Science: A Response to Peter Harrison," *History of Science* 47 (2009): 79–113, here 83, 95; Henry, "Medicine and Pneumatology," 37.

preserve intrinsic sources of motion in secondary causes that reflect the communicative nature of a living (not only willing) God. He feared that recent advances in mechanical philosophy would undermine both a proper understanding of creaturely activity implied in the Genesis creation account and God's communication, by analogy, of his life, wisdom, and goodness with the created order.

Copernicanism

One of the most celebrated conflicts of the early modern era about motion was the question of heliocentricism, or Copernicanism, as it came to be identified.[14] In the Netherlands, the conflict over Copernicanism became closely associated with Cartesianism. The Voetian party—so named for following the teaching of the Dutch Reformed theologian Gisbetus Voetius, who opposed Descartes—denounced Copernicanism, while the Dutch Cartesians defended Copernicanism.[15] As Vermij has shown, the nature of these debates had less to do with the merits of Galileo's mathematical data and experimental confirmation than with the place of Copernicanism in Cartesian philosophy. After heliocentric cosmology became integrated into the larger theoretical project of Cartesian natural philosophy, Copernicanism became a symbol for "competing philosophical schools" with all their theological (and political) ramifications.[16] Although it is true that Voetians (until Bernhardinus de Moor [1709–1780]) opposed Copernicanism on biblical grounds, Voetius did not consider the issue as a matter of first importance.[17] For Voetius, the more general metaphysical questions that mechanical philosophy raised about the causal activity of creatures and the validity of substantial form were a greater concern than the more particular question of the earth's motion.[18]

In England, the reception of Copernicanism likewise produced competing theological positions. As we observed in the previous chapter, John Wilkins, an outspoken advocate for Copernicanism, resisted the use of Scripture as a rule for philosophical truths. In opposition to Wilkins, Alexander Ross argued against Copernicanism in a similar manner to the Voetian party that Scripture does contain philosophical truths, and, in the interest of preserving the unity of

---

14. For an overview of the theological debate surrounding early modern Copernicanism, see Howell, *God's Two Books*.

15. For a full account, see Vermij, *Calvinist Copernicans*.

16. Vermij, *Calvinist Copernicans*, 6.

17. Goudriaan, *Reformed Orthodoxy and Philosophy*, 125–33.

18. Van Ruler, *Crisis of Causality*, 25.

truth, the literal sense of Scripture should correct philosophical theory.[19] Others were less polemically engaged. Edward Leigh, for example, while personally favoring geocentrism, noted even-handedly the arguments both for and against Copernicanism.[20]

Baxter shared the Voetians' appeal to the tradition of Mosaic physics, yet his reaction to mechanical philosophy also contrasted with them in important ways. Baxter's response to mechanical philosophy was already in place in the late 1660s before he became aware of Spinoza's *Tractatus*. Unlike later Voetians, he therefore engaged the topic of motion in mechanical philosophy prior to, and independently of, the threat of necessitarianism that later Voetians associated with Cartesian laws of motion.[21] Furthermore, in contrast to both Voetius's and Ross's vigorous anti-Copernicanism, Baxter rarely discussed the matter. In his *Methodus theologiae*, Baxter offers an explanation for the limited scope of his polemic and his relative silence on astronomy. In his estimation, a theological treatment of creation should focus on issues raised in Genesis 1 and treat many other matters of physics—including astronomy and the generation and corruption of mixtures—only in passing. The topic of the motion and activity of creatures, he thought, was a matter much more related to Genesis 1, and of greater relevance for understanding the human soul.[22] He reiterated this position in the *Church Directory*, where he stated that although Scripture is not a "perfect Rule" for physics or metaphysics, it is "no Rule" for astronomy and other arts.[23] While Baxter therefore shared with the Voetians a concern for integrating Genesis 1 with the principles of natural philosophy (Mosaic physics), he did not appear to be concerned with the question of the motion of the earth in relation to such passages as Psalms 19 or 104.[24] His position is therefore distinct from the anti-Copernican literalism of the Voetians and Ross.

---

19. Shapiro, *John Wilkins*, 52–54; Grant McColley, "The Ross-Wilkins Controversy," *Annals of Science* 3, no. 2 (1938): 153–89; Francis R. Johnson, *Astronomical Thought in Renaissance England: A Study of the English Scientific Writings from 1500 to 1645* (Baltimore: The Johns Hopkins Press, 1937), 277–82.

20. Edward Leigh, *A Systeme or Body of Divinity* (London: A. M., 1662), 300 (marginal note). I am grateful to Richard Muller for this reference.

21. Cf. Goudriaan, *Reformed Orthodoxy and Philosophy*, 94–96, 110–13. A comparison between later nonconformist responses to Spinoza (William Bates and John Howe) and Baxter might reveal a changing reception of Descartes in light of the threat of Spinoza's necessitarianism. Their responses are briefly discussed in Wallace, *Shapers*, 178–80; and Colie, "Spinoza in England," 188–89 (on Howe only).

22. *MT*, I.141, 152.

23. *CD*, III.886 (q. 130).

24. For the intense debate over these passages between the Voetians and Cartesians, see Vermij, *Calvinist Copernicans*, 256–67.

Although Baxter's remarks on Copernicanism are scarce, he was aware of the opinions of Copernicus and Tycho Brahe, which represented major positions for heliocentrism and geocentrism. In the 1670s and 1680s, when Baxter weighed in on the controversy, Copernicus and Brahe were recognized as plausible alternatives, even though, in the estimation of Boyle, the "greater part" of the *virtuosi* favored Copernicanism.[25] Robert Hooke, writing in favor of the earth's motion, conceded that "there is somewhat of reason on both sides," so that the controversy "remains undetermined, Whether the Earth move above the Sun, or the Sun about the Earth; and all the Arguments alledged either on this or that side, are but probabilities at best, and admit not of a necessary and positive conclusion."[26] Matthew Hale, representing a more conservative opinion, maintained that Ptolemy, Copernicus, and Tycho "solve the *Phaenomena* very near equally."[27] For his part, Baxter briefly addressed the hypotheses of Copericus and Tycho in his *Methodus theologiae* in the context of critical remarks on Descartes's *Principia*. Descartes was of the opinion that although Ptolemy's hypothesis did not fit the appearances in light of recent empirical observations, the hypotheses of Copernicus and Tycho "explain the phenomena equally well." Of the latter two options, Descartes described Copernicus as "somewhat simpler and clearer," despite Tycho's attempts to alter it to fit better the "very truth of the thing" (*ipsam rei veritatem*), that is, the "common sense of mankind."[28] Baxter chided Descartes for generally preferring a clear hypothesis to one that seemed to fit better with reality.[29] Although Baxter's criticism of Descartes here points to greater sympathy with Tycho, and places him in the company of those whom Hooke regarded as

---

25. According to a comment of Boyle from the 1680s, "the greater part by far of the modern *Virtuosi*, that are any thing versed in astronomy, favour the doctrine of *Copernicus*, as it is improved by the discoveries made by the help of the telescope." See Robert Boyle, *The Christian Virtuoso, The Second Part* (1744), in *The Works of Robert Boyle* (London: Pickering & Chatto, 2000), 12:438. On the dating of Boyle's work, see p. xlix.

26. Robert Hooke, *An Attempt to Prove the Motion of the Earth from Observations* (London: T. R., 1674), 3–4. Cf. Robert S. Westman, *The Copernican Question: Prognostication, Skepticism, and Celestial Order* (Berkeley: University of California Press, 2011), 509, who writes of Hooke's state of the controversy: "No fuller characterization can be found of the Copernican question at this historical moment."

27. Matthew Hale, *Difficiles Nugae: Or, Observations Touching the Torricellian Experiment* (London: W. Godbid for William Shrowsbury, 1674), 5–6.

28. Descartes, *Principia philosophiae*, III, §17–18 (AT 8:85; *Principles of Philosophy*, trans. Valentine Rodger Miller and Reese P. Miller [Dordrecht: D. Reidel, 1983], 90 [hereafter Miller]). There are also differences between Descartes and Copernicus, which are discussed in Garber, *Descartes' Metaphysical Physics*, 181–88; and Stephen Gaukroger, *Descartes' System of Natural Philosophy* (Cambridge: Cambridge University Press, 2002), 136–42.

29. *MT*, I.150–51, citing Descartes, *Principia philosophiae*, III, §17.

under the "prejudice of common converse,"[30] his remark also made an important methodological claim. In the face of competing hypotheses, Baxter implied that greater weight should be given to reality (*rei veritatem*) over the clarity of the hypothesis. And since even Descartes recognized that Copernicus and Tycho both solve the phenomena "equally well," Baxter thought Descartes's rationale for choosing Copernicus over Tycho was indicative of his problematic preference for clarity of speculation over consideration of reality and sense experience.[31]

In his polemics with Henry More, Baxter clearly came out against the opinion of Copernicus. In continuity with his general position that Scripture is "no Rule" for astronomy,[32] Baxter's reasoning was based primarily on rational rather than biblical criteria. Baxter had considered arguments of Hale in a manuscript in which the latter, according to Baxter, opposed Copernicus. Hale's arguments, Baxter related in a response to More, had moved him toward a denial of the earth's motion. Baxter expressed uncertainty regarding More's support for the earth's motion and pled his own "ignorance" on the matter:

> Your Assurance of the *Earth's Motion*, assureth not me: I have seen a M.S. of your Antagonist's Judge *Hale*, that inclineth me to deny it; and nothing more than the Igneous nature of the Sun, to which Motion is natural, and the torpid nature of Earth; God making every thing fit for its use. But of this, as my judgment is of little value, so I profess Ignorance.[33]

This anti-Copernican remark is consistent with Baxter's preference, stated earlier in opposition to Descartes's *Principia*, for hypotheses which do justice to reality (*rei veritatem*). Given the hypotheses of Copernicus and Tycho, which even Descartes granted solve the phenomena nearly equally, Baxter preferred the hypothesis that made most sense of his view that element of fire (the sun) is active and the element of earth is passive. For Baxter, considerations of natural philosophy cast the deciding vote between plausible astronomical theories.

Baxter's preference for geocentrism must also be balanced with a recognition of his enthusiasm for experimental discoveries, including Galileo's telescopic observations and Gilbert's experiments on magnets.[34] In fact, Baxter himself used

---

30. Hooke, *An Attempt*, 1.

31. Baxter's close disciple Thomas Doolittle, who was reading Baxter's *Methodus theologiae*, similarly rejected Copernicus on the basis of sense experience. See Doolittle, *Earthquakes Explained and Practically Improved* (London: John Salusbury, 1693), 8–10.

32. *CD*, III.886 (q. 130).

33. Baxter, *Of the Nature of Spirits*, 40.

34. *RCR*, 350–51.

a telescope to confirm some of Galileo's planetary observations and as a result was convinced that other planets were made of the same element as earth (without connecting these observations with the motion of the earth).[35] Such interests in empirical inquiry are consistent with the priority he accorded to sense perception, as well as his remark that "now as the best Philosophers think that experiments *de facto* must be premised to the Theory."[36] With respect to the discipline of astronomy, he had no problem recommending Gassendi's Copernican *Institutio astronomica* (1647), a widely used astronomical textbook in both England and New England.[37] He also referred the reader to Gassendi's views on the possible habitability of the moon.[38] While Baxter himself denied the earth's motion on account of Hale, he also shared with the *virtuosi* of the Royal Society an enthusiasm that "[a]lmost all Arts and Sciences are encreasing neerer towards Perfection. Ocular demonstrations by the *Telescope*, and sensible experiments, are daily multiplyed."[39]

While Baxter's openness to the empirical advances of his age may stand in contrast with his Voetian brethren in the Netherlands, he still shared reservations with them about mechanical philosophy's more general principles touching substance and motion. Baxter was mainly concerned with how mechanical philosophy would alter conceptions of agency and motion in both living creatures and God. We will address Baxter's response to these problems below, but first let us situate Baxter's general conception of motion in its intellectual context.

The Nature of Motion

For Aristotle and his early modern commentators, motion referred not merely to a change of place, or local motion, but rather to a broad conception of change as process from a beginning to an end. This process of change always had reference to some power (*potentia*) that begins the change and its manifested act (*actus*). Since various kinds of things manifest various forms of change, the concept of motion itself varied depending on the nature of things that changed. For Aristotle, change applied to four of his ten categories. Given four basic categories of being that undergo alteration—place, quantity, quality, substance—Aristotle identified four main kinds of motion, namely change of place (local motion), change of quantity

---

35. RCR, 572.

36. Richard Baxter, *The Nonconformists Plea for Peace* (London: Benjamin Alsop, 1679), 289.

37. CD, III.923 (q. 174); Feingold, "Mathematical Sciences and New Philosophies," 405–6; Burden, "Academical Learning," 192–93; Mel Gorman, "Gassendi in America," *Isis* 55, no. 4 (1964): 409–17.

38. RCR, 388 (marginal note).

39. RCR, 351.

(augmentation and diminution), change of quality (alteration), and (less properly) change of substance (generation and corruption).[40] Among the kinds of motion, he thought local motion was primary and more general than the others due to the fact that augmentation or alteration do not happen without a change of place.[41]

The mechanical philosophers were united in their opposition to a complex concept of motion dependent on various kinds of forms and qualities. Descartes repeatedly objected to the obscurity and complexity of the Aristotelian definition of motion as "the actuality of a thing in potentiality insofar as it is in potentiality."[42] Like Descartes, Gassendi rejected the hylomorphism of the scholastics and along with it substantial and qualitative changes as distinct categories of motion.[43] In place of a variety of kinds of motion, mechanical philosophy reduced the concept of motion to local motion. This was different from the Aristotelian theory of the priority of local motion, for rather than requiring local motion as a *sine qua non* for other changes, mechanical philosophy explained all changes only by local motion itself.[44] The conception of local motion, moreover, was also radically altered as mechanical philosophy removed the concept of an end or terminus of local motion. For Aristotelian philosophy, in the absence of a continuing force, whether internal or external to a thing, motion tends toward rest and comes to a stop. By contrast, for Descartes, once something is in motion, it will continue to move infinitely unless stopped from without; it has a point of departure but no end, no *terminus ad quem*.[45] As Henry More paraphrased Descartes's doctrine, "That what Matter there is in any part of Matter is necessarily there, and there continues, till some other part of Matter change or diminish its Motion, is plain from the lawes of Motion set down by *Des-Cartes* in his *Principia Philosophiae*."[46]

With a reduction of motion to local motion, causal activity became reducible to the collisions of material particles as they change location. There were of course differences among mechanical philosophers as to the exact proximate source of local motion. For Gassendi, atoms were inherently active or endowed

---

40. Aristotle, *Physics*, III.1 (201a5–8), in *Complete Works*, 1:343; Des Chene, *Physiologia*, 22–26; Ariew and Gabbey, "Scholastic Background," 1:440.

41. Aristotle, *Physics*, IV.1 (208a31), VII.2 (243a10), in *Complete Works*, 1:355, 409; Ariew and Gabbey, "Scholastic Background," 440–41.

42. Garber, *Descartes' Metaphysical Physics*, 157–59, 194.

43. Gassendi, *Syntagma philosophicum*, II, sec. 1, lib. 5, cap. 6, in *Opera*, 1:362–64; Margaret J. Osler, "Whose Ends? Teleology in Early Modern Natural Philosophy," *Osiris*, 2nd Series, 16 (2001): 151–68, at 159.

44. Alan Gabbey, "New Doctrines of Motion," in *CHSP*, 1:649.

45. Des Chene, *Physiologia*, 256.

46. Henry More, *The Immortality of the Soul* (London: J. Flesher, 1659), 122.

with a principle of motion by God at creation. These atoms then formed into larger clusters of molecules and *semina*, which through more complex local motions produced the "texture" that underlies the phenomena of qualities, powers, and generation of individual substances.[47] For Descartes, by contrast, matter was an inert *res extensa*, whose motion was imposed on it from without by God according to certain laws of motion. While we will return to Baxter's specific remarks on Descartes's laws of motion below, we should observe that his laws of motion functioned (in his own words) as "secondary and particular causes of different motions" and thus, together with God as the cause of the laws, replaced the function of substantial forms as secondary causes under God.[48] With the important exception of the human soul, both the atomist and Cartesian accounts of motion thus excluded an intrinsic source of causality in things that was not in principle reducible to material particles and local motion. It was precisely this denial of substances with intrinsic sources of motion other than local motion—which in scholastic philosophy were explained by substantial forms and real qualities—that most agitated Voetius in his early encounter with Cartesianism.[49]

Like Voetius, Baxter's response to the elimination of substantial form as a principle of motion was overwhelmingly negative. According to his own account, both he and Matthew Hale "both greatly disliked the Principles of *Cartesius* and *Gassendus* (much more of the Bruitists, *Hobs* and *Spinosa*); especially their Doctrine *de Motu*, and their obscuring, or denying *Nature it self*, even the *Principia Motus*, the *Virtutes formales*, which are the Causes of Operations."[50] It was their denial that inherent substantial powers or virtues (*virtutes formales*) constitute the principles of motion (*principia motus*) that he found most objectionable. In Baxter's estimation, in place of *principia motus*, they "substitute only former *motion*," with the result that "the *nature* of things is mostly out of themselves in the extrinsick mover."[51] With this main objection (to be discussed more below), Baxter aligned

---

47. LoLordo, *Pierre Gassendi*, 152–207.

48. Descartes, *Principia philosophiae*, II, §37 (AT 8:62; Miller, 59); Garber, *Descartes' Metaphysical Physics*, 274–75: "What Descartes chooses in their [substantial forms] place is God, who will act not only as the general conservator of the world, but as the *direct* cause of motion and change in the world." The relative role of secondary causes as agents of motion in relation to God in Descartes's philosophy is still a matter of debate. See Helen Hattab, "Concurrence or Divergence? Reconciling Descartes' Physics with His Metaphysics," *Journal of the History of Philosophy* 45, no. 1 (2007): 49–78.

49. Van Ruler, *Crisis of Causality*, 172–87, 201–6, 298–301.

50. Baxter, *Additional Notes*, 6.

51. RCR, 519.

himself with the Aristotelians who rooted causes intrinsically in individuals rather than in largely relational external factors.[52]

At the same time, Baxter's negative evaluation of mechanical philosophy did not entail a wholly uncritical embrace of Aristotelianism. Not only did he embrace aspects of the new astronomy of Galileo and Gassendi and accept a limited role for corpuscular explanation in the realm of passive nonliving things (see chapter 4), he also expressed dissatisfaction with "the order and number of *Aristotle's* ten predicaments," as well as Aristotle's description of the predicament of quality as ambiguous—a "*name* too general and defective to signifie the nature of them aright."[53] Moreover, he believed that his own time had seen genuine progress with respect to the nature of local motion. "The doctrine of *Motion* is much improved by our late Philosophers," Baxter wrote.[54] The "late Philosophers" to whom Baxter referred were, of course, neither Descartes nor Gassendi. Who were they? One to whom he only briefly refers is John Wallis (1616–1703), Savilian professor of geometry at Oxford and one of the founding members of the Royal Society, whose publications on laws of impact in the *Philosophical Transactions* of the Royal Society in 1668 were followed by *Mechanica, sive, De motu tractatus geometricus* (1670).[55] However, Baxter was more interested in the *Tractatus physicus de motu locali* (1646) of the Jesuit Honoré Fabri (c.1607–1688), which he cites repeatedly. Fabri had incorporated new ideas of motion into his physics, and his works were reviewed and cited by the *Philosophical Transactions* of the early Royal Society.[56] In Fabri's discussion of impetus (*de impetu*) and downward natural motion (*de motu naturali deorsum*), according to Baxter, "the nature of Motion is more exactly handled than by the Epicureans or Cartesians; though little is said *de vi moventis* [of the force of the thing that moves], in comparison of what is said *de impetu mobilis* [of the impetus of the thing that is moved]." Baxter had read the first two chapters of Fabri's

---

52. On the broader shift away from individually located intrinsic causation, see Keith Hutchison, "Individual, Causal Location, and the Eclipse of Scholastic Philosophy," *Social Studies of Science* 21 (1991): 321–50.

53. *RCR*, 537. Baxter complained that Aristotle's category of quality contained *heterogenea*, wished to add the category of "order" to Aristotle's categories (*TKL*, 22), and considered writing a logic textbook (*MT*, I.153). Cf. Packer, *Redemption*, 76–77.

54. *RCR*, 31.

55. *CD*, III.923 (q. 174); *ODNB*, s.v. "Wallis, John (1616–1703)."

56. Michael Elazar, *Honoré Fabri and the Concept of Impetus: A Bridge Between Conceptual Frameworks* (Dordrecht: Springer, 2011), xi–xii; Gemma Murray, William Harper, and Curtis Wilson, "Huygens, Wren, Wallis, and Newton on Rules of Impact and Reflection," in *Vanishing Matter and the Laws of Motion: Descartes and Beyond*, ed. Dana Jalobeanu and Peter R. Anstey (New York: Routledge, 2011), 153–91, at 154.

Tractatus physicus de motu locali quite carefully, as appears from his summary of specific points from pages of chapter 2 on the cause of local motion.[57]

Fabri's discussion of motion was one of many responses to Galileo's theory of free fall, according to which the uniform acceleration of falling bodies is held to increase in distance according to the series of odd numbers 1, 3, 5, 7, 9, and so on.[58] Since Galileo refrained from discussing the causality of his mathematically descriptive account of free fall, a variety of philosophers vied to integrate a mathematical description of the uniform acceleration of bodies with a causal account of that acceleration. Fabri's response in 1646 came after that of Gassendi's *De motu impresso a motore translato* (1642).[59] Against the mechanical externalization of causality to impact, Fabri drew upon a late medieval theory of impetus, or internal quality causing downward local motion, which he reinterpreted as the formal cause of motion. He also rejected the Aristotelian natural motion of levity. Along with this modification of Aristotelian local motion, Fabri proposed an alternative mathematical series of accelerating free fall to that of Galileo that built on the foundation of impetus and (he claimed) preserved the experimental results of Galileo's observations. Fabri's *Tractatus* thus attempted to assimilate new observations about local motion into a nonmechanical theory of the intrinsic cause of local motion. Remarkably, even as Fabri proposed an alternative causal foundation to mechanical philosophers, the outcome of his theory of motion came quite close to the Cartesian law of the conservation of rectilinear motion (essentially the modern principle of inertia).[60] It was certainly the anti-mechanical implications of

---

57. *RCR*, 519. Cf. *MT*, "Praefatio," [A5r]; *CD*, III.923 (q. 174); Baxter, *Additional Notes*, 5. Baxter attributes the *Tractatus physicus de motu locali* (Lyon: Joannes Champion, 1646) to Petrus Mousnerius, student of Fabri, who transcribed Fabri's lectures. The attribution of authorship on the title page of this work reads, "*Auctore* Petro Movsnerio *Doctore Medico*: cvncta excerpta *Ex praelectionibus* R. P. Honorati Fabry, *Societatis* Iesv." Thus, although Fabri's doctrine was properly the source of this work, Baxter understandably attributed it to Mousnerius.

58. Galileo Galilei, *Two New Sciences*, trans. Stillman Drake (Toronto: Wall & Thompson, 1989), 153–54, 167–70. Cf. Michael Elazar and Rivka Feldhay, "Honoré Fabri S. J. and Galileo's Law of Fall: What Kind of Controversy?," in *Controversies within the Scientific Revolution*, ed. Marcelo Dascal and Victor D. Boantza (Philadelphia: John Benjamins Publishing Company, 2011), 13–32, at 15.

59. Paolo Galluzzi, "Galileo and *l'Affaire Galilée* of the Laws of Motion," in *Galileo in Context*, ed. Jürgen Renn (Cambridge: Cambridge University Press, 2001), 239–75; Carla Rita Palmerino, "Two Jesuit Responses to Galileo's Science of Motion: Honoré Fabri and Pierre Le Cazre," in *The New Science and Jesuit Science: Seventeenth Century Perspectives*, ed. Mordechai Feingold (Dordrecht: Kluwer, 2003), 187–227.

60. Elazar, *Honoré Fabri*; Elazar and Feldhay, "Honoré Fabri," 13–32. Ezazar emphasizes Fabri's assimilation of new science of motion against older studies, which, following Alexander Koyré and Anneliese Maier, saw a radical antithesis between Fabri's theory of impetus and modern accounts of inertia. See David C. Lukens, "An Aristotelian Response to Galileo: Honoré Fabri, S. J. (1608–1688) on the Causal Analysis of Motion" (PhD diss.,

Fabri's treatise on local motion that attracted Baxter to it. For Baxter, Fabri's theory presented an example of a viable alternative to the philosophies of Gassendi and Descartes that harmonized with his own concern to preserve internal principles of causality against the relegation of causality to external factors.[61]

While Baxter was interested in contemporary theories of local motion such as that of Fabri, the heart of his polemic was over the causality of living and active things with a principle of self-motion. We turn next, then, to Baxter's defense of what he often refers to as "active nature" and also, less frequently, as "substantial form." After this, we will examine Baxter's response to Descartes's laws of motion, which he saw as a popular mechanical alternative to the activity of substantial forms, before turning finally to Baxter's engagement with Henry More's adaptation of Cartesian mechanism.

Substantial Form

By the late 1660s and early 1670s, when Baxter wrote down most of his thoughts on substance, the Aristotelian hylomorphic notion of substance as composed of matter and form had come under severe criticism for a couple of decades, and Robert Boyle's attack on substantial forms was hot off the press.[62] "We read great disputes both for & ag^t substantiall formes," noted Baxter (ca. 1669).[63] A great part of Voetius's objection to Descartes's philosophy, expressed just a few decades earlier, centered on Descartes's rejection of Aristotelian substantial form.[64] Other thinkers, including Baxter, took a more eclectic approach. Daniel Sennert combined an atomist explanation of the elements with the notion of substantial form.[65] Baxter's younger contemporary Leibniz, while early in life adopting mechanical philosophy, later found that the "ultimate reasons for mechanism" and the laws of motion "could not be found in mathematics but that I should have to return to metaphysics." This compelled Leibniz to modify his natural philosophy by reintroducing a concept of substantial form in order to better account for

---

University of Toronto, 1979); and Stillman Drake, "Impetus Theory and Quanta of Speed before and after Galileo," *Physis* 16 (1974): 47–75.

61. Cf. *RCR*, 519.

62. Robert Boyle, *The Origine of Formes and Qualities, (According to the Corpuscular Philosophy,) Illustrated by Considerations and Experiments* (Oxford: H. Hall, 1666).

63. DWL BT XIX.351, fol. 28r.

64. Verbeek, *Descartes and the Dutch*, 14–19; Van Ruler, *Crisis of Causality*, 32–35, 59–61, 167–98. On Descartes, see Garber, *Descartes' Metaphysical Physics*, 94–116.

65. Newman, *Atoms and Alchemy*, 85–125; Michael, "Daniel Sennert on Matter and Form," 272–99.

the metaphysical foundations of unity and motion in substances.[66] Matthew Hale, who discussed such matters with Baxter in person, granted that some forms previously thought to be substantial might be "various Modifications of *Matter*," while others might have "some middle Nature," but found substantial form necessary to account for "Life, Sense, Intellection, Volition, and the like."[67] Baxter shared these concerns about the metaphysical necessity for the concept of substantial form. Although he conceded the explanatory validity of Boyle's corpuscularism in a limited part of the inanimate realm, he considered it especially necessary to preserve a conception of substantial form for the realm of living creatures. But since his concept of active nature was broader than life and included the nature of fire, he also defended the possibility of nonliving principles of motion, as we shall see in his reply to Henry More.

From a metaphysical perspective, Baxter thought the concept of form was necessary to account for the activity, specification, and unity of composite substances. He describes substantial form as both specifying and animating a composition:

> The *Substantial* Form is the principal, most active, predominating *Substance* in the composition: Such is the human Soul in the human being, & the Souls of bruits in brute beasts (whatever many may growl at against this). This thing is different from the body; & it is not inappropriate for this *Form*, inasmuch as it is a separable spiritual Substance, to receive its own specific *Form*.[68]

Elsewhere, Baxter states that "form" is "that peculiar nature, consisting in certain powers or virtues, by which, as essential to it, that being is specifically differenced from others: which some call an essential quality, and some a substantial quality, and some a substantial form, because it is the perfection and essential nature of the substance *in specie*, and not another substance besides it."[69]

---

66. Daniel Garber, "Leibniz on Form and Matter," *Early Science and Medicine* 2, no. 3 (1997): 326–52, at 327–28; Garber, *Leibniz: Body, Substance, Monad* (Oxford: Oxford University Press, 2011), 48–54; Paul Bartha, "Substantial Form and the Nature of Individual Substance," *Studia Leibnitiana* 25, no. 1 (1993): 43–54.

67. Matthew Hale, *The Primitive Origination of Mankind* (London: William Godbid, 1677), 9–10, 27–28.

68. MT, I.137: "Forma *Substantialis* est *Substantia* in composito principalis, maximè activa, praedominans: Talis est Anima humana in homine, & Anima brutorum in brutis, (Quicquid contra hoc nonnulli ogganiant.) Haec est Res altera à corpore; & non est inconveniens hujus *Formae* utpote Substantiae spiritualis separabilis, dari *Formam* suam specificam."

69. RCR, 536.

In composite substances, the union of the substantial form with the rest of the substance provides order and unity for the parts of the composite. Baxter refers to this resulting "order of parts" as the "relative form" (*forma relativa*) or "respective form" (*forma respectiva*).[70] He also says that "form" is "oft taken for *substantiae figura,* and oft for the contexture of corporeal parts making it receptive of Motion, oft for the union of the moving and moved parts."[71] This sense of form as the "order of parts" can be found in both inanimates and animates. For "inanimate machines," the form as the order of parts is simply the "weight or other principle of motion."[72] For animates, the relative form is merely the "mode" of the substantial form. In setting forth a distinction between substantial and relative form, Baxter cites Franco Burgersdijck's division between substantial form, which "perfects and informs" matter, and accidental form, which is a "unity by accident."[73] Baxter thus regarded his "relative form" as close to the scholastic concept of *unum per accidens.* He also illustrates this difference by distinguishing a plurality of forms: the form of the body (*formam corporis*), the form of the soul (*formam animae*), and the form of man (*formam hominis*). He identifies the form of the body as the order of parts "apt to receive a soul," and the form of man as "the *state* of the *parts contemperate* and *ordered.*[74] As Burton has persuasively argued, Baxter's espousal of a plurality of forms in humanity, with the soul perfecting the form of the body, is close to the position of Scotus and is "most likely influenced by the Scotist tradition."[75] Baxter could also have derived such a view from his reading of early modern authors such as Sennert and Julius Caesar Scaliger.[76]

From a theological perspective, substantial form provided a philosophically useful concept that appeared to fit well (according to its defenders) with the Genesis account of creation. When Voetius attacked the Cartesian denial of substantial form, he was mostly interested in preserving a conception of creation in which God created essentially distinct "kinds" endowed with their own proper

---

70. *MT,* I.6 (*forma relativa*), 137 (*forma respectiva*), 140 (*forma relativa*).

71. Baxter, *Of the Nature of Spirits,* 83–84.

72. *MT,* I.137.

73. *RCR,* 536–37, citing Franco Burgersdijck, *Institutionum Metaphysicarum,* 3rd ed. (London, 1653), I.xxv.6 (p. 162): "*Forma substantialis* est quae materiam complet eamque informat, atque ita constituit substantiam corpoream. *Forma accidentalis,* est addimentum, completae substantiae inhaerens, & cum illa constituens ens concretum, atque unum per accidens."

74. *RCR,* 537. Cf. DWL BT II.23, fol. 54v.

75. Burton, *Hallowing of Logic,* 150–52. Cf. Richard Cross, *The Physics of Duns Scotus: The Scientific Context of a Theological Vision* (Oxford: Clarendon Press, 1998), 62–71.

76. Emily Michael, "Daniel Sennert on Matter and Form," 275–86.

qualities and acts.[77] Baxter, who shared the same theological motivation as Voetius for a Mosaic physics, agreed that the kinds mentioned in Genesis were equivalent to the concept of substantial form. In his summary of the "Physicks" of Genesis 1, Baxter referred to the kinds of plants as "specifick forms."[78] Yet his interest in substantial form was focused on its role as a principle of activity and motion. He thus often calls substantial form by the synonyms "active nature," "active form," and "essential virtue," and describes the substantial form as "the principal, most active, predominating *Substance* in the composition."[79] Likewise, Baxter states, "there are Essential *Virtues* called *substantial Forms*, or *active Natures*."[80]

While Baxter agreed with others such as Voetius that the substantial form is the principle of activity, he also held distinctive views regarding the origin and nature of forms. A popular explanation for the origin of substantial forms among Aristotelian philosophers was that they were educed from (or latent in) the potency of matter in some way.[81] Sennert observed that "most of the Schoolmen and their followers have fiercely maintained this Opinion,"[82] and Voetius was among them.[83] This theory of eduction was a favorite whipping boy of anti-Aristotelians like Gassendi, who objected that on the Aristotelian account one cannot derive an active principle like form from a purely passive principle like matter.[84] On this point, Baxter noted his disagreement with the Aristotelian theory, summarized in the dictum "form is drawn from matter" (*forma educitur a materia*), in a letter to Glanvill.[85] Yet like others, such as Sennert and Hale, the reason for this criticism was not philosophical but theological—God initially created forms, which thereafter have a divinely given power of multiplication in accordance with Genesis

77. Van Ruler, *Crisis of Causality*, 59–61; Goudriaan, *Reformed Orthodoxy and Philosophy*, 117, 119–21. See also Han van Ruler, "'Something, I Know Not What'. The Concept of Substance in Early Modern Thought," in *Between Imagination and Demonstration. Essays in the History of Science and Philosophy Presented to John D. North*, ed. Lodi Nauta and Arjo Vanderjagt (Leiden: Brill, 1999), 365–93.

78. *RCR*, 415.

79. *MT*, I.137.

80. *TKL*, 253.

81. Cf. Des Chene, *Physiologia*, 139–44.

82. Daniel Sennert, *Thirteen Books of Natural Philosophy* (London: Peter Cole, 1660), 469.

83. Goudriaan, *Reformed Orthodoxy and Philosophy*, 115.

84. LoLordo, *Pierre Gassendi*, 43–44; Robert Boyle, *Origine of Formes and Qualities, (According to the Corpuscular Philosophy) Illustrated by Considerations and Experiments*, 2nd ed. (Oxford: H. Hall, 1667), 73–78. Cf. Schmaltz, *Descartes on Causation*, 45–46; and Dennis Des Chene, *Spirits and Clocks: Machine & Organism in Descartes* (Ithaca, NY: Cornell University Press, 2001), 154–55.

85. Baxter to Glanvill, 18 Nov. 1670 (DWL BC II.139r).

1:22, 28: "be fruitful and multiply." Baxter stated, "We do not say that these Powers or formal Virtues are educed from the *Potency of Matter*, but active & generative principles, & spiritual & active substances with their formal virtues, are from the Will & blessing of the Creator, [and] they themselves as it were communicate with bodies, & operate on them."[86] Baxter thus represents an alternative explanation for the origin of forms that departs from the dominant scholastic account, even while still retaining forms over against the outright rejection by Glanvill and others.

The extent to which Baxter was willing to depart from traditional views of substantial form is vividly illustrated in his manuscript "Of the Nature and Immortality of Humane Soules" (ca. 1669) and the further correspondence with Hale on it (ca. 1672–1673). In this manuscript, Baxter utilized his distinction between substantial and relative forms to express the extent to which he could accommodate a mechanical understanding of vegetative and sensitive forms. Every animate being, according to Baxter, has both an *active nature* constituting its substantial form and an *order* or *temperament* of parts that together make up a particular species. Whereas traditional Aristotelians assumed that every subspecies of living things, such as a horse or a dog, has its own particular substantial form, Baxter speculated that the specific differences within the genera of vegetative and sensitive forms might be explained by the various contextures of their parts.[87] This position (stated around 1669) would appear to be a departure from his view, expressed just a few years earlier in *Reasons*, that plants and animals have "specifick forms," "proper species," or "specifying differences."[88] Baxter evidently felt the force of mechanical objections to Aristotelian forms and opened up the category of subordinate forms to mechanical explanation. As he explained to Hale, "I was not willing to goe further from o[u]r new oppugners of *formes*, then I needes must."[89] In making this concession, Baxter effectively shifted the issue of subordinate forms to the category of uncertain matters, as a thing "unknowne to mortalls."[90] To Hale he

---

86. *MT*, I.141: "Non dicimus Potentias hasce seu Virtutes formales è Potentia Materiae eductas esse; sed ex Creatoris Voluntate & benedictione, esse principia activa & generativa, & substantias spirituales & activas cum suis virtutibus formalibus, se ipsas corporibus quasi communicare, & in illa operari." Cf. *RCR*, 416; *MT*, I.125; Sennert, *Thirteen Books of Natural Philosophy*, 18–20, 422–23, 461, 468–73; Hale, *A Discourse of the Knowledge of God*, 101, 147–48.

87. DWL BT XIX.351, fols. 27v–28v, 85r. He notes that Daniel Sennert, in his *Hypomnemata physica*, is among those who hold that "every plant hath moreover its specifike forme, & so hath every animal, by wch they differ from each other" (fols. 84v–85r).

88. *RCR*, 208, 415, 511–12, 520. Cf. *CD*, IV.171.

89. LPL MS 3499, fol. 93v.

90. DWL BT XIX.351, fol. 85r: "But whether God hath further differenced Plants among themselves, & Animals (Sensitive only) among themselves, by an essentiall formall Virtue in their severall soules, or only by ye various contexture, temp[er]ament, & motion of & in

admitted that he was uncertain whether God had "founded this difference" of "distinct subordinate species" in the diversity of matter or in "ye diversity of y^e *formall virtues* or *soule*." Both opinions are possible: "I thinke y^t God can do either: And if he can, I know not wch he doth."[91]

Baxter's uncertainty about subordinate species was qualified by a number of important certainties. Baxter was certain that "God himselfe made y^m of different species at ye first [creation]," that God made them from previously created elements, and that God gave them the power of multiplication.[92] He was also uncompromising in his affirmation of the generic differences between plants, animals, and humans. He was certain that even if the differences between apples, pears, lemons, turnips, and so forth resulting in various colors, tastes, shapes, smells, and so forth might be explained by their various "mixtures," these mixtures could never account for the difference in powers among vegetative, sensitive, and rational forms, which are eminently above any compound mixture.[93] These caveats regarding the origin and nature of subordinate forms illustrate important lines that Baxter was unwilling to cross as he sought a limited accommodation with mechanical philosophy. The creation of a hierarchy of vital powers was among these points. The preservation of the specific differences within the genera of plants and animals mattered less to him than the preservation of essential differences between vegetative, sensitive, and rational forms, and the inclusion of a hierarchy of powers within the rational soul.

In correspondence with Hale, Baxter appears to have backpedaled from his earlier concession on subordinate forms in response to Hale's criticism. Hale thought the possibility of a material explanation for subordinate forms conceded too much and urged Baxter against that opinion.[94] Baxter was apparently persuaded by Hale's remarks, and replied, "But upon consideration of w^t you say, & also considering how improbable it is, y^t God who maketh such wonderfull diversityes among bodies, should not also make great diversityes among spirits, I do more incline to yo[u]r opinion than ye other."[95] With this remark, Baxter indicated a preference for his earlier affirmation of "specifick forms" found in the *Reasons*.

---

ye Corporeall particles to wch they are united, & by ye Matters various reception of ye solar (or fiery) influxe, is a thing I thinke unknowne to mortalls. Our distribution therefore is certaine: But his [Sennert] is uncertaine, & not contradictory to o[ur]s if it were certaine."

91. LPL MS 3499, fol. 93v.

92. DWL BT XIX.351, fol. 28r.

93. DWL BT XIX.351, fol. 29r.

94. LPL MS 3499, fol. 93r, 94r.

95. LPL MS 3499, fol. 93v.

Even so, he did not retract his uncertainty regarding subordinate forms in print. In his *Methodus theologiae*, Baxter placed among the "uncertainties" of creation the question of whether vegetative and sensitive souls are specified by a diversity of forms or by material textures.[96] Baxter's correspondence with Hale thus demonstrates a certain fluidity to Baxter's views on subordinate forms during the years 1669–1672 when he was drafting "Of the Nature and Immortality of Humane Soules" and the *Methodus theologiae.*

With respect to the relation of forms and powers, Baxter disagreed with the Thomists who thought the powers or virtues of form are really distinct from the form itself. Rather, he sided with the Scotists who taught that the powers differ formally but not really from the essence of the form or soul.[97] Baxter's conviction that the soul is the image of the triune God—a *"Trinity in Unity of Essence"*— certainly played a part in his mature argument in favor of the Scotists against the Thomists. If powers are essentially the same with the form, then there would be a closer resemblance to the Trinity.[98] Yet he inclined toward this Scotist opinion at an early date, well before his explicitly Trinitarian agenda took shape.[99] In any case, Baxter's continuities with Scotist views on the nature and plurality of forms demonstrates that even though he was quite eclectic in his approach to substantial form, he still considered debates between Thomists and Scotists relevant to his own formulation.

Given his own acceptance of substantial form, Baxter reacted strongly against its denial by Descartes and Gassendi. Historians of philosophy now recognize a variety of philosophical positions held by early modern philosophers on the nature of matter, ranging from Descartes's "strict" mechanical perspective, whereby mechanical action is restricted to direct contact by inert matter, to what is sometimes considered a less strict mechanical perspective, represented by Gassendi's inclusion of intrinsic activity in matter.[100] Baxter appears to have been attuned to certain differences in this respect. He recognized, for example, differences between

---

96. *MT*, I.126–27 (nos. 29–30).

97. Baxter devotes an entire *disputatio* in the *Methodus theologiae* to the question, "Are the Soul's faculties or Natural Powers the soul's essential form itself?" See *MT*, I.164–75; with discussion in Burton, *Hallowing of Logic*, 159–64. He refers to this disputation often, e.g., *MT*, I.134; *End of Doctrinal Controversies*, x. Cf. Des Chene, *Life's Form*, 143–51; Katherine Park, "The Organic Soul," in *The Cambridge History of Renaissance Philosophy*, ed. Charles B. Schmitt, Quentin Skinner, and Eckhard Kessler (New York: Cambridge University Press, 1988), 464–84, at 477–78.

98. Cf. Baxter, *MT*, I.134, 165–67; and Burton, *Hallowing of Logic*, 163.

99. Baxter, *Reduction of a Digressor*, 126–27.

100. See chapter 1 above; and Antonia LoLordo, "The Activity of Matter in Gassendi's Physics," *Oxford Studies in Early Modern Philosophy* 2 (2005): 75–103.

Descartes and Gassendi on whether matter is inherently active or inert.[101] Yet this recognition did not stop him from lumping Descartes and Gassendi together into the same camp of "innovators," since he saw their denial of substantial form, with its inherent powers (or virtues), as resulting in a similar problem. "Besides the *substance* of simple *acts* as such, and besides an act," wrote Baxter, "it is indubitable that there is ACTIVE VIRTUE. Therefore they are mad who contend that there is nothing else in the entire nature of things beyond *Matter & Motion*."[102] Elsewhere he singled out the "errors of certain innovators" (*neotericorum*) concerning motion. "The ignorance & denial of active virtues has thrown the Epicureans and other modern Philosophers headlong into a multitude of errors."[103] Despite painting Descartes and Gassendi with the same broad brush as "Epicureans" and "innovators," as we shall see, in the details of his polemic Baxter showed familiarity with their differences and tried to exploit those differences to his advantage.

Baxter used a number of different arguments to defend the existence of substantial forms (or active natures). In general, he tried to cast doubt on the assumptions of his opponents in order to make the existence of intrinsic principles of motion more plausible. The arguments he employed to defend substantial forms were drawn from both theology proper (i.e., the attributes of God in relation to second causes) and the nature of secondary causes. We will first discuss Baxter's arguments from God's attributes and then address the remaining philosophical arguments regarding secondary causes.

As we discussed in the previous chapter, Baxter held that God's attributes have an analogical relation to creatures. He assumes this analogical relation when he discusses the relation of God's attributes to the nature of secondary causes. Baxter argues that since God is an active and living God, his creation should likewise have an analogous activity and life. Since active virtue "is without doubt found *in God himself*, it must not be entirely denied to *Being* [*Esse*]." It is a "vile and contemptible" conception of God, and "by no means the perfect Image of Divine *Vitality*, or *Activity*, & *Love*," to assert that he makes only inert matter without any active principle in things. God was neither unable to make active natures because he is omnipotent, nor unwilling to make them since he desired to communicate his goodness to creatures.[104] Since even creatures "generate their like," one should

---

101. As Baxter summarizes Gassendi's view, "[I]t is the *contexture of the most subtle Atomes which is the form and first mover in physical* beings . . . that God moved those Atomes, and also put a moving inclination into them" (*RCR*, 504, citing Gassendi, *Opera*, 1:337a).

102. *MT*, I.133: "Simplicium *Activorum* praeter *substantiam*, quâ *talem*, & *actum*, datur proculdubio VIRTUS ACTIVA. Delirant igitur qui in tota rerum naturâ praeter *Materiam* & *Motum* nil aliud esse contendunt."

103. *MT*, I.141.

104. *MT*, I.133–34.

expect that God also communicates a variety of perfections beyond matter: "God is essential infinite Life, Wisdom and Love: and can he, or would he make nothing liker to himself than dead Atomes?"[105]

A second argument derives from God's attributes of wisdom and goodness. In a completely mechanical world, God's omnipotence figures prominently since God acts as the first mover and preserver of all things. However, Baxter argues, God is not merely an omnipotent creator of being and motion; he is also a God of wisdom and goodness. "It is also manifest in the effect," writes Baxter, "that it is not a *meer motion* of the *first* Cause, which appeareth in the *being* and *motions* of the Creature." An effect also has a tendency and order to an end. God's goodness is shown in the tendency or inclination of things to certain ends or attractive goods, while his wisdom is shown in the order that those things have in the attaining of those ends. Thus, "that *Wisdom* and *Goodness* do eminently appear in them all, in their beings, natures, differences, excellencies, order and ends, as well as *Motion* the effect of *Power*."[106] In this argument, Baxter combines God's analogical relationship to creation with the three primary attributes of power, wisdom, and goodness that he thought reflected the Trinity (see chapter 4).

With such theological arguments, Baxter demonstrates not a one-sided appeal to God's omnipotence associated in modern secondary literature with voluntarism. Instead, he quite clearly justifies his opposition to the displacement of intrinsic secondary causes with reasons taken from God's life, wisdom, and goodness. Whether or not it is true, as many scholars have argued, that voluntarism was an important theological factor in the rise of modern science,[107] Baxter's position contradicts those who have argued that "the Calvinist God in His remote majesty resembles the watchmaker God of the mechanical universe,"[108] or that "the Reformers' view of God rendered Aristotelian essentialism pointless by denying that essences contribute causality or purpose to nature."[109] In fact, Baxter's analogical thinking, although demonstrating more eclecticism than his Reformed predecessors, nevertheless aligns in many respects with their typically Thomistic

---

105. Baxter, *Nature and Immortality of the Soul*, 55.

106. *RCR*, 503–6.

107. See the recent exchange: Peter Harrison, "Voluntarism and Early Modern Science," *History of Science* 40 (2002): 63–89; Henry, "Voluntarist Theology," 79–113; Peter Harrison, "Voluntarism and the Origins of Modern Science: A Reply to John Henry," *History of Science* 47 (2009): 223–31. Cf. Francis Oakley, "Christian Theology and the Newtonian Science: The Rise of the Concept of the Laws of Nature," *Church History* 30, no. 4 (1961): 433–57; Funkenstein, *Theology and the Scientific Imagination*, 117–201; Osler, *Divine Will and the Mechanical Philosophy*, 48–56.

108. Westfall, *Science and Religion*, 5.

109. Deason, "Reformation Theology," 178.

analogical approach to understanding God.[110] For Baxter at least, the theological assumption of God's analogical relation to creatures constitutes a more important factor in the evaluation of mechanical philosophy than the question of the relative priority of God's intellect or will.

Beyond these arguments from God's attributes, Baxter provided numerous reasons to doubt that matter and motion alone are a sufficient explanation for the kind of intrinsic causality traditionally attributed to substantial forms. The main point of his first argument is that change of motion indicates an intrinsic source of motion—a power or inclination to motion that lies behind particular motions. In order for mechanical philosophy to be true, reasons Baxter, all differences in motions would have to be accounted for either by an external agent or the configuration of matter in the recipient. However, neither of these is sufficient to account for all the differences in moving bodies. External agency is not sufficient to account for diversity of motions, since the uniform motion from an external agent such as the sun results in a variety of motions.[111] A different configuration of bodies in the recipients is likewise not sufficient, since there should still be an equal proportion between antecedent and subsequent motion. Yet in fact we often recognize a disproportion between antecedent and subsequent motion when there is a sudden change. This sudden change indicates a power beyond motion either to move or restrain motion.[112]

Furthermore, according to Baxter, the notion of matter put forth by Gassendi has problems explaining phenomena. Gassendi posited a unique theory of weight (*pondus*) or innate mobility (*mobilitas ingenita*) in his atoms, by which atoms produce the phenomena of gravity by hooking onto and drawing bodies away from their previous position.[113] But why, asks Baxter, do these atoms pull things toward the earth so powerfully when there are presumably just as many pulling up from the sun's attraction? Why do the upward atoms not pull things up? Or why do the downward-pulling atoms pull some things quickly down but not other objects like birds and feathers?[114] Moreover, Baxter observes that Gassendi's concept of *mobilitas ingenita* indicates an active power that generates motion. If so, then there are innate powers beyond already-existing motion and matter, which militates against a purely mechanical philosophy and increases the plausibility of other active principles in nature.[115]

---

110. See chapter 4; and Muller, "Not Scotist," 127–50.

111. *RCR*, 506.

112. *RCR*, 507.

113. LoLordo, *Pierre Gassendi*, 142.

114. *RCR*, 507–8.

115. *RCR*, 508–9.

Another line of argument is that there seem to be potential sources of motion—that is, sources of motion distinct from already existing motion. He defends the scholastic concept of *conatus* (inclination) as a potentiality for motion.[116] There are objects that are not presently moving but that we can sense as inclined to move. Baxter provides the example of holding one hundred pounds of lead in one's hand. We feel the lead inclining to move even while it is at rest.[117] Another potential source of motion is habit (*habitus*). A habit is not merely actual motion but rather consists of the potential to act; it is an "inclination for acting." When anyone with a special skill or knowledge suspends his or her thoughts, the ability does not go away even if there is no act of the habit.[118]

In addition to arguments from the change and sources of motion, Baxter argued that matter and motion alone could not account for the hierarchy of being characterized by essential differences of genus and species. The variety of effects evident in the world—the descent of gravity, the ascent of fire, the carnivorous or herbivorous natures of animals, the distinctive shapes and odors of plants, etc.—all indicate differences in kind that are not reducible to changes in matter and motion.[119] For Baxter, one of the greatest difficulties mechanical philosophy has is explaining how faculties of sensation can arise out of matter and motion. Assuming the proportionality between cause and effect—"nothing gives that which it does not have, either formally or eminently" (*Nihil dat quod non habet, vel formaliter vel eminenter*)—Baxter objects to the claim that sensation is somehow the result of matter and motion.[120] Neither atoms nor motion have sense, and it is impossible for any mixture of insensible things to create something sensible. Both Scaliger and Sennert, Baxter thought, had already written various objections to deriving sensation from matter, motion, or mixture, but among the explanations of mechanical philosophers, "we can meet with no account of it yet worth reading: not by *Cartesius*, not by [Henricus] *Regius* or [Claudius] *Berigardus*, not by *Gassendus*, nor any other that we can get and read." Although Baxter did not elaborate any further, he did single out Regius's explanation of animal sensation as particularly unconvincing.[121]

---

116. Cf. Leijenhorst, *Mechanisation of Aristotelianism*, 196–201, on Hobbes's reinterpretation of *conatus* as actual motion.

117. *RCR*, 510.

118. *RCR*, 511.

119. *RCR*, 511–12. This argument precedes his concession on subordinate forms, discussed above.

120. *RCR*, 513.

121. *RCR*, 513–14, citing Henricus Regius, *Philosophica naturalis* (Amsterdam: Apud Ludovicum & Danielem Elzevirios, 1661), IV.iii (p. 267).

Baxter also attacked Descartes's reduction of bodies to divisibility, shape, and mobility. He saw the "foundations of Descartes' hodgepodge of errors" in his geometrical account of body, [122] and argued that this constitutes a poor substitute for a concept of substance inclusive of qualities. He contested Descartes's account of body first by drawing attention to the inconclusive state of the knowledge of bodies. Baxter points to general ignorance concerning many *differentia* of substances, whether of spirits or bodies. Among these matters of ignorance, Baxter includes the differencing characteristics (*differentiis*) of passive bodies, the nature of gravity, projectiles, penetrability, and individuation. Speculation regarding such matters was still a matter of uncertainty, and although "certain modest conjectures" could be made about them, existing conclusions regarding them and systems built on such conclusions should not be trusted.[123] In a similar way, Baxter argues that Descartes's reduction of bodies to the properties of divisibility, shape, and mobility are assertions based on matters that remain highly uncertain. "But what sort of person will believe that there are no other qualities of matter or accidents [than those] unknown to Descartes? Or what sort of person will believe that so many things must be believed while [someone] is ignorant of them and the remainder have not been fully proved?"[124] In particular, Baxter takes exception to Descartes's argument that the difference between liquids and solids could be explained simply by the motion (liquid) or rest of their particles (solid). Baxter also questions how it could be proved that "water in a marble or air in a balloon is as hard as marble itself? or even that their particles do not rest beside each other?"[125] He also argues that, given Cartesian principles, we should expect that denser things such as stones or dirt, if only finely pulverized, could become sun, light, or sensitive souls, and likewise if the latter were only made more dense (*per solam incrassationem*) they could become stones or dirt.[126] Baxter clearly assumes such conclusions were absurd.

Baxter further added that Descartes's geometrical concept of body had a problem accounting for the unity of bodies. In this objection, Baxter echoed the concerns of Voetius before him and Leibniz after him. Voetius argued that without

---

122. *MT*, I.150, citing Descartes, *Principia philosophiae*, II, §64 (AT 8:78–79).

123. *MT*, I.150.

124. *MT*, I.150: "Quis autem credet, nullas alias materiae qualitates esse, aut accidentia nulla Cartesio incognita? Aut tam multa ignoranti, in caeteris non solidè probatis, credendum esse?"

125. *MT*, I.150: "Quomodo autem potest probare aut aquam marmore inclusam, aut aerem in vesicâ, tam durum esse quam ipse Marmor? aut etiam earum particulas non juxta se mutuo quiescere?" Baxter cites Descartes, *Principia philosophiae*, II, §54 (AT 8:71). On this topic, see Gaukroger, *Descartes' System*, 130–34.

126. *MT*, I.150.

a notion of substantial form, one would be hard-pressed to explain individuality—a concern that later philosophical development demonstrated to be remarkably prescient.[127] Leibniz himself returned to a concept of substantial form in part because he saw that Cartesian philosophy could not account for "real unity."[128] Descartes had stated that "our reason certainly cannot discover any bond which could join the particles of solid bodies more firmly together than does their own rest." Rather than substance, Descartes claimed that rest constitutes the bond uniting particles.[129] In response to this claim, Baxter asks whether it is possible that the "entire world of passive things," as long as they are at rest, is one thing without an individuation of its parts? Conversely, if particles are always moving, does this imply that objects such as the sun are not a unity? In short, "are there as many Suns as fine Atoms, or what is the glue of particles that never rest?" Baxter concludes that if Descartes would have understood more "theologically or platonically" and recognized "spiritual substances with their formal virtues," he would have understood "more rightly the principles of individuation."[130] By understanding "platonically," Baxter may be referring to the relative superiority over Descartes of "Plato's Philosophy wch acknowledgeth ye spirituall nature to be the mover of the corporeall."[131] He certainly regarded Plotinus's understanding of the soul as containing "a great deal of doctrine in it, much wiser and wholesome than that of Epicurus and the Atomists."[132] Whatever Baxter meant, it is clear that he regarded Descartes's account of the unity of bodies as inferior to his own understanding of substantial forms that animate and unite passive reality.

As we have seen, although substantial form played a variety of functions in early modern Aristotelian philosophy, Baxter's central focus was the role of substantial form in explaining sources of motion. In general, he tried to show that substantial forms provide a better explanation for the motion of living and active things than the explanations of mechanical philosophers. Beyond this defense of substantial form, however, Baxter also specifically objected to Descartes's alternative theory of laws of motion. Particularly in the *Methodus theologiae*, Baxter made a point of attacking Descartes's laws, and it is to this polemic that we now turn.

---

127. Van Ruler, "'Something, I Know Not What,'" 365–93.

128. Garber, "Leibniz on Form and Matter," 334–37.

129. Descartes, *Principia philosophiae*, II, §55 (AT 8:71; Miller, 70).

130. *MT*, I.150: "aut tot sunt Soles quot Atomi subtiles, aut quodnam est gluten particularum nunquam quiescentium. At si vel Theologicè vel Platonicè magis saperes; & substantias spirituales cum Virtutibus suis formalibus magis agnosceres, principia individuationis rectiùs teneres."

131. Baxter to Glanvill, 18 Nov. 1670 (DWL BC II.139r).

132. *RCR*, 575.

Descartes's Laws of Motion

Most modern people take it for granted that there are general "laws of nature" or "laws of motion" according to which natural phenomena can be explained and predicted in a physical or specifically mathematical (as opposed to moral) sense. However, this concept of physical laws of nature is of distinctly Western origin, and arguably rose to prominence in the seventeenth century through the influence of Descartes's *Principia philosophiae*. Before Descartes, theologians and philosophers had referred to laws of nature to indicate some providentially ordained regularity in nature (e.g., the sun rises or bees make honey), which was typically related to the concept of God as a legislator (e.g., Job 28:26) and the existence of nonspecific secondary causes. But the concept was not used in a precise physical sense to indicate the foundations of natural philosophy until the seventeenth century.[133] As John R. Milton observes, "The idea that one of the main aims—perhaps *the* main aim—of a natural philosopher should be the discovery of the laws governing the natural world emerged clearly for the first time during the seventeenth century."[134] This alteration in the foundation of natural philosophy would also have profound implications for natural theology, inasmuch it contributed to the development of eighteenth-century physico-theology, which shifted the conception of wisdom in nature away from analogical relations in a ladder of being (*scala naturae*) toward the divinely ordained machinery of efficient causes and material parts (see chapter 4). As William Paley later argued, God set down "general laws of matter," and these "exhibit demonstrations of his wisdom."[135]

Descartes's laws of nature, first adumbrated in the posthumously published *Le Monde* but reaching maturity and first published in the *Principia*, consisted of three fundamental principles.[136] The first law set forth the principle of the persistence of motion: "each thing, as far as it is in itself [*quantum in se est*], always

---

133. John Henry, "The Theological Origins of the Concept of Laws of Nature and Its Subsequent Secularization," in *Laws of Nature, Laws of God? Proceedings of the Science and Religion Forum Conference, 2014*, ed. Neil Spurway (Newcastle: Cambridge Scholars Publishing, 2015), 65–90, esp. 66–67. There is still debate among historians as to why a conception of laws of nature rose to prominence in the seventeenth century. For a good introduction to recent literature, see John Henry, "Metaphysics and the Origins of Modern Science: Descartes and the Importance of the Laws of Nature," *Early Science and Medicine* 9, no. 2 (2004): 73–114.

134. John R. Milton, "Laws of Nature," in *CHSP*, 1:680.

135. William Paley, *Natural Theology: Or, the Evidences of the Existence and Attributes of the Deity*, 2nd ed. (London: R. Faulder, 1802), 43. He also speaks of "laws of mechanism" (22), "laws which govern the communication of motion" (43), and "laws of motion" (550).

136. In what follows, I discuss the account from the Latin *Principia*, since this is the version that Baxter and his contemporaries were familiar with. For a description of the laws in *Le Monde*, see Garber, *Descartes' Metaphysical Physics*, 198–99.

remains in the same state; and that consequently, when it is once moved, it always continues to move."[137] The second law stated that all motion moves rectilinearly: "all movement is, of itself, along straight lines; and consequently, bodies which are moving in a circle always tend to move away from the center of the circle which they are describing."[138] The third law set forth rules for the collision of bodies: "a body, upon coming in contact with a stronger one, loses none of its motion; but that, upon coming in contact with a weaker one, it loses as much as it transfers to that weaker body."[139] All of Descartes's laws were rooted in God as the "universal and primary cause," who on account of his immutable nature "always maintains in [matter] an equal quantity of motion."[140] Although this latter "conservation" principle, as it is often referred to, was not one of Descartes's laws properly so-called, it was a fundamental premise of the particular laws. Thus the relation between God's immutability and the nature of motion (a fundamentally theological assumption) undergirded all particular motions. Through the general conservation of the quantity of motion, the laws shared in the idea that motion is persistent: it persists in its existing state (Law 1), its direction (Law 2), and its total quantity after collisions (Law 3).[141]

The general laws Descartes set forth in the *Principia* were highly influential in the latter half of the seventeenth century. Their importance can hardly be overstated. One scholar has recently remarked, "[T]he laws of nature are the lynch-pin of Cartesian and other mechanical philosophies."[142] While Descartes's particular rules governing the collisions of bodies were criticized by following generations, his general views on the conservation and persistence of motion were adopted by subsequent natural philosophers, including Newton. As Milton observes, "The actual laws proposed by Descartes proved unsatisfactory, though the general principle of inertia embodied in his first two laws has become the cornerstone of all subsequent dynamics."[143] Laws 1 and 2 from Descartes's *Principia*, when taken together, closely resemble Newton's first law of motion from his *Principia*,

---

137. Descartes, *Principia philosophiae*, II, §37 (AT 8:62; Miller, 59). The phrase *quantum in se est* has roots in Lucretius's *De rerum natura*. See Cohen, " 'Quantum in se est,' " 143–44.

138. Descartes, *Principia philosophiae*, II, §39 (AT 8:63; Miller, 60).

139. Descartes, *Principia philosophiae*, II, §40 (AT 8:65; Miller, 61).

140. Descartes, *Principia philosophiae*, II, §36 (AT 8:61; Miller, 57–58). In his argument for each of the three laws, Descartes states that they follow from divine immutability. See *Principia philosophiae*, II, §37, §39, §42 (AT 8:62, 63, 66; Miller, 59, 60, 62).

141. Garber, *Descartes' Metaphysical Physics*, 203–4.

142. Henry, "Theological Origins," 68.

143. Milton, "Laws of Nature," 699; cf. Heyd, *Between Orthodoxy and the Enlightenment*, 129–35.

albeit with a new account of force and no reference to God's immutability.[144] There were also highly influential late-seventeenth century Cartesians—such as Jacques Rohault, whose *Traité de physique* (1671) was still in use in nonconformist academies in the mid-eighteenth century—who, while more empirically oriented than Descartes, nonetheless preserved the metaphysical ground of the conservation principle and laws of motion in the nature of God.[145] The influence of Descartes's laws is especially evident in the early Royal Society, where over the course of the 1660s, discussion of laws of motion increased dramatically,[146] leading to a debate over collisions (1668–1670). This debate, as a recent historian has concluded, "started from a Cartesian program for a mathematical physics" before broadening into a larger metaphysical debate over the nature of bodies and the role of hypothetical deduction in scientific experiment.[147] Even though Baxter began writing his *Methodus theologiae* simultaneously, he provides no indication that he was aware of this debate. Yet Baxter's focus on Descartes's laws in the *Methodus theologiae* indicates that he was certainly aware of the importance of this aspect of Descartes's *Principia* and its contemporary influence.

In the *Methodus theologiae*, Baxter responded to two main points of Descartes's laws. The first concerned the theological grounding of Descartes's laws in God's immutability.[148] The second and more detailed discussion involved Descartes's

---

144. Isaac Newton, *Mathematical Principles of Natural Philosophy*, trans. Andrew Mott and Florian Cajori, 2 vols. (Berkeley: University of California Press, 1966), 13: "Every body continues in its state of rest, or of uniform motion in a right line, unless it is compelled to change that state by forces impressed upon it." Cf. Garber, *Descartes' Metaphysical Physics*, 230; Cohen, "'Quantum in se est,'" 131–55; Alexandre Koyré, "Newton and Descartes," in *Newtonian Studies* (Chicago: University of Chicago Press, 1968), 53–114, at 66–79; J. Bruce Brackenridge, *The Key to Newton's Dynamics: The Kepler Problem and the Principia* (Berkeley: University of California Press, 1995), 17–24. In the estimation of Brackenridge, Galileo "contributed far less to [Newton's] thought than Descartes" (22).

145. Jacques Rohault, *Rohault's System of Natural Philosophy, Illustrated with Dr. Samuel Clarke's Notes taken mostly out of Sir Isaac Newton's Philosophy*, trans. John Clarke, 3rd ed. (London: James, John, and Paul Knapton, 1735), 1:45–46, 48; Nausicaa Elena Milani, "Motion and God in XVIIth Century Cartesian Manuals: Rohault, Régis and Gadroys," *Noctua* 2, no. 1–2 (2015): 481–516. On the English reception of Rohault, see Minhea Dobre, "Rohault's *Traité de physique* and its Newtonian Reception," in *The Circulation of Science and Technology*, ed. A. Roca-Rosell (Barcelona: SCHCT-IEC, 2012), 389–94; and McLachlan, *English Education*, 46, 69, 131, 147, 301.

146. Friedrich Steinle, "From Principles to Regularities: Tracing 'Laws of Nature' in Early Modern France and England," in *Natural Law and Laws of Nature in Early Modern Europe*, ed. Lorraine Daston and Michael Stolleis (Farnham: Ashgate, 2008), 215–31, at 220–22.

147. Dana Jalobeanu, "The Cartesians of the Royal Society: The Debate Over Collisions and the Nature of Body (1668–1670)," in *Vanishing Matter and the Laws of Motion: Descartes and Beyond*, eds. Dana Jalobeanu and Peter R. Anstey (New York: Routledge, 2011), 103–29, at 120.

148. Descartes, *Principia philosophiae*, II, §36.

first law of motion, or what may be called the principle of inertia.[149] This latter discussion included as a corollary a critique of Descartes's idea of rest.[150] We will first address Baxter's response to the theological foundations of the laws and then turn to Descartes's first law.

Like the Dutch theologians Melchior Leydekker (1642–1721) and Antonius Driessen (1684–1748), Baxter found Descartes's argument for the foundation of his laws in God's immutability to be problematic. Yet unlike them, given the probable composition of his remarks in 1669 before his encounter with Spinoza, Baxter did not filter his interpretation through the lens of Spinoza.[151] Even so, he understood Descartes's laws to impinge negatively on God's freedom. With respect to Descartes's argument that God's immutability implies that there must always be the same total quantity of motion in the world, Baxter responds that this "foundation" (*fundamentum*) of Descartes "is groundless, and without proof; & if it were granted, it is nothing to the case." A basic problem with Descartes's assumption, according to Baxter, is that it portrays God's activity not as an intelligent agent but more as a natural element like fire. Against Descartes's understanding of divine immutability, Baxter insists, "God does not work as *fire*, in the manner of mere nature, *ad ultimum posse*; but according to the choice *of Intellect & free will*."[152]

Baxter also thinks Descartes's argument from immutability to the conservation of total motion is open to various objections. There are many things that do not follow simply because God is immutable. On the one hand, God's activity in the world after creation does not alter his immutability; on the other hand, just because God is immutable it does not follow that the world is eternal. In Baxter's words, "He is neither mutable if after the world was created he performs things, which he did perform from eternity: Nor does the eternity of the world either in eternity past [*à parte ante*] or in eternity future [*à parte post*] follow from the immutability of God." Moreover, given that changes of motion in particular things do not alter God's immutability, Baxter asks, "how would a change of motion in the

---

149. Descartes, *Principia philosophiae*, II, §37–38.

150. Descartes, *Principia philosophiae*, II, §26.

151. Cf. Goudriaan, *Reformed Orthodoxy and Philosophy*, 95–96, 110–11.

152. MT, I.145: "Cartesii fundamentum, '*quod ab Immutabilitate Divina sequitur eandem Motûs quantitatem* (ita *gradum* vocat) *semper in tota rerum universitate esse*,' gratis dictum, non probatum; & si daretur, nihil ad Causam est. Deus enim non operatur ut *ignis*, per modum merae naturae, ad ultimum posse; sed ad *Intellectus* & *liberi arbitrii* delectum." His citation appears to paraphrase Descartes, *Principia philosophiae*, II, §36, which includes the similar phrase "eandem semper in totâ rerum universitate esse posse" (AT 8:61).

Universe make God more liable to change than a change of motion in *particular things*?"[153]

While Baxter raised objections to Descartes's foundational principle of preserving the total quantity of motion by appeal to divine immutability, he was most concerned with Descartes's removal of creaturely causality and transferring the source of all activity to God alone. The "falsehood that we attack," writes Baxter, is that "*God alone* is provided with *Natural Motive Virtue*, & thus (as if he were *the Soul of the World*) moves all things *only* by *himself*, & communicated *no Active Nature* or *Virtue to created things* for moving themselves and others."[154] Baxter of course recognized that Descartes held that the human mind was an active nature beside God, but he still thought that Descartes everywhere supposed that "at least as far as all natural motion" the "entire World is a *passive inanimate Body*."[155] As he writes elsewhere,

> So that *Nature* with the *Cartesians* is nothing at all, but God's first moving act at the creation: as if he caused motion, without any moving created principle: and as if *spirits* and *fire* had no more moving a *nature* or *principle* than clay; but only that their *matter* was either in the creation more moved by God, or since by a knock from some other mover, put into motion, by which accidental motion clay or water may be made *fire*.[156]

This view of a passive world and an active God, Baxter thinks, is open to the objection of being inconsistent. It arbitrarily posits motion in God while removing it from creatures. Why assume that all the power of motion resides in God but not all other substances? With their admission that at least God has the power of motion, "the somatists inevitably kill their entire case."[157] For once God's power is

---

153. *MT*, I.145: "Neque mutabilis est si ea operatur post mundum conditum, quae non operatus est ab aeterno: Neque mundi aeternitas vel à parte ante vel à parte post, ab immutabilitate Dei sequetur. Et quare mutatio motûs in Universitate magis Deum mutabilitatis reum perageret, quam mutatio motus in rebus particularibus?" Cf. *CD*, III.726: "If learned men be but perverted in their apprehensions of some one Attribute of God (as those that think his *Goodness* is nothing but his *Benignity*, or proneness to *do good*, or that he is a Necessary agent doing good *ad ultimum posse*, &c.) what abundance of horrid and impious consequents will follow?"

154. *MT*, I.145: "At id falsum quod oppugnamus est, *Deum solum* esse *Virtute Motivâ Naturali* praeditum, & ita (quasi *Anima Mundi* esset) omnia movere *solum* per *seipsum*, & *nullam rebus Conditis Naturam Activam* seu *Virtutem* se & alia movendi communicasse."

155. *MT*, I.145.

156. *RCR*, 519, marginal note.

157. *MT*, I.236–37: "Totam suam Causam inevitabiliter somatistae jugulant, dum necesse habent *Potentiam, Virtutem* seu *Vim* in Deo ipso causâ primâ fateri."

admitted as a source of motion, there is no good reason to deny the communication of God's power to creatures. To deny activity in nature is "a debaseing of God" and equivalent to denying God's communicative nature.[158]

Of the three laws of nature that Descartes set forth after grounding the quantity of motion in God's immutability, Baxter focuses on Descartes's idea of the persistence of motion as it related to his first law. Although Baxter "omit[s] a great number of Descartes' doubtful & erroneous assertions concerning motion," he discusses this law in particular since it seems to replace the need for intrinsic principles of motion with the idea that motion persists "as far as it is in itself [*quantum in se est*]."[159] That this law was among Baxter's chief concerns is clear from his letter to Glanvill, in which he warned that Descartes's principles "by wch he would make a first push of ye Deity to serve for ever, & a continued effect to be wthout a continuation of ye true causality, & would make all subservient spirituall movers, needles, yea de facto exclude y^m," and would render intellectual natures "uselesse as to ye corporeall motions in ye world."[160]

Baxter summarizes the principle of inertia in the following way: "If a thing was once put in motion, it will be moved to infinity unless it is hindered." This principle he ascribes not only to Descartes, but also to Gassendi.[161] Elsewhere he attributes the opinion generally to the "Somatists," a term inclusive of Hobbes, Descartes, and Gassendi: "The com[m]on doctrine of ye Somatists is, y^t they [atoms] are moved by something els, & y^t everything moved will continue moving till it is stopt."[162] Baxter explains this view at greater length in his *Catholick Theologie*:

> After these come *Hobbs*, *Cartesius* and *Gassendus*, with a swarm of *Epicureans*, (a Sect commonly despised even in *Cicero*'s time, and yet called *Wits* in ours by men that have no more wit than themselves); and some of these say, that Motion needeth no continued cause at all, any more than *non-movere*: But when a thing is in motion, it will so continue, because it

---

158. DWL BT 19.351, fols. 3v–4r: "All ye question then is whether *this Virtue* be *God alone*. And 1° it is a debaseing of God to thinke y^t he *maketh* no nobler a nature in all ye world than *passive matter*: & y^t his workes have no nobler a principle of action than an engine made by ye invention of man. That he who delighteth in his Image, & is Com[m]unicative, should com[m]unicate no measure of *self-moving Vitall Virtue* to any Creature? How incredible is this?"

159. *MT*, I.146. Cf. Descartes, *Principia philosophiae*, II, §37 (AT 8:62; Miller, 59).

160. Baxter to Glanvill, 18 Nov. 1670 (DWL BC II.139r).

161. *MT*, I.144. The marginal note reads, "Ita & Cartes. & Gassend. ut postea." Gassendi is thought to have formulated the concept of inertia prior to Descartes, whereas Descartes developed a consistent theory. See, e.g., Peter Anton Pav, "Gassendi's Statement of the Principle of Inertia," *Isis* 57, no. 1 (1966): 24–34.

162. DWL BT 19.351, fol. 138v.

is its state, without any other continued cause than the *motion* it self. And so they may as well say (and some do) that when a thing is in *Being*, it will so continue till it be positively annihilated, without any continued causation of *its being*. As if *esse & existere* were nothing more than *non esse*; and *agere* were no more noble a *mode* of Entity than *non agere*, and so needed no more (that is, no) *Cause*. (For *non esse & non agere* need no Cause:) When this distraction is worn out and shamed, the next Age will reproach us for attempting the confutation of it; And yet the *Wits* of this delirant Age have not the wit to *understand* a *Confutation*.[163]

To this proposition of Descartes and other "Somatists," Baxter responds that a passive thing will only be moved as long as there is a continuous cause moving it. Therefore, contrary to Descartes, Baxter thinks that if a cause ceased, rather than continuing to move to infinity, the effect would cease as well.[164] To say that an effect once caused could continue for an eternal duration, writes Baxter, is to "deny principles known in themselves [*Principia per se nota*]," for an effect that continues after a cause ceases would no longer be an effect.[165]

In another place, Baxter addresses the objection that the motion of projectiles and gravity provides an example of continued motion separate from the mover. He replies that in such cases there still must be a "neerer cause" that "goeth along with y^e *mobile*" even after the "remote cause" ceases. "But if y^e *next cause cease*, ye effect must cease: For els it must be independant, & so be God. There is a *nisus vel conatus ad motum* [striving or tendency to motion] wch is a sort of *Actus* though not *Actio*; such as is in a bended bow, or ye spring of a watch."[166] Baxter is ambivalent about whether to attribute the continued motion of projectiles to an impressed force (*vis impressa*), propelling air (*aer propellens*), or fiery power (*ignea vis*), although he insists that some cause is necessary for a continued effect. He also states that motion always requires an active power, whether this is from a natural intrinsic (active nature moving itself) or an extrinsic agent (active operating on a passive nature). This latter point of course follows the Aristotelian division of motion and the argument that both natural and violent kinds of motion require a mover.[167] We can infer from Baxter's remarks that he believed Descartes's notion of inertia, by positing an infinite motion that continues to persist *quantum*

---

163. *CT*, I/3.38.

164. *MT*, I.144, 146.

165. *MT*, I.144.

166. DWL BT 19.351, fols. 40r–40v.

167. *MT*, I.145. Cf. Aristotle, *Physics*, VIII.4 (255b32–256a3), in *Complete Works*, 1:427.

in se est, broke apart an essential relation between cause and effect, thereby implying the "absurd" notion of an independent effect that continues without a cause.[168]
And if an effect could continue independently, God's "first push" might provide
a suitable explanation for causality in the world without the need for continued
proximate causes, including spiritual ones.

As a close corollary to the persistence of motion, Baxter also finds Descartes's
notion of rest problematic. While his disagreement with the persistence of motion
centers on Descartes's argument in *Principia* II.3–38, his disagreement over the
nature of rest centers on *Principia* II.26. In that place, Descartes argues that
just as much action is necessary to bring about rest as to bring about motion.
In Descartes's mechanical universe, both motion and rest are different states
that equally persist in things unless other external motions change their state.
For Baxter, by contrast, without an active cause, things would come to a rest.
Consequently, rest itself requires no cause. In other words, in Baxter's more
Aristotelian view, in which motion tends toward rest, rest is simply nonmotion or
a negative mode of motion.[169]

The particular focus of Baxter's polemic against Descartes's first law of motion
illustrates that for Baxter the root problem with mechanical philosophy involved
the denial of the intrinsic activity of things that had been hitherto explained by the
concept of substantial form. Baxter targeted Descartes's first law and the grounding of the laws in divine immutability and ignored the second and third laws
dealing with rectilinear motion and collision. This choice of focus demonstrates
the importance Baxter placed on the analogical relation between God and living
creatures, whose intrinsic activity reflected God's power, wisdom, and goodness.
Baxter feared that the conception that Descartes presented of God and the principle of inertia in the first law would destroy the basic relation between God and
the world that Baxter's own theology envisioned. In place of a living world filled
with activity that reflected a living God, Baxter thought Descartes's world was life-
less and reflected a God who alone was active but (inexplicably) incommunicative
of his active nature.

Henry More's "Mixt Mechanicall Philosophy"

Whereas Descartes had substituted substantial forms with his laws of motion to
account for secondary causation, Henry More adapted Descartes's philosophy

---

168. Cf. DWL BT 19.351, fols. 138v–139r: "Though ye conceit y^t motion needeth no more cause
than *not-to-be-moved*, or y^t ye effect will continue when ye Causation ceaseth, are both absurd."

169. *MT*, I.145; cf. *CT*, II.32, 89. The same point is made in Samuel Gott, *The Divine History
of the Genesis of the World Explicated and Illustrated* (London: E. C. & A. C. for Henry Eversden,
1670), 91.

to his own Neoplatonic philosophy, resulting in a unique "mixt Mechanicall Philosophy."[170] Early in his career, More had held a view of the world closely aligned with Neoplatonism, according to which an animating world soul exists alongside particular subordinate animating principles in individuals. Thus, in his *Psychodia Platonica* (1642) and *Conjectura Cabbalistica* (1653), he espoused a hierarchy in creation of distinct material, seminal (vegetative), sensitive (animal), and intellectual forms. Even planets and stars had distinctive forms.[171] More initially adapted Descartes's theory of physical motion within this Platonic framework.[172] Between *The Immortality of the Soul* (1659) and *Enchiridion metaphysicum* (1671), a simplified and mature theory took shape. He came to ascribe the activity of the material and vegetative realms to the activity of the world soul, or "Spirit of Nature," thereby stripping particular self-animating forms down to only animal and human souls.[173] He explained the remainder of the material and vegetative realm by a combination of Descartes's laws and the activity of the Spirit of Nature. He thought that Descartes's laws were true, but limited and insufficient to account for a variety of phenomena, including the unity of bodies and action at a distance (e.g., gravity, magnetism, and tides). Such phenomena, More argued, require a nonmaterial principle, and this principle was the Spirit of Nature, a kind of "Spirit of the Causal Gaps," as Alan Gabbey puts it.[174] Thus, a blend of Descartes's laws and the Spirit of Nature replaced explanations from intrinsic formal causes for a significant part of the world.

Baxter, it must be observed, regarded More's mixed mechanical philosophy as far more tolerable than the philosophies of Descartes and Gassendi. At the conclusion of his unpublished "Of the Nature and Immortality of Humane Soules," Baxter recommended Henry More's *Enchiridion metaphysicum* as an "excellent" recent book where readers could "find fuller satisfaction about Im[m]ateriall beings, or spirits."[175] However, this did not constitute a blanket endorsement of More's views. He expressed disagreement not only with More's theory of the soul, as we shall see (chapter 6), but also the partial evacuation of intrinsic causality

170. More to Henry Hyrne, 21 Aug. 1671, as cited in Reid, *Metaphysics of Henry More*, 299.

171. Reid, *Metaphysics of Henry More*, 313–23.

172. Reid, *Metaphysics of Henry More*, 283–87.

173. Reid, *Metaphysics of Henry More*, 329–37.

174. Gabbey, "Henry More and the Limits of Mechanism," 24; Gabbey, "*Philosophia Cartesiana Triumphata*," 171–250; Reid, *Metaphysics of Henry More*, 287–301.

175. DWL BT 19.351, fol. 143v.

entailed by his mixed mechanical philosophy. Although Baxter discussed the related general topic of world soul in multiple places,[176] in the course of their exchange in 1682 (see chapter 2), Baxter engaged directly with More's understanding of motion and the Spirit of Nature. John Henry has referred to "Baxter's philosophical sophistication" in his reply to More, but since Henry was interested in Baxter's reception of Francis Glisson, he did not directly analyze this section on motion.[177] Given the late date of this exchange, Baxter's response to More represents his mature opinion of More's philosophy as expressed in the *Enchiridion metaphysicum*.

As part of his attack on Baxter, More took issue with Baxter's view that self-motion is not exclusive to spiritual beings. Baxter had remarked, "I dare not say that a Self-moving Principle is proper to a Spirit." Whereas Baxter thought that a whole range of forms, both living and nonliving, could have to one degree or another intrinsic sources of motion, More restricted intrinsic sources of motion to life. Accordingly, he thought that Baxter's affirmation of a nonspiritual self-moving principle implied the attribution of life to the elements, thereby falling into the errors of Tommaso Campanella and Francis Glisson, who held that matter was alive.[178] For More, as we already observed, the nonliving realm was governed by external sources of motion, whether these were mechanical laws or the influence of the Spirit of Nature. Thus, to admit a kind of self-motion in this mechanical realm that is not the Spirit of Nature would overturn his framework, not to mention the apologetic strategy of appealing from gaps in Descartes's mechanical theory to a spiritual principle. Baxter's affirmation of nonspiritual intrinsic sources of motion undermined a position More had been advocating for two decades, so Baxter's arguments, as John Henry notes, "must have been especially annoying to More."[179]

Since Baxter was not committed to a fully mechanical explanation of the nonliving realm (although he also allowed for corpuscular explanations of a part), he did not see a problem with admitting some self-motion among nonliving things. In reply to More's objection Baxter first defends himself and then argues that More's restriction of self-motion to life has yet to be proved. These arguments resemble in many respects those of his colleague Matthew Hale, with whom he conversed at

---

176. DWL BT 19.351, fols. 22v–27r, 30r–30v, 41r–41v, 43v, 45v, 47r–48r, 72v–78v, 85v, 93v, 104v, 109v–110r, 120v; Baxter, *An End of Doctrinal Controversies*, xiii–xix; *MT*, I.136–37, 142; *RCR*, 11–12, 379, 494, 586.

177. Baxter, *Of the Nature of Spirits*, 33–40. Cf. Henry, "Medicine and Pneumatology," 36, discussing Baxter, *Of the Nature of Spirits*, 28–29.

178. More, *Answer to a Letter*, 7–8.

179. Henry, "Voluntarist Theology," 95.

length about the nature of spirits and motion.[180] In his own defense, Baxter states that a kind of nonspiritual self-motion is entirely plausible. As an example, Baxter observes that gravity "and other aggravative motion of Passives" could just as well be explained as "an Essential self-moving Principle." Furthermore, this opinion has been widely held: "Few men I think have thought otherwise."[181] Baxter argues that the aggregative motion (*motus aggregativus*) caused by gravity, "which is only the tendency of the *parts* to the *whole*, that they may there *rest from motion*," could be explained equally by either intrinsic or extrinsic principles. "I do but say I am ignorant whether Gravitation be from the Motion of a Spirit thrusting down the Stone, &c. or from an Essential Principle in the Matter." Baxter even concedes to More, "I am most inclined to your Opinion" about a spiritual explanation for gravitation. But he thinks, given the "stream of Dissenters" who have argued for gravity as an essential principle, it "obligeth such a one as I am to more modesty than must be expected from one of your degree."[182]

Baxter next challenged More's assumption that self-motion must be restricted to living things. To More's statement that "*self-motion* certainly is an effect" of life,[183] Baxter responds that More's assertion that "there is no *self-motion* but by *Life*" remains undemonstrated. "I never yet saw your proof, that God is able to make no self-mover but vital! And if he *can*, how know I that he *doth not*?"[184] With these words, Baxter intimates that More's partial adoption of mechanical philosophy has closed him off to alternative explanations of motion that are theoretically equally viable. He presses More further on alternatives to his theory of gravity, which More had ascribed to the Spirit of Nature.[185] There are three equally valid arguments for gravity, argues Baxter: (1) Francis Glisson's "principle *in the Matter*"; (2) an "Essential *Compounding* Principle" such as a soul; and (3) an extrinsic agent alone.[186] Baxter also argues that More's mixed mechanical philosophy is open to the charge of inconsistency. Since More admits that "subordinate particular Moving Principles" besides a world soul are necessary for animals, then why would it be

---

180. Matthew Hale, *Observations Touching the Principles of Natural Motions* (London: W. Godbid, 1677), 26–35. Cf. John Henry, "Occult Qualities and the Experimental Philosophy: Active Principles in Pre-Newtonian Matter Theory," *History of Science* 24 (1986): 335–81, at 355; and Cromartie, *Sir Matthew Hale*, 203–6. On the relationship of Baxter and Hale, see chapter 2.

181. Baxter, *Of the Nature of Spirits*, 33.

182. Baxter, *Of the Nature of Spirits*, 34.

183. More, *Answer to a Letter*, 8.

184. Baxter, *Of the Nature of Spirits*, 35.

185. Cf. More, *Answer to a Letter*, 9–10, citing Henry More, *Enchiridion metaphysicum: sive, de rebus incorporeis succincta & luculenta dissertatio* (London: E. Flesher, 1671), cap. 13.

186. Baxter, *Of the Nature of Spirits*, 37.

implausible to suppose subordinate principles, other than a world soul, for gravity or fire?[187] Baxter concludes his point by observing "two things I see not proved" from More's *Enchiridion metaphysicum* on gravitation (ch. 13): "1. That there are not particular Moving Principles subordinate to the more Universal. 2. That the God of Nature hath not put into the passive Elements, a strong inclination of the parts to union with the whole, and to aggregative Motion when forcibly separated."[188]

Among the authorities Baxter cites in favor of the possibility of intrinsic principles of motion are not only Glisson's recent *Tractatus de natura substantiae energetica* (1672) but also the famous English physicist William Gilbert's *De magnete* (1600). Gilbert believed with "many others," Baxter noted approvingly, "that the whole *Tellus* [earth] hath one Active Principle."[189] Baxter's citation of Gilbert was a clever move, for it enlisted an experimentalist of similar stature to Francis Bacon against mechanical philosophy. Gilbert was widely regarded in the seventeenth century as a model of experimental philosophy, for he had discovered terrestrial magnetism while rejecting the traditional Aristotelian cosmological division of corruptible terrestrial and perfect superlunary realms, and his work facilitated the adoption of Copernicanism. But Gilbert also viewed earth as a giant magnet possessed with immaterial attractive power, a theory that conflicted with a corpuscular model.[190] Whereas John Wilkins's early works from 1640 had favored Gilbert's theory, and even enlisted him in support of Copernicanism, in subsequent decades Gilbert's theory was transformed by mechanical philosophy.[191] Early mechanical philosophers including Descartes, Gassendi, Digby, and Charleton "clearly found magnetism an embarrassment" but were able to supply "little hard experimental evidence" for a mechanical explanation.[192] In the early years of the Royal Society, Henry Power drew directly on Charleton's explanation of magnetism as material effluvia (i.e., streams of material particles), which are "not bare Qualities, but indeed Corporeal Atoms,"[193] and his line of thought was followed by Boyle and Hooke. Hooke argued at great length for magnetic corpuscles, although

---

187. Baxter, *Of the Nature of Spirits*, 38–39.

188. Baxter, *Of the Nature of Spirits*, 39.

189. Baxter, *Of the Nature of Spirits*, 37–38. Cf. *RCR*, 351, 560; *MT*, I.126 (no. 24), where this notion is placed among the "uncertainties" of creation.

190. Stephen Pumfrey, "Gilbert, William (1544–1603)," in *The Dictionary of Seventeenth-Century British Philosophers*, ed. Andrew Pyle (Bristol: Thoemmes Press, 2000), 1:334–38; J. A. Bennett, "Cosmology and the Magnetical Philosophy, 1640–1680," *Journal for the History of Astronomy* 12 (1981): 165–77.

191. Bennett, "Cosmology," 168–69.

192. Pumfrey, "Mechanizing Magnetism," 3.

193. Power, *Experimental Philosophy*, 155; cf. Charleton, *Physiologia*, 403–4: "Art. 8. The Magnetique Virtue, a *Corporeal* Efflux." Charleton also speaks of "Magnetical Atoms" (388).

he admitted as late as 1686 that the cause of magnetism remained an intractable problem.[194] By appealing to Gilbert's theory of magnetism against More's denial of nonliving active principles, Baxter was calling attention to a respectable philosophical precedent by a revered experimentalist, on a matter recognized by mechanical philosophers as a thorny subject. Gilbert's theory of magnetism as an intrinsic principle of activity, as Baxter was aware, did not oblige More's mixed mechanical philosophy.

Baxter's response to More is significant in many respects. It concretely illustrates Baxter's opposition not only to the mechanization of living forms, but also the mechanization of a significant part of the nonliving material realm. This highlights the critical nature of his acceptance of Boyle's corpuscularism (see chapter 4), which while significant as a concession to new philosophical developments, did not to Baxter's mind entail the abandonment of nonliving active principles such as fire, magnetism, and gravity. The exchange also shows that Baxter believed many different explanations for certain phenomena like gravity were equally plausible, and by contrast, More's a priori exclusion of intrinsic causal explanations for all such phenomena revealed an overly confident view toward uncertain matters. For Baxter, More's version of mechanical philosophy illustrated a narrowing of possible explanations contradicted by authorities such as Gilbert and Glisson, who carried great weight in English experimental and medical circles.

Conclusion

As Aristotelian physics came increasingly under attack in the seventeenth century, alternative ideas of motion challenged not only older ideas of celestial phenomena but also the foundations of physics in general. In many areas, Baxter demonstrated a remarkable openness to this shifting philosophical landscape. He embraced new planetary observations of Galileo, directed readers to Gassendi's astronomy, referred approvingly to William Gilbert's *De magnete*, and cited innovative treatises on the nature of motion by Honoré Fabri and John Wallis. As we observed in the previous chapter, he also integrated aspects of Boyle's corpuscular theory into his understanding of a number of elements.

However, to this positive reception of recent philosophical trends Baxter joined a fierce polemic against mechanical philosophers' denial of substantial form and a

---

Pumfrey, "Mechanizing Magnetism," 4, produces manuscript evidence for Power's dependence on Charleton.

194. Pumfrey, "Mechanizing Magnetism," 5–22. Cf. Robert Hooke, "A Discourse of the Magnetical Variation, read July 7th. 1686," in *The Posthumous Works of Robert Hooke* (London: Sam. Smith and Benj. Walford, 1705), 484.

spirited rebuttal of Henry More's specific denial of nonspiritual active principles. For Baxter, substantial forms not only provided philosophical expression to a hierarchy of being implied by Genesis 1, but even more importantly they accounted for activity in nature. The affirmation of this intrinsic activity was essential to Baxter's view of God and creation, and it was of greater consequence than empirical discoveries or new views of astronomy. To Baxter, an essentially active and living God created essentially active and living creatures, and mechanical philosophy broke apart this analogical relationship. Accordingly, Baxter's polemic focused on those aspects of mechanical philosophy, including Descartes's concept of inertia (his first law of motion), that he believed undermined either God's analogical and communicative nature or the activity of substantial forms as secondary causes.

6

The Incipient Materialism
of Mechanical Philosophy

IN PREVIOUS CHAPTERS, we observed that the doctrine of the soul was of particular concern to Baxter. In Baxter's theology, the human soul constitutes the greatest reflection of the living and triune God. In the present chapter, we will examine the extension of Baxter's polemics beyond the nature of motion in general to the nature of the soul. More specifically, we will explore his suspicion of problematic tendencies accompanied by the rise of mechanical philosophy as they pertain to the question of the soul's immortality and the danger of materialism.

The existing literature on Baxter's polemics with respect to the soul focuses on his debate with Henry More. These studies are more interested in how Baxter sheds light on More's views with respect to the nature of the soul than with the thought of Baxter in light of his own development.[1] As a result, they neglect crucial manuscript evidence of Baxter's engagement with mechanical theories of the soul, which predates the More correspondence. An examination of these manuscripts reveals Baxter's awareness of the heterodox potential of a strand of mechanical philosophy flourishing among professional physicians. John Henry has drawn attention to the heterodox potential of new medical theories, including Thomas Willis's *De anima brutorum* (1672), but he concluded that "More and Cudworth were alone in taking issue with medical speculations."[2] This conclusion requires revision in light of additional manuscript evidence. As the present chapter will demonstrate, Baxter singled out Willis's *De anima brutorum* as an especially problematic application of mechanical philosophy, and this sentiment was shared by Matthew Hale. Baxter's unpublished critique, written in 1672, was perhaps the

---

1. Henry, "A Cambridge Platonist's Materialism," 183–88; Henry, "Medicine and Pneumatology," 32–42; Crocker, *Henry More*, 170–76; Fouke, *Enthusiastical Concerns*, 225–27.

2. Henry, "Matter of Souls," 113.

earliest reaction of a theologian to Willis, but certainly not the only one.[3] Although Willis's *De anima brutorum* has become increasingly recognized as an important backdrop to eighteenth-century conceptions of the "material soul,"[4] Baxter's theological response has not yet received the attention of scholars.

The present chapter addresses two distinct issues that nevertheless both involve Baxter's negative evaluation of the impact of mechanical philosophy on questions pertaining to the soul. First, we will draw attention to the sharp contrast between the material and immaterial generated by the rise of mechanical philosophy, and show that Baxter expressed doubt as to the method of proving the soul's immortality from such a contrast. Against this background, we will show that Baxter thought that this method weakened rather than strengthened the defense against materialism, as illustrated by Baxter's remarks on Henry More's "slippery ground" and Gassendi's "feeble" proofs for the immortality of the soul. The second issue consists of Baxter's response to Thomas Willis's *De anima brutorum* (1672), who drew on Gassendi's atomism to argue for the corporeality of animal souls. Through an examination of Baxter's hitherto completely neglected manuscript against Willis's *De anima brutorum*, we will show that Baxter understood Willis's arguments as filled with heterodox potential. In Baxter's opinion, Willis's Gassendian arguments for material animal souls could be extended to the human soul. In this sense, we can speak of Baxter's fear regarding the incipient materialism of mechanical philosophy. The title of Rosenfield's classic historical study of the Cartesian mechanization of life nicely encapsulates this fear: *From Beast-Machine to Man-Machine.*[5]

Mechanical Philosophy and the Immaterial Soul

Except for unorthodox mortalists, the demonstration of the immortality of the soul was a universal concern in the seventeenth century. Among the many proofs that circulated prior to the rise of mechanical philosophy was that from the immateriality of the soul. If the human soul could be demonstrated to contain a purely incorporeal and incorruptible operation (in the intellect) in contrast to the corruptible

---

3. Norman Fiering, *Moral Philosophy at Seventeenth-Century Harvard: A Discipline in Transition* (Chapel Hill: The University of North Carolina Press, 1981), 222n24.

4. Charles T. Wolfe and Michaela van Esveld, "The Material Soul: Strategies for Naturalizing the Soul in an Early Modern Epicurean Context," in *Conjunctions of Mind, Soul and Body from Plato to the Enlightenment*, ed. Danijela Kambaskovic (Dordrecht: Springer, 2014), 371–421; Ann Thomson, "Animals, Humans, Machines and Thinking Matter," *Early Science and Medicine* 15 (2013): 3–37.

5. Leonora Cohen Rosenfield, *From Beast-Machine to Man-Machine: Animal Soul in French Letters from Descartes to La Mettrie* (New York: Oxford University Press, 1941).

body, so these authors reasoned, it would follow that the soul continued to exist after bodily death. The arguments of Aquinas, in one scholar's estimation, "are representative of what became the standard arguments for later Aristotelians."[6] The works of Reformed authors that circulated in early seventeenth-century England likewise reflected this line of argument, although they also produced other arguments such as that from natural desires or inclinations that cannot be fulfilled in the present life.[7]

With the exception of Hobbes, mechanical philosophers continued to argue for the soul's immortality by means of its immateriality. However, as Daniel Garber argues, their explanation of bodily change in terms of size, shape, and motion exclusive of the concept of Aristotelian form resulted in a "significant transformation" on the "question of the separability and immortality of the soul." Garber continues, "For the mechanist, whose conception of body does not include form, it is not a question of the detachability of some *constituent* of body [as for the Aristotelian]; it is a question of what (if anything) we must *add* to body, a question of establishing the limits of what can be explained in terms of body alone, and what must be posited over and above body."[8] Another way to put this is that Aristotelian hylomorphism assumed a universe filled with a hierarchy of forms, and from this assumption, many philosophers argued for a *uniquely distinct* immaterial and immortal form, characterized by faculties and operations not entirely dependent upon matter. By contrast, those inclined in the direction of mechanical philosophy assumed a simplified account of body explained in terms of matter and motion, and therefore tended to argue for the separability of the soul by establishing an incorporeal substance not explainable in mechanical terms. In this new line of argument, there is a symbiotic relationship between mechanical philosophy and proofs for the soul's immortality, with the limits of the former aiding in the demonstration of the latter.

Of the early English writers who adapted proofs for the soul's immortality and incorporeality to the new mechanical philosophy, among the most influential were Kenelm Digby, Henry More, Walter Charleton, and Edward Stillingfleet. These authors to varying degrees drew on the physical doctrines of Descartes, Gassendi,

---

6. Daniel Garber, "Soul and Mind: Life and Thought in the Seventeenth Century," in *CHSP*, 1:761.

7. See Pierre de La Primaudaye, *The Second Part of the French Academie* (London: G. B[ishop] R[alph] N[ewbery] R. B[arker], 1594), 526–93; Mornay, *Trunesse*, ch. 14; and Weemes, *Portraiture*, 44–46, obviously reproducing arguments from Aquinas's *Summa contra gentiles*, II.72, with the same illustration of swallows and spiders.

8. Garber, "Soul and Mind," 762.

and Hobbes.[9] Stillingfleet, for example, prefaced his proofs for the soul's immortality by stressing the need "to finde out such peculiar *properties* in the *soul* of *man*, which cannot be *salved* on *supposition* there were nothing else but *matter* and *motion* in the world," and to show that "there is a *principle* in man higher then *matter* and *motion*."[10] Henry More took a distinctive line of argument, in which he maintained that incorporeal substance is indivisible ("indiscerpible"), penetrable, and self-moving in contrast to corporeal substance, which is divisible, impenetrable, and inert.[11] More also maintained the existence of animal souls, and given his argument that immateriality implies immortality, he was willing to concede the possibility that animal souls were somehow also immortal.[12] The influence of this new line of thought, involving a strict contrast between incorporeal substance and mechanical bodies, on later seventeenth- and eighteenth-century philosophy and theology was profound. At the beginning of the eighteenth century, the famous freethinker Anthony Collins (1676–1729) observed, "The principal Argument for the *Natural Immortality of the Soul* is founded on the Supposition of its Immateriality; and therefore great Endeavours have been made use of to prove the Soul an Immaterial Being."[13]

While he did not immediately respond to these works, Baxter kept a close eye on them. In *The Saints Everlasting Rest*, published shortly after Digby's *Two Treatises*, Baxter referred the reader to Digby's treatise on the immortality of the soul along with Alexander Ross's polemical response, *The Philosophicall Touch-Stone* (1645), containing the traditional arguments.[14] Of the two authors, Baxter preferred the

---

9. Kenelm Digby, *Two Treatises* (Paris: Gilles Blaizot, 1644), 393–420; Henry More, *An Antidote against Atheism* (London: Roger Daniel, 1653), I.xi (pp. 35–42); More, *Immortality of the Soul*, I.xi (pp. 75–84), II.i (pp. 109–22); Charleton, *Immortality of the Human Soul*, 78–124; Stillingfleet, *Origines Sacrae*, 411–18. On Digby and More, see Garber, "Soul and Mind," 769–71, 776–78; and on More, see Reid, *The Metaphysics of Henry More*, 357. Emily Michael and Fred S. Michael, "Gassendi on Sensation and Reflection: A Non-Cartesian Dualism," *History of European Ideas* 9 (1988): 583–95, at 590–93, argue for a similarity, if not influence, of Gassendi's arguments for the soul's immateriality on Charleton, Stillingfleet, Glanvill, Boyle, and Zachary Mayne.

10. Stillingfleet, *Origines Sacrae*, 412.

11. More, *Immortality of the Soul*, I.v.1 (pp. 24–25), I.xi.3 (p. 77); cf. Garber, "Soul and Mind," 777; and Reid, *Metaphysics of Henry More*, 185–200, 357.

12. More, *Immortality of the Soul*, 302–7; Henry More, *An Antidote against Atheism*, 2nd ed. (London: J. Flesher, 1655), 353–54; cf. Reid, *Metaphysics of Henry More*, 365–66.

13. Anthony Collins, *A Letter to the Learned Henry Dodwell; Containing Some Remarks on a (pretended) Demonstration of the Immateriality and Natural Immortality of the Soul*, 2nd ed. (London: A. Baldwin, 1709), 6.

14. *SER2*, II.278 (II.vii.4), marginal note: "See Sir *Ken. Digby* of the Immort. of the soul, And *Ab. Rosse* his Philosophical Touchstone in Ans. to it."

arguments of Ross, as is indicated by a parenthetical comment: "Beside all those Arguments for the souls Immortality, which you may read in *Alex. Rosse* his Philosophical Touchstone, Part last."[15] However, during the interregnum, likely in reaction to the scriptural arguments of Christian mortalists such as Richard Overton's *Mans Mortallitie* (1643),[16] Baxter engaged exclusively with arguments from Scripture to counter the "Socinians & many others of late among us."[17] His adversaries at this point were not philosophers but heterodox Christians: "It is a lamentable case that the brutish opinion of the souls mortality, should find so many patrons professing godliness!"[18] Accordingly, Baxter drew at this point on Calvin's *Psychopannychia* (1545), among others.[19]

Sometime in the intervening years leading up to the publication of the *Reasons* in 1667, Baxter's focus shifted to the philosophical arguments of Gassendi, More, and others. As we already noted in chapter 2, the appendix to the *Reasons* was written to counter the spread of Gassendi's and Hobbes's philosophy, which he believed were "inclining men to Sadducism."[20] Likewise, while Baxter and Hale resided in Acton (ca. 1667–1669), they conversed "especially about the Nature of Spirits and superior Regions; and the Nature, Operations and Immortality of mans Soul."[21] In both the *Reasons* and in his manuscript "Of the Nature and Immortality of Humane Soules," written shortly thereafter (ca. 1669–1672), Baxter raised objections to the method of arguing for the soul's immortality from its immateriality. Already in the body of the *Reasons*, even prior to his polemics against mechanical philosophy, Baxter indicated his discontent with this method of argument:

> And I shall pass by those arguments which are commonly fetcht from the
> Souls immateriality, and the independence upon matter, and other such

15. *SER2*, II.299 (II.x.1). Cf. Ross, "The Conclusion, wherein is asserted the *Soules Immortality*, and Objections answered," in *The Philosophicall Touch-stone*, 108–31.

16. Norman T. Burns, *Christian Mortalism from Tyndale to Milton* (Cambridge, MA: Harvard University Press, 1972); Ann Thomson, *Bodies of Thought* (Oxford: Oxford University Press, 2008), 42–44.

17. *SER2*, II.298–304 (II.x). On the early modern association between Socinianism and mortalism, see Thomson, *Bodies of Thought*, 39–41.

18. *SER2*, II.304.

19. *SER2*, II.303, marginal note, citing Calvin, *Psychopannychia* (Strasbourg: W. Rihelium, 1545); Christian Becmann, *Exercitationes theologicae* (Servestae, 1639), Exercitatio XXIV; and John Rainolds, *Censura librorum apocryphorum Veteris Testamenti, adversus Pontificios, inprimis Robertum Bellarminum* (Oppenheim, 1611), Praelectiones 3, 79, and 80.

20. *Rel. Bax.*, III.61.

21. Baxter, *Additional Notes*, 5; cf. *Rel. Bax.*, III.47.

like, which are commonly to be found in Physicks and Metaphysicks, as being not such as my present method leadeth me to; and shall make use of such as are the necessary consectaries of the certain Truths already proved![22]

It is not clear whether at this early stage, just prior to his polemics against mechanical philosophy, he had in mind the approach of traditional Aristotelians or the mechanical philosophers, or both. What is clear is that he found moral arguments, upon which he elaborates at length, more conducive to his apologetic method than the so-called physical arguments.[23]

Baxter received confirmation of his suspicion of the proof from immateriality from Hale. Long before he conversed with Baxter on the nature of spirits, Hale viewed the demonstrability of immateriality as inaccessible to natural reason apart from supernatural revelation, and, even after having been first supernaturally revealed, at best a "probable" argument to "rectified reason."[24] Moreover, Hale held that even if one were to grant the immateriality of the soul, it would not necessarily follow that the soul is immortal.[25] While Baxter expressed similar sentiments in his *Reasons* just prior to his friendship with Hale, after they began discussing the nature of spirits in 1667, Baxter emphasized the difficulty of rational argument for the soul's immortality in his *More Reasons* (1672).[26] The basic agreement between Hale and Baxter is confirmed by the fact that Hale commended Baxter for distancing himself from proofs based on immateriality: "In my apprehention y[o]u have done well in disintangling of y[ou]rself from that comon supposition of the absolute immateriality of the soule."[27]

The development of Baxter's thinking about the nature and immortality of the soul was clearly moving in a direction divergent from that of the more mechanically inclined theologians and philosophers. While the demonstration of the soul's immateriality was taking on added importance among mechanical philosophers as they accentuated the contrast between matter and spirit, Baxter was, as Hale put it, "disintangling" himself from that line of argument.

---

22. *RCR*, 119.

23. *RCR*, 119–56.

24. Hale, *A Discourse of the Knowledge of God*, 40–41. This was written when Hale was thirty or thirty-one years old (ca. 1639–41). See the preface to Hale, *Discourse*, fol. a2r; and Cromartie, *Sir Matthew Hale*, 141.

25. Hale, *A Discourse of the Knowledge of God*, 41.

26. Baxter, *More Reasons*, 145–47.

27. Hale to Baxter [undated, ca. 1672–1673] (LPL MS 3499, fol. 65v).

Henry More's "Slippery Ground" and Pierre Gassendi's "Feeble" Proofs

In the appendix to the *Reasons*, Baxter turned his attention to the new approach of demonstrating an incorporeal substance over against a corporeal substance. Here he objects to laying "the stress of this Controversie [on the soul's immortality] upon that difference" between a corporeal and incorporeal substance, since the difference is in fact a lot more difficult to conceive than most take for granted.[28] Among the authors to whom Baxter clearly objects here is Henry More, whose particular conception of spirits as extended, penetrable, and indiscerpible Baxter singles out for censure:

> For my part I profess, that as my understanding is fully satisfied by the op-
> erations and effects, that there are such invisible potent substances, which
> we call *Angels* and *Spirits*, so it is utterly unsatisfied in the common prop-
> erties of *Penetrability* and *Impenetrability, Extension,* or *discerptibility,* and
> *indiscerptibility* or *indivisibility,* as the Characters to know them by.[29]

This position, Baxter continues, is "too slippery a ground for any man to satisfie himself or others by."[30] Hale concurred with Baxter in this judgment of More. In his *Additional Notes* on the life of Hale, Baxter observes that both he and Hale shared this opinion: "We were neither of us satisfied with the notions of *Penetrability* and *Indivisibility,* as sufficient differences."[31]

To Baxter, the position adopted by More was "slippery ground" because it rested the immortality of the soul not on the essential, formal powers of the soul, but rather on ambiguous, accidental properties deriving from a faulty division of being into material and immaterial. The division between immaterial and mate- rial is not nearly so clear cut, argues Baxter. Matter "being but a *pars intelligibilis* or inadequate conception of a thing, is not to be a *Genus* in any predicament," but rather, along with form, is an aspect of substance.[32] Likewise, the lowest forms of incorporeality are only gradually distinct from higher forms of corporeality. One

---

28. *RCR,* 525.

29. *RCR,* 530. More is not named here, but the use of terms is a clear indication of who Baxter has in mind. Cf. *MT,* I.155: "qui substantias spirituales à materialibus per *penetra-bilitatem* & *indivisibilitatem* sufficienter discernendas asserunt, praesumpta ferè & incognita loquuntur."

30. *RCR,* 531.

31. Baxter, *Additional Notes,* 15.

32. *RCR,* 531.

indication of this ambiguity is that even moderns who argue for distinct proper-ties of corporeality and incorporeality disagree among themselves as to what these properties are.[33] For his part, Baxter thinks that the highest forms of incorporeality (with the exception of God), such as angels, probably have "a purer subtile sort of bodies" or metaphysical matter (*materiam metaphysicam*), as an "abundance of our writers of Physicks, Metaphysicks and Logick, do tell us."[34] At best, the properties of penetrability and indivisibility identified by More are only "accidental proper-ties" that do not address the "formal difference" or "formal virtues" of the human soul.[35] Moreover, Baxter argues, the spiritual and material aspects of things are not known in themselves but rather from their operations and effects.[36] In at least this second argument, there is apparently an appeal to the Aristotelian principle that powers are known by their acts.[37]

While in the *Reasons* Baxter clearly objected to the construction of the argu-ment from immateriality in general and that of More in particular, only later did he explain that the "slippery ground" he referred to includes the danger of materi-alism. In "Of the Nature and Immortality of Humane Soules," Baxter singled out Gassendi's approach for its "strong temptation" to materialism:

> I do not insist on ye com[m]on proofe from ye Im[m]ateriality of their acts <so much or in y^t man[n]er as some do.> Not contradicting y^m, but confess-ing y^t I understand y^m not; And I doubt, y^t to lay the stresse of so important a point as ye naturall proofe of ye Soules Im[m]ortality, uppon a medium wch no wits can reach but such as are subtiler than mine, will be almost as strong a temptation to p[er]swade men to judge it mortall, as a direct argu-mentation for its mortality may: And I have observed ~~not only Gassendus, but~~ divers ~~others~~ who laid downe first such principles as tend to inferre y^t ye soule is nothing but *moved atomes*, yet after plead for its *Im[m]ortality*, principally by this argument from ye Im[m]ateriality of its acts, so feebly &

---

33. *RCR*, 525–28; cf. DWL BT XIX.351, fol. 10v.

34. *RCR*, 527–29; cf. DWL BT XIX.351, fol. 129r (Appendix C); *MT*, I.153, 155. He assem-bled an impressive array of patristic, medieval, and contemporary authors to support this claim, among them Tertullian, Arnobius, Origen, Lactantius, Basil, Augustine, Gregory the Great, Theodoret, Bede, John Damascene, Faustus of Riez, Julius Caesar Scaliger, Richard Crakanthorpe, and Christoph Scheibler (*RCR*, 528–30; DWL BT XIX.351, fol. 125v; DWL BT IV.87, fol. 231v; Baxter, *Of the Nature of Spirits*, 11–12). See discussion in Burton, *Hallowing of Logic*, 139–43, who argues (perhaps too narrowly) for a Franciscan influence. Baxter's earliest indication of a source for this opinion is Zanchi. See *SER2*, II.299 (II.x.1).

35. DWL BT XIX.351, fol. 129v.

36. Baxter, *Reasons*, 527, 533.

37. Cf. Des Chene, *Life's Form*, 23, 120, 125.

unconcludingly or obscurely as y^t I could not but suspect prevarication for worldly ends.[38]

In his letter to Joseph Glanvill, written around the same time, Baxter likewise stated that while he did not publicly "accuse [Descartes or Gassendi] as excluding all immaterial beings," yet he still suspected otherwise of Gassendi:

> Though I never printed any such thing, I here say privately to you, I much feare that Gassendus did in this prevaricate. 1° From Sorberius & Hobbs's words wch I cited 2° From ye thinness of his plea for ye soule's Immortality, 3° But above all from his principles wch seem to make ag^t it.[39]

With his suspicion of Gassendi's "prevarication" and "feeble" or "thin" proofs, Baxter most likely had in mind that in his mature *Syntagma philosophicum*, Gassendi's so-called physical argument for the soul's immortality consisted of the simple argument: "The rational soul is immaterial; therefore it is also immortal."[40]

Baxter thought that Gassendi prevaricated because his proofs were not only "slender," but also "downright contradictory to his physicall theorems."[41] Exactly what was "contradictory" about Gassendi's philosophy Baxter did not clarify. Yet he may have had in mind a particular argument from Gassendi's *Syntagma philosophicum*, which he criticized repeatedly. In a chapter demonstrating that the "first principle of action" (*primum agendi principium*) in secondary causes is corporeal, Gassendi argued that only corporeal principles can generate corporeal acts and likewise the soul as incorporeal can only generate incorporeal acts:

> [S]ince physical actions are corporeal, they may not be able to be elicited except by a physical and corporeal principle. And . . . one cannot grasp how, if [such a principle] should be incorporeal, it would be so effectively applied to a body that it would impress an impulse on it; since it cannot make contact with it, being itself without the sense of touch or mass by which it may touch. . . . But since the human soul is incorporeal, and yet acts on its own body, and impresses motion on itself; we say that the human soul in

---

38. DWL BT XIX.351, fols. 4r–4v. The reference to Gassendi is crossed out in the manuscript.

39. Baxter to Glanvill, 18 Nov. 1670 (DWL BC II.138r–138v).

40. Gassendi, *Opera*, 2:628a: "Anima Rationalis immaterialis est; igitur est & immortalis." This physical proof is the second of three arguments (faith, physics, morals). Cf. Osler, "Baptizing Epicurean Atomism," 178; Osler, *Divine Will and the Mechanical Philosophy*, 71; and Olivier René Bloch, *La philosophie de Gassendi: Nominalisme, matérialisme et métaphysique* (La Haye: Martinus Nijhoff, 1971), 398.

41. DWL BT XIX.351, fol. 132r.

its proper place, as it is an Intellect, or Mind, and indeed incorporeal, does not elicit acts, unless they are Intellectual, or mental & incorporeal: And as it is sentient, vegetative, & endowed with the motive force of bodies, and thus corporeal, it elicits corporeal actions—and first moves its own body and then also by its mediation moves another object.[42]

This argument, in Baxter's estimation, would lead to the conclusion that all incorporeal agents, including even God, angels, and human souls, "must be corporeall, or els can[n]ot move things corporeall."[43] Late in life, Baxter went so far as to write, "*Gassendus* seemeth to except *God* from corporeity, & calls ye world but *Indefinite*, & not *Infinite*: But as he taketh all other spirits to be corporeall, so it is plaine by ye tenor of his reasoning y^t this is but to avoid *odium*, & y^t he taketh *God* to be *corporeall* & ye world to be *Infinite*."[44] Baxter thus seemed to think that Gassendi's own principles conflicted with incorporeal agency in general.

While it is clear that Baxter found Gassendi's argument from the soul's immateriality to its immortality wanting and internally inconsistent, it is not immediately clear what about the argument itself he objected to, particularly since in many respects Gassendi used traditional proofs for the soul's immateriality not unlike Aquinas[45]—arguments Baxter himself recognized as "common proofs" that he is not "contradicting."[46] Be that as it may, Baxter notes some deficiencies with Gassendi's arguments from immaterial *acts* and *objects*.[47] First, immaterial acts do not necessarily prove an immaterial agent, for even the acts of material things are immaterial. Second, the fact that there are immaterial objects does not necessarily prove that the agent is immaterial, just as we do not infer that the soul is material

---

42. Gassendi, *Syntagma philosophicum*, II, sec. 1, lib. 4, cap. 8, in *Opera*, 1:334b: "Physicae actiones corporeae cùm sint, nisi à Principio Physico, corporeóque elici non possint. Et . . . capere non licet, quomodo, si incorporeum sit, ita applicari corpori valeat, ut illi impulsum imprimat; quando ipsum contingere, careus ipsa tactu, seu mole, qua tangat, non potest. . . . Anima autem humana incorporea cùm sit, & in ipsum tamen corpus suum agat, motúmque ipsi imprimat; dicimus suo loco Animam humanam, quà est Intellectus, seu Mens, atque adeò incorporea, non elicere actiones, nisi Intellectualeis, seu Mentaleis, & incorporeas; & qua est sentiens, vegetans, praeditáque vi corporum motrice, atque adeò corporea est, elicere actiones corporeas, ac tum corpus proprium, tum ipsius quoque interventu alienum movere."

43. DWL BT XIX.351, fol. 140r (incorrectly labeled fol. 199), citing Gassendi, *Opera*, 1:334b. Baxter also cites this passage from Gassendi in *RCR*, 541–42; and *MT*, I.146.

44. DWL BT IV.87, fol. 232v.

45. Cf. Garber, "Soul and Mind," 772.

46. DWL BT XIX.351, fol. 4r.

47. Baxter likely has in view Gassendi, *Opera*, 2:440b–442b. Cf. Bloch, *La philosophie de Gassendi*, 400–405; Osler, "Baptizing Epicurean Atomism," 173–75.

simply from its having material objects. Baxter seems to admit that the objects of the soul can provide a good argument, "But w^t these objects are is ye question."[48] This latter point indicates that he was more interested in what kind of (immaterial) objects the soul relates to than the fact that it has immaterial objects per se. In other words, it seems that Baxter's problem with Gassendi's argument from immateriality is that the argument does not go far enough in specifying the nature of the objects to which the soul relates.

A clearer picture of the deficiencies of Gassendi that Baxter had in mind emerges by the contrast with Baxter's own positive argument for the soul's immortality. Toward the end of his manuscript "Of the Nature and Immortality of Humane Soules," Baxter provides a brief "sum[m]e" of his "natural Reasons for ye soules im[m]ortality." There he states, as he did in the *Reasons*, that the soul's acts indicate powers essential to humanity as such. Moreover, he adds, in these powers there is a "capacity & inclination" toward knowing more truth and enjoying more goodness "than it attaineth to in this world; even to desire & seeke an everlasting p[er]fection, in ye p[er]fect Knowledge, Love & Praise of God."[49] Elsewhere in the same work, he states even more clearly, "Nothing is more evident than y^t Humane nature desireth Im[m]ortality: These desires come not from Art or force."[50] Thus, Baxter argues for the immortality of the soul from essential human inclinations that are oriented to the perfection of the soul's faculties.

In the previous section of the same manuscript, Baxter provides an indication of the sources that were influential to his own view. After noting the disputed question among scholastics "whether Heaven be *finis hominis naturalis* or *sup[er]naturalis*," Baxter observes that they only disagree on whether God is *clearly* seen, but they are in agreement with respect to the natural inclination for the end. He goes on to cite Francesco Silvestri da Ferrara's (1474–1528) commentary on Aquinas's *Summa contra gentiles*, Aquinas's *Summa contra gentiles* and *Summa theologiae*, and

---

48. DWL BT XIX.351, fol. 4v: "1° As *Im[m]ateriality* respects y^e *Agent*, it is ye thing in question, whether y^e *Agent* be im[m]ateriall, & therefore not to be begd, but proved. 2° As *Im[m]ateriality* is attributed to the *Act* as such, so *all Acts* even of Materiall *Substances* are Im[m]ateriall: For to *Act* is not *Matter*, but a *Mode* of *Materiall* or *Im[m]ateriall* agents. 3° If it be y^e *Object* or *Terminus* here wch are called *Im[m]ateriall*, ye soule hath *materiall objects* & *Termini*, & yet is not thereby proved materiall. But it hath also *Im[m]ateriall objects*, y^e *Knowledge* & *Volition* of wch I thinke will prove it to be Incorporeall or Im[m]ateriall in ye Common Sense. ~~But w^t these objects are is ye question. [?How] farre universalls are such objects, is ye difficulty wch I am professing to passe by, & to lay no great stresse <on>:~~"

49. DWL BT XIX.351, fol. 118r. In this section, he also directs the reader to the *Reasons* for a complementary view: "Abundance more I have said in my Reasons of the Christian Religion wch I must not here repeat" (fols. 119r–119v).

50. DWL BT XIX.351, fol. 112v. The following pages contain a detailed explanation of how sin affects this disposition.

Juan de Rada's (ca. 1545–1608) *Controversiae theologicae.*[51] In his *Dying Thoughts*, Baxter likewise remarks, "*Aquinas*, and many others took it for the chief Natural proof of the Souls Immortality, that Man by Nature desireth not only to know Effects, and second Causes, but to rise up to the *Knowledge* of the *first Cause*; and therefore was made for such Knowledge in the state of his Perfection."[52] Baxter thus assumes together with many scholastics, including Aquinas, that the faculties of the soul have an inclination for perfection beyond what is attainable in this life, and this inclination is an important, if not the chief, argument for the soul's immortality.

This short digression on the importance that Baxter placed on the soul's inclination toward unattainable perfection provides an illuminating contrast with Gassendi. In contrast to Gassendi and others who were concerned with demonstrating that the soul is immaterial, Baxter was relatively uninterested in the specific (material or immaterial) *properties* of the soul, which he regarded as merely accidental. He was instead interested in the soul's powers inasmuch as they manifest essential inclinations toward their *ends* or perfections. He disliked proofs for the soul's immateriality mostly for their insufficiency and uncertainty in clarifying the essential powers and inclinations of the soul. As he later conceded to More, "I tell you still I deny not your *Penetrability* and *Indiscerpibility*, though I lay not the stress on them as to *Certainty* and *Importance*, as you do."[53] For Baxter, the growing importance placed on proofs for immortality from the soul's immateriality, by overshadowing proofs from the soul's powers and inclinations, constituted "slippery ground" and a "strong temptation" to materialism.

Despite Baxter's objections and fears, the soul's immateriality grew to occupy a central place in controversy about the soul's immortality. Had Baxter lived to read

---

51. DWL BT XIX.351, fol. 116v: "And note, y^t ye doubt is not whether a felicity in ye p[er]fectest knowledge & Love of God wch nature is capable of (not determining w^t y^t is) be mans naturall end; But only *An Deus clare visus sit finis hominis naturalis?* Ferrariensis Cont. Gent. c. 51 owneth it, *Quod appetitu et desiderio naturali voluntatis naturaliter cupimus videre Deum: Nam visis effectibus cognoscimus Deum esse; ex quo accendimur desideris videndi causam primam*. And Aquin. hath ye like, 1 q. 12 a. 1. et in prolog sent. et cont. gent. 3. c. 50. It is Radas first controversie." See Francis de Sylvestris, *Commentaria in libros quatuor contra gentiles S. Thomae de Aquino* (Rome: sumptibus et typis Orphanotrophii a. S. Hieronymo Aemiliani, 1897), 3:261–70 (on *Summa contra gentiles*, III.51); Aquinas, *Summa theologiae*, Ia, q. 12, art. 1 (cited in Sylvestris, *Commentaria*, 3:262, 268); Aquinas, *Summa contra gentiles*, III.50 (cited in Sylvestris, *Commentaria*, 3:262); and Juan de Rada, *Controversiae theologicae inter S. Thoman et Scotum, super quatuor libros sententiarum* (Cologne: Joannes Crithius, 1620), 1:110b, who cites all the same passages as Baxter from Sylvestris and Aquinas. Baxter's first point of reference appears to be Rada.

52. Richard Baxter, *Richard Baxter's Dying Thoughts upon Phil. 1.23.* (London: Tho. Snowden, 1683), 149.

53. Baxter, *Of the Nature of Spirits*, 32–33.

Anthony Collins's response to Samuel Clarke, he would have found his fears justified. Clarke made the immateriality of the soul his main argument for immortality. To this, Collins simply replied that even if one granted the soul's immateriality, "the Soul would not then be prov'd to be naturally Immortal; and consequently all the pains taken to prove the Soul Immaterial, signify nothing."[54] Although the response of Collins struck at the heart of Clarke's apologetic, it did not touch that of Baxter, who distanced himself from the approach represented by Clarke.

Pierre Gassendi, Thomas Willis, and the Material Soul

While Baxter's polemic against proofs from the soul's immateriality reflected his dissatisfaction with the accentuated contrast between the material and immaterial in the thought of mechanical philosophers, he also saw the threat of materialism in the mechanization of the organic realm of vegetative and sensitive souls. Descartes, as is well known, subjected life, including animals, to mechanical explanation.[55] Baxter, along with others, including Henry More and Ralph Cudworth, feared the Cartesian application of mechanical philosophy to souls and asserted the necessity of immaterial forms or self-moving principles for animals.[56] However, Baxter focused his polemic regarding the mechanization of the soul on the thought of Gassendi as manifested specifically in Thomas Willis's *De anima brutorum* (1672). Our present concern is therefore with Gassendi and his impact on Thomas Willis.

Gassendi offered a sophisticated account of material souls. In place of an immaterial form that actualizes the living thing, he posited a theory of seeds (*semina*). These *semina* were complex textures of moving atoms that have superadded powers of *scientia* and *industria*, which account for the specific development of living organisms. Gassendi described these seminal powers either as evolving in Lucretian fashion from moving atoms or as added to matter through immediate divine creation, and, although he did not clearly commit to either position, he seems to have inclined toward the Lucretian explanation. It is clear, however, that even in a Lucretian evolutionary account, Gassendi viewed God as providentially ordering the growth of seminal powers from atoms.[57] Given the intermediate superadded powers that Gassendi attributed to *semina*, his theory was less

54. Collins, *A Letter*, 6, 13.

55. Garber, *Descartes' Metaphysical Physics*, 111–16; Rosenfield, *From Beast-Machine to Man-Machine*, 3–26.

56. Cf. Reid, *Metaphysics of Henry More*, 285; Henry, "The Matter of Souls," 106–8.

57. LoLordo, *Pierre Gassendi*, 184–202.

reductionist than that of Descartes. At the same time, Gassendi conceptualized his *semina* according to mechanical analogies. He thought human ignorance about the nature of *semina* is analogous to an ignorant woodsman who encounters a clock for the first time. Gassendi also spoke of each *semina* as a "little machine" (*machinula*) containing "innumerable little machines [*machinulae*], each with its own little motions."[58] Despite Gassendi's complex theory of *semina*, he still understood vegetative and animal souls, along with their faculties, as material. He arrived at this conclusion by arguing that the soul is a kind of subtle material fire. Just as qualities of fire such as light and heat can arise out of material fire, so sensation can arise out of a material soul.[59] Gassendi's line of argument for a material animal soul would be extended by English members of the medical community, including Willis.

During the 1650s and 1660s, members of the Oxford medical community, most likely as a result of mingling with other scientific groups at Oxford, became increasingly favorable toward mechanical philosophy, including the works of Gassendi.[60] We have already observed the importance of Walter Charleton's transmission of Gassendian ideas onto English soil (chapter 2). Charleton was among the earliest members of the medical community to suggest that active matter could account for the faculties of animals.[61] Willis also drew inspiration from Gassendi while breaking new ground with sophisticated experimental studies and corpuscularian explanations of physiology. Willis integrated mechanical and chemical concepts—a kind of "corpuscularian chemistry"—and applied them to the study of physiology.[62] He was particularly important for the reinterpretation of "animal spirits" as the product of chemical compounds.[63] In his *Diatribae duae medicophilosophicae* (1659), which gained him considerable international fame, Willis explained a variety of phenomena, including plant growth and animal digestion, in terms of the rearrangement of small corpuscular chemical compounds—a process he referred to as "fermentation."[64] After receiving an appointment as Sedleian

---

58. Gassendi, *Opera*, 2:267a, with trans. in Adelmann, *Marcello Malpighi*, 2:806. Cf. LoLordo, *Pierre Gassendi*, 201.

59. LoLordo, *Pierre Gassendi*, 202–7.

60. Frank, *Harvey*, 90–114.

61. Charleton, *Physiologia*, 272. Cf. Thomson, "Animals," 13.

62. Frank, "Thomas Willis," 114–20; Frank, *Harvey*, 28–29, 165 et passim.

63. Antonio Clericuzio, "The Internal Laboratory. The Chemical Reinterpretation of Medical Spirits in England (1650–1680)," in *Alchemy and Chemistry in the 16th and 17th Centuries*, ed. Piyo Rattansi and Antonio Clericuzio (Dordrecht: Kluwer, 1994), 51–83, esp. 67, 72.

64. Thomas Willis, "De fermentatione," in *Diatribae duae*, 17, 20–32; cf. Frank, *Harvey*, 165–66.

Professor of Natural Philosophy at Oxford in 1660, he began new lectures on neu-roanatomy and psychology, which were taken down by his students John Locke and Richard Lower.[65] In his first two major works on the brain and neuroanatomy, *Cerebri anatome* (1664) and *Pathologiae cerebri* (1667), Willis explained muscular contraction in terms of the explosion of "nitrosulphureous particles," which he partially supported with the authority of Gassendi.[66] He concluded his studies on the brain with *De anima brutorum* in 1672, which Oldenburg promoted in the Royal Society's *Philosophical Transactions* and his correspondence. Of this work, Robert Frank observes, "As in his two previous neurophysiological works, Willis gave detailed corpuscular explanations of nerve function and dysfunction, but-tressed by many cases and postmortem results, some of them going back to his Oxford days."[67]

Although Willis is remembered today chiefly by medical historians for his con-tribution to the history of neuroanatomy,[68] he and his *De anima brutorum* were arguably of much greater importance to the pre-history of eighteenth-century materialism than is commonly recognized.[69] Locke is famous for his suggestion that God may have "given to some Systems of Matter fitly' disposed, a power to

---

65. Frank, "Thomas Willis," 120–29. The original lectures are found in Kenneth Dewhurst, ed., *Thomas Willis's Oxford Lectures* (Oxford: Sandford Pub., 1980).

66. Frank, *Harvey*, 222–23. Willis, *Pathalogiae cerebri, et nervosi generis specimen* (Oxford, 1667), 5–6 writes that the *Clarissimi Gassendi* "openly favors our hypothesis and in a certain way supplied the occasion of it," and cites Gassendi, *Syntagma philo-sophicum*, II, sec. 3, lib. 2, cap. 1. Cf. Alfred Meyer and Raymond Hierons, "On Thomas Willis's Concepts of Neurophysiology," *Medical History* 9 (1965): 1–15, at 6; and Frank, *Harvey*, 223.

67. Frank, *Harvey*, 248.

68. Meyer and Hierons, "On Thomas Willis's Concepts," 1–15 and 142–55; Alastair Compston, "A Short History of Clinical Neurology," in *Brain's Diseases of the Nervous System*, ed. Michael Donaghy, 12th ed. (Oxford: Oxford University Press, 2009), ch. 1; Daniel A. Casey, "Neuroscience, Metaphysics and *Cerebri Anatome cui Accessit Nervorum Descriptio et Usus*," *International Journal of History and Philosophy of Medicine* 1 (2011): 15–19; Wes Wallace, "The Vibrating Nerve Impulse in Newton, Willis and Gassendi: First Steps in a Mechanical Theory of Communication," *Brain and Cognition* 51 (2003): 66–94.

69. See Wolfe and van Esveld, "The Material Soul," 387–92, 397, 407, 411; Thomson, *Bodies of Thought*, 79–86; Thomson, "Animals," 14–18; Clericuzio, "Internal Laboratory," 72–73; John W. Yolton, *Thinking Matter: Materialism in Eighteenth-Century Britain* (Minneapolis: University of Minnesota Press, 1983), 163, 169; and Richard Allen, *David Hartley on Human Nature* (Albany, NY: SUNY Press, 1999), 107. Note also Friedrich Albert Lange, *History of Materialism*, trans. Ernest Chester Thomas, 2nd ed. (London: Kegan Paul, Trench, Trübner, 1892), 2:68: "Lamettrie ... studied industriously Willis's epoch-making book on the Anatomy of the Brain [*Cerebri anatome*], and took from it all that could serve his purpose."

perceive and think,"[70] which became a point of debate between materialists and immaterialists throughout the eighteenth century.[71] While scholars have argued based on only scant evidence whether or not Locke derived various aspects of his philosophy directly from Gassendi,[72] a more likely and proximate Gassendian influence for Locke's conception of the soul is Willis's *De anima brutorum*.[73] Locke took detailed notes of Willis's lectures circa 1663–1664, which Willis subsequently expanded and published as *De anima brutorum*.[74] In these lectures taken down by Locke, Willis made the Gassendian point, later to be reiterated in the *De anima brutorum*, that the "nature and constitution of the *animus sensitivus*" is reducible

---

70. John Locke, *An Essay Concerning Human Understanding*, ed. Peter Nidditch (Oxford: Clarendon Press, 1975), IV.iii.6 (540).

71. Yolton, *Thinking Matter*, 14–28. The meaning of Locke's statement is a matter of ongoing debate; see, recently, Patrick J. Connolly, "Lockean Superaddition and Lockean Humility," *Studies in History and Philosophy of Science* 51 (2015): 53–61.

72. Among the scholars who have argued for Gassendi's influence on Locke, see Richard I. Aaron, *John Locke*, 3rd ed. (Oxford: Clarendon Press, 1971), 34; Antoine Adam, "L'influence de Gassendi sur le mouvement des idées à la fin du XVII siècle," in *Actes du Congrès du Tricentenaire de Pierre Gassendi* (Paris: Presses universitaires de France, 1957), 7–11; Edward Driscoll, "The Influence of Gassendi on Locke's Hedonism," *International Philosophical Quarterly* 12, no. 1 (1972): 87–110; Richard Kroll, "The Question of Locke's Relation to Gassendi," *Journal of the History of Ideas* 45 (1984): 339–59; Emily Michael and Fred S. Michael, "The Theory of Ideas in Gassendi and Locke," *Journal of the History of Ideas* 51 (1990): 379–99; Michael and Michael, "A Note on Gassendi in England," 297–99; Rolf W. Puster, *Britische Gassendi-Rezeption am Beispiel John Lockes* (Stuttgart-Bad Cannstatt: Frommann-Holzboog: 1991); Thomas M. Lennon, *The Battle of the Gods and Giants: The Legacies of Descartes and Gassendi, 1655–1715* (Princeton, NJ: Princeton University Press, 1993), ch. 3; M. R. Ayers, "The Foundations of Knowledge and the Logic of Substance: The Structure of Locke's General Philosophy," in *Locke's Philosophy: Content and Context*, ed. G. A. J. Rogers (Oxford: Clarendon, 1994), 49–73, at 54–56; Lisa T. Sarasohn, *Gassendi's Ethics: Freedom in a Mechanistic Universe* (Ithaca, NY: Cornell University Press, 1996), 168–97; and Rainer Specht, "À propos des analogies entre les théories de la connaissance sensible chez Gassendi et Locke," in *Gassendi et l'Europe, 1592–1792*, ed. Sylvia Murr (Paris: J. Vrin, 1997), 237–43. John R. Milton, convincingly in my estimation, casts doubt on arguments for direct Gassendian influence beyond some topics in physics, due to the scarcity of evidence. See Milton, "Locke at Oxford," 37–39; and Milton, "Locke and Gassendi," 87–109.

73. John P. Wright, "Locke, Willis, and the Seventeenth-Century Epicurean Soul," in *Atoms, Pneuma, and Tranquillity: Epicurean and Stoic Themes in European Thought*, ed. Margaret J. Osler (Cambridge: Cambridge University Press, 1991), 239–58. Much like Willis, Locke's interest in mechanical philosophy in the 1660s stemmed from the discipline of chemistry, "and in the borderland between medicine and natural philosophy" (Milton, "Locke at Oxford," 39–40). On Locke's close links during the 1660s with the medical community, including Willis, see Jonathan Craig Walmsley, "John Locke on Respiration," *Medical History* 51 (2007): 453–76; and Frank, *Harvey*, 49–51, 58–60, 186–88, 195–96.

74. Dewhurst, "Sedleian Professor of Natural Philosophy," in *Thomas Willis's Oxford Lectures*, 42–45; Dewhurst, "Oxford Lectures of Dr. Thomas Willis," in *Thomas Willis's Oxford Lectures*, 51.

to a contexture of atoms: "This [*animus sensitivus*] seems to consist of a contexture of animal spirits and is a sort of aetherial man made up of the most subtle atoms being coextensive with our body."[75] Since his student days at Oxford, Locke was certainly exposed to a Gassendian conception of the nature of the soul through Willis, and he showed continued interest in Willis's conception of the soul after the publication of *De anima brutorum.*[76]

Willis opened the *De anima brutorum* with a preface that consisted almost entirely of an apology for the corporeity of the sensitive soul, thereby indicating the controversial nature of his two physiological and pathological discourses.[77] The first chapter sets forth his general motivations and surveys the major opinions on the nature of the sensitive soul "both ancient and modern." Willis's motivations, as he presents them, are twofold: first, to gain a better knowledge of diseases through a detailed physiology; and second, by defining the limits of the corporeal soul, to show the difference of the rational "Superior and Immaterial" soul by way of contrast.[78] In his survey of the major opinions, Willis observed that the opinion of Epicurus is "of late revived in our Age, which introduces the Soul plainly Corporeal, and made out of a knitting together of subtil Atoms." Willis saw most of the modern mechanical philosophers, including Gassendi, Descartes, and Digby, as building on this "Epicurean" foundation. "Upon this Hypothesis of the *Epicureans*, as it were its basis, the Philosophers of this latter Age have built

---

75. Dewhurst, ed., *Thomas Willis's Oxford Lectures*, 125.

76. Locke owned Willis's *Diatribae duae* (1660), *Cerebri anatome* (1664), *Pathologiae cerebri* (1667), and *Opera omnia* (1682), which contained the *De anima brutorum*. See John Harrison and Peter Laslett, *The Library of John Locke*, 2nd ed. (Oxford: Clarendon Press, 1971), 265 (no. 3165). In a notebook entry from 1698, Locke notes that both Willis and Gassendi hold that the "soul of brutes and the sensitive [soul] of humanity is material": "Animam brutorum et sensitivam hominis esse materialem v: Bacon Advancem' 208. 209. Willis de Anima Brut: Gassendi Phys: §3 l.1 c.11. M.S. 7/34." For this citation, see Milton, "Locke and Gassendi: A Reappraisal," 93, who observes that the "M.S." refers to a M[atthew] S[mith], *A Philosophical Discourse of the Nature of Rational and Irrational Souls* (London, 1695), 7, which cites these sources from Bacon, Willis, and Gassendi. Milton rightly observes that M. S.'s reference to Gassendi's *Syntagma philosophicum*, Pars 2, "§3 l.1 c.11." does not exist, but he wrongly attributes the reference to bk. 11, ch. 1. The correct reference, as Willis has it in *De anima brutorum*, 116, is sec. 3, bk. 9, ch. 2. Wright, "Locke, Willis," 243, takes Locke's citation as evidence of "Locke's interest in the Epicurean doctrine of the soul."

77. Thomas Willis, *De anima brutorum quae hominis vitalis ac sensitiva est, exercitationes duae* (Oxford, 1672), "Praefatio ad Lectorem"; Thomas Willis, *Two Discourses Concerning the Soul of Brutes, which is that of the Vital and Sensitive of Man*, trans. S. Pordage (London: Thomas Dring, 1683), "The Preface to the Reader." At the time of his response, Baxter only had access to the original Latin edition. All English translations are from the Pordage edition unless otherwise indicated.

78. Willis, *De anima*, 1–2; *Two Discourses*, 1. This second motivation places Willis in the tradition of immaterial arguments for the soul's immortality addressed above.

all their doctrines of the Soul [ψυχολογίας *suas*], tho very divers, and I may almost say opposite."[79]

Of all the modern "Epicureans," Willis singled out Gassendi as his obvious favorite. Gassendi had taken from Lucretius a distinction between *anima* (the irrational part of the human soul responsible for life and sensation) and *animus* (the rational part), yet in contrast to Lucretius, he held that the rational *animus* was located in the head (not the chest) and incorporeal (not corporeal).[80] Willis agreed with Gassendi's division.[81] Thus, like Gassendi, Willis held to an incorporeal rational soul and a corporeal (fiery) sentient soul. After having noted that both Lucretius and Gassendi think the sentient soul composed of atoms is "not much different from those [atoms] out of which fire is [composed]," Willis agreed with Gassendi's conclusion that the soul is "therefore to be a Certain Flame, or a Species of most thin fire, which as long as it lives, or remains inkindled, so long the Animal lives."[82] The only deficiency Willis observed in Gassendi's account is how such a corporeal flame could "produce the Acts of the animal Faculty." This "most difficult Problem" of the transition from corporeal fire to sentient activity, in Willis's estimation, "this most Learned Man [Gassendi] came to, and pass'd over its Knot as it were purposely in that place."[83] Willis then turned immediately in the second chapter to providing the explanation that Gassendi had declined to give.

Of the sixteen chapters in part one of *De anima brutorum*, Baxter directed his comments exclusively to chapters 2 (*Animam bruti esse corpoream & igneam*; "That the Soul of the Brute is Corporeal and Fiery") and 6 (*De scientia seu cognitione brutorum*; "Of the Science or Knowledge of Brutes"). His objections to chapter 6 are roughly twice the length as his objections to chapter 2. Baxter's response to these chapters effectively addressed larger metaphysical questions relating to the nature of the sensitive soul, while passing over the detailed anatomy of most of Willis's other chapters. Although Baxter had already conceded some ground to mechanical philosophy in the explanation of inanimate elements and substantial forms (see chapters 4–5), when Baxter encountered Willis's *De anima brutorum*, he discovered arguments that, like those of Gassendi and Descartes, broke down

79. Willis, *De anima*, 4–5; *Two Discourses*, 2–3.

80. See Gassendi, *Opera*, 2:237b, 445–46; with discussion in Osler, "Baptizing Epicurean Atomism," 167–70.

81. See Willis, *De anima*, "Praefatio" and 116–18; *Two Discourses*, "Preface" and 40–41, citing Gassendi, *Opera*, 2:444a. Cf. Wright, "Locke, Willis," 245. Walter Charleton later agreed in this division. See Booth, *'A Subtle and Mysterious Machine,'* 156.

82. See Gassendi, *Syntagma philosophicum*, II, sec. 3, lib. 3, cap. 3, in *Opera*, 2:251a; cited in Willis, *De anima*, 8; *Two Discourses*, 4.

83. Willis, *De anima*, 8; *Two Discourses*, 4.

the boundaries of the most generic differences in the hierarchy of being. This was a line Baxter was unwilling to cross. We will first examine Baxter's response to chapters 2 and 6 of Willis's *De anima brutorum*. Next we will show how Baxter viewed the arguments of Willis (and by extension Gassendi) as a slippery slope to materialism.

Chapter 2 of *De anima brutorum* consists of two general sets of arguments. First, Willis introduces some miscellaneous arguments for the animal soul's corporeality. Second, he argues more specifically for the corporeal nature of the animal soul based on its identity with fire, which he takes to be corporeal. Baxter responds to each of these arguments in turn. One of the first miscellaneous arguments Willis gives for the soul's corporeality is from the difference between heaven and earth. Whereas immaterial beings (God and angels) are prone to the air and heaven, corporeal beings, with the exception of humans, are prone to the earth. For Willis, it "seems more agreeable" to the "Oeconomie of the World" that the heavenly things are purely immaterial and the earthly things are purely material.[84] Against this, Baxter states that it is "much more agreeable to yᵉ harmony of Gods evident op[er]ations" that "all things here below are full of incorporeall spirits!" On the earth, declares Baxter, there is "no *unmixed* passive matter," and it is "not a world of Carkasses," but rather highly animated. He then turns the tables on Willis. If one grants Willis's premise that aether (i.e., the fiery element) is "meerly a body," why should spirits be "confined to yᵉ aethereall, yᵗ is, yᵉ *bodily* regions? If you allow *bodies* to be *there with spirits*, why not *spirits* to be *here* also *with bodies*[?]"[85]

For the remaining miscellaneous arguments, Willis maintains that souls are material and divisible from the fact that various animal acts arise from various members of the body at the same time, which would not happen unless the soul is something extended with many parts. Moreover, some animals, such as worms and eels, continue to move after they are cut into pieces, showing that their soul is divisible.[86] To these arguments, Baxter first responds that an immaterial soul can be present instantaneously in various members of the body, just as the sun's light fills the air in a moment. Next, he responds that this "would as well hold agᵗ the Rationall Soule, as yᵉ Sensitive in man: For besides yᵗ you can never prove yᵗ they are not rather diverse faculties of one soule, than divers soules."[87]

---

84. Willis, *De anima*, 10; *Two Discourses*, 4–5.

85. DWL BT XIX.351, fols. 134v–135r. Baxter presents the idea that the ethereal fiery element is material (bodily) for the sake of argument, a view not his own but rather one he attributes to Gassendi and Willis.

86. Willis, *De anima*, 10–11; *Two Discourses*, 5. The continued motion of dissected worms and similar animals was a traditional problem for Aristotelians. See Des Chene, *Life's Form*, 178.

87. DWL BT XIX.351, fols. 135r–135v.

Willis's most detailed and main argument for the soul's corporeality is from the soul's "fiery nature." Both Willis and Baxter, like many of their contemporaries, agree that the soul consists of, in Willis's words, "a certain fiery nature, and its Act or Substance is either a Flame or a Breath, neer to, or a-Kin to Flame."[88] Baxter, however, objects to Willis's Gassendian assertion that both fire and the soul can be reduced to atoms in motion. Willis defines the "essence" of fire as "an heap of most subtil Contiguous particles, and existing in a swift motion, and with a continued generation of some, renewed by the falling off of others." The "food" of fire and also the soul is "Sulphur or some other nitrous thing in the Air," which, once sufficiently agitated, forms both fire and soul.[89] To this, Baxter replies that it is "unproved & improbable" to suppose that fire or the sensitive soul would exist by mere motion, with the addition and subtraction of fuel (*pabulum*), but without the intrinsic cause of a "*formall selfacting virtue.*" As Baxter remarks, "Therefore ye inference, y^t *thus ye soule of Bruites* (&y^e *sensitive in man*) is *but a heape of such agglomerated subtile atomes*, without mentioning any *essentiall Vitall Virtue*, is to speake *atomes*, rather than *Sense* about *Sensitive Soules.*" Baxter stresses that, while he is "uncertaine" whether the "*firy part*" of animal spirits are "*corporeall atomes,*" yet it is "*most certaine*" that the sensitive soul is not corporeal.[90]

After these comments on chapter 2 of Willis's *De anima brutorum*, Baxter turned to chapter 6 on the knowledge of animals. He briefly responds to Willis's argument that if brutes had immaterial souls, then they would reason like humans, with the retort reminiscent of his critique of the immaterial proofs discussed above: "Do you thinke *soules* differ from bodies in nothing but their *im[m]ateriality* (a word least understood by us)?" They differ, Baxter says, rather in their natural powers, where brutes know in a sensitive way and humans know in a rational way.[91] With this brief rejoinder out of the way, Baxter turns to Willis's main arguments, which

---

88. See Willis, *De anima*, 11; *Two Discourses*, 5, who lists numerous ancients and moderns who held this belief. On Baxter, see chapter 4.

89. Willis, *De anima*, 12–13; *Two Discourses*, 5–6. Willis may have borrowed directly from Gassendi's *Syntagma philosophicum* at this point: he describes the animal soul as consisting of particles "most subtle, and highly active, which, as a flower arising out of the crasser mass [*subtilissimis, & maximè activis constare, quae tanquam flos, è crassiori massâ emergentes*], do mutually come together." Gassendi had a nearly identical description of the animal soul as "like the flower of matter [*florem materiae*] with a special disposition, condition, and symmetry holding among the crasser mass [*massam crassiorem*] of the parts of the body. . . . Such a substance seems to be made of a most subtle texture, extremely mobile or active corpuscles [*contexturam subtilissimorum, & summè mobilium, actuosorúmve corpusculorum*], not unlike those of fire or heat." (Gassendi, *Opera*, 2:250b; translation in Osler, "Baptizing Epicurean Atomism," 169). As far as I am aware, this textual similarity has gone unnoticed.

90. DWL BT XIX.351, fol. 136r.

91. Willis, *De anima*, 95–96; *Two Discourses*, 32. DWL BT XIX.351, fol. 137r.

continue in the same vein as chapter 2. In chapter 6, Willis labors to demonstrate that the powers of sensation in animals can arise out of the contexture of atoms that he had asserted was the essence of the soul in chapter 2. There are two main arguments to which Baxter responds, again each in turn.

Willis's first main argument is that just as fire can erupt from various materials, so likewise sensation can emerge from insensible matter. We see, argues Willis, "that there is not much more difference between an insensible and a sensible Body, than between a thing unkindled, and a thing kindled; and yet we ordinarily see, this [kindled thing] to be made from that [unkindled thing]; why therefore in like manner, may we not judge a sensible thing, or Body to be made out of an insensible?"[92] Baxter responds that the difference between something kindled and sensation is a difference "in *kind*, & not in degree of ye same kind. An *Ant* that hath *sense* is lesse than a mountaine y^t is *sensles*, & yet is of another & more noble species." Moreover, Baxter argues, matter and motion do not produce fire merely of themselves. There is an "*Active-essentiall Virtue* of *fire*, wch is *toto genere* distinct from ye meere *Passive elements*," and this virtue of fire is evoked from the air and wood and other materials, where it is already diffused.[93] Baxter then concludes his rebuttal of this point with a summary of Willis's argument:

> So y^t yo[ur] Argum^t runs thus: If passive matter & motion without ye agents *essentiall Virtue*, may cause Motion, Light & Heate, then ye same without a sensitive Agents essentiall virtue, may cause sensation: But &c. The Anteced^t is notoriously false; The consequence can[n]ot be proved, were ye anteced^t true. And therfore ye Conclusion [is] false.[94]

Baxter thus disagrees with Willis in two respects: the reduction of fire to matter and motion, and the analogy from the material cause of fire to the material cause of sensation.

Willis's second argument to which Baxter responds is that since the animated body is a great specimen of "truly Divine Workmanship, for certain Ends and Uses," God by a "Law of Creation" or divine "institution" makes the soul's faculties result from the mixing together of the body and soul. Willis provides an analogy: just as in "Mechanical things" and human arts such as musical instruments, "the Workmanship Excels the matter" (*materiam superavit opus*), so also

---

92. Willis, *De anima*, 96; *Two Discourses*, 33.

93. DWL BT XIX.351, fols. 137r–138r.

94. DWL BT XIX.351, fol. 138r.

in the sensitive soul do the faculties of imagination and appetite excel the matter.[95] Baxter notes the ambiguity of this divine institution (*Dei instituto*) claimed by Willis. The divine institution can refer to any of three options, according to Baxter:

(1) God himself is "yᵉ *only vitall-virtue* of sensation"; or
(2) God has given to the whole body-soul compound something which is in neither of its parts; or
(3) "*sense & appetite* is caused *without* any such *sensitive virtue* at all, formally or eminently so called" (i.e., sense is caused only by atoms).[96]

If the first option is true and it is possible that God directly causes sensation without a sensitive power, Baxter reasons, then the same might apply to intellectual powers, and God might cause intellection without a corresponding human intellectual faculty. The result would be that "yᵉ Sadducees were in yᵉ right ~~(& I thinke Gassendus meant as they)~~ yᵗ there were neither Angels nor spirits, but God & bodies were all yᵉ universe." If Willis means the second option, then it "will contradict both com[m]on reason, & yo[ur] [Willis's] owne principles," since the parts cannot give to the whole what "they have not *formally* or *eminently*." If Willis claims the third option, then Baxter asks for the proof which is so far lacking.[97] Finally, to Willis's analogy of mechanical instruments such as clocks and musical instruments, Baxter argues that the makers and users of these instruments impose meaning on them; these instruments do not gain harmony and order simply by matter and motion.[98]

Having set forth Baxter's specific criticisms of Willis, we now turn to Baxter's larger argument that the materialization of the animal soul could easily lead to a similar materialization of the rational human soul. Baxter addresses this topic directly in a few places in "Of the Nature and Immortality of Humane Soules." In the postscript, he writes, "Gassendus & such others as make Sensitive Soules to be *meere Fire* (wᶜʰ he taketh to be a Body), prepare men strongly to thinke yᵉ same of *Intellective Soules*."[99] The reason that a material animal soul is a preparative for

---

95. Willis, *De anima*, 98–99; *Two Discourses*, 33–34. This is not unlike Locke's suggestion of "superadded" perception and thought by divine institution. See Wright, "Locke, Willis," 254–55; and Yolton, *Thinking Matter*, 14–18.

96. DWL BT XIX.351, fol. 140r.

97. DWL BT XIX.351, fols. 140r–140v.

98. DWL BT XIX.351, fols. 140v–141r. Baxter had already responded to this objection prior to reading Willis. See DWL BT XIX.351, fol. 11r; and *RCR*, 514–15.

99. DWL BT XIX.351, fol. 131v. Cf. Hale, *Primitive Origination*, 48–49.

materialism is, to put it briefly, that it breaks the metaphysical axiom that the effect cannot be greater than the total cause.[100] Baxter uses this axiom on many occasions, and particularly in the context of arguing against the attribution of higher functions of the soul to matter and motion. One of Baxter's early questions and answers is as follows:

> Q. *Why may not all Intellection & Volition be the effects of subtile matter wch itselfe hath no Intellective nature, but by meere motion uppon the subtile corporeall particles within us (of the same kind) may have such effects?*
>
> A. Because no effect can transcend the power of the totall cause: & nothing can give that to another, which it hath not itselfe, either formally or eminently. If therfore ye subtile matter mencioned, have itselfe no Power of Intellection or Volition, nor yet y^t matter wch it is supposed to move, it is impossibile y^t their motions can be sufficient to cause Intellection & Volition.[101]

According to this axiom, as Baxter argues again, "No *effect* can be more excellent than y^e *totall cause*, though severall *partiall causes* may contribute all their excellencies to ye effect." The effect must be contained either formally or eminently in the total cause.[102] It is this principle that Baxter sees Willis violating when he argues that sensation is somehow produced from matter and motion.[103] If in the case of sensation a formally more excellent effect could come from several less eminent causes, Baxter thinks, one might go beyond both Gassendi and Willis and argue that the rest of the human faculties, including the intellect, could be produced from matter and motion. In fact, at least one famous philosopher, Anthony Collins, later argued in precisely this way. According to Collins, the "Composition or Modification of a Material System"—also called "Texture"—could give rise to a power that is not in any of the individual particles. Just as a rose is only made up of material particles, but those particles together produce "that agreeable Sensation we experience," the same "may be the case of Matter's thinking." The power of thinking may either derive necessarily from the combination of material particles

---

100. A total cause is that cause that suffices in itself to produce the entire effect. See, e.g., Pierre Godard, *Lexicon philosophicum* (Paris, 1675), 1:73: "Totalis, quae secundùm se par est toti effectui producendo, v.g. sol respectu diei." Cf. the useful discussion in Leijenhorst, *Mechanisation of Aristotelianism*, 204–5.

101. DWL BT XIX.351, fol. 11r.

102. DWL BT XIX.351, fol. 11v.

103. DWL BT XIX.351, fol. 140r.

or be superadded to them by God.[104] For Baxter, the line from Gassendi to Willis would lead logically to an argument such as that of Collins.

After penning his critique of Willis, Baxter sent it to Matthew Hale. Baxter observed in general, "The more I read Gassendus & Willis yᵉ more I am confirmed agᵗ their doctrine, though I am too ignorant of a better." Although disagreeing with Glisson's account of living matter (*materia omnis est essentialiter vitalis*), Baxter found it preferable to that of Willis: "I take his [Glisson's] booke to be one of yᵉ most considerable yᵗ hath appeared (to me)."[105] Baxter reiterated his belief that admission of the principle that matter could transmute into higher spiritual forms would have disastrous consequences for the conception of higher orders of life: "so yᵗ wᶜʰ was once a clod or stone may be thought by degrees to be made first water, then aire, than fire, then vegetable, then sensible then rationall, & then an angell." If this evolutionary picture is admitted, it would lead men to think of themselves as animals: "And this will tempt men to thinke yᵗ penaltyes will be by a Pythagorean transmutation of men into beasts againe."[106] Baxter observed on a personal note that arguments represented by Willis had been among his "greatest temptations" to materialism not only for others but also for himself:

I thinke yᵉ com[m]on asserting sensitive soules in bruites & men to be a evanide modes (they being so neere kin to ye Rationall, as to have Analogicall Reason) is one of yᵉ greatest snares yᵗ com[m]only tempteth men to thinke yᵉ Intellectuall souls to be as evanide: I am sure it hath bin one of yᵉ greatest temptations to me.[107]

For his part, Hale agreed with the main lines of Baxter's critique of Willis. In Hale's opinion, "And the explication of sensation by those fancyes of mechanisme and atomes is a vaine unintelligible and affected explication w[i]thout any so much as tolerable evidence for it: And the reasons given for it are so farr

---

104. Collins, *A Letter*, 11–12. This is elaborated with a discussion of texture in Anthony Collins, *A Reply to Mr. Clark's Defence of His Letter to Mr. Dodwell* (London, 1707), 12–18. Cf. Yolton, *Thinking Matter*, 24, 40–41; and William Uzgalis, "Anthony Collins on the Emergence of Consciousness and Personal Identity," *Philosophy Compass* 4, no. 2 (2009): 363–79.

105. LPL MS 3499, fol. 105v. For a comparison of Glisson and Willis, see Giglioni, "Genesis of Francis Glisson's Philosophy of Life," 285–87.

106. LPL MS 3499, fol. 100v.

107. LPL MS 3499, fol. 113v. Compare Baxter's early account of his temptation to infidelity, which includes the assumption that "that any Man should dream that the World was made by a Conflux of Irrational Atoms, and Reason came from that which had no Reason, or any Inferiour Being was independent" (*Rel. Bax.*, I.22).

from reason that they are not tolerable explications."[108] To this comment of Hale, Baxter replied, "I rejoice y^t you thinke as hardly as I do of their meere mechanicall Reasons of sensation, from Matter, figure, motion &c."[109] Baxter's final word consists of a passing remark, which is difficult not to read as an allusion to Willis. He speaks of "an Anatomist that is but an Atomist, and can say no more of the body of a man, but that it is made up of *Atoms*, or at most, can only enumerate the similar parts."[110]

Conclusion

Most of those who embraced mechanical philosophy were, apart from Hobbes, just as interested as earlier theologians and philosophers to refute mortalism. In so doing, they accentuated the contrast between the corporeal and incorporeal realms, and put renewed stress on arguments for the soul's immortality from its immateriality. Baxter disagreed with this trend. He thought in their eagerness to show that the soul is immaterial, mechanical philosophers neglected the better rational argument from the inclinations of the soul's faculties to perfection unattainable in this life. By contrast, those rational proofs for immortality resting on the demonstration of the soul's immateriality and typified by Gassendi constituted "slippery ground" or "feeble" proofs, and increased the temptation of materialism.

For many mechanical philosophers, the contrast between the corporeal and incorporeal also included the materialization of lower irrational powers of the soul. Willis and Gassendi, both of whom adopted Lucretius's distinction between the irrational *anima* and rational *animus*, but differed from ancient Epicureanism in holding that the *animus* was incorporeal, viewed the *anima*, consisting of both vegetative and sensitive faculties, as corporeal. This materialization of the animal soul, Baxter objected, was a slippery slope to complete materialism. In addition to providing a point-by-point rebuttal of two chapters from Willis's *De anima brutorum*, Baxter objected that the arguments of Gassendi and Willis for the production of sensitive faculties by matter and motion, "prepare men strongly to thinke ye same of *Intellective Soules*."[111]

Baxter died in 1691. He therefore did not live to read either Locke's suggestion that God might have "given to some system of matter, fitly disposed, a power to

---

108. LPL MS 3499, fol. 114r. Cf. Hale, *Primitive Origination*, 48–49.

109. LPL MS 3499, fol. 113v.

110. *TKL*, 143.

111. DWL BT XIX.351, fol. 131v.

perceive and think," or Collins's further arguments in favor of this suggestion and against the validity of proofs for the soul's immortality from its immateriality. Yet Baxter anticipated and feared the kind of arguments exemplified by Collins. We can only wonder how he might have reacted to a new generation of "our Epicureans who dreame y^t they are but *aliunde-moved-atomes*."[112]

---

112. DWL BT XIX.351, fols. 7r–v.

7

From "Epicurean" Physics to Ethics

SINCE MECHANICAL PHILOSOPHY brought about an intellectual sea change in views about the natural physical world, Baxter's most vigorous polemics were aimed at the topics of motion and the soul discussed in previous chapters. However, the seventeenth century also witnessed what has been referred to as a "revolution" in moral philosophy.[1] Whereas older scholarship identified Hugo Grotius as inaugurating a "modern" school of natural law,[2] the theory of a Grotian revolution has come under severe criticism,[3] and recent scholarship argues for major change occurring in the later seventeenth century, chronologically following the rise of mechanical philosophy.[4] With this shift in the historiographical

1. Cf. Merio Scattola, "Scientific Revolution in the Moral Sciences: The Controversy between Samuel Pufendorf and the Lutheran Theologians of the Late Seventeenth Century," in *Controversies within the Scientific Revolution*, ed. Marcelo Dascal and Victor D. Boantza (Amsterdam: John Benjamins, 2011), 251–75.

2. See especially Richard Tuck, "The 'Modern' Theory of Natural Law," in *The Languages of Political Theory in Early-Modern Europe*, ed. Anthony Pagden (Cambridge: Cambridge University Press, 1987), 99–119.

3. Terence Irwin, *The Development of Ethics: A Historical and Critical Study* (Oxford: Oxford University Press, 2008), 2:70–99; Merio Scattola, "*Scientia Iuris* and *Ius Naturae*: The Jurisprudence of the Holy Roman Empire in the Seventeenth and Eighteenth Centuries," in *A History of the Philosophy of Law in the Civil Law World, 1600–1900*, ed. Damiano Canale, Paolo Grossi, and Hasso Hofmann, A Treatise of Legal Philosophy and General Jurisprudence 9 (Dordrecht: Springer, 2009), 1–41, at 18–21; Johann P. Sommerville, "Selden, Grotius, and the Seventeenth-Century Intellectual Revolution in Moral and Political Theory," in *Rhetoric and Law in Early Modern Europe*, ed. Victoria Kahn and Lorna Hutson (New Haven, CT: Yale University Press, 2001), 318–44; Brian Tierney, *The Idea of Natural Rights: Studies on Natural Rights, Natural Law, and Church Law, 1150–1625* (Atlanta: Scholars Press, 1997), 317–24.

4. Scattola, "Scientific Revolution," 251–75; Scattola, "Before and After Natural Law: Models of Natural Law in Ancient and Modern Times," in *Early Modern Natural Law Theories: Contexts and Strategies in the Early Enlightenment*, ed. T. J. Hochstrasser and P. Schröder (Dordrecht: Kluwer, 2003), 1–30; Scattola, "*Scientia Iuris* and *Ius Naturae*," 1–41.

landscape, the connections between mechanical philosophy and ethics take on added importance. Some of the main contributors to the Christian Epicurean revival such as Gassendi and Charleton also wrote on ethics.[5] Moreover, natural philosophy and metaphysics are increasingly recognized as integral to the moral and political thought of both Hobbes and Spinoza.[6] Recent scholarship argues that Samuel Pufendorf is closer to Hobbes than traditionally thought.[7] While observing that Ralph Cudworth linked a revival of voluntarist ethics to "the physiological hypotheses of Democritus and Epicurus," Francis Oakley argues that "natural law theories are by no means insulated from changes in the temperature and pressure of natural philosophy and scientific thinking, but reflect or presuppose congruent concepts of nature."[8]

Baxter likewise saw a connection between changing theory in the physical and ethical realms. Although fear of radical philosophies was widespread in the late seventeenth century, Baxter's polemics are of interest against the backdrop of his largely negative evaluation of mechanical philosophy. Whereas many of Baxter's contemporaries favored the philosophy of Gassendi or Descartes while distancing themselves from Hobbes and Spinoza, Baxter saw the views of Hobbes and Spinoza regarding law and human choice as a consistent radicalization of "Epicurean" principles associated with mechanical philosophy. In this respect, we can observe a parallel with Baxter's critique of the incipient materialism of mechanical philosophy discussed in the previous chapter—the danger of materialism represented by Gassendi and Willis finds its ethical counterpart in Hobbes and Spinoza.

Just as a proper understanding of Baxter's response to changing concepts of motion and the soul required attention to his own approach to natural philosophy,

---

5. Lisa T. Sarasohn, "Motion and Morality: Pierre Gassendi, Thomas Hobbes and the Mechanical World-View," *Journal of the History of Ideas* 46, no. 3 (1985): 363–79; Sarasohn, *Gassendi's Ethics.*

6. Alan Cromartie, "*The Elements* and Hobbesian Moral Thinking," *History of Political Thought* 32, no. 1 (2011): 21–47; Donald Rutherford, "Spinoza's Conception of Law: Metaphysics and Ethics," in *Spinoza's* Theological-Political Treatise: *A Critical Guide*, ed. Yitzhak Y. Melamed and Michael A. Rosenthal (Cambridge: Cambridge University Press, 2010), 143–67; Don Garrett, "Spinoza's Ethical Theory," in *The Cambridge Companion to Spinoza*, ed. Don Garrett (Cambridge: Cambridge University Press, 1996), 267–314, at 270–72; Aaron Garrett, "Was Spinoza a Natural Lawyer?," *Cardozo Law Review* 25, no. 2 (2003): 627–41, at 635; Andre Santos Campos, *Spinoza's Revolutions in Natural Law* (New York: Palgrave Macmillan, 2012), 8–12.

7. Fiammetta Palladina, "Pufendorf Disciple of Hobbes: The Nature of Man and the State of Nature: The Doctrine of *socialitas*," *History of European Ideas* 34 (2008): 26–60.

8. Francis Oakley, *Natural Law, Laws of Nature, Natural Rights: Continuity and Discontinuity in the History of Ideas* (New York: Continuum, 2005), 70.

so also an understanding of his polemics with respect to the domain of ethics requires attention to his ethical theory, and specifically his understanding of natural law. Unfortunately, even the most thorough study of Baxter's ethics to date entirely ignored the most complete source for Baxter's natural law theory, the *Methodus theologiae*.[9] Baxter's engagement with Spinoza has similarly been read without attention to his larger theoretical concerns regarding natural philosophy and natural law. Rosalie Colie portrayed Baxter as drawing merely on Spinoza's *Tractatus theologico-politicus* and, besides the problem of necessitarianism, only concerned with defending patriarchy in the family and government,[10] when in fact Baxter engaged also with Spinoza's *Ethics* and *Tractatus politicus* while discussing the more fundamental questions of Spinoza's definition of natural right, its relation to natural philosophy, and its implications for promises and covenants in society.

The present chapter will make a modest attempt at a more complete, albeit brief, examination of Baxter's sources. After situating Baxter within a wider tradition of reflection on natural law, we will turn to his polemics against Hobbes and Spinoza. We will first demonstrate that Baxter formulated a theory of natural law that reflected many traditional questions raised by medieval theologians and cultivated within the Reformed theological tradition. While maintaining broad continuities with the larger medieval and Reformed tradition, Baxter openly aligned his view with Francisco Suárez's *De legibus* and reflected a similar twofold emphasis on the divine will as the ground of the obligation of natural law (voluntarism) and a divinely given natural order reflective of divine wisdom (intellectualism) as the ground of the content of natural law. Against this background, we will show not only that Baxter viewed the philosophies of Spinoza and Hobbes as an unfortunate consequence of mechanical philosophy, but more specifically as raising the specter of necessitarianism and a naturalistic concept of natural law unhinged from a divinely legislated and theologically oriented moral order. Since Baxter framed his response to Spinoza's necessitarianism in light of Hobbes and used Spinoza's theories of natural law and political society as a basis for his mature evaluation of Hobbes, the present chapter gives relatively greater attention to either Spinoza or Hobbes according to the topic under consideration.

---

9. Phillips, "Between Conscience and the Law," 106. Other studies suffer from similar neglect of the *Methodus theologiae*. See Walter Douglas, "Politics and Theology in the Thought of Richard Baxter," *Andrews University Seminary Studies* 15, no. 2 (1977): 115–26; Walter Douglas, "Politics and Theology in the Thought of Richard Baxter. Part II," *Andrews University Seminary Studies* 16, no. 1 (1978): 305–12.

10. Colie, "Spinoza in England," 190–92.

Baxter and Reformed Natural Law Theory

In his influential survey of medieval political thought, Otto von Gierke classified medieval theories of natural law into those of the (older) realists and (later) nominalists. While realists such as Aquinas and his followers found the essence of law in God's eternal reason, "which dictates were unalterable even by God himself," the nominalists such as Ockham, Gerson, and d'Ailly "saw in the Law of Nature a mere divine Command, which was right and binding merely because God was the law-giver."[11] In creating this classification, which he likely derived from Francisco Suárez,[12] Gierke assumed that voluntarism and nominalism seemed to entail each other. Such a conceptual wedding, together with the well-known influence of late medieval nominalism on Luther, allowed later historians of natural law theory to construct a narrative of continuity between Protestantism and late medieval nominalist natural law theory, and straightforward discontinuity between Protestantism and Thomist natural law theory. Alexander d'Entrèves, like Heinrich Rommen before him, thus supposed that "the notion of the moral law as the expression of the divine will passed over from the Nominalists to the Reformers—to Wycliff, and later on to Luther and Calvin." Moreover, he took it as "obvious" that a Thomist conception of natural law "would have been out of place in the Reformers' theology, and actually they found little or no room for it."[13] Whereas d'Entrèves and Rommen painted with a broad brush, others have applied this narrative in a more detailed fashion to later generations of Protestants. One scholar has argued that in contrast to Richard Hooker's Thomist natural law theory, "the magisterial Protestant Reformers and their disciplinarian progeny stand squarely in the camp of the medieval voluntarists and nominalists."[14]

---

11. Otto von Gierke, *Political Theories of the Middle Ages*, trans. F. W. Maitland (Cambridge: Cambridge University Press, 1900), 172–73.

12. As observes Francis Oakley, *Politics and Eternity: Studies in the History of Medieval and Early-Modern Political Thought* (Leiden: E. J. Brill, 1999), 222.

13. Alexander Passerin d'Entrèves, *Natural Law: An Introduction to Legal Philosophy* (New Brunswick, NJ: Transaction Publishers, 1994), 70. Cf. Heinrich A. Rommen, *The Natural Law: A Study in Legal and Social History and Philosophy*, trans. Thomas R. Hanley (St. Louis: B. Herder, 1949), 60: "The so-called Reformers had drawn the ultimate conclusions from Occamism with respect to theology. Contemptuous of reason, they had arrived at a pregnant voluntarism in theology as well as at the doctrine of *natura deleta*, of nature as destroyed by original sin. Thereby the traditional natural law became speculatively impossible."

14. Lee W. Gibbs, "Book I," in *The Folger Library Edition of The Works of Richard Hooker*, ed. W. Speed Hill, vol. 6/1, *Of the Laws of Ecclesiastical Polity* (Cambridge, MA: Belknap Press, 1993), 81–124, at 103. Gibbs cites Gierke, Rommen, and d'Entrèves at 103n36. For further examples, see the literature cited in Stephen Grabill, *Rediscovering the Natural Law in Reformed Theological Ethics* (Grand Rapids, MI: Eerdmans, 2006), 55–56; and Frederick C. Beiser, *The*

There are a number of problems with this line of scholarship. First, Gierke's assumption that late medieval nominalist natural law theory was a matter of "mere Divine Command" or "merely because God was the law-giver" makes that theory appear highly arbitrary and fails to do justice to the stability of the moral order that was in fact maintained. As medieval historians such as William Courtenay, Francis Oakley, and Heiko Oberman have shown, late medieval nominalists used the distinction between God's absolute and ordained power (*potentia absoluta et ordinata*) dialectically to emphasize the contingency and dispensability of the created (moral) order (*potentia absoluta*) while also maintaining the immutability and indispensability of the natural law due to God's self-limitation (*potentia ordinata*). Thus, while God could occasionally dispense with moral precepts, humanity could not dispense with the reliable moral order maintained by God's ordained power.[15]

A second and more important problem with the argument for strong continuity between nominalist natural law theory and Protestantism is that it rests on a narrow reading of Protestant sources. It is true that, as scholars have long noted, Calvin's voluntarist remarks resemble the late medieval stress on God's freedom, although probably resembling Scotus more than Ockham.[16] Yet Calvin also detested the "hypothetical separation of God's power from his justice" and expressly repudiated the late medieval understanding of God's absolute power for this reason, which makes arguments for late medieval continuity difficult to sustain.[17] Moreover, when scholars make generalizations about Protestantism based on a small sampling of Reformers (typically Luther and Calvin), while overlooking their contemporaries and successors, they neglect the fact that multiple medieval traditions often fed into the teachings of various Reformers, including (to various degrees) the intellectualist approach of Aquinas. There were Reformers who were Thomistically trained, including Martin Bucer, Peter Martyr Vermigli, and Girolamo Zanchi, who were highly influential on the development of the Reformed branch of Protestantism. This Thomistic influence is likely responsible for the fact that many later Reformed theologians employ the

---

Sovereignty of Reason: The Defense of Rationality in the Early English Enlightenment (Princeton, NJ: Princeton University Press, 1996), 41–45.

15. Francis Oakley, "Medieval Theories of Natural Law: William of Ockham and the Significance of the Voluntarist Tradition," *Natural Law Forum* 6 (1961): 65–83. See also the literature cited by Grabill, *Rediscovering*, 61–66.

16. Grabill, *Rediscovering*, 66–69; David C. Steinmetz, *Calvin in Context*, 2nd ed. (Oxford: Oxford University Press, 2010), 49; Georges de Lagarde, *Recherches sur l'esprit politique de la réforme* (Paris: Auguste Picard, 1926), 166–67.

17. Steinmetz, *Calvin in Context*, 48. Cf. Richard A. Muller, *Divine Will and Human Choice: Freedom, Contingency, and Necessity in Early Modern Reformed Thought* (Grand Rapids, MI: Baker Academic, 2017), ch. 7.

distinction of God's absolute and ordained power in the classical manner of Aquinas.[18] As John Patrick Donnelly has argued with respect to the medieval roots of Protestant scholasticism, "they tend to go back to the *via antiqua* and Thomism." Moreover, in Donnelly's estimation, "Protestant fruit grows quite well on the Thomist tree, even better than on the bad nominalist tree. In this light the intrinsic connections between Protestantism and nominalism become less important or even questionable."[19]

In fact, when sixteenth- and seventeenth-century Reformed theologians looked for useful medieval approaches to the question of natural law and ethics, many turned to Aquinas's *Summa theologiae* as a resource. Calvin's contemporary Wolfgang Musculus, who in many respects favored medieval Franciscan precedents, nonetheless followed Aquinas in defining the natural law as a participation in the eternal law.[20] Girolamo Zanchi, professor of theology at Heidelberg and one of the most influential figures in the development of Reformed scholasticism, drew heavily on Aquinas for his discussion of eternal and natural law.[21] Whereas various modern studies suppose that Calvin passed on a nominalist bias, some of his brightest students, who knew him face to face, saw things differently. Lambert Daneau and Franciscus Junius, both students of Calvin, saw no difficulty in drawing on Aquinas. Daneau, professor of theology first at Geneva and then Leiden, identified Aquinas as among the "purer scholastics" and praised his identification of the precepts of justice with the Decalogue in *Summa theologiae* IIaIIae, q. 122.[22] Daneau also cited Aquinas heavily on anthropological matters, and directed his readers to Aquinas's exposition of conscience: "On *synteresis* and conscience see

---

18. Francis Oakley, "The Absolute and Ordained Power of God in Sixteenth- and Seventeenth-Century Theology," *Journal of the History of Ideas* 59, no. 3 (1998): 437–61, at 459, agreeing with Herman Bavinck, *Reformed Dogmatics*, ed. John Bolt (Grand Rapids, MI: Baker Academic, 2004), 2:249.

19. John Patrick Donnelly, "Calvinist Thomism," *Viator* 7 (1976): 441–55, at 454.

20. Wolfgang Musculus, *Loci communes in usus sacrae theologiae candidatorum parati* (Basel: Johann Herwagen, 1560), 44: "Est autem naturae, lumen ac dictamen illud rationis quo inter bonum & malum discernimus. Thomas dicit, Lex naturae nihil est aliud, quam participatio legis aeternae in rationali creatura." Cf. Richard Bäumlin, "Naturrecht und obrigkeitliches Kirchenregiment bei Wolfgang Musculus," in *Für Kirche und Recht: Festschrift für Johannes Heckel zum 70. Geburtstag*, ed. Siegfried Grundmann (Cologne: Böhlau, 1959), 120–43; and Jordan J. Ballor, *Covenant, Causality, and Law: A Study in the Theology of Wolfgang Musculus* (Göttingen: Vandenhoeck & Ruprecht, 2012), 226–27.

21. Girolamo Zanchi, *On the Law in General*, trans. Jeffrey J. Veenstra (Grand Rapids, MI: CLP Academic, 2012). Cf. Kalvin Budiman, "A Protestant Doctrine of Nature and Grace as Illustrated by Jerome Zanchi's Appropriation of Thomas Aquinas" (PhD diss., Baylor University, 2011), 105–59.

22. Lambert Daneau, *Ethices christianae libri tres* (Geneva: Eustache Vignon, 1577), 182r–v: "puriores Scholastici sentiunt. Thomas 2.2^{ae}. quaest. 122."

Thomas in *Prima Primae*, 79, artic. 12. & 13."[23] In his *De politiae Mosis observatione*, Franciscus Junius, a student of Calvin and Beza at Geneva and later professor of theology at Heidelberg and Leiden, followed a basically Thomistic division of the kinds of law (eternal, natural, human, divine) and, as Musculus and Zanchi, defined the natural law as reason's participation in the eternal law.[24]

The positive reception of Aquinas's natural law theory continued into the seventeenth century and included the Puritans. In his popular *De conscientia*, the Puritan William Ames described natural law, using terminology reminiscent of (if not borrowed from) Aquinas, as the impression of eternal law on human nature: "the natural law is the same as what is ordinarily called eternal law. But it is called eternal, insofar as it is in God himself from eternity, while [it is called] natural insofar as it is implanted and impressed in human nature by the author of nature."[25] In the same work, Ames followed "the best of the scholastics" in defining conscience as the "act of the practical judgment"—a clearly Thomist position— explicitly over against other scholastics, including Scotus and Bonaventure, who identified conscience as a habit.[26] This Thomistic view of conscience as an act was recognized by Robert Sanderson as the "most common opinion" of Reformed theologians.[27] Near the end of the seventeenth century, when Francis Turretin summarized the state of the question on the dispensability of the moral law, he observed that, while a minority of Reformed theologians adhere to the opinion of Scotus that God may dispense with second-order precepts relating to the contents of the second table of the Decalogue, the "common opinion of the [Reformed]

---

23. Lambert Daneau, *Isagoges christianae pars quinta, quae est de homine* (Geneva: Eustache Vignon, 1588), 15r.

24. Franciscus Junius, *De politiae Mosis observatione*, 2nd ed. (Leiden: Christopher Guyotius, 1602), 11–34. English translation: *The Mosaic Polity*, trans. Todd M. Rester, ed. Andrew M. McGinnis (Grand Rapids, MI: CLP Academic, 2015), 37–57.

25. William Ames, *De conscientia et eius iure, vel casibus* (Amsterdam: Joan. Janssonius, 1631), V.i.6: "Jus naturale, vel lex naturalis est eadem quae dici solet lex aeterna. Sed aeterna dicitur, quatenus est in ipso Deo ab aeterno: naturalis aute[m] quatenus indita est, & impressa naturae hominum ab authore naturae." Cf. Thomas Aquinas, *Summa theologiae*, IaIIae, q. 91, art. 2. Contra Lee W. Gibbs, "The Puritan Natural Law Theory of William Ames," *Harvard Theological Review* 64, no. 1 (1971): 37–57, who views Ames as similar to Ockham and late medieval nominalism based on Ames's description of law as "made by commanding or forbidding" (41) and employment of the *potentia absoluta/ordinata* distinction (42). Against this, see Oakley, "Absolute and Ordained Power," 459, who reads Ames's use of *potentia absoluta/ordinata* as similar to that of Aquinas. The description of law as "commanding or forbidding" is not indicative of voluntarism; cf. Aquinas, *Summa theologiae*, IaIIae, q. 90, art. 1.

26. Ames, *De conscientia*, I.i.5–6. Cf. Aquinas, *Summa theologiae*, Ia, q. 79, art. 13.

27. Robert Sanderson, *Bishop Sanderson's Lectures on Conscience and Human Law*, trans. Christopher Wordsworth (Lincoln: James Williamson, 1877), 14.

orthodox" follows Aquinas against Scotus and Ockham in holding the indispensability of the entire moral law because it is based on God's own nature.[28] It is now apparent that, as Reformed theologians in the early modern era developed theories of natural law in conversation with various medieval options, they generally found more affinity with the approaches of medieval realists including Aquinas and Scotus than late medieval nominalist natural law theory.[29]

Baxter shared with his Reformed predecessors and contemporaries a strong interest in natural law. The concept of natural law is ubiquitous in his writings. If we were to collect every reference of Baxter to the "law of nature" or "*lex naturalis*"— used of course in an ethical sense—the list of works cited would approximate his entire corpus. Baxter clearly viewed the natural law as of both doctrinal and practical import, as the concept is foundational to his discussion of both the old and new covenants in his *Methodus theologiae*, and it underlies his arguments for both subjection and resistance to rulers in *A Holy Commonwealth* (1659). The main outlines of his thought on natural law were already present in his *Unreasonableness of Infidelity* (1655), and he appears to have maintained basic continuity with his early discussion throughout his later works. Although the most systematic presentation of the natural law is of course found in the *Methodus theologiae*, his discussion in that work contains few indications of the sources from which he derives his natural law doctrine. However, through a comparison between the *Methodus theologiae* and Baxter's other occasional writings, where he is more transparent about his source material, we can derive a clear picture of how Baxter fits into the landscape of seventeenth-century natural law discourse.

Before proceeding to distinctive features of Baxter's formal definition of natural law, a few words are in order about general continuities between Baxter's discussion and that of the Reformed tradition. Since the patristic era, theologians had held that the law of nature, while obscured by the noetic effects of sin since the fall of Adam, had been republished in the Scriptures, principally in the Decalogue but also by Christ.[30] This basic schema of an ontologically prior natural law with a subsequent supernatural republication was more systematically developed by the medieval scholastics, and continued to be affirmed by both the Lutheran and Reformed traditions, albeit with an emphasis on the noetic effects of sin.[31] However, this traditional

---

28. Turretin, *Institutio*, XI.ii.10–11. Cf. Grabill, *Rediscovering*, 171–73.

29. So concludes Grabill, *Rediscovering*, 190–91.

30. R. W. Carlyle and A. J. Carlyle, *A History of Mediaeval Political Theory in the West*, 3rd ed. (Edinburgh: William Blackwood & Sons, 1930), 1:104–5; Fred D. Miller, Jr., "Early Jewish and Christian Legal Thought," in *A History of the Philosophy of Law from the Ancient Greeks to the Scholastics*, ed. Fred. D. Miller, Jr. (Dordrecht: Springer, 2007), 181–82.

31. See John Witte Jr., *Law and Protestantism: The Legal Teachings of the Lutheran Reformation* (Cambridge: Cambridge University Press, 2002), ch. 4; Witte, *The Reformation of Rights: Law,*

Christian approach gradually fell out of favor following Pufendorf, when natural law became disjoined from the history of revelation and increasingly based not on continuity with the original state of innocence and mankind's eternal end, but rather on the de facto fallen state and mere self-preservation of the present physical life.[32]

Baxter, like other post-Reformation Reformed scholastics, falls broadly into the aforesaid patristic and medieval schema. His discussion in the *Methodus theologiae* begins with a discussion of law in general, where he sets forth the relation of natural law to God's rule of creation, the state of innocence, and mankind's final beatification. Subsequent sections of the *Methodus theologiae* explain, respectively, the relation of the natural law to the Mosaic law and Christ's doctrine. In his *Christian Directory*, Baxter states that the natural law "is indeed partly *presupposed* in the Law supernatural, and partly *rehearsed* in it, but never *subverted* by it."[33] Likewise, in reply to the question whether Scripture and natural law may ever contradict each other, he states that, just as obscure Scriptural texts should be explained in light of other plain texts (a typical Augustinian and Reformed hermeneutical rule),[34] so also "dark and doubtful" knowledge of the natural law should not be explained contrary to Scripture, nor should obscure texts of Scripture be explained contrary to a clear truth of the natural law. When attempting to harmonize natural law with revealed Scripture, writes Baxter, it should always be kept in mind that "*natural evidence* hath this advantage, that it is, 1. first in order, 2. and most *common* and received by all; But *supernatural evidence* hath this advantage, that it is for the most part the more *clear* and satisfactory."[35] Thus, the ontological priority and universal scope of the natural law distinguish it from an often more particular, albeit more perspicuous, Scriptural revelation.

This distinction also happens to be part of a broader assumption, also shared with many Reformed scholastics, of a general continuity between grace and nature. Like other Reformed theologians, Baxter was fond of the Thomistic maxim "grace presupposes nature."[36] This general assumption surely supports his view that natural law is "first in order" in relation to Scriptural revelation. Another

---

Religion, and Human Rights in Early Modern Calvinism (Cambridge: Cambridge University Press, 2007), 156–69; Grabill, Rediscovering, 88–90, 145–47, 165, 168.

32. Scattola, "Before and After Natural Law," esp. 16–17; cf. Sell, Philosophy, Dissent and Nonconformity, 56.

33. CD, II.495.

34. See, e.g., Confessio Helvetica Posterior, II.i (Creeds of Christendom, ed. Schaff, 3:239); Westminster Confession of Faith, I.ix (Creeds of Christendom, ed. Schaff, 3:605).

35. CD, III.908 (q. 159).

36. CD, III.907 (q. 158); cf. Phillips, "Between Conscience and the Law," 175–76.

traditional assumption that supports his view that the natural law is "most common and received by all" is the doctrine of common notions. Baxter often refers to common notions of the natural law, implanted by God in all minds, which enable all people to have at least some rudiments of the knowledge of right and wrong.[37] Since almost the beginning of the Reformation, when Melanchthon affirmed the existence of common notions in his *Loci communes* (1521), this epistemic teaching had become a commonplace of Protestant exegesis of the *locus classicus* on natural law, Romans. 2:14–15.[38] It is quite possible that Baxter drew on Andrew Willet's exegesis of Romans, for in his early *Saints Everlasting Rest* he cites Willet as an authority on the interpretation of the natural knowledge of God in Romans 1.[39] Be that as it may, it is clear that the general contours of Baxter's thought on natural law fall within the Reformed tradition's commitment to the ontological priority of the natural law, the existence of common notions implanted in the human mind, and the continuity of nature and grace manifested in the republication of the natural law in Scripture. Moreover, these aspects of his natural law doctrine reflect a broadly catholic approach to the natural law shared with the larger medieval tradition.

Within this generally traditional approach to natural law, there were of course major differences over the grounding of the natural law in relation to God's intellect and will, resulting in variant definitions of the natural law. On the one hand, Aquinas gave priority to the divine intellect, and thus defined natural law as a participation in the eternal law and reason of God. On the other hand, late medieval nominalists following Ockham stressed the non-necessity of the created moral order through their dialectic of God's absolute and ordained power, with the result that the natural law was grounded primarily in God's will. In the early modern era, Francisco Suárez tried to split the difference by rooting the content of the natural law in the divine intellect but the obligating force in the divine will.[40] Suárez

---

37. A particularly lengthy discussion is found in Baxter, *More Reasons*, 118–69.

38. Philip Melanchthon, *Loci communes theologici* (1521), trans. Lowell J. Satre, in *Melanchthon and Bucer*, ed. Wilhelm Pauck (London: Westminster Press, 1969), 50–51. Cf. Charlotte Methuen, "*Lex Naturae* and *Ordo Naturae* in the Thought of Philip Melanchthon," *Reformation and Renaissance Review* 3 (2000): 110–25; John Calvin, *Commentaries on the Epistle of Paul the Apostle to the Romans*, trans. and ed. by John Owen (Edinburgh: Calvin Translation Society, 1849), 96–97; Peter Martyr Vermigli, *Most Learned and Fruitful Commentaries . . . upon the Epistle of S. Paul to the Romans*, trans. Sir Henry Billingsley (London: John Daye, 1568), 31. Cf. Grabill, *Rediscovering*, 95, 110–11, on Calvin and Vermigli. The doctrine appears in later commentaries, e.g., Willet, *Romanes*, 117–18, and is affirmed by Hale, *Of the Law of Nature*, 41–42, 150–51.

39. *SER2*, II.282. Cf. Willet, *Romanes*, 59–60, 117–18.

40. Oakley, *Politics and Eternity*, 222.

thereby attempted to wed his theological voluntarism to an essentialist, or realist, view of the natural law.

In his own resolution to this disputed question, Baxter drew heavily on Suárez. In a number of places, he praises Suárez's *De legibus* in no uncertain terms. In the preface to the *Methodus theologiae*, he recommends the *De legibus* as "among the best" books on the nature of law.[41] This sentiment is reiterated in his *Catholick Theologie*, where he states, "It is of great use for a Divine who handleth Gods Laws to understand the nature of Laws in *genere* (as *Suarez in praef. de Legib.* sheweth; which book is one of the best on that Subject that is extant among us)."[42] Thus, although Baxter did draw on Grotius in other matters, the most important source for Baxter's thought on natural law was not Grotius, as J. I. Packer seems to imply, but rather Suárez.[43] At least in England, Baxter's esteem for Suárez's *De legibus* was shared by many of his contemporaries. Baxter observed that "the Authors of Politicks and Laws, (especially Suarez *de Legibus* and Azorius) I find are commonly read by Lawyers."[44] Matthew Hale, for example, followed many features of Suárez's natural law theory.[45]

Baxter's definition of law reflects that of Suárez. In the *Methodus theologiae*, Baxter defines law as "a sign of the Ruler's Will, the Right of subjects, or the Duty of the one who institutes, as the Norm of duty and judgment; or the Authoritative institution of Duty, viz. of duty and reward or penalty, for the ends of governance (or as the Instrument of Governance)."[46] This identification of law with a sign emanating from the ruler's will was most likely derived from Suárez. In his earlier *A Holy Commonwealth*, Baxter presented a nearly identical definition of law as the *Methodus theologiae*, but also cited the following passage from Suárez's *De legibus*: "I assert, with respect to the application of the term 'law', that it seems to have been used primarily to denote the external rule of the person commanding, and the sign making manifest his will."[47] The authority of Suárez was supplemented

---

41. *MT*, "Praefatio," [A5r].

42. *CT*, I/1.53; cf. II.270.

43. Packer, *Redemption*, 121, does not mention Suárez. Phillips, "Between Conscience and the Law," 170–71, correctly observes scholastic influences, but not Suárez.

44. Baxter, *Second Part*, 129.

45. Hale, *Of the Law of Nature*, xxxv–xxxvi, xxxviii–xl, xliv–xlv, xlvii–xlviii, 7–8, 63, 90, 112–13, 192. For other examples, see ibid. xv–xvi.

46. *MT*, I.259: "Est signum Voluntatis Rectoris, subditorum Jus, vel Debitum instituentis, ut Norma officii & judicii; vel Authoritativa institutio Debiti, *viz.* officii & praemii vel poenae, ad fines regiminis, (vel ut Instrumentum Regiminis.)."

47. Baxter, *A Holy Commonwealth*, 320, citing Francisco Suárez, *Tractatus de legibus et legislatore Deo*, I.v.25 (*Opera omnia* [Paris: L. Vivès, 1856], 5:22). See also *CT*, I/1.52. Translations

by a similar citation from Gabriel Biel's (d. 1495) *Sentences* commentary.[48] In his *Catholick Theologie*, Baxter also provided a smattering of citations from the *Sentences* commentary of Pierre d'Ailly (1350–1420).[49] Since Suárez also cited these same places, it is highly probable that Baxter simply repeated citations he found in Suárez.[50] Baxter clearly favored the late medieval voluntarist emphasis on law as formally an expression of the will, but did so while drawing on Suárez's *De legibus*.

Due to his voluntarist perspective, in which God's law is properly an external sign of God's will, Baxter also excluded other traditionally Thomist elements of natural law doctrine from his definition of law. Aquinas, and indeed many Reformed theologians, had included the archetypal Platonic ideas in God's mind under the category of law as "eternal law," and the hierarchy of human inclinations built into human nature and reflective of that archetype—whether living, sensitive, or rational—under the category of "natural law."[51] Baxter recognizes that many take law in these senses, but he thinks such definitions of law are only metaphorical or improper, since law is properly an objective sign from a ruler's will rather than either the internal intention of the lawgiver or the subjective reception or disposition in the ruled subject.[52] Indeed, Baxter repeatedly denies that there is an "eternal law" in any proper sense, thereby distancing himself from the Thomist definition.[53]

---

of Suárez's *De legibus* are taken from *Selections from Three Works of Francisco Suárez, S. J.: De legibus, ac deo legislatore, 1612; Defensio fidei catholicae, et apostolicae adversus anglicanae sectae errores, 1613; De triplici virtute theologica, fide, spe, et charitate, 1621,* 2 vols. (Oxford: Clarendon Press/London: H. Milford, 1944).

48. Baxter, *A Holy Commonwealth*, 320, citing Gabriel Biel, *Commentarii doctissimi in IIII. sententiarum libros* (Brescia: T. Bozzola, 1574), III, d. 37, q. un.

49. *CT*, I/1.51–52, citing Pierre d'Ailly, *Quaestiones super libros Sententiarum Petri Lombardi* ([Lyon]: Nicolaus Wolf, 1500), I, q. 14 A and F.

50. Suárez, *De legibus*, I.v.8, I.v.19, I.v.20 (citing Biel, III *Sent.*, d. 37, q. un.), II.vi.4, II.xv.3 (citing d'Ailly, I *Sent.*, q. 14). Suárez's manner of citation is exactly the same as that found in Baxter. Cf. Suárez, *De legibus*, I.v.20: "[Biel, III *Sent.*, d. 37, q. un.] dixisset esse *signum verum creaturae rationali notificativum, rectae rationis dictantis, ligari eam,* etc." (*Opera*, 5:21); with Baxter, *A Holy Commonwealth*, 320: "So *Gabriel*, 3. d. 37. q. un. calls it *signum verum creaturae rationali notificativum, rectae rationis dictantis, ligari eam,* &c."

51. Aquinas, *Summa theologiae*, IaIIae, qq. 93, 94; Anthony J. Lisska, "The Philosophy of Law of Thomas Aquinas," in *A History of the Philosophy of Law from the Ancient Greeks to the Scholastics*, ed. Fred. D. MillerJr. (Dordrecht: Springer, 2007), 288–99; Ernest F. Kevan, *The Grace of the Law: A Study in Puritan Theology* (London: Carey Kingsgate Press, 1964), 66–67; Grabill, *Rediscovering*, 136–38.

52. Baxter, *A Holy Commonwealth*, 317–20; *MT*, I.259, 263; Baxter, *Second Part*, 12; *RCR*, 70–72.

53. *CT*, I/1.52; Baxter, *A Holy Commonwealth*, 317; *MT*, I.259. Baxter was also critical of the common ascription of "ideas" or "forms" to God on account of the infinite transcendence

Despite Baxter's voluntarism and discontinuity with Thomists in his formal definition of law, in his larger description of law he maintains important continuities with a more Thomistic approach. While he does not admit that eternal law is in fact a law, he does admit that as the eternal law is understood simply as God's wisdom and goodness, it is "the Principle of all just Laws."[54] In *A Holy Commonwealth*, he states, "When I say a Law is a sign of the Lawgivers Will, I imply his understanding signified also: As Right, it proceedeth from the Legislators Intellect, and as Imposed, it proceedeth from his Will, and so is to be received by the Intellect and will of the subject for Regulation and Obligation or Obedience." In his explanation of this position, Baxter notes the "great controversie whether it be the *Reason* or the *Will* as signified that informeth Laws," with Aquinas and others on the intellectualist side and Ockham and others on the voluntarist side. He refers to Suárez's handling of the controversy, and approves of Suárez's solution: "but doubtless many of [the scholastics] hold as [Suárez] doth, and as the plain truth is, that it is both [intellect and will]."[55]

Just as Baxter arrived at a Suárezian position with respect to the ultimate grounding of the natural law in both God's intellect and will, he also mirrored Suárez (and Aquinas) in grounding the content of the natural law in the nature and inclinations of creatures. The grounding of the natural law generally in nature is evident in his formal definition of natural law as "*The visible and intelligible world, or universal Nature of things* (namely of Creatures and Divine Acts or Changes) *so far as the instruments of Divine Government establish his will in signifying the duty of subjects.*"[56] For Baxter, the essence of God, humanity, and other creatures, together with their various relations to each other, lay the foundations for natural law. Thus he could write as early as 1655, "The whole Law of nature (which was such to innocent man) did *necessarily* result from the Nature of man as Related to God and his fellow-subjects; and as placed in the midst of such a world of objects; and so is legible *in rerum natura.*"[57] He also thinks that Scripture assumes a strong relation between morality and nature, or as he put it, "Morality always presupposeth nature." This is why, in Baxter's estimation, the Scriptures begin

---

of God's form and mode of intellection. See *CT*, I/1.18–19 Cf. Burton, *Hallowing of Logic*, 259–60.

54. *RCR*, 69.

55. Baxter, *A Holy Commonwealth*, 323; cf. Suárez, *De legibus*, II.vi. See also *MT*, I.259.

56. *MT*, I.264: "*Mundus visibilis & intelligibilis, seu universa rerum Natura* (scilicet Creaturarum & Actionum seu Mutatio num Divinarum) *quatenus ut instrumenta Divini Regiminis, voluntatem ejus significando, subditorum debitum instituunt.*"

57. Baxter, "Advertisement," in *Unreasonableness*, a6v (par. 12).

with an account of the creation of the world and humanity, and this account is presupposed in Scripture's moral precepts. In Job and the Psalms, meditation on our nature leads to praise of the creator, for example, in Psalm 139:14: "I will praise thee, for I am fearfully and wonderfully made: Marvellous are thy works; and that my soul knoweth right well."[58]

Baxter was aware of those who, in a similar manner to Aquinas, identify the natural law with natural inclinations. But like Suárez, he argues that the ascription of "law" to inclinations is improper since they make known one's duty but do not formally establish it. Yet he still affirms the existence of a hierarchy of inclinations in passive, vegetative, sensitive, and intellectual natures. For Baxter, the specific "natural human inclination that is called the Law of Nature" is found in the intellect (a disposition for understanding truths), the will (a disposition for moral virtues), and the executive power (a disposition for the execution of good acts).[59] The "very nature of humanity, with natural dispositions and virtues to obedience and to higher things" are not formally speaking the law of nature, but are its "sign and object" by which God's will is made known.[60] Thus, despite Baxter's quibbles over the formal definition of natural law, he arrives at a position not far removed from that of a Thomist: God's wisdom ultimately grounds the natural law, while a hierarchy of inclinations reflecting a divinely established hierarchy of being provide the proximate way in which the natural law is manifested and discovered. The voluntarist modification to this basic framework accords with Suárez's *De legibus*.

Since Baxter, like Suárez, believes the content of natural law is proximately grounded in the essential natures of things (*in natura rerum*), his discussion of the potential mutability of the natural law is based on the corresponding mutability of human nature. For Baxter, natural rights are immutable to the extent that the natures or circumstances of things are immutable. Thus, he writes, "*Natural* rights are not *all immutable*; but to the extent that the *natures of things*, which are the *Foundations* of right, can *be changed*, to that extent the right itself can be said to have a *mutable nature*."[61] Indispensable obligations arising from rational human nature are founded on relations to God, each other, and oneself. "All these have their necessary Original with our natures, by Resultancy therefrom," writes

---

58. Baxter, *Mischiefs of Self-Ignorance*, 4–5. Cf. *MT*, "Praefatio," [A5r].

59. *MT*, I.263. For further elaboration on inclinations, see *CD*, I.183 (I.iii, "Appendix"). Cf. Suárez, *De legibus*, I.i.2 on the metaphorical application of "law" to inclinations.

60. *MT*, I.264.

61. *MT*, I.264: "Jura *naturalia* non sunt *omnia immutabilia*; sed in quantum *mutari* possunt *rerum naturae* quae juris sunt *Fundamenta*, in tantum jus ipsum *naturae mutabile* dici potest." Cf. *RCR*, 72–73; and Richard Baxter, *The Judgment of Non-conformists about the Difference between Grace and Morality* ([London], 1676), 53–54.

Baxter, "and God cannot (that is he will not, because he is perfect) Dispense with them; nor yet reverse them but by destroying our natures, which stand so related, and are the foundation thereof." Indispensible duties to love God, others, and self cannot be annihilated even by God as long as human nature exists.[62] Other natural rights that depend on certain circumstances, and are founded on "mutable Accidents, Relations, Moods," only remain indispensible as long as the accidents remain. However, "God can destroy the Obligation, by changing and destroying those Relations and Accidents" with respect to "this or that particular person, by a change of the person or thing; but not dispense with it *rebus sic stantibus*."[63] In other words, the immutability of natural law follows from the natures of things, but circumstances play a large role in the application of natural law in the concrete, and a change in circumstance can alter the applicability of natural law.

Baxter speaks of the basic duties to love God, self, and others as immutable, but he also provides a number of illustrations of the mutability of natural law due to a change of object or circumstances. These concern circumstances attached to human relations of authority, marriage, and property, and therefore relate to the obligations of magistrates, subjects, spouses, and children. According to Baxter, if there were no poverty, there would not be an obligation to give to the poor. Baxter states, for example, that while sleeping with one's sister would normally be a violation of the natural law, in the case of Adam's immediate children it would not have violated natural law.[64] A change in relation or accidents also underlies exceptions to precepts of the Decalogue. Baxter adduces the traditional scholastic examples of God commanding Abraham to kill his son and commanding the Israelites to plunder the Egyptians. The example of Abraham is justified on account of the command coming from "the Lord of Life and of all the world," while the example of plundering the Egyptians is justified because "the absolute Owner of the World had by his Precept altered the Propriety."[65] In the same way, he states that God can "dissolve most of the obligations" of the fifth (honor parents), sixth (murder), seventh (adultery), and eighth commandments (theft).[66] But apart from "some rare or supernatural declaration of the will of God," the natural law expressed in the second table of the Decalogue remains "ordinarily unchanged" and "are seconds

62. Baxter, "Advertisement," in *Unreasonableness*, a7r (par. 13). Cf. *MT*, I.264.

63. Baxter, "Advertisement," in *Unreasonableness*, a7v (par. 14).

64. *MT*, I.264.

65. Baxter, *Judgment of Non-conformists about the Difference between Grace and Morality*, 55; cf. Baxter, "Advertisement," in *Unreasonableness*, a6v–a7v (par. 12–14).

66. Baxter, "Advertisement," in *Unreasonableness*, a7v (par. 14). Baxter's enumeration of the commandments of course follows the Reformed tradition.

in point of *immutable Obligation* to the first (mentioned) sort (our natural duty to God)."[67]

Baxter's distinction between immutable and mutable natural law duties comes remarkably close to Francis Turretin's distinction between absolute and relative indispensable duties. According to Turretin, relative indispensable duties can be altered in particular cases by a (divinely ordered) change of circumstance.[68] Since Baxter formulated his views independently from Turretin, it is probable that Baxter simply followed the Thomist Salamancan tradition represented by Suárez in this matter. Suárez, Molina, and others, following the general reasoning of Aquinas's *Summa theologiae*, IaIIae, q. 100, art. 8, argued that while there are not changes to the principles of justice inherent in the natural law and the precepts of the Decalogue, God may alter the circumstances such that obligations do not apply in particular cases.[69] Suárez also distinguished between absolutely immutable precepts (toward God) and mutable precepts (toward humanity).[70] If, as we have good reason to believe, Baxter agreed with Suárez, his position would fall into the mainstream of post-Reformation Reformed orthodoxy. As Turretin observed, the Thomist view regarding the indispensability of the Decalogue "is the more common opinion of the orthodox."[71]

One of the frequently debated early modern ethical topics was the Euthyphro problem—the question whether something is good because God wills it or whether God wills it because it is good.[72] Leibniz was of the opinion that, although some early Reformed theologians favored an arbitrary basis for justice and goodness, "the Reformed theologians of today usually reject this teaching, as do all our own [Lutheran] theologians and most of those of the Roman church as well."[73] Baxter's response to the Euthyphro problem not only agrees with the majority perspective

---

67. Baxter, *Judgment of Non-conformists about the Difference between Grace and Morality*, 55.

68. Turretin, *Institutio*, XI.ii.6–11.

69. Suárez, *De legibus*, II.xv.20, II.xv.26; Aquinas, *Summa theologiae*, IaIIae, q. 100, art. 8 *ad* 3; Frank Bartholomew Costello, *The Political Philosophy of Luis de Molina, S. J. (1535–1600)* (Rome: Institutum Historicum S. J., 1974), 210–16.

70. Suárez, *De legibus*, II.xv.21–24.

71. Turretin, *Institutio*, XI.ii.11.

72. Oakley, *Natural Law*, 67–69; Oakley, *Politics and Eternity*, 219; Irwin, *Development of Ethics*, 2:251–52, 257, 321, 373–74, 386, 452–54; Petter Korkman, "Voluntarism and Moral Obligation: Barbeyrac's Defence of Pufendorf Revisited," in *Early Modern Natural Law Theories: Contexts and Strategies in the Early Enlightenment*, ed. T. J. Hochstrasser and P. Schröder (Dordrecht: Kluwer, 2003), 195–225.

73. Gottfried Wilhelm Leibniz, *Philosophical Papers and Letters*, trans. and ed. Leroy E. Loemker, 2nd ed. (Dordrecht: Kluwer Academic, 1989), 561, as noted in Irwin, *Development of Ethics*, 2:321.

identified by Leibniz; it is also specifically consistent with his stated preference for Suárez's *via media* that derived the nature of right from God's intellect and its obligation from God's will.

Baxter addressed the Euthyphro problem briefly in his *Unreasonableness of Infidelity* and then again in his *Catholick Theologie* in response to Samuel Rutherford's critique of John Cameron. Whereas Cameron had argued that some things are good or evil per se and God could not command them to be otherwise, Rutherford objected that Cameron's position limited God's freedom and came close to Arminians such as Thomas Jackson who held that the goodness of creatures is logically antecedent to any exercise of the divine will.[74] Baxter's solution to the Euthyphro problem tries to avoid both the intellectualism associated with Jackson's Arminian position and the extreme voluntarism associated with Ockham. Against the Ariminians, he argues that universals in creation such as love, justice, and goodness cannot exist apart from actual individuals, so that one cannot speak of the actual existence of eternal good or evil with respect to creatures apart from God's will, which effects creation. Yet Baxter maintains that it is possible to speak of God's eternal knowledge of such good and evil, as well as the eternal truth of the hypothetical proposition that if humanity exists, justice must also exist. Against the nominalism of d'Ailly and Ockham, Baxter argues that, once God creates, the natural law follows from the nature of things (*ex naturai rei*) and could not be otherwise than it is. Baxter specifically criticizes Ockham's supposition that God could command someone to hate him as involving a contradiction. He also argues that "God's own eternal perfection hath in it that root of humane virtue (truth, justice, &c.) which therefore analogically have the same name (our holiness being Gods image)," and as proof of this points out that without an analogical relation between human virtue and God's perfection we could not have any assurance that God's word is true.[75] Baxter's solution to the Euthyphro problem therefore affirms both the dependence of the natural law on God's will (things are

74. Samuel Rutherford, *Exercitationes apologeticae pro divina gratia* (Amsterdam: Henricus Laurentius, 1636), II.iii.11–13 (pp. 351–59), citing Thomas Jackson, *A Treatise of the Divine Essence and Attributes* (London: M. F. for Iohn Clarke, 1628), 149–52 and John Cameron, *Praelectionum in selectora quaedam Novi Testamenti loca Salmurii habitarum* (Saumur: Cl. Girard and Dan. Lerpinerius, 1628), 2:140–43. The objections to Cameron are repeated in Samuel Rutherford, *Disputatio scholastica de divina providentia* (Edinburgh: George Anderson, 1649), 317–24. See the summary of Rutherford's response to Cameron in Simon J. G. Burton, "Samuel Rutherford's *Euthyphro* Dilemma: A Reformed Perspective on the Scholastic Natural Law Tradition," in *Reformed Orthodoxy in Scotland: Essays on Scottish Theology 1560–1775*, ed. Aaron Clay Denlinger (London: Bloomsbury Academic, 2015), 123–39, at 125–27.

75. *CT*, I/1.110–11 with marginal notes; cf. Baxter, "Advertisement," in *Unreasonableness*, a7v–a8r (par. 15); and *RCR*, 69–70.

good because God wills them) and the realism of the natural law following from the actual creation which is rooted in God's eternal perfection (God wills things because they are good).

Just as Baxter affirms that much of the content of the natural law is ontologically rooted in a hierarchy of inclinations, so likewise he affirms that there are a hierarchy of good ends that people ought to pursue. The good of the soul is greater than the good of the body. The good of the many is greater than that of the few. The greatest good is God's will. In all things, everlasting good is greater than temporary good, and universal good is greater than particular good.[76] Such basic assumptions inform any number of Baxter's casuistical remarks. For example, he thinks that the welfare of magistrates and pastors ought to be more highly regarded since they are of greater importance to the common good.[77] And since the eternal good of the soul is greater than the temporal good of body, and the soul depends on knowledge for its welfare, knowledge that is useful for human salvation should be promoted above all.[78] It is this hierarchy of goods, derived ultimately from God's immutable nature and founded on the proximate goodness of creatures, which Baxter found threatened by Hobbes and Spinoza.

The Specter of Necessitarianism

To his contemporaries, Hobbes represented a twofold threat. On the one hand, his reduction of causality to local motion and subsequent explanation of human volition as a product of a chain of necessary causes undermined free choice necessary for human responsibility.[79] On the other hand, his reduction of the natural law from the principle of self-preservation was seen as a threat to the existing conception of the moral order.[80] Hobbes's contemporaries, aware of a revival of Epicureanism and anxious to refute any turn toward Epicureanism in ethics (if not in physics), painted Hobbes's ethics as Epicurean. By this, many had in mind Hobbes's derivation of justice from the will of individuals who conferred upon the

---

76. Richard Baxter, *How to do Good to Many* (London: Rob. Gibs, 1682), 5–6.

77. *CD*, IV.63 (IV.x.21).

78. Baxter, *How to do Good to Many*, 16–17.

79. On the physical basis for Hobbes's necessitarianism, see Leijenhorst, *Mechanisation of Aristotelianism*, 211–17; and Thomas Pink, "Suarez, Hobbes and the Scholastic Tradition in Action Theory," in *The Will and Human Action: From Antiquity to the Present Day*, ed. Thomas Pink and Martin Stone (London: Routledge, 2004), 127–53.

80. Hale, *Of the Law of Nature*, xli–xlii, 43; Johann P. Sommerville, *Thomas Hobbes: Political Ideas in Historical Context* (New York: St. Martin's Press, 1992), 49; Mintz, *Hunting of Leviathan*, 143–46.

state the authority to decide right and wrong in the interest of self-preservation.[81] As Spinoza's works became available in England in the 1670s, he was interpreted along similar lines as Hobbes.[82] Like Hobbes, he was also read through an Epicurean lens. As one scholar has recently noted, Spinoza's *Ethics* was "certainly received as an Epicurean work, by Leibniz, amongst others."[83]

Since both Hobbes and Spinoza were closely associated with the philosophies of Gassendi and Descartes, English divines and philosophers who favored mechanical philosophy sought to distance themselves from the dangerous religious and ethical conclusions associated with Hobbes while simultaneously arguing for the usefulness of mechanical philosophy even in the realm of ethics. Latitudinarian divines such as Joseph Glanvill and Richard Cumberland were anxious "to prove that mechanical principles, or the science of matter in motion, could support forms of morality that were not Hobbesian [i.e. determinist]."[84] Cumberland, in his *De legibus naturae* (1672), defined natural law in a traditional Ciceronian manner as a dictate of reason for the common good, but then labored to explain the content of the natural law from the physical consequences of moral acts by means of the empirical observations of mechanical philosophy. In this way, he hoped to show that mechanical philosophy could buttress more traditional morality rather than leading to Hobbesian mechanical determinism.[85] Baxter shared concerns similar to his English contemporaries. Like them, he worried both about the problem of necessitarianism and about innovative conceptions of natural law. Yet unlike many of his English contemporaries, Baxter emphasized continuities between these problems and mechanical philosophy. Baxter first encountered the problem of necessitarianism in Hobbes, but, after reading Spinoza's works in the 1670s, he extended his initial critique of Hobbes to Spinoza.

Beginning with his *Reasons* (1667), Baxter linked Hobbes's necessitarianism with mechanical philosophy. He argued that the denial of active natures and qualities is consistent with Hobbesian necessitarianism and a denial of morality. According to Baxter, the reduction of nature to quantity, figure, motion, and

---

81. Mayo, *Epicurus in England*, 122–27.

82. Colie, "Spinoza in England," 183–219.

83. Wilson, "Epicureanism," 98.

84. Parkin, *Science, Religion and Politics*, 181.

85. Richard Cumberland, *A Treatise of the Laws of Nature*, ed. Jon Parkin, trans. John Maxwell (Indianapolis: Liberty Fund, 2005), I.iii (p. 291): "That the Whole of *moral Philosophy*, and of the Laws of Nature, is ultimately resolv'd into *natural Observations* known by the Experience of all Men, or into Conclusions of true *Natural Philosophy*"; and I.iv (p. 292): "*the common Good is the supreme Law*." Cf. Parkin, *Science, Religion and Politics*, 89–90, 109–13, 173–203, and for Cumberland's likely influence on Samuel Clarke and Richard Bentley, see 187.

position would logically remove the character of good and evil from actions, since it would replace explanations of human choice based on powers, habits, and dispositions with the necessity of mere motion. Baxter writes, "For if there be no *power, habits* or *dispositions*, antecedent to motion, but *motion* it self is all, then there is one and the same account to be given to all actions, good and bad, I did it because I was irresistibly moved to it, and could no more do otherwise than my pen can choose to write." In such a mechanical universe, moral laws are no better than "tacklings in the engine which necessitateth," and "whatsoever is done amiss, is as much imputable to God the first mover, as that which is done well."[86] That Baxter had Hobbes in mind in these comments is indicated by his concluding comment: "I refer you to the foresaid writing of Bishop *Bromhal* against Mr. *Hobs,* allowing you to make the most you can of his Reply."[87] Baxter later observed that Hobbes teaches that "*Volition is necessitated by superiour or natural Causes* as much as any motion in a Clock or Watch, and that it is unconceivable that any *Act* or *Mode* of Act can be without a *necessitating efficient cause.*"[88]

When Baxter became familiar with Spinoza's *Tractatus theologico-politicus* (1670), he applied his earlier critique of Hobbes and the necessitarian implications of mechanical philosophy to Spinoza as well. Although the *Ethics* presented the clearest case for Spinoza's necessitarianism, a careful reader could glean necessitarian doctrine from the *Tractatus theologico-politicus.* Spinoza said that "the universal laws of nature according to which all things happen and are determined, are nothing other than the eternal decrees of God and always involve truth and necessity."[89] Even before he had a chance to read Spinoza's *Opera posthuma* (1677), Baxter was drawing parallels between Hobbes and Spinoza as similarly problematic for their subversion of morality via a shared understanding of physical motion and necessity. In his *Catholick Theologie* he stated that the doctrines of Hobbes and Spinoza would result in the "subversion of all morality as distinct from physical motion, and consequently of all true religion."[90] A few

---

86. *RCR*, 520–21.

87. *RCR*, 521. On the debate, see Vere Chappell, ed., *Hobbes and Bramhall on Liberty and Necessity* (Cambridge: Cambridge University Press, 1999); and J. Mark Beach, "The Hobbes-Bramhall Debate on the Nature of Freedom and Necessity," in *Biblical Interpretation and Doctrinal Formulation in the Reformed Tradition: Essays in Honor of James A. De Jong,* ed. Arie C. Leder and Richard A. Muller (Grand Rapids, MI: Reformation Heritage Books, 2014), 231–61.

88. *CT*, I/3.39.

89. Benedict de Spinoza, *Theological-Political Treatise* [hereafter *TTP*], ed. Jonathan Israel, trans. Michael Silverthorne and Jonathan Israel (Cambridge: Cambridge University Press, 2007), III.3 (pp. 44–45); also IV.1 (p. 57); VI.3 (pp. 82–83); XVI.4 (p. 197); XIX.8 (p. 241).

90. *CT*, II.152; cf. *CT*, I/3.108.

years later, when commenting on Spinoza's *Tractatus theologico-politicus*—prior to reading the *Ethics* in *Opera posthuma*[91]—Baxter identified Spinoza's philosophy as necessitarian and as rooted in an "Epicurean" philosophy of "God and Nature":

> And the root of all this mans [Spinoza's] inhumanity is his Epicurean principles of Philosophy about God and *Nature,* supposing God to be but the *Eternal necessary necessitating first cause of all things and motions, as the Sun is of light and heat, who can do no more, nor less than he doth,* moving the world as a Clock or Watch by meer invariable necessity, that never did or can do a miracle, or alter the necessitating course of nature: And that man hath no self determining free-will at all, but is moved as necessarily as an Engine; And that God is no governour, nor hath no Laws (but mens) nor no *Justice,* nor *Mercy,* these being not to be attributed to him, but only natural motion or necessitation; And that he that lyeth, murdereth, stealeth, rebelleth is equally moved to it by God, as good: and therefore it is but our narrow minds and ignorance, that taketh one thing to be better or worse than another, or to be sin or duty, save in respect to our commodity and the will of the strongest.[92]

Baxter's rhetoric here points back to the appendix to the *Reasons* with its general critique of "Epicurean" mechanical philosophy and its specific objections to Hobbes's necessitarianism.

In addition, Baxter's description of Spinoza's view of God as analogous to the sun that necessarily lights and heats is significant. For in his *Methodus theologiae,* as we saw in chapter 5, Baxter objected to Descartes's grounding of the laws of motion in God's immutability using the same analogy. Even before he was aware of Spinoza, Baxter wrote against Descartes, "God does not work as *fire,* in the manner of mere nature, *ad ultimum posse;* but according to the choice *of Intellect & free will.*"[93] Perhaps this similarity is one reason Baxter referred to Spinoza as "Cartesian."[94] But there is further evidence that Baxter

---

91. Cf. Baxter, *Second Part,* 111: "The marrow of *Spinosa's Opera posthuma* which I read not till after the writing of what is before." The earlier pages of *Second Part* cited below were written before Baxter became acquainted with Spinoza's *Ethics.*

92. Baxter, *Second Part,* 6.

93. *MT,* I.145: "Deus enim non operatur ut *ignis,* per modum merae naturae, ad ultimum posse; sed ad *Intellectus & liberi arbitrii* delectum."

94. Baxter, *Second Part,* "The Preface," a4v: "Is it the new Philosophers; such Cartesians as Spinosa, and such as Hobbes that you prefer?"

associated Spinoza with Cartesianism. In a statement embedded in Baxter's "summ" of "Judgments against these pernicious principles" of Spinoza's *Tractatus theologico-politicus*,[95] Baxter derides the "impudency in them that pretend to Cartesian *clarity* and *certainty* in all that they receive." While those such as Spinoza pretend to Cartesian certainty, Baxter avers, they are at the same time so confident about their knowledge about God, his operations, and nature that they claim,

> Liberty of will is inconsistent with Gods nature, that he never doth a miracle, nor altereth the course of the smallest particle in nature, nor doth nothing in the world which is not the necessary effect of natural second causes, as well as of his own will, as he put them in a set course of motion from eternity, or from the creation.[96]

But, Baxter retorts, those such as Spinoza lack the requisite epistemic certainty for their "dreams"—such things "are certainly unknown to them to be so."[97] By identifying Spinoza's necessitarian philosophy with Cartesianism, Baxter paralleled the conservative anti-Cartesian Dutch theologians, who likewise saw Spinoza as an outgrowth of Cartesian principles. By contrast, Dutch Cartesians argued that Spinoza's philosophy differed sharply from Descartes, who did not confound God and creation or matter and spirit.[98]

Yet Baxter's identification of Spinoza as "Cartesian" should not be taken as exclusive of Hobbesian continuity. We already observed Baxter drawing parallels between Hobbes and Spinoza's *Tractatus theologico-politicus*. In the mid-1670s, Baxter said that Hobbes's necessitarianism had been "improved by *Benedictus Spinosa*, an Apostate Jew in his *Tractatus Politico-theologicus*."[99] After Spinoza's *Opera posthuma* appeared, Baxter read through the entire *Ethics*, including scholia and appendices. He summarized thirty-five objectionable points culled from the *Ethics* in a "marrow," and prefaced this summary with the general comment, "To

---

95. Baxter, *Second Part*, 8.

96. Baxter, *Second Part*, 14.

97. Baxter, *Second Part*, 14.

98. Jonathan Israel, "The Early Dutch and German Reaction to the *Tractatus Theologico-Politicus*: Foreshadowing the Enlightenment's More General Spinoza Reception?," in *Spinoza's* Theological-Political Treatise: *A Critical Guide*, ed. Yitzhak Y. Melamed and Michael A. Rosenthal (Cambridge: Cambridge University Press, 2010), 72–100; Kato, "*Deus sive Natura*," 139–40, 181, 188.

99. *CT*, II.152.

which *Hobbes* much agreeth."[100] Among the points from Baxter's summary are the following:

> 8. Every thing and act is necessarily determined of God, and nothing can suspend that determination, nor is any thing Contingent; every Volition of man is necessitated by the Divine nature, as all other things are; and no will is free.
>
>   9. It is not, nor ever was possible that any thing should be otherwise than it comes to pass.[101]

Baxter consistently identified Spinoza's teaching with that of Hobbes, and specifically the problem of necessitarianism. Moreover, this identification of the *Ethics* with Hobbes's necessitarianism strengthens the likelihood that Baxter had Hobbes also in mind when he spoke of Spinoza's *Tractatus theologico-politicus* as containing "Epicurean" principles regarding "God and Nature." Although such a reading of Spinoza as an "improved" version of Hobbes might only be due to shared radical conclusions, it is not unthinkable that Baxter could also have seen genuine continuities between the respective natural philosophies of Hobbes and Spinoza. For despite the prevailing understanding of Spinoza as drawing on Cartesian mechanism, Daniel Garber has recently argued that "when we look more closely at Spinoza's actual statements about natural philosophy, I think we have reason to believe that Spinoza's inspiration is more likely Hobbes than Descartes."[102] Moreover, Baxter was not alone in regarding Spinoza as continuous with Hobbes's philosophy—this opinion was shared by Leibniz and Johann Georg Graevius, among others.[103] Although Baxter did not elaborate much further on the problem of necessitarianism, it clearly figured throughout his polemics as a prominent concern in the application of mechanical philosophy to ethics. And

---

100. Baxter, *Second Part*, 111. This summary is discussed below.

101. Baxter, *Second Part*, 111. These correspond to Spinoza, *Ethics*, Ip29, Ip32, Ip33.

102. Daniel Garber, "Natural Philosophy in Seventeenth-Century Context," in *The Oxford Handbook of Hobbes*, ed. A. P. Martinich and Kinch Hoekstra (Oxford: Oxford University Press, 2016), 106–33, here 123. Cf. William Sacksteder, "How Much of Hobbes Might Spinoza Have Read?," *The Southwestern Journal of Philosophy* 11, no. 2 (1980): 25–39, who also suggested a number of parallels.

103. Mogens Laerke, "G. W. Leibniz's Two Readings of the *Tractatus Theologico-Politicus*," in *Spinoza's Theological-Political Treatise: A Critical Guide*, ed. Yitzhak Y. Melamed and Michael A. Rosenthal (Cambridge: Cambridge University Press, 2010), 101–27, here 120, 124–26; Edwin Curley, "Homo Audax: Leibniz, Oldenburg and the TTP," in *Leibniz' Auseinandersetzung mit Vorgängern und Zeitgenossen*, ed. Ingrid Marchlewitz and Albert Heinekamp (Stuttgart: Franz Steiner Verlag, 1990), 277–312. I am grateful to Albert Gootjes for this observation.

for our purposes, it is significant that he saw the necessitarianism of Hobbes and Spinoza as an outgrowth of a similar "Epicurean" philosophy of nature.

The Problem of Naturalistic Natural Law

Besides the problem of necessitarianism, Baxter objected to the teaching of Hobbes and Spinoza on natural law. He saw their teaching in general as introducing a kind of naturalistic or secular theory of right that legitimized the pursuit of selfish ends. Late in life, Baxter summarized the problem in the following way: "It is a Monster of inhumanity in the Doctrine of the Sadducees, Spinosa, Hobbes, and their bruitish followers, that they set up Individual self interest as a mans chiefest end and object of rational Love and desire; and own no Good, but that which Relatively is Good to me, that is, either my personal life and pleasure as the end, or other things as a means thereto."[104] Such polemics of course rehearse typical objections shared by contemporaries to the elevation of the principle of self-preservation above other ends. As Hale observed, in an obvious critique of Hobbes, some philosophers "have shrunk up the Laws of Nature into a very narrow Compass and have made in effect self preservation the only Cardinall Law of human Nature."[105]

Baxter focused his polemic on Spinoza's concept of natural law in *Tractatus theologico-politicus*, which he later extended to Spinoza's *Ethics* and *Tractatus politicus*. He also observed a certain degree of continuity with Hobbes's *De cive*, but given the recent appearance of Spinoza's works in the 1670s, Baxter drew more attention to Spinoza and connected Spinoza's understanding of natural law in particular to "Epicurean" philosophical principles. The fact that Baxter focused on Spinoza's understanding of natural law, particularly in chapter 16 of *Tractatus theologico-politicus*, is remarkable. For it has recently been observed that Spinoza's seventeenth-century critics focused on his denial of miracles and Mosaic authorship of the Pentateuch, while tending to ignore the ethical topics of natural law and political theory that were actually central to Spinoza's argument.[106] Baxter's polemic thus engages a central feature of Spinoza's philosophy

---

104. Baxter, *Church-History*, "The Preface," A2r.

105. Hale, *Of the Law of Nature*, 43. Cf. Hobbes, *De cive*, I.7; Hobbes, *Leviathan*, XIV.1–3.

106. Laerke, "G. W. Leibniz's Two Readings," 122. Cf. Johann Melchior, *Epistola ad amicum, continens censuram. Libri cui titulus:* Tractatus theologico-politicus (Utrecht: C. Noenaert, 1671), who relegates discussion of *Tractatus Theologico-Politicus*, chapters 16–20 to a two-page appendix (pp. 46–48), while focusing on chapters 1–15. I am grateful to Albert Gootjes for drawing my attention to this example. See also J. J. V. M. De Vet, "On Account of the Sacrosanctity of the Scriptures: Johannes Melchior against Spinoza's *Tractatus theologico-politicus*," *Lias* 18 (1991): 229–61, at 230.

that was often ignored by his contemporaries. If the "root" of Spinoza's errors lay in his "Epicurean principles of Philosophy about God and *Nature*," including an "Eternal necessary necessitating first cause of all things and motions,"[107] then for Baxter we might say that the radical naturalization of natural law constitutes the fruit of these principles.

In the sixteenth chapter of *Tractatus theologico-politicus*, Spinoza made the radical claim that right (*ius*) in a state of nature is coextensive with natural power. According to Spinoza, natural right ought to be conceived along the lines of possibility within nature analogously to bigger fish eating smaller fish. In Spinoza's words, "For it is certain that nature, considered wholly in itself, has a sovereign right to do everything that it can do, i.e., the right of nature extends as far as its power extends."[108] This understanding of natural law assumes his overall conception of nature and natural law in a physical or metaphysical sense, and scholars have argued that Spinoza's comments on the foundation of natural law in chapter 16 ought to be read in light of his comments on the nature of law in general in the opening sections of chapter 4.[109] At the beginning of chapter 4, Spinoza states that law can be taken in an "absolute sense" for the "fixed and determined way" all things behave, "depending upon either natural necessity or a human decision."[110] This yields a twofold understanding of law as based either on natural necessity or human agency, where the former sense of necessity is more basic.[111] Spinoza's understanding of natural right in chapter 16 is predicated on the more basic sense of law as natural necessity. Therefore, when explaining that natural right is coextensive with power, he argues that "since it is the supreme law of nature that each thing strives to persist in its own state so far as it can ... it follows that each individual thing has a sovereign right to do this, i.e. (as I said) to exist and to behave as it is naturally determined to behave."[112]

In addition to natural right, Spinoza distinguishes law in a secondary sense as the dictates or laws of reason. While "all humans are born and for the most part live" under natural right[113]—and likewise live according to desire, power,

---

107. Baxter, *Second Part*, 6.

108. Spinoza, *TTP*, XVI.2 (p. 195).

109. Rutherford, "Spinoza's Conception of Law," 143–67; Garrett, "Was Spinoza a Natural Lawyer?," 627–41.

110. Spinoza, *TTP*, IV.1 (p. 57).

111. Rutherford, "Spinoza's Conception of Law," 143–48.

112. Spinoza, *TTP*, XVI.2 (pp. 195–96). Cf. Rutherford, "Spinoza's Conception of Law," 148–49.

113. Spinoza, *TTP*, XVI.4 (p. 197).

self-conservation, passions, and the "sole impulse of appetite"[114]—the wise man lives by the "laws of reason."[115] The wise man's laws of reason appear to correspond to laws based on human agency, which people prescribe in order to live a "better and safer life" and promote "men's true interests."[116] The transition from the state of nature to civil society is explained in terms of a transition from natural right to living according to laws of reason; individuals curb their power and appetites, which they have by natural right, in favor of collective power and rules, which reflect the dictates and laws of reason.[117] Although Spinoza uses familiar terms such as natural right and laws of reason, he both accommodates their meaning to a necessitarian world order and detaches their meaning from God as a transcendent legislator whose nature and prescriptive will establish the ontological foundation and sanction for natural law. In fact, Spinoza argues that the notion of God as legislator is a defective sort of knowledge (i.e., not in accord with reality) on the grounds that God's intellect and will are not really distinct, with the result that whatever God wills happens by necessity of divine decree and excludes the possibility underlying obedience or disobedience to a legislator.[118]

As we observed in chapter 2, Baxter made use of Spinoza's works in order to demonstrate that radical philosophy, rather than nonconformity, constituted a threat to political order amid the conspiracy theories regarding plots against the crown that circulated in the late 1670s. He therefore sought to demonstrate that Spinoza's understanding of natural law and civil society sows seeds of sedition. To begin, Baxter pieced together his own summary of the logical progression of the sixteenth chapter of *Tractatus theologico-politicus*. For Spinoza, Baxter observes, natural right "extendeth as far as power," and the "chief" law of nature is that "every thing do its utmost to continue in its own state, having no respect to any other, but only to it self." In the state of nature, people live "by the only Laws of Appetite, and that by the highest Right."[119] Natural right is therefore "not determined by sound reason, but by Lust and power," and people in general, being born in ignorance, are "no more bound this while to live by the Laws of a sound mind (or reason) than a Cat the Laws of Lions." In this state of nature, furthermore,

---

114. Spinoza, *TTP*, XVI.3 (p. 196).

115. Spinoza, *TTP*, XVI.2 (p. 196).

116. Spinoza, *TTP*, IV.1 (p. 57), XVI.5 (p. 197). Cf. Rutherford, "Spinoza's Conception of Law," 149–50.

117. Spinoza, *TTP*, XVI.5 (pp. 197–98).

118. Spinoza, *TTP*, IV.8–9 (pp. 62–63); also *TTP*, XIX.8 (p. 241). Cf. Edwin Curley, "The State of Nature and Its Law in Hobbes and Spinoza," *Philosophical Topics* 19, no. 1 (1991): 97–117, at 110.

119. Baxter, *Second Part*, 2–3, paraphrasing Spinoza, *TTP*, XVI.2 (pp. 195–96).

anything that one finds profitable or desirable for himself is "lawful for him by the highest right of nature to desire it and take it" even by force or fraud. The law of nature "under which all are born, and for the most part live, forbiddeth nothing, but that which no man desireth and which no man can do."[120] The law of nature, which is "so firmly written in mans nature, that it is to be numbred with the eternal verities," bids each individual to seek greater good over the lesser good, and avoid the greater evil over the lesser evil, as far as it concerns himself.[121] This paraphrase of Spinoza's doctrine of natural right is remarkably close to the original. However, Baxter does omit Spinoza's contrasting account of how the dictates of reason are instrumental for the formation of a peaceful society,[122] focusing instead exclusively on Spinoza's provocative understanding of natural right.

Baxter continues with his summary by observing the effect of Spinoza's doctrine of natural right on his theory of political society set forth in chapters 16 and 19 of *Tractatus theologico-politicus*. According to Spinoza, since by natural right every one seeks the greater good and avoids the greater evil, people only enter into a civil covenant from "fear of greater evil or hope of greater good." In order to avoid a greater evil, we can make false promises and we can break past promises that we deem mistaken in retrospect. The result is that "Covenants can have no force but for our profit's sake, which being taken away, the Covenant is taken away and remaineth void."[123] Spinoza also holds that the one with the greatest power has the greatest right and "is bound by no Law," while subjects must follow even absurd commands because such constitutes a lesser evil.[124] Since those living in a state of nature live according to appetite, justice and charity only come into existence and gain the force of law from the authority of the state and the ruler's will. Even religion "hath the force of Law or Right only by [rulers'] Decree."[125]

Spinoza's understanding of natural law is diametrically opposed to that of Baxter. It is hardly surprising that Baxter objected to nearly every aspect of Spinoza's theory of natural law. As we observed above, Baxter understood God as a legislator and grounded the obligatory force of the natural law in God's will. He also understood the description of the natural law as arising from the nature of things in the created order, including inclinations of the mind and will. Spinoza's rejection of the concept of God as legislator, as well as his identification of natural law with appetite and power, stands in stark contrast to Baxter's largely Suárezian

---

120. Baxter, *Second Part*, 3, paraphrasing Spinoza, *TTP*, XVI.3–4 (pp. 196–97).

121. Baxter, *Second Part*, 3, paraphrasing Spinoza, *TTP*, XVI.6 (p. 198).

122. Spinoza, *TTP*, XVI.5 (p. 197).

123. Baxter, *Second Part*, 3–4, paraphrasing Spinoza, *TTP*, XVI.7 (p. 199).

124. Baxter, *Second Part*, 4, paraphrasing Spinoza, *TTP*, XVI.8 (p. 200).

125. Baxter, *Second Part*, 7, paraphrasing Spinoza, *TTP*, XIX.1–5 (pp. 238–40).

natural law theory. We thus find Baxter accusing Spinoza of condoning bare self interest and the will of the stronger, "openly dissolving and deriding all divine obligations," and of theoretically allowing for murder, theft, lying, and adultery if they could be shown to advance an individual's personal good. By advocating that "no man is to be trusted by another any further than he thinketh it good for himself," Spinoza releases consciences and dissolves the obligations of subjects to their rulers. The result is that "if Princes ever set up Epicurisme, Atheisme, and Infidelity, they shall set up Rebellion with it, and expose their lives to every man that hath but list to venture upon a secret or open assault."[126]

There are especially two points that Baxter seems to have detested in Spinoza's understanding of natural law. One is the preference given to individual good over the common good. "This Atheistical Politician," Baxter writes of Spinoza, "who alloweth every man to prefer himself before all the world, doth make that in Princes, which all men have called Tyranny, to be the very Law of Nature."[127] A second point is the identification of natural law with appetite. For Baxter, human desires and passions are violent, desperate, and subject to cunning and temptations. In Baxter's opinion, Spinoza's identification of natural law with appetite is closely related to the dissolution of "the bond of oaths and divine commands." Baxter thinks even Spinoza recognized the problem of dissolving consciences from divine commands since he makes "Religion a necessary humane project for keeping Vulgar Wits in obedience."[128]

At the conclusion of his critique of *Tractatus theologico-politicus*, Baxter summed up the problem with Spinoza's natural law doctrine in twelve points. The first three points involve the identity of natural law with appetite, by which Spinoza makes reason serve sensuality and makes the "vituosity of man to be his natural Law." The next two points involve the replacement of God as a "moral Governour" with the "unalterable engine called the universe," which results in the identification of possibility with goodness. The rest of Baxter's points list unsavory results that follow from these premises concerning natural law and necessitarianism, such as making duty to parents, king, and country a means to personal gain, and even allowing for killing and breaking oaths if it serves personal gain. Baxter wraps up this summary by noting that Spinoza removes fear of punishment and "hope for any reward from God in this life or in the life to come," with the result that "Epicurean Physics are the sole Philosophy, and morality is nothing but a vulgar deceit."[129] There is no doubt that Baxter saw the

---

126. Baxter, *Second Part*, 5.

127. Baxter, *Second Part*, 16.

128. Baxter, *Second Part*, 18.

129. Baxter, *Second Part*, 19.

Tractatus theologico-politicus as an outgrowth of Spinoza's "Epicurean" natural philosophy.

After Baxter had written the foregoing critique of the *Tractatus theologico-politicus*, he read Spinoza's *Ethics* and *Tractatus politicus* in the *Opera posthuma*. He did not offer a specific critique of these later works, but instead summarized key points from them into a "marrow" for the reader.[130] Nonetheless, even selection involves interpretation,[131] and the specific points on ethics and natural law that Baxter selected for inclusion in this summary are indicative of Baxter's view of the most objectionable points in Spinoza's mature philosophy. After summarizing points from the first two books of Spinoza's *Ethics*, in which Baxter identified the necessitarianism of the *Ethics* (as we observed above), Baxter highlighted problematic ethical positions from books 3 and 4. Among these are the identification of goodness and virtue with the pursuit of personal profit and preservation,[132] the denial of humility and repentance as virtues,[133] and the right of anyone to use any means necessary to avoid apparent evil and pursue apparent good.[134] From Spinoza's *Tractatus politicus*, Baxter highlighted similar themes as the *Tractatus theologico-politicus*: the identification of natural right and natural law with power and appetite,[135] the legitimacy of breaking promises and covenants upon a change of mind,[136] the relegation of sin and justice to matters of state,[137] and the subjects' duty to obey rulers apart from considerations of justice and injustice.[138]

---

130. Baxter, *Second Part*, 111–13 (nos. 1–35), summarizing Spinoza, *Ethics*, Ip6, Ip8, Ip13, Ip14, Ip14c1–2, Ip15, Ip15s, Ip16, Ip22, Ip23, Ip25s, Ip29, Ip30, Ip32, Ip33, Ip34, I Appendix, IIp11, IIp11c, IIp13, IIp15, IIp36dem, IIIp39s, IVp20, IVp24, IVp25, IVp26, IVp28, IVp31, IVp42, IVp53, IVp54, IVp63, IVp67, IVp68, IV Appendix cap. 4, IV Appendix cap. 8, IV Appendix cap. 31, Vp18, Vp18c, Vp19dem, Vp21, Vp23, Vp36c, Vp36s, Vp37. Baxter, *Second Part*, 113–16 (nos. 36–55), summarizing Spinoza, *Tractatus Politicus*, II.2–9, II.12, II.14, II.18–19, II.23, III.5, III.10, III.13–14, IV.6, VI.5, VI.8, VI.40.

131. Charles A. Beard, "That Noble Dream," in *The Varieties of History*, ed. Frank R. Stern (Cleveland: World Publishing Co., 1956), 314–28.

132. Baxter, *Second Part*, 112 (nos. 17–20); cf. Spinoza, *Ethics*, IIIp39s, IVp20, IVp24, IVp25.

133. Baxter, *Second Part*, 113 (nos. 24–25); cf. Spinoza, *Ethics*, IVp53, IVp54.

134. Baxter, *Second Part*, 113 (no. 29); cf. Spinoza, *Ethics*, IV Appendix cap. 8.

135. Baxter, *Second Part*, 113–14 (nos. 36–41); cf. Spinoza, *Tractatus Politicus*, II.2–8, in *Complete Works*, trans. Samuel Shirley, ed. Michael Morgan (Indianapolis: Hackett, 2002), 683–85.

136. Baxter, *Second Part*, 115 (nos. 44, 51); cf. Spinoza, *Tractatus Politicus*, II.12, III.14, in *Complete Works*, 686, 694–95.

137. Baxter, *Second Part*, 115 (nos. 46–47); cf. Spinoza, *Tractatus Politicus*, II.18–19, II.23, in *Complete Works*, 688–89.

138. Baxter, *Second Part*, 115 (no. 48); cf. Spinoza, *Tractatus Politicus*, III.5, in *Complete Works*, 691.

Beginning with his early reading of *Tractatus theologico-politicus*, and continuing with his reading of the *Ethics* and *Tractatus politicus*, Baxter recognized that Spinoza identified natural law with power and appetite. He viewed this innovative concept of natural law as integrally related to his principles of natural philosophy, which turned a divinely legislated teleological hierarchy of goods into a necessitarian and natural-istic ethic. For Baxter, Spinoza's identification of natural law with appetite legitimized the pursuit of lesser temporal ends apart from higher eternal ones, and removed any restraint towards those lesser objects. This evaluation is evident in Baxter's remark that Spinoza "make[s] man but an Ingenious Beast, and his Reason to be given him but to serve his Appetite, and sensitive Life."[139] Moreover, since appetite does not in itself provide the criteria of what is lawful, "those *lower Ends* when *alone*, will be a constant *sin themselves*." If such a philosophy were to prevail, wrote Baxter, people would no longer live out of hope or fear of a life to come, with the result that they would lose motivation to live an honest and holy life. Thus, "We see in the brut-ish Politicks of *Benedictus Spinosa*, in his *Tract. Theol. Polit.* whither the Principles of *Infidelity* tend."[140]

When Baxter penned his "marrow" that summarized Spinoza's *Opera post-huma*, Baxter remarked that Hobbes "much agreeth" with Spinoza.[141] Shortly after this "marrow," Baxter also outlined the principles of Hobbes's *De cive* in the format of select citations from that work on the state of nature, natural right, the law of nature, covenants, the nature of sovereignty and subjection, and sedition.[142] One of the major differences between Hobbes and Spinoza noted by modern scholars concerns their concept of covenants: Spinoza argued that individuals retain their natural rights following covenants and criticized Hobbes's view that one can hand over one's right to a sovereign. The practical result is that Spinoza, unlike Hobbes, retains the possibility of resistance when sovereigns no longer serve the utility of subjects.[143] Baxter's citations from Hobbes indicate that he was aware of this dif-ference,[144] but aside from these passages, he saw basic continuity between Hobbes

---

139. Baxter, *Second Part*, 7.

140. Baxter, *Richard Baxter's Dying Thoughts*, 5.

141. Baxter, *Second Part*, 111.

142. Baxter, *Second Part*, 123–26.

143. Justin Steinberg, "Spinoza's Political Philosophy," *The Stanford Encyclopedia of Philosophy* (Winter 2013 Edition), accessed May 6, 2016, http://plato.stanford.edu/archives/win2013/entries/spinoza-political/.

144. See Baxter, *Second Part*, 125–26, citing passages from Hobbes against resistance and sedition.

and Spinoza, and thus wrote, "I pass by the rest [of Hobbes's *De cive*], it being mostly the same with *Spinosa's*."[145]

Baxter's critique of Hobbes targeted some distinctive features of *De cive* while also criticizing views that could also apply to Spinoza. He opposed Hobbes's famous notion that the state of nature is a state of war. By contrast, Baxter argued that human beings would naturally exist in a state of love, and in the present fallen condition, due to God's common grace, mankind is naturally sociable.[146] Baxter also objected to Hobbes's distinctive view that subjects can give up their right of resistance to a sovereign. On the contrary, Baxter emphasized the possible resistance to kings and human law on account of the prior obligation to God: "It is wickedness to obey man against Gods Law, more than to obey a Justice against the King," and "It's not seditious but necessary to tell men of Gods future judgement, against those that obey men against God."[147] Some of Baxter's remarks on *De cive* could apply equally to Spinoza. These include Baxter's opinion that to "make Kings independent on Gods Laws, is to subvert their foundation,"[148] whereas "Mans natural state is a state of due subjection to God as universal King" and "Mans Laws could make no duty or sin but as empowered by Gods Law."[149] Like Spinoza's description of natural right, Baxter also viewed Hobbes as subverting a divinely ordained hierarchy of goods (God, common good, soul, and body). Against Hobbes he asserts, "The ends of this order [of God's law] are first the fulfilling of the will of God as universal King, and next the common good, and next our own of soul and body, and not only our own corporeal peace and pleasure."[150]

This problem of legitimating self-interest was a constant concern of Baxter, and likely irritated him more than any other aspect of the ethics of Hobbes and Spinoza. Throughout his works, he reiterated that corrupted self-interest is among the worst evils besetting the human condition. Although Baxter admitted that God instilled in humanity a natural inclination for individual self-preservation, he complained that this inclination for self-preservation had been "lamentably made

145. Baxter, *Second Part*, 127.

146. Baxter, *Second Part*, 127 (no. 5). The Aristotelian point regarding humanity's sociable nature was also made against Hobbes by Hale, *Of the Law of Nature*, 86, 94–96, 198.

147. Baxter, *Second Part*, 128.

148. Baxter, *Second Part*, 128.

149. Baxter, *Second Part*, 126.

150. Baxter, *Second Part*, 127.

inordinate by o[ur] fall, & natures depravation." The depths of this problem are as deep as they are difficult to comprehend:

> But no man, I thinke, hath yet p[er]fectly understood, how much this is growne inordinate by yᵉ fall: I suspect it is not yᵉ least p[ar]t of yᵉ unhappy knowledge of Good & Evill, wᶜʰ we did then acquire. The very sum[m]e of o[ur] sin & misery is, yᵗ we fell from GOD to SELFE: not to Individuation, but to an *overmuch Inclination* to o[ur] Individuall SELFE as o[ur] *Center, object* & *End*; & to an alienation from God to whom each Holy Soule Inclineth as its *Center, End,* and *ultimate object.*"[151]

When one compares such a statement with Baxter's polemics, it is obvious that Baxter believed that by legitimating the problematic (postlapsarian) natural tendency of preferring oneself to others, Hobbes and Spinoza were overturning a central tenet of Christian ethics.[152]

Conclusion

The second half of the seventeenth century witnessed the emergence of new natural law theories at roughly the same time as the rise of mechanical philosophy. Many theologians identified some of the more radical ethical theories, including those of Hobbes and Spinoza, with the revival of Epicureanism. Baxter also participated in this trend. His own positive formulation of the natural law owed a great deal to Francisco Suárez's *De legibus*. From this Suárezian perspective, Baxter criticized Hobbes and Spinoza as departing from traditional points of natural law, such as the priority of the common good, and establishing a naturalistic moral order in its place, which either identified natural law with appetite (Spinoza) or bodily peace (Hobbes). With Baxter we do not find an attempt to mediate between Hobbes and mechanical philosophy as we do with some of his contemporaries. Rather, Spinoza is represented in a purely polemical manner as one for whom "Epicurean Physics are the sole Philosophy" and whose natural law theory has its "root" in "Epicurean principles of Philosophy about God and *Nature,*" while

---

151. DWL BT XIX.351, fol. 105r. Cf. Baxter, *Two Disputations of Original Sin,* 75–76.

152. Baxter was aware of Spinoza's denial of original sin, which included the assertion that "it was not in the power of the first man to use reason aright, and that, like us, he was subject to passions" (Spinoza, *Tractatus Politicus,* II.6, in *Complete Works,* 684). Cf. Baxter, *Second Part,* 114 (no. 39).

Hobbes is presented as one who "much agreeth" with Spinoza on the same matters. For Baxter, these radical philosophers represented a dangerous ethical outgrowth of the mechanical philosophy—namely, a necessitarian worldview that destroys both human choice and divine providence, and a moral universe turned on its head, in which natural law is severed from any divine telos, the soul serves either appetite or body, the common good serves the individual, and might makes right.

8

Conclusion

ALTHOUGH BAXTER HAS long been recognized for his practical divinity as among
the greatest Puritans, his standing as a major theological and philosophical mind
of the seventeenth century, as George Park Fisher observed long ago, has been
rather "poorly appreciated."[1] As the present volume has hoped to demonstrate,
Baxter in fact possessed a mastery of scholastic theology and philosophy while
staying current with the new philosophies of the era. His relationships with Boyle,
Glanvill, More, and Hale placed him in close proximity to changing philosophical currents. Glanvill, as Baxter's younger contemporary, sought to win favor
with Baxter before parting ways in their estimation of mechanical philosophy,
while More paid Baxter the respect of disputing with him in print, and Hale, who
had privileged access to Baxter's manuscript "Of the Nature and Immortality of
Humane Soules," praised it as "the best and most perspicuous of any thinge that
I ever read of that subject."[2]

Throughout this study we have had occasion to observe time and again the
eclectic nature of Baxter's theology and appropriation of philosophical notions. As
one scholar has well remarked, "Perhaps the best way to describe his theology is
to say that it is eclectic."[3] To this we should add that his eclecticism is heavily indebted to medieval and early modern scholasticism, both Catholic and Protestant.
Baxter drew on multiple traditions and individuals for different doctrinal topics,
and even within a particular doctrine, such as the analogy of being, he appropriated aspects of various traditions to suit his needs. Whereas his discussion of the

---

1. Fisher, "Writings of Richard Baxter," 324.

2. LPL MS 3499, fol. 65v.

3. Boersma, *A Hot Pepper Corn*, 27.

relation of revelation to reason, his apologetics, and his doctrine of the analogy of being draws positively on Aquinas, his discussion of the plurality of forms, the powers of the soul, and the nature of the will reflects a strongly Scotist perspective. We might even say that, while the bridge between the natural and supernatural is paved with much Thomist doctrine, the voluntarist traffic running back and forth across it is heavily Scotist. With respect to the doctrine of natural law, Baxter clearly favored Suárez's *De legibus*, which eclectically melded a more voluntarist perspective with the intellectualism of Aquinas.

As with his theology, Baxter's approach to philosophy advocated an eclectic view. In his own thought, this eclecticism is related both to problems he saw with postlapsarian reason and to a broadly Thomist view of apologetic method. Throughout his works, Baxter stressed the uncertainty characteristic of discursive fallen reason as it moves further away from knowledge derived from the senses and first principles of the mind, and as a result was reticent to endorse the conclusions of any philosophical sect, either from antiquity or contemporary proponents of mechanical philosophy. In terms of his broader relation to his theological tradition, an important backdrop is the largely Calvinist tradition of so-called Mosaic physics. An eclectic approach to philosophy is inherent in this tradition, of which Baxter is an illustrative case. While many others in the Netherlands participated in this tradition, particularly the followers of Voetius, Baxter manifests a less Aristotelian, and even more eclectic, branch of this family tree. This eclecticism is especially evident in Baxter's reception of Campanella's primalities and Boyle's corpuscularism. In his reception of such philosophies, prior theological and philosophical considerations, whether congruence with Trinitarian theology or the philosophical affirmation of activity in nature, frame the acceptable limits of Baxter's philosophical eclecticism.

Incidentally, our findings demonstrate the necessity of manuscript research in Baxter studies. The printed works alone are not sufficient for a full comprehension of Baxter's thought.[4] Without an examination of his manuscripts, we would not be aware at all of his debt to Boyle's corpuscularism or his response to Willis. We would also not appreciate the importance of Hale's contribution to Baxter's intellectual development, and we would have an impoverished understanding of his remarks on Gassendi and More, among many other ideas. There are many unpublished treatises that yet require examination for a full understanding of Baxter's thought and development—and even in the correspondence, particularly with other theologians, there are lengthy treatments of various doctrines.

---

4. This conclusion disagrees with the assessment of Orme, *Life*, 2:441; and Packer, *Redemption*, 11.

In a recent study, one scholar observes that the response to Cartesianism in the Netherlands took on various forms at Leiden and Utrecht, where, despite the common problem of Cartesianism, different issues nonetheless dominated the polemical agenda.[5] Even though many common concerns rose to the surface in multiple geographical locations, the response to Cartesianism, and mechanical philosophy more generally, was affected by both local context and the subjective importance placed on particular doctrines by individual theologians and philosophers. In the case of Baxter, his polemics ought to be understood in light of the relatively more positive reception of Gassendi—alongside Descartes—on English soil, the rise of the Royal Society, and the promotion of mechanical philosophy by a number of Latitudinarian divines. In this context, Baxter holds a unique place. He was perhaps the earliest polemicist against Hobbes in the interregnum and among the earliest polemicists against mechanical philosophy in the context of the rise of the Royal Society. Baxter's correspondence with Glanvill in 1670 and More in the 1680s illustrate his difference from the theological alliance with mechanical philosophy characteristic of these Latitudinarian divines. Moreover, his interest in the topics of motion and the soul reflect the importance of natural philosophy to the shifting intellectual landscape in late seventeenth-century England.

Baxter's polemics with respect to mechanical philosophy demonstrate similarities with, and distinctive differences from, the Voetian polemics in the Netherlands. Despite sharing with Voetius a tradition of Mosaic physics, Baxter showed little interest in the question of Copernicanism as a theological problem, and separated the issue of astronomy from the question of substance and motion more generally, although due in part to the influence of Hale, he favored an anti-Copernican perspective. Moreover, Baxter shared with many of his contemporaries an enthusiasm for experimental discovery. In continuity with the Voetians, Baxter was concerned about laws of motion and substantial forms, although given his limited accommodation of Boyle's corpuscularism for inorganic substance and subordinate forms, Baxter's doctrine of substantial form was not entirely traditional. His polemics with regard to issues of substance, causality, and motion reveal a desire to preserve a hierarchy of being and affirm the intrinsic activity of creatures, whose vital natures and activity he believed to be an analogy of the power, wisdom, and goodness of the living God. In addition, Baxter expressed a concern, with most of his contemporaries in England and the Continent, about the dangers of Hobbes's and Spinoza's philosophy. Like the anti-Cartesian Dutch theologians, Baxter highlighted continuity between these radical philosophies and mechanical philosophy and chose to describe Spinoza's philosophy as rooted in

---

5. Goudriaan, *Jacobus Revius*, 10.

"Epicurean principles of Philosophy about God and *Nature*."[6] Baxter's response to Spinoza is also distinctive in that, unlike most of his contemporaries who focused on topics such as Spinoza's denial of miracles and Mosaic authorship of the Pentateuch, Baxter engaged directly with the ethical topics of natural law and political theory that constituted the central argument of Spinoza's *Tractatus theologico-politicus*.

While in the Netherlands the question of Descartes's philosophy dominated the polemical agenda, Gassendi received a relatively greater reception in England. Baxter registered this Gassendian influence on English philosophy in the attention he gave to the nature and immortality of the soul, both with respect to Gassendi and more specifically Willis's *De anima brutorum*. In light of the importance of Gassendi and Willis as possible influences on the development of Locke, as well as Willis's importance for eighteenth-century concepts of the "material soul,"[7] Baxter's polemics against Willis take on added significance. In this respect, whereas Voetius predicted with some acuity certain philosophical problems concerning the notion of substance that would become apparent with Spinoza,[8] Baxter's prediction that the material soul of Gassendi and Willis would be a temptation to a more complete materialism sounds, with the benefit of hindsight, remarkably prophetic.

Given Baxter's importance to the history of Puritanism, the very fact that he raised theoretical objections to Descartes's first law of motion ought to call into question a strong correlation between Puritanism in general and the rise of modern science. While the question of Puritanism's relation to new philosophy and science requires further study, it is no longer possible to assert with Charles Webster that "Puritans as a whole felt that the 'new philosophy' was consistent with the reformed Christian faith."[9] Rather, with the proviso that acceptance of new philosophical trends cut across confessional boundaries, the present study suggests that a stronger correlation existed between "new philosophy" and leading Anglican Latitudinarians than the leading Puritan theologians of the later seventeenth century. Accordingly, due weight needs to be given to the contemporary testimony of the Latitudinarian S. P., who observed that in the interregnum, new philosophy "was as great a bug-beare to the Presbyterians as a Crosse or Surplisse," and that such divines held that "*Philosophy* and *Divinity* are so interwoven by the School-men, that it cannot be safe to separate them; new *Philosophy* will bring in *new Divinity*; and freedom in the one will make men desire a liberty

---

6. Baxter, *Second Part*, 6.

7. Wolfe and van Esveld, "The Material Soul," 371–421.

8. Van Ruler, " 'Something, I Know Not What,' " 365–93.

9. Webster, *Great Instauration*, 498.

in the other."[10] More than two decades later, as Baxter neared the end of his life, he demonstrated a similar concern to those interregnum divines when he complained that his *Methodus theologiae* was neglected by "yᵉ multitude of younger students uncapable of things very accurate & methodicall, (& crying downe Aristotle & the Schoolmen to hide their ignorance of their Learning)."[11] Only now, with the benefit of hindsight, Baxter intimated that the new philosophical climate was actually contributing to the neglect of scholastic theology.

At the same time, given Baxter's eclecticism and the epistemological priority placed on sense perception, which not only allowed for significant modifications to older Aristotelian philosophy but also included a certain openness to the results of empirical inquiry through new tools such as the telescope, it is probable that this very eclecticism contributed to a transition away from Aristotelian views, particularly in the realm of astronomy. In evaluating the relation between Puritanism and the rise of modern science, this study demonstrates a need to distinguish matters of a more theoretical nature—what we might refer to today as matters of worldview or metaphysics—which relate to substance and causality, from other matters of a more empirical nature. While a case can be made that Puritanism contributed positively to the growing use of scientific instruments and experiments,[12] the theoretical premises of mechanical philosophy, as Baxter's polemics attest, encountered considerable resistance. As Richard Foster Jones once perceptively noted, Baxter "argues strenuously against the latter [mechanical philosophy], but is favorably disposed toward the former [experiment]."[13]

As far as Baxter's relation to subsequent Puritan and nonconformist tradition is concerned, the present study points to an important discontinuity in attitudes toward philosophy. Within several decades of Baxter's death, two tendencies emerged among nonconformist theologians: either avoidance of new philosophical developments, as represented by Thomas Ridgley (1667–1734) and John Gill (1697–1771), or a more accommodating attitude, as represented by Isaac Watts (1674–1748) and Philip Doddridge (1702–1751).[14] Baxter would not likely have appreciated either trend. His *Methodus theologiae* included various "philosophical elucidations" on ontology and the soul, and he was wary of ignorance in philosophical

---

10. P[atrick], *A Brief Account*, 14, 22–23.

11. DWL BT VII.229, fol. 68v [written ca. 1683–1691].

12. Cf. Webster, *Great Instauration*, 126–29, 243–44; Burden, "Academical Learning," 182.

13. Jones, *Ancients and Moderns*, 323n2.

14. Muller, "Philip Doddridge," 70–71. Cf. Wykes, "Contribution of the Dissenting Academy," 118–21. On Watts, see John Hoyles, *The Waning of the Renaissance, 1640–1740: Studies in the Thought and Poetry of Henry More, John Norris and Isaac Watts* (The Hague: Martinus Nijhoff, 1971), 149–250.

matters that he thought would lead to loss of "defensive skills" necessary to combat ignorant use of philosophy, heretics, and unbelievers.[15] But he also thought that "Philosophers are all still in very great darkness,"[16] "the sacred Scriptures are now too much undervalued, and Philosophy much overvalued by many both as to *Evidence* and *Usefulness*,"[17] and it is "better to ignore many Philosophical matters, than even one article of faith."[18] Given this position, as well as his persistent hostility to Descartes and Gassendi, we can speculate that Baxter's sympathies would have remained with those theologians and nonconformist tutors who remained highly cautious in the face of philosophical innovation.

The nonconformist leader who probably best approximated Baxter's views is Thomas Doolittle, who as a teenage convert of Baxter at Kidderminster always regarded Baxter as his spiritual father,[19] and whose private academy at Islington was commended by Baxter to Philip Henry.[20] Like Baxter, Doolittle appears to have entertained mechanical explanations of the inorganic realm while maintaining a more conservative stance on the nature of the soul and metaphysics. He was reading a mix of old and new authors, referring to Aquinas on the topic of motion, and Aristotle, Zanchi, David Derodon, Henricus Regius, and Jacques Rohault on the material causes of earthquakes.[21] He held that there were vegetative, sensitive, and rational souls, echoed Baxter's threefold division of the rational soul into active power, understanding, and will,[22] and defended the reliability of sense perception.[23] Doolittle was cognizant of the limitations of both reason and will in theology, but regarded philology and the philosophical disciplines of logic, metaphysics, and jurisprudence as requirements for theology. Doolittle's curriculum, which has been characterized as "narrow and somewhat old-fashioned,"[24] used Andreas Frommenius's *Synopsis Metaphysica* (1658) and encouraged students to read Baxter's *Reasons of the Christian Religion*, *Catholick Theologie*, and *Methodus theologiae*, alongside other Reformed authorities (Ames, Crocius, Calvin, and

---

15. *MT*, I.152.

16. *CD*, III.919 (q. 173, §15).

17. *CD*, III.922 (q. 174).

18. *MT*, I.152.

19. J. William Black, "Doolittle, Thomas," in *ODNB*.

20. Burden, "A Biographical Dictionary," 143.

21. Doolittle, *Earthquakes Explained*, 2, 52–57.

22. Thomas Doolittle, *A Complete Body of Practical Divinity* (London: John and Barham Clark, 1723), 51–52.

23. Doolittle, *Earthquakes Explained*, 9.

24. Burden, "Academical Learning," 69.

Wendelin for dogmatics; Le Blanc, Cameron, Davenant, Placeus, Amyraut, et al. for polemics).[25] This is a reading list that mirrored Baxter's own recommendations, and no doubt it would have greatly pleased him.[26]

Issac Watts tried to preserve many traditional logical and metaphysical concepts, but formed a far more positive evaluation of Descartes and Gassendi than Baxter. Watts studied under the nonconformist tutor Thomas Rowe (ca. 1657–1705), who introduced his students to the Cartesian Port Royal logic, attacked substantial forms, and espoused a Cartesian account of the soul as "Unextended Thinking Substance."[27] Like Rowe, whom he praised in an ode subtitled "Free Philosophy,"[28] Watts dismissed substantial forms while promoting laws of motion as expressed in the "corpuscular philosophy, improved by Descartes, Mr. Boyle, and Sir Isaac Newton."[29] Although Watts referred to vegetative, animal, and human "powers," and retained many traditional kinds of causes (universal and particular, remote and proximate, univocal and equivocal, efficient and final), he also set aside material and formal causality "as not properly causes."[30] He accepted Locke's critique of scholastic essences, and while he retained the term "form," he reinterpreted form as the combination of mechanical "primary or real qualities" (shape, motion, quantity, situation) and secondary qualities (modifications or dispositions of the primary).[31] Watts attributed the origin of his "freedom of thought" to reading Descartes's *Principia philosophiae* and went on to say, "That great man [Descartes], in some of his writings, pointed out the road to true philosophy, by reason, and experiment, and mathematical science. . . . Gassendus and the Lord Bacon went a little before him; Mr. Boyle followed after; and they all carried on the noble design of freeing the world from the long slavery of Aristotle and substantial forms and occult qualities, and words without ideas."[32] This rhetoric is a far cry from that of Baxter, who remarked that Descartes and Gassendi "differ as much from true Philosophers, as a Carkass or a Clock from a living man."[33]

Philip Doddridge, who is generally regarded as "Baxterian" and promoted Baxter's practical works to later generations, likewise acquired a disposition

25. Burden, "Academical Learning," 236–38.

26. Cf. *CD*, III.924 (nos. 18–19), 927 (no. 11).

27. Burden, "Academical Learning," 176–77, 223–24.

28. Watts, "Free Philosophy," in *Works* (London: John Barfield, 1810), 4:466.

29. Isaac Watts, *Works*, 5:340; cf. 5:47, 112, 120–21, 590–91, on substantial forms.

30. Watts, "A Brief Scheme of Ontology," ch. 10, in *Works*, 5:644, 651; cf. *Works*, 5:611.

31. Watts, *Works*, 5:610–11.

32. Watts, preface to "Philosophical Essays," in *Works*, 5:500.

33. *CD*, III.919 (q. 173, §15).

against older scholastic philosophy under the influence of his tutor John Jennings (c.1687–1723).[34] Whereas Baxter could state in his *Methodus theologiae* that, by comparison with ancient and modern philosophers, "I found no better philosophers than the scholastics,"[35] Doddridge referred dismissively to both the scholastic logic of Franco Burgersdijck as "unmeaning Jargon"[36] and Baxter's *Methodus theologiae* as "unintelligible."[37] Doddridge, in continuity with Watts, divided being in a Cartesian manner into body as an "extended solid being" and spirit as a "thinking being."[38] His main interlocutors on pneumatology were Descartes, Locke, and Watts.[39] On the topic of the immortality of the soul, Doddridge drew eclectically on Baxter's *Reasons*. He agreed with Baxter on the use of moral proofs but employed the proof from immateriality despite Baxter's objections.[40] Although Doddridge read Baxter's *Reasons* extensively, and must surely have been aware of Baxter's criticism of Descartes and Gassendi contained therein, he did not share Baxter's sense of apprehension about the "false Philosophy" of his age.[41]

The most famous American Puritan, Jonathan Edwards, likewise illustrates discontinuity with Baxter in his evaluation of philosophy. The editor of Edwards's philosophical writings observes that he "never appeals to the virtues, qualities, or entelechies of natural bodies in his explanations, nor distinguishes between natural and violent motions, nor even adopts the divisions of things into various natural kinds in the manner of the scholastic textbooks."[42] Like his contemporary Doddridge, Edwards acquired a bias against Aristotelian logic and metaphysics at the hands of his tutors, and his course of studies included Cartesian logic and mechanical natural philosophy. In continuity with this education, Edwards

---

34. Burden, "A Biographical Dictionary," 294–98.

35. *MT*, "Praefatio," [A5r]: "nullos meliores inveni Philosophos quam Scholasticos."

36. Strivens, *Philip Doddridge*, 69.

37. Doddridge, *Correspondence*, 1:397 (29 May 1724).

38. Doddridge, *Course of Lectures*, 2–3, citing Descartes's *Principia philosophiae*, I, §7, 11, 53 (AT 8:7, 8, 25) on body and spirit. Doddridge observes, "Dr. *Watts* maintains the same opinion" as the Cartesians on "primary and essential properties of body and spirit." Cf. Watts, *Works*, 5:521–27, citing the "Cartesians" on extension and thought (525).

39. Doddridge, *Course of Lectures*, 3–42.

40. See Doddridge, *Course of Lectures*, 199–209, who at 207 cites and rejects Baxter, *RCR*, 523–33.

41. Cf. *RCR*, 588: "I think that in this age, it is one of the devils chief designs, to assault Christianity by false Philosophy." For citations to Baxter's *Reasons*, see Doddridge, *Course of Lectures*, 72, 144, 157, 200, 203, 207, 288, 290, 314, 321, 402, 456, 540, 593.

42. Wallace E. Anderson, "Introduction," in *The Works of Jonathan Edwards* (New Haven, CT: Yale University Press, 1980), 6:47.

initially espoused a mechanical understanding of nature characterized by material substance (atoms with properties of size, shape, and divisibility), "laws of motion and gravitation," and thinking substance. Edwards revised this inherited dualistic account of matter and mind into an idealistic monism of mind as "the only real and substantial beings," but his idealism is only comprehensible in light of his early immersion in mechanical philosophy.[43] For Edwards, mechanical philosophy had become the "old way" or how things are "vulgarly thought," a perspective which ought to be subsumed within an idealist framework.[44] In this, as well as in his arguably deterministic view of human choice resulting from an acceptance of new definitions of causality, necessity, and contingency,[45] Edwards represents a striking departure from the scholastic Puritanism of Baxter. Indeed, inasmuch as Edwards's determinism derives from a Hobbesian account of freedom and volition via Locke,[46] he approximates a philosophical position criticized by Baxter as a radical and unacceptable conclusion of mechanical philosophy.

As the contrast between Baxter and later leaders in his tradition illustrates, the relation of Puritanism and Reformed theology to the rise of mechanical philosophy was highly variegated. Whereas Baxter represents an eclecticism sympathetic to, and highly conversant with, medieval and early modern scholastic theology and philosophy, even while critically engaged with new philosophical trends, subsequent generations increasingly took the results of mechanical philosophy as a given or starting point. The result of this philosophical transition is of great methodological consequence. Baxter recommended dozens of medieval and early modern scholastics in his *Christian Directory*,[47] and his works are peppered with references to scholastics who directly informed his views on God, the world, and

---

43. Rehnman, "Towards a Solution," 142–53.

44. Jonathan Edwards, "The Mind," no. 34, in *Works*, 6:353–54: "yet we may speak in the old way, and as properly and truly as ever: God in the beginning created such a certain number of atoms, of such a determinate bulk and figure, which they yet maintain and always will; and gave them such a motion, of such a direction, and of such a degree of velocity; from whence arise all the natural changes in the universe forever in a continued series. Yet perhaps all this does not exist anywhere perfectly but in the divine mind." Cf. Rehnman, "Towards a Solution," 154–55.

45. See Muller, "Jonathan Edwards and the Absence of Free Choice," 3–22; with response by Paul Helm, "Jonathan Edwards and the Parting of the Ways?," *Jonathan Edwards Studies* 4, no. 1 (2014): 42–60; and again, Richard A. Muller, "Jonathan Edwards and Francis Turretin on Necessity, Contingency, and Freedom of Will. In Response to Paul Helm," *Jonathan Edwards Studies* 4, no. 3 (2014): 266–85; Paul Helm, "Turretin and Edwards Once More," *Jonathan Edwards Studies* 4, no. 3 (2014): 286–96. Muller is supported by Philip John Fisk, *Jonathan Edwards's Turn from the Classic-Reformed Tradition of Freedom of the Will* (Göttingen: Vandenhoeck & Ruprecht, 2016), 40.

46. Muller, "Jonathan Edwards and Francis Turretin," 269–72.

47. *CD*, III.925, 928 (q. 174).

the human soul. By contrast, Doddridge's discussion of God and the soul in his *Course of Lectures* is dominated by citations to Locke, Cartesians, Latitudinarians, and other sympathizers of mechanical philosophy, and while he occasionally refers to Francis Turretin and Herman Witsius, one searches in vain for a reference to Aquinas or Scotus.[48] Both Baxter and Doddridge display great erudition, but, despite the latter's reputation for "free inquiry" and the consideration of "authors on both sides of every question,"[49] the relevant authors and questions have shifted noticeably, and thereby the range of opinions entertained by Doddridge has also diminished considerably.

Did "new philosophy" entail new theology, as interregnum divines feared? Did the Gassendian or Cartesian variants of mechanical philosophy in some way entail the radical philosophies of Hobbes or Spinoza? Should the theologian ignore, resist, or conform to mechanical philosophy? These were important questions raised in the course of the seventeenth century, which elicited a range of responses. While many opposed radical variants of mechanical philosophy and argued that the philosophies of Gassendi and Descartes did not entail new theology or radical philosophical conclusions, Baxter remained unconvinced. In a variety of works, including *Christian Directory, Methodus theologiae*, and *Reasons*, he strongly and repeatedly warned an educated Christian readership to exercise great caution with respect to Gassendi and Descartes alongside Hobbes. Although he was acutely aware of the need for philosophical reform and provided a model for a limited accommodation to mechanical philosophy, he saw in the philosophies of Gassendi and Descartes the seeds of radical philosophy and the potential for theological heterodoxy. Moreover, he made this evaluation with a grasp of sources and arguments reflective of a rich and erudite mind, and not simply as a practical or devotional theologian. The fact that this evaluation of mechanical philosophy by an erudite Puritan was not shared by many later theologians in Baxter's own tradition illustrates a remarkable discontinuity in early modern intellectual history. This discontinuity warrants greater scholarly attention, and such examinations must take into account the genius and foresight of Baxter's critical engagement with mechanical philosophy.

---

48. Doddridge, *Course of Lectures*, 1–103. Note that this is a posthumous edition in which the editor had a hand in adding references to authors (fol. A2r).

49. Joseph Priestley, *Theological and Miscellaneous Works*, ed. John Towill Rutt (London: G. Smallfield, 1831), I/1, 23–24. Cf. Job Orton, *Memoirs of the Life, Character and Writings of the late Reverend Philip Doddridge* (Salop: J. Cotton and J. Eddowes, 1766), 101, 127.

Chronology of Baxter's Post-Restoration Writings on Philosophy

Date of Composition	Title
June 1665	Baxter to Robert Boyle, 14 June 1665 (Boyle, *Correspondence*, 2:473)
Jan.–Oct. 1666	*Reasons of the Christian Religion* (1667)
Oct. 1666–Mar. 1667	"The Conclusion, Defending the Soul's Immortality against the Somatists or Epicureans, and other Pseudophilosophers," in *Reasons*, 489–604[1]
ca. 1669	"Cap. 4. Οντολογίαν sive *Entium Natura*, Ordo, Finis; Totius Philosophiae, &c. compendium / Elucidationes Philosophicae: ubi quaedam contra Cartesium Gassendum, &c.," in *Methodus theologiae christianae*, 1:131–53 (as titled in the table of contents)[2]

1. This was composed after the completion of the body of the work on 16 Oct. 1666 (p. 489). The prefaces were written 31 Oct. 1666. *Reasons* was ready for publication and recorded in the Stationers' Register on 12 Mar. 1667. [London Stationers' Company], *A Transcript of the Registers of the Worshipful Company of Stationers* (London, 1913), 2:374.

2. Baxter began work on the tables of the *Methodus theologiae* in 1668–1669 ("Praefatio," in *MT*, [A5r]). A draft of this "Scheme of Creation" was complete and sent to Matthew Hale for comments in late 1669 (*Rel. Bax.*, III.70). Baxter finished "all the Schemes, and half the Elucidations" of the *Methodus theologiae* at the end of 1669 and early 1670 ("Praefatio," in *MT*, [A6r]). He refers to his "scheme" containing "some principles of philosophy of my own" in a letter to Glanvill, 18 Nov. 1670 (DWL BC II.139r).

Date of Composition	Title
ca. 1669	"Of the Nature and Immortality of Humane Soules" [excluding preface and postscript] (DWL BT XIX.351, 10r–124r)[3]
November 1670	Baxter to Glanvill, 18 Nov. 1670 (DWL BC II.138r–139v)
ca. 1671	"Quest. 158. Should not Christians take up with Scripture wisdom only, without studying Philosophy and other Heathens humane Learning?"; "Quest. 173. What particular Directions for Order of Studies, and Books should be observed by young Students?," in *A Christian Directory* (1673), III.907–8, 917–20[4]
Dec. 1671–Jan. 1672	*More Reasons for the Christian Religion* (1672)[5]
1672	Preface (fols. 1r–9v)[6] and "A Postscript / Considerations of some passages wch concerne w^t is before asserted in Dr Willis his Learned Tractate *de Anima Brutorum, quae Hominis Vitalis et Sensitiva est*," in "Of the Nature and Immortality of Humane Soules" (DWL BT 19.351, fols. 125r–143v)[7]

3. The manuscript refers to early disputations of the *Methodus theologiae* (I.v [pp. 164–75]; and I.xiv [pp. 278–333]), which were composed between late 1669 and early 1670, placing the *terminus a quo* in 1669 (DWL BT XIX.351, fol. 38v). In the postscript, written in 1672, Baxter states that Thomas Willis's *De anima brutorum* (1672) appeared "three yeares after the writing of this" (i.e., the body of the text), which dates the body to ca. 1669 (DWL BT XIX.351, fol. 129r).

4. All except for the ecclesiastical cases of conscience (III.771–929) were written ca. 1664–1665 ("Advertisements," A2r; cf. *Rel. Bax.*, I.122; III.61; Richard Baxter, *The Divine Life* [London: Francis Tyton and Nevil Simmons, 1664], 291). The ecclesiastical cases of conscience, written later, cite John Wallis's *Mechanica* (1670), Samuel Gott's *Divine History* (1670), and Henry More's *Enchiridion metaphysicum* (1671), but do not cite Willis's *De anima brutorum* (1672), or Francis Glisson's *De natura substantiae energetica* (1672) (*CD*, III.919, 923, 925), placing the date of composition no earlier than 1671 but prior to Baxter's 1672 postscript "Of the Nature and Immortality of Humane Soules" against Willis's *De anima brutorum* (1672).

5. The epistle dedicatory is dated 17 Jan. 1672 (A3v). The first part is dated 28 Dec. 1671 (p. 77). The second part is dated 16 Jan. 1672 (p. 169).

6. The title page and preface refer to Baxter's *More Reasons* (17 Jan. 1672), which dates them to sometime after January 1672 (DWL BT XIX.351, fols. 1r, 8v).

7. This response to Thomas Willis's *De anima brutorum* (1672)—which appeared around January 1672 ([London Stationers' Company], *Transcript of the Registers*, 2:438)—was written in 1672 no later than Christmas of that year, at which time Matthew Hale made comments on it (Lambeth MS 3499, fol. 82r). But Hale had at that time "longe since perused" Baxter's treatise (ibid. fol. 82r), suggesting a date earlier in 1672. Hale's letter containing the comments is dated "1 January 1672" [i.e., 1673] (Lambeth MS 3499, fol. 115r).

Date of Composition	Title
ca. 1672–1673	*A Treatise of Knowledge and Love Compared* (Part I, chs. 1–10)[8]
ca. 1673	Baxter's comments in response to Sir Matthew Hale's comments on Baxter's "Of the Nature and Immortality of Humane Soules" (LPL MS 3499, fols. 63r–115r)
September 1673	Baxter to Sir Matthew Hale, 20 Sept. 1673 (Lambeth MS 3499, fol. 81v)
ca. 1675	*Catholick Theologie* (1675)
ca. 1676	"The principles of Spinosa and such Bruitists against Government and Morality recited, and confuted, and the fundamental reasons of Government asserted" (ch. 1), in *The Second Part of the Nonconformists Plea for Peace* (1680), 1–22[9]
ca. 1677–1680	"The marrow of *Spinosa's Opera posthuma* which I read not till after the writing of what is before. To which *Hobbes* much agreeth," in *The Second Part of the Nonconformists Plea for Peace* (1680), 111–16
ca. 1679	*Additional Notes on the Life and Death of Sir Matthew Hale* (1682)[10]
November 1681	Baxter to More, 17 Nov. 1681, in Richard Baxter, *Of the Nature of Spirits; Especially Mans Soul. In a Placid Collation with the Learned Dr. Henry More* (1682).

---

8. In the preface to the reader (3 Aug. 1689), Baxter mentions the book was "written long ago" (a2r). On p. 98, Baxter refers to the Great Ejection of 1662 as having happened ten years prior, dating at least the first ten chapters (pp. 1–117) to ca. 1672. He cites Francis Glisson's *De natura substantiae energetica* (1672) in this section (pp. 20, 28), along with his own *More Reasons* (p. 69), placing the *terminus a quo* in 1672. He also refers to his *Catholick Theologie* (1675) as forthcoming (p. 96), placing the *terminus ad quem* no later than 1675. The latter part was written sometime after *Catholick Theologie* (1675), which he refers the reader to on p. 267.

9. According to the preface (A2r), some sections were written in 1668, others when *The Judgment of Non-conformists, of the Interest of Reason, in Matters of Religion* (1676) was printed. This chapter belongs to this latter group, and was written before Baxter had read Spinoza's *Opera posthuma* (1677) (p. 111).

10. According to Baxter's prefatory note, this was written two years before Gilbert Burnet's *The Life and Death of Sir Matthew Hale* (1681).

Date of Composition	Title
March 1682	*Of the Nature of Spirits; Especially Mans Soul. In a Placid Collation with the Learned Dr. Henry More* (1682)[11]
March 1682	*The Nature and Immortality of the Soul Proved. In Answer to one who professed perplexing Doubtfulness* (1682) [published together with *Of the Nature of Spirits*][12]
August 1682	Reply to an unknown doubter, in continuation of *The Nature and Immortality of the Soul Proved* (1682) (DWL BT II.23, fols. 47–79)[13]
1686	"~~REVIVED ORIGENISME~~ <The State of soules> moderately examined.... Written by the provocation of Dʳ H. More And published by yᵉ provocation of Mʳ Th. Beverley" (DWL BT IV.87, fols. 226r–255v)[14]

UNDATED MSS

"ATHEISME, BEASTIALITY & INFIDELITY Confuted" [fragment] (DWL BT VI.204, fols. 281–83).

"Of the Nature & Immortality of Mans Soule" (DWL BT III.73, fol. 320).

---

11. Printed as a response to Henry More, *An Answer to a Letter of a Learned Psychopyrist Concerning the True Notion of a Spirit* (London: S. Lownds, 1681), in *Saducismus Triumphatus: Or, Full and Plain Evidence Concerning Witches and Apparitions*, 2nd ed. (London: Tho. Newcomb, 1682).

12. The work is dated "14 Mar. 1681" [i.e., 1682].

13. A date of 5 Aug. 1682 is given by Roger Thomas, *The Baxter Treatises* (London: Dr. Williams's Trust, 1959), 18.

14. The preface, dated 16 May 1690, states, "This book was written when I lay in Prison for writing my Paraphrase on yᵉ New Testament" (DWL BT IV.87, fol. 227v).

APPENDIX B

Richard Baxter to Joseph Glanvill, 18 November 1670

Worthy Sr[1]

I have two messages to send you by these lines. 1° Some gentlemen of quality and parts coming purposely to me, to heare w^t more instances I could give them of Apparitions and witches than I have printed, (telling me of ye very great increase of Sadducees that will beleive no other evidences, & importuning me (in vaine) to print the instances I gave you), where Mr Mompessons story (published by you) was mentioned on y^e by, they assured me that it goeth currantly now among the Sadducees (at court and the Innes of Court) that Mr Mompesson hath confessed that it was all his own jugling done onely that he might be taken notice of &c. I intreate you (from y^m) to acquaint him with ye report, & wish him if it be false (not for his own honour so much as for their sakes that are hardened by it) to publish some vindication or contradiction.

2° I am requested by ye widdow of Mr Joseph Allein (who hath a friend neere me, y^t came lately from her) to intreate you to send either to her or to me a Latine manuscript of his in your possession (for my neighbour is one that had a hand in transcribing it, and on his report I have a desire to see it, and shee also desireth to possesse it.)[2] If you send it to me rather than to her, If you send it to Nevil

---

1. DWL BC II.138r–139v.

2. Joseph Alleine's manuscript, *Theologia philosophica*, described by Baxter as "a body of *Natural Theology*," was never printed and is now lost. See Richard Baxter, "Introduction," in *The Life & Death of that Excellent Minister of Christ, Mr. Joseph Allein* (London: J. Darby, 1672), 27–28.

Simmons bookseller at ye 3 Crownes neere Holborne Conduit, it is like to come safe to me.

Though these two be all ye busynes I would trouble you w^th, yet having got your two late bookes (& received a third not long before as your guift) I may not omit to return you thanks for your very great respects to me therein expressed. And as for y^t passage of mine wch you chide me for, I will not enter into an altercation lest it prove troublesome; but only tell you 1° That I no where cast any reflexion of Atheisme on Gassendus or Cartesius. Nor accuse them as excluding all immateriall beings. 2° That ye first objection y^t I answer is "That matter and motion may do also that wch we ascribe to soules" not "to God" where I say y^t Gassendus writeth for Immateriall humane soules, ["]w^tever against Cartesius /fol. 138v/ or elsewhere he writeth wch seemeth injurious to this doctrine"³ 3° That I never gave ye least intimation y^t Cartes denyeth our soules Im[m]ortality, who so copiously defendeth it. 4° Though I never printed any such thing, I may say privately to you, I much feare that Gassendus did in this prevaricate. 1° From Sorberius & Hobbs's words wch I cited⁴ 2° From ye thinness of his plea for ye soules Immortality, 3° But above all from his principles wch seeme to make ag^t it. 5° If it could be done w^thout any thing like contending between us, I should be glad of your help, particularly to shew me how the passage cited by me pag. 541. & 504. are consistent wth an incorporaall soule in man?⁵ If no incorporeall being can be so applyed to a body as to impell it or move it? If all physicall actions be corporeal and can be elicite by no other than a corporeall principle? If because an incorporeall being cannot touch a body w^thout <for want> of *Tactus* & *Moles*, therefore it cannot impell it? If [?] our soules no way move our bodyes at all, but only act Immanently by Intellection, & so no Volitions or executive powers of them move ye corporeall spirits or sense? If our soules as sensitive are bodyes, and also as Motive of ye body? If it be known only by faith that Angels and Devils are at all Incorporeall? judge you of ye Consequencies. And if nothing can move another thing that is not it selfe in motion, nor a spirit move a Body, doth not this inferre that (not only no Angels nor ye soules of men can move a body, but that God himselfe cannot move it, unlesse he be a moving corporeall substance? And therefore when he saith, y^t God is here to be excepted, and giveth no reason for it, but because he is "*infinitae virtutis, et ubiq[ue] praesens*,"⁶ doth not this Generall assertion so expressely contradict this (God being ye most spirituall of spirits) as plainly to shew that the great wit of Gassendus could speake this but to put off reproach?

---

3. *RCR*, 495.

4. *RCR*, 495.

5. *RCR*, 541, 504.

6. Pierre Gassendi, *Opera omnia* (Lyon: Laurentius Anisson & Joan. Bapt. Devenet, 1658), 1:334.

But this is nothing to my open Controversy with him; But that wch I entreate your helpe in is, to tell me those reasons by wch you will justify him, in his opinion, y^t there <are> no spirits in *rerum natura* which move or actuate bodyes, or can move them? And y^t only faith and not reason telleth us that Angels or Daemons are Spirits? And whether I did not justly answer these speeches among those that /fol. 139r/ set up matter and motion as sufficient to all ye visible action in ye world without any incorporeall soules or spirits? 6° You your selfe make it a principle of Sadducisme to deny ye sensitive nature to be Immateriall: But Gassendus and Cartesius do both deny it: And make bruites to be meere corporeall engines; yea and one of them at least, saith ye same of ye sensitive soule of man: Therefore by you they are charged with ye principles of Sadducisme, if I understand you. 7° And why may I not dispute these particulars ag^t y^m (without wch you thinke your selfe that our Immortality cannot be defended), even in ye same papers where I name worse men, as long as I accuse them of no worse?

8° And (wth submission to your greater perspicuity) I confes y^t ye very principles of cartes himselfe, in Regius, (Lipstorpius, du Hamel, &c.)[7] by wch he would make a first push of ye Deity to serve for ever, & a continued effect to be wthout a continuation of ye true causality, & would make all subservient spirituall movers, needles, yea de facto exclude y^m, seemeth to me a very poor childish precarious toy insufficient to prove ye sensitive soule to be a body, or ye Intellectuall created nature, to be uselesse as to ye corporeall motions in ye world; And I thinke y^t Plato's Philosophy wch acknowledgeth ye spirituall nature to be the mover of the corporeall, is so much more manly, as y^t there is no comparison. And yet I told you so much of my opinion ag^t Aristotle's predicam^t of Qualityes, and his doctrine of educted formes, y^t you needed <not> have supposed me to have defended them. I judg y^t spirits are ye Active Natures y^t move ye passive (call y^m Atomes or w^t you will) under God; & yet y^t such spirits incorporale are ye forme of Matter; And y^t as simple beings they are (without composition) intellectually distinguishable into substance & forme; And y^t this forme is a *Virtus Essentialis*. But why do I begin to talke to you of these matters, why require so many more words? I have some principles of Philosophy of my own, a scheme of which I was almost going to enclose and send you.[8] /fol. 139v/ But I must shorten worke and not make more. Beleive I pray you, that I wrote not this as offended at your publick reprehension, being most offended wth mens touchynes that cannot beare such reproofes. I rest your very much obliged freind

Nov. 18. 1670.   Ri: Baxter.

---

7. Henricus Regius (1589–1679), Daniel Lipstorp (1631–1684), Jean-Baptiste Du Hamel (1624–1706).

8. This "scheme" is almost certainly a reference to a draft of "Cap. 4. Οντολογίαν sive Entium Natura, Ordo, Finis; Totius Philosophiae, &c. compendium," in *MT*, I.131–53 (as titled in the table of contents). Cf. *Rel. Bax.*, III.70.

Richard Baxter on Thomas Willis, De anima brutorum *(1672)*

A Postscript[1]

Considerations of some passages wch concerne w^t is before asserted in Dr Willis his Learned Tractate *de Anima Brutorum, quae Hominis Vitalis et Sensitiva est*

The Preface

Reader, I am bold here to suppose all truly Learned men to be so hearty Lovers of Truth, if it is for this y^t they study, write & live; & therfore y^t this very eminent Learned man will take it for no injury to be contradicted, if it have ye least tendencie to ye fuller discovery of truth: wch it may have if I erre, seeing it as with so much & excellent company, as y^t whoever shall openly dissent from y^m, oweth ye world, such evidence of reason for it, as if we can but draw it out, will make us all wiser than we have for many ages bin.

And let it not be offensive y^t I goe no further from him, & insist not more on ye notion of Im[m]ateriality: It is only y^e *essentiating formall Virtue* of spirits (even *sensitive*) y^t I defend; wch is necessary to those effects wch we p[er]ceive, besides meere *Matter, figure, site* &c & *forced motion*: I meddle not much with ye notion of Im[m]ateriality even as to Intellectuall spirits, for ye reasons oft here rendered. The Platonists thought soules had a kind of Bodies, & yet studyed ye doctrine of spirits above all sects. Their Marsilius Ficinus

---

1. DWL BT XIX.351, fols. 125r–143v.

& Mich. Psellus whom he publisheth were of yᵉ same /fol. 125v/ mind. Yea so were no small number of yᵉ Fathers of yᵉ foure first ages at yᵉ least. The Schoolmen thinke yᵗ Tertullian & others of yᵐ yᵗ were of yᵗ mind, did meane by a *Body* only a *Substance.* Zanchy seeketh to confute this opinion as to Tertullian, but not strongly enough: But wᵗever Tertullian thought, yᵗ answer will not serve for others. That Augustine himselfe was for some Corporeity of spirits, Zanchy sheweth by many citations, li. 2° de Angel. cap. 3. pag. 67. And before him Origen, Lactantius, yea & Basil: His friend Greg. Nazianz. is dubious. Zanchy saith yᵉ Schoolmen have neither Reason nor authority save Dionysius as for the contrary. And yᵗ yᵉ Author *de eccliast. dogmat.* & Gregor. Magn: Theodoret, Beda &c incline yᵗ way; & with Damascene many say yᵗ *In respect of God yᵉ Angels are corporeall, & in respect of us, they are not*: wᶜʰ yields yᵉ cause.²

Faustus Rheg[ius] wrote a booke to prove this to be yᵉ com[m]on sense of yᵉ Fathers before him:³ And in yᵉ *Script. Veter. Theolog. Galliae* he hath an Epistle ad Benedictum Paulinum on severall questions about yᵉ soule, where he openeth his mind, excepting God only from Corporeity: By wᶜʰ he sheweth yᵗ by *Corporeity* he meant not meere *substantiality*: For few deny God to be a *substance*, however they thinke yᵗ *substance* spoken of God & of yᵉ Creatures is aequivocall. And Faustus his Reasons are such as these, /fol. 126r/ *Quod temporibus non includitur, nec locorum terminis coercetur, quod soli Dei competit, hoc tantum incorporeum esse cognosce: sicut unus Doctor eximius disserens cuidam sciscitanti ubi esset Deus, respondit ita, Deus non alicubi est: Quod alicubi est continetur loco; Quod continetur loco corpus est:—omnis caro corpus, non omne corpus caro: non solum Anima, sed etiam Angelorum invisibilis substantia caelestisq[ue] sicut localibus spatiis continetur, ita auctore suo corporea esse, et comprehensibilis approbatur: Quid est enim nisi Corporeum, quod de sup[er]nis sedibus p[ro]turbatum loco cessit? Quid est quod sensit ruinam? &c. vid.* pag. 137. 138.⁴

Wᵗ Claudian: Mam[m]ertus hath written in confutation of Faustus, & how ~~yet~~ he himselfe, thought yᵗ Incorporeall Angells had yet Bodyes of Fire, & how Caesarius &c have spoken to yᵉ same purpose, I have allready mentioned in yᵉ Append. to yᵉ Reas. of Christ: Relig: p. 528 529. And Zanchius himselfe, though he professe to be no determiner of yᵉ case as being to him uncertaine, yet declareth his opinion for a pure sort of Corporeity of Angels.

For my owne p[ar]t I have there & herre told you why I no further meddle with it (as beyond my reach) than to distinguish *Spirits* from those grosser sub- /fol. 126v/

2. Girolamo Zanchi, *De operibus Dei intra spacium sex,* II.iii, in *Omnium operum theologicorum* (Geneva: S. Crispin, 1619), 3:66–69.

3. Faustus of Riez, "Epistula III" (*CSEL* 21:168–81; PL 58:837–45).

4. Faustus of Riez, "Incipit epistola sancti Faustini ad Benedictum Paulinum," in *Veterum aliquot Galliae theologorum scripta* (Paris: Sebastian Nivell, 1586), 134–41; "Epistula V" (*CSEL* 21:183–95; *PL* 58:845–50).

stances wch we call *Bodyes* & *Matter*, by their incomprehensible *Purity* of substance, & their *Formall Virtues* or *Powers* discerned plainly in their operations.

And yet I will not deny to Dr Harvy or any of his mind, but y^t all Creatures, even ye noblest spirits are Second Causes, & in some sort Instruments of ye first; & therfore y^t they do more than their owne power alone is sufficient for; & therfore y^t there is something in ye effect above the nobility of ye Second Cause: yea y^t without it they can do nothing: And all this is evident, as in every thing, so notably in ye vegetative oper-ations, where ye soule doth fabricate its owne *domicilium*, but ignorantly, not <as> all knowing w^t it doth; nor doth ye soule of ye wisest man know how he concocteth his owne food; nor is nutrition or augmen<ta>tion caused by our knowledge: wch yet undoubtedly is knowingly caused & governed by ye Supream (if not other sup[er]ior) Cause: so y^t ye soule must needs op[er]ate herein *p[er] modum instrumenti*, where all effects have somewhat above ye power of ye second cause.

But then let us consider 1° That as every wise artificer, so much more God, doth fit his In- /fol. 127r/ strument to its prop[er] worke. And yet Gods Instruments be not only Inanimate & forcibly moved Instruments; but also Creatures p[ar]ticipating of his Image, in Life, or self-moving power: And therefore though God is ye first mover, yet we are under him self-movers, yea & free determiners of our owne acts. 2° And as in this life Creatures are evidently diversifyed *essentially* in their owne natures & *formes*, & not only Accidentally in their received *motion*, so God changeth not simple essences (as far as can be proved) but will continue ye Natures wch he has made: And though without him we can be or do nothing, yet we have reason to expect ye same sustentation & concurse from him hereafter as now.

It is true y^t ye sun alone *shineth* not or moveth not, but God {?} {[?&] {?} ye sun; & y^t ye soule alone understandeth not, but God, & ye soule. But it is as true y^t ye sun *moveth, illuminateth, heateth* & ye soule *Liveth, understandeth, willeth*, not as a lifelesse pen doth write, but by an intrinsicke essentiall Virtue, w^{ch} /fol. 127v/ it hath here, & shall have hereafter, derivatively from & dependantly on God, who also doth & will actuate us according to ye nature he hath given us.

And as for ye Somatists opinion, wch plainly tendeth to this, y^t there is no essentially Active nature but God, but all ye world is only *God & Passive matter*, God ye prop[er] soule & mover, & passive Matter diversifyed only by various divisions, magnitudes, shape, site & motion, without any essentially self-moving Life, there is so much long agoe written ag^t it, by multitudes of Authors y^t I will not here further trouble my selfe & you with it, than to mind you how much it is ag^t all y^t exp[er]ience wch by such powers as God hath given us to judge by, man is capable of about such things; & y^t its all unproved on their parts: As for ye Atheisticall sort y^t thinke this matter is eternally moved by chance, wth<out> God, a first-moving cause, I think y^m not /fol. 128r/⁵ the worthy of a Confutation.

/fol. 129r/

---

5. Top of page: "A Postscript, considering some passages which concerne what is before asserted, in Dr Willis his very Learned Tractate *De Anima Brutorum quae Hominis Vitalis et et Sensitiva est.*"

Ch. 1[6]

Three yeares after the writing of this,[7] there is come forth a Learned Treatise of Dr Willis <his> writing *de Anima Brutorum* In wch cap. 2 he conjectureth ye sensitive soules of bruites & men to be *corporeall Fire*, & not im[m]ateriall. I suppose I may without offence first state my owne sence of ye Case as plainly as I can; & then consider how far it is concerned in his arguings.

1° I do againe professe, y^t though I take not spirits to be compounded of various substances, yet y^t there is necessary an Intellectuall distinguishing of their *Materia Metaphysica* as Schibler & many others call it from their *Differencing Formes*. And y^t when we call spirits *Im[m]ateriall*, we do not meane y^t they are not *substances*: Therfore though we com[m]only use ye word *substance* for *matter & forme* together, yet for want of another word I mostly use it for y^t wch in spirits answereth to *Matter* in bodies, as distinct from ye forme: wch also I sometime call *spirituall* or *metaphysicall matter*. For I concerne not how any *Virtus* or *Potentia Activa* can subsist purely of itselfe, without being *substantiae alicuius Virtus*.

2° I doubt not but there are divers species of spirits: 1° Because we see God delight so much in ye diversity of inferior species of animals. 2° Because it is proved by ye diversity of their op[er]ations.

3° The composition of *spirituall substantiality* & *forme* being not a composition of substance & substance, nor properly of /fol. 129v/ *res et res*, but an Intellectuall distinguishing of objective *conceptus* wch goe to ye full definition of ye thing, doth not at all inferre any danger of a dissolution of spirits.

4° To give mans understanding a cleare definition of the said spirituall matter or substantiality, as it differeth from ye most pure corporeall matter, without taking in y^e *Formall difference*, I thinke impossible. Some have fixed it uppon *Penetrability* & *Indivisibility*; wch are not inconsiderable I confesse: But as they are in y^{m}selves lyable to much dispute; so they give us but a kind of Accidentall difference. How spirits penetrate bodies, or are penetrated by bodies we apprehend not clearly: And seeing spirits are *multiplyed*, whether God can[n]ot *divide* a spirit, we do not satisfactorily know. And Dr More in *Metaph.* hath copiously asserted their extension according to their prop[er] nature. That they are substances of ye greatest *Purity* its easy to conceive: And y^t Purity adapted to ye p[er]fection & use of their formall virtues. ~~And unles fire be a spirit I may adde y^t their substance is Insensible,~~ But ye bare names of *Im[m]ateriall* & *Materiall* satisfie no mans understanding, y^t doth not thinke *Im[m]ateriality* to be *Nothingnes*,

---

6. Top of page: "Postscript: [?] the [??] pag Ch. 1."

7. DWL BT XIX.351, fols. 1–124r.

or els y^t ye notion of *virtus vel potentia-activa*, is ~~not~~ y^e *conceptus adaequatus* of a spirit: or unles he otherwise be taught to know how *spirituall-substantiality*, & ye purest corporeall *materiality* differ. And if this gratifie Mr Hobbes, much good may it do him.

5° As we must have therfore a *Formall no-* /fol. 130r/ *tion* of a spirit, if we will difference it from Bodyes, so there must be some *Com[m]on Forme* of a *spirit* as a *spirit*; & a *speciall differencing forme*, by w^{ch} *one spirit* differeth from *another*.

6° The Forme of a spirit is its *Essentiall Virtue* or *Active Power, force & inclination*: wch by some is falsly called an *Accident*. That this *Virtue* is an *Essentiall forme* I have elswhere proved in a peculiar disputation,[8] & ye Scotists have proved long agoe, not withstanding some mens pretended confutations.

7° The com[m]on forme of a spirit as such, is *Virtus-Activa-Vitalis: Vitall-Activity* or to be *Essentiall-Life*: or A *Virtue-naturall* of *vitall-action*. In ye word *Virtus*, I comprehend ye three notions, of *Potentia-activa, Vis et Inclinatio*, wch all goe to make it up.

8° A meere *Body* or *Matter* is meerly *passive*, & hath no *self-moving power*; but if it be moved it is moved by another; wch is *originally* by some *Active spirituall being*.

9° Meere *Bodyes* are distinguished but by their magnitude, shape, site, weight, motion & contexture &c. of wch see Mr Boile of formes.[9]

10° God in nature hath stablished all *passive matter* in a threefold species of contexture, called *Aire, water & earth*: whose threefold contexture hath formed y^m into a threefold *Receptivity* of y^e *Igneous & spirituall Influxe*; in wch their difference consisteth.

11° These *three Passive elements* are no where found *unmixt*; nor without a participation of *fire*, & its effects uppon them.

12° The *Active-spirituall* natures or substances /fol. 130v/ under God ye Creator, are also three: 1° Intellectuall Spirits; 2° Sensitive Spirits; 3° Fiery or Vegetative Spirits.

13° The *speciall Forme of each one of these*, is its *proper virtue*; wch in each one is *Three in one*, as an *Image* of y^e *Divine Trinity* of *Active principles*.

14° The Forme of y^e *Intellectuall Spirit* is to be *A Virtue, most-Vitall-Active, Intellective Volitive, in ye Purest Substance*.

15° The forme of y^e *Sensitive Spirit*, is to be *A Virtue, more-Vitall-Active, sensitively-apprehensive, & sensitively Appetitive*, in a Purer Substance.

---

8. *MT*, I.164–75 (cap. 5). The disputation is entitled, "Utrum Animae facultates seu Potentiæ Naturales (Activa-Vitalis, scilicet Intellectiva, Volitiva) sint ipsa animae forma essentialis? Aff. Non accidentia."

9. Robert Boyle, *The Origine of Formes and Qualities, (According to the Corpuscular Philosophy,) Illustrated by Considerations and Experiments* (Oxford: H. Hall, 1666).

16° The forme of the Vegetative Spirit is to be a *Virtue, Vitall-Active, Discretive,* & *Attractive* (analogically, [?Appetitive] perceptive & *Appetitive*) in *a Pure Substance.*

17° All these *formall Virtues* are certainly knowne to us by their op[er]ations.

18° But operating in Bodyes, their op[er]ations are named by us, & knowne to us, not simply as they are *Agentis Actus,* but compoundedly as they connote ye effects on bodies. And so their Acts were they out of bodies might possibly deserve some other name.

19° Yet y^e *Power* or *Virtue* being their essence, never ceaseth, nor is it ever like to be idle or in vaine. The *noblest Active nature,* wch is *Essentiall Life,* will *not die,* nor be *unactive,* nor have *Action below y^t nobility* of its *nature,* wch it expresseth by its operation in bodies.

20° It seemeth to me most probable, y^t y^e *Vegetative Spirit* is nothing but *Fire* itselfe: But mortalls can[n]ot reach a certainty herein: nor do I affirme it. /fol. 131r/

21° Whether ye diversity of Vegetables be from a *diverse contexture* of y^e *receptive matter* of y^e *seed & plant;* or from a *sub-specifique difference* in y^e *vegetative fierie formes,* is past our reach.

22° The *fierie substance* in its com[m]oner op[er]ation (out of Vegetables) is informed by A *Virtue* of *naturall Activity* (or *Motion*), *Illumination* & *Calefaction;* By wch alone it is probable ye three *Vegetative op[er]ations* are produced.

23° They y^t reduce all to *Motion alone* contradict experience, & p[er]forme not their pretensions of solving all ye phaenomena of nature.

24° It seemeth to me no absurdity <*de nomine*> to say y^t *Fire* is a *Spirit:* But if any will call it a *Body* & *materiall,* I will not dispute y^e *name,* if we agree in y^e *definition.*

25° If *Fire* be not a *Spirit,* it is either *Quid medium* between a *spirit* & *body,* or a *Body* of so *pure* & *virtuous* a nature, as will tell us how hard if not impossible it is, to have right distinguishing conceptions of ye highest corporeall & ye Lowest spirituall nature. Certainly it is a substance wch is as it were y^e *nexus* or *vinculum* of ye Corporeall & more spirituall natures, & a kind of soule to all y^e *Passive world:* And for my part I must incline to call it prop[er]ly a Spirit.

26° That it is *Sensible,* contradicteth not this: For 1° Its yet unresolved whether it be *It selfe,* or only *Its Effects* wch we *see* & *feele*—viz, motion, Light, & heate as they are modes of ye Passive Recipient, rather than as either *substance, virtue* or *Act* of ye Agent. 2° And /fol. 131v/ why may not a *Sensitive Spirit* have y^e *Sight* or *Sense* of a *Sensitive Spirit* as its *object?* as well as an *Intellective Spirit, Intelligere spiritum intellectivum.* w^t absurdity is it, for every active substance to have a substance of ye same species for its object? Its more doubtfull whether it be not ye very *Spiritum Sensitivum* wch we do *first sentire,* before we sense other inferior objects?

27° But remember y^t by *fire* I meane not y^t composition of various things, wch we call a *flame,* a *coale,* a *candent matter* &c. & wch ye vulgar call *Fire:* But y^t *pure Virtuous Substance* wch in this is y^e *Active principle* of *Motion, Light* & *Heate.* And wch is by others called aether.

28° All *fire* is of one *Nature*, ~~at least~~ *genericall*: whether solar, culinary, or y^t wch is ye mobile spirits in o[ur] blood, & in all vegetables, & goeth through this world.

29° If y^e *Vegetative Life* be *meere Fire* (wch is probable, though not sure) yet so is not y^e *Sensitive*: For its op[er]ations shew a *formall Virtue specifically* distinct from *meere fire*. *Meere fire* sheweth us no Virtue in its op[er]ations, but *Motive, Illuminative & Calefactive*; & such effects only are done by it, as these there can do. But *Sensation* is an effect w^ch *totâ specie* transcendeth these.

30° The same I say of y^e *Intellectuall Soule*, & its transcendent operations.

31° Gassendus & such others as make Sensitive Soules to be *meere Fire* (wch he taketh to be a Body), prepare men strongly to thinke ye same of *Intellective Soules*. /fol. 132r/ And when after he cometh to plead for ye Immortality & difference of humane soules, his Reasons are so slender, & so downright contradictory to his physicall theorems, y^t he wrongeth his Reader by forcing his judgment upon this dilemma, y^t either ye Learned Rationall Gassendus knew not when he did palpably contradict his owne Philosophy, or els y^t he did prevaricate for his reputation with men, & durst not assert y^t corporeity & evanide nature of humane soules, wch indeed he held.

32° It is needfull that (as allwaies, so) here, wee confound not ye controversies *de nomine* & *de re*. The name of *Fire* or *aether* is taken from, or given to, either y^e *substance* or *igneous Matter*, or y^e *Virtue* wch is y^e *forme*. If it be meant only of y^e *Matter* (whether *physicall* or *spirituall* I determine not) then either *All Spirits* have the same *Substance* as *Fire*, or *not*. If not, then *Sensitive Spirits* have not ye same substance as fire. If yea; then all y^t would follow it but y^t *Fire* is ye Com[m]on *Substance* or Metaphysicall Matter of all Spirits (Created), wch yet by ~~[?a]~~ specifying *formes* differ among y^mselves. And these things are much unknowne to man. Though many of ye Fathers seemed so to thinke.

33° But *Forma denominat*: That is not to be called *Fire*, much lesse, *meere fire*, wch hath a nobler higher forme; no more y^n a man is to be called a meere bruit. For y^e *forme* of *Fire* as such, & of a Sensitive Animal as Sensitive, specifically differ.

34° And it is most consonant to Reason, observing ye harmony of Gods workes, to /fol. 132v/ thinke, y^t nobler *Formes* have nobler *Bodies*. And therefore y^t though y^e *Substance* of all Spirits be Pure, yet y^e *Substance* of one y^t hath a nobler Forme, may be Purer & more excellent, than ye Substance of another wch hath a lesse noble forme. And so y^t y^e *firey Substance*, & y^e *Sensitive* & y^e *Intellective*, agree indeed in ye generall y^t they are all *pure* & *spirituall*, but differ in *degrees* of *Purity* & *Spirituality*: Even as *earth, water* & *Aire*, agree in ye generall of being *meere passive matter* or *elements*; & yet differ specifically in contexture & degrees of crassitude, or tenuity.

35° And so as to y^e *Formes*, though y^e *Virtus-Activa-Vitalis*, be ye common Forme of spirits, as spirits; yet (though penury allow us <no> distinguishing names ~~[?]~~) y^e *virtus-Activa-vitalis* of ye Intellectuall Substance, & y^e *Virtus-Activa-Vitalis* of ye sensitive nature, & y^t of ye Vegetative or Igneous, are all so farre distinct in degrees of excellency, as y^t with ye rest of y^e *Formall virtue* doth constitute *distinct species.*

36° If any will say y^t ["]all *Fire* hath y^e *Virtue* or *faculty* of *Sensification*, & of *Intellection & Volition*, though on fuell it exercise only y^e *Motive, illuminative & Calefactive* virtue, & on Vegetables only ye Motive, *Discretive*, & *Attractive* or uniting virtue" affirmers must prove: And nothing is to be held y^t hath not some evidence. They may as well say y^t a stone feeleth, because I can[n]ot disprove it. /fol. 133r/

37° If any thinke it probable y^t ye sun hath either a *Sensitive* or *Intellective forme* or *virtue*, nothing would follow were it sure, but y^t ~~either~~ ye sun is not meere *fire*, but either *Fire* of a *Sensitive* or *Intellective* Species, (as *Man* is an *Animal*) or els a *compound being* of a *fierie Substance* & a *Sensitive* or *Intellective Soule*. wch still is above ye nature of meere fire. For neither *culinary* nor *vegetative* fire shew ye least signes of *Sensation* or *Intellection* (w^{t}ever Campanella say *de Sensu Rerum*). And it is not rationall to judge, y^t God would preserve a nature y^t hath noble faculties (of *sense* & *reason*) & yet never give y^m occasion to exercise y^m, but be as if they had no such *faculties.* God maketh nothing in vaine.

38° The Question then wch I engage my selfe in (to prove ye affirmative) is, *whether, that Pure Substance wch is a Sensitive Soule, in bruites or men, have not essentially a Virtus formalis, Sensitivè-Vitaliter Agendi, sensitivè apprehendendi, et sensitivè appetendi, specifically distinguishing it from meere Fire, & from ye Vegetative Spirits.* And consequently whether y^e *Intellective Soule* have not also its *nobler specifying Forme.* As to ye question, whether man have one, two or three soules, I will not intermixe it with this dispute.

39° And to prevent vaine answers, be it knowne, y^t to avoid mistakes, I acknowledge y^t ye words, "*Forme*" & "*Life*" are /fol. 133v/ both ambiguous: And y^t "*Forme*" sometimes signifyeth y^e *informing Principle Constitutive* & *Active*; & sometime only y^e *Relation* or *Union* of y^t *Principle* to or with ye other parts: so *Life* is some-time taken for ye vitall-*Principle*; & sometimes for ye state of ye Composition by y^e *Union* of y^t *Principle* with ye rest. But I here take *forme* & *Life*, in the first sense physically, & not in the later *Relatively.* Let not *words* then be a quarrell.

40° And lastly be it knowne y^t I so distinguish between y^e *formes* of *simple* & of *compound* beings, as y^t in *simple beings* I call only y^e *virtus-specifica*, the *forme*, wch is but a partiall conception of ye Simple Substance, & not *res in re*, nor sepa-rable: But in *Compound Substances* I call y^e *whole Substance* of y^e *Informing Active Principle* y^e *forme* conteining its owne prop[er] *Metaphysicall matter & forme.* E.g. *Forma hominis est Anima <intellectualis> (totâ substantia animalis)*: At *forma Animae, est tantum Virtus specifica Vitalis, Intellectiva, Volitiva.*

And so much for ye understanding of w^t I do assert & w^t I do oppose, wch is espe-cially ye Somatists, who thinke y^t *matter* & *motion* do all y^t is done, without essentiall *formall virtues*: not charging this on ye Learned Author, but considering so much of his words as seeme to be ag^t my tene[n]ts. /fol. 134r/

Ch. 2. Dr Willis Reasons weighed

In his second Ch. y^t *Anima Bruti* is *corporea et Ignea*; & not *Incorporea substantia aut forma*, he giveth divers reasons to prove: As 1° from ye vanity of other opinions: as Plato's *Anima mundi*, & Origens *Mundus animarum*; (wch yet are far more rationall y^n ye doctrine of ye Epicureans.)

But saith he "*ubinam tot myriades animarum—aut quid agent?*"[10] Resp. Will soules take up more roome & be more troublesome than bodies? *ubinam erunt tot myriades atomorum—aut quid agent?* If there be roome on earth, there is more elswhere. you take not yo[ur] corporeall soules to be an[n]ihilated. where then will they be? But y^e *Quid agent* is a question unfit for men on earth to answer or to aske.

He addeth ["]*cum AEgyptus olim, infliction Divina pulicum, muscarum, &c examinibus infestabatur—haud facile conceptu erit, undenam tot Animae subito devocari, et in quae munia eaedem mox sep[ar]atae deputari poterint.*"[11] Resp. As if corporeall matter were quicklyer calld together than spirits? I thinke a stone would be longer coming hither from ye sun, than a sunbeame is. And you can as ill tell w^t yo[ur] dissolved atomes shall be imployed in. And why may they not be resolved into an *Anima huius Systematii* as an extinguished Candle into ye com[m]on fire, without any deperdition or dishonour?

2° He addeth "*Porrò cum coelum Dei opt. Max. regia, angelos, geniosq[ue] et labe omni puras animas sibi incolas vendicet, terra vero tanquam sentina quae-* /fol. 134v/ *dam foeces rerum et mole sua ruentia corpora hauriat,—ad concinnam mundi oeconomiam com[m]odius videbitur, im[m]ortalia omnia*—(humane soules excepted) *aetheri adscribere, Animalia verò reliqua, ventri obnoxia, et in terram prona, glebae huic addicere; ita ut eorum animas cum corporibus nasci et interire, et pura puta corpora esse, dicantur.*["][12]

Resp. On ye contrary, how much more agreeable to ye harmony of Gods evident op[er]ations is it, to conceive y^t all things here below are full of incorporeall spirits! I meane all y^t are animated. When we see y^t no *unmixed* passive matter is found on earth, & y^t this is not a world of Carkasses, & ye grave where bodies are only interred;

---

10. Thomas Willis, *De anima brutorum quae hominis vitalis ac sensitiva est, exercitationes duae* (Oxford: Ric. Davis, 1672), 9. [Thomas Willis, *Two Discourses concerning the Soul of Brutes, which is that of the Vital and Sensitive of Man*, trans. S. Pordage (London: Thomas Dring, 1683), 4: "yet where do so many Myriads of Souls ... what do they?"]

11. Willis, *De anima*, 9–10. [Willis, *Two Discourses*, 4: "when of old, *Egypt* was infested by Divine Punishment, with Swarms of Fleas, Flyes ... and Insects ... it is not easily to be Conceived, form whence so many Souls were so suddenly Called, and into what places, the same being by and by separated, could be placed."]

12. Willis, *De anima*, 10. [Willis, *Two Discourses*, 4–5: "Moreover, as Heaven, the Kingly Palace of the Great God, challenges for it self Angels, *Gen.* 2. and pure Souls, free from all spot, to be its Inhabitants: but the Earth, as it were a Certain sink, draws forth and extracts the feces of things, and from its bulk, ruinous Bodies; it seems more agreeable to the fitted Oeconomie of the World, that all immaterial things ... should be ascribed to the Air; but the other Animals, Condemned to the belly, and prone to the Earth, to this Globe; so that

But y^t ye Active fiery nature itselfe (not easily proved corporeall) doth passe through all, & is as an *Anima Telluris*, & animateth every seed & plant: And when we see y^t ye world is made for ye use of Intellectual agents: And find y^t here we have much to do with Angels & Devils y^{m}selves: And know y^t ye universe is as one Body animated, at least *p[er] partes*, & y^t God is here & every where, & more than an universall soule. To dreame then y^t spirits & bodies are so locally separated (while ye very locality of spirits is so much disputed) as y^t This world must be only for Bodys (except man) & another world for soules, is a most improbable conceipt: when spirits & bodyes are so com[m]ixt through all.

And seeing you take aether itselfe /fol. 135r/ to be meerly a body, why must spirits be confined to y^e *aethereall*, y^t is, y^e *bodily* regions? If you allow *bodies* to be *there with spirits*, why not *spirits* to be *here* also *with bodies*[?]

But w^t if these soules are but fire? Are they annihilated? Why so, any more than earth? If not, why should you *glebae addicere ignem?* At least ye Sun is a fitter originall & center to addict it to. And w^t meane you by *Interire?* If you meane *an[n]ihilation* it is most absurd. If you meane *separation* from y^t body, its unquestionable, & so *humane soules* might be said *interire?* If you meane y^t it is *formaliter* a *Soule* or *Life* no longer, I answer, Thats past doubt, if by a Soule or Life, you meane y^t principle w^{ch} *actually animateth* y^t body, or y^e *union of ye parts*. But if you meane a Vitall *principle* w^{ch} *did animate* a *body* & whose nature & essentiall Virtue continueth ye same, so it doth not *interire*, but still live.

Next p. 10 he argueth y^t ye soules of bruites & ye inferior soules of men are *Materiall* & *Divisible*, ["]*quia plures ac diversos actus animalis simul a diversis corporis membris obiri cernimus*["]; e.g. *videre, audire &c.*[13] Resp. But is it proved or probable y^t an Incorporeall Indivisible spirit can[n]ot be present *im[m]ediatiore suppositi et virtutis*, in all parts of ye body as well as another body can? And can it <[?not]> op[er]ate as /fol. 135v/ powerfully as dead unactive Matter? When you have proved sand or atomes more extensive & op[er]ative than ye beames of ye Sun, wch in a moment passing thence fill all ye aire to ye earth, I will next believe y^t spirits wch are nobler than fire, are lesse able also for this office, than ye atomes of bodily divisible matter.

The next reason is from the separation of the soules parts in dissected animals.[14] Resp. The answer to this is given before,[15] & I will not repeat it: but only adde, y^t

---

the Souls of these, may be said to be born and dye with their Bodies, and to be altogether Corporeal."]

13. Willis, *De anima*, 10. [Willis, *Two Discourses*, 5: "because we perceive many and diverse animal Acts, to arise at once, from diverse members and parts of the Body: For examples sake; in the same instant, that the Eye sees, the Ear hears."]

14. Willis, *De anima*, 10–11.

15. Cf. DWL BT XIX.351, fol. 56v: "It is hard to prove y^t ye soule of a bruite is divisible: or y^t it extrudeth itselfe *ad p[ar]tes materia* any otherwise than y^e *Rationall* doth, wch is but by an

This would as well hold ag^t the Rationall Soule, as ye Sensitive in man: For besides y^t you can never prove y^t they are not rather diverse faculties of one soule, than divers soules. I suppose you thinke not ye Rationall Soule is only in ye head: And then, w^t if ye Head of a malefactor, be suddenly carryed as far as you can reasonably imagine before it & ye body <die?> is not y^t Soule as likely to be divided as ye Sensitive?

The description of y^e *Essence of fire* p. 12 is prooflesse & unprobable; That it is *aggeries* ["]*particularium subtilium contiguarum*["], is no better: That it is ["]*in motu pernici*["], is true if by *Motus* be meant Action. But as long as y^e *Cause* of this *Motus* is left out, wch is a *formall selfacting virtue* nothing is said to purpose. w^t is said *de* ["]*continua quarundam genesi, aliarumq[ue] decessu*["], is no better.[16] If by y^e *genesis* be /fol. 136r/ <meant> ye inception of matter not before existent, like a new creation, & by *decessus* be meant *an[n]ihilation*, it is intollerable. But if (as I understand it) he meane ye turning of some other matter or element into fire, & turning fire againe into other elements, it is utterly unproved & improbable, y^t ye addition & subtraction of y^e *pabulum*, doth any such thing.

And when he saith y^t ["]*Ignis et flamma tantum quoad magis et minus differunt*["],[17] it is no better, than to say, y^t *Anima et Homo tantum quoad magis et minus differunt* when one is a *Simple Substance*, & ye other a *Compounded*.

Therefore ye inference, y^t thus y^e *soule of Bruites* (&y^e *sensitive in man*) is *but a heape of such agglomerated subtile atomes*, without mentioning any *essentiall Vitall Virtue*, is to speake *atomes*, rather than *Sense* about *Sensitive Soules*.

We deny not but y^t a *fiery nature* is in every *animal*; & y^t it being *never alone*, its *first composition* is with y^e *airy matter* in those wch we call y^e *Spirits*. But whether y^e *firy* part of these *spirits* be *corporeall atomes* is uncertaine, but y^t the *Sensitive Soule* is not such is *most certaine*.

And w^t meane you by ["]*tenuesq[ue] in auras evanescere apta*["]? p. 14.[18] Not *an[n]ihilation*. If it turne into *aire*, it was aire before; or how prove you a transmutation of elements (wch Gassendus will not grant). If you meane y^t it is still *fire inter auras termes*, then it hath still all ye Virtues of fire. And /fol. 136v/ when you say of *soules* & *fire*, ["]*quamprimum a motu omni cessat, illico non est*["],[19] had you said, *non est*

---

indivisible presence with ye whole, & an op[er]ation uppon ye increasing p[ar]ts: or if it do, yet whether it *cause* ye increase or nutrition of those members to wch it is so extended."

16. Willis, *De anima*, 12. [Willis, *Two Discourses*, 5: "most subtil Contiguous particles, and existing in a swift motion, and with a continued generation of some, renewed by the falling off of others."]

17. Willis, *De anima*, 12. [Willis, *Two Discourses*, 6: "the forms of Fire and Flame (which differ only in more or less)."]

18. Willis, *De anima*, 14. [Willis, *Two Discourses*, 6: "being apt . . . to vanish away into Air."]

19. Willis, *De anima*, 14. [Willis, *Two Discourses*, 6: "as soon as it Ceaseth from all motion, it is no more."]

anima [?] *huius corporii, et non est flam[m]a,* it had bin true: but this is *Ignis* still, & ye former is *spiritus Sensitivus still*: And why God can[n]ot redintegrate *eandem numero Substantiam Compositam,* I know not, when no part is an[n]ihilated. Nor yet why he can[n]ot [?move] it.

Ch. 3. The 6th Ch. *De Scientia Brutorum* considered

The 6th Ch. is most considerable to my purpose. 1° Pag. 95 you take it as proved or granted wch is not proved & is most denyed, y^t ["]*objecti impressio, spiritus animales introrsum pellens et peculiari quodam ritu modificans, sensationem infert*["].[20] Whereas 1° An *Object,* meerly as *an object* is but *passive* & *terminative,* & *impresseth nothing* on y^e *sense* itselfe; though y^e *solar-motive-effective-influxe* or op[er]ation may: And 2° no *motion* of the said *spirits* is sufficient to cause *sensation* without a *sensitive essentiall forme.*

2° When you make it another thing *se p[er]cipere sentire,* I think y^t *sentiendo p[er] cipio me sentire,* & y^t it is all one; Though there is also another kind of p[er]ception following in y^e *sensus com[m]unis, phantasie* & *passions.* Pag. 96. You thinke if ye soules of Bruites were *Im[m]ateriall,* & subsist after ye bodies, they would *understand* & *reason* as well as men & learne arts & sciences, because to both ["]*eadem prorsus sit conformatio* /fol. 137r/ *organorum animalium*["].[21]

Resp. <I am glad of so excellent an Anatomists concession.> Do you thinke *soules* differ from bodies in nothing but their *im[m]ateriality* (a word least understood by us)? The grand difference is their *Formall Virtues* or *Naturall powers,* by wch also *one spirit* differeth from *another.* Therfore y^e *Sensitive Soule,* though I thinke as truly *im[m]ateriall* as y^e *rationall,* (though not of ye same *degree* of *purity* or substantiall excellence) Learneth not *arts* & *sciences,* because it hath not y^e *essentiall Virtue* of *Intellection,* but only of *Sensation.*

But I come to y^t for wch only I meddle with this Author, viz., his proofes y^t sensation may be wrought by ye motion aforesaid of his passive atomes. This is his chosen proving instance "*Inter corpus insensile ac sensile haud multo magis discrimen esse quam inter inaccensum, accensumq[ue]: et tamen hoc, ex illo, fieri passim cernimus: quidni pariter existimemus, sensile fieri ex insensile*["].[22]

---

20. Willis, *De anima,* 95. [Willis, *Two Discourses,* 32: "an Impression of an Object driving the Animal spirits inwards, and harmonizing them by a certain peculiar manner, causes sensation."]

21. Willis, *De anima,* 96. [Willis, *Two Discourses* 32: "there is altogether the same Conformation of the Animal Organs."]

22. Willis, *De anima,* 96. [Willis, *Two Discourses,* 33: "there is not much more difference between an insensible and a sensible Body, than between a thing uninkindled, and a thing kindled; and yet we ordinarily see, this to be made from that; why therefore in like manner, may we not judge a sensible thing, or Body to be made out of an insensible?"]

Resp. 1° The difference between *accension* & *sensation* is in *kind*, & not in degree of yᵉ same kind. An *Ant* that hath *sense* is lesse than a mountaine yᵗ is *sensles*, & yet is of another & more noble species.

2° *Sensation* & *accension* differ *tota specie ǫ genere [?ra]ther*; And wᵗ shew of proofe give you yᵗ yᵉ same Virtue or Causality is enough for one, wᶜʰ produc- /fol. 137v/ eth yᵉ other? Could you prove yᵗ yᵉ burned candle *feeleth*, or yᵗ yᵉ Coales are hurt, or yᵗ yᵉ loudest fiercest Gunpowder & Guns, have any *paine* or *sensitive* pleasure, you said something: But when all yᵉ flames of AEtna, or all yᵉ force of Thunder & light-ening can make neither stones nor earth nor water nor pulverized matter even to an Alcohol, nor yᵉ invisible aire itselfe to *feele*, you must give us another instance before you can prove wᵗ you attempt.

Or at least when you can[n]ot prove yᵗ ever any *meere passive matter* was by *motion* turned into a *sensitive soule*. Give us either a proofe, or something to make this seeme a probable thing.

3° And I turne yo[ur] instance agᵗ yo[ur] selfe. There was never any *accension* proved to be made by meere *Passive matter* & *motion*: but only by yᵉ *Active-essentiall Virtue* of *fire*, wᶜʰ is *toto genere* distinct from yᵉ meere *Passive elements*. But you say yᵗ *inaccensum* is turned into *accensum*: No wonder: for *inaccensum* & *accensum* are both far enough from yᵉ nature of fire wᶜʰ kindleth or burneth; if by *accensum* you meane yᵉ *fuel* only, further than there is antecedently *fire* in yᵗ fuel. But where no *accension* is caused on yᵗ fuel but only by *an Agent* /fol. 138r/ wᶜʰ hath *essentially* a *Virtus-Motiva, illuminativa et calefactiva*, in like man[n]er no *sensation* will be p[er]formed, but by a *spirit* wᶜʰ hath a *formall Sensitive Virtue*. Though *passive matter* may be yᵉ fuel of yᵉ one, & the *terminus* of yᵉ other (wᶜʰ yet is dubious).

If you say yᵗ yᵉ *motion* of two stickes, will set yᵐ on fire, I answer, yᵗ is because 1° The aire is full of dissipated fire, wᶜʰ enflameth when contracted, & 2° There is fire in yᵉ *wood* & in all materialls, wᶜʰ needs but excitation & evocation.

But you say yᵗ ["]*Torpida ac inertia sine igne—im[m]ota jacent: quamprimum verò ab incentivo admoto flam[m]am concipiunt, mox eorum particulae rapidissimè com[m] otae, ac velut animatae, lumen cum calore et luce producunt*["].[23] Resp. But not yᵉ least *sensation*: And yᵗ they produce *this* no wonder, when it is yᵉ very *nature of fire* so to do.

So yᵗ yo[ur] Argumᵗ runs thus: If passive matter & motion without yᵉ agents *essentiall Virtue*, may cause Motion, Light & Heate, then yᵉ same without a sensitive Agents essentiall virtue, may cause sensation: But &c. The Antecedᵗ is notoriously false; The consequence can[n]ot be proved, were yᵉ antecedᵗ true. And therfore yᵉ Conclusion [is] false.

---

23. Willis, *De anima*, 96–97. [Willis, *Two Discourses*, 33: "torpid and sluggish, lye unmoved without fire. . . . But as soon as they have taken flame, from some incentive being put to it, by and by their Particles being rapidly moved, and as it were animated, produce a shining with Heat and Light."

But p. 97 you seeme to come neerer me, /fol. 138v/ you deny ["]*Materiam e quâ, res naturales constant esse mere passivam, et non moveri nisi ab alio*["]—And say that ["]*Atomi, quae sublunarium materies sunt, plurimae adeo sunt activae et ἀυτοκίνητος ut nusquam diu subsistant.*"[24] Resp. 1° Either you meane this of all *matter* or but of *some*. If of all, then yᵉ case is altered indeed: For we have no *meere passive matter* left, but all is *selfmoving*, & so wᵗ ever yᵉ *Matter* be, hath somewᵗ of yᵉ *Virtue of Spirits*. But if it be *some*, as "*plurimae*" intimateth, then why *those* & not yᵉ *rest?* Those "*plurimae*" are *selfmovers* either by their *parvitude* & *shape*, or by their *formall Virtue & Active Nature*, or by some *Active nature compounded with* yᵐ to make one *compound substance*. The com[m]on doctrine of yᵉ Somatists is, yᵗ they are moved by something els, & yᵗ every-thing moved will continue moving till it is stopt: But this is not to be a *selfmover*: & so is nothing to o[ur] case: For we deny not but *passive matter* may be *moved* by another thing. Though yᵉ conceit yᵗ motion needeth no more cause than /fol. 139r/ *not-to-be-moved*, or yᵗ yᵉ effect will continue when yᵉ Causation ceaseth, are both absurd) But this opinion confesseth a *Virtus motiva* in yᵉ first mover (of wᶜʰ more elsewhere).

And I suppose you meane not yᵗ every Atome is a compound of *fire* & *passive* matter, & is moved by yᵉ fiery part: For then it is not yᵉ passive but yᵉ Active p[ar]t of yᵉ compounded atome wᶜʰ is yᵉ selfmover. If it be only yᵉ *parvitude* & *shape* yᵗ you suppose to be yᵉ selfmoving cause, you will speake without either reason or exp[er]ience, & agᵗ both wᵗ Reason can be given why shape or parvitude should be a moving cause: wᵗ proofe of any such thing in yᵉ world? Indeed an atome of pulverized marble is easily<er> moved than a rocke: but it hath no more power to move itselfe.

But if you say yᵗ yo[ur] *atomi plurimae* have a *selfmoving Virtue* wᶜʰ others have not, wᵗ is yᵗ *virtue?* An *accident*, or their *Naturall forme?* If yᵉ former, wᵗ is it? If mutable & separable it will cause no constancy in yᵉ motion: If p[er]manent, it is some *forme* or *naturall property*: /fol. 139v/ And so you will come to yᵗ wᶜʰ I assert: And why then are not those *selfmoving atomes specifyed* & *distinguished* by yᵗ *selfmoving virtue*, from yᵉ rest of yᵉ atomes yᵗ have no such power & *named* accordingly? And then we shall come neerer in this controversie.

The truth is there are but two causes of motion wᶜʰ Reason can assigne: either an *Active-nature* or *Virtue* in yᵉ mover, or els yᵉ premotion & impulse of some other thing. And those yᵗ are for yᵉ later only agᵗ *Active Virtues* 1° do make all motion in yᵉ world to be violent, & none prop[er]ly naturall: 2° They deny all yᵉ noblest essences in nature; even all Active natures, & leave none but passive (~~among~~ <to> creatures) They deny Fire to be fire; They deny yᵉ Sensitive Soule; & on their grounds teach men to deny yᵉ Rationall: The *names* they retaine & yᵉ *essences* they deny. 3° And when they have all done they must confesse yᵉ Being of a *Virtus motiva* distinct from matter

---

24. Willis, *De anima*, 97. [Willis, *Two Discourses*, 33: "that Matter, out of which Natural things are made, is meerly passive, and cannot be moved, unless it be moved by another thing.... Atoms, which are the matter of sublunary things, are so very active and self-moving, that they never stay long."]

& motion, or els they can never assigne a Reason of yᵉ beginning or first cause of motion. They must confesse yᵗ Gods Life, & Power is a cause of yᵉ [?worlds] creatures motion: yea if they take God to be nothing but yᵉ subtilest Atomes eternally in act (wᶜʰ must be at yᵉ bottome of Gassendus'es principles, or at yᵉ end), yet in order of nature, yᵉ eternall *virtus-movendi*, must /fol. [139b]r²⁵/ be antecedent to yᵉ *motus* (as they yᵗ thinke yᵉ world eternall, thinke yet it is but an eternall effect:) or at least yᵉ *virtus et Actus* must be conjunct, & it is must be a powerfull vitall Act: [?as well] sure few that call God Allmighty & Living, & wise & Good, do thinke yᵗ he no otherwise differeth in his Being from a stone, but by subtilty of matteriall atomes, & meere motion.

Gassendus saith ["]*capere non licet quomodo si incorporeum sit, ita applicari corpori valeat, ut illi impulsum imprimat, quando neq[ue] ipsum contingere, careus ipsa tactu, seu mole qua tangat non potest*[,"]²⁶ with more to yᵉ same purpose, wᶜʰ doth inferre yᵗ not only mens soules & Angels, but God himselfe, must be corporeall, or els can[n]ot move things corporeall.

But if it be certaine yᵗ God hath a *Virtus motiva* distinct *ab ipso motu*, I aske whether it can seeme probable to a wise enquirer yᵗ this God never com[m]unicated any *vitall moving virtue* to any of his creatures, but only *matter, motion* & yᵉ *effects?* Whether he yᵗ saith thus disgrace not yᵉ glorious workes of God, by mortifying yᵉ whole world, & turning it into a dead engine, & denying any created prop[er] Life? & consequently dishono[ur] not yᵉ Great Creator? Whether it be not likelyest yᵗ God fitteth every nature to its use, & therfore giveth prop[er] *Life*, or *Active power* where he expecteth or causeth *vitall action?* And whether all exp[er]ience tell us not, yᵗ we o[ur] selves & all living creatures have an *Active power* distinct from /fol. [139b]v/ *motion* itselfe? He yᵗ can sit still & rise & walke when he will, yᵗ can speake or be silent, & can begin an interrupted motioned freely, is not moved merely by violent motion of anothers impulse, but by a vitall principle freely used.

So much on yᵉ by, I put in, for a *Vital moving* power. whether yᵉ selfmoving power wᶜʰ yᵉ Author giveth to most or many atomes be such or not, I know not. I am <sure> Gassendus is forced to confesse a *nisus vel conatus movendi*; distinct from motion, which continueth when motion ceaseth, & reneweth it.²⁷

But all this is still farre off from yᵉ cause in hand. The question is whether yᵉ selfmoving power of Atomes, with their motion & shape &c will cause *Sensation* without a *Vitall Sensitive Virtue?* The strongest motion of yᵉ aire by winds, yᵉ quickest & strongest motion of gunpowder & aire by Canons, causeth not sensation in any nature before insensible: prove yᵗ ever any meere motion did it in yᵉ world, & you shall carry yᵉ cause: But till then, you have said nothing.

---

25. Incorrect foliation "199" in bottom right corner of MS.

26. Pierre Gassendi, *Opera omnia* (Lyon: Laurentius Anisson & Joan. Bapt. Devenet, 1658), 1:334b.

27. Cf. *RCR*, 508, citing Gassendi, *Opera*, 1:336a: "Unum omnino supponere par est; nempe quanta cumque fuit Atomis mobilitas ingenita, tantam constanter perseverare, adeò ut

And if you confesse really in many Atomes a *selfmoving power*, as not *moved* by another, why may you not as well confesse a *Vitall-Power* of *Sensation*?

Pag. 98 ye Cause of *imagination* & *appetite* is enquired of (when yet ye Cause of *Sense* itselfe is ye maine difficulty & undiscovered) And you confesse you can[n]ot find it in body or soule or any material subject alone /fol. 140r/ ["]*cui talis potentia ἐνεργετικὴ κὶ ἀυτοκίνητος attribui debet. At verò quando corpus animatum sum[m]o et verè Divino artificio in certos quosdam fines ac usus fabricatum considero, nil vetat dicere, creationis lege, sive Dei opt. Max. instituto, ita comparatum esse ut ex anima et corpore simul commissis, ejusmodi facultatum confluentia resultet*["]—.[28]

Resp. 1° If you had first proved ye atomes by meere motion to cause *Sense*, I would ye easilyer believe they might cause *imagination* & *appetite*. But y^{t}s yet undone.

2° That it is caused *Dei instituto* is no question: but ye question is *how* God causeth it? Either you meane y^t *God himselfe* in all ye creatures, is y^e *only vitall-virtue* of sensation? or else y^t *ex lege Creationis* he hath com[m]unicated or given such a *Virtue* to y^e *Creature itselfe* as its *owne Nature*? or els y^t *sense* & *appetite* is caused *without* any such *sensitive virtue* at all, formally or eminently so called. If you meane ye first, you take all ye world to be a lifeles corps of atomes of itselfe, & God to be ye only life, soule or spirit of & in ye world (of sensitives.) And if it be once proved y^t it is only God without a created *Sensitive Virtue* y^t causeth *Sense* in Sensitives, ye same reason would p[er]suade men, y^t it is only God y^t without any *created Intellective vitall virtue* doth cause Intellection too. And then ye Sadducees were in ye right (~~& I thinke Gassendus meant as they~~) y^t there were neither Angels nor spirits, but God & bodies were all ye universe.

If you meane ye second, y^t ye Creator hath put a *Sensitive Nature* into /fol. 140v/ ye Compound, wch is in neither of ye parts of y^{m}selves, y^t will contradict both com[m]on reason, & yo[ur] owne principles: That any *power* should be found in y^e <nature of y^e> *compositum*, wch is not in ye nature of *one* or *both* ye parts is impossible, seeing it hath nothing to constitute it, but those parts, wch can give nothing wch they have not *formally* or *eminently*. If neither *soule* nor *body*, have a *Vital-Sensitive nature* or *Virtue*, y^e *compositum* can have no[~~?ne~~] [?such] nature, but only w^t another (God) may be to it.

And you make y^e *selfmoving power* yo[ur]selfe to be in *some* of ye Atomes, & by y^m com[m]unicated to other parts: Therefore if you did acknowledge any

---

inhiberi quidem Atomi, ne moveantur valeant, at non, ne perpetuò quasi connitantur, conentúrve se expedire, motúmque suum instaurare."

28. Willis, *De anima*, 98. [Willis, *Two Discourses*, 33: "I cannot readily detect, in this, or in that, or in any material subject, any thing, to which may be attributed such a Power, with a self-moving energy: But indeed, when I consider the animated Body, made by an Excellent and truly Divine Workmanship, for certain Ends and Uses, nothing hinders me from saying, That it is so framed by the Law of Creation, or by the Institution of the most Great God, that from the Soul and Body mixed together, the same Kind of Confluence of the Faculties doth result."]

sensitive-vitall-power in yᵉ whole, in conformity to yo[ur]selfe, its like you would place it primarily in yᵉ *Active Atomes*.

But if you meane yᵗ yᵉ Creator by *meere motion*, of *subtile matter* causeth *sense, imagination* & *appetite*, without giving a *sensitive-nature* to yᵉ *parts* or *whole*, it is yo[ur] proofe yᵗ we still expect.

Yo[ur] next proving instance is of *a clocke wᶜʰ measureth time* &c: And yᵉ next of *musicall instruments causing melodie*; Both wᶜʰ I have before answered, & formerly in my Append. to yᵉ Reas. of Christ. Relig.²⁹

2° Wᵗ is there in any of these engines or organes, wᶜʰ hath yᵉ least resemblance to *sense*? in *kind*, or *excellency* of nature? wᵗ is there in a clocke but matter & motion? & wᵗ doth it but move in yᵉ order wᶜʰ an Intellectuall Agent placed it in? It hath neither *knowledge* nor *sense* of its owne motion, [?much] nor of *sun* or *time* or yᵉ *thoughts* of him yᵗ useth it. It is yᵉ *Man* & not yᵉ clocke to whom yᵉ measuring of time is to be ascribed: It doth nothing beside bare /fol. 141r/ motion, wᶜʰ every stone hath in descending, but *p[er] modum signi*; to be a memorative & Indicant signe to yᵉ user: And I can make yᵉ same use of things allready existent & in motion, without yᵉ least interposition of art. I can measure an houre by numbering my pulses: I can make use of preexistent things for a dyall; By yᵉ sun in my chamber, & by yᵉ shaddow of a tree, or of a peg on my ho<u>se side, allowing for yᵉ variations of time. And yet it doth not follow yᵗ *Matter* & *Motion* are sufficient to *sensation*, & *sensitive appetite*, because *Reason* can make such use *of signes*, whether naturall or artificiall.

The like I say of Musicke. The Harmony is in yᵉ *Hearer*, & yᵉ *order* of motion wᶜʰ caused <it> was contrived by humane understanding. Wᵗ is there equivalent to *Sensation* in all this? If you can prove 1° yᵗ matter & motion ever made such an engine, without yᵉ art of an understanding spirit, 2° or yᵗ this engine is understood & used by any but a *Living Soule*, 3° or yᵗ this engine feeleth wᵗ it doth; you will do your worke. But if it be nothing but com[m]on matter fitted & ordered to such naturall motion by a Rationall mind, wᶜʰ it shall make use of as an Indicant & memorative signe, or wᶜʰ shall by yᵉ order please yᵉ phantasie or mind of yᵉ maker or user, this indeed extolleth Reason above *Sense*, but doth not equall this order of lifeles motion to *Life* & Sense at all.

And if yᵉ *Fire* or *aether* have so great a Causalitie in all motion as G.G newly, & as *Le Grand* /fol. 141v/ senior, & as Telesius, Campanella &c thought, all yᵗ you prove by engines is but this; yᵗ there is no motion of passive bodyes but by yᵗ firey principle, wᶜʰ hath essentially a *Moving Virtue* & is a Vitall principle (its like) in Vegetatives: Therefore its as likely yᵗ there is no *Sensation* but from yᵗ wᶜʰ hath essentially a *Sensitive Virtue*. Though I take yᵉ *descensus gravium, & every motus passivorum aggregativus* to be so unserchable as to its cause yᵗ we can[n]ot knowingly ascribe it to yᵉ aethereall principle. But when there is no other motion in all yᵉ world besides

---

29. *RCR*, 514–15.

this aggregative (by wch the parts do seeke a closure) wch is lyable to doubt, whether it proceed from ye operation of the *Natures* wch by an *essentiall forme* or *Virtue* are *Active*, I will not be he y^t shall deny y^t of *all motion*, wch I am <in> doubt of whether it be <to be> denyed of *any* of y^m all: Nor will I solve ye phaenomena of nature by denying all ye very *being of nature* (as it is *principium motus*) nor by dissolving ye world, & dreaming all its most *excellent vitall parts* into *nothing*, excepting only the higher faculties of mans soule.

Where you adde p. 99 *"Verum anima bruti, vix sui, aut suarum facultatum moderatrix["]* &c;[30] Do but really grant y^e *Faculties*, & we easily grant y^t they are not ye moderaters of y^mselves intellectually: w^t sup[er]ior Intelligences or spirits do by y^m I know not; but I know y^t God is ye chiefe if not only Intellec- /fol. 142r/ tuall Moderator of them. But they *Feele* themselves by a *Sensitive Essence*, though they *moderate not intellectually* their owne sensations.

But I am stopt & allmost recall all y^t seemeth to oppose you: For you next adde *"Hoc revera tenet de Brutis imp[er]fectioribus, quorum animis sive naturis, actionum ab ijs edendarum typi, sive orbitae, quas rarò aut nunquam transiliunt, inscribuntur, quaeq[ue]—non tam agunt, quam aguntur. Attamen p[er]fectioribus quibusdam Brutis, quorum actiones, ad plures, et praestantiores usus ordinantur, et typi originalis longe plures in sunt, et eorum animis, typos variandi, ac inter se componendi facultas quaedam attribui debet: ipsa nimirum brutalis natura[liter] ita dotata, ut circa res quasdam necessarias cognoscens et Activa fuerit["]* &c.[31]

I thought you had treated in generall of y^e *soules of bruites* before: The exception y^t you now make I thinke is of no lesse than All: All are of one *sensitive kind*, though differing by an inferior sort of specification. And in some degree they have all, y^t which you ascribe to some. And w^t you meane by *"Anima brutalis naturaliter dotata"* I will trouble you no further to enquire, but say, y^t if you meane it of either a *Formall Virtue*, or an *Inseparable property* in y^t pure /fol. 142v/ substance wch we call y^e *soule*, & not *meerly* a violent or accidentall motion from a premoved bodyes impulse, or some exterior cause, it is as much as ye interest of my now-defended principles do require. But if you meane anything els, I shall not pretent to understand it, much lesse to confute it, till I am enabled & constreined by yo[ur] owne explication.

---

30. Willis, *De anima*, 99. [Willis, *Two Discourses*, 34: "But the Soul of the Brute, being scarce moderatrix of its self, or of its Faculties."]

31. Willis, *De anima*, 99–100. [Willis, *Two Discourses*, 34: "This indeed holds good, concerning the more imperfect Brutes, in whose Souls or Natures are inscribed the types or ways of the Actions to be performed by them, which they rarely or never transgress or go beyond.... *They do not so much act, as are acted*: yet in some more perfect Brutes, whose Actions are ordained to many and more noble Uses, there are far more Original Types, and to their Souls there ought to be attributed a certain faculty of Varying their Types, and of Composing them in themselves; for the Brutal Soul it self, being so gifted naturally, as she is Knowing and Active, concerning some things necessary for it."]

And if any thinke, y^t a defense of ye spirituality & p[er]petuity of Sensitive Soules, do<th> rather tend to discourage than comfort us, about ye state of Intellectuall Soules, I am not of their opinion: And though God have not told us w^t use he will make of ye separated soules of bruites, because it is of no necessity or use to us to know it; It sufficeth me to p[er]ceive y^t its more than probable, that they continue ye same simple essences, & neither lose all being by annihilation, nor their *essentiall virtues* by a perdition of their specifique nature: But all y^t to Reason is left doubtfull is but whether they are still *individualls*, or fall into one com[m]on spirit, as an extinguished Candles-fire into ye com[m]on fired-aire; & also whether by ye Pythagorean transition & circumvolution of spirits, they will be againe imbodyed & when; wch we are not at all concerned to know. But our case is more fully revealed to us by God, not only by Scripture, but by ye light of nature & humane experience. /fol. 143r/

And I am ye more concerned in ye point because o[ur] owne soules as sensitive do undergoe ye same doome with those of bruites: And though I take it for utterly uncertaine whether we have one, two or three (as is aforesaid),[32] yet I thinke it most probable y^t we have one, or at least, y^t ye Intellective & Sensitive are ye same, y^e *lower Virtues* in ye same substance, being [2] subordinate to the higher.

The Lord teach us to use well ye Faculties wch we have, & a little time will open to us ye mysteries of their nature. God never meant to teach me his Artifice of *making men* or *soules*; And I can know nothing but y^t wch I was made to know: And when I read many voluminous pretensions of men, that take on y^m confidently to know w^t they know not, & call their presumptions by ye name of Philosophy & Physicks, I am forced to confesse y^t I am ignorant of w^t they pretend to know, & am quiet in my ignorance, when I find y^t I was not made to know it. But practically to know how to *use* both *soule* & *body* to please God, & for my owne & others happynes, is my *duty* & my *interest*, & y^t wch I was made for, & y^t wch I find both possible & delightfull. /fol. 143v/

The Reader y^t will find fuller satisfaction about Im[m]ateriall beings, or spirits, may have much in two new excellent bookes: Dr Mores *Metaphysicks*,[33] & Mr Sam: Got's *Divine History* (my worthy friend who is lately passed from a holy life on earth, to a perfect glorious life in heaven, before he could so review & perfect that booke as he intended.[)][34]

If any ag^t my notion of *substantiality* or *metaphysicall materiality* of spirits, shall say, y^t If not created spirits, yet at least GOD is *Pura-Virtus-in-Actu*, or *Potentia-Actus*,

---

32. DWL BT XIX.351, fols. 50r–v, 58r–59v; and above, fol. 133r.

33. Henry More, *Enchiridion metaphysicum: sive, de rebus incorporeis succincta & luculenta dissertatio* (London: E. Flesher, 1671).

34. Samuel Gott, *The Divine History of the Genesis of the World Explicated and Illustrated* (London: E. C. & A. C. for Henry Eversden, 1670).

sine substantialitate, & y^t *Virtus Infinita in Actu* is y^e *conceptus adaequatus* of his essence (& ye essence of a spirit leaving out *Infinite*) without ye notion of *Substance* as being too grosse, I shall confesse y^t he taketh the only way to confute my conception. And I dare not say y^t y^e *existence* of a meere *Virtus in Actu* without a substance is Impossible: But I must say y^t ye notion is not com[m]on among Divines, who call God a *Substance*; And y^t I can<not> reach a satisfying conception of it: Though I confesse y^t it is never ye unliker to be Gods essence because man cannot conceive it. But these things are higher than my understanding was made to reach: And therfore I rather reverence & adore & confesse my ignorance, than dispute them.

Bibliography

I. MANUSCRIPTS

Dr. Williams's Library, London
  Baxter Treatises (MS 59, vols. 7–13; MS 61, vols. 1–6, 11–18)
              Reference is to volume, item, and folio numbers, cited according
              to the consecutive sequence of 22 volumes as classified by Roger
              Thomas, *The Baxter Treatises* (London: Dr. Williams's Trust, 1959), 4a.
  II.23,   fols. 47–79 [Reply to an unknown doubter, 5 August 1682; in contin-
              uation of *The Nature and Immortality of the Soul Proved. In Answer to*
              one who professed perplexing Doubtfulness (1682)]
  III.73,   fols. 320r–v "Of the Nature & Immortality of Mans Soule. / The
              Contents of The first Part. . . . The Contents of the 2^d Part ag^t
              Atheisme. . . . The Contents of the 3^d Part ag^t Bestiality. . . . The
              Contents of the 4th Part ag^t Infidelity. . . ." [table of contents only]
  IV.87,   fols. 226–55 "~~REVIVED ORIGENISME~~ <The State of soules> mod-
              erately examined. . . . Written by the provocation of Dr H. More And
              published by ye provocation of M^r Th. Beverley"
  IV.96,   fols. 322–48 "Of the NATURE & IMMORTALITY of HUMANE
              SOULES" [incomplete copy of 19.351, fols. 10r–57r]
  VI.194,   fols. 13–14 [Theses on the nature of God]
  VI.204,   fols. 281–83 "ATHEISME, BEASTIALITY & INFIDELITY Confuted;
              or / A cleare proofe of The Deity[,] The Immortality of mans soule[,]
              The Gospell of Christ / In a Dialogue betweene PAUL & Sr ELYMAS
              DIVES / The first part: ~~against Athei~~" [fragment]
  VII.229,   fol. 68 "A BREVIATE OF PACIFYING THEOLOGIE / written for
              Distinct Knowledge of sacred truth / The Ending of perverse doc-
              trinall controversies / By Richard Baxter A Lover of Truth, <Love>
              & Peace. / To be read by those students who use his writings next
              after his *Family Catechisme*, before his *Catholicke Theologie, Directory*
              & Methodus Theologiae." [fragment]

XIX.351,   fols. 1–143 "Of the NATURE & IMMORTALITY of HUMANE
                SOULES / The first part. / which supposeth what is written in
                my *Reasons of the Christian Religion*; & my *More Reasons* for it.
                / By Richard Baxter / with a postscript, considering some pas-
                sages in Dr Willis his Learned Tractate *de Anima Brutorum, qua
                Hominis vitalis et sensitive est*"

Baxter Correspondence (MS 59, vols. 1–6)
                Reference is to volume and folio numbers.
I.170–71   Joseph Glanvill to Baxter, [ca. February 1663]
I.172   Joseph Glanvill to Baxter, February 1662
I.174–75   Joseph Glanvill to Baxter, 4 August 1662
I.177   Joseph Glanvill to Baxter, 21 January 1663
II.138r–139r   Baxter to Joseph Glanvill, 18 November 1670
III.272r–273r   Baxter to Thomas Hill, 8 March 1652
III.284r   Henry More to Baxter, 10 February 1682
III.286r   Henry More to Baxter, 25 September 1681

Lambeth Palace Library, London
MS 3499,   fols. 63r–v [Matthew Hale to Richard Baxter, undated fragment]
MS 3499,   fols. 64r–77r "De Anima To Mr B[axter]."
MS 3499,   fols. 78r–115r "De An[ima] Transactions between me & M^r
                B[axter]." [fol. 81v: Richard Baxter to Matthew Hale, 20 Sept.
                1673; fols. 82r–115r: Matthew Hale to Richard Baxter, 1 Jan. 1673,
                with Baxter's undated notes on Hale in margins and verso pages]

II. PRINTED PRIMARY SOURCES

Alsop, Vincent. *A Vindication of the Faithful Rebuke to a False Report*. London: John
    Lawrence, 1698.

Alsted, Johann Heinrich. *Physica harmonica*. Herborn, 1616.

———. *Scientiarum omnium encyclopaediae*. 4 vols. Lyon: J. A. Huguetan & M. A.
    Ravaud, 1649.

———. *Theologia naturalis*. Frankfurt: Antonius Hummius, 1615.

———. *Triumphus bibliorum sacrorum*. Frankfurt: Bartholomaeus Schmidt, 1625.

Alting, Jacob. *Opera omnia theologica analytica, exegetica, practica, problematica &
    philologica*. Amsterdam: Gerardus Borstius, 1686.

Ames, William. *De conscientia et eius iure, vel casibus*. Amsterdam: Joan.
    Janssonius, 1631.

Anderson, John. *A Dialogue between a Curat and a Country-Man*. Edinburgh, 1728.

Anton, Paul. *De autoritate ecclesiae, qua mater est, positiones theologicae*.
    Leipzig: Christopher Gunther, 1690.

Aristotle. *The Complete Works of Aristotle*. Edited by Jonathan Barnes. 2 vols.
    Princeton, NJ: Princeton University Press, 1984.

Ashe, Simeon. *Gray Hayres Crowned with Grace.* London: A. M., 1655.

Aslakssøn, Cort. *Physica et ethica mosaica.* Hanoviae, 1613.

Augustine. *Confessions.* Translated by Maria Boulding. Hyde Park, NY: New City Press, 1997.

Bacon, Francis. *New Organon.* Translated by Fulton H. Anderson. Indianapolis: Bobbs–Merrill, 1960.

Baron, Robert. *Ad Georgii Turnebulli Tetragonismum pseudographum apodixis catholica.* Aberdeen: Edward Raban, 1631.

Baron, William. *An Historical Account of Comprehension, and Toleration. From the Old Puritan to the New Latitudinarian; with their continued Projects and Designs, in Opposition to our more Orthodox Establishment.* London: J. Chantry and Church Simmons, 1706.

Bates, William. *Considerations on the Existence of God and the Immortality of the Soul.* London: J. D. for Brabazon Aylmer, 1676.

———. *A Funeral Sermon for the Reverend, Holy and Excellent Divine, Mr. Richard Baxter.* London: Brab. Aylmer, 1692.

Baxter, Richard. *An Accompt of all the Proceedings of the Commissioners of both Perswasions.* London, 1661.

———. *Additional Notes on the Life and Death of Sir Matthew Hale.* London: Richard Janeway, 1682.

———. *Against the Revolt of a Foreign Jurisdiction, Which would be to England its Perjury, Church-ruine, and Slavery.* London: Tho. Parkhurst, 1691.

———. *The Arrogancy of Reason against Divine Revelations, Repressed.* London: T. N. for Tho. Underhill, 1655.

———. *Calendar of the Correspondence of Richard Baxter.* Edited by N. H. Keeble and Geoffrey F. Nuttall. 2 vols. Oxford: Clarendon Press, 1991.

———. *Catholick Communion Defended against both Extreams.* London: Tho. Parkhurst, 1684.

———. *Catholick Theologie: Plain, Pure, Peacable: For the Pacification of the Dogmatical Word-Warriours.* London: Robert White, 1675.

———. *The Certainty of Christianity without Popery.* London: Nevil Simons, 1672.

———. *A Christian Directory: Or, A Summ of Practical Theologie, and Cases of Conscience.* London: Robert White, 1673.

———. *Church-History of the Government of Bishops and Their Councils Abbreviated.* London: B. Griffin, 1680.

———. *Confirmation and Restauration.* London: A. M. for Nevil Simmons, 1658.

———. *The Crucifying of the world, by the Cross of Christ.* London: Joseph Cranford, 1658.

———. *The Cure of Church-Divisions.* London: Nevil Symmons, 1670.

———. *The Defence of the Nonconformists Plea for Peace.* London: Benjamin Alsop, 1680.

———. *The Divine Life.* London: Francis Tyton and Nevil Simmons, 1664.

———. *An End of Doctrinal Controversies*. London: John Salusbury, 1691.

———. *The English Nonconformity as under King Charles II and King James II truly stated and argued*. London: Tho. Parkhurst, 1689.

———. *Full and Easie Satisfaction which is the True and Safe Religion*. London: Nev. Simmons, 1674.

———. *Gildas Salvinus; The Reformed Pastor*. London: Robert White for Nevil Simmons, 1656.

———. *The Glorious Kingdom of Christ*. London: T. Snowden, for Thomas Parkhurst, 1691.

———. *A Holy Commonwealth, or, Political Aphorisms, Opening the true Principles of Government*. London: Thomas Underhill and Francis Tyton, 1659.

———. *How to do Good to Many*. London: Rob. Gibs, 1682.

———. *Humble Advice: Or the Heads of those things which were offered to Many Honourable Members of Parliament by Richard Baxter at the End of his Sermon, Decemb. 24. at the Abby in Westminster*. London: Thomas Underhill and Francis Tyton, 1655.

———. "Introduction." In *The Life & Death of that Excellent Minister of Christ, Mr. Joseph Allein*, 12–28. London: J. Darby, 1672.

———. *The Judgment of Non-conformists about the Difference between Grace and Morality*. [London], 1676.

———. *The Judgment of Non-conformists, of the Interest of Reason, in Matters of Religion*. London, 1676.

———. *A Key for Catholicks*. London: R. W. for Nevil Simmons, 1659.

———. *The Life of Faith*. London: R. W., 1670.

———. *Methodus Theologiae Christianae*. London: M. White & T. Snowden, 1681.

———. *The Mischiefs of Self-Ignorance, and the Benefits of Self-Aquaintance*. London: R. White, 1662.

———. *More Proofs of Infants Church-membership and Consequently their Right to Baptism*. London: Nevil Simmons, 175.

———. *More Reasons for the Christian Religion and No Reason Against It*. London: Nevil Simmons, 1672.

———. *Naked Popery*. London: N. Simmons, 1677.

———. *The Nature and Immortality of the Soul Proved. In Answer to one who professed perplexing Doubtfulness*. London: B. Simons, 1682.

———. *The Nonconformists Plea for Peace*. London: Benjamin Alsop, 1679.

———. *Of the Immortality of Mans Soul, And the Nature of it, and other Spirits*. London: London: B. Simons, 1682.

———. *Of Justification*. London: R. W. for Nevil Simmons, 1658.

———. *Of the Nature of Spirits; Especially Mans Soul. In a Placid Collation with the Learned Dr. Henry More*. London: B Simmons, 1682.

———. *A Paraphrase on the New Testament with Notes, Doctrinal and Practical*. London: B. Simmons and Tho. Simmons, 1685.

————. *Poetical Fragments*. London: T. Snowden, 1681.

————. *The Practical Works*. 4 vols. London: Thomas Parkhurst, 1707.

————. *The Practical Works of Richard Baxter*. Edited by William Orme. 23 vols. London: James Duncan, 1830.

————. *The Reasons of the Christian Religion*. London: R. White, 1667.

————. *The Reduction of a Digressor: or Rich. Baxter's Reply to George Kendall's Digression in his Book against Mr. Goodwin*. London: A. M. for Thomas Underhill, 1654.

————. *Reliquiae Baxterianae: Or, Mr. Richard Baxter's Narrative of the most Memorable Passages of his Life and Times*. Edited by Matthew Sylvester. London: T. Parkhurst et al., 1696.

————. *Richard Baxter's Answer to Dr Edward Stillingfleet's Charge of Separation*. London: Nevil Simmons, 1680.

————. *Richard Baxter's Dying Thoughts upon Phil. 1.23*. London: Tho. Snowden, 1683.

————. *The Saints Everlasting Rest*. 2nd ed. London: Thomas Underhill, 1651.

————. *The Saints Everlasting Rest*. Abridged by Benjamin Fawcett. Salop: J. Cotton and J. Eddowes, 1759.

————. *The Scripture Gospel Defended*. London: Tho. Parkhurst, 1690.

————. *The Second Part of the Nonconformists Plea for Peace*. London: John Hancock, 1680.

————. *A Treatise of Knowledge and Love Compared*. London: Tho. Parkhurst, 1689.

————. *The True and Only Way of Concord of all the Christian Churches*. London: John Hancock, 1680.

————. *The True History of Councils Enlarged and Defended*. London: T. Parkhurst, 1682.

————. *Two Disputations of Original Sin*. London: Robert Gibbs, 1675.

————. *Universal Redemption of Mankind*. London: John Salusbury, 1694.

————. *The Unreasonableness of Infidelity*. London: R. W. for Thomas Underhill, 1655.

Becmann, Christian. *Exercitationes theologicae*. Servestae, 1639.

Biel, Gabriel. *Commentarii doctissimi in IIII. sententiarum libros*. 5 vols. Brescia: T. Bozzola, 1574.

Birch, Thomas. *The History of the Royal Society of London*. 4 vols. London: A. Millar, 1756–1757.

————. *The Life of the Most Reverend Dr. John Tillotson*. 2nd ed. London: J. and R. Tonson et al., 1753.

Blackmore, Richard. *Creation. A Philosophical Poem. Demonstrating the Existence and Providence of a God*. London: S. Buckley, 1712.

Boyle, Robert. *Certain Physiological Essays*. London: Henry Herringman, 1661.

————. *The Correspondence of Robert Boyle*. Edited by Michael Hunter and Antonio Clericuzio. 6 vols. Burlington, VT: Pickering & Chatto, 2001.

————. *A Disquisition about the Final Causes of Natural Things*. London: H. C. for John Taylor, 1688.

————. *Essays of the Strange Subtilty, Great Efficacy, Determinate Nature of Effluviums*. London: W. G. for M. Pitt, 1673.

————. *The Origine of Formes and Qualities, (According to the Corpuscular Philosophy,)* *Illustrated by Considerations and Experiments.* Oxford: H. Hall, 1666.

————. *The Origine of Formes and Qualities, (According to the Corpuscular Philosophy)* *Illustrated by Considerations and Experiments.* 2nd ed. Oxford: H. Hall, 1667.

————. "Tryals Proposed by Mr. Boyle to Dr. Lower, to be Made by Him, for the Improvement of Transfusing Blood out of One Live Animal into Another." *Philosophical Transactions* 1, no. 22 (1665–1666): 385–88.

————. *The Works of Robert Boyle.* 14 vols. London: Pickering & Chatto, 1999–2000.

Brine, John. *A Vindication of some Truths of Natural and Revealed Religion.* London: Aaron Ward, 1746.

Brucker, Johann Jakob. *Historia critica philosophiae.* 2nd ed. 6 vols. Leipzig, 1766–1767.

————. *The History of Philosophy.* Translated by William Enfield. 2 vols. London: J. Johnson, 1791.

Burgersdijck, Franco. *Idea philosophiae, tum moralis, tum naturalis.* Oxford: Ioh. Lichfield, 1631.

————. *Institutionum logicarum.* Cambridge, 1637.

————. *Institutionum Metaphysicarum.* 3rd ed. London, 1653.

Burnet, Gilbert. *An Exposition of the Thirty-nine Articles of the Church of England.* London: R. Roberts, 1699.

————. *History of My Own Time.* Edited by Osmund Airy. 2 vols. Oxford: Clarendon Press, 1897.

————. *A Supplement to Burnet's* History of My Own Time. Edited by H. C. Foxcroft. Oxford: Clarendon Press, 1902.

Calamy, Edmund. *A Continuation of the Account.* 2 vols. London: R. Ford, 1727.

————. *An Historical Account of My Own Life.* Edited by John Towill Rutt. 2 vols. London: Henry Colburn, 1830.

Calvin, John. *Commentaries on the first book of Moses, called Genesis.* 2 vols. Translated by John King. Edinburgh: Calvin Translation Society, 1847–1850.

————. *Commentaries on the Epistle of Paul the Apostle to the Romans.* Translated and edited by John Owen. Edinburgh: Calvin Translation Society, 1849.

————. *Institutes of the Christian Religion.* 2 vols. Edited by John T. McNeill. Translated by Ford Lewis Battles. Philadelphia: Westminster Press, 1960.

————. *Psychopannychia.* Strasbourg: W. Rihelium, 1545.

————. *Treatises against the Anabaptists and against the Libertines.* Edited and translated by Benjamin Farley. Grand Rapids, MI: Baker, 1982.

Cameron, John. *Praelectionum in selectora quaedam Novi Testamenti loca Salmurii habitarum.* 3 vols. Saumur: Cl. Girard and Dan. Lerpinerius, 1628.

Campanella, Tommaso. *Metaphysica.* 1638. Reprint, Torino: Bottega D'Erasmo, 1961.

Cavendish, Margaret. *Philosophicall Fancies.* London: Tho. Roycroft, 1653.

Charleton, Walter. *The Darkness of Atheism Refuted by the Light of Nature: A Physico–Theologicall Treatise.* London, 1652.

————. *Epicurus's Morals.* London: W. Wilson, 1656.

————. *The Immortality of the Human Soul, Demonstrated by the Light of Nature.* London: William Wilson, 1657.

————. *Physiologia Epicuro–Gassendo–Charltoniana: Or a Fabrick of Science Natural, Upon the Hypothesis of Atoms, Founded by Epicurus, Repaired by Petrus Gassendus, Augmented by Walter Charleton.* London: Thomas Newcomb, 1654.

Clifford, Samuel. *An Account of the Judgment of the Late Reverend Mr. Baxter.* London: John Lawrence, 1701.

Collins, Anthony. *A Letter to the Learned Henry Dodwell; Containing Some Remarks on a (pretended) Demonstration of the Immateriality and Natural Immortality of the Soul.* 2nd ed. London: A. Baldwin, 1709.

————. *A Reply to Mr. Clark's Defence of His Letter to Mr. Dodwell.* London, 1707.

Comenius, Johann Amos. *Naturall Philosophy Reformed by Divine Light; or, A Synopsis of Physicks.* London, 1651.

————. *A Reformation of Schooles.* London: Michael Sparke, 1642.

Cumberland, Richard. *A Treatise of the Laws of Nature.* Edited by Jon Parkin. Translated by John Maxwell. Indianapolis: Liberty Fund, 2005.

Cumming, John. *A Funeral Sermon on Occasion of the Death of the Late Reverend and Learned Mr. Benjamin Robinson.* London: John Clark, 1724.

D'Ailly, Pierre. *Quaestiones super libros Sententiarum Petri Lombardi.* [Lyon]: Nicolaus Wolf, 1500.

Daneau, Lambert. *Ethices christianae libri tres.* Geneva: Eustache Vignon, 1577.

————. *Isagoges christianae pars quinta, quae est de homine.* Geneva: Eustache Vignon, 1588.

————. *Physice christiana, sive, christiana de rerum creatarum origine, & usu disputatio.* 4th ed. Geneva: Ex officina Vignoniana, 1602.

Davenant, John. *Animadversions Written by the Right Reverend Father in God, John Lord Bishop of Sarisbury, upon a Treatise Intituled, Gods Love to Mankinde.* London: John Partridge, 1641.

————. *Dissertationes duae.* Cambridge: Roger Daniel, 1650.

————. *Expositio epistolae D. Pauli ad Colossenses.* Cambridge: Thomas and John Buck, 1630.

————. *An Exposition of the Epistle of St. Paul to the Colossians.* Translated by Josiah Allport. 2 vols. London: Hamilton, Adams, & Co., 1831–1832.

Descartes, René. *Meditations, Objections, and Replies.* Edited and translated by Roger Ariew and Donald Cress. Indianapolis: Hackett, 2006.

————. *Oeuvres de Descartes.* Edited by Charles Adam and Paul Tannery. 13 vols. Paris: Léopold Cerf, 1897–1913.

————. *The Philosophical Writings of Descartes.* Translated by John Cottingham, Robert Stoothoff, and Dugald Murdoch. 3 vols. Cambridge: Cambridge University Press, 1985–1991.

————. *Principles of Philosophy.* Translated by Valentine Rodger Miller and Reese P. Miller. Dordrecht: D. Reidel, 1983.

Digby, Kenelm. *Two Treatises*. Paris: Gilles Blaizot, 1644.

Doddridge, Philip. *The Correspondence and Diary of Philip Doddridge*. 5 vols. Edited by J. D. Humphreys. London: Henry Colburn & Richard Bentley, 1829–1831.

———. *A Course of Lectures on the Principle Subjects in Pneumatology, Ethics, and Divinity*. London: J. Buckland et al., 1763.

Doolittle, Thomas. *A Complete Body of Practical Divinity*. London: John and Barham Clark, 1723.

———. *Earthquakes Explained and Practically Improved*. London: John Salusbury, 1693.

———. *The Lord's Last-Sufferings Shewed in the Lords Supper*. London: John Dunton, 1682.

Duns Scotus, John. *Opera omnia*. 26 vols. Paris: Vives, 1891–1895.

———. *Philosophical Writings*. Translated and edited by Alan Wolter. Indianapolis: Hackett, 1987.

Edwards, Jonathan. *The Works of Jonathan Edwards*. 26 vols. New Haven, CT: Yale University Press, 1957–2008.

Edwards, Thomas. *The Paraselene Dismantled of her Cloud. Or, Baxterianism Barefac'd*. London: Will. Marshal, 1699.

Elys, Edmund. *Animadversiones in aliqua C. Jansenii, Guillielmi Twissi Richardi Baxteri, et Gerardi de Vries, dogmata*. London: E. P., 1706.

Enty, John. *A Preservative Against Several Abuses and Corruptions of Reveal'd Religion*. Exon: Andrew Brice, 1730.

Evelyn, John. *An Essay on the First Book of T. Lucretius Carus De rerum natura*. London: Gabriel Bedle and Thomas Collins, 1656.

Fabri, Filippo. *Philosophia naturalis Ioan. Duns Scoti, ex quatuor libris sententiarum et quodlibetis collecta*. Venice: Bertonus, 1606.

Fabri, Honoré. *Tractatus physicus de motu locali*. Lyon: Joannes Champion, 1646.

Faustus of Riez. "Incipit epistola sancti Faustini ad Benedictum Paulinum." In *Veterum aliquot Galliae theologorum scripta*, 134–41. Paris: Sebastian Nivell, 1586.

Ferguson, Robert. *The Interest of Reason in Religion*. London: Dorman Newman, 1675.

———. *A Sober Enquiry into the Nature, Measure, and Principles of Moral Virtue*. London: D. Newman, 1673.

Fletcher, John. *A Vindication of the Rev. Mr. Wesley's Last Minutes*. Bristol: W. Pine, 1771.

Fowler, Edward. *Principles and Practices of Certain Moderate Divines of the Church of England*. London: Lodowick Lloyd, 1670.

Galilei, Galileo. *Two New Sciences*. Translated by Stillman Drake. Toronto: Wall & Thompson, 1989.

Gassendi, Pierre. *Opera omnia*. 6 vols. Lyon: Laurentius Anisson & Joan. Bapt. Devenet, 1658.

Gipps, Thomas. *Tentamen novum continuatum*. London: Tho. Warren, 1699.

Glanvill, Joseph. *A Blow at Modern Sadducism*. London: E. C., 1668.

———. *Essays on Several Important Subjects in Philosophy and Religion*. London: J. D., 1676.

———. *ΛΟΓΟΥ ΘΡΗΣΚΕΙΑ: Or, A Seasonable Recommendation and Defence of Reason in the Affairs of Religion*. London: J. M., 1670.

———. *Philosophia Pia, Or, A Discourse of the Religious Temper, and Tendencies of the Experimental Philosophy, which is profest by the Royal Society*. London: J. Macock, 1671.

———. *Plus Ultra: Or, the Progress and Advancement of Knowledge since the Days of Aristotle*. London: James Collins, 1668.

———. *Scepsis Scientifica: Or, Confest Ignorance, the Way to Science*. London: E. Cotes, 1665.

———. *Some Discourses, Sermons, and Remains*. London: Henry Mortlock, 1681.

———. *The Vanity of Dogmatizing*. London: E. C., 1661.

Glisson, Francis. *De natura substantiae energetica*. London: E. Flesher, 1672.

Goclenius, Rodolphus. *Lexicon philosophicum*. Frankfurt: Matthew Becker, 1613.

Godard, Pierre. *Lexicon philosophicum*. 2 vols. Paris, 1675.

Gott, Samuel. *The Divine History of the Genesis of the World Explicated and Illustrated*. London: E. C. & A. C. for Henry Eversden, 1670.

Hale, Matthew. *Difficiles Nugae: Or, Observations Touching the Torricellian Experiment*. London: W. Godbid for William Shrowsbury, 1674.

———. *A Discourse of the Knowledge of God, and of our Selves*. London: B. W. for William Shrowsbery, 1688.

———. *Observations Touching the Principles of Natural Motions*. London: W. Godbid, 1677.

———. *Of the Law of Nature*. Edited by David S. Sytsma. Grand Rapids, MI: CLP Academic, 2015.

———. *The Primitive Origination of Mankind*. London: William Godbid, 1677.

———. *The Works, Moral and Religious*. Edited by Thomas Thirwall. 2 vols. London: H. D. Symonds, 1805.

Hall, Thomas. *Vindiciae Literarum, The Schools Guarded*. London: W. H., 1654.

Hobbes, Thomas. *Leviathan*. Edited by Richard Tuck. Cambridge: Cambridge University Press, 1996.

———. *On the Citizen*. Translated and edited by Richard Tuck and Michael Silverthorne. Cambridge: Cambridge University Press, 1998.

Holzfus, Barthold. *Dissertatio theologica, de libero hominis arbitrio . . . praeside Bartholdo Holtzfus*. Frankfurt: Christopher Zeitler, 1707.

Hooke, Robert. *An Attempt to Prove the Motion of the Earth from Observations*. London: T. R., 1674.

———. *Micrographia*. London: Jo. Martin, and Ja. Allestry, Printers to the Royal Society, 1665.

———. *The Posthumous Works of Robert Hooke*. London: Sam. Smith and Benj. Walford, 1705.

Hooker, Richard. *The Folger Library Edition of The Works of Richard Hooker*. Edited by
    W. Speed Hill. 6 vols. Cambridge, MA: Belknap Press, 1977–1993.

Howe, John. *The Living Temple, or, A Designed Improvement of that Notion, that a Good
    Man is the Temple of God*. London: John Starkey, 1675.

———. *The Living Temple, Part II. Containing Animadversions on Spinoza, and a
    French Writer pretending to Confute him*. London: Thomas Parkhurst, 1702.

Iredell, Francis. *Remarks upon some Passages*. Dublin: S. Powell, 1726.

Jackson, Thomas. *A Treatise of the Divine Essence and Attributes*. London: M. F. for
    Iohn Clarke, 1628.

Junius, Franciscus. *De politiae Mosis observatione*. 2nd ed. Leiden: Christopher
    Guyotius, 1602.

———. *The Mosaic Polity*. Translated by Todd M. Rester. Edited by Andrew M.
    McGinnis. Grand Rapids, MI: CLP Academic, 2015.

Keckermann, Bartholomaeus. *Systema ethicae*. London, 1607.

Kettner, Friedrich Ernst. *Exercitationes historico-theologicae de religione prudentum*.
    [Jenae]: Bielke, 1701.

Kippis, Andrew. "Doddridge (Philip)." In *Biographia Britannica*, 2nd ed., 5:266–315.
    London, 1793.

La Primaudaye, Pierre de. *The Second Part of the French Academie*. London: G.
    B[ishop] R[alph] N[ewbery] R. B[arker], 1594.

Le Grand, Jean–François. *Dissertationes philosophicae et criticae*. Paris: Petrus
    Menard, 1657.

Leibniz, Gottfried Wilhelm. *Philosophical Papers and Letters*. Translated and edited by
    Leroy E. Loemker. 2nd ed. Dordrecht: Kluwer Academic, 1989.

Leigh, Edward. *A Systeme or Body of Divinity*. London: A. M., 1662.

———. *A Treatise of Divinity Consisting of Three Books*. London: E. Griffin, 1646.

Locke, John. *An Essay Concerning Human Understanding*. Edited by Peter Nidditch.
    Oxford: Clarendon Press, 1975.

Lower, Richard. "The Method Observed in Transfusing the Blood out of One Animal
    into Another." *Philosophical Transactions* 1, no. 20 (1665–1666): 353–58.

Manlove, Timothy. *The Immortality of the Soul Asserted and Practically Improved*.
    London: R. Roberts, 1697.

Maresius, Samuel. *Collegium theologicum*. 6th ed. Geneva: Joannes Antonius et
    Samuel de Tournes, 1662.

Maxwell, John. *A Discourse Concerning God*. London: W. Taylor, 1715.

Mede, Joseph. *Diatribae pars IV. Discourses on Sundry Texts of Scripture*. London: J.
    F. for John Clark, 1652.

Melanchthon, Philip. *Loci communes theologici*. In *Melanchthon and Bucer*. Edited by
    Wilhelm Pauck. Translated by Lowell J. Satre. London: Westminster Press, 1969.

Melchior, Johann. *Epistola ad amicum, continens censuram. Libri cui titulus:* Tractatus
    theologico-politicus. Utrecht: C. Noenaert, 1671.

Micraelius, Johannes. *Lexicon philosophicum terminorum philosophis usitatorum.* Jena: J. Mamphrasius, 1653.

More, Henry. "Annotations." In *Two Choice and Useful Treatises: the One Lux Oritentalis; Or An Enquiry into the Opinions of the Eastern Sages Concerning the Praeexistence of Souls. Being a Key to unlock the Grand Mysteries of Providence. In Relation to Man's Sin and Misery* [by Joseph Glanvill]. *The Other, A Discourse of Truth, By the late Reverend Dr. Rust, Lord Bishop of Dromore in Ireland. With Annotations on them both* [by Henry More]. London: J. Collins and S. Loundes, 1682.

———. *An Answer to a Letter of a Learned Psychopyrist Concerning the True Notion of a Spirit.* London: S. Lownds, 1681. [Printed in *Saducismus Triumphatus: Or, Full and Plain Evidence Concerning Witches and Apparitions.* 2nd ed. London: Tho. Newcomb, 1682.]

———. *An Antidote against Atheism.* London: Roger Daniel, 1653.

———. *An Antidote against Atheism.* 2nd ed. London: J. Flesher, 1655.

———. *Democritus Platonissans, or, An Essay upon the Infinity of Worlds out of Platonick Principles.* Cambridge: Roger Daniel, 1646.

———. *Enchiridion metaphysicum: sive, de rebus incorporeis succincta & luculenta dissertatio.* London: E. Flesher, 1671.

———. *The Immortality of the Soul.* London: J. Flesher, 1659.

Mornay, Philippe de. *A Worke Concerning the Trunesse of Christian Religion.* London: George Purstowe, 1617.

Mosley, Nicholas. *ΨΥΧΟΣΟΦΙΑ: or, Natural and Divine Contemplations of the Passions & Faculties of the Soul of Man.* London: Humphrey Mosley, 1653.

Musculus, Wolfgang. *In epistolam apostoli Pauli ad Romanos commentarii.* Basel: ex officina Hervagiana, 1562.

———. *Loci communes in usus sacrae theologiae candidatorum parati.* Basel: Johann Herwagen, 1560.

Newton, Isaac. *Mathematical Principles of Natural Philosophy.* Translated by Andrew Mott and Florian Cajori. 2 vols. Berkeley: University of California Press, 1966.

Nye, Stephen. *The Doctrine of the Holy Trinity, and the Manner of our Saviour's Divinity.* London: Andrew Bell, 1701.

———. *The Explication of the Articles of the Divine Unity, the Trinity, and Incarnation.* London: John Darby, 1703.

———. *Institutions, Concerning the Holy Trinity, and the Manner of our Saviour's Divinity.* London: J. Nutt, 1703.

Orton, Job. *Memoirs of Life, Character and Writings of the Late Reverend Philip Doddridge, D. D. of Northampton.* Salop: J. Cotton and J. Eddowes, 1766.

Paley, William. *Natural Theology: Or, the Evidences of the Existence and Attributes of the Deity.* 2nd ed. London: R. Faulder, 1802.

Palmer, Samuel (d. 1813). Preface to *The Reformed Pastor; A Discourse on the Pastoral Office,* by Richard Baxter, iii–xv. London: J. Buckland, 1766.

Palmer, Samuel (d. 1724). *A Vindication of the Learning, Loyalty, Morals, and Most Christian Behaviour of the Dissenters toward the Church of England.* London: J. Lawrence, 1705.

Pareus, David. *In divinam S. Pauli apostoli Romanos epistolam commentarius.* Frankfurt: Jona Rhodius, 1608.

Parker, Samuel. *A Free and Impartial Censure of the Platonick Philosophie.* Oxford: W. Hall, 1666.

———. *Tentamina physico-theologica de Deo.* London: A. M., 1665.

Patrick, Simon. *A Brief Account of the new Sect of Latitude–Men, Together with some reflections upon the New Philosophy. By S. P. of Cambridge. In answer to a Letter from his Friend at Oxford.* London, 1662.

———. *A Friendly Debate between a Conformist and Non-Conformist.* London, 1669.

Peter Lombard. *Libri quatuor Sententiarum.* Paris: Jacob Du-puys, 1574.

Peter of Aquila. *Scotellus. Ubi non tantum ad Scoti subtilitates, sed etiam ad D. Thomae, reliquorumque scholasticorum doctrinam facilis via paratur.* Paris: Nicolaum Nivellium, 1585.

Plotinus. *Plotini Platonicorum coryphaei opera quae extant omnia per Marsilium Ficinum.* Basel: Ludovicus Rex, 1615.

Polanus von Polansdorf, Amandus. *Syntagma theologiae christianae.* Hanau, 1610.

Power, Henry. *Experimental Philosophy.* London, 1664.

Prideaux, John. *Hypomnemata logica, rhetorica, physica, metaphysica, pneumatica, ethica, politica, oeconomica.* Oxford: Leonar. Lichfield, 1650.

Priestley, Joseph. *Theological and Miscellaneous Works.* Edited by John Towill Rutt. 25 vols. London: G. Smallfield, 1817–1832.

Rada, Juan de. *Controversiae theologicae inter S. Thoman et Scotum, super quatuor libros sententiarum.* 4 vols. Cologne: Joannes Crithius, 1620.

Rainolds, John. *Censura librorum apocryphorum Veteris Testamenti, adversum Pontificios, inprimis Robertum Bellarminum.* 2 vols. Oppenheim, 1611.

Ray, John. *The Wisdom of God Manifested in the Works of Creation.* London, 1691.

Regius, Henricus. *Philosophica naturalis.* Amsterdam: Apud Ludovicum & Danielem Elzevirios, 1661.

Reitz, Johan Henrich. *Historie der Wiedergebohrnen.* Vol. 3. [Itzstein]: [Haug], 1717.

Reyner, Edward. *A Treatise of the Necessity of Humane Learning for a Gospel-Preacher.* London: John Field, 1663.

Richard of St. Victor. *Opera.* Cologne: Apud Ioannem Gymnicum, 1621.

Rivet, André. *Catholicus orthodoxus.* Geneva: Jacob Chouet, 1644.

[Robinson, Benjamin]. *A Plea for the Late Accurate and Excellent Mr. Baxter.* London: J[ohn] Lawrence, 1699.

Rohault, Jacques. *Rohault's System of Natural Philosophy, Illustrated with Dr. Samuel Clarke's Notes taken mostly out of Sir Isaac Newton's Philosophy.* Translated by John Clarke. 3rd ed. 2 vols. London: James, John, and Paul Knapton, 1735.

Rolle, Samuel. *A Sober Answer to the Friendly Debate Betwixt a Conformist and a Nonconformist*. London, 1669.

Ross, Alexander. *Arcana Microcosmi: Or, the hid Secrets of Mans Body disclosed*. London: Thomas Newcomb, 1651.

———. *The Philosophicall Touch-stone*. London: James Young, 1645.

Rutherford, Samuel. *Disputatio scholastica de divina providentia*. Edinburgh: George Anderson, 1649.

———. *Exercitationes apologeticae pro divina gratia*. Amsterdam: Henricus Laurentius, 1636.

Salden, Willem. *De libris, varioque eorum usu et abusu libri duo*. Amsterdam: H. & T. Boom, 1688.

———. *Otia theologica*. Amsterdam: H. & T. Boom, 1684.

Sanderson, Robert. *Bishop Sanderson's Lectures on Conscience and Human Law*. Translated by Christopher Wordsworth. Lincoln: James Williamson, 1877.

Schaff, Philip, ed. *The Creeds of Christendom*. 3 vols. New York: Harper & Brothers, 1877.

Scheibler, Christopher. *Metaphysica*. Geneva: Jacob Stoer, 1636.

Sennert, Daniel. *Thirteen Books of Natural Philosophy*. London: Peter Cole, 1660.

S[mith], M[atthew]. *A Philosophical Discourse of the Nature of Rational and Irrational Souls*. London, 1695.

Sorbière, Samuel. *Relation d'un voyage en Angleterre*. Cologne: Pierre Michel, 1666.

Spencer, Thomas. *The Art of Logick, Delivered in the Precepts of Aristotle and Ramus*. London: John Dawson, 1638.

Spinoza, Benedict de. *Complete Works*. Translated by Samuel Shirley. Edited by Michael Morgan. Indianapolis: Hackett, 2002.

———. *Theological–Political Treatise*. Edited by Jonathan Israel. Translated by Michael Silverthorne and Jonathan Israel. Cambridge: Cambridge University Press, 2007.

Sprat, Thomas. *The History of the Royal Society, for the Improving of Natural Knowledge*. London: T. R., 1667.

———. *Observations on Monsieur de Sorbier's Voyage into England*. London: John Martyn, 1665.

Stanley, Thomas. *The History of Philosophy. The First Volume*. London: Humphrey Moseley and Thomas Dring, 1655.

———. *The History of Philosophy, The Second Volume*. London: Humphrey Moseley and Thomas Dring, 1656.

———. *The History of Philosophy, The Third and Last Volume, in Five Parts*. London: Humphrey Moseley and Thomas Dring, 1660.

Stillingfleet, Edward. *Origines Sacrae*. London: R. W., 1662.

Suárez, Francisco. *On Efficient Causality: Metaphysical Disputations 17, 18, and 19*. Translated by Alfred J. Freddoso. New Haven, CT: Yale University Press, 1994.

———. *On the Formal Cause of Substance: Metaphysical Disputation XV.* Translated by John Kronen and Jeremiah Reedy. Milwaukee, WI: Marquette University Press, 2000.

———. *Opera omnia.* 28 vols. Paris: L. Vivès, 1856–1866.

———. *Selections from Three Works of Francisco Suárez, S. J.: De legibus, ac deo legislatore, 1612; Defensio fidei catholicae, et apostolicae adversus anglicanae sectae errores, 1613; De triplici virtute theologica, fide, spe, et charitate, 1621.* 2 vols. Oxford: Clarendon Press/London: H. Milford, 1944.

Sylvestris, Francis de. *Commentaria in libros quatuor contra gentiles S. Thomae de Aquino.* 4 vols. Rome: sumptibus et typis Orphanotrophii a. S. Hieronymo Aemiliani, 1897.

Thomas Aquinas. *On the Truth of the Catholic Faith: Summa Contra Gentiles.* Translated by Anton C. Pegis, James F. Anderson, Vernon J. Bourke, and Charles J. O'Neil. 4 vols. Garden City, NY: Doubleday Image Books, 1955.

———. *Opera omnia iussu Leonis XIII. O. M. edita.* Rome, 1882–.

———. *The Power of God.* Translated by Richard J. Regan. Oxford: Oxford University Press, 2012.

———. *Summa contra gentiles.* In *Opera omnia,* vols. 13–15.

———. *Summa theologiae.* In *Opera omnia,* vols. 4–12.

———. *Summa theologica.* Translated by the Fathers of the English Dominican Province. 5 vols. 1911; repr., Westminster, MD: Christian Classics, 1981.

Thorndike, Herbert. *The Theological Works of Herbert Thorndike.* 6 vols. Oxford: John Henry Parker, 1844–1856.

Turretin, Francis. *Institutio theologiae elencticae.* 3 vols. Geneva, 1679–1685.

Twisse, William. *Vindiciae gratiae, potestatis ac providentiae Dei.* Amsterdam: Joannes Janssonius, 1648.

Mastricht, Petrus van. *Novitatum Cartesianarum gangraena.* Amsterdam: Janssoons van Waesberghe, 1677.

Vedel, Nicolaus. *Rationale theologicum seu de necessitate et vero usu principiorum rationis ac philosophiae in controversiis theologicis libri tres.* Geneva: Jacob Chouet, 1628.

Vermigli, Peter Martyr. *In epistolam S. Pauli apostoli ad Romanos.* Zürich, 1559.

———. *Most Learned and Fruitful Commentaries . . . upon the Epistle of S. Paul to the Romans.* Translated by Sir Henry Billingsley. London: John Daye, 1568.

Voetius, Gisbertus. *Exercitia et bibliotheca studiosi theologiae.* Utrecht: Willem Strick, 1644.

———. *Selectarum disputationum theologicarum.* 5 vols. Utrecht: Johannes a Waesberge, 1648–1669.

Wallis, John. *Mechanica, sive, De motu, tractatus geometricus.* London: G. Godbid, 1670.

[War]d, [Set]h. *Vindiciae Academiarum.* Introduction by [Joh]N. [Wilkin]S. Oxford: Leonard Lichfield, 1654.

Watts, Isaac. *Dissertations Relating to the Christian Doctrine of the Trinity, The Second Part.* London: J. Clark and R. Hett, 1725.

———. *Works.* 6 vols. London: John Barfield, 1810.

Weemes, John. *The Portraiture of the Image of God in Man.* 3rd ed. London: Thomas Cotes for John Bellamie, 1636.

White, Thomas. *Sciri, sive, sceptices & scepticorum jure disputationis exclusio.* London, 1663.

Wilkins, John. *A Discourse Concerning a New Planet. Tending to Prove, That 'Tis Probable Our Earth Is One of the Planets.* London: R. H. for John Maynard, 1640.

Williams, Daniel. *Discourses on Several Important Subjects.* Vol. 5. London: James Waugh, 1750.

———. *An End to Discord.* London: John Lawrence and Tho. Cockeril, 1699.

Willis, Thomas. *De anima brutorum quae hominis vitalis ac sensitiva est, exercitationes duae.* Oxford: Ric. Davis, 1672.

———. *Diatribae duae medico-philosophicae.* London: Tho. Roycroft, 1659.

———. *Pathalogiae cerebri, et nervosi generis specimen.* Oxford, 1667.

———. *Two Discourses Concerning the Soul of Brutes, which is that of the Vital and Sensitive of Man.* Translated by S. Pordage. London: Thomas Dring, 1683.

Willet, Andrew. *Hexapla: that is, A Six-fold Commentarie upon the most Divine Epistle of the holy Apostle S. Paul to the Romanes.* London: Cantrell Legge, 1611.

Wilson, John. *The Scriptures Genuine Interpreter Asserted.* [London]: T. N. for R. Boulter, 1678.

Wittich, Christoph. *Dissertationes duae quarum prior de S. Scripturae in rebus philosophicis abusu.* Amsterdam: L. Elzevirius, 1653.

———. *Theologia pacifica.* 3rd ed. Leiden: C. Boutesteyn, 1683.

Wülfer, Daniel. *De physica christiana exercitio.* Nürnberg: Christophor Gerhard, 1656.

Zanchi, Girolamo. *Omnium operum theologicorum.* Geneva, 1619.

———. *On the Law in General.* Translated by Jeffrey J. Veenstra. Grand Rapids, MI: CLP Academic, 2012.

III. SECONDARY SOURCES

Aaron, Richard I. *John Locke.* 3rd ed. Oxford: Clarendon Press, 1971.

Aarsleff, Hans. "John Wilkins." In *Dictionary of Scientific Biography,* edited by Charles C. Gillispie, 14:361–81. New York: Charles Scribner's Sons, 1976.

Adam, Antoine. "L'influence de Gassendi sur le mouvement des idées à la fin du XVII siècle." In *Actes du Congrès du Tricentenaire de Pierre Gassendi,* 7–11. Paris: Presses universitaires de France, 1957.

Adelmann, Howard B. *Marcello Malpighi and the Evolution of Embryology.* 5 vols. Ithaca, NY: Cornell University Press, 1966.

Albury, W. R. "Halley's Ode on the *Principia* of Newton and the Epicurean Revival in England." *Journal of the History of Ideas* 39, no. 1 (1978): 24–43.

Allen, Phyllis. "Scientific Studies in the English Universities of the Seventeenth Century." *Journal of the History of Ideas* 10, no. 2 (1949): 219–53.

Allen, Richard. *David Hartley on Human Nature*. Albany, NY: SUNY Press, 1999.

Anstey, Peter R. "Boyle on Seminal Principles." *Studies in History and Philosophy of Science* 33 (2002): 597–630.

———. *The Philosophy of Robert Boyle*. New York: Routledge, 2000.

Ariew, Roger. "Les *Principia* et la *Summa Philosophica Quadripartita*." In *Descartes: Principia Philosophiae (1644–1994)*, edited by Jean Robert Armogathe and Giulia Belgioioso, 473–89. Naples: Vivarium, 1996.

Ariew, Roger, and Alan Gabbey. "The Scholastic Background." In *CHSP*, 1:425–53.

Arthur, Richard. "Beeckman, Descartes and the Force of Motion." *Journal of the History of Philosophy* 45, no. 1 (2007): 1–28.

Ashcraft, Richard. "Latitudinarianism and Toleration: Historical Myth versus Political History." In *Philosophy, Science, and Religion 1640–1700*, edited by Richard Kroll, Richard Ashcraft, and Perez Zagorin, 151–77. Cambridge: Cambridge University Press, 1992.

Ashworth, E. J. "Analogy and Equivocation in the Thirteenth-Century: Aquinas in Context." *Mediaeval Studies* 54 (1992): 94–135.

———. "Analogy, Univocation, and Equivocation in Some Early Fourteenth-Century Authors." In *Aristotle in Britain during the Middle Ages*, edited by John Marenbon, 233–47. Belgium: Brepols, 1996.

Axtell, James L. "The Mechanics of Opposition: Restoration Cambridge v. Daniel Scargill." *Bulletin of the Institute of Historical Research* 38 (1965): 102–11.

Ayres, Lewis. *Augustine and the Trinity*. Cambridge: Cambridge University Press, 2010.

Ayers, M. R. "The Foundations of Knowledge and the Logic of Substance: The Structure of Locke's General Philosophy." In *Locke's Philosophy: Content and Context*, edited by G. A. J. Rogers, 49–73. Oxford: Clarendon, 1994.

Ballor, Jordan J. *Covenant, Causality, and Law: A Study in the Theology of Wolfgang Musculus*. Göttingen: Vandenhoeck & Ruprecht, 2012.

Barth, Timotheus A. "Being, Univocity, and Analogy According to Duns Scotus." In *John Duns Scotus, 1265–1965*, edited by John K. Ryan and Bernardine M. Bonansea, 210–62. Washington, DC: Catholic University of America Press, 1965.

Bartha, Paul. "Substantial Form and the Nature of Individual Substance." *Studia Leibnitiana* 25, no. 1 (1993): 43–54.

Baschera, Luca. "Aristotle and Scholasticism." In *A Companion to Peter Martyr Vermigli*, edited by T. Kirby, E. Campi, and F. A. James III, 133–59. Leiden: Brill, 2009.

———. "Total Depravity? The Consequences of Original Sin in John Calvin and Later Reformed Theology." In *Calvinus clarissimus theologus*, edited by Herman J. Selderhuis, 37–58. Göttingen: Vandenhoeck & Ruprecht, 2012.

Bäumlin, Richard. "Naturrecht und obrigkeitliches Kirchenregiment bei Wolfgang Musculus." In *Für Kirche und Recht: Festschrift für Johannes Heckel zum 70. Geburtstag*, edited by Siegfried Grundmann, 120–43. Cologne: Böhlau, 1959.

Bavinck, Herman. *Reformed Dogmatics*. Edited by John Bolt. 4 vols. Grand Rapids, MI: Baker Academic, 2003–2008.

Beach, J. Mark. "The Hobbes-Bramhall Debate on the Nature of Freedom and Necessity." In *Biblical Interpretation and Doctrinal Formulation in the Reformed Tradition: Essays in Honor of James A. De Jong*, edited by Arie C. Leder and Richard A. Muller, 231–61. Grand Rapids, MI: Reformation Heritage Books, 2014.

Beard, Charles A. "That Noble Dream." In *The Varieties of History*, edited by Frank R. Stern, 314–28. Cleveland: World Publishing Co., 1956.

Beiser, Frederick C. *The Sovereignty of Reason: The Defense of Rationality in the Early English Enlightenment*. Princeton, NJ: Princeton University Press, 1996.

Bennett, J. A. "Cosmology and the Magnetical Philosophy, 1640–1680." *Journal for the History of Astronomy* 12 (1981): 165–77.

Berryman, Sylvia. *The Mechanical Hypothesis in Ancient Greek Natural Philosophy*. Cambridge: Cambridge University Press, 2009.

Birrell, T. A. Introduction to *A Brief Account of the New Sect of Latitude–Men*, by Simon Patrick, i–vi. 1662; repr., Los Angeles: University of California, 1963.

Bizer, Ernst. "Die reformierte Orthodoxie und der Cartesianismus." *Zeitschrift für Theologie und Kirche* 55 (1958): 306–72.

———. "Reformed Orthodoxy and Cartesianism." Translated by Chalmers MacCormick. *Journal for Theology and the Church* 11 (1965): 20–82.

Black, J. William. "Doolittle, Thomas." In *ODNB*.

Blair, Ann. "Mosaic Physics and the Search for a Pious Natural Philosophy in the Late Renaissance." *Isis* 91, no. 1 (2000): 32–58.

Bloch, René. *La philosophie de Gassendi: Nominalisme, Matérialisme et Métaphysique*. La Haye: Martinus Nijhoff, 1971.

Boersma, Hans. *A Hot Pepper Corn: Richard Baxter's Doctrine of Justification in Its Seventeenth-Century Context of Controversy*. Zoetermeer: Uitgeverij Boekencentrum, 1993.

Bonansea, Bernardino M. *Tommaso Campanella: Renaissance Pioneer of Modern Thought*. Washington, DC: The Catholic University of America Press, 1969.

Booth, Emily. *'A Subtle and Mysterious Machine': The Medical World of Walter Charleton (1619–1707)*. Dordrecht: Springer, 2005.

Boyle, G. D. *Richard Baxter*. London: Hodder and Stoughton, 1883.

Brackenridge, J. Bruce. *The Key to Newton's Dynamics: The Kepler Problem and the Principia*. Berkeley: University of California Press, 1995.

Brown, Montague. "Augustine and Aristotle on Causality." In *Augustine: Presbyter Factus Sum*, edited by Joseph T. Lienhard, Earl C. Muller, and Roland J. Teske, 465–76. New York: Peter Lang, 1993.

Brown, Theodore. *The Mechanical Philosophy and the 'Animal Oeconomy.'* New York: Arno Press, 1981.

Brundell, Barry. *Pierre Gassendi: From Aristotelianism to a New Natural Philosophy*. Dordrecht: Kluwer Academic, 1987.

Budiman, Kalvin. "A Protestant Doctrine of Nature and Grace as Illustrated by Jerome Zanchi's Appropriation of Thomas Aquinas." PhD diss., Baylor University, 2011.

Burden, Mark. "Academical Learning in the Dissenters' Private Academies." PhD diss., University of London, 2012.

———. "A Biographical Dictionary of Tutors at the Dissenters' Private Academies, 1660–1729." London: Dr. Williams's Centre for Dissenting Studies, 2013. http://www.qmulreligionandliterature.co.uk/wp-content/uploads/2015/11/bd.pdf.

Burnham, Frederic B. "The Latitudinarian Background to the Royal Society, 1647–1667." PhD diss., The Johns Hopkins University, 1970.

———. "The More-Vaughan Controversy: The Revolt against Philosophical Enthusiasm." *Journal of the History of Ideas* 35, no. 1 (1974): 33–49.

Burns, Norman T. *Christian Mortalism from Tyndale to Milton.* Cambridge, MA: Harvard University Press, 1972.

Burton, Simon J. G. "Faith, Reason, and the Trinity in Richard Baxter's Theology: Incipient Rationalism or Scholastic *Fides Quarens Intellectum?*" *Calvin Theological Journal* 49 (2014): 85–111.

———. *The Hallowing of Logic: The Trinitarian Method of Richard Baxter's* Methodus Theologiae. Leiden: Brill, 2012.

———. "Samuel Rutherford's *Euthyphro* Dilemma: A Reformed Perspective on the Scholastic Natural Law Tradition." In *Reformed Orthodoxy in Scotland: Essays on Scottish Theology 1560–1775,* edited by Aaron Clay Denlinger, 123–39. London: Bloomsbury Academic, 2015.

Buzon, Frédéric de. "Beeckman, Descartes and Physico–Mathematics." In *The Mechanization of Natural Philosophy,* edited by Daniel Garber and Sophie Roux, 143–58. Dordrecht: Springer, 2013.

Calloway, Katherine. *Natural Theology in the Scientific Revolution: God's Scientists.* London: Pickering & Chatto, 2014.

Campos, Andre Santos. *Spinoza's Revolutions in Natural Law.* New York: Palgrave Macmillan, 2012.

Čapková, Dagmar. "The Reception Given to the *Prodromus pansophiae,* and the Methodology of Comenius." *Acta Comeniana* 7 (1987): 37–59.

Carlyle, R. W., and A. J. Carlyle. *A History of Mediaeval Political Theory in the West.* 3rd ed. 6 vols. Edinburgh: William Blackwood & Sons, 1928–1936.

Carré, Meyrick H. *Phases of Thought in England.* Oxford: Clarendon Press, 1949.

Casey, Daniel A. "Neuroscience, Metaphysics and *Cerebri Anatome cui Accessit Nervorum Descriptio et Usus.*" *International Journal of History and Philosophy of Medicine* 1 (2011): 15–19.

Cervenka, Jaromír. *Die Naturphilosophie des Johann Amos Comenius.* Hanau: Werner Dausien, 1970.

Chappell, Vere, ed. *Hobbes and Bramhall on Liberty and Necessity.* Cambridge: Cambridge University Press, 1999.

Clericuzio, Antonio. *Elements, Principles and Corpuscles: A Study of Atomism and Chemistry in the Seventeenth Century.* Dordrecht: Kluwer Academic, 2000.

———. "Gassendi, Charleton and Boyle on Matter and Motion." In *Late Medieval and Early Modern Corpuscular Matter Theories,* edited by Christoph Lüthy, John E. Murdoch, and William R. Newman, 467–82. Leiden: E. J. Brill, 2001.

———. "The Internal Laboratory. The Chemical Reinterpretation of Medical Spirits in England (1650–1680)." In *Alchemy and Chemistry in the 16th and 17th Centuries,* edited by Piyo Rattansi and Antonio Clericuzio, 51–83. Dordrecht: Kluwer, 1994.

———. "L'atomisme de Gassendi et la philosophie corpusculaire de Boyle." In *Gassendi et l'Europe, 1592–1792,* edited by Sylvia Murr, 227–35. Paris: J. Vrin, 1997.

———. "A Redefinition of Boyle's Chemistry and Corpuscular Philosophy." *Annals of Science* 47 (1990): 561–89.

Clucas, Stephen. "The Atomism of the Cavendish Circle. A Reappraisal." *The Seventeenth Century* 9, no. 2 (1994): 247–73.

———. "Corpuscular Matter Theory in the Northumberland Circle." In *Late Medieval and Early Modern Corpuscular Matter Theories.* Edited by Christoph Lüthy, John E. Murdoch, and William R. Newman, 181–207. Leiden: E. J. Brill, 2001.

Cohen, I. Bernard. "'Quantum in se est': Newton's Concept of Inertia in Relation to Descartes and Lucretius." *Notes and Records of the Royal Society of London* 19, no. 2 (1964): 131–55.

Colie, Rosalie L. *Light and Enlightenment: A Study of the Cambridge Platonists and the Dutch Arminians.* Cambridge: Cambridge University Press, 1957.

———. "Spinoza in England, 1665–1730." *Proceedings of the American Philosophical Society* 107, no. 3 (1963): 183–219.

Compston, Alastair. "A Short History of Clinical Neurology." In *Brain's Diseases of the Nervous System,* 12th ed., edited by Michael Donaghy, 1–15. Oxford: Oxford University Press, 2009.

Connolly, Patrick J. "Lockean Superaddition and Lockean Humility." *Studies in History and Philosophy of Science* 51 (2015): 53–61.

Cook, Harold J. "The New Philosophy in the Low Countries." In *The Scientific Revolution in National Context,* edited by Roy Porter and Mikuláš Teich, 115–49. Cambridge: Cambridge University Press, 1992.

Cope, Jackson I. "'The Cupri-Cosmits': Glanvill on Latitudinarian Anti-Enthusiasm." *The Huntington Library Quarterly* 17, no. 3 (1954): 269–86.

———. *Joseph Glanvill: Anglican Apologist.* St. Louis: Washington University, 1956.

Copleston, Frederick C. *A History of Philosophy.* Vol. 3, *Late Medieval and Renaissance Philosophy.* London: Burns, Oates & Washbourne, 1953.

Costello, Frank Bartholomew. *The Political Philosophy of Luis de Molina, S. J. (1535–1600).* Rome: Institutum Historicum S. J., 1974.

Crocker, Robert. *Henry More, 1614–1687: A Biography of the Cambridge Platonist.* Dordrecht: Kluwer, 2003.

Cromartie, Alan. "*The Elements* and Hobbesian Moral Thinking." *History of Political Thought* 32, no. 1 (2011): 21–47.

———. *Sir Matthew Hale 1609–1676: Law, Religion and Natural Philosophy.* Cambridge: Cambridge University Press, 1995.

Cross, Richard. *Duns Scotus.* Oxford: Oxford University Press, 1999.

———. *The Physics of Duns Scotus: The Scientific Context of a Theological Vision.* Oxford: Clarendon Press, 1998.

———. "Where Angels Fear to Tread: Duns Scotus and Radical Orthodoxy." *Antonianum* 76 (2001): 7–41.

Curley, Edwin. "Homo Audax: Leibniz, Oldenburg and the TTP." In *Leibniz' Auseinandersetzung mit Vorgängern und Zeitgenossen,* edited by Ingrid Marchlewitz and Albert Heinekamp, 277–312. Stuttgart: Franz Steiner Verlag, 1990.

———. "The State of Nature and Its Law in Hobbes and Spinoza." *Philosophical Topics* 19, no. 1 (1991): 97–117.

Dauben, Joseph W. "Merton Thesis." In *Reader's Guide to the History of Science,* edited by Arne Hessenbruch, 469–71. Chicago: Fitzroy Dearborn, 2000.

Daugirdas, Kęstutis. "*Ratio recta scripturae interpres*: The Biblical Hermeneutics of Simon Episcopius before 1634 and Its Impact." *Bulletin annuel de l'Institut d'histoire de la Réformation* 32 (2010–2011): 37–49.

Deason, Gary B. "Reformation Theology and the Mechanistic Conception of Nature." In *God and Nature: Historical Essays on the Encounter between Christianity and Science,* edited by David C. Lindberg and Ronald L. Numbers, 167–91. Berkeley: University of California Press, 1986.

Debus, Allen G. "The Webster–Ward Debate of 1654: The New Philosophy and the Problem of Educational Reform." In *L'univers á la Renaissance: Microcosme et macrocosme,* 33–51. Brussels: Presses Universitaires de Bruxelles, 1970.

Demoss, David, and Daniel Devereux. "Essence, Existence, and Nominal Definition in Aristotle's 'Posterior Analytics' II 8–10." *Phronesis* 33, no. 2 (1988): 133–54.

D'Entrèves, Alexander Passerin. *Natural Law: An Introduction to Legal Philosophy.* New Brunswick, NJ: Transaction Publishers, 1994.

Des Chene, Dennis. *Life's Form: Late Aristotelian Conceptions of the Soul.* Ithaca, NY: Cornell University Press, 2000.

———. *Physiologia: Natural Philosophy in Late Aristotelian and Cartesian Thought.* Ithaca, NY: Cornell University Press, 1996.

———. *Spirits and Clocks: Machine & Organism in Descartes.* Ithaca, NY: Cornell University Press, 2001.

De Vet, J. J. V. M. "On Account of the Sacrosanctity of the Scriptures: Johannes Melchior against Spinoza's *Tractatus theologico–politicus.*" *Lias* 18 (1991): 229–61.

Dewhurst, Kenneth, ed. *Thomas Willis's Oxford Lectures.* Oxford: Sandford Pub., 1980.

Dijksterhuis, E. J. *The Mechanization of the World Picture.* Translated by C. Dikshoorn. Oxford: Oxford University Press, 1961.

Dillenberger, John. *Protestant Thought and Natural Science*. Garden City, NY: Doubleday, 1960.

Dobre, Minhea. "Rohault's *Traité de physique* and its Newtonian Reception." In *The Circulation of Science and Technology*, edited by A. Roca–Rosell, 389–94. Barcelona: SCHCT–IEC, 2012.

Donnelly, John Patrick. *Calvinism and Scholasticism in Vermigli's Doctrine of Man and Grace*. Leiden: Brill, 1976.

———. "Calvinist Thomism." *Viator* 7 (1976): 441–55.

Douglas, Alexander. *Spinoza and Dutch Cartesianism: Philosophy and Theology*. Oxford: Oxford University Press, 2015.

———. "Spinoza and the Dutch Cartesians on Philosophy and Theology." *Journal of the History of Philosophy* 51, no. 4 (2013): 567–88.

Douglas, Walter. "Politics and Theology in the Thought of Richard Baxter." *Andrews University Seminary Studies* 15, no. 2 (1977): 115–26.

———. "Politics and Theology in the Thought of Richard Baxter. Part II." *Andrews University Seminary Studies* 16, no. 1 (1978): 305–12.

Drake, Stillman. "Impetus Theory and Quanta of Speed before and after Galileo." *Physis* 16 (1974): 47–75.

Draper, John W. *History of the Conflict between Religion and Science*. New York: Appleton, 1874.

Dray, J. P. "The Protestant Academy of Saumur and Its Relations with the Oratorians of Les Ardilliers." *History of European Ideas* 9, no. 4 (1988): 465–78.

Driscoll, Edward. "The Influence of Gassendi on Locke's Hedonism." *International Philosophical Quarterly* 12, no. 1 (1972): 87–110.

Droge, Arthur. *Homer or Moses? Early Christian Interpretations of the History of Culture*. Tübingen: J. C. B. Mohr, 1989.

Dumont, Stephen. "Scotus's Doctrine of Univocity and the Medieval Tradition of Metaphysics." In *Was ist Philosophie im Mittelalter?*, edited by Jan Aertsen and Andreas Speer, 193–212. Berlin: De Gruyter, 1998.

———. "Transcendental Being: Scotus and Scotists." *Topoi* 11 (1992): 135–48.

Eaton, William R. *Boyle on Fire: The Mechanical Revolution in Scientific Explanation*. London: Continuum, 2005.

Ehrlich, Mark E. "Mechanism and Activity in the Scientific Revolution: The Case of Robert Hooke." *Annals of Science* 52, no. 2 (1995): 127–51.

Elazar, Michael. *Honoré Fabri and the Concept of Impetus: A Bridge Between Conceptual Frameworks*. Dordrecht: Springer, 2011.

Elazar, Michael, and Rivka Feldhay. "Honoré Fabri S. J. and Galileo's Law of Fall: What Kind of Controversy?" In *Controversies within the Scientific Revolution*, edited by Marcelo Dascal and Victor D. Boantza, 13–32. Philadelphia: John Benjamins Publishing Company, 2011.

Emory, Gilles. *The Trinitarian Theology of Saint Thomas Aquinas*. Translated by Francesca Aran Murphy. Oxford: Oxford University Press, 2007.

Erdmann, Johann Eduard. *A History of Philosophy*. Translated by W. S. Hough. 2nd ed. 3 vols. London: Swan Sonnenschein & Co., 1891.

Ernst, Germana. *Tommaso Campanella: The Book and the Body of Nature*. Translated by David L. Marshall. Dordrecht: Springer, 2010.

Fabian, Bernard. "Ein Apologet der Royal Society: Joseph Glanvill." In *Die Philosophie des 17. Jahrhunderts*, vol. 3, bk. 2, *England*, edited by Jean–Pierre Schobinger, 435–41. Basel: Schwabe, 1988.

Feingold, Mordechai. "Isaac Barrow: Divine, Scholar, Mathematician." In *Before Newton: The Life and Times of Isaac Barrow*, edited by Mordechai Feingold, 1–104. Cambridge: Cambridge University Press, 1990.

———. "The Mathematical Sciences and New Philosophies." In *The History of the University of Oxford*, vol. 4, *Seventeenth–Century Oxford*, edited by Nicholas Tyacke, 359–448. Oxford: Clarendon Press, 1997.

Fiering, Norman. *Moral Philosophy at Seventeenth–Century Harvard: A Discipline in Transition*. Chapel Hill: The University of North Carolina Press, 1981.

Fisch, Harold. "The Scientist as Priest: A Note on Robert Boyle's Natural Theology." *Isis* 44, no. 3 (1953): 252–65.

Fisher, George Park. "The Theology of Richard Baxter." *Bibliotheca Sacra and American Biblical Repository* 9 (1852): 135–69.

———. "The Writings of Richard Baxter." *Bibliotheca Sacra and American Biblical Repository* 9 (1852): 300–329.

Fisk, Philip John. *Jonathan Edwards's Turn from the Classic–Reformed Tradition of Freedom of the Will*. Göttingen: Vandenhoeck & Ruprecht, 2016.

Fouke, Daniel. *The Enthusiastical Concerns of Dr. Henry More: Religious Meaning and the Psychology of Delusion*. Leiden: Brill, 1997.

Frank, Robert G., Jr. *Harvey and the Oxford Physiologists*. Berkeley: University of California Press, 1980.

———. "Thomas Willis and His Circle: Brain and Mind in Seventeenth–Century Medicine." In *The Languages of Psyche: Mind and Body in Enlightenment Thought*, edited by G. S. Rousseau, 107–46. Berkeley: University of California Press, 1990.

French, Roger. *William Harvey's Natural Philosophy*. Cambridge: Cambridge University Press, 1994.

Fuchs, Thomas. *The Mechanization of the Heart: Harvey and Descartes*. Translated by Marjorie Grene. Rochester, NY: The University of Rochester Press, 2001.

Funkenstein, Amos. *Theology and the Scientific Imagination: From the Middle Ages to the Seventeenth Century*. Princeton, NJ: Princeton University Press, 1986.

Gabbey, Alan. "Cudworth, More and the Mechanical Philosophy." In *Philosophy, Science, and Religion 1640–1700*, edited by Richard Kroll, Richard Ashcraft, and Perez Zagorin, 109–27. Cambridge: Cambridge University Press, 1992.

———. "Henry More and the Limits of Mechanism." In *Henry More (1614–1687): Tercentenary Studies*, edited by Sarah Hutton and Robert Crocker, 19–35. Dordrecht: Kluwer, 1990.

————. "*Philosophia Cartesiana Triumphata*: Henry More (1646–1671)." In *Problems of Cartesianism*, edited by Thomas M. Lennon, John N. Nicholas, and John W. Davis, 171–250. Toronto: McGill–Queens University Press, 1982.

————. "The *Principia Philosophiae* as a Treatise in Natural Philosophy." In *Descartes: Principia Philosophiae (1644–1994)*, edited by Jean Robert Armogathe and Giulia Belgioioso, 517–29. Naples: Vivarium, 1996.

————. "What Was 'Mechanical' about 'The Mechanical Philosophy'?" In *The Reception of the Galilean Science of Motion in Seventeenth–Century Europe*, edited by Carla Rita Palmerino and J. M. M. H. Thijssen, 11–23. Springer: Kluwer Academic, 2004.

Gallagher, David. "Thomas Aquinas on the Will as Rational Appetite." *Journal of the History of Philosophy* 29 (1991): 559–84.

Galluzzi, Paolo. "Galileo and *l'Affaire Galilée* of the Laws of Motion." In *Galileo in Context*, edited by Jürgen Renn, 239–75. Cambridge: Cambridge University Press, 2001.

Garber, Daniel. "Descartes, Mechanics, and the Mechanical Philosophy." *Midwest Studies in Philosophy* 26 (2002): 185–204.

————. *Descartes' Metaphysical Physics*. Chicago: The University of Chicago Press, 1992.

————. *Leibniz: Body, Substance, Monad*. Oxford: Oxford University Press, 2011.

————. "Leibniz on Form and Matter." *Early Science and Medicine* 2, no. 3 (1997): 326–52.

————. "Natural Philosophy in Seventeenth-Century Context." In *The Oxford Handbook of Hobbes*, edited by A. P. Martinich and Kinch Hoekstra, 106–33. Oxford: Oxford University Press, 2016.

————. "Physics and Foundations." In *The Cambridge History of Science*, edited by Katherine Park and Lorraine Daston, vol. 3, *Early Modern Science*, 21–69. Cambridge: Cambridge University Press, 2006.

————. "Remarks on the Pre-history of the Mechanical Philosophy." In *The Mechanization of Natural Philosophy*, edited by Daniel Garber and Sophie Roux, 3–26. Dordrecht: Springer, 2013.

————. "Soul and Mind: Life and Thought in the Seventeenth Century." In *CHSP*, 1:759–95.

Garber, Daniel, and Béatrice Longuenesse, eds. *Kant and the Early Moderns*. Princeton, NJ: Princeton University Press, 2008.

Garrett, Aaron. "Was Spinoza a Natural Lawyer?" *Cardozo Law Review* 25, no. 2 (2003): 627–41.

Garrett, Don. "Spinoza's Ethical Theory." In *The Cambridge Companion to Spinoza*, edited by Don Garrett, 267–314. Cambridge: Cambridge University Press, 1996.

Gascoigne, John. *Cambridge in the Age of the Enlightenment: Science, Religion and Politics from the Restoration to the French Revolution*. Cambridge University Press, 1989.

———. "Isaac Barrow's Academic Milieu: Interregnum and Restoration Cambridge." In *Before Newton: The Life and Times of Isaac Barrow*, edited by Mordechai Feingold, 250–90. Cambridge: Cambridge University Press, 1990.

———. "A Reappraisal of the Role of the Universities in the Scientific Revolution." In *Reappraisals of the Scientific Revolution*, edited by David C. Lindberg and Robert S. Westman, 207–60. Cambridge: Cambridge University Press, 1990.

Gaukroger, Stephen. *The Collapse of Mechanism and the Rise of Sensibility: Science and the Shaping of Modernity*. Oxford: Clarendon Press, 2010.

———. *Descartes' System of Natural Philosophy*. Cambridge: Cambridge University Press, 2002.

Gelbart, Nina R. "The Intellectual Development of Walter Charleton." *Ambix* 18, no. 3 (1971): 149–68.

Gibbs, Lee W. "Book I." In *The Folger Library Edition of The Works of Richard Hooker*, edited by W. Speed Hill, vol. 6/1, *Of the Laws of Ecclesiastical Polity*, 81–124. Cambridge, MA: Belknap Press, 1993.

———. "The Puritan Natural Law Theory of William Ames." *Harvard Theological Review* 64, no. 1 (1971): 37–57.

Gierke, Otto von. *Political Theories of the Middle Age*. Translated by F. W. Maitland. Cambridge: Cambridge University Press, 1900.

Giglioni, Guido. "The Genesis of Francis Glisson's Philosophy of Life." PhD diss., Johns Hopkins University, 2002.

———. "Pansychism versus Hylozoism: An Interpretation of Some Seventeenth-Century Doctrines of Universal Animation." *Acta Comeniana* 11 (1995): 25–45.

Gill, Mary Louise. *Aristotle on Substance: The Paradox of Unity*. Princeton, NJ: Princeton University Press, 1989.

Gillespie, Neal C. "Natural History, Natural Theology, and the Social Order: John Ray and the 'Newtonian Ideology.'" *Journal of the History of Biology* 20, no. 1 (1987): 1–49.

Gilson, Étienne. *The Christian Philosophy of St. Thomas Aquinas*. Translated by L. K. Shook. New York: Random House, 1956.

Gootjes, Nicolaas H. "Calvin on Epicurus and the Epicureans: Background to a Remark in Article 13 of the Belgic Confession." *Calvin Theological Journal* 40 (2005): 33–48.

Gordon, Alexander. *Heads of English Unitarian History*. London: Philip Green, 1895.

Gorham, Geoffrey. "Newton on God's Relation to Space and Time: The Cartesian Framework." *Archiv für Geschichte der Philosophie* 93 (2011): 281–320.

Gorman, Mel. "Gassendi in America." *Isis* 55, no. 4 (1964): 409–17.

Goudriaan, Aza. *Jacobus Revius: A Theological Examination of Cartesian Philosophy: Early Criticisms (1647)*. Leiden: Brill, 2002.

———. *Reformed Orthodoxy and Philosophy, 1625–1750: Gisbertus Voetius, Petrus van Mastricht, and Anthonius Driessen*. Leiden: Brill, 2006.

———. "The Synod of Dordt on Arminian Anthropology." In *Revisiting the Synod of Dordt (1618–1619)*, edited by Aza Goudriaan and Fred van Lieburg, 81–106. Leiden: Brill, 2011.

———. "Theology and Philosophy." In *A Companion to Reformed Orthodoxy*, edited by Herman J. Selderhuis, 27–63. Leiden: Brill, 2013.

Grabill, Stephen. "Natural Law and the Noetic Effects of Sin: The Faculty of Reason in Francis Turretin's Theological Anthropology." *Westminster Theological Journal* 67 (2005): 261–79.

———. *Rediscovering the Natural Law in Reformed Theological Ethics.* Grand Rapids, MI: Eerdmans, 2006.

Gregory, Brad S. *The Unintended Reformation: How a Religious Revolution Secularized Society.* Cambridge, MA: Harvard University Press, 2012.

Grene, Marjorie. "Aristotelico-Cartesian Themes in Natural Philosophy: Some Seventeenth-Century Cases." *Perspectives on Science* 1, no. 1 (1993): 66–87.

Griffin, Martin I. J., Jr. *Latitudinarianism in the Seventeenth-Century Church of England.* Annotated by Richard H. Popkin. Edited by Lila Freedman. Leiden: E. J. Brill, 1992.

Hall, A. Rupert. "Cambridge: Newton's Legacy." *Notes and Records of the Royal Society of London* 55, no. 2 (2001): 205–26.

Hampton, Stephen. *Anti-Arminians: The Anglican Reformed Tradition from Charles II to George I.* Oxford: Oxford University Press, 2008.

Harrison, C. T. "The Ancient Atomists and English Literature of the Seventeenth Century." *Harvard Studies in Classical Philology* 45 (1934): 1–79.

———. "Bacon, Hobbes, Boyle, and the Ancient Atomists." *Harvard Studies and Notes in Philology and Literature* 15 (1933): 191–218.

Harrison, John, and Peter Laslett. *The Library of John Locke.* 2nd ed. Oxford: Clarendon Press, 1971.

Harrison, Peter. *The Bible, Protestantism, and the Rise of Natural Science.* Cambridge: Cambridge University Press, 1998.

———. "Curiosity, Forbidden Knowledge, and the Reformation of Natural Philosophy in Early Modern England." *Isis* 92, no. 2 (2001): 265–90.

———. *The Fall of Man and the Foundations of Science.* Cambridge: Cambridge University Press, 2007.

———. "Voluntarism and Early Modern Science." *History of Science* 40 (2002): 63–89.

———. "Voluntarism and the Origins of Modern Science: A Reply to John Henry." *History of Science* 47 (2009): 223–31.

Hattab, Helen. "Concurrence or Divergence? Reconciling Descartes' Physics with His Metaphysics." *Journal of the History of Philosophy* 45, no. 1 (2007): 49–78.

Helm, Paul. "Jonathan Edwards and the Parting of the Ways?" *Jonathan Edwards Studies* 4, no. 1 (2014): 42–60.

———. "Turretin and Edwards Once More." *Jonathan Edwards Studies* 4, no. 3 (2014): 286–96.

Henry, John. "A Cambridge Platonist's Materialism: Henry More and the Concept of Soul." *Journal of the Warburg and Courtauld Institutes* 49 (1986): 172–95.

———. "Charleton, Walter." In *ODNB*.

———. "Die Rezeption der atomistischen Philosophie." In *Die Philosophie des 17. Jahrhunderts*, vol. 3, bk. 2, *England*, edited by Jean-Pierre Schobinger, 270–82. Basel: Schwabe, 1988.

———. "The Matter of Souls: Medical Theory and Theology in Seventeenth-Century England." In *The Medical Revolution of the Seventeenth Century*, edited by Roger French and Andrew Wear, 87–113. Cambridge: Cambridge University Press, 1989.

———. "Medicine and Pneumatology: Henry More, Richard Baxter, and Francis Glisson's *Treatise on the Energetic Nature of Substance*." *Medical History* 31 (1987): 15–42.

———. "Metaphysics and the Origins of Modern Science: Descartes and the Importance of the Laws of Nature." *Early Science and Medicine* 9, no. 2 (2004): 73–114.

———. "Occult Qualities and the Experimental Philosophy: Active Principles in Pre-Newtonian Matter Theory." *History of Science* 24 (1986): 335–81.

———. *The Scientific Revolution and the Origins of Modern Science*. 3rd ed. New York: Palgrave Macmillan, 2008.

———. "The Scientific Revolution in England." In *The Scientific Revolutions in National Context*, edited by Roy Porter and Mikuláš Teich, 178–209. Cambridge: Cambridge University Press, 1992.

———. "The Theological Origins of the Concept of Laws of Nature and Its Subsequent Secularization." In *Laws of Nature, Laws of God? Proceedings of the Science and Religion Forum Conference, 2014*, edited by Neil Spurway, 65–90. Newcastle: Cambridge Scholars Publishing, 2015.

———. "Voluntarist Theology at the Origins of Modern Science: A Response to Peter Harrison." *History of Science* 47 (2009): 79–113.

Heppe, Heinrich. *Reformed Dogmatics*. Edited by Ernst Bizer. Translated by G. T. Thomson. London: Allen & Ulwin, 1950.

Hervey, Helen. "Hobbes and Descartes in the Light of Some Unpublished Letters of the Correspondence between Sir Charles Cavendish and Dr. John Pell." *Osiris* 10 (1952): 67–90.

Hessayon, Ariel. *'Gold Tried in the Fire'. The Prophet Theaurau John Tany and the English Revolution*. Burlington, VT: Ashgate, 2007.

Heyd, Michael. *"Be Sober and Reasonable": The Critique of Enthusiasm in the Seventeenth and Early Eighteenth Centuries*. Leiden: Brill, 1995.

———. *Between Orthodoxy and the Enlightenment: Jean-Robert Chouet and the Introduction of Cartesian Science in the Academy of Geneva*. The Hague: Martinus Nijhoff, 1982.

———. "From a Rationalist Theology to Cartesian Voluntarism: David Derodon and Jean-Robert Chouet." *Journal of the History of Ideas* 40, no. 4 (1979): 527–42.

———. "The Reaction to Enthusiasm in the Seventeenth Century: Towards an Integrative Approach." *The Journal of the History of Ideas* 53, no. 2 (1981): 258–80.

———. "Un rôle nouveau pour la science: Jean–Alphonse Turrettini et les débuts de la théologie naturelle à Genève." *Revue de théologie et philosophie* 112 (1980): 25–42.

Hirai, Hiro. "Le concept de semence de Pierre Gassendi entre les théories de la matière et les sciences de la vie au XVIIᵉ siècle." *Medicina nei Secoli* 15, no. 2 (2003): 205–26.

Hochschild, Joshua P. *The Semantics of Analogy: Rereading Cajetan's* De nominum analogia. Notre Dame, IN: University of Notre Dame Press, 2010.

Hooykaas, Reijer. *Religion and the Rise of Modern Science.* Edinburgh: Scottish Academic Press, 1972.

Hornberger, Theodore. "Samuel Lee (1625–1691), a Clerical Channel for the Flow of New Ideas to Seventeenth-Century New England." *Osiris* 1 (1936): 341–55.

Hotson, Howard. *Johann Heinrich Alsted (1588–1638): Between Renaissance, Reformation, and Universal Reform.* Oxford: Clarendon Press, 2000.

Howell, Kenneth J. *God's Two Books: Copernican Cosmology and Biblical Interpretation in Early Modern Science.* Notre Dame, IN: University of Notre Dame Press, 2002.

Hoyles, John. *The Waning of the Renaissance, 1640–1740: Studies in the Thought and Poetry of Henry More, John Norris and Isaac Watts.* The Hague: Martinus Nijhoff, 1971.

Hunter, Michael. "Ancients, Moderns, Philologists, and Scientists." *Annals of Science* 39 (1982): 187–92.

———. "How Boyle Became a Scientist." *History of Science* 33 (1995): 59–103.

———. *Establishing the New Science: The Experience of the Early Royal Society*, 45–72. Woodbridge: Boydell Press, 1989.

———. *Science and Society in Restoration England.* Cambridge: Cambridge University Press, 1981.

Hutchison, Keith. "Individual, Causal Location, and the Eclipse of Scholastic Philosophy." *Social Studies of Science* 21 (1991): 321–50.

Hutton, Sarah. "Edward Stillingfleet and Spinoza." In *Disguised and Overt Spinozism around 1700*, edited by Wiep van Bunge and Wim Klever, 261–74. Leiden: E. J. Brill, 1996.

———. "Thomas Jackson, Oxford Platonist, and William Twisse, Aristotelian." *Journal of the History of Ideas* 39, no. 4 (1978): 635–52.

Irwin, Terence. *The Development of Ethics: A Historical and Critical Study.* 3 vols. Oxford: Oxford University Press, 2007–2009.

Isler, Hansruedi. *Thomas Willis, 1621–1675: Doctor and Scientist.* New York: Hafner, 1968.

Israel, Jonathan I. "The Early Dutch and German Reaction to the *Tractatus Theologico-Politicus*: Foreshadowing the Enlightenment's More General Spinoza Reception?" In *Spinoza's* Theological-Political Treatise: *A Critical Guide*, edited by

Yitzhak Y. Melamed and Michael A. Rosenthal, 72–100. Cambridge: Cambridge University Press, 2010.

———. *Enlightenment Contested: Philosophy, Modernity, and the Emancipation of Man, 1670–1752*. Oxford: Oxford University Press, 2006.

———. *Radical Enlightenment: Philosophy and the Making of Modernity, 1650–1750*. New York: Oxford University Press, 2001.

Jacquot, Jean. "Sir Charles Cavendish and His Learned Friends." *Annals of Science* 8 (1952): 13–28, 175–92.

Jalobeanu, Dana. "The Cartesians of the Royal Society: The Debate Over Collisions and the Nature of Body (1668–1670)." In *Vanishing Matter and the Laws of Motion: Descartes and Beyond*, edited by Dana Jalobeanu and Peter R. Anstey, 103–29. New York: Routledge, 2011.

Johnson, Francis R. *Astronomical Thought in Renaissance England: A Study of the English Scientific Writings from 1500 to 1645*. Baltimore: The Johns Hopkins Press, 1937.

Jones, Howard. *The Epicurean Tradition*. London: Routledge, 1980.

Jones, Richard Foster. *Ancients and Moderns: A Study of the Rise of the Scientific Movement in Seventeenth-Century England*. 2nd ed. St. Louis: Washington University, 1961.

Jorink, Eric. "Reading the Book of Nature in the Seventeenth-Century Dutch Republic." In *The Book of Nature in Early Modern and Modern History*, edited by Klaas van Berkel and Arjo Vanderjagt, 45–68. Leuven: Peeters, 2006.

Joy, Lynn Sumida. *Gassendi the Atomist: Advocate of History in an Age of Science*. Cambridge: Cambridge University Press, 1987.

Kaledin, Arthur Daniel. "The Mind of John Leverett." PhD diss., Harvard University, 1965.

Kaiser, Christopher. "Calvin's Understanding of Aristotelian Natural Philosophy: Its Extent and Possible Origins." In *Calviniana: Ideas and Influence of Jean Calvin*, edited by Robert V. Schnucker, 77–92. Kirksville, MO: Sixteenth Century Essays and Studies, 1988.

Kargon, Robert. *Atomism in England from Hariot to Newton*. Oxford: Clarendon Press, 1966.

———. "Thomas Hariot, the Northumberland Circle and Early Atomism in England." *Journal of the History of Ideas* 27, no. 1 (1966): 128–36.

———. "Walter Charleton, Robert Boyle and the Acceptance of Epicurean Atomism in England." *Isis* 55, no. 2 (1964): 184–92.

Kato, Yoshiyuki. "*Deus sive Natura*: The Dutch Controversy over the Radical Concept of God, 1660–1690." PhD diss., Princeton Theological Seminary, 2013.

Keeble, N. H. "Autobiographer as Apologist: *Reliquiae Baxterianae* (1696)." *Prose Studies* 9, no. 2 (1986): 105–19.

———. "Baxter, Richard." In *ODNB*.

———. *Richard Baxter: Puritan Man of Letters*. Oxford: Clarendon Press, 1982.

Kennedy, Rick. "The Alliance between Puritanism and Cartesian Logic at Harvard, 1687–1735." *Journal of the History of Ideas* 51, no. 4 (1990): 549–72.

———. "Thomas Brattle and the Scientific Provincialism of New England, 1680–1713." *New England Quarterly* 63, no. 4 (1990): 584–600.

Kevan, Ernest F. *The Grace of the Law: A Study in Puritan Theology.* London: Carey Kingsgate Press, 1964.

King, Christine. "Philosophy and Science in the Arts Curriculum of the Scottish Universities in the 17th century." PhD diss., University of Edinburgh, 1974.

Klauber, Martin I. "Reason, Revelation, and Cartesianism: Louis Tronchin and Enlightened Orthodoxy in Late Seventeenth-Century Geneva." *Church History* 59, no. 3 (1990): 326–39.

———. "The Use of Philosophy in the Theology of Johannes Maccovius (1578–1644)." *Calvin Theological Journal* 30, no. 2 (1995): 376–91.

Klinck, Dennis R. "*Vestigia Trinitatis* in Man and His Works in the English Renaissance." *Journal of the History of Ideas* 42, no. 1 (1981): 13–27.

Kochiras, Hylarie. "The Mechanical Philosophy and Newton's Mechanical Force." *Philosophy of Science* 80, no. 4 (2013): 557–78.

Korkman, Petter. "Voluntarism and Moral Obligation: Barbeyrac's Defence of Pufendorf Revisited." In *Early Modern Natural Law Theories: Contexts and Strategies in the Early Enlightenment*, edited by T. J. Hochstrasser and P. Schröder, 195–225. Dordrecht: Kluwer, 2003.

Koyré, Alexandre. *Newtonian Studies.* Chicago: University of Chicago Press, 1968.

Kroll, Richard W. F. *The Material Word: Literate Culture in the Restoration and Early Eighteenth Century.* Baltimore: The Johns Hopkins University Press, 1991.

———. "The Question of Locke's Relation to Gassendi." *Journal of the History of Ideas* 45 (1984): 339–59.

Kroll, Richard, Richard Ashcraft, and Perez Zagorin, eds. *Philosophy, Science, and Religion in England 1640–1700.* Cambridge: Cambridge University Press, 1992.

Labrousse, Elizabeth. *Pierre Bayle.* 2 vols. La Haye: M. Nijhoff, 1963–1964.

Laerke, Mogens. "G. W. Leibniz's Two Readings of the *Tractatus Theologico-Politicus*." In *Spinoza's* Theological-Political Treatise: *A Critical Guide*, edited by Yitzhak Y. Melamed and Michael A. Rosenthal, 101–27. Cambridge: Cambridge University Press, 2010.

Lagarde, Georges de. *Recherches sur l'esprit politique de la réforme.* Paris: Auguste Picard, 1926.

Laird, John. "L'Influence de Descartes sur la philosophie anglaise du xvi siècle." *Revue Philosophique de la France et de l'Étranger* 123, no. 5–8 (May–August 1937): 226–56.

Lamont, William. *Puritanism and Historical Controversy.* London: UCL Press, 1996.

———. *Richard Baxter and the Millenium: Protestant Imperialism and the English Revolution.* London: Croom Helm, 1979.

Lamprecht, S. P. "The Role of Descartes in Seventeenth-Century England." In *Studies in the History of Ideas*, 3:181–240. New York: Columbia University Press, 1935.

Lane, A. N. S. Introduction to *The Bondage and Liberation of the Will: A Defense of the Orthodox Doctrine of Human Choice against Pighius*, by John Calvin, xiii–xxxiv. Edited by A. N. S. Lane. Translated by G. I. Davies. Grand Rapids, MI: Baker, 1996.

Lange, Friedrich Albert. *History of Materialism*. Translated by Ernest Chester Thomas. 2nd ed. 3 vols. London: Kegan Paul, Trench, Trübner, 1892.

Laudan, Laurens. "The Clock Metaphor and Probabilism: The Impact of Descartes on English Methodological Thought, 1650–65." *Annals of Science* 22, no. 2 (1966): 73–104.

Leijenhorst, Cees. *The Mechanisation of Aristotelianism: The Late Aristotelian Setting of Thomas Hobbes' Natural Philosophy*. Leiden: Brill, 2002.

———. "Space and Matter in Calvinist Physics." *The Monist* 84, no. 4 (2001): 520–41.

Leinonen, Markku. "*De Physica Mosaica Comeniana*: The Academic Thesis of Anders Lundbom." *Acta Comeniana* 15–16 (2002): 107–25.

Lennon, Thomas M. *The Battle of the Gods and Giants: The Legacies of Descartes and Gassendi, 1655–1715*. Princeton, NJ: Princeton University Press, 1993.

Levitin, Dmitri. *Ancient Wisdom in the Age of the New Science: Histories of Philosophy in England, c. 1640–1700*. Cambridge: Cambridge University Press, 2015.

———. "Rethinking English Physico-theology: Samuel Parker's *Tentamina de Deo* (1665)." *Early Science and Medicine* 19 (2014): 28–75.

Lewis, Rhodri. "Of 'Origenian Platonisme': Joseph Glanvill on the Pre-existence of Souls." *Huntington Library Quarterly* 69, no. 2 (2006): 267–300.

Lisska, Anthony J. "The Philosophy of Law of Thomas Aquinas." In *A History of the Philosophy of Law from the Ancient Greeks to the Scholastics*, edited by Fred. D. Miller Jr., 285–310. Dordrecht: Springer, 2007.

LoLordo, Antonia. "The Activity of Matter in Gassendi's Physics." *Oxford Studies in Early Modern Philosophy* 2 (2005): 75–103.

———. *Pierre Gassendi and the Birth of Early Modern Philosophy*. Cambridge: Cambridge University Press, 2007.

[London Stationers' Company]. *A Transcript of the Registers of the Worshipful Company of Stationers*. 3 vols. London, 1913–1914.

Longo, Mario. "A 'Critical' History of Philosophy and the Early Enlightenment." In *Models of the History of Philosophy*, vol. 2, *From the Cartesian Age to Brucker*, edited by Gregorio Piaia and Giovanni Santinello, 477–577. Dordrecht: Springer, 2011.

Lukens, David C. "An Aristotelian Response to Galileo: Honoré Fabri, S. J. (1608–1688) on the Causal Analysis of Motion." PhD diss., University of Toronto, 1979.

Lüthy, Christoph. *David Gorlaeus (1591–1612): An Enigmatic Figure in the History of Philosophy and Science*. Amsterdam: Amsterdam University Press, 2012.

Lynch, William T. *Solomon's Child: Method in the Early Royal Society of London*. Stanford: Stanford University Press, 2001.

Macintosh, J. J. "Robert Boyle on Epicurean Atheism and Atomism." In *Atoms, Pneuma, and Tranquillity: Epicurean and Stoic Themes in European Thought*, edited by Margaret J. Osler, 197–219. Cambridge: Cambridge University Press, 1991.

Makin, William E. A. "The Philosophy of Pierre Gassendi: Science and Belief in Seventeenth-Century Paris and Provence." 2 vols. PhD diss., The Open University, 1985.

Mann, William E. "Duns Scotus on Natural and Supernatural Knowledge of God." In *The Cambridge Companion to Duns Scotus*, edited by Thomas Williams, 238–62. Cambridge: Cambridge University Press, 2003.

Manzo, Silva A. "Francis Bacon and Atomism: A Reappraisal." In *Late Medieval and Early Modern Corpuscular Matter Theories*, edited by Christoph Lüthy, John E. Murdoch, and William R. Newman, 209–43. Leiden: E. J. Brill, 2001.

Marshall, John. *John Locke: Resistance, Religion and Responsibility*. Cambridge: Cambridge University Press, 1994.

Martin, Hugh. *Puritanism and Richard Baxter*. London: SCM Press, 1954.

Matthews, Steven. *Theology and Science in the Thought of Francis Bacon*. Burlington, VT: Ashgate, 2008.

Mayo, Thomas. *Epicurus in England (1650–1725)*. Dallas: The Southwest Press, 1934.

McColley, Grant. "The Ross-Wilkins Controversy." *Annals of Science* 3, no. 2 (1938): 153–89.

McGahagan, Thomas A. "Cartesianism in the Netherlands, 1639–1676: The New Science and the Calvinist Counter Reformation." PhD diss., University of Pennsylvania, 1976.

McGrath, Gavin John. "Puritans and the Human Will: Voluntarism within Mid-Seventeenth Century English Puritanism as Seen in the Works of Richard Baxter and John Owen." PhD diss., University of Durham, 1989.

McKenzie, Edgar C. "British Devotional Literature and the Rise of German Pietism." PhD diss., University of St. Andrews, 1984.

McLachlan, Herbert. *English Education under the Test Acts: Being the History of the Non-conformist Academies 1662–1820*. Manchester: Manchester University Press, 1931.

McLelland, Joseph C. Translator's introduction to *Philosophical Works: On the Relation of Philosophy to Theology*, by Peter Martyr Vermigli, xix–xli. Translated and edited by Joseph C. McLelland. Kirksville, MO: Truman State University Press, 1996.

McMahon, Susan. "Constructing Natural History in England (1650–1700)." PhD diss., University of Alberta, 2001.

Meer, Jitse M. van der, and Richard J. Oosterhoff. "God, Scripture, and the Rise of Modern Science (1200–1700): Notes in the Margin of Harrison's Hypothesis." In *Nature and Scripture in the Abrahamic Religions: Up to 1700*, edited by Jitse M. van der Meer and Scott Mandelbrote, 2:363–96. Leiden: Brill, 2008.

Mendelsohn, Everett. *Heat and Life: The Development of the Theory of Animal Heat*. Cambridge, MA: Harvard University Press, 1964.

Mercer, Christia. "The Seventeenth-Century Debate between the Moderns and the Aristotelians: Leibniz and *Philosophia Reformata*." In *Leibniz' Auseinandersetzung mit Vorgängern und Zeitgenossen*, edited by Ingrid Marchlewitz and Albert Heinekamp, 18–29. Stuttgart: Franz Steiner Verlag, 1990.

Merton, Robert K. "Puritanism, Pietism, and Science." *The Sociological Review* 28, no. 1 (1936): 1–30.

———. "Science, Technology and Society in Seventeenth Century England." *Osiris* 4 (1938): 360–632.

———. *Science, Technology & Society in Seventeenth Century England*. New York: Harper & Row, 1970.

Methuen, Charlotte. "*Lex Naturae* and *Ordo Naturae* in the Thought of Philip Melanchthon." *Reformation and Renaissance Review* 3 (2000): 110–25.

Meyer, Alfred, and Raymond Hierons. "On Thomas Willis's Concepts of Neurophysiology." *Medical History* 9 (1965): 1–15, 142–55.

Michael, Emily. "Daniel Sennert on Matter and Form: At the Juncture of the Old and the New." *Early Science and Medicine* 2, no. 3 (1997): 272–99.

Michael, Emily, and Fred S. Michael. "Gassendi on Sensation and Reflection: A Non-Cartesian Dualism." *History of European Ideas* 9 (1988): 583–95.

———. "A Note on Gassendi in England." *Notes and Queries* 37, no. 3 (1990): 297–99.

———. "The Theory of Ideas in Gassendi and Locke." *Journal of the History of Ideas* 51 (1990): 379–99.

Milani, Nausicaa Elena. "Motion and God in XVIIth Century Cartesian Manuals: Rohault, Régis and Gadroys." *Noctua* 2, no. 1–2 (2015): 481–516.

Miller, Fred D., Jr. "Early Jewish and Christian Legal Thought." In *A History of the Philosophy of Law from the Ancient Greeks to the Scholastics*, edited by Fred. D. MillerJr., 167–85. Dordrecht: Springer, 2007.

Miller, Perry. *The New England Mind: From Colony to Province*. Cambridge, MA: Harvard University Press, 1953.

———. *The New England Mind: The Seventeenth Century*. New York: Macmillan, 1939.

Milton, John R. "Laws of Nature." In *CHSP*, 1:680–701.

———. "Locke and Gassendi: A Reappraisal." In *English Philosophy in the Age of Locke*, edited by M. A. Stewart, 87–109. Oxford: Clarendon Press, 2000.

———. "Locke at Oxford." In *Locke's Philosophy: Content and Context*, edited by G. A. J. Rogers, 29–47. Oxford: Clarendon Press, 1994.

———. "Locke, John." In *ODNB*.

Mintz, Samuel I. *The Hunting of Leviathan*. Cambridge: Cambridge University Press, 1962.

Morgan, John. *Godly Learning: Puritan Attitudes towards Reason, Learning, and Education, 1560–1640*. Cambridge: Cambridge University Press, 1986.

Müller, Patrick. *Latitudinarianism and Didacticism in Eighteenth Century Literature: Moral Theology in Fielding, Sterne, and Goldsmith*. Frankfurt am Main: Peter Lang, 2009.

Muller, Richard A. *After Calvin: Studies in the Development of a Theological Tradition.* Oxford: Oxford University Press, 2003.

———. "Diversity in the Reformed Tradition: A Historiographical Introduction." In *Drawn into Controversie: Reformed Theological Diversity and Debates within Seventeenth-Century British Puritanism,* edited by Michael A. G. Haykin and Mark Jones, 11–30. Göttingen: Vandenhoeck & Ruprecht, 2011.

———. *Divine Will and Human Choice: Freedom, Contingency, and Necessity in Early Modern Reformed Thought.* Grand Rapids, MI: Baker Academic, 2017.

———. "God and Design in the Thought of Robert Boyle." In *The Persistence of the Sacred in Modern Thought,* edited by Chris L. Firestone and Nathan A. Jacobs. 87–111. Notre Dame, IN: University of Notre Dame Press, 2012.

———. "Jonathan Edwards and the Absence of Free Choice: A Parting of Ways in the Reformed Tradition." *Jonathan Edwards Studies* 1, no. 1 (2011): 3–22.

———. "Jonathan Edwards and Francis Turretin on Necessity, Contingency, and Freedom of Will. In Response to Paul Helm." *Jonathan Edwards Studies* 4, no. 3 (2014): 266–85.

———. "Not Scotist: Understandings of Being, Univocity, and Analogy in Early-Modern Reformed Thought." *Reformation & Renaissance Review* 14, no. 2 (2012): 127–50.

———. "Philip Doddridge and the Formulation of Calvinistic Theology in an Era of Rationalism and Deconfessionalization." In *Religion, Politics and Dissent, 1660–1832: Essays in Honour of James E. Bradley,* edited by Robert D. Cornwall and William Gibson, 65–84. Farnham: Ashgate, 2010.

———. *Post-Reformation Reformed Dogmatics.* 2nd ed. 4 vols. Grand Rapids, MI: Baker Academic, 2003.

———. "Scholasticism, Reformation, Orthodoxy, and the Persistence of Christian Aristotelianism." *Trinity Journal* NS 19, no. 1 (1998): 81–96.

———. "Thomas Barlow on the Liabilities of 'New Philosophy'. Perceptions of a Rebellious *Ancilla* in the Era of Protestant Orthodoxy." In *Scholasticism Reformed: Essays in Honour of Willem J. van Asselt,* edited by Maarten Wisse, Marcel Sarot, and Willemien Otten, 179–95. Leiden: Brill, 2010.

———. *Unaccommodated Calvin: Studies in the Formation of a Theological Tradition.* New York: Oxford University Press, 2000.

Murray, Gemma, William Harper, and Curtis Wilson. "Huygens, Wren, Wallis, and Newton on Rules of Impact and Reflection." In *Vanishing Matter and the Laws of Motion: Descartes and Beyond,* edited by Dana Jalobeanu and Peter R. Anstey, 153–91. New York: Routledge, 2011.

Newman, William R. *Atoms and Alchemy: Chymistry and the Experimental Origins of the Scientific Revolution.* Chicago: University of Chicago Press, 2006.

Nicolson, Marjorie. "The Early Stage of Cartesianism in England." *Studies in Philology* 26 (1929): 356–74.

Norton, David Fate. "The Myth of 'British Empiricism.'" *History of European Ideas* 1, no. 4 (1981): 331–44.

Nuttall, Geoffrey F. *Richard Baxter*. Stanford, CA: Stanford University Press, 1965.

———. *Richard Baxter and Philip Doddridge: A Study in a Tradition*. London: Oxford University Press, 1951.

———. "A Transcript of Richard Baxter's Library Catalogue: A Bibliographical Note." *Journal of Ecclesiastical History* 2, no. 2 (1951): 207–21 and 3, no. 1 (1952): 74–100.

Oakley, Francis. "The Absolute and Ordained Power of God in Sixteenth- and Seventeenth-Century Theology." *Journal of the History of Ideas* 59, no. 3 (1998): 437–61.

———. "Christian Theology and the Newtonian Science: The Rise of the Concept of the Laws of Nature." *Church History* 30, no. 4 (1961): 433–57.

———. "Medieval Theories of Natural Law: William of Ockham and the Significance of the Voluntarist Tradition." *Natural Law Forum* 6 (1961): 65–83.

———. *Natural Law, Laws of Nature, Natural Rights: Continuity and Discontinuity in the History of Ideas*. New York: Continuum, 2005.

———. *Politics and Eternity: Studies in the History of Medieval and Early-Modern Political Thought*. Leiden: E. J. Brill, 1999.

Ogilvie, Brian W. "Natural History, Ethics, and Physico-Theology." In *Historia: Empiricism and Erudition in Early Modern Europe*, edited by Gianna Pomata and Nancy G. Siraisi, 75–103. Cambridge, MA: MIT Press, 2005.

Olson, Richard. "On the Nature of God's Existence, Wisdom, and Power: The Interplay Between Organic and Mechanistic Imagery in Anglican Natural Theology." In *Approaches to Organic Form: Permutations in Science and Culture*, edited by Frederick Burwick, 1–48. Dordrecht: D. Reidel, 1987.

Orme, William. *The Life and Times of Richard Baxter: With a Critical Examination of His Writings*. 2 vols. London: James Duncan, 1830.

Orton, Job. *Memoirs of the Life, Character and Writings of the late Reverend Philip Doddridge*. Salop: J. Cotton and J. Eddowes, 1766.

Osler, Margaret J. "Baptizing Epicurean Atomism: Pierre Gassendi on the Immortality of the Soul." In *Religion, Science, and Worldview: Essays in Honor of Richard S. Westfall*, edited by Margaret J. Osler and Paul L. Farber, 163–83. Cambridge: Cambridge University Press, 1985.

———. "Becoming an Outsider: Gassendi in the History of Philosophy." In *Insiders and Outsiders in Seventeenth–Century Philosophy*, edited by G. A. J. Rogers, Tom Sorell, and Jill Kraye, 23–42. New York: Routledge, 2010.

———. "Descartes and Charleton on Nature and God." *Journal of the History of Ideas* 40, no. 3 (1979): 445–56.

———. *Divine Will and the Mechanical Philosophy: Gassendi and Descartes on Contingency and Necessity in the Created World*. Cambridge: Cambridge University Press, 1994.

———. "Fortune, Fate, and Divination: Gassendi's Voluntarist Theology and the Baptism of Epicureanism." In *Atoms, Pneuma, and Tranquillity: Epicurean and Stoic Themes in European Thought*, edited by Margaret J. Osler, 155–74. Cambridge: Cambridge University Press, 1991.

———. "The Intellectual Sources of Robert Boyle's Philosophy of Nature: Gassendi's Voluntarism and Boyle's Physico-Theological Project." In *Philosophy, Science, and Religion 1640–1700*, edited by Richard Kroll, Richard Ashcraft, and Perez Zagorin, 178–98. Cambridge: Cambridge University Press, 1992.

———. "Religion and the Changing Historiography of the Scientific Revolution." In *Science and Religion: New Historical Perspectives*, edited by Thomas Dixon, Geoffrey Cantor, and Stephen Pumfrey, 71–86. Cambridge: Cambridge University Press, 2010.

———. "Whose Ends? Teleology in Early Modern Natural Philosophy." *Osiris*, 2nd Series, 16 (2001): 151–68.

Pacchi, Arrigo. "Die Rezeption der cartesischen Philosophie." In *Die Philosophie des 17. Jahrhunderts*, vol. 3, bk. 1, *England*, edited by Jean-Pierre Schobinger, 293–97. Basel: Schwabe, 1988.

Packer, J. I. "The Redemption and Restoration of Man in the Thought of Richard Baxter." PhD diss., Oxford University, 1954.

———. *The Redemption & Restoration of Man in the Thought of Richard Baxter: A Study in Puritan Theology*. Vancouver: Regent College Publishing, 2003.

Palladina, Fiammetta. "Pufendorf Disciple of Hobbes: The Nature of Man and the State of Nature: The Doctrine of *socialitas*." *History of European Ideas* 34 (2008): 26–60.

Palmerino, Carla Rita. "Two Jesuit Responses to Galileo's Science of Motion: Honoré Fabri and Pierre Le Cazre." In *The New Science and Jesuit Science: Seventeenth Century Perspectives*, edited by Mordechai Feingold, 187–227. Dordrecht: Kluwer, 2003.

Park, Katherine. "The Organic Soul." In *The Cambridge History of Renaissance Philosophy*, edited by Charles B. Schmitt, Quentin Skinner, and Eckhard Kessler, 464–84. New York: Cambridge University Press, 1988.

Parkin, Jon. "Hobbism in the Later 1660s: Daniel Scargill and Samuel Parker." *The Historical Journal* 42, no. 1 (1999): 86–96.

———. *Science, Religion and Politics in Restoration England: Richard Cumberland's De legibus naturae*. Woodbridge: The Boydell Press, 1999.

———. *Taming the Leviathan: The Reception of the Political and Religious Ideas of Thomas Hobbes in England 1640–1700*. Cambridge: Cambridge University Press, 2007.

Partee, Charles. *Calvin and Classical Philosophy*. Leiden: Brill, 1977.

Pav, Peter Anton. "Gassendi's Statement of the Principle of Inertia." *Isis* 57, no. 1 (1966): 24–34.

Penner, Sydney. "Final Causality: Suárez on the Priority of Final Causation." In *Suárez on Aristotelian Causality*, edited by Jakob Leth Fink, 122–49. Leiden: Brill, 2015.

Petry, M. J. "Burgersdijk's Physics." In *Franco Burgersdijk (1590–1635): Neo-Aristotelianism in Leiden,* edited by E. P. Bos and H. A. Krop, 83–118. Amsterdam: Rodopi, 1993.

Philip, Robert. "An Essay on the Genius, Works, and Times of Richard Baxter." In *The Practical Works of Richard Baxter,* edited by Robert Philip, 1:xxi–lx. London: George Virtue, 1838.

Philipp, Wolfgang. "Physicotheology in the Age of Enlightenment: Appearance and History." *Studies on Voltaire and the Eighteenth Century* 57 (1967): 1233–67.

Phillips, James McJunkin. "Between Conscience and the Law: The Ethics of Richard Baxter (1615–1691)." PhD diss., Princeton University, 1958.

Pink, Thomas. "Suarez, Hobbes and the Scholastic Tradition in Action Theory." In *The Will and Human Action: From Antiquity to the Present Day,* edited by Thomas Pink and Martin Stone, 127–53. London: Routledge, 2004.

Pollock, John. *The Popish Plot: A Study in the History of the Reign of Charles II.* London: Duckworth and Co., 1903.

Poole, William. "Sir Robert Southwell's Dialogue on Thomas Burnet's Theory of the Earth: 'C & S discourse of Mr Burnetts Theory of the Earth' (1684): Contexts and an Edition." *The Seventeenth Century* 23, no. 1 (2008): 72–104.

Popkin, Richard H. "Gassendi, Pierre." In *The Encyclopedia of Philosophy,* edited by Paul Edwards, 3:269–73. New York: The Macmillan Co., 1967.

———. "The Philosophy of Bishop Stillingfleet." *Journal of the History of Philosophy* 9, no. 3 (1971): 303–19.

Powicke, Frederick J. *The Reverend Richard Baxter under the Cross (1662–1691).* London: Jonathan Cape, 1927.

———. "Story and Significance of the Rev. Richard Baxter's '*Saints' Everlasting Rest.*'" *Bulletin of the John Rylands Library* 5 (1920): 445–79.

Prior, Moody E. "Joseph Glanvill, Witchcraft, and Seventeenth-Century Science." *Modern Philology* 30, no. 2 (1932): 167–93.

Prost, Joseph. *La philosophie à l'académie protestante de Saumur (1606–1685).* Paris: Paulin, 1907.

Pumfrey, Stephen. "Mechanizing Magnetism in Restoration England—The Decline of Magnetic Philosophy." *Annals of Science* 44 (1987): 1–22.

———. "Gilbert, William (1544–1603)." In *The Dictionary of Seventeenth-Century British Philosophers,* edited by Andrew Pyle, 1:334–38. Bristol: Thoemmes Press, 2000.

Puster, Rolf W. *Britische Gassendi-Rezeption am Beispiel John Lockes.* Stuttgart-Bad Cannstatt: Frommann-Holzboog, 1991.

Raven, C. E. *John Ray, Naturalist: His Life and Works.* Cambridge: Cambridge University Press, 1942.

Reid, Jasper. *The Metaphysics of Henry More.* Dordrecht: Springer, 2012.

Reif, Mary Richard (Patricia). "Natural Philosophy in Some Early Seventeenth Century Scholastic Textbooks." PhD diss., Saint Louis University, 1962.

Rehnman, Sebastian. "Alleged Rationalism: Francis Turretin on Reason." *Calvin Theological Journal* 37, no. 2 (2002): 255–69.

———. *Divine Discourse: The Theological Methodology of John Owen.* Grand Rapids, MI: Baker Academic, 2002.

———. "Towards a Solution to the 'Perennially Intriguing Problem' of the Sources of Jonathan Edwards' Idealism." *Jonathan Edwards Studies* 5, no. 2 (2015): 138–55.

Reill, Peter Hans. "The Legacy of the 'Scientific Revolution': Science and the Enlightenment." In *The Cambridge History of Science*, vol. 4, *The Eighteenth Century*, edited by Roy Porter, 23–43. Cambridge: Cambridge University Press, 2003.

Rémusat, Charles de. *Histoire de la philosophie en Angleterre depuis Bacon jusqu'à Locke.* 2nd ed. 2 vols. Paris: Didier et cie, 1875.

Ridings, Daniel. *The Attic Moses: The Dependence Theme in Some Early Christian Writers.* Göteborg: Acta Universitatis Gothoburgensia, 1995.

Rivers, Isabel. *Reason, Grace, and Sentiment: A Study of the Language of Religion and Ethics in England, 1660–1780.* 2 vols. Cambridge: Cambridge University Press, 1991–2000.

Rogers, G. A. J. "Charleton, Gassendi, et la reception de l'atomisme." In *Gassendi et l'Europe, 1592–1792*, edited by Sylvia Murr, 213–25. Paris: J. Vrin, 1997.

———. "Descartes and the English." In *The Light of Nature: Essays in the History and Philosophy of Science Presented to A. C. Crombie*, edited by J. D. North and J. J. Roche, 281–302. Dordrecht: M. Nijhoff, 1985.

———. "Gassendi and the Birth of Modern Philosophy." *Studies in History and Philosophy of Science* 26, no. 4 (1995): 681–87.

———. "Locke and the Latitude-Men: Ignorance as a Ground of Toleration." In *Philosophy, Science, and Religion 1640–1700*, edited by Richard Kroll, Richard Ashcraft, and Perez Zagorin, 230–52. Cambridge: Cambridge University Press, 1992.

Rogers, G. A. J., Tom Sorell, and Jill Kraye, eds. *Insiders and Outsiders in Seventeenth-Century Philosophy.* New York: Routledge, 2010.

Rommen, Heinrich A. *The Natural Law: A Study in Legal and Social History and Philosophy.* Translated by Thomas R. Hanley. St. Louis: B. Herder, 1949.

Rosenfield, Leonora Cohen. *From Beast-Machine to Man-Machine: Animal Soul in French Letters from Descartes to La Mettrie.* New York: Oxford University Press, 1941.

Rother, Wolfgang. "Zur Geschichte der Basler Universitätsphilosophie im 17. Jahrhundert." *History of Universities* 2 (1982): 153–91.

———. "The Teaching of Philosophy at Seventeenth-Century Zurich." *History of Universities* 11 (1992): 59–74.

Ruler, J. A. (Han) van. *The Crisis of Causality: Voetius and Descartes on God, Nature, and Change.* Leiden: E. J. Brill, 1995.

———. "'Something, I Know Not What'. The Concept of Substance in Early Modern Thought." In *Between Imagination and Demonstration. Essays in the History of*

Science and Philosophy Presented to John D. North, edited by Lodi Nauta and Arjo Vanderjagt, 365–93. Leiden: Brill, 1999.

Russell, John L. "Cosmological Teaching in the Seventeenth-Century Scottish Universities, Part 1." *Journal for the History of Astronomy* 5 (1974): 122–32.

Rutherford, Donald. "Spinoza's Conception of Law: Metaphysics and Ethics." In *Spinoza's Theological-Political Treatise: A Critical Guide*, edited by Yitzhak Y. Melamed and Michael A. Rosenthal, 143–67. Cambridge: Cambridge University Press, 2010.

Sacksteder, William. "How Much of Hobbes Might Spinoza Have Read?" *The Southwestern Journal of Philosophy* 11, no. 2 (1980): 25–39.

Sailor, Danton B. "Moses and Atomism." *Journal of the History of Ideas* 25, no. 1 (1964): 3–16.

Sarasohn, Lisa T. *Gassendi's Ethics: Freedom in a Mechanistic Universe*. Ithaca, NY: Cornell University Press, 1996.

———. "Motion and Morality: Pierre Gassendi, Thomas Hobbes and the Mechanical World-View." *Journal of the History of Ideas* 46, no. 3 (1985): 363–79.

———. "Thomas Hobbes and the Duke of Newcastle: A Study in the Mutuality of Patronage before the Establishment of the Royal Society." *Isis* 90, no. 4 (1999): 715–37.

Saveson, J. E. "Differing Reactions to Descartes among the Cambridge Platonists." *Journal of the History of Ideas* 21 (1960): 560–67.

Scattola, Merio. "Before and After Natural Law: Models of Natural Law in Ancient and Modern Times." In *Early Modern Natural Law Theories: Contexts and Strategies in the Early Enlightenment*, edited by T. J. Hochstrasser and P. Schröder, 1–30. Dordrecht: Kluwer, 2003.

———. "*Scientia Iuris* and *Ius Naturae*: The Jurisprudence of the Holy Roman Empire in the Seventeenth and Eighteenth Centuries." In *A History of the Philosophy of Law in the Civil Law World, 1600–1900*, edited by Damiano Canale, Paolo Grossi, and Hasso Hofmann, 1–41. A Treatise of Legal Philosophy and General Jurisprudence 9. Dordrecht: Springer, 2009.

———. "Scientific Revolution in the Moral Sciences: The Controversy between Samuel Pufendorf and the Lutheran Theologians of the Late Seventeenth Century." In *Controversies within the Scientific Revolution*, edited by Marcelo Dascal and Victor D. Boantza, 251–75. Amsterdam: John Benjamins, 2011.

Schaffer, Simon. "Regeneration: The Body of Natural Philosophers in Restoration England." In *Science Incarnate: Historical Embodiments of Natural Knowledge*, edited by Christopher Lawrence and Steven Shapin, 83–120. Chicago: University of Chicago Press, 1998.

Schmaltz, Tad M. *Descartes on Causation*. Oxford: Oxford University Press, 2008.

Schmidt-Biggemann, Wilhelm. "Robert Fludd's Kabbalistic Cosmos." In *Platonism at the Origins of Modernity: Studies on Platonism and Early Modern*

Philosophy, edited by Douglas Hedley and Sarah Hutton, 75–92. Dordrecht: Springer, 2008.

Schmitt, Charles B. *Aristotle and the Renaissance*. Cambridge, MA: Harvard University Press, 1983.

Scholder, Klaus. *The Birth of Modern Critical Theology: Origins and Problems of Biblical Criticism in the Seventeenth Century*. Translated by John Bowden. London: SCM Press, 1990.

Scriba, Christoph J. "The Autobiography of John Wallis." *Notes and Records of the Royal Society* 25 (1970): 17–46.

Secada, Jorge. *Cartesian Metaphysics: The Late Scholastic Origins of Modern Philosophy*. Cambridge: Cambridge University Press, 2000.

Sell, Alan P. F. *Philosophy, Dissent and Nonconformity*. Cambridge: James Clarke & Co, 2004.

———. *Testimony and Tradition: Studies in Reformed and Dissenting Thought*. Eugene, OR: Wipf & Stock, 2005.

Serjeanston, Richard. "Herbert of Cherbury before Deism: The Early Reception of the *De veritate*." *The Seventeenth Century* 16, no. 2 (2001): 217–38.

Shapiro, Barbara J. *John Wilkins, 1614–1672: An Intellectual Biography*. Berkeley: University of California Press, 1969.

———. "Latitudinarianism and Science in Seventeenth-Century England." *Past and Present* 40 (July 1968): 6–41.

———. *Probability and Certainty in Seventeenth-Century England: A Study of the Relationships between Natural Science, Religion, History, Law, and Literature*. Princeton, NJ: Princeton University Press, 1983.

———. "The Universities and Science in Seventeenth Century England." *The Journal of British Studies* 10, no. 2 (1971): 47–82.

Sharp, Lindsay. "Walter Charleton's Early Life 1620–1659, and Relationship to Natural Philosophy in Mid-Seventeenth Century England." *Annals of Science* 30 (1973): 311–40.

Shields, Christopher. "Aristotle." In *The Stanford Encyclopedia of Philosophy* (Fall 2015 Edition). Accessed July 25, 2016. http://plato.stanford.edu/archives/fall2015/entries/aristotle/.

Sinnema, Donald. "Aristotle and Early Reformed Orthodoxy: Moments of Accommodation and Antithesis." In *Christianity and the Classics: The Acceptance of a Heritage*, edited by Wendy Helleman, 119–48. New York: University Press of America, 1990.

Sleigh, Robert, Jr., Vere Chappell, and Michael Della Rocca. "Determinism and Human Freedom." In *CHSP*, 2:1195–278.

Smith, Gerard. *Freedom in Molina*. Chicago: Loyola University Press, 1966.

Sommerville, Johann P. "Selden, Grotius, and the Seventeenth-Century Intellectual Revolution in Moral and Political Theory." In *Rhetoric and Law in Early Modern*

Europe, edited by Victoria Kahn and Lorna Hutson, 318–44. New Haven, CT: Yale University Press, 2001.

———. *Thomas Hobbes: Political Ideas in Historical Context.* New York: St. Martin's Press, 1992.

Southgate, B. C. "'Forgotten and Lost': Some Reactions to Autonomous Science in the Seventeenth Century." *Journal of the History of Ideas* 50, no. 2 (1989): 249–68.

Specht, Rainer. "À propos des analogies entre les theories de la connaissance sensible chez Gassendi et Locke." In *Gassendi et l'Europe, 1592–1792,* edited by Sylvia Murr, 237–43. Paris: J. Vrin, 1997.

Spiller, Michael R. G. *"Concerning Natural Experimental Philosophie": Meric Casaubon and the Royal Society.* The Hague: Martinus Nijhoff, 1980.

———. "Die Opposition gegen die Royal Society." In *Die Philosophie des 17. Jahrhunderts,* vol. 3, bk. 2, *England,* edited by Jean-Pierre Schobinger, 442–53. Basel: Schwabe, 1988.

Spurr, John. "'Latitudinarianism' and the Restoration Church." *The Historical Journal* 31, no. 1 (1988): 61–82.

Stanglin, Keith. *Arminius on the Assurance of Salvation: The Context, Roots, and Shape of the Leiden Debate, 1603–1609.* Leiden: Brill, 2007.

Stebbins, Sara. *Maxima in minimis: zur Empirie- und Autoritätsverständnis in der physikotheologischen Literatur der Frühaufklärung.* Frankfurt am Main: P. D. Lang, 1980.

Steinberg, Justin. "Spinoza's Political Philosophy." In *The Stanford Encyclopedia of Philosophy* (Winter 2013 Edition). Accessed May 6, 2016. http://plato.stanford. edu/archives/win2013/entries/spinoza-political/.

Steinle, Friedrich. "From Principles to Regularities: Tracing 'Laws of Nature' in Early Modern France and England." In *Natural Law and Laws of Nature in Early Modern Europe,* edited by Lorraine Daston and Michael Stolleis, 215–31. Farnham: Ashgate, 2008.

Steinmetz, David C. "Calvin as Biblical Interpreter among the Ancient Philosophers." *Interpretation* 63, no. 2 (2009): 142–53.

———. *Calvin in Context.* 2nd ed. Oxford: Oxford University Press, 2010.

Stewart, M. A. *Independency of the Mind in Early Dissent.* London: The Congregational Memorial Trust, 2004.

Stimson, Dorothy. "Ballad of Gresham Colledge." *Isis* 18, no. 1 (1932): 103–17.

Stoeffler, F. Ernest. *The Rise of Evangelical Pietism.* Leiden: E. J. Brill, 1965.

Stone, M. W. F. "The Nature and Significance of Law in Early Modern Scholasticism." In *A History of the Philosophy of Law from the Ancient Greeks to the Scholastics,* edited by Fred. D. Miller, Jr., 335–65. Dordrecht: Springer, 2007.

Strivens, Robert. *Philip Doddridge and the Shaping of Evangelical Dissent.* Farnham: Ashgate, 2015.

Syfret, R. H. "Some Early Reactions to the Royal Society." *Notes and Records of the Royal Society* 7, no. 2 (1950): 207–58.

Sykes, Norman. *From Sheldon to Secker: Aspects of English Church History 1660–1768.* Cambridge: Cambridge University Press, 1959.

Sytsma, David S. "'As a Dwarfe set upon a Gyants shoulders': John Weemes (ca. 1579–1636) on the Place of Philosophy and Scholasticism in Reformed Theology." In *Die Philosophie der Reformierten,* edited by Günter Frank and Herman J. Selderhuis, 299–321. Melanchthon-Schriften der Stadt Bretten 12. Stuttgart: Frommann-Holzboog, 2012.

———. "Calvin, Daneau, and *Physica Mosaica*: Neglected Continuities at the Origins of an Early Modern Tradition." *Church History and Religious Culture* 95, no. 4 (2015): 457–76.

———. "General Introduction." In Matthew Hale, *Of the Law of Nature,* edited by David S. Sytsma, ix–lv. Grand Rapids, MI: CLP Academic, 2015.

———. "The Harvest of Thomist Anthropology: John Weemes's Reformed Portrait of the Image of God." ThM thesis, Calvin Theological Seminary, 2008.

———. "The Logic of the Heart: Analyzing the Affections in Early Reformed Orthodoxy." In *Church and School in Early Modern Protestantism: Essays in Honor of Richard A. Muller on the Maturation of a Theological Tradition,* edited by Jordan J. Ballor, David S. Sytsma, and Jason Zuidema, 471–88. Leiden: Brill, 2013.

———. "Thomas Aquinas and Reformed Biblical Interpretation: The Contribution of William Whitaker." In *Aquinas among the Protestants,* edited by David VanDrunen and Manfred Svensson. Hoboken: Wiley-Blackwell, forthcoming.

Tanzella-Netti, G. "The Two Books Prior to the Scientific Revolution." *Annales Theologici* 18 (2004): 51–83.

Thiel, Udo. "The Trinity and Human Personal Identity." In *English Philosophy in the Age of Locke,* edited by M. A. Stewart, 217–43. Oxford: Clarendon Press, 2000.

Thom, Paul. *The Logic of the Trinity: Augustine to Ockham.* New York: Fordham University Press, 2012.

Thomson, Ann. "Animals, Humans, Machines and Thinking Matter." *Early Science and Medicine* 15 (2013): 3–37.

———. *Bodies of Thought.* Oxford: Oxford University Press, 2008.

Thomas, Keith. *Religion and the Decline of Magic.* London: Weidenfeld and Nicolson, 1971.

Thomas, Roger. *The Baxter Treatises: A Catalogue of the Richard Baxter Papers (Other than the Letters) in Dr. Williams's Library.* Dr. Williams's Library Occasional Paper 8. London: Dr. Williams's Trust, 1959.

———. "The Break-Up of Nonconformity." In *The Beginnings of Nonconformity,* 33–60. London: James Clarke, 1964.

———. "Parties in Nonconformity." In *The English Presbyterians: From Elizabethan Puritanism to Modern Unitarianism,* 93–112. Boston: Beacon Press, 1968.

———. "Presbyterians in Transition." In *The English Presbyterians: From Elizabethan Puritanism to Modern Unitarianism,* 113–74. Boston: Beacon Press, 1968.

Tierney, Brian. *The Idea of Natural Rights: Studies on Natural Rights, Natural Law, and Church Law, 1150–1625.* Atlanta: Scholars Press, 1997.

Trueman, Carl R. "Lewis Bayly (d. 1631) and Richard Baxter (1615–1691)." In *The Pietist Theologians: An Introduction to Theology in the Seventeenth and Eighteenth Centuries,* edited by Carter Lindberg, 52–67. Malden, MA: Blackwell, 2005.

———. "A Small Step towards Rationalism: The Impact of the Metaphysics of Tommaso Campanella on the Theology of Richard Baxter." In *Protestant Scholasticism: Essays in Reassessment,* edited by Carl R. Trueman and R. Scott Clark, 181–95. Carlisle: Paternoster, 1999.

———. "Reformed Orthodoxy in Britain." In *A Companion to Reformed Orthodoxy,* edited by Herman Selderhuis, 261–91. Leiden: Brill, 2013.

———. "Richard Baxter on Christian Unity: A Chapter in the Enlightening of English Reformed Orthodoxy." *Westminster Theological Journal* 61 (1999): 53–71.

Tuck, Richard. "The 'Modern' Theory of Natural Law." In *The Languages of Political Theory in Early-Modern Europe,* edited by Anthony Pagden, 99–119. Cambridge: Cambridge University Press, 1987.

Tulloch, John. *Rational Theology and Christian Philosophy in England in the Seventeenth Century.* 2nd ed. 2 vols. Edinburgh: W. Blackwood, 1874.

Tyacke, Nicholas. "From Laudians to Latitudinarians: A Shifting Balance of Theological Forces." In *The Later Stuart Church, 1660–1714,* edited by Grant Tapsell, 46–67. Manchester: Manchester University Press, 2012.

Uzgalis, William. "Anthony Collins on the Emergence of Consciousness and Personal Identity." *Philosophy Compass* 4, no. 2 (2009): 363–79.

Van Asselt, Willem J. *Introduction to Reformed Scholasticism.* Translated by Albert Gootjes. Grand Rapids, MI: Reformation Heritage Books, 2011.

Van Asselt, Willem J., J. Martin Bac, and Roelf T. te Velde, eds. *Reformed Thought on Freedom: The Concept of Free Choice in Early Modern Reformed Theology.* Grand Rapids, MI: Baker Academic, 2010.

Van Berkel, Klaas. *Isaac Beeckman on Matter and Motion: Mechanical Philosophy in the Making.* Baltimore: The Johns Hopkins University Press, 2013.

Van den Berg, Johannes. "Between Platonism and Enlightenment: Simon Patrick (1625–1707) and His Place in the Latitudinarian Movement." *Dutch Review of Church History* 68, no. 2 (1988): 164–79.

———. *Religious Currents and Cross-Currents: Essays on Early Modern Protestantism and the Protestant Enlightenment.* Edited by Jan de Bruijn, Pieter Holtrop, and Ernestine van der Wall. Leiden: Brill, 1999.

Van den Brink, Gisbert. "A Most Elegant Book: The Natural World in Article 2 of the Belgic Confession." *Westminster Theological Journal* 73, no. 2 (2011): 273–91.

Van Helden, Albert. "The Birth of the Modern Scientific Instrument." In *The Uses of Science in the Age of Newton,* edited by John G. Burke, 49–84. Berkeley: University of California Press, 1983.

————. "Galileo, Telescopic Astronomy, and the Copernican System." In *Planetary Astronomy from the Renaissance to the Rise of Astrophysics, Part A: Tycho to Newton*, edited by René Taton and Curtis Wilson, 81–105. Cambridge: Cambridge University Press, 1995.

Vanzo, Alberto. "Empiricism and Rationalism in Nineteenth-Century Histories of Philosophy." *Journal of the History of Ideas* 77 (2016): 253–82.

Venn, John. *Alumni Cantabrigienses*. 6 vols. Cambridge: Cambridge University Press, 1922–1954.

————. *Biographical History of Gonville and Caius College, 1349–1897*. 3 vols. Cambridge: Cambridge University Press, 1897–1901.

Verbeek, Theo. *Descartes and the Dutch: Early Reactions to Cartesian Philosophy, 1637–1650*. Carbondale, IL: Southern Illinois University Press, 1992.

————. "From 'Learned Ignorance' to Scepticism: Descartes and Calvinist Orthodoxy." In *Scepticism and Irreligion in the Seventeenth and Eighteenth Centuries*, edited by Richard H. Popkin and Arjo Vanderjagt, 31–45. Leiden: E. J. Brill, 1993.

————. "Tradition and Novelty: Descartes and Some Cartesians." In *The Rise of Modern Philosophy*, edited by Tom Sorrell, 167–96. Oxford: Clarendon Press, 1993.

Vermij, Rienk H. "The Beginnings of Physico-Theology: England, Holland, Germany." In *"Grenz-Überschreitung". Wandlungen der Geisteshaltung, dargestellt an Beispielen aus Geographie und Wissenschaftshistorie, Theologie, Religions– und Erziehungswissenschaft, Philosophie, Musikwissenschaft und Liturgie. Festschrift zum 70. Geburtstag von Manfred Büttner*, edited by Henyo Kattenstedt, 173–84. Bochum: Brockmeyer, 1993.

————. *The Calvinist Copernicans: The Reception of the New Astronomy in the Dutch Republic, 1575–1750*. Amsterdam: Koninklijke Nederlandse Academie van Wetenschappen, 2002.

Wallace, Dewey D. *Shapers of English Calvinism, 1660–1714*. Oxford: Oxford University Press, 2011.

Wallace, Wes. "The Vibrating Nerve Impulse in Newton, Willis and Gassendi: First Steps in a Mechanical Theory of Communication." *Brain and Cognition* 51 (2003): 66–94.

Walmsley, Jonathan Craig. "John Locke on Respiration." *Medical History* 51 (2007): 453–76.

Weber, Max. *The Protestant Ethic and the Spirit of Capitalism*. Translated by Talcott Parsons. New York: Charles Scribner's Sons, 1958.

Webster, Charles. *The Great Instauration: Science, Medicine and Reform, 1626–1660*. New York: Holmes & Meier, 1976.

————. "Henry Power's Experimental Philosophy." *Ambix* 14 (1967): 150–78.

Weisheipl, James. "The Interpretation of Aristotle's *Physics* and the Science of Motion." In *The Cambridge History of Later Medieval Philosophy*, edited by Norman Kretzmann, Anthony Kenny, and Jan Pinborg, 521–36. Cambridge: Cambridge University Press, 1982.

——. "Scholastic Method." In *New Catholic Encyclopedia*, 2nd ed., 12:747–49. Washington, DC: Catholic University of America, 2003.

Westfall, Richard S. "The Foundations of Newton's Philosophy of Nature." *British Journal for the History of Science* 1 (1962–1963): 171–82.

——. *Science and Religion in Seventeenth-Century England*. New Haven, CT: Yale University Press, 1958.

Westman, Robert S. *The Copernican Question: Prognostication, Skepticism, and Celestial Order*. Berkeley: University of California Press, 2011.

White, Andrew D. *History of the Warfare of Science with Theology in Christendom*. 2 vols. London: Macmillan, 1896.

Williams, Arnold. *The Common Expositor: An Account of the Commentaries on Genesis 1527–1633*. Chapel Hill: The University of North Carolina Press, 1948.

Williamson, George. "The Restoration Revolt against Enthusiasm." *Studies in Philology* 30, no. 4 (1933): 571–603.

Wilson, Catherine. *Epicureanism at the Origins of Modernity*. Oxford: Oxford University Press, 2008.

——. "Epicureanism in Early Modern Philosophy: Leibniz and His Contemporaries." In *Hellenistic and Early Modern Philosophy*, edited by Jon Miller and Brad Inwood, 90–115. Cambridge: Cambridge University Press, 2003.

——. *The Invisible World: Early Modern Philosophy and the Invention of the Microscope*. Princeton, NJ: Princeton University Press, 1995.

Witte, John, Jr. *Law and Protestantism: The Legal Teachings of the Lutheran Reformation*. Cambridge: Cambridge University Press, 2002.

——. *The Reformation of Rights: Law, Religion, and Human Rights in Early Modern Calvinism*. Cambridge: Cambridge University Press, 2007.

Wojcik, Jan W. "The Theological Context of Boyle's *Things above Reason*." In *Robert Boyle Reconsidered*, edited by Michael Hunter, 139–55. Cambridge: Cambridge University Press, 1994.

Wolfe, Charles T., and Michaela van Esveld. "The Material Soul: Strategies for Naturalizing the Soul in an Early Modern Epicurean Context." In *Conjunctions of Mind, Soul and Body from Plato to the Enlightenment*, edited by Danijela Kambaskovic, 371–421. Dordrecht: Springer, 2014.

Wood, P. B. "Methodology and Apologetics: Thomas Sprat's *History of the Royal Society*." *British Journal for the History of Science* 13 (1980): 1–26.

Wright, John P. "Locke, Willis, and the Seventeenth-Century Epicurean Soul." In *Atoms, Pneuma, and Tranquillity: Epicurean and Stoic Themes in European Thought*, edited by Margaret J. Osler, 239–58. Cambridge: Cambridge University Press, 1991.

Wykes, David L. "The Contribution of the Dissenting Academy to the Emergence of Rational Dissent." In *Enlightenment and Religion: Rational Dissent in Eighteenth-Century Britain*, edited by Knud Haakonssen, 99–139. Cambridge: Cambridge University Press, 1996.

Yazawa, Reita. "John Howe on Divine Simplicity: A Debate Over Spinozism." In *Church and School in Early Modern Protestantism: Studies in Honor of Richard A. Muller on the Maturation of a Theological Tradition*, edited by Jordan J. Ballor, David S. Sytsma, and Jason Zuidema, 629–40. Leiden: Brill, 2013.

Yolton, John W. *Thinking Matter: Materialism in Eighteenth-Century Britain*. Minneapolis: University of Minnesota Press, 1983.

Zaret, David. "The Use and Abuse of Textual Data." In *Weber's Protestant Ethic: Origins, Evidence, Contexts*, edited by Hartmut Lehmann and Guenther Roth, 245–72. Washington, DC: German Historical Institute, 1993.

Zedler, Johann Heinrich. "Moses Vielwissenheit." In *Grosses vollständiges Universal Lexicon aller Wissenschafften und Künste*, 21:1888–97. Halle & Leipzig: J. H. Zedler, 1739.

Index